Managing the Web of Things

Linking the Real World to the Web

Managing the Web of Things
Linking the Real World to the Web

Edited by

Quan Z. Sheng
Department of Computing, Macquarie University, Australia

Yongrui Qin
School of Computing and Engineering, University of Huddersfield, United Kingdom

Lina Yao
School of Computer Science and Engineering, University of New South Wales, Australia

Boualem Benatallah
School of Computer Science and Engineering, University of New South Wales, Australia

MK

MORGAN KAUFMANN PUBLISHERS

AN IMPRINT OF ELSEVIER

elsevier.com

Library of Congress Cataloging-in-Publication Data
A catalog record for this book is available from the Library of Congress

British Library Cataloguing-in-Publication Data
A catalogue record for this book is available from the British Library

ISBN: 978-0-12-809764-9

For information on all Morgan Kaufmann publications
visit our website at https://www.elsevier.com/books-and-journals

Working together
to grow libraries in
developing countries

www.elsevier.com • www.bookaid.org

Publisher: Todd Green
Acquisition Editor: Todd Green
Editorial Project Manager: Lindsay Lawrence
Production Project Manager: Punithavathy Govindaradjane
Designer: Matthew Limbert

Typeset by VTeX

CONTENTS

PART 3 DATA INTEGRATION AND ANALYTICS

PART 4 APPLICATIONS, SECURITY AND SOCIAL IMPACT

LIST OF CONTRIBUTORS

Fabrizio Amarilli
Fondazione Politecnico di Milano, Milano, Italy

Francesco Amigoni
Dipartimento di Elettronica, Informazione e Bioingegneria, Politecnico di Milano, Milano, Italy

Claudio Anliker
Communication Systems Group, Department of Informatics, University of Zurich, Zurich, Switzerland

Muhammad Ali Babar
Software and Systems Section, IT University of Copenhagen, Copenhagen, Denmark
Centre for Research in Engineering Software Technologies, School of Computer Science, The University of Adelaide, Adelaide, SA, Australia

Reem Bahgat
Computer Science Department, Cairo University, Cairo, Egypt

Boualem Benatallah
School of Computer Science and Engineering, University of New South Wales, Sydney, NSW, Australia

Jean-Marie Bonnin
Institute Mines-Telecom/TELECOM Bretagne, Network, Multimedia and Security Department, Cesson Sévigné, France

Kayla M. Booth
The College of Information Sciences and Technology, The Pennsylvania State University, University Park, PA, United States

Ahmed Bouabdallah
Institute Mines-Telecom/TELECOM Bretagne, Network, Multimedia and Security Department, Cesson Sévigné, France

Hongming Cai
School of Software, Shanghai Jiao Tong University, Shanghai, China

Adriana Caione
Department of Innovation Engineering, University of Salento, Lecce, Italy
VidyaSoft s.r.l., Spin-off company of Salento University, Lecce, Italy

Philippe Capdepuy
Génération Robots, Bruges, France

Muhammad Aufeef Chauhan
Software and Systems Section, IT University of Copenhagen, Copenhagen, Denmark
Department of Applied Mathematics and Computer Science, Technical University of Denmark, Lyngby, Denmark

Charalampos Chelmis
Ming Hsieh Department of Electrical Engineering, University of Southern California, Los Angeles, CA, United States

Suparna De
Institute for Communication Systems (ICS), Department of Electrical and Electronic Engineering, University of Surrey, Surrey, United Kingdom

Elizabeth V. Eikey
The College of Information Sciences and Technology, The Pennsylvania State University, University Park, PA, United States

Saad El Jaouhari
Institute Mines-Telecom/TELECOM Bretagne, Network, Multimedia and Security Department, Cesson Sévigné, France

Alessandro Fiore
Department of Innovation Engineering, University of Salento, Lecce, Italy
VidyaSoft s.r.l., Spin-off company of Salento University, Lecce, Italy

Maria Grazia Fugini
Dipartimento di Elettronica, Informazione e Bioingegneria, Politecnico di Milano, Milano, Italy

Ilias Gerostathopoulos
Fakultät für Informatik, Software & Systems Engineering Research Group, Technische Universität München, München, Germany

Amelie Gyrard
Insight Centre for Data Analytics, IoT Unit, National University of Ireland, Galway, Ireland

Jean-Paul Jamont
Laboratoire LCIS, Université Grenoble Alpes, Valence, France

El-Mehdi Khalfi
Laboratoire LCIS, Université Grenoble Alpes, Valence, France

Sherif Khattab
Computer Science Department, Cairo University, Cairo, Egypt

Nicolas Le Sommer
Laboratoire IRISA, Université de Bretagne Sud, Vannes, France

Xue Li
School of Information Technology and Electrical Engineering, University of Queensland, Brisbane, QLD, Australia

Luca Mainetti
Department of Innovation Engineering, University of Salento, Lecce, Italy
VidyaSoft s.r.l., Spin-off company of Salento University, Lecce, Italy

Luigi Manco
Department of Innovation Engineering, University of Salento, Lecce, Italy
VidyaSoft s.r.l., Spin-off company of Salento University, Lecce, Italy

Lionel Médini
Univ Lyon, Université Claude Bernard Lyon 1, CNRS, LIRIS UMR5205, F-69622, Villeurbanne, France

Klaus Moessner
Institute for Communication Systems (ICS), Department of Electrical and Electronic Engineering, University of Surrey, Surrey, United Kingdom

Michael Mrissa
Univ Lyon, Université Claude Bernard Lyon 1, CNRS, LIRIS UMR5205, F-69622, Villeurbanne, France

Anne H.H. Ngu
Department of Computer Science, Texas State University, San Marcos, TX, United States

Michel Occello
Laboratoire LCIS, Université Grenoble Alpes, Valence, France

Pankesh Patel
ABB Corporate Research, Bangalore, KN, India

Viktor K. Prasanna
Ming Hsieh Department of Electrical Engineering, University of Southern California, Los Angeles, CA, United States

Christian Prehofer
Fakultät für Informatik, Software & Systems Engineering Research Group, Technische Universität München, München, Germany

Yongrui Qin
School of Computing and Engineering, The University of Huddersfield, Huddersfield, United Kingdom

Muhammad Rizwan Saeed
Ming Hsieh Department of Electrical Engineering, University of Southern California, Los Angeles, CA, United States

Corinna Schmitt
Communication Systems Group, Department of Informatics, University of Zurich, Zurich, Switzerland

Martin Serrano
Insight Centre for Data Analytics, IoT Unit, National University of Ireland, Galway, Ireland

Ali Shemshadi
School of Computer Science, The University of Adelaide, Adelaide, SA, Australia

Quan Z. Sheng
Department of Computing, Macquarie University, Sydney, NSW, Australia

Burkhard Stiller
Communication Systems Group, Department of Informatics, University of Zurich, Zurich, Switzerland

Mehdi Terdjimi
Univ Lyon, Université Claude Bernard Lyon 1, CNRS, LIRIS UMR5205, F-69622, Villeurbanne, France

Lionel Touseau
Laboratoire IRISA, Université de Bretagne Sud, Vannes, France

Eileen M. Trauth
The College of Information Sciences and Technology, The Pennsylvania State University, University Park, PA, United States

Athanasios V. Vasilakos
Department of Computer Science, Electrical and Space Engineering, Luleå University of Technology, Luleå, Sweden

Roberto Vergallo
Department of Innovation Engineering, University of Salento, Lecce, Italy
VidyaSoft s.r.l., Spin-off company of Salento University, Lecce, Italy

Xianzhi Wang

School of Computer Science and Engineering, University of New South Wales, Sydney, NSW, Australia

Lina Yao

School of Computer Science and Engineering, University of New South Wales, Sydney, NSW, Australia

Mina Younan

Computer Science Department, Minia University, Minia, Egypt

Gian Piero Zarri

STIH Laboratory, Sorbonne University, Paris, France

Yuchao Zhou

Institute for Communication Systems (ICS), Department of Electrical and Electronic Engineering, University of Surrey, Surrey, United Kingdom

ABOUT THE EDITORS

Quan Z. (Michael) Sheng is currently a full Professor and Head of Department of Computing, at Macquarie University. Prof. Sheng has more than 10 years' research and development experience in the Internet of Things (IoT) and related areas such as service-oriented computing, radio frequency identification (RFID), sensor networks, and big data analytics. He has published more than 280 publications in these areas and is one of the top-ranked authors in the "World Wide Web" research area according to Microsoft Academic Search. Prof. Michael Sheng is the recipient to a number of prestigious awards including ARC Future Fellowship in 2014, Chris Wallace Award for Outstanding Research Contribution (2012), and Microsoft Research Fellowship (2003).

Yongrui Qin is currently a Lecturer at School of Computing and Engineering, University of Huddersfield, United Kingdom. His main research interests include the Internet of Things, Graph Data Management, Data Stream Processing, Data Mining, Information Retrieval, Semantic Web, Computer Networks, and Mobile Computing. Dr. Qin has published more than 40 refereed technical papers, including publications in prestigious journals, such as IEEE Trans. on Parallel Distributed Systems, World Wide Web Journal, Journal of Network and Computer Applications, and IEEE Internet Computing, as well as top international conferences, such as SIGIR, EDBT, CIKM, WISE, DASFAA, and SSDBM.

Lina Yao is currently a Lecturer at School of Computer Science and Engineering, the University of New South Wales. Her research interest lies in Data Mining, Internet of Things Analytics, Ubiquitous Computing, and Service Computing. Her work has published in a wide range of prestigious journals such as ACM Trans. on Intelligent Systems and Technology (TIST), ACM Trans. on Internet Technology (TOIT), IEEE Transactions on Parallel and Distributed Systems (TPDS), IEEE Trans. on Knowledge Discovery and Engineering (TKDE), IEEE Internet Computing, ACM Trans. on Knowledge Discovery (TKDD) and IEEE Trans. on Services Computing (TSC), as well as top international conferences such as SIGIR, ICDM, UbiComp, CIKM and ICSOC. She is the recipient of Australian Research Council Discovery Early Career Researcher Award (2015) and is recognized as Inaugural Vice Chancellor's Women's Research Excellence Award (2015).

Boualem Benatallah is currently a Scientia Professor at the School of Computer Science and Engineering, the University of New South Wales. Prof. Benatallah's research focuses on Web service protocol analysis and management, enterprise services integration, large scale data sharing, cloud computing, and the Internet of Things (IoT). He is the leader of the Service Oriented Computing research group and has more than 220 research papers in leading international journals and conference proceedings. Prof. Benatallah's research has been heavily cited by his international peers. He has more than 14,000 citations with an H-index of 52, according to Google Scholar.

PREFACE

Over the years, the World Wide Web has gone through many transformations, from traditional linking and sharing of computers and documents (i.e., "Web of Data"), to the current connection of people (i.e., "Web of People"), and to the emerging connection of billions of physical objects (i.e., "Web of Things"). Web of Things (WoT) aims to connect everyday objects, such as coats, shoes, watches, ovens, washing machines, bikes, cars, even humans, plants, animals, and changing environments, to the Internet to enable communication/interactions between these objects. The ultimate goal of WoT is to enable computers to see, hear and sense the real world. It is predicted by Ericsson that the number of Internet-connected things will reach 50 billion by 2020. Electronic devices and systems exist around us providing different services to the people in different situations: at home, at work, in their office, or driving a car on the street. WoT also enables the close relationship between human and opportunistic connection of smart things. To realize the goals of WoT and to fully exploit its potentials, building and managing the Web of Things at the global scale has created numerous challenges, as well as tremendous opportunities, to many stakeholders, including research institutions, companies, governments, and international organizations. There is an urgent need to capture related technology trends, so as to guide and help all these stakeholders to actively contribute to the promising future of WoT. WoT provides an Application Layer that simplifies the creation of the Internet of Things (IoT) applications and aims to enable real-world objects to be part of the World Wide Web, which can be achieved on top of connecting them together at a global scale in IoT. This book provides a consolidated and holistic coverage of engineering, management and analytics that advances the fundamental understanding of the Web of Things building blocks in terms of concepts, models, languages, productivity support techniques, and tools. This enables effective exploration, understanding, assessing, comparing, and selecting WoT models, languages, techniques, platforms, and tools.

Meanwhile, there is a scarcity of texts on how to manage large-scale of things over the Web. This book aims to fill this gap and serve as a primary point of reference by compiling the newest developments and advances in the area of the Web of Things. It offers a comprehensive and systematic presentation of methodologies, technologies and applications that enable efficient and effective management of things over the Web, thereby helping academic researchers, practitioners, graduate students, and governments unveil the potentials of WoT.

This book is the collection of 15 chapters that focus on the most recent developments in the field of the Web of Things. The covered new advances range from modelling, searching, data analytics, to software building, applications and social impact. Hence, this book provides a comprehensive view of the latest developments and trends in this nascent area. From the book, the reader will be able to gain up-to-date knowledge and experience on how to manage things over the Web. This can help them accelerate their research on the Web of Things (for researchers), gain immediate experiences on building the Web of Things systems (for practitioners), and support policy and decision making (for industries and government agencies).

This book would not have been possible without the help of many people. We would like to thank them for their tremendous efforts. We would like to thank all authors of the book chapters for their high quality contributions to this book. We would also like to thank our book chapter reviewers for their hard work in providing professional reviews to all the book chapters, which helped improve the quality of all book chapters significantly. We are very grateful to the people at Morgan Kaufmann for their hard work and continuous help and assistance throughout the book-editing process.

Quan Z. Sheng
Sydney, Australia

Yongrui Qin
Huddersfield, England

Lina Yao
Sydney Australia

Boualem Benatallah
Sydney, Australia

January 2017

PART

MODELING AND SEARCHING

1

ONTOLOGIES AND CONTEXT MODELING FOR THE WEB OF THINGS

Suparna De, Yuchao Zhou, Klaus Moessner

*Institute for Communication Systems (ICS), Department of Electrical and Electronic Engineering,
University of Surrey, Surrey, United Kingdom*

CHAPTER POINTS

- This chapter presents a taxonomy and survey of the current state-of-the-art in WoT ontologies.
- The developed taxonomy considers the ontologies in a two-layered approach: cross-domain that include models of WoT elements, such as device, entity, service, location and domain models that represent WoT application areas, classified into environmental and user-oriented areas.

1.1 INTRODUCTION

The Internet of Things (IoT) is envisaged to impact significantly the lives of citizens and offer new business opportunities through digital innovation in the integration of the physical and digital worlds. The first step in the IoT vision has been interconnectivity between physical world objects. The main drivers for further IoT development are enabling things-to-things communications and integration of things data with applications to lead the way towards context-aware solutions and smart cyber-physical systems. This has led to the next step of connecting things to the Web; leading to the emergence of the Web of Things (WoT). The WoT principles are not limited to Web access, but extend to *"Web Linking for resource description and discovery, resource directories and security"* [29], through Internet Engineering Task Force (IETF) protocols such as Constrained Application Protocol (CoAP) [52] and lightweight HTTP implementations. The WoT enables interaction of things and systems through Application Programming Interfaces (APIs) exposing things data and metadata. However, true integration is hampered by the fact that *"many devices do not speak the same language and cannot exchange data across different gateways and smart hubs"* [53]. To illustrate, the data generated by things about their ambient environment may have a

Managing the Web of Things. DOI: 10.1016/B978-0-12-809764-9.00002-0

defined structure in a known format (e.g. JSON/CSV/XML), but the data models and schemas adopted are different and not always compatible. Additionally, they may be represented in different units and include additional information. This leads us to the 'interoperability' challenge, which has been recognised by industry alliance bodies such as the Alliance for Internet of Things Innovation (AIOTI)[1] and in the European IoT research roadmap [61] as key to achieving *"convergence in the long term"* [53]. Recent research has led to the unanimous conclusion that semantic technologies can be the driver for integration and interoperability [66,29,39], by enabling the semantic annotation of IoT devices and data. This has been termed as the progression towards a semantic Web of Things (SWoT) in the literature [29], as the basis for achieving a common understanding of the various entities forming part of the IoT. This evolution is recognised as a seamless extension of the IoT towards achieving wide-scale interoperability and a move towards horizontal open systems and platforms that can support multiple applications. A recent report [6] on interoperability for the WoT, by industry and standards experts, highlights the role of semantic interoperability to unlock value across the different domains (such as cities, factories, retail environments etc.) of the WoT.

Specifically, the use of semantic Web-based modelling techniques (RDF models and OWL ontologies) can enable a homogeneous and scalable means to access WoT information. Ontologies can capture the various facets in a common, formalised structure as well as the inter-relationships between the things to form the domain knowledge of the WoT. Semantic interoperability can enable the use of things/objects and data across application domains as well as data exchange across the value chain [53]. However, given the massive scale of the things involved in the IoT, the *"creation of a unitary ontology to define all the resources and manage all the aspects related to them seems to be impossible"* [39]. The semantic annotations need to capture the capabilities of the heterogeneous objects forming part of the WoT in order to enable their search and discovery, the location of these objects (as part of a set of context features) as well as the information they can provide [61]. This leads to the need for domain specific ontologies. Practitioners also need knowledge of the existence of the various domain specific ontologies and an assessment of the applicability of these towards applications such as search and discovery, data analytics and data fusion in different domains such as smart cities, assisted living, home automation etc. Thus, it becomes quite important to have a clear framework in place that facilitates a clear use of the different available ontologies from a data and context-awareness perspective. In addition to the four ontology design principles of lightweight-ness, completeness, compatibility and modularity as identified in [67], various requirements for the elements to be modelled by WoT specific ontologies have been identified [39,72,29,67]:

- WoT ontologies need to address the representation of not only the thing specific (such as sensors, devices, actuators, smart objects) heterogeneity of the WoT with

---

[1] AIOTI: Alliance for Internet of Things Innovation, www.aioti.eu.

the necessary level of abstraction, but also capture the distributed environment context in which they operate.
- Since WoT smart objects provide services individually or in cooperation, this also needs to be taken into account.
- The data generated by smart objects needs to be precisely and effectively modelled so that it can be represented, reasoned upon and used to drive higher-level processes such as data manipulation and fusion.
- The semantic representations should facilitate extensible annotations, i.e. from minimal to elaborate descriptions.
- With WoT objects typically being energy-constrained and operating in dynamic environments, capturing the notion of quality of the available services and generated data assumes importance.
- With mobile objects increasingly contributing as data sensors in the WoT, associating the generated data with the location of sensing and the object identity becomes crucial so that the data can be corroborated and combined to generate knowledge about the ambient environment state.

A number of ontologies and context models have been proposed by the research community addressing different parts of the above requirements, leading to a substantive body of ontological models that can be candidates for a wide variety of WoT applications. A survey and analysis of current ontologies is presented in this book chapter. Additionally, we will focus on a definition of a taxonomy to capture the various elements of the WoT as modelled by the various available ontologies. An analysis of the available ontological models in terms of different facets and domain applicability will also be presented through a mix of comparison measures.

The remainder of this chapter is organised as follows: based on the requirements identified above, we developed the taxonomy for the survey of ontology modelling efforts in the WoT in Section 1.2, along with a number of measures for comparing the surveyed ontologies. Sections 1.3–1.4 detail the specific approaches from existing state of the art that propose ontologies that fit into the defined classification model. Where applicable, the ontologies are described in the context of the European research projects within which they were defined. A discussion of the findings and future outlook is presented in Section 1.5, before providing concluding remarks in Section 1.6.

1.2 TAXONOMY AND COMPARISON FRAMEWORK

Existing studies surveying WoT ontologies include a survey of existing IoT ontologies and vocabularies along five identified conceptual groups [36] of sensors/actuators; global and local coordinates; communication endpoint; observations, features of interest, units and dimensions; and vendor, version, deployment time. The authors only aim at identifying ontologies that can be used to semantically describe a specific set of real world devices that include a weather station, fan and an electric meter, with

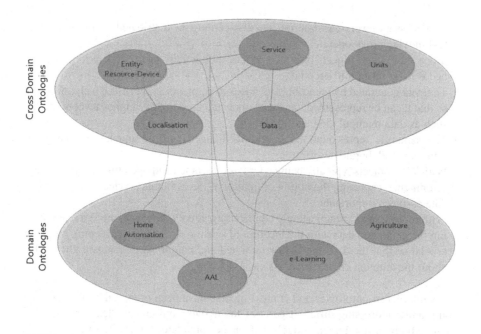

FIGURE 1.1

Multi-layered perspective of WoT ontologies

the service perspective notably missing as well as ontologies capturing data. Prominent device/sensor, data and service ontologies are listed in [39], whereas [25] discusses ontologies proposed for describing sensors and those covering WoT domains such as smart cities, ambient assisted living (AAL) and generally cyber-physical systems. A review of some of the existing ontology models and their comparison along the aspects of dynamics, concepts modelled, scale and mobility is presented in [70]. However, these approaches are limited by the absence of a classification and comparison scheme and a comprehensive listing of available WoT ontologies. The taxonomy proposed in this book chapter extends the ontology categories outlined in [39], while taking cognizance of the features commented upon in [70].

Existing research on ontologies for the WoT defines models for the various entities forming part of the WoT, viz. devices, services, sensors etc. either in isolation or as part of an interconnected suite of ontologies. In addition, there are ontologies that cover the allied context representation tasks. The taxonomy developed in this chapter considers a two layered approach: cross-domain and domain-specific ontologies, as shown in Fig. 1.1. A similar demarcation is also outlined in the WoT semantic interoperability report [6]. The cross-domain ontologies consist of WoT concepts that are shared across the domains and vertical application silos. These include the core WoT elements as identified in the literature, including things, sensors, services etc. as well as shared concepts related to quantities, units and location. The domain ontolo-

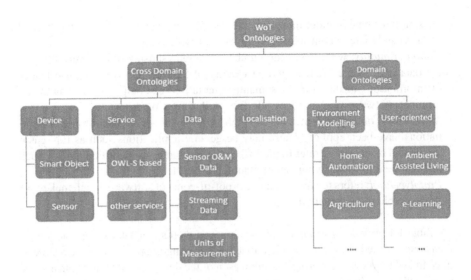

FIGURE 1.2

Classification of the WoT ontologies

gies, on the other hand, relate to specific application domains, such as smart home, ambient assisted living (AAL), etc. and often reference the cross domain ontologies. Moreover, the cross domain ontologies are classified into four perspectives: (1) device models, including smart object or resource models and more specific sensor ontologies, (2) service ontologies, that cover the provision of WoT device functionalities as services, (3) data ontologies, that represent the semantic annotation of both instantaneous and streaming data and (4) localisation ontologies, that capture both indoor and outdoor locations, such as geographical features. The domain ontologies provide the context to the cross domain models. These are classified according to two main perspectives: (1) environment models, that cover home/office/public buildings environment and the agriculture domain and (2) user-oriented ontologies, focussing on user activity recognition, ambient intelligence and WoT-enabled learning scenarios. The developed taxonomy is presented in Fig. 1.2.

To gain a quick while in-depth overview of the various models, we define a number of dimensions against which the existing works can be compared. These are explained as follows:

- *Modelled concepts*: indicates the elements modelled in the ontology
- *Language*: specifies the modelling language formalism, e.g. RDF, OWL
- *Links to domain ontologies*: refers to possible ontology relationships that link to existing third-party ontologies covering different domains such as location, units of measurement for data etc. Referring to existing domain ontologies offers the

possibility of having more interconnected device descriptions, by forming Linked Data [8] and thereby contributing to the Web of Data vision

- *Notion of quality*: with increasing number of mobile sensing units contributing to the data pool of the WoT, including Quality of Service (QoS) and QoI (Quality of Information) attributes in the semantic annotations can help applications to discriminate between WoT services offering similar functionalities
- *Application domain*: indicates the application domain to which the ontology instantiations have been applied. These may be generic applications such as for sensor search and discovery or refer to the IoT application areas as identified in [62], such as smart health, smart living, smart manufacturing etc.
- *Prototype/tool*: refers to any applicable proof-of-concept software which makes use of the ontology instantiations

Table 1.1 provides a summary of the surveyed works against the comparison dimensions outlined above. It is evident that most existing approaches define a suite of inter-linked ontologies covering a combination of the device, service and data aspects along with possibly the physical locations that the device inhabits.

1.3 CROSS DOMAIN MODELS

1.3.1 DEVICE ONTOLOGIES

Most of the ontologies in the WoT are drawn from early efforts in the Wireless Sensor Network (WSN) area to model sensors and actuators. However, recently, efforts have been made to extend the semantic efforts to model WoT-specific elements, including *things* and the functionalities they provide. Since sensors still represent a sizeable section of the things in the WoT, the semantic modelling efforts for them are presented in a separate section.

1.3.1.1 *WoT Smart Object Ontologies*

With the IoT domain providing the possibility of everyday objects providing real world data to the Internet, the associated models should include metadata describing the objects to provide context to the descriptions.

One of the first EU research initiatives in the IoT area, the IoT-A project,[2] defined the IoT domain model [7], identifying the main concepts of the IoT and the inter-relationships between them. A semantic model [20] for entities, resources and services was also proposed, with resources forming the software representation of device functionalities. The focus of interactions by human users or software agents was identified to be the 'entity'. An entity is modeled to have attributes that tie it to the domain (i.e. observable or actionable features), location attributes as well as

---

[2]Internet of Things Architecture, http://www.iot-a.eu/public.

Table 1.1 Comparison of WoT Cross-Domain and Domain Ontologies

Ontology	Modelled Concepts	Language	Links to Domain Ontologies	Notion of Quality	Application Domain	Prototype or Tool
oneM2M Base ontology [42]	Thing, device, service	OWL-DL	–	no	Domain independent	Illustrative mappings defined to SSN and SAREF ontologies
IoT-A ontology [20]	Entity, resource, service	OWL-DL	DBpedia, FOAF, OWL-S, QUDV, QUDT	no	Associations between objects and services, service composition and search	Sense2Web platform
Jin et al. [32]	Device, resource, service	OWL	FOAF, GeoNames	no	Quality rating of services, service selection	–
Chun et al. [15]	Entity, device, resource, service, event	OWL		no	Service event recognition	IoT-DS (directory service)
PT-SOA [74]	Physical thing, Service	OWL	–	no	Emergency rescue	–
iCore Virtual Object (VO) [34]	VO, ICT, non-ICT objects	OWL	–	yes	VO composition	Ambient Assisted Living demonstrator
Christophe et al. [14]	VO	OWL	FOAF, GeoNames	no	VO search	–
VO (Zhou et al.) [71]	VO, O&M data	OWL-DL	WGS84, Geohash	no	O&M data discovery	Web-based GUI for O&M data discovery
SSN [16]	Sensor, system, observation, feature	OWL-DL	DOLCE-Ultralite	no	Sensing for manufacturing, WoT infrastructures, SWE linked data infrastructure	SPITFIRE FP7 project event model, semantic sensor Web, SemsorGrid4Env[a] environment management framework

(continued on next page)

Table 1.1 (continued)

Ontology	Modelled Concepts	Language	Links to Domain Ontologies	Notion of Quality	Application Domain	Prototype or Tool
CSIRO sensor ontology [41]	Sensor deployment, operation	OWL	OWL-S	yes	data integration, search, classification and workflows	–
OntoSensor [50]	Sensor, capabilities, measures	OWL	IEEE SUMO, ISO 19115, SensorML, GML	no	extended by service oriented sensor data ontology [35]	–
Semantic Actuator Network (SAN) [56]	actuator	OWL-DL	SSN, QU	no	Earthquake emergency	part of the Earthquake Emergency (EEM) ontology
Actuator ontology [64]	actuator	OWL	–	no	Actuator discovery and invocation	policy-based home care system
IoT.est service ontology [67]	Service, test, platform, location, QoS, QoI	OWL-DL	IoT-A entity, resource ontologies, OWL-S, WGS84, CF-features	yes	Sensor service discovery, service composition	–
Qu et al. [45]	Service, status, location	OWL	OWL-S	no	selection, combination and control of entity services	–
ForwarDS-IoT service ontology [24]	Sensor, actuator, service	OWL	OWL-S	no	Discovery services	ForwarDS-IoT discovery service
Linked USDL [60]	Service, business entity	RDF	–	no	Enterprise IT integration	–
SSD ontology [28]	Service, server profile	OWL	–	no	Automated WoT service deployment	–
Service oriented sensor data ontology [35]	Sensor service	OWL	OntoSensor, SUMO, GML	no	Service query	–

Table 1.1 (continued)

Ontology	Modelled Concepts	Language	Links to Domain Ontologies	Notion of Quality	Application Domain	Prototype or Tool
IoT-based service integration ontology (IIO) [51]	Service, topic, user	OWL	–	no	Smart office	Integrated Semantic Service Platform
Wang et al. [65]	Sensor observation data	RDF	DBpedia	no	Reasoning for weather conditions at specific locations	–
SemSOS O&M-OWL [27]	Sensor O&M data	RDF	–	no	Weather condition reasoning	SemSOS tool
SensorData [3]	Sensor O&M data	RDF	NASA SWEET	no	–	–
LinkedSensorData [43]	Sensor O&M data	RDF	GeoNames	no	Weather (hurricane and blizzard observations in the United States)	Semantic Sensor Web application
Barnaghi et al. [5]	Sensor O&M data	RDF	DBPedia, GeoNames	no	Sensor metadata publication, query	Linked Sensor Data platform (sensor description publication and visualisation)
LSM [38]	Sensor O&M data	RDF	DBPedia, GeoNames	no	Sensor data discovery	Linked Sensor middleware
SEEK Extensible Observation Ontology (OBOE) [12]	Sensor O&M data	OWL-DL	–	no	coastal ecosystems	ontology link[b]
Stream Annotation Ontology (SAO) [37]	Sensor O&M data streams	OWL-DL	–	yes	Smart city traffic use case	–
Barnaghi et al. [4]	Sensor O&M data streams	OWL-DL	DBPedia, GeoNames	no	Sensor data clustering	–

(continued on next page)

Table 1.1 *(continued)*

Ontology	Modelled Concepts	Language	Links to Domain Ontologies	Notion of Quality	Application Domain	Prototype or Tool
NASA SWEET	Representation, Process, Phenomena, Matter, Realm, Human Activities, Property, State, Relation	OWL, RDF	–	no	Sensor observations annotation, mobile applications	Projects such as Trickscity[c], SemSerGrid4Env
QUDV	Data, Unit, Scale, Quantity, Dimension	OWL	–	no	Entity, resource attribute annotation References to QUDV instances in IoT-A entity and resource ontology, IoT.est service ontology	–
QUDT	Unit, Dimension, Quantity	OWL, RDF	–	no	Entity, resource, unit of measurement annotation	Water quality vocabulary [54], IoT-A entity and resource ontology, IoT.est service ontology
UO	Quality, Unit	OBO, OWL, RDF	part of the Phenotype and Trait Ontology (PATO) framework[d]	no	–	Beta Cell Genomics database, BioAssay Ontology, Electrophysiology Ontology, ISA software suite, Neural Electromagnetic Ontologies
OM	Unit of Measure, System of Units, Quantity, Measure, Measurement Scale, Dimension	OWL2	–	no	–	TI Food and Nutrition[e]

Table 1.1 *(continued)*

Ontology	Modelled Concepts	Language	Links to Domain Ontologies	Notion of Quality	Application Domain	Prototype or Tool
MUO	BaseUnit, ComplexDerivedUnit, DerivedUnit, MetricUnit, PhysicalQuality, Prefix, QualityValue, SIUnit, SimpleDerivedUnit, UnitOfMeasurement	RDF	–	no	–	–
Indoor location ontology [19]	Indoor locations such as place, premises	OWL-DL	–	no	Associations between physical things and WoT services	–
Indoor location ontology [63]	Indoor locations in a university campus	OWL-DL	–	no	Sensor service discovery	–
GeoNames	geographical features	OWL	–	no	Location specification in other ontologies through linked data	–
CityGML	virtual 3D city model	OWL-DL	–	no	City level location specification in other ontologies	–
DBpedia Place	cities and region features	RDF	–	no	Location specification in other ontologies through linked data	–
WGS84	Latitude, longitude, altitude	RDF	–	no	Geo-coordinate tagging in many ontologies	–
DogOnt [9]	Home structural elements, appliances	RDF, OWL	–	no	Smart home	Power consumption estimation in smart homes

(continued on next page)

Table 1.1 (*continued*)

Ontology	Modelled Concepts	Language	Links to Domain Ontologies	Notion of Quality	Application Domain	Prototype or Tool
SAREF [17]	Appliances, their functions and services, energy profile	RDF	WGS84, OWL-Time	no	Reference ontology for smart appliances	–
Home environment ontology [33]	Home structural elements, appliances, computing and peripheral devices	OWL	–	no	Dynamic home environment status	intelligent home service framework (iHSF)
BOnSAI [58]	Building, location, devices (hardware and communication protocol)	OWL	CoDAMoS	yes	Smart building (automation)	Smart IHU project
Chahuara et al. [13]	Rooms in a home, objects, status	OWL2	–	no	Home automation	Voice reactive smart home
ThinkHome [47]	Building structure, energy providers, resources, comfort	OWL-DL	–	no	Energy efficiency of white and brown goods	ThinkHome project (energy efficiency and thermal comfort)
SmartHomeWeather [57]	Weather report, source, weather phenomena	OWL2	Measurement Units Ontology (MUO), OWL-Time, WGS84	no	Rule reasoning to monitor weather values over time	–
Phenonet [30]	Crop trials (crop, treatment, plot, genotype)	OWL	Automatic Weather Station ontology, CF ontology, QU, SSN	no	Agriculture Meteorology	Phenonet-OpenIoT middleware

Table 1.1 (continued)

Ontology	Modelled Concepts	Language	Links to Domain Ontologies	Notion of Quality	Application Domain	Prototype or Tool
Context-aware infrastructure and functional activity ontology [68]	location, sensors, object, context human posture, functional activity	RDF	–	no	Human activity recognition	ontology based activity recognition (OBAR) system, part of a Recommender Management Framework
Efthymiou et al., [21]	Computational entity, event, activity, person, location, environment	OWL	–	no	Smart classroom	-
Assisted Living ontology [75]	Person, health, time and core (activity ontology) [21]	OWL	W3C time ontology, activity ontology of Efthymiou et al., [21]	no	Activity recognition	Daily living assistance component
User profile ontology [55]	User profile (capability, interest, preference, education, health), context, location, activity	OWL	–	no	Reasoning to provide customised support for daily activities	MobileSAGE project (assistance services to people with dementia)
IMS-LD [59]	Learning objects (devices), learner activity record	–	–	no	e-learning	–
u-learning object model [31]	Learner, tutor, device, content object	–	–	no	e-learning	Self-directed u-learning service

a *http://www.semsorgrid4env.eu/.*
b *https://sonet.ecoinformatics.org/semtools-svn/ontologies.*
c *https://bioportal.bioontology.org/ontologies/SWEET.*
d *https://bioportal.bioontology.org/ontologies/PATO.*
e *http://www.tifn.nl.*

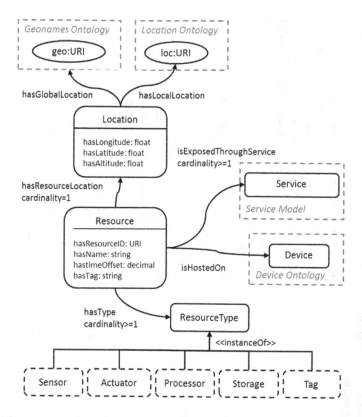

FIGURE 1.3

IoT-A Resource Model, see De et al. [20]

type and identifier specifications. Also captured are optional temporal features and links to known vocabularies for specifying ownership. The resources provide some form of physical access to the entity. The resource model specifies resource types (e.g. sensor/actuator/gateway node), the location of the corresponding device as well as a link to the service model that exposes the resource capabilities. The location can be defined in terms of the geographical coordinates, to an external ontology instance such as that in GeoNames[3] or through an URI to a local location ontology, such as that which provides detailed location description of rooms and buildings in a campus [18]. A simplified version of the resource model proposed in [20] is shown in Fig. 1.3.

A similar device and entity model is proposed in [32] and in [15] with resources identified as the computational element of a device and categorised as on-device or network resource to represent events in an IoT environment.

---

[3]GeoNames ontology, http://www.geonames.org/ontology/documentation.html.

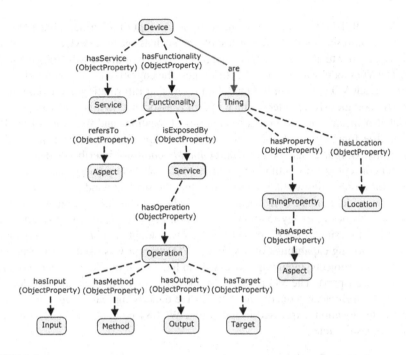

FIGURE 1.4

Main concepts in oneM2M Base ontology, derived from oneM2M technical specification TS-0012 [42]

A domain independent ontology from the oneM2M standards initiative is the oneM2M Base ontology [42], shown in Fig. 1.4, that features a *Thing* as its root concept. A root class thing represents an entity in the oneM2M system, and its refinement, the Device class represents a thing which can interact electronically with the environment. A device has 1 or more *functionalities* (i.e. capabilities) which are exposed to the network through *services*. The functionality may in turn relate to actuation on the environment (*controllingFunctionality*) or sensing real world aspects (*measuringFunctionality*).

In contrast to the entity-resource modelling constructs reviewed above, Zhu et al. [74] define a PT-SOA ontology for physical things (PTs) and services in the cyber-physical domain, where they model the PTs as providers (and recipients) of services. The PT ontology has 4 classes: *physical profile* to depict the things physical properties, any constituent PT and components; *operation profile* to specify the resources required for its operation, control mechanisms, maintenance and physical constraints when providing services; *context* to depict the dynamic state of the PT and the *scheduled service* specification for scheduling the PT to serve multiple requests to its provided services.

The EU ICT-FP7 project iCore[4] defined the concept of a Virtual Object (VO) as the virtual representation of a real world object, such as sensors, devices, or everyday objects, in order to abstract the technical heterogeneity of the possible objects in the IoT. The VO model was defined [34] to support the cognitive management of virtual objects. Each VO concept in the model represents an Information and Communication Technologies (ICT) object, which in turn is associated to a non-ICT object. The model also specifies the VO function in terms of locations and functions of the ICT object. The functions of ICT objects are further expressed as *Input*, *Output*, *Cost*, and *Utility*. *Output* is also bound with *OutputMetadata* to describe its data. A similar VO concept is also outlined by Christophe et al. [14] who present a semantic model for representing virtual objects, to define the structure and capabilities of objects. The model reuses FOAF vocabulary to indicate the owner of objects, and links to the GeoNames ontology to show the location of the corresponding smart space. A simplified version of the iCore VO ontology was adopted in [71], focussing on the data provisioning capabilities of a VO. The VO concept was used to represent different sensing objects, including those with no fixed locations (e.g. sensors mounted on public transport). The VO metadata proposed in this work includes the VO ID, name, type, a Boolean property indicating if the underlying real world object is mobile and the location, expressed in terms of a WGS84 modelled latitude, longitude and a geohash[5] value.

1.3.1.2 *Sensor Ontologies*

Early modelling efforts for sensor and actuator networks were driven by the Sensor Web Enablement (SWE) initiative [10] of the Open Geospatial Consortium (OGC) which defined a set of XML schemas and standards aimed at discovering Web accessible sensor networks and archived data. The widely accepted sensor ontology, which builds upon the SWE initiatives, is the SSN ontology [16] from the W3Cs Incubator Group on Semantic Sensor Networks[6] to describe sensors and sensor networks. The SSN ontology describes sensors from a number of perspectives [26], including those representing: a) *Sensor*: definition of a sensor, to include anything that can estimate or calculate the value of a phenomenon, the sensing procedure and what is being sensed, b) *System*: to model systems of sensors and their deployment, c) *Feature*: the property being sensed and, d) *Observation*: observation values and their metadata. The different modules of the SSN ontology are shown in Fig. 1.5. The SSN ontology, however, does not include modelling aspects for features of interest, units of measurement and domain knowledge that are related to sensor data and need to be associated with the observed data to support autonomous data communications and efficient reasoning and decision making processes. Extensions to other components in the IoT domain are not specified in the ontology.

---

[4]Internet Connected Objects for Reconfigurable Ecosystems (iCore), http://www.iot-icore.eu.
[5]Geohash, http://geohash.org/.
[6]http://www.w3.org/2005/Incubator/ssn/.

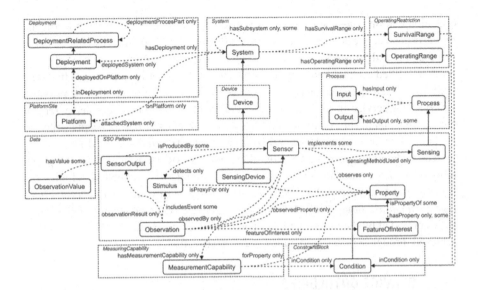

FIGURE 1.5

The SSN ontology and conceptual modules, see W3C SSN-XG report [69]

The CSIRO sensor ontology [41] was the precursor of the W3C SSN sensor ontology. It provides a semantic description of sensors in terms of the sensor grounding (platform, dimensions, calibration, power-source and access mechanism) and operation specification (operation, process and results). Concepts for sensor measurements are not part of the ontology. Moreover, similar to the SSN ontology, concepts for domain knowledge, units of measurement, location etc. are not included. Thus, more modelling concepts are needed to link the sensor descriptions to sensor measurements and then to the real-world objects in the WoT domain. Previous sensor description models include OntoSensor [50] which constructs an ontology-based descriptive specification model for sensors by excerpting parts of SensorML [11] descriptions and extending the IEEE Suggested Upper Merged Ontology (SUMO).[7] However, it does not provide a descriptive model for observation and measurement data.

In contrast to generic thing or device ontologies which may be applied to sensor or actuator instantiations, a number of recent research initiatives have specifically looked at modelling actuators and their functionalities by extending the SSN ontology. The Semantic Actuator Network (SAN) ontology [56] proposes the *Actuator-Stimulus-Operation* modelling pattern as analogous to the *Sensor-Stimulus-Operation* pattern of the SSN ontology. According to this model, an actuator is an object that modifies an environment property by producing a stimulus. The *Operation* concept describes the dynamic description of an actuator by defining the actuator

---

[7]http://www.ontologyportal.org/.

operation that modifies the property of a specific *feature of interest*. The *feature* and *property* perspective are the same as in the SSN ontology, with the only change being that features and properties are 'changed by actuators instead of being' sensed.

A simplified actuator ontology for home care systems has been proposed by Wang et al. [64] where an actuator is modelled as a refinement of a *Device* and provides a *Service*. A service in turn supports a number of *Operations* which have zero or more *Parameters*. The *Actuator* class is further sub-classed into concepts suited to the home domain, such as *Alarm*, *DVDPlayer*, *Light*, *MobilePhone*, and *TV*.

The wide adoption of the SSN ontology and its extensions as well as the possibility of semantic annotation of generic objects through the available ontologies can lay credence to the claim that *"the solutions for the representation of 'things' have reached a mature stage"* [26]. However, to address the heterogeneity of the functionalities provided by the things, a higher abstraction level is required. This is typically achieved through services, as detailed in the next section.

1.3.2 SERVICE ONTOLOGIES

To facilitate the development of large-scale, loosely coupled WoT applications, researchers have been applying service-oriented principles to decouple the sensing/actuating functionalities of the WoT things and their hosts. The main tenet has been to abstract the things functionalities and capabilities in terms of standard service interfaces to support uniform service operations.

1.3.2.1 *OWL-S Based Ontologies*

The semantic annotation methodology of Web Services has been adopted in the WoT domain by researchers to expose services offered by the smart objects. The modelled services provide functionalities to provide information about entities they are associated with or to manipulate the physical properties of the related entities or their surrounding environment. The OWL-S model for SOAP/WSDL services is based on the Profile-Process-Grounding pattern and much of the complexity stems from the process modelling. Semantic modelling efforts in the WoT area apply a modified version of the OWL-S modelling constructs, which is referred to as the profile-model-grounding design pattern, where the profile and grounding are adapted from OWL-S and refined to fit RESTful services and the model excludes process modelling and is based on the atomic service modelling in OWL-S and RESTful service modelling in hREST. The service profile represents the non-functional aspects of the service; what the service is. The service model defines the functional aspects of the service to describe its behaviour and the grounding describes the access details of the service.

The IoT-A project applied the OWL-S principles to service modelling as part of their entity-resource-service ontology suite. The service model [20] represents the functionalities provided by the resource in terms of the IOPE (input, output, precondition, effect) terms. The input and output types are detailed by linking to defined

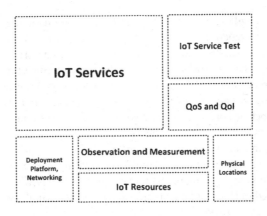

FIGURE 1.6

IoT.est service description ontology modules, see Wang et al. [67]

concepts in the QU ontologies.[8] The service model also specifies the service area (i.e. the observed area for 'sensing services' and the operation area for 'actuating services') and the service schedule (to specify time constraints on service availability).

Similar service ontology models have been proposed in [32] and applied to calculating service cost for service selection and in [15] for identifying service related events in IoT environments.

The IoT.est project[9] focussed on the senor-as-a-service paradigm [44] and proposed a semantic IoT service description model for knowledge representation [67]. The design aims to balance the trade-off between being lightweight and completeness in addition to focussing on modularity. They adopt the design pattern of [18] for modelling in the WoT domain, and provide a service model which can be accessed through SOAP/WSDL and RESTful services. The service model applies the OWL-S [40] principles to define a service profile which includes the service name, category, QoS and location; a service model which defines the operations allowed on the service; and the grounding which describes the interaction elements, (e.g. endpoint addresses and communication protocols), and captures the RESTful resources (e.g. Input/Output parameters and the corresponding access URLs). Quality of Service (QoS) and Quality of Information (QoI), are also modelled, including relationships that link to the 'service' class. The defined ontology also incorporates test features to enable automated test case creation and execution. The designed test model enables model-based testing of IoT service capabilities and automated test data creation. The various modules of the service ontology are shown in Fig. 1.6.

---

[8]Library for Quantity Kinds and Units: schema, based on QUDV model OMG SysML, Version 1.2, https://www.w3.org/2005/Incubator/ssn/ssnx/qu/qu-rec20.html.

[9]Internet of Things Environment for Service Creation and Testing (IoT.est), http://ict-iotest.eu/iotest/.

The OWL-S specification also forms the basis of the dynamic service ontology proposed in [45] to model transactions in the IoT domain. The service profile element of OWL-S is expanded with a *ServiceStatus* class to describe the current status of entity services. The *ServiceStatus* class is defined in terms of a *name* (as string), *location* (as latitude, longitude or other physical locations), *current status* (which can take 3 values: atomic, composite or simple status), *complicating count* (representing the number of concurrent services) and *waiting sequence* (representing the transactions waiting on the entity). The *ServiceStatus* class instance values support the selection, combination and control of entity services.

The semantic information model in the *ForwarDS-IoT* discovery service [24] also applies the profile-model-grounding pattern of OWL-S to describe services. The Service class is linked to both the Sensor and Actuator classes in the information model through the *exposes* property.

In contrast to the above approaches, the PT-SOA ontology model [74] applies the OWL-S constructs of process-profile-grounding as is. The *Service* class is linked to a PT instance through the *providedBy* and *appliedTo* properties, as a service is provided by a physical thing and may also be applied to, i.e. influence, another thing. The conventional OWL-S ontology is extended with the *context precondition* and *context effect* classes to specify the dynamic requirements and subsequent effects of each service of a PT.

1.3.2.2 *Other Service Ontologies*

Thoma et al. [60] outline a service description for sensor node services in an RDF version of USDL (Unified Service Description Language). The main focus of the semantic annotation of sensor nodes and network services is their integration with enterprise IT systems. The description model specifies the interaction protocol (including input and output parameters), the service model, provider details, links to the service executable, legal conditions and the service providing business entity. The Semantic Service Description (SSD) ontology [28] aims to support the translation of platform-specific configuration into semantic metadata to achieve interoperability between services offered by physical objects and deployment platforms. The proposed ontology has a main concept of *ServiceObject* which is defined in terms of 3 main classes: *Property*, *Capability* and *Server Profile*. Each class property value is defined as a key-value pair. The Property class describes the static properties of the underlying object, the capability class describes the data provided by the service in terms of its name, data type, data unit and condition. The server profile contains classes and properties describing the server name, URL and the available server actions such as deploy, uninstall and update. Each action comprises of HTTP methods such as GET, POST, PUT, UPDATE, user request destination, HTTP header and content.

The work presented in [35] proposes an ontology-based model for service oriented sensor data and networks. The ontology consists of three main classes: *ServiceProperty*, *LocationProperty*, and *PhysicalProperty*. *ServiceProperty* explains the functionality of a service, while properties in the other two components describe contextual and physical characteristics of the sensor nodes in wireless sensor network architecture. The system, however, does not specify how sensor data will be described and interpreted in a sensor network application.

The service ontology defined as part of the IoT-based service integration ontology (IIO) [51] represents services in a smart city. It is represented in terms of a *Topic*, defined by developers and used to distinguish between service offerings in the city. The service class is further defined in terms of the *Method* concept (Create, Read, Update, Delete methods) to reference WoT resources, URLs and repositories to reference the service platform, and links to the *User* class.

1.3.3 DATA ONTOLOGIES

As the next step to the semantic modelling of the physical objects of the WoT and their capabilities exposed as services, it is necessary to review the information available from such resources, either as a result from their interactions or from the observation of the ambient environment. Data ontologies in the WoT mainly describe Observation and Measurement (O&M) data, mostly focusing on how data is generated, what the data is and what real world phenomena or features may be related to the data. In addition, metadata on when and where the data is generated is usually included. This section presents both data ontologies designed for annotating instantaneous and streaming O&M data.

1.3.3.1 *Observation and Measurement Data Ontologies*

A number of works have looked at extending the syntactic XML OGC schemas to semantic models to link the domain knowledge to external schemas and enable cross-domain query and reasoning. Annotation of observation data with external temporal and geographical concepts using the Linked Data principles is demonstrated in [65]. In this work, observations are annotated with time (at which they occurred) and location concepts published by DBpedia.[10] This work does not address annotating a series of observations and its subsequent storage or querying over past data. In the Linked Sensor Middleware (LSM) and in [5], sensor data is annotated using relevant links to concepts in DBpedia and GeoNames. However, in these approaches, the focus is on provisioning the sensed data through common interfaces.

Semantic data models to manage sensor data are also presented in [27,43,3] with ontology models based on OGCs O&M standard. The models defined in [27,43] attach a time stamp to each observation using OWL-time ontology.[11] The key concepts modelled in the SemSOS O&M-OWL ontology [27] are observation, process, feature (abstraction of real-world entity) and phenomenon (property of a feature that can be sensed or measured). The observation location, result data and sampling time are also captured. The O&M concepts are aligned to SensorML and the feature and phenomenon concepts pertain to the weather domain. In [43], the authors retrieve observational data from a number of weather stations in the US and develop a method

---

[10]wiki.dbpedia.org/.

[11]http://www.w3.org/TR/owl-time/.

to convert this raw textual data into RDF. The model captures the time, location and type attributes of the observation data. Location information is linked to concepts in GeoNames to enable answering queries related to location of sensors near a place name. The *SensorData* ontology [3] defines a semantic form of the OGC SWE common data model. Each SWE data record encompasses the quantity being measured and associates it with instances of the NASA SWEET ontology[12] to specify measurement units. A similar approach to separate the observations from the entity being observed is presented in the SEEK Extensible Observation Ontology (OBOE) [12], which has a core observation ontology, units extension, and a further extension for domain use (coastal ecosystems). Each observation is modelled to have a measurement, with an example provided for a coastal ecosystem domain. The concepts in the OBOE ontology would require to be extended to include generic features of possible IoT smart objects. Also, placeholders to include sensor descriptions from other ontologies would be required.

The VO ontology in [71] incorporates *Information* elements to represent the O&M data sensed by the VOs. Each information instance has a *name* and *semanticURI* that specifies the type of the observed feature (e.g. temperature) in terms of an instance in an external domain model, for instance, the vocabulary of climate and forecast features (CF) taxonomy.[13] The actual O&M data is represented through a literal *value*, its unit of measurement drawn from vocabularies such as the ontology, the time the measurement was recorded and the location of measurement as specified by a geohash string.

1.3.3.2 *Semantic Annotation for Sensor Data Streams*

As pointed out in a recent survey of WoT search techniques [73], much of the work on sensor data streams has focused on using sensor Data Stream Management Systems (DSMS) that employ continuous queries over the data streams. However, a couple of recent works have investigated semantic annotation of sensor streams.

The O&M data attributes modelled in [4] include ID, timestamp, value, unit (using SWEET ontology), datatype, location (expressed as a geohash) as well as links to external metadata (such as DBpedia and GeoNames).

The Stream Annotation Ontology (SAO) [37] extends the SSN ontologys observation concept through the *StreamData* class that captures *segment* or *points* of the O&M stream, linked to time intervals or time instants.

1.3.3.3 *Units of Measurement Ontologies*

A discussion of WoT data ontologies is incomplete without presenting the ontology efforts for describing units of measurement that are vital for representing data measurements. Unit of Measurement (UoM) is one important aspect of sensor observation data as it helps to avoid ambiguous information from sensor values and provides explicit meaning to the sensed data.

---

[12]http://sweet.jpl.nasa.gov/ontology.

[13]Climate and Forecast Features, http://www.w3.org/2005/Incubator/ssn/ssnx/cf/cf-feature.

NASAs Semantic Web for Earth and Environment Terminology (SWEET) defines concepts of Representation, Realm, Phenomena, Processes, Human Activities, Matter, etc. It also defines Property, State, and Relation to express relationships between the concepts. Units are defined in NASA SWEET by using Unidatas UDUnits,[14] providing conversion factors between various units [46]. Unlike NASA SWEET, W3C Quantities, Units, Dimensions and Values (QUDV)[15] focuses more on data-related concepts. It defines modules of Data, Unit, Scale, Quantity, and Dimension for expressing values. Multiple Classes and Properties are defined under related modules for detailed expression. Focusing on terminology used in science and engineering, Quantities, Units, Dimensions and Data Types Ontologies (QUDT[16]) aims to provide a consistent vocabulary, which can be used by both human and machines, while maintaining extensibility. In order to enable interoperability and data exchange between information systems without ambiguities, it defines three main classes of *Dimension*, *Quantity* and *Unit*. The simple Units Ontology (UO) [23] is defined and classified with respect to different kinds of unit, such as acceleration unit, density unit, etc. Similarly, Ontology of Units of Measure and Related Concepts (OM) [49] also defines classes based on quantity and related kinds. An early ontological effort for representing units was the Measurement Units Ontology (MUO)[17] that follows the Unified Code for Units of Measure (UCUM) [22], and defines basic classes such as *BaseUnit*, *DerivedUnit*, etc. and relationships (e.g. *derivesFrom*, *numericalValue*, etc.). A survey of other UoM ontologies is described in [48].

1.3.4 LOCALIZATION MODELS

A number of generic location models at different levels of granularity (city-wide, buildings) have been proposed to support the modelling of the core WoT elements outlined in the preceding sections and to provide location context to the modelled entities.

The indoor location ontology in [19] is used to describe a *place* and its location relatively to others, to allow reasoning on adjacency, access etc. the *place* concept is further refined into *building*, *premise* and *floor*. These concepts are formally defined in terms of logical OWL-DL predicates, e.g. a *building* is defined as a place not contained in any other place and containing at least one *floor*. *Premises* are further refined into *Room*, *House*, *Shop* etc. Properties interlinking the various place concepts are also defined, including those defining containment, adjacency (including directions), access and inclusion. A similar indoor location ontology is defined in [63] representing buildings, floors, laboratories and meeting rooms in a university campus. For representing wider, city-scale location features, the GeoNames geographical database is an important source as it provides user-friendly location names or geographical

---

[14]http://www.unidata.ucar.edu/software/udunits/.
[15]https://www.w3.org/2005/Incubator/ssn/ssnx/qu/qu.
[16]http://www.qudt.org/.
[17]http://idi.fundacionctic.org/muo/.

coordinates of geographical features and captures the associated contextual information on region containment and distance among locations. Following the linked data principles, ontology instances in other domain independent models (e.g. device, service etc.) can refer to GeoNames place names through the unique URI to enable semantic reasoning related to relative positioning. The WGS84 RDF model [2] is a simple vocabulary for representing latitude, longitude and altitude information of a geographical point.

The CityGML ontology[18] is an OWL version of the CityGML standard that has created by generating the classes, properties and axioms from the CityGML XML schemas, which aim at representing virtual 3D city models. The city space representation is based on the Geography Markup Language version 3.1.1 (GML3) and includes concepts for land use, vegetation, tunnel, transportation, water body, bridge, building etc. The DBpedia RDF dataset also hosts unique semantic identifiers and descriptions for cities and region features around the world as instances of the *Place* concept in the DBpedia ontology, containing properties defining region containment as a hierarchy of places and other information. The DBpedia instances can also enable location-aware semantic reasoning in WoT applications.

1.4 DOMAIN MODELS
1.4.1 ENVIRONMENT MODELS

This section presents ontologies that model the home/office/public buildings environment along with associated applications and influencing factors such as energy efficiency and thermal control of building elements. Also presented is the ontology that extends the SSN sensor ontology to the agriculture domain.

1.4.1.1 *Home Automation*

The domotics application domain has been the focus of a number of research applications and modelling efforts due to increasing numbers of 'smart' home appliances being shipped that can interact among themselves and overall, contribute to the 'smart home' vision.

The DogOnt ontology [9] supports device and network independent description of homes, including both 'controllable' (i.e. appliances) and 'structural' (e.g. room, garden, garage) elements. Defined properties link these elements to their *functionality*, defined in terms of notification, query and control functionalities, state and communication components. The Smart Appliances REFerence (SAREF) ontology[19] [17] has been proposed to abstract the communication protocol heterogeneity and energy profiles of appliances in the smart home domain. It contains the generic concepts derived

---

[18]http://cui.unige.ch/citygml/2.0/.
[19]http://ontology.tno.nl/saref/.

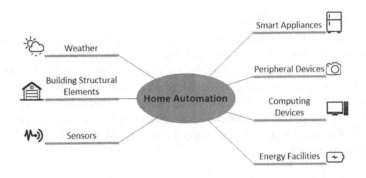

FIGURE 1.7

Themes in Home Automation ontologies

from the semantic annotation of other assets (standards, protocols, devices, datamodels etc.) in the smart appliances domain. It has a core concept of a *Device* which represents objects found in households, public buildings and offices. Each device offers *functions* through associated *commands*. A *function* is presented to the network through a *Service*, which specifies the input and output parameters. Each *device* is also characterized by an *Energy/Power profile* to optimize energy efficiency within a building environment. The home environment ontology proposed by Joo et al. [33] models home structural elements such as door, window, boiler etc. as well as a number of appliances that may be found in a typical home, including appliances (fridge, toaster, microwave oven), peripheral devices (camera, microphone etc.), computing devices (PC, home server, set-top box etc.) and sensing devices (e.g. location and security sensor). The developed home ontology is used to support service classification and execution as part of the intelligent home service framework (iHSF). The smart Building Ontology for Ambient Intelligence (BOnSAI) [58] includes concepts for functionality (services) of devices along with their communication protocol specification, environment, users and context. A simplified model of different types of rooms in a home, objects located in these different rooms along with their current state is modelled in [13].

In contrast to the above ontologies that focus on the smart objects within the home environment, the 'ThinkHome' ontology [47] has an energy and user comfort focus, with concepts defined for the building structure, actor (human user and software agent), comfort, energy providers, process and resource. The ontology enables the self-regulation of the cooling system according to a defined schedule. The 'SmartHomeWeather' ontology [57] facilitates predictive control of home elements such as window opening, garden irrigation etc. The weather ontology models the weather report and its source, the weather state and weather phenomena (such as wind, temperature, cloud cover, humidity, precipitation, sun position etc.). As presented above, the domotics area has received a substantive research attention and has been the driver for a number of semantic modelling efforts. The different themes captured in the different models are depicted in Fig. 1.7.

1.4.1.2 *Agriculture Meteorology*

The Phenonet ontology [30] extends the SSN ontology to the agriculture meteorology domain and links sensor descriptions and data to information about crop trials. The Phenonet part of the ontology defines the main concepts of *crop*, the *Treatment* and its type, the crop *genotype* and the *plot* characteristics, including *soilSlice*. The *SamplingFeature* class links the samples from the plot and *soilSlice* class to the ssn:Sensor class. The ontology facilitates automatic annotation of sensor data streams, enables discovery of resource from trial data sets and provides a standard way to publish crop trial experiments data.

1.4.2 USER-ORIENTED MODELS

This section presents ontology efforts that focus on human activities, including learning scenarios and the home care (or assisted living) scenarios.

1.4.2.1 *Ambient Assisted Living (AAL)*

Most of the ontology modeling efforts in the AAL domain have focused on activity recognition and ambient intelligence, with some also aiming to capture user modeling and personalization. The context-aware infrastructure ontology and the functional activity ontology have been proposed as part of the ontology based activity recognition (OBAR) system [68]. Concepts such as location, sensors, object and context are modelled in the infrastructure ontology to provide context to the *Human Posture* and *Functional Activity* classes of the functional activity ontology. The system applies Semantic Web Rule Language (SWRL) reasoning to infer 13 activities, including 'eating & drinking', 'take a bath' etc. and a range of human postures such as 'standing', 'sitting' or 'lying down'.

Real-time activity recognition is the focus on the ontology presented in Efthymiou et al., [21] which represents concepts such as *Computational entity*, *Person*, *Activity*, *Simple Event* and *Environment*. Information obtained from sensors is stored in the *Computational entity* class, with the knowledge inferred from reasoning on the stored data applied to the *Simple Event* class. Events are *included in* an *Activity*, which has a beginning and end time. The *Person* class is linked to the *Activity* class through the *participates in* property.

The Assisted Living ontology [75] defines a number of modules covering different aspects, including *Person Profile* encompassing the persons habits, impairment and preferences; *Health* encompassing disease, its symptoms and treatment aspects; W3C time ontology; and a *Core* ontology that is imported from the activity recognition ontology of [21]. The ontology modules enable rule-based and case-based reasoning to deduce activities and take into account a persons health.

The user profile ontology [55] in the MobileSage project is aimed at user modelling and personalisation reasoning to provide assistance services to people with dementia. The profile aspects are modelled through five classes: *CapabilityProfile*, *InterestProfile*, *PreferenceProfile*, *EducationProfile* and *HealthProfile*. The ambient environment is modelled through *Context*, *Location* and *Activity* classes.

1.4.2.2 *IoT-Enabled e-Learning*

The IMS Learning Design (IMS-LD) ontology [59] provides a semantic representation of learning resources and smart objects, while taking into account the learners activities. The ontology defines *Learning Objects* as addressable digital or physical learning resources, which could take the form of Web resources or physical resources attached with IoT devices such as sensors, actuators or tags. Smart *Learning Objects* are abstracted as virtual objects which have properties describing their functionalities, location and status. The *Learning Record Store* models the data collected as a result of the learners activity and use of the *Learning Objects*. The associated xAPI ontology adds semantic meaning to the collected data.

A different perspective is captured in the *u-learning* object model [31], which captures the relationships between the learner, the learning resources and the educational content. The core concept is that of a *service object* that links to the *Learner, Device object* and *Content object* classes. The *Content object* can be text/image/video/audio and is further defined through metadata such as an *object profile, attribute container,* time and location.

1.5 DISCUSSION AND OUTLOOK

This section presents a discussion of the findings from the review of the existing work and an outlook towards the future direction of WoT ontology modelling based on the authors experience in knowledge modelling in the WoT field over the course of several IoT related European projects. The discussion section is structured following the classification defined in this chapter.

1.5.1 CROSS-DOMAIN ONTOLOGY MODELS

The abstraction of the physical world things provides access to the data already produced by the things, while decoupling the physical things and the data they generate. The abstraction process also facilitates data processing steps such as aggregation, which could not be possible at the physical thing level. The service abstractions enable access to the virtual things as Web services or RESTful services. The review of the entity, virtual thing (resource), service and data ontologies reveals that most research works define semantic models for a combination of these concepts. Fig. 1.8 depicts how these crucial WoT concepts are interrelated.

As far as sensor ontologies are concerned, the SSN ontology is now the de-facto standard and starting point for all modelling efforts in the sensor domain, as evidenced by its wide adoption and numerous extensions, as listed in [1]. The ontologies for representing things have also reached a critical mass and the concepts in different ontology modelling efforts have begun to converge. An important development allied to the data ontologies, and which is related to an issue that is going to gain prominence as the data sources in the WoT continue to grow, is the W3C provenance

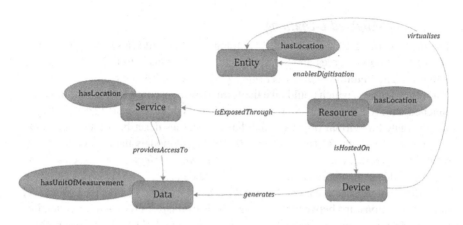

FIGURE 1.8

WoT concepts and inter-relationships

ontology.[20] The ontology models concepts which can help to uniquely identify and trace the data source generators. The ontology can be crucial in deciding whether data can be trusted and how it should be integrated with other diverse information sources.

1.5.2 DOMAIN-ORIENTED ONTOLOGY MODELS

The drive towards smart cities has motivated a number of research works and modelling efforts in allied domains such as smart home, AAL and smart appliances. Also receiving research attention are modelling efforts in buildings representation along with the energy profile and usage in buildings. The importance of domain ontologies as providing the core resource for reasoning about a domain and context is evident from the developed applications and prototypes that make use of these ontologies.

As also depicted in Fig. 1.2 through the dotted lines, we do not claim completeness of the presented categorisation and review of domain ontologies. The domains reviewed here include those that have received substantial research modelling efforts (e.g. home automation and AAL), or have formed part of large trials (e.g. agriculture meteorology). Other specific domains that have been modelled included some specific airports (e.g. Rome Fiumicino[21] and Malpensa[22] airports), smart grids[23] and

---

[20]https://www.w3.org/TR/prov-o/.

[21]http://jpo.imp.bg.ac.rs/cascade/airport-ontology/FCO/airportOntologyFCO_TBox.owl.

[22]http://jpo.imp.bg.ac.rs/cascade/airport-ontology/MXP/airportOntologyMXP_TBox.owl.

[23]http://ns.cerise-project.nl/energy/def/cim-smartgrid.

smart environments.[24] The READY4SmartCities project[25] maintains a catalogue of ontologies and datasets relevant to the smart cities and smart home domain.

1.5.3 OUTLOOK

The study presented in the previous sections shows that ontology modelling efforts have largely concentrated on the active objects of the WoT, i.e. devices, specifically sensors (and to some extent actuators), the data produced by such objects and the abstraction of their interaction methods through service models. The other focus has been on conversion of existing syntactic models, such as those in XML, into their semantic form, as evidenced by the body of sensor related ontologies drawing on the OGC XML schemas. However, future modelling efforts need to take into account the emergence of smart tags, such as printed electronic sensors and dynamic QR codes, that can attach to passive objects to enable them to form part of the WoT. The ontologies would need to take into account the dynamic capabilities of the smart tags, such as their different encoding and scanning processes, their reactions to environmental factors such as temperature, humidity, light and the possible reaction states they can undergo. Ontology models for smart tags can allow everyday passive objects to form part of the WoT and open up new mass-market applications such as evidence of tampering in logistics, product provenance etc. by enabling semantic reasoning of their status and captured data.

1.6 CONCLUSIONS

A good practice in ontology modelling for the WoT has been to publish the metadata as linked data, which links to other data items in different sources (e.g., domain knowledge bases and existing linked data cloud). Regarding the storage of the ontology instances, especially with regard to those of the data ontologies, a combination of centralised and distributed methods is suitable with the WoT object and service metadata in a centralised repository and the more dynamic data streams in distributed stores. To encourage the use of ontologies by practitioners and application developers, ontology designers also need to consider developing annotation tools that can make the task of creating semantic annotations of WoT objects and provisioned services, according to the defined ontologies, easier. The annotation tools need to support the CRUD (Create, Read, Update, Delete) methods which translate into publishing, reading, updating and deleting WoT concept descriptions and can ideally be implemented through a graphical user interface, as achieved in [20]. Also of importance is the ability to create linkages to existing ontology instance or data repositories in accordance with the linked data principles.

---

[24] http://casas.wsu.edu/owl/cose.owl.

[25] http://www.ready4smartcities.eu.

REFERENCES

[1] SSN applications. https://www.w3.org/community/ssn-cg/wiki/SSN_Applications, 2012.

[2] National geospatial-intelligence agency. World geodetic system 1984 (wgs-84). http://www.w3.org/2003/01/geo/wgs84_pos, 2005.

[3] Barnaghi P, Meissner S, Presser M, Moessner K. Sense and sens'ability: semantic data modelling for sensor networks. In: ICT mobile summit. 2009.

[4] Barnaghi P, Wang W, Dong L, Wang C. A linked-data model for semantic sensor streams. In: Green computing and communications (GreenCom), 2013 IEEE and Internet of things (iThings/CPSCom). IEEE international conference on and IEEE cyber, physical and social computing. August 2013. p. 468–75.

[5] Barnaghi Payam, Presser Mirko, Moessner Klaus. Publishing linked sensor data. In: Proceedings of the 3rd international conference on semantic sensor networks, vol. 668. 2010. p. 1–16.

[6] Bassbouss Louay, Kraft Andreas, Bauer Martin, Logvinov Oleg, Ben Alaya Mahdi, Longstreth Terry, Bhowmik Rajdeep, Martigne Patrica, Brett Patrica, Mladin Catalina, Chakraborty Rabindra, Monteil Thierry, Dadas Mohammed, Murdock Paul, Davies John, Nappey Philippé, Diab Wael, Raggett Dave, Drira Khalil, Roes Jasper, Eastham Bryant, Serrano Martin, El Kaed Charbel, Seydoux Nicolas, Elloumi Omar, Simmon Eric, Girod-Genet Marc, Subramaniam Ravi, Hernandez Nathalie, Swetina Joerg, Hoffmeister Michael, Underwood Mark, Jiménez Jaime, Wang Chonggang, Kanti Datta Soumya, Whitehead Cliff, Khan Imran, Zhang Yongjing, Kim Dongjoo. In: Semantic interoperability for the web of things. Murdock Paul, editor. August 2016.

[7] Bassi Alessandro, Bauer Martin, Fiedler Martin, Kramp Thorsten, van Kranenburg Rob, Lange Sebastian, Meissner Stefan. Enabling things to talk. Springer-Verlag; 2013.

[8] Bizer Christian, Heath Tom, Berners-Lee Tim. Linked data – the story so far. Int J Semantic Web Inf Syst 2009;5(3):1–22.

[9] Bonino Dario, Corno Fulvio. Modeling, simulation and emulation of intelligent domotic environments. Autom Constr 2011;20(7):967–81.

[10] Botts Mike, Percivall George, Reed Carl, Davidson John. Sensor web enablement: overview and high level architecture. Technical report. Open Geospatial Consortium (OGC); 2007.

[11] Botts Mike, Robin Alexandre. Opengis sensor model language (sensorml) implementation specification. Technical report. Open Geospatial Consortium Inc.; January 2007. OGC white paper.

[12] Bowers Shawn, Madin Joshua S, Schildhauer Mark P. A conceptual modeling framework for expressing observational data semantics. In: Conceptual modeling – ER 2008. Berlin, Heidelberg: Springer; 2008. p. 41–54.

[13] Chahuara Pedro, Portet François, Vacher Michel. Context aware decision system in a smart home: knowledge representation and decision making using uncertain contextual information. In: The 4th international workshop on acquisition, representation and reasoning with contextualized knowledge (ARCOE-12). August 2012. p. 52–64.

[14] Christophe B, Verdot V, Toubiana V. Searching the 'web of things'. In: 2011 fifth IEEE international conference on semantic computing (ICSC). September 2011. p. 308–15.

[15] Chun S, Seo S, Oh B, Lee KH. Semantic description, discovery and integration for the internet of things. In: 2015 IEEE international conference on semantic computing (ICSC). IEEE; February 2015. p. 272–5.

[16] Compton Michael, Barnaghi Payam, Bermudez Luis, García-Castro Raúl, Corcho Oscar, Cox Simon, Graybeal John, Hauswirth Manfred, Henson Cory, Herzog Arthur, Huang Vincent, Janowicz Krzysztof, Kelsey W David, Phuoc Danh Le, Lefort Laurent, Leggieri Myriam, Neuhaus Holger, Nikolov Andriy, Page Kevin, Passant Alexandre, Sheth Amit, Taylor Kerry. The SSN ontology of the W3C semantic sensor network incubator group. J Web Semant: Sci, Serv Agents World Wide Web 2012;17:25–32.

[17] Daniele Laura, den Hartog Frank, Roes Jasper. Study on semantic assets for smart appliances interoperability. Technical report. TNO; March 2015.

[18] De S, Barnaghi P, Bauer M, Meissner S. Service modelling for the internet of things. In: 2011 federated conference on computer science and information systems (FedCSIS). IEEE; September 2011. p. 949–55.

[19] De Suparna, Christophe Benoit, Moessner Klaus. Semantic enablers for dynamic digital–physical object associations in a federated node architecture for the internet of things. Ad Hoc Netw 2014;18:102–20.

[20] De Suparna, Elsaleh Tarek, Barnaghi Payam, Meissner Stefan. An internet of things platform for real-world and digital objects. Scalable Comput: Pract Exp 2012;13(1):45–57.

[21] Efthymiou V, Koutraki M, Antoniou G. Real-time activity recognition and assistance in smart classrooms. ADCAIJ: Adv Distrib Comput Artif Intel J 2013;1(1):9–22.

[22] Schadow G, McDonald CJ, Suico JG, Föhring U, Tolxdorff T. Units of measure in clinical information systems. J Am Med Inform Assoc March 1999;6(2):151–61.

[23] Hoehndorf Robert, Gkoutos Georgios V, Schofield Paul N. The units ontology: a tool for integrating units of measurement in science. Database, October 2012. Oxford.

[24] Gomes Porfirio, Cavalcante Everton, Rodrigues Taniro, Batista Thais, Deli. A federated discovery service for the internet of things. In: Proceedings of the 2Nd workshop on middleware for context-aware applications in the IoT. Vancouver, BC, Canada: ACM; 2015. p. 25–30.

[25] Gyrard Amelie. Designing cross-domain semantic web of things applications. PhD thesis. Telecom ParisTech; April 2015.

[26] Hachem Sara. Service-oriented middleware for the large-scale mobile internet of things. PhD thesis. University of Versailles Saint-Quentin-en-Yvelines; February 2014.

[27] Henson Cory A, Pschorr Josh K, Sheth Amit P, Thirunarayan Krishnaprasad. Semsos: semantic sensor observation service. In: Proceedings of the 2009 international symposium on collaborative technologies and systems, CTS '09. 2009.

[28] Hur K, Jin X, Lee KH. Automated deployment of iot services based on semantic description. In: 2015 IEEE 2nd world forum on internet of things (WF-IoT). December 2015. p. 40–5.

[29] Jara Antonio J, Olivieri Alex C, Bocchi Yann Bocchi, Jung Markus, Kastner Wolfgang, Skarmeta Antonio F. Semantic web of things: an analysis of the application semantics for the iot moving towards the iot convergence. Int J Web Grid Serv April 2014;10(2/3):244–72.

[30] Jayaraman PP, Palmer D, Zaslavsky A, Georgakopoulos D. Do-it-yourself digital agriculture applications with semantically enhanced iot platform. In: 2015 IEEE tenth international conference on intelligent sensors, sensor networks and information processing (ISSNIP). April 2015. p. 1–6.

[31] Jeong K, Kim HS, Chong I. Knowledge driven composition model for woo based self-directed smart learning environment. In: 2015 international conference on information networking (ICOIN). January 2015. p. 537–40.

[32] Jin Xiongnan, Chun Sejin, Jung Jooik, Lee Kyong-Ho. A fast and scalable approach for iot service selection based on a physical service model. Inf Syst Front 2016:1–16.

[33] Joo I, Park J, Paik E. Developing ontology for intelligent home service framework. In: 2007 IEEE international symposium on consumer electronics. June 2007. p. 1–6.

[34] Kelaidonis D, Somov A, Foteinos V, Poulios G, Stavroulaki V, Vlacheas P, et al. Virtualization and cognitive management of real world objects in the internet of things. In: 2012 IEEE international conference on green computing and communications (GreenCom). IEEE; November 2012. p. 187–94.

[35] Kim JH, Kwon H, Kim DH, Kwak HY, Lee SJ. Building a service-oriented ontology for wireless sensor networks. In: Seventh IEEE/ACIS international conference on computer and information science, 2008. ICIS 08. May 2008. p. 649–54.

[36] Kolchin Maxim, Klimov Nikolay, Andreev Alexey, Shilin Ivan, Garayzuev Daniil, Mouromtsev Dmitry, Zakoldaev Danil. Ontologies for web of things: a pragmatic review. In: Knowledge engineering and semantic web. Cham: Springer International Publishing; 2015. p. 102–16.

[37] Kolozali S, Bermudez-Edo M, Puschmann D, Ganz F, Barnaghi P. A knowledge-based approach for real-time iot data stream annotation and processing. In: Internet of things (iThings), 2014 IEEE international conference on, and green computing and communications (GreenCom), IEEE and cyber, physical and social computing (CPSCom), IEEE. September 2014. p. 215–22.

[38] Le-Phuoc Danh, Nguyen-Mau Hoan Quoc, Parreira Josiane Xavier, Hauswirth Manfred. A middleware framework for scalable management of linked streams. J Web Seman: Sci, Serv Agents World Wide Web 2012;16:42–51. The Semantic Web Challenge 2011.

[39] Manate B, Munteanu VI, Fortis TF. Towards a smarter internet of things: semantic visions. In: 2014 eighth international conference on complex, intelligent and software intensive systems (CISIS). July 2014. p. 582–7.

[40] Martin David, Burstein Mark, Hobbs Jerry, Lassila Ora, McDermott Drew, McIlraith Sheila, Narayanan Srini, Paolucci Massimo, Parsia Bijan, Payne Terry, Sirin Evren, Srinivasan Naveen, Sycara Katia. Owl-s: semantic markup for web services. W3C Member Submission, November 2004.

[41] Neuhaus H, Compton M. The semantic sensor network ontology: a generic language to describe sensor assets. In: Pre-conference workshop on challenges in geospatial data harmonisation (AGILE 2009). 2009. p. 1–33.

[42] oneM2M partners. Base ontology. Technical report, oneM2M, June 2016. Technical specification TS-0012-V-0.10.0.

[43] Patni H, Henson C, Sheth A. Linked sensor data. In: Proc. international symposium on collaborative technologies and systems (CTS). 2010. p. 362–70.

[44] Perera Charith, Zaslavsky Arkady, Christen Peter, Georgakopoulos Dimitrios. Sensing as a service model for smart cities supported by internet of things. Trans Emerg Telecommun Technol January 2014;25(1):81–93.

[45] Qu Chao, Liu Fagui, Tao Ming, Deng Dacheng. An OWL-S based specification model of dynamic entity services for internet of things. J Ambient Intell Humaniz Comput 2016;7(1):73–82.

[46] Raskin Rob, Pan Michael. Semantic web for Earth and environmental terminology (sweet). In: Proc. of the workshop on semantic web technologies for searching and retrieving scientific data. 2003.

[47] Reinisch Christian, Kofler MarioJ, Iglesias Félix, Kastner Wolfgang. Thinkhome energy efficiency in future smart homes. EURASIP J Embed Syst 2010;2011(1):1–18.

[48] Rijgersberg H, Wigham M, Top JL. How semantics can improve engineering processes: a case of units of measure and quantities. Adv Eng Inform 2011;25(2):276–87. Information mining and retrieval in design.

[49] Rijgersberg Hajo, van Assem Mark, Top Jan. Ontology of units of measure and related concepts. Semant Web January 2013;4(1):3–13.

[50] Russomanno DJ, Kothari C, Thomas O. Sensor ontologies: from shallow to deep models. In: Thirty-seventh southeastern symposium on system theory. 2005.

[51] Ryu Minwoo, Kim Jaeho, Yun Jaeseok. Integrated semantics service platform for the internet of things: a case study of a smart office. Sensors 2015;15(1):2137.

[52] Shelby Z, Hartke K, Bormann C. Constrained application protocol (coap). RFC 7252 18. Internet Engineering Task Force (IETF); March 2013.

[53] Shiao Maria. Internet of things standardisation and architectures – workshop report. Technical report. Alliance for Internet of Things Innovation (AIOTI); 2015.

[54] Simons BA, Yu J, Cox SJD. Defining a water quality vocabulary using qudt and chebi. In: 20th international congress on modelling and simulation. December 2013.

[55] Skillen K, Chen L, Nugent CD, Donnelly MP, Solheim I. A user profile ontology based approach for assisting people with dementia in mobile environments. In: Annual international conference of the IEEE engineering in medicine and biology society, EMBC. 2012. p. 6390–3.

[56] Spalazzi L, Taccari G, Bernardini A. An internet of things ontology for earthquake emergency evaluation and response. In: 2014 international conference on collaboration technologies and systems (CTS). May 2014. p. 528–34.

[57] Staroch Paul. A weather ontology for predictive control in smart homes. Master's thesis. Vienna University of Technology; August 2013.

[58] Stavropoulos Thanos G, Vrakas Dimitris, Vlachava Danai, Bassiliades Nick. Bonsai: a smart building ontology for ambient intelligence. In: Proceedings of the 2Nd international conference on web intelligence, mining and semantics, vol. 30. New York, NY, USA: ACM; 2012. p. 30.

[59] Taamallah Aroua, Khemaja Maha. Designing and experiencing smart objects based learning scenarios: an approach combining ims ld, xapi and iot. In: Proceedings of the second international conference on technological ecosystems for enhancing multiculturality, TEEM '14. New York, NY, USA: ACM; 2014. p. 373–9.

[60] Thoma M, Sperner K, Braun T. Service descriptions and linked data for integrating wsns into enterprise it. In: 2012 third international workshop on software engineering for sensor network applications (SESENA). June 2012. p. 43–8.

[61] Vermesan Ovidiu, Friess Peter, Guillemin Patrick, Gusmeroli Sergio, Sundmaeker Harald, Bassi Alessandro, Jubert Ignacio, Mazura Margaretha, Harrison Mark, Eisenhauer Markus, Doody Pat. Internet of things strategic research roadmap. In: Internet of things – global technological and societal trends. Series in communications. River Publishers; 2011. p. 9–52.

[62] Vermesan Ovidiu, Friess Peter, Guillemin Patrick, Sundmaeker Harald, Eisenhauer Markus, Moessner Klaus, Arndt Marilyn, Spirito Maurizio, Medagliani Paolo, Giaffreda Raffaele, Gusmeroli Sergio, Ladid Latif, Serrano Martin, Hauswirth Manfred, Baldini Gianmarco. Internet of things – strategic research and innovation agenda. In: Internet of things applications – from research and innovation to market deployment. Series in communications. River Publishers; 2014. p. 7–142.

[63] Wang W, De S, Cassar G, Moessner K. Knowledge representation in the internet of things: semantic modelling and its applications. Automatika – J Control, Measurement, Electron, Comput Commun October 2013;54(4):388–400.

[64] Wang Feng, Turner Kenneth J. An ontology-based actuator discovery and invocation framework. In: An ontology-based actuator discovery and invocation framework in home care systems. Berlin, Heidelberg: Springer; 2009. p. 66–73.

[65] Wang Wei, Barnaghi Payam. Semantic annotation and reasoning for sensor data. In: Barnaghi Payam, Moessner Klaus, Presser Mirko, Meissner Stefan, editors. Smart sensing and context: Proceedings of the 4th European conference. Berlin, Heidelberg: Springer; 2009. p. 66–76.

[66] Wang Wei, De Suparna, Cassar Gilbert, Moessner Klaus. An experimental study on geospatial indexing for sensor service discovery. Expert Syst Appl 2015;42(7):3528–38.

[67] Wang Wei, De Suparna, Toenjes Ralf, Reetz Eike, Moessner Klaus. A comprehensive ontology for knowledge representation in the internet of things. In: IEEE 11th international conference on trust, security and privacy in computing and communications. IEEE Computer Society; June 2012. p. 1793–8.

[68] Wongpatikaseree K, Ikeda M, Buranarach M, Supnithi T, Lim AO, Tan Y. Activity recognition using context-aware infrastructure ontology in smart home domain. In: 2012 seventh international conference on knowledge, information and creativity support systems (KICSS). November 2012. p. 50–7.

[69] Semantic Sensor Network XG. Report work on the SSN ontology. https://www.w3.org/2005/Incubator/ssn/wiki/Report_Work_on_the_SSN_ontology, June 2011.

[70] Xu Wenyi. Modeling and exploiting the knowledge base of web of things. PhD thesis. Paris VI: Universite Pierre et Marie Curie; July 2015.

[71] Zhou Y, De S, Wang W, Moessner K. Enabling query of frequently updated data from mobile sensing sources. In: 13th IEEE international conference on ubiquitous computing and communications (IUCC 2014). IEEE Computer Society; December 2014.

[72] Yachir Ali, Djamaa Badis, Mecheti Ahmed, Amirat Yacine, Aissani Mohamed. A comprehensive semantic model for smart object description and request resolution in the internet of things. Proc Comput Sci 2016;83:147–54. The 7th international conference on ambient systems, networks and technologies (ANT 2016) / The 6th international conference on sustainable energy information technology (SEIT-2016) / affiliated workshops.

[73] Zhou Yuchao, De Suparna, Wang Wei, Moessner Klaus. Search techniques for the web of things: a taxonomy and survey. Sensors 2016;16(5):600.

[74] Zhu W, Zhou G, Yen IL, Bastani F. A pt-soa model for cps/iot services. In: 2015 IEEE international conference on web services (ICWS). IEEE; June 2015. p. 647–54.

[75] Zografistou Dimitra. Support for context-aware healthcare in ambient assisted living. Master's thesis. Heraklion: University of Crete; October 2012.

ACKNOWLEDGEMENTS

This work is supported by the collaborative European Union and Ministry of Internal Affairs and Communication (MIC), Japan, Research and Innovation action, iKaaS under EU Grant number 643262. The first author also acknowledges funding support from the TagItSmart! collaborative project supported by the European Horizon 2020 programme, contract number: 688061.

THE ANATOMY OF AN INTENT BASED SEARCH AND CRAWLER ENGINE FOR THE WEB OF THINGS

2

Ali Shemshadi*, Quan Z. Sheng[†], Yongrui Qin[‡]

School of Computer Science, The University of Adelaide, Adelaide, SA, Australia*
Department of Computing, Macquarie University, Sydney, NSW, Australia[†]
School of Computing and Engineering, University of Huddersfield, Huddersfield, United Kingdom[‡]

CHAPTER POINTS

- Provides a detailed view of the WoT search and crawler engine.
- Addresses heterogeneous data sources in our architecture.
- Identifies the trends and existing status of the WoT on the Internet.
- Showcases an use case of intent based search for flights data that is collected from WoT in real-time.

2.1 INTRODUCTION

Web of Thing (WoT) is a new paradigm in designing Web pages and making them suitable for the dissemination of the data that originates from things rather than people. WoT is one of the enabling technologies which facilitate the dissemination of things data affordable and efficient. Thus, the number of everyday physical objects which use WoT is sharply increasing. WoT is one of the main enablers of the emerging paradigms such as the Internet of Things (IoT). WoT enables the IoT paradigm to be applied in a variety of areas of applications including healthcare, mining industry, environmental sensing, transportation and logistics, and so on [8,24]. For example, through the use of the WoT infrastructure, users can track the location and schedule of aeroplanes in real-time.[1]

With the increasingly diverse range of resources on the Internet, identifying, crawling and searching of the data that is disseminated by WoT remains a challenge.

---

[1] http://www.flightradar24.com.

Managing the Web of Things. DOI: 10.1016/B978-0-12-809764-9.00003-2

Today, the options for this purpose are extremely limited. To the best of our knowledge, the only working example of the WoT search engine is *Thingful*[2] and none of the WoT search engines in the literature have been deployed for real-world or large-scale data. Furthermore, the Thingful initiation itself is still limited and significant progress is needed to expand this area. One instance of such limitations is the public availability of the collected data. For example, Thingful provides access to its data only via a dedicated UI. Another example of the limitations is the quick expiration of the data due to the highly dynamic nature of the IoT [29,28]. *Graph of Things*[3] is another interesting project which aims to provide live things data in real-time, which is still limited and can be potentially expanded in terms of scope and capabilities.

There is another search engine, namely Shodan[4] which also claims to be a search engine for IoT. The main difference between Shodan and WoT search engines such as Thingful, is that Shodan is basically designed as a search engine for hackers. It identifies and hacks into password protected devices connected to the Internet. However, it does not support the Web interface at all. Moreover, servers and routers as well as other Internet-connected devices have been archived with their IP addresses in its database. The website itself does not process sensor outputs. Due to its large and broad scope, catching everyday objects on this website is still difficult while servers and network devices constitute the majority of the things in its database. Due to ethical issues and scope matters, we do not include Shodan in our study.

The Intent based search, which is also known as intent oriented, is a popular trend in designing new search engines [48]. The existing approaches propose to either identify the intent of the search based on a set of features [14] or diversify the search results based on the known set of intentions [6]. For example, when a user searches for a product with given brand we can assume that they are looking to buy it as the same user has done it multiple times in the pas. On the other hand, the second approach can diversify the results over the set of possible intentions such as purchasing, reading reviews or finding similar products. However, the challenging issue in intent based search for WoT is to identify the set of possible intentions in the first place. One way to tackle this challenge, is to analyze the users and the contextual features of the things data. In the context of the previous example, the first step is to identify the possible/popular use cases for the page that contains product information. Then we would be able to apply different approaches to index the search intentions and prepare the results.

In this chapter, we conduct an extensive study on the current status of the WoT search and crawling and conduct an experiment to emphasize its applications in real-world scenarios. Our main contributions are summarized as follows:

[2]http://www.thingful.net.
[3]http://graphofthings.org.
[4]https://www.shodan.io.

- We propose a novel crawler and search engine, namely ThingSeek, that enables the collection of data from heterogeneous data sources. We address the needs of the future WoT search engines in our architecture. We demonstrate that how the data that is flowing between the frontend and the backend of WoT resources.
- We identify different data sources and crawl them. We use our ThingSeek crawler to collect a large dataset of things data. To address the intent based search, we propose the case scenario of flight delay analysis which can emphasize the application of WoT in our lives everyday.
- We study the general user interests on things data by using a real world query log dataset from an WoT search engine. We also analyze the characteristics of the collected things data including spatio-temporal distributions of things, data dynamics, and data quality.
- Based on the collected real-world things data and our analysis, we discuss future research challenges and identify open research problems to shed light on the future WoT research and development.

The rest of this paper is organized as follows. We provide a motivating scenario for WoT search in Section 2.2. We discuss the potential places to look for WoT over the Internet in Section 2.3. In Section 2.4, we discuss the best practices that we learn in things data acquisition and in Section 2.5 we demonstrate how the search engine can present the data for the users. In Section 2.6, we showcase an intention of search in flights data and demonstrate a possible use case for this data. Then in Section 2.7, we present the analytical results of the collected things data. We discuss some of the opportunities for further IoT research in Section 2.8. In Section 2.9, we overview the related works and Section 2.10 concludes the paper.

2.2 MOTIVATING SCENARIO

We use the scenario illustrated in Fig. 2.1 to inspire the role of future engines for crawling and searching the WoT.

In our scenario, we focus on two types of users including *smart devices* and *human users*. Specifically, two types of search queries can be identified in this scenario, which are described as follows:

- **Correlation based search**: based on Yao et al. [45], searching and recommending things using heterogeneous correlations is a promising and interesting trend in WoT research. This type of search queries can be used by both smart devices and human clients to find the things of interest.
- **Intent based search**: another trend in WoT research emphasizes the role of the knowledge that is acquired from things in real-world applications. Ragget proposes intent based search as a promising research opportunity for WoT search [30]. Accordingly, this would provide the footpath for smarter search in IoT. Thus, application specific search queries can be manipulated to improve the effectiveness

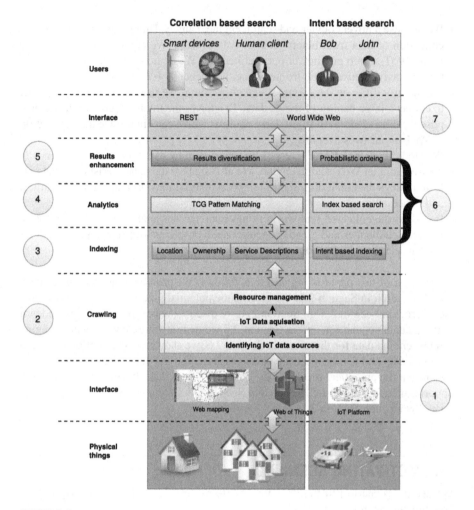

FIGURE 2.1

Motivating scenario for WoT search

of WoT search in application. Yet, this type of query is mainly useful for human clients only as the knowledge or domain specific applications cannot be easily deployed by things.

We describe each part of the motivating scenario of Fig. 2.1 as follows:

1. Initially, sensor enabled physical things propagate their data such as sensor readings and meta-data through different mediums on the Internet. This includes, real-time maps, real time Web pages which use WoT technology and WoT platforms. A crawler engine in the next level would only have access to the visible

WoT data sources on the Internet. The following steps are all activated by a user's request, which is submitted to the system as a search query. The format of the search query can be different based on the particular application.

2. A crawler engine identifies data sources and crawls them based on a pre-constructed crawling pattern. The purpose of the crawling pattern is to specify the amount of resources required to crawl the data. In addition, due to the heterogeneity of the data sources and deployed technologies, the crawler must be tuned to support, then integrate the used data formats.

3. Due to the lack of interconnection between data sources on the Internet, heterogeneous correlations are identified and used to construct networks of things. The key elements in the data, which enable us to create edges, are location, ownership meta-data and descriptive tags.

4. Pattern matching is the core of our analytic engine. It has a number of applications in our scenario. For example, it can be used to find matches for complex queries on correlation graphs. Furthermore, given the Things Correlations Graphs (TCG) from the previous steps, pattern matching can be applied to identify matching nodes from different data sources to form a larger enterprise TCG.

5. Smart devices have limited resources in terms of processing power and memory. In addition, providing unprocessed sets of all existing things that match a query, is not useful for human clients. Thus, in our scenario, the size of the search result is limited to contain k things only. Due to the ambiguity in the purpose of the search, we can select either a set of k closest things, k things with closest owners, k things that have the closest set of tags or a diversified result set. Results diversification can improve the quality of results in this stage, before they are presented to the users.

6. Alternatively, human users may use the search engine to either find things or search the knowledge that is acquired by the sensory data over the Internet. In this scenario, considering a case where a client is looking for things, two human users (John and Bob) searches for the flights to a specific destination. Assuming that they find at least two options with different airlines, they may pick one randomly. Assume that John's flight encounters a delay on the specified day and as he knows John, he wishes that he had booked the same flight as Bob. Thus, by predicting and indexing flight delays, the search engine can enable Bob to select the flight with possibility of delay.

7. Final results can be tailored and presented to the users based on the intent of search or types of things. For instance, a smart device receives a message that contains the list of top k things and a human client can receive a visualized result set instead.

This motivating scenario poses several major concerns including: (i) due to the limited capacity of machine users, the size of the response should be limited to k and thus, preparing the best response may require finding the most relevant and/or diversifying the things in the result set; (ii) based on the previous issue, given that the WoT resources are presented in singular form and are not correlated to each other, we are interested in digging the correlations and establishing a heterogeneous network of things using a scalable approach; and (iii) we are specifically interested to deploy the role of the WoT search engine in two use cases including taxi ridesharing and flight delay analysis.

2.3 IDENTIFYING DATA SOURCES

The interactions with IoT can be realized in Machine-to-Machine (M2M) as well as Machine-to-Human (M2H) [43]. The M2M approach is mainly used for smart things and enabled by predefined APIs, e.g., RESTful APIs [16,5]. In contrast, M2H can include almost every object that are connected to the Internet and enabled using current Web protocols and existing IoT middleware. Pioneering IoT cloud services such as Xively,[5] Paraimpu [26], ThingSpeak[6] and Sen.se[7] are some of the examples of IoT dedicated cloud services which provide infrastructure to store and share things data for various types of sensors. Nowadays, there are numerous examples of websites which focus on a specific type of applications such as tracking aircrafts,[8] marine traffic,[9] traffic jams[10] or Raspberry Pi board.[11]

The number of cloud IoT platforms with open access data is limited and thus, identifying them is not difficult. For WoT enabled data sources, one can check the traces of existing WoT packages such as the ones from WeIO,[12] WoT Code Forge[13] and WoT Project Directory.[14]

In principle, not all things data appears in the form of Web Mapping and not every Web based map is related to things data. Web based maps have been used for a variety of purposes including presenting things data. From our experience, those Web pages that visualize things data have the following requirements: 1) containing an interactive map; 2) being publicly available; 3) being real-time; 4) being real-world; and 5) being within valid ranges.

IoT is usually updated in real-time and vintage maps are not very useful in this case. The real-world data is a key to find real physical things, thus, maps of virtual worlds such as game maps do not provide things data. Finally, key features of the data should contain proper values. Maps with encrypted data cannot be very useful for things data collection.

---

[5]www.xively.com.
[6]www.thingspeak.com/.
[7]https://sen.se/mother.
[8]flightradar24.com.
[9]www.marinetraffic.com.
[10]www.waze.com/livemap.
[11]rastrack.co.uk.
[12]http://we-io.net.
[13]https://github.com/webofthings.
[14]https://github.com/webofthings/webofthings-projects-directory/wiki/Web-of-Things-Projects-Directory.

Based on the features of things data, which are mentioned above, we use the following procedure to identify the data sources: 1) the Web page should contain an interactive map; 2) data is presented inside the XMLHttpRequest (XHR) response of the requests that the page makes; 3) the response in the XHR may continuously be updated; and 4) data contains coordinates which are within the valid boundaries.

We leverage Web Mapping such as Google Maps which is the most dominant way of visualizing spatial data on the Web, to achieve the goal. Thus, we limit our search scope to the sources which contain a map. We use a set of keywords to narrow our search results to find such sources such as "*real-time map of [application]*", "*live map of [application]*" and "*tracker map of [application]*". In the search query, the term "application" can be replaced with any application of IoT such as *flight*. We also include some of the available IoT platforms such as Xively[15] to the initial set of data sources.

2.3.1 WOT ENABLED PLATFORMS

The WoT concept describes approaches, frameworks and programming patterns that allow things to share their data through the World Wide Web. Currently, WoT is an active research area with a range of challenges and opportunities including security, resilience, intent oriented search, legal implications and so on [30]. Backed by existing WoT packages,[16] these data sources create mashups to publish things data. One of the most popular WoT packages is the WoTKit [4]. Although some WoT packages have been used by IoT cloud services, we distinguish them from other cloud services (e.g., Xively) that are not developed based on the WoT. WoT can be applied in both of the traditional server (such as WeIO examples[17]) and the cloud based (such as SenseTecnic[18]) environments.

2.3.2 WEB MAPPING ENABLED DATA SOURCES

Web Mapping is the process of using online maps to browse and visualize geospatial data in a Web environment (e.g., Google Maps) [11]. Web Mapping is more than just Web cartography. There exist a wide variety of use cases for Web Mapping presentation of the data. In fact, we realize that a considerable number of Web pages with maps are providing things data and thus, include them in our list of data sources. The main categories of such data sources are as follows:

---

[15] https://xively.com/.

[16] https://github.com/webofthings.

[17] http://github.com/nodesign/weio/tree/master/examples.

[18] https://wotkit.sensetecnic.com/wotkit/.

- *Real-time Transportation Information Services*: Real-time tracking services (e.g., FlightRadar24[19] and Arrivebus[20]) are designed to process and share the coordination of public transport services generated by embedded GPS devices. Unlike IoT cloud platforms, these services are often publicly available and data is visualized via Web Mapping. The most dynamic attributes of the objects in these networks are location-related including latitude and longitude.
- *Urban Crowdsensing Services*: Urban crowdsourcing services provide a platform for people to report and share their observations of things around them. For example, Waze[21] provides a mobile phone application for users to report their locations, traffic jams, roadworks or police attendances. Although the collected data from this type of platforms is not originated from embedded physical sensors, the information is still related to physical or virtual things that people observe around themselves. Most often, the data is available through a Web based map.
- *Public Environmental Sensing Services*: These services include platforms that share the data originated by environmental sensors such as weather stations and pollution metrics. The data is available through a Web based map interface available to public.

2.4 THINGSEEK CRAWLER ENGINE

To minimize the required amount of work when collecting data from a new source, we have broken down the crawling procedure into a certain set of steps in a unified framework.

Fig. 2.2 illustrates the main features of the ThingSeek crawler engine. In the first step, a URL generator initializes the queue of queries. Each entry in the queue is supplied with certain parameters to construct a query to a page or a specific location. The parameters can be the time window, the boundaries of the querying region and/or other parameters. Then for each entity in the queue, a reader function reads the selected part of the page, and the contents are converted to a set of vectors and refined using a refiner. The data for each subset is separately held until all subsets are refined where we merge all of the subsets of the resource's data. In this step, a specific enricher can be used to collect the missing information, if any, from other sources. This can, for example, fill the incomplete fields such as IP address by acquiring them from Shodan. Finally, the collected data from different sources are integrated and stored on a distributed backend.

Due to the size and dynamics of the sensor-generated data, things data sources often provide a subset of their data with a call to their API. Thus, pagination techniques such as location-based queries are deployed to present the data. We use the same

---

[19]http://flightradar24.com.
[20]http://www.arrivabus.co.uk/journeyplanner/help/en?tpl=livemap.
[21]https://www.waze.com.

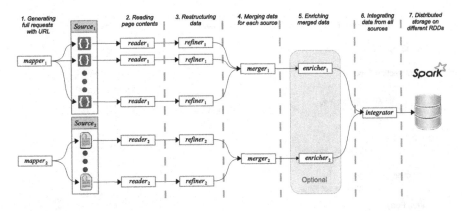

FIGURE 2.2

Architecture of the ThingSeek crawler engine

mechanism through implementing the URL generator. The URL generator plays a key role in adjusting the workload on the data source. It converts a set of spatial segments to a sequence of queries which can be submitted via the API of the data source. Thus, a highly populated area can be placed multiple times in the processing queue while an empty area may appear only once (or not appear) in the queue. For example, through a URL generator, URL b will be repeated three times for others during a scan as it contains more dynamic objects than others:

$$\begin{bmatrix} a:1 & b:3 \\ c:1 & d:1 \end{bmatrix} \implies [a, b, c, b, d, b] \tag{2.1}$$

We have developed ThingSeek using a set of tools to collect, process and visualize the dataset. Some of the tools we used are as follows: R programming language, SparkR, Apache Spark 1.4.1 and Rails framework.

To show how the data can be collected from a given data source, we can refer to Fig. 2.3. As shown, the data is flowing between two main parts: a frontend which resides on user's side and a backend which resides on the server. The frontened, generates the queries and send them to the service through a pre-designed API. The queries are for example the existing records within a given area. The queries are resolved through the given model and the data is extracted from the database. Then, it is send to the user and a javascript function updates the given div on user's page. The API address and the structure of the XMLhttpRequest that is sent to the server can be identified and used by the crawler engine.

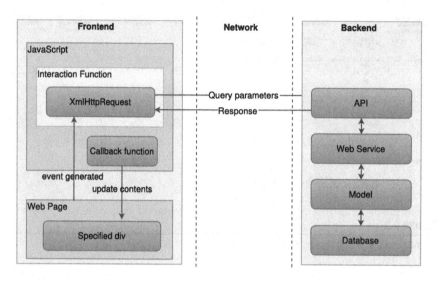

FIGURE 2.3

Architecture of a WoT resource

2.5 THINGSEEK SEARCH ENGINE

In this section, we demonstrate the functionality of the proposed ThingSeek framework.

2.5.1 SEARCH BY HUMAN USERS

Through a Web-based user interface, a human user uses the search engine to acquire information from sensors. For example, a user would like to get information from nearby weather sensors. Fig. 2.4 shows a screen shot of our Web-based interface where each red spot denotes an object in the result set. Users can use the query panel to generate new queries and the result can be shown as a list of sensors or through an interactive map as shown. However, users would be more interested in acquiring knowledge from the data streams rather than finding the sensors. Thus, we added an interactive plot maker to generate real-time plots.

2.5.2 SEARCH BY SMART MACHINES

In this scenario, we consider a smart object querying our search engine. We developed a Machine-to-Machine (M2M) interface based on the architecture in Fig. 2.6 to enable things to use CoAP to connect to our server and submit their queries. To use the interface, on the client side, users can use any of CoAP implementations on

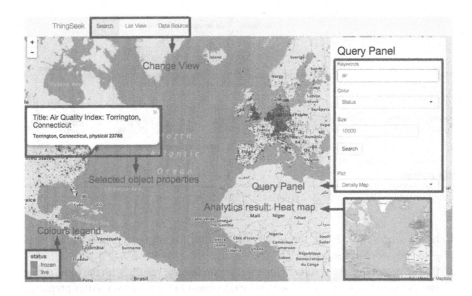

FIGURE 2.4

ThingSeek Web based visualization

CoAP website[22] to send a GET or POST message to our server. The message payload contains keywords followed the desired number of the result set at the end. The server would provide the results in response.

2.5.3 QUERY RESULTS PREPARATION

2.5.3.1 Human User

In this section, we propose our approach for query resolution and the indexing approach to enable large-scale search for IoT. Fig. 2.5 shows the procedure of retrieving query results in ThingSeek. As the figure shows, the query processing workflow works as follows.

1. Queries, which are formed as pairs of keywords and locations, are fed into the system. The query structure is inspired from the Thingful search engine.
2. The Queries are processed in two steps: location based filtering and keyword based filtering and finally the results are updated with the most recent values before being presented to the user.
3. We use approximate values based on indexed data in the location filtering step. The location filtering is facilitated using the R-Tree data structure to enhance the flexibility and the performance of the system.

---

[22]http://coap.technology/.

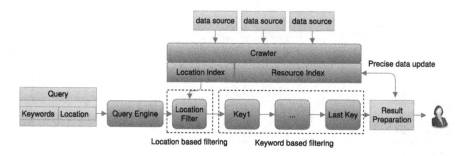

FIGURE 2.5

Query resolution and indexing in ThingSeek framework

4. In the keyword filtering, the results of location filtering are processed for each given keyword accordingly.
5. Before presenting the results to the user, we update the results with the most recent values using the data source index for each object in the result set. After preparing the final result set, we update the result continuously when presenting to the user. This would provide a better user experience of real-time data.

Due to the highly dynamic nature of the things data, analytical result may change promptly. In addition, raw things data are often meaningless and not very useful by themselves. Thus, we also designed a Web-based interface to visualize the things data as well as query the things data.

2.5.3.2 *Smart Objects Interface*

As objects are becoming smarter, they become the main producers and consumers of information. Thus, we created an interface for smart objects to enable them to query the dataset. To cope with the existing standards, we used Constrained Application Protocol (CoAP), which is a protocol for simple electronic devices to allow them to communicate interactively over the Internet. We initialize a CoAP based REST-ful interface for smart objects to search for things in our database. Although CoAP contains a discovery tool, its scope is limited and lacks flexibility.

Fig. 2.6 compares our architecture with CoAP discovery and illustrates how the ThingSeek's machine interface serves queries. For example, a smart air conditioning system searches objects related to air or weather to plan its cooling strategy. As shown, with the use of CoAP, a querying object can only enquire objects on the same network via distributing discovery messages to all objects on the network. Following this, the issuer gets objects' responses if they match to the query. However, this approach can limit the scope and effectiveness of the search. To resolve this issue, in our ThingSeek architecture, the smart object uses a service to send its query directly to the search engine with a POST or GET message. Due to the power, network and computing limits of things, ThingSeek should respond the query with a number of messages containing only a small number of results. In this regard, we use the *ECS*

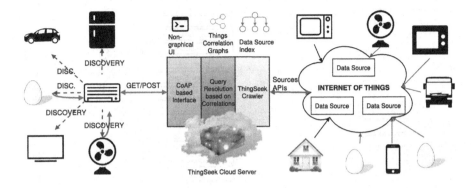

FIGURE 2.6

Query resolution for smart things in ThingSeek framework

approach [33] (Extract-Cluster-Select) to provide the best response with limited size. The ECS approach extracts co-location (objects in the same location or very close to each other) and co-owned (objects with the same owner) correlations between things and forms a unified Things Correlation Graph. Then, the nodes are clustered into k groups and finally a number of things from each cluster are selected and returned. It is designed to rank objects based on their correlations and responds the query with a limited number of the top-k results based on the weight of their correlations with the query issuer. Finally, the URI of the corresponding data source is located and crawled to get the latest sensor readings. If the object is not found in the index, the latest cached records will be supplied.

2.6 THINGSEEK IN APPLICATION: FLIGHT DELAY ANALYSIS

In the previous chapters we already presented a number of examples of the search results for searching things. In this chapter, we present results for a novel application in the aviation industry. Specifically we focus on flight delay analysis. For our case study, we use three different data sources including a real-time flight data, air quality index and real-time weather data. While finding the trajectories of aeroplanes in real-time can be interesting for aviation professional, value added results such as flight delay predictions can be widely used.

The results of our study fall into two categories. First, a search result can provide the list of contextual features that can be identified based on the selected things data sources. Secondly, additional results can precisely show that the extent of effectiveness for a given feature such as *temperature*. We briefly present the results as follows.

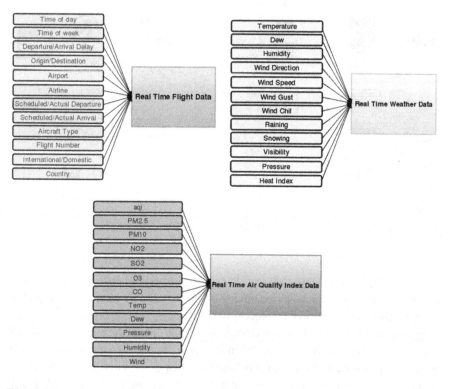

FIGURE 2.7

Features affecting flight delays from each source

2.6.1 MODEL FEATURES

Due to the heterogeneity of things data, the semi-structured or unstructured sensor reading data that is provided by different data sources can widely vary based on our selection of the dataset. An intra-source feature model is an interesting showcase to demonstrate the correlation between different data sources. Accordingly, Fig. 2.7 shows the list of the features that we have extracted from our case study.

In order to provide a clearer image, we describe the characteristics of each feature in Table 2.1.

2.6.2 FEATURE ANALYSIS RESULTS

For this case study, we select seven airports from the largest cities of China. The cities are: Beijing (PEK), Shanghai (SHA), Guangzhou (CAN), Wuhan (WUH), Chengdu (CTU), Harbin (HRB), and Dalian (DLC). In our case study, we collect the data of all flights between these cities. The distribution of the number of flights varies according to the city size and the population number. The airlines operate the flight between

Table 2.1 Feature Description for Flight Delay Search

Source	Feature	Description
Flight	Time of day	Represents the time of the flight during the day.
	Day of week	Represents the day of the flight during the week.
	Departure/Arrival Delay	Represents the departure delay and the arrival delay of the flight in minutes.
	Origin/Destination	Represents the origin airport, city, country of the flight.
	Airport	Represents the airport where the flight departs or arrives.
	Airline	Represents the airline that operates the flight.
	Scheduled/Actual Departure	Represents the scheduled/actual departure time of the flight.
	Scheduled/Actual Arrival	Represents the scheduled/actual arrival time of the flight.
	Aircraft Type	Represents the airplane type of the flight.
	Flight Number	Represents the flight number.
	International/Domestic	Represents if the flight domestic or international.
Weather	Temperature	Represents the current temperature of the weather at the airport where the flight departs or arrive.
	Dew	Represents the dew at the airport.
	Humidity	Represents the Humidity at the airport.
	Wind Direction	Represents the Wind Direction at the airport.
	Wind Speed	Represents the Wind Speed at the airport.
	Wind Gust	Represents the Wind Gust at the airport.
	Wind Chill	Represents the Wind Chill at the airport.
	Raining	Represents the Raining at the airport.
	Snowing	Represents the Snowing at the airport.
	Visibility	Represents the Visibility at the airport.
	Pressure	Represents the Pressure at the airport.
	Heat Index	Represents the Heat Index at the airport.
Air Quality	aqi	Represents the air quality index at the airport.
	PM2.5	Represents Particulate Matter 2.5 micrometers. It is a for particles found in the air, including dust, dirt, smoke, etc.
	PM10	Represents particulate matter 10 micrometers or less in diameter
	NO2	Represents the chemical compound Nitrogen dioxide.
	SO2	Represents the chemical compound Sulfur dioxide.
	O3	Represents the Ozone.
	CO	Represents the Carbon monoxide.

identification.row	identification.number.default	identification.number.alternative	status.live	status.text
2938392811	CA1855	CA1855	FALSE	Scheduled
2934625405	CA1855	CA1855	FALSE	Scheduled
2930890219	CA1855	CA1855	FALSE	Scheduled
2930890220	CA1855	CA1855	FALSE	Scheduled
2920607116	CA1855	CA1855	FALSE	Scheduled
2916225693	CA1855	CA1855	FALSE	Scheduled
2912409039	CA1855	CA1855	FALSE	Scheduled
2908630624	CA1855	CA1855	FALSE	Scheduled
2904833455	CA1855	CA1855	FALSE	Scheduled

FIGURE 2.8

Example of the flight records

winddir	windspeedmph	humidity	tempf	rainin	baromin	dewptf	weather
-999	0.0	72	87	-999	29.85	79	Partly Cloudy
290	2.3	75	88	-999	29.82	81	Partly Cloudy
230	5.8	72	80	-999	29.80	72	Partly Cloudy
270	9.2	73	86	-999	29.79	78	Scattered Clouds
270	5.8	42	93	-999	29.71	72	Scattered Clouds
230	2.3	43	93	-999	29.71	73	Scattered Clouds
230	17.3	77	89	-999	29.72	83	Mostly Cloudy
-999	0.0	71	83	-999	29.77	75	Mist

FIGURE 2.9

Example of the weather records

these cities are: China Air (CA), Shanghai Airlines (FM), China Eastern Airlines (MU), China Southern Airlines (CZ), Juneyao Airlines (HO), Hainan Airlines (HU), Xiamen Airlines (MF), Sichuan Airlines (3U), Shandong Airlines (SC), Chongqing Airlines(OQ), Grand China Air (CN), Shenzhen Airlines (ZH), Spring Airlines (9C), Tibet Airlines (TV), Beijing Capital Airlines (JD), Chengdu Airlines (EU).

In our study we focus on China, where environmental factors can be concerning due to the industrial development. We get around 14,000 records for more than 800 flights between the selected cities. Fig. 2.8 shows a screenshot of a few records from the flights dataset.

We also crawl 2091 records for weather data from public and private weather stations. Fig. 2.9 shows a screenshot from a number of records in our dataset.

We also collect 3084 records for air quality data near the airports. Fig. 2.10 shows a screenshot from a number of records.

The following results would be shown to the user after a search for the flights data. Fig. 2.11 compares the delay at departure for different airlines. Therefore, the user can easily identify the airlines which have the least and the most delay in real-time.

lat	lon	aqi	utime	sutime	stamp
14.349366683822	100.56853549578	21	Friday 28th August 08:00	2015-08-28 06:00:00	1440716400
14.683085094818	100.87513981078	49	Friday 28th August 08:00	2015-08-28 06:00:00	1440716400
14.523536277394	100.92917127159	17	Friday 28th August 09:00	2015-08-28 07:00:00	1440720000
14.040299305494	100.60873959621	-	Sunday 16th August 21:00	2015-08-16 19:00:00	1439726400
14.976785802969	102.10219652705	-	Thursday 27th August 10:00	2015-08-27 08:00:00	1440637200
14.5995124	120.9842195	108	Friday 28th August 08:00	2015-08-28 07:00:00	1440716400
14.6714904	120.93984669999998	166	Friday 28th August 08:00	2015-08-28 07:00:00	1440716400
14.65	120.96666700000003	98	Friday 28th August 09:00	2015-08-28 08:00:00	1440720000
14.554729	121.02444519999995	-	Tuesday 25th August 14:00	2015-08-25 13:00:00	1440478800

FIGURE 2.10

Example of the air quality records

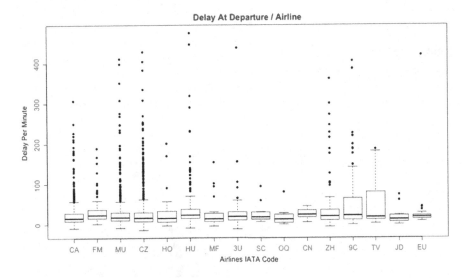

FIGURE 2.11

Delay at departure performance for airlines

Another interesting output from this case study is shown in Fig. 2.12, which can be used by the user to identify the airports which have the least and the most amount of delay for the flights departing from them.

Finally, Fig. 2.13 shows the results of a multiple linear regression analysis which shows the identified features and the extent that each feature contributes towards the delay at departure from the our dataset. These results are prepared and displayed in almost real-time and would enable the users to not only find things from performing search in IoT, but also acquire more knowledge and deploying it for their application.

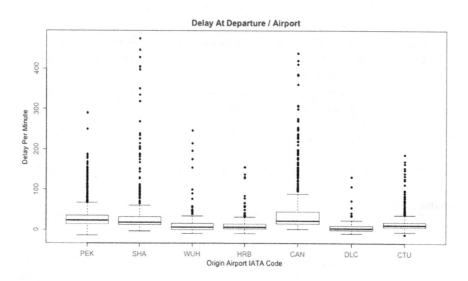

FIGURE 2.12

Delay at departure performance for airports

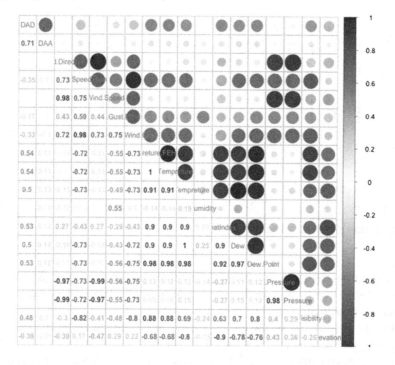

FIGURE 2.13

Results of the correlation analysis

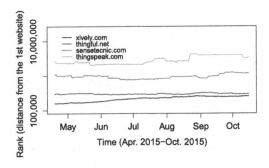

FIGURE 2.14

Ranking of the popular IoT services

2.7 **THINGS DATA ANALYSIS**

In this section, we present the result and statistical analysis of things data and queries collected during multiple routine crawling rounds. We investigate the results from user-related and things-related points of view and then we compare the distribution of IoT and queries data.

2.7.1 **USER INTERESTS**

We investigate user interests from different angles including *Popularity Trends*, *Search Queries Statistics* and comparing the *Things vs Query Distribution*.

2.7.1.1 *Popularity Trends*

A glimpse into IoT keyword trends over Google Trends,[23] suggests that the public interest towards IoT with its most popular abbreviations has been steadily increasing over the past few years.

To further understand this trend, we select some of the most cited IoT platforms (i.e., Xively, ThingSpeak, sensetecnic.com, and Thingful) from the literature and compare their popularity using Alexa Web Ranking.[24] Fig. 2.14 shows the results for the selected websites during six months from 16 Apr., 2015 to 15 Oct., 2015. Accordingly, the popularity of cloud based IoT platforms (e.g., Xively) have been gradually decreasing throughout the last six months while the popularity of Thingful search engine has been increasing during the same period. Clearly, a powerful search engine for IoT can help attract users' interests.

---

[23]http://trends.google.com/.
[24]http://www.alexa.com.

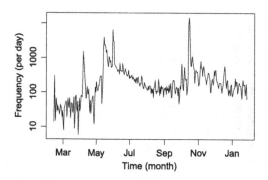

FIGURE 2.15

Query frequency per day in Thingful

2.7.1.2 *Search Queries Statistics*

Analyzing real-world WoT search queries can provide valuable insights for the design and development of future WoT search engines. To get the statistics, we use a dataset of search queries from the Thingful search engine. Fig. 2.15 shows the number of WoT search queries per day. It has been gradually increasing through the time and the average number of queries have been tripled since the beginning. However, in three points of time, during May, June and October, 2014, an abrupt increase in the number of queries per day can be observed. One of the reasons for such increase can be the introduction of new features by the search engine such as embedding and the release of the beta version. This also denotes that any novel improvement in this area can attract many users in a relatively short period of time.

According to the query logs, 84.9% of queries are associated with keywords. An investigation over the popular keywords yields Table 2.2. The category is selected from Thingful's predefined categories including Energy, Home, Health, Environment, Flora and Fauna, Transport, Experiment, Miscellaneous. Apparently, environmental sensing related keywords such as "air quality" and "radiation" have been very popular amongst users.

The category analysis in Table 2.2 shows that for the majority of the queries, transportation related keywords constitute less than 3% of the search queries. On the other hand, keywords that are related to the environmental scanning, constitute more than 67% of the search queries. Thus, in assigning computing resources, environmental data sources should receive more attention. That is, more effort is needed to make the environmental data sources updated and in this way, we can use our computing resources more efficiently.

	Keyword	Freq	Category	%
	Keyword	**Freq**	**Category**	**%**
1	air quality	71,700	environment	61.7
2	sensor	3348	misc.	2.8
3	ship	1851	transport	1.6
4	radiation	1825	environment	1.5
5	earthquake	1601	environment	1.4
6	gamma	1131	environment	1.0
7	weather	876	environment	0.8
8	shark	851	flora and fauna	0.7
9	temperature	581	environment	0.5
10	camera	397	home	0.3
11	car	392	transport	0.3
12	iphone	271	home	0.2
13	fridge	259	home	0.2
14	webcam	255	home	0.2
15	aircraft	247	transport	0.2
16	sharks	245	flora and fauna	0.2
17	energy	242	energy	0.2
18	food	239	home	0.2
19	netatmo	216	environment	0.2
20	coffee	177	home	0.2
21	traffic	168	transport	0.1
22	transport	166	transport	0.1
23	cars	163	transport	0.1
24	raspberry pi	159	experiment	0.1
–	other keywords	28,771	–	24.6
–	Total	116,131	–	100

Table 2.2 Most Popular Keywords and Their Categories

2.7.2 DATA CHARACTERISTICS

Things data is semi-structured as the popular format in things data transmission is JSON. To provide a more detailed vision over things data characteristics, we investigate *data source types* and the *dynamics* and the *quality* of things data.

To grasp a more detailed image of IoT clouds and WoT, Table 2.3 shows WoT and IoT clouds and the number of non-private things which use these technologies.

2.7.2.1 Spatial and Temporal Distribution of Things

Understanding the spatial and temporal distribution of IoT and query updates is valuable for identifying the existing gaps, which can help in predicting the trends of searches and updates. To model the spatial gaps between IoT and queries, we use the Earth Mover's Distance (EMD) measure. EMD describes the normalized minimum amount of work required to transform one distribution to the other. In our case,

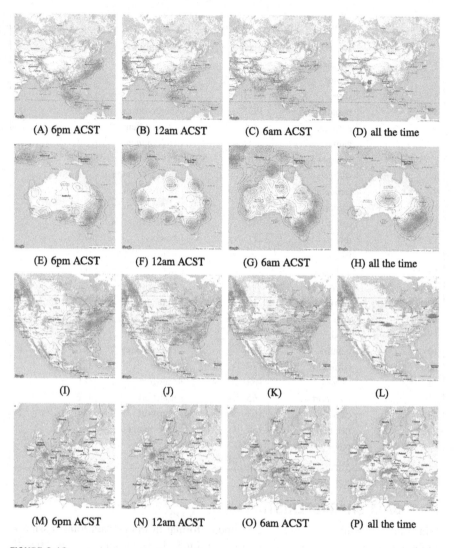

FIGURE 2.16

Heat map for things (A,B,C,E,F,G,I,J,K) and user queries (D,H,L)

given the two distributions matrices of things, d_1 and d_i, which have been taken in timestamps t_1 and t_i respectively, we want to measure the amount of changes in the latter distribution (d_i) from the initial distribution d_1 using $EMD(d_1, d_i)$ measure. Therefore, we can monitor the changes in distribution over the time.

We summarize the two datasets into a list of density indices shown in Fig. 2.17. The length and width of each record density index is 5 degrees of longitude and 5

Table 2.3 WoT vs. IoT cloud services		
Data Source	**Public Sensors (Things)**	**Type**
Xively	67,000	IoT Cloud
WoTkit	4065	WoT
ThingSpeak	3571	WoT
WikiBeacon	30,052	WoT
ISMN[a]	2080	WoT

^a *International Soil Moisture Network*

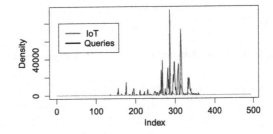

FIGURE 2.17

Comparison of the densities of the two datasets

degrees of latitude, respectively. The EMD yields 0.4338619 for an image of things data and the whole queries dataset.

In the next step, we want to know whether the patterns in Fig. 2.16 and changes in the distribution of things recur over the time. Thus, we perform the same analysis over a period of time on how the spatial distribution of things changes through the time. In particular, we use the emdist [38] implementation to approximate the EMD score for each transition. Fig. 2.18 shows the EMD score for a given period of time in 48 timestamps which we have collected within 48 hours. The curve shows that in each given timestamp t_i, the value of $EMD(t_1, t_i) \in [0, 1]$. Thus, the EMD score for t_1 is 0 since there is no difference between the distribution matrix in t_1 and itself. Shortly, a huge amount of change is observed between t_2 to t_5 and later the EMD score continuously decreases as the distribution returns to its initial status. The very same pattern recurs on the next period of time. As a result, we understand that the geospatial distribution of things goes back to its original state over a period of time (in this case, after 24 hours). This result can assist in setting up new strategies for saving computing resources when updating the things dataset. For example, during an update process, we can scan the areas with higher densities more often than the lesser dense areas.

2.7.2.2 *Data Dynamics*

Things data are widely regarded as highly dynamic and volatile [29]. Although several approaches have been proposed to tackle various problems caused by the

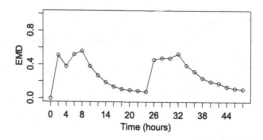

FIGURE 2.18

EMD score for things data during 48 hours

	id	Title	Private	Status	Updated	Value
Table 2.4 **Example of Selected Parameters from a Set of Readings of a Specific Sensor in Xively**						
1	1213	house	false	public	2015-06-10T13:01:59.997058Z	77.46
2	1213	house	false	public	2015-06-10T20:31:00.777699Z	78.56
3	1213	house	false	public	2015-06-11T03:50:00.136106Z	79.5

dynamic nature of IoT, no other work investigates the real-world things data on their dynamics. With our first-hand dataset collected, we observe the following interesting aspects on things data:

- Only a small portion of things data changes frequently. This finding can be easily checked by measuring the number of things and the amount of data that is being updated (new sensor reading during the next IoT scan). For instance, Fig. 2.19 shows the ratio of things which have updated their previous readings from nearly 70,000 objects on the Xively network, which is a part of our things dataset. The ratio of updated rows $r \in [0, 1]$, is obtained from the following equation:

$$r(i, j) = \frac{|diff(d_i, d_j)|}{max(|d_i|, |d_j|)} \qquad (2.2)$$

where if D is the domain of sensor readings, $d_i \in D$ denotes sensor readings in timestamp i, $diff : D \times D \rightarrow N^+$ is a function which returns the new rows in d_j and also $j > i$. Here, the time difference between each $j - 1$ and j is 6 hours. As shown, up to 23% of objects have new sensor outputs during the experiment. Furthermore, only a small part of each tuple gets updated each time. Table 2.4 shows an example from the Xively platform. We only select a small subset of the attributes (77 attributes in the original version) for the illustration purpose. As it shows, only the *value* attributed is being updated every time.
- Frequencies of updates for the same object from different data sources can be highly variant. For instance, with every flight tracker website the sensor readings

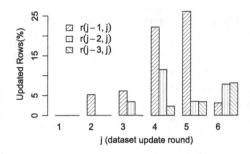

FIGURE 2.19

Ratio of the rows with new sensor outputs

for flights are updated several times per second, while in MarineTraffic the sensor readings for ships and vessels are updated every three minutes.

- Similar to the geographical distribution of objects, IoT dynamics may follow patterns over the time. As Fig. 2.19 shows, the ratio of updated values decreases when increasing the number of steps. This indicates that many of the updated tuples return to their initial values after a while. For example, an air quality egg, which is an egg shaped device to measure indoor temperature and air quality, may report the similar temperature in 24 hours.

2.7.2.3 *Data Quality*

We observe that different data sources, may share the data that is being generated by the same sensors. One of the interesting points in the integration of things data would be knowing the redundancy. Also consistency of the redundant data will be an interesting topic for researchers.

Table 2.5 shows a list of redundant sources of things data and the type of the things that they cover. We select a few data sources which seem to be more popular from three different categories: *flight tracking* and *marine traffic tracking*. Every object from these sources is associated with an identifier which can distinguish it from other objects. We merge the data from all websites in each category to get the ratio of inclusiveness. This measure denotes the rate of the objects which exist in the data source and the union set of objects for the corresponding category.

For the captured flight data, the objects information from different sources is quite different. There are two main reasons associated with this issue. The first reason is the delay in updating the information. The second reason is the loss of some values for some flights. For example, the flight registration is provided by a data source while the same attribute for the same flight is not set in other websites. For the marine traffic tracking websites, we observe that the majority of niche websites are using the same techniques and data as the source website. No delay is observed while the ratio of overlapped data is higher than flight trackers.

Table 2.5 Transportation Data Sources with Overlapping Set of Objects

Appli-cation	URL	Scope	Novel Data	Inclu-siveness	Delay
Flight tracking	http://www.flightradar24.com	World-wide	✓	99.99%	–
	https://flightaware.com/live/		✓	0.01%	✓
	https://planefinder.net		✓	0.01%	✓
	http://www.radarbox24.com		✓	0.01%	✓
	http://www.radarvirtuel.com		✓	0.01%	✓
	http://tinyurl.com/klmliv	Airline	✓	0.01%	✓
	http://tinyurl.com/perthliv	Airport	✓	0.01%	✓
Marine traffic tracking	http://www.marinetraffic.com	World-wide	✓	100%	–
	http://www.shipspotting.com/ais/		✓	0.01%	✓
	http://ship.gr/map/index.htm		✗	100%	✗
	http://www.cruisemapper.com	Cruise	✓	0.01%	✗
	http://www.cruisin.me/cruise-ship-tracker/		✗	100%	✗

2.7.3 WOT VS. USER INTERESTS

As mentioned, the analysis of the distribution of things and queries can lead to finding more efficient strategies for storing and retrieving things data.

Our observation shows that in many cases, there is a huge difference between the distribution of the queries and the distribution of the things data. Figs. 2.16(D), 2.16(H) and 2.16(P) show the local distribution of the queries from Thingful in Asia, Australia and the Europe, respectively. We do not include other continents such as the Americas and the Africa as their results do not add new information on top of the selected regions. As the figures show, in each region most of the queries are focused on specific regions such as India, East Coast of Australia and London.

We also investigate the distribution of the things and its changes over the time in each region separately. We randomly pick a 12-hour time frame and conduct the analysis over three snapshots all over the world. Due to the space limit, we select three snapshots and investigate the distribution of the things in each region. The first snapshot is during evening, the second is during early morning and the third is around noon. The snapshots are all based on the Australian Central Standard Time (ACST). In Asia, during the afternoon most of the things are concentrated on East Asia (Fig. 2.16(A)) while later in the morning the concentration of the things trans-fers to the South West Asia (Fig. 2.16(B)). In the next snapshot, the concentration moves towards South East Asia again (Fig. 2.16(C)). A large part of this change is due to the existing large ratio of flight data comparing to the other types of things data in Asia. However, in Asia, no record demonstrates a good match between the distribu-tion of things and the distribution of the queries, while most queries are concentrated on India (see Fig. 2.16(D)).

In Australia, things are mostly concentrated on the east coast of Australia during evening time (Fig. 2.16(E)) which is a good match for the distribution of the queries (Fig. 2.16(H)). Later as Figs. 2.16(F) and 2.16(G) show, many things are present in other places as well as around the capital cities of Sydney and Melbourne. Thus, a huge gap exists between the distribution of things and queries in this region. However, unlike Asia, the distribution of the things partially matches with the distribution of the queries over the two cities.

In the US, the snapshots demonstrate the change of distribution throughout the time during daylight. The distribution of things continuously spreads from the east coast to the west coast as Figs. 2.16(I), 2.16(J) and 2.16(K) illustrate. However, there is a loose connection between the queries distribution 2.16(L) and things distribution over the New York.

The situation is quite different in Europe. As Figs. 2.16(M), 2.16(N) and 2.16(O) show, a large number of things are constantly concentrated over London area and partially over Germany which is a very good match with the distribution of the queries in this part of the world (Fig. 2.16(P)).

In overall, results show that the distribution of the things trajectories in Asia is mostly around the East Asia while the distribution of queries is utmost around South Asia, which creates a gap between the supply and the demand of data in terms of geographical distribution. Another evidence which also shows that this result is plausible, comes from Google Trends. It suggests that IoT is more popular in India rather than East Asia as well. Thus, enormous amount of resources could be saved through saving update frequency for objects located in East Asia.

2.8 DISCUSSIONS

In this section, we provide further discussions on the challenges and opportunities for IoT research and development.

2.8.1 CHALLENGES IN WOT DATA DISCOVERY

Things data discovery is important towards establishing the next step in the life of the Internet. Since the early days of IoT, several technologies have been specifically proposed to share things data. There have been several successful stories for cloud based IoT platforms such as Xively and Paraimpu. They are often designed to provide global support for almost any type of sensors or actuators.

However, the community of users does not restrict themselves to what these IoT platforms provide. An increasing number of techniques are being used to publish sensory data on the Web. The number of sensors, various types of applications and the increasing demand for real time data have driven to reinvent various techniques which are previously used for other purposes (e.g., Web Mapping). In this case, a large number of niche websites have been developed to publish the data that are generated by specific sensors or for specific applications. In fact, the volume of the publicly available information provided by these websites is much more than the general purpose IoT cloud platforms. However, identifying these websites is similar to finding a needle in haystack as there is no comprehensive list of such websites, many of which have been created recently after the success of similar applications such as the flight trackers.

Another challenge is the structure of the data that is provided on the Web. For a large portion of the websites, the data should be collected from the deep Web. For example, to obtain the results from a flight tracker website, several parameters need to be set and passed. Otherwise, a small subset of the data or an empty set will be provided by the server. In some cases, authentication may also be required as a part of the process when accessing the data.

Unlike other types of the information on the Web, things data mostly are presented in a structured or semi-structured format. The structure of the data widely varies from one website to another. In addition, in many cases, the parameter names are not self descriptive and these parameters need to be demystified manually.

2.8.2 OTHER CHALLENGES

Our dataset can be used for a variety of purposes in the IoT research and development, including correlation discovery between things [44], things data storage [21,15], context aware computing for IoT [25] by merging sensor readings from different sources such as environmental and transportation sensors, point of interest recommendation [46] and other active IoT research areas which may need real-world data.

2.8.2.1 *Data Integration*

Continuous retrieval of things data is very challenging. Some of the sources demand authentication before providing the access. In many cases, data for the same object (e.g., an aircraft) is being broadcasted by different data sources. Furthermore, in some cases, each available source may only provide partial information for an object. The similar issue affects merging data for the same resource. For example, the results of parsing objects data for a single resource have different length and parameters which need to be integrated at the end. Lastly, many data sources limit their response length due to load balancing concerns. We do not fully resolve all challenges in the integration but rather, we use an efficient approach to integrate the data from different sources for the purpose of our research. However, the integration of things data is more challenging than what is believed and more research in this area is required in the future.

2.8.2.2 *Scalability*

Collecting, processing and storing WoT data can be a time consuming procedure, particularly if the size of the dataset is large. As the number of sources and objects increases, which might count in billions, using one instance of the crawler would be very inefficient. In particular, dramatic difference between the update rate of different data sources which also partially depends on their size, can be challenging. Furthermore, technical failures of one resource may affect collecting data from other data sources in the same chain. Thus, we use a distribution strategy to coordinate different instances of the crawler running on different machines.

2.8.2.3 *Archiving WoT Data*

WoT is the main channel for disseminating Big Data generated by things. The volume, velocity and the variety of the data generated by things are enormous. The amount of the data that is already being published from 20 things data sources on the Web, which we estimate to be more than 100 TB a day, is already comparable to the amount of data that is being generated by users on social networks. With the rapid growth of the IoT, in the near future, new techniques will be required to effectively and efficiently process and store things data.

Currently, to the best of our knowledge, there is no popular website for archiving the publicly available things data. In this regard, the traditional approaches need to be revised for the new era of the IoT. The result can be valuable to many core applications such as WoT search while we compromise on some issues to make the impossibles possible. For instance, we discover that based on the changes in the geographical distribution of objects, a crawling strategy can be issued to capture the most updated data in the least amount of time. Through creating spatial and per resource indexes, the process can also become more optimized.

2.8.3 RESEARCH ISSUES

Based on our observation, correlation based search for WoT search and data management services should tackle the following issues:

- **Discovery.** Indeed, there is no universal directory of IoT connected devices due to a number of reasons. Firstly, IoT is not a unified network or platform as heterogeneous types of sensory data are publicized using a variety of technologies and thus, it is not straightforward to identify things data sources on the Internet. Secondly, most works on WoT search have used simulated or small scale datasets and, as yet, the current status of IoT is not investigated by other works [49]. Thirdly, given the security and privacy concerns of the IoT, the majority of sensory data sources are kept private and not revealed to the public, making it impossible to collect and process that data.
- **Correlation extraction.** The heterogeneity of the nodes of the IoT network implies a variety of correlations which can be defined across those nodes. However, unlike the traditional Web documents, which are correlated using hyperlinks, all of the correlations in IoT are implicit and none is explicitly demonstrated. Given the scale of the streaming sensory data in IoT, it would be very complex to capture all types of correlations on the fly. Moreover, in correlation based WoT search the correlation of the querying user with other nodes is required to provide the best results.
- **Network matching.** It is defined as finding the top-k matches in a data graph for a given subgraph. Network matching is a core function that lies at the heart of things data management and querying due to a number of reasons. Firstly, open linked data and service descriptions are widely deployed for Wireless Sensor Network as well as the IoT [36,12]. Resource Description Framework (RDF) descriptions are useful in providing semantic foundations for the dynamic networks of things, where

each node is provided with a set of descriptions [3]. Secondly, merging different networks to create an enterprise correlation graph is a challenging task. Having the network of networks where each sub-network is a collection of things in IoT, finding the best matches to integrate all networks is NP-Hard. Thirdly, in the IoT, things may have more than one service description and very often, different things can share the same description. Thus, assigning unique labels to things based on their service description in a semantic network is not viable in the real-world.

- **Query resolution for smart machines.** Due to the limits in the processing power and memory of the smart machines, the size of the response to the query made by a smart machine should be limited. Thus, only a subset of the result set should be returned to the machine user. In this case, as well as other scenarios when the user is a human being, a good result subset is a subset of correlated things. One example is the search locality concept where only things in the same area are returned as a result. However, due to the heterogeneity of the correlations in the IoT, a combination of the correlations can be selected to prepare the result set. In this case, rather than returning the things that are locally correlated with the query maker, we need to balance the correlations in order to get the best result set. However, due to the lack of things data, this problem yet has not been studied in detail.

- **Intent based search.** Intent based search is proposed as one of the strong application areas for searching the IoT [30]. It is difficult to identify the users' search intention only by using the query keywords and the ambiguity can cause high degree of fuzziness in the result set [35]. Modelling the user's intention can vary significantly across different applications. Given a sub-scenario of taxi ridesharing, taxi search engines, which are equivalent to ridesharing applications, are designed to find the nearest taxi. However, the intention of users in this case is not only to find the nearest taxi, but rather find the most economical taxi which can be booked conveniently, while traditionally it is assumed that when the nearest taxi is found, it is then booked. Considering the consequences of selecting taxis that cannot be easily booked can change the solution fundamentally and thus, increase the complexity of finding the optimal taxi.

- **Knowledge acquisition from things data.** In addition to acquiring the most relevant things in query results or finding the most optimal solution for an intention search, from the motivating scenario we know that users are more interested in acquiring knowledge from sensory data. In the case of flight tracking and management, one of the major intentions of flight data analysis is to understand the parameters that affect flight delays in order to predict flight delays beforehand. However, previous work in this area either consider only one dataset and/or rely on using historical data [37]. Nowadays there are a variety of online tools available. For instance, flight tracking software such as the website FlightRadar24 [1] are currently very popular. Using the real-time sensory data from heterogeneous data sources requires more complex and deeper analysis of the parameters that affect flight delays.

2.9 **RELATED WORK**

Over the past few years, the WoT has received increasing attention from researchers and practitioners. In the earlier days, Atzori et al. [2] offers an initial survey on the IoT research. Accordingly, there exist manifold definitions of the IoT paradigm within the research community. Each definition may view this paradigm from a specific angle including things oriented, Internet oriented and semantic oriented definitions. More specifically, based on all these definitions, a wide variety of networking and sharing technologies have been used to enable the future IoT including but not limited to the Web of Things (WoT) [30], RFID, Near-Field Communication (NFC), middleware and the Wireless Identification and Sensing Platform (WISP).[25]

Some researchers have claimed that the IoT is implemented with the technologies specifically designed for the purpose of being deployed in IoT [40]. Thus, it is argued that the IoT already exists but only a small number of experiments and as a result, yet many researchers consider as inaccessible [40]. Restricting IoT with this point of view is contrary to the spirit of open systems at the heart of the original Internet standards. Moreover, within the technologies which have been applied to facilitate IoT, open Web technologies including HTML, Ajax, HTTPS, OpenID and structured data apply equally well to IoT. However, yet there is no advanced mechanism to be able to effectively search and retrieve things from the Web.

The very diverse range of the objects, approaches and technologies used to implement IoT have contributed in broadening the definition of this paradigm. For instance, the IoT can be realized through deploying an RFID ecosystem consisting of objects tagged with numerous RFID labels [41]. Another option is to build the IoT using smart objects [17] which in turn can be divided into activity-aware, policy-aware and process-aware smart objects.

Currently WoT search is a trending research direction [42] with stress over some major goals such as real-time search [23], context-awareness [25] and relationship support [22].

Researchers have complained about the lack of real-world things data in the past [44]. Although some of the previous works have claimed testing their proposed solutions for large scale things data, such as meta-heuristic [9] or context aware sensor search [25], all these previous works mainly deal with small or simulated datasets. To the best of our knowledge, no work has ever collected or analyzed large scale things data. In addition, none of the existing works use real WoT search query dataset. Moreover, we could not find any other work that has deployed or analyzed a large real-world IoT query dataset for mining user interests in the IoT domain. By combining the user interests and the things data, we can analyze the gap of what people look for and what currently the WoT presents.

To illustrate the future of search engines, [7] identified some of the challenging issues for searching within IoT as search locality and real-time search. Furthermore,

---

[25]http://wisp.wikispaces.com/.

based on IoT characteristics such as networked interconnection, real-time, semantic coherence and spontaneous interaction will result in raising issues such as architectural design, search locality, scalability and real-time for designing and implementing WoT search engines [13]. However, due to the existing differences in the nature of Web of Things (WoT) with the IoT, WoT may even strike additional different challenges.

In order to design the next generation of search engines, many components of current search engines from data collection methods to user experience and semantics should be redesigned. In this section, some of the previous initiations in this area are categorized and reviewed. MAX [47], Microsearch [34] and Snoogle [39] are developed based on this idea. In keyword search approach, keywords are extracted from a given term and top query results are ranked based on a score derived from the percentage of similarity between the given query term and the keyword-based description on sensors. The result is a list of sensors and thus, it might not be very useful particularly for human users.

In the following, we also address the works that are related to flight delay analysis. Flight delay is not a new problem, and it has been considered by many researchers. In [27] the authors analyzed the time factor influence of the flight delay in twenty airports in the US. They observed the changes of the delay rate using historical data. Their investigation aim was to predict the delay of each period based on their mode. They used ANOVA and k-means clustering model in order to demonstrate the periodic of the delay rate. After that they applied the Fast Furious Transform to find the period of the delay. Although their model was able to predict accurately for the first airport they were studying, they found out that their model should be improved in order to be applied to the other 19 airports. However, they did not consider the airline influence.

Liu and Yang studied in [18] the flight delay propagation in the flight chain. So they proposed a new algorithm that could estimate the delay from the beginning in order to determine how much time the flights in chain could be delayed. Authors of [18] did not focus on the potential causes of the delay. They only modelled the problem utilizing the Bayesian Network.

Liu and Ma (2009) [20] analyzed how flight delay is influenced by delay propagation using Bayesian Network. First, they investigated the correlation between the departure delay and the arrival delay at a particular airport. They found that the majority of delays happens in the period between 8 am and 9 pm. They measured the delays as light, medium, or heavy. They proposed that cancelling flights when there is a heavy delay in the chin will relief the problem. Even though cancelling the flights will definitely help other subsequent flights in the chain to be on-time, other factors that may cause the flight delay should be taken in account.

In the study in [37], authors studied the major factors that contribute to flight delay. They developed a model to predict the flight delay using historical records of Denver International Airport. Basically, their model considers two types of delays. First is daily propagation patterns that might be caused by crew connection problems, propagated delay from previous flights, or other factors. Second is seasonal trend where weather or seasonal demand have impact on it. However, as in [27] predicting the status of the flight in the future would require additional dynamic resources that could enrich the model.

In [19] the authors looked at how the arrival delay could be propagated and impact the other subsequent flights in the stream. They believe all these types of delay only happen in busy hub-airports. They created three models. First, they had a propagation model after they investigated the relationships among flights. After that, they came up with an arrival delay model using Bayesian Network. Then they discussed the propagation delay in the hub-airport. They claim that the arrival delay is the source that mainly cause the departure delay.

Geng in his paper [10] provided statistical analysis of the flight delay. He listed all potential factors that may cause the flight delay. Some of these factors are airports, airlines, passengers, public safety, weather, fuel, departure control system, and air force. All these factors are actually play a role on the flight delay. Then he discussed some countermeasures in order to deal with the flight delay.

Another study [32] focused on study the flight delay problem based on the random flight point delays. They used series analysis on airline data and presented an influence factor model of the random flight points. The basic idea of this model is to combine the Bayesian Network with the Gaussian Matrix Model using expectation maximization algorithm. This model can predict the delay of the downstream.

As the best of our knowledge, there is no study has considered the real-time data to investigate the flight delay. In [27] the authors recommend for the future work to combine the analysis of historical data with real time data. That would predict the on-time performance of any airport. Our work will consider the real time data to predict the performance of individual flights.

Rebollo and Balakrishnan [31] presented a new model to predict the flight delay. They consider the temporal and the spatial delay states as explanatory variables. Their approach is to predict the delay sometime in the future between 2 to 24 hours. They use the Random Forest algorithm to do so. Although this model predicts the flight status in the future, the aforementioned interval seems too short because people require time more than that when they book their flights.

2.10 CONCLUSION

In this chapter, we overview the analytical architecture of a search and crawler engine framework, namely ThingSeek, which enables us to crawl, process and search things data that is disseminated by technologies such as WoT. Technically, our framework is capable of supporting other technologies in addition to WoT but we are interested in the cases that implement WoT. We discuss how the data sources can be selected. Moreover, we discuss the technical approach in collecting and integrating the data.

However, using the ThingSeek crawler, we also provide a statistical overview of things data. We provide a user interface that can be used by two different types of users including human users and smart machines. Furthermore, we use this architecture to address the needs of users in domain specific applications such as flight delay analysis. We provide an analytical discussion for the possible future directions in this area and the challenges that need to be tackled in related research.

REFERENCES

[1] Flight radar 24 live air traffic. https://www.flightradar24.com. Accessed 1 July 2016.

[2] Atzori L, Iera A, Morabito G. The internet of things: a survey. Comput Netw 2010;54(15):2787–805.

[3] Bandyopadhyay D, Sen J. Internet of things: applications and challenges in technology and standardization. Wirel Pers Commun 2011;58(1):49–69.

[4] Blackstock M, Lea R. Iot mashups with the wotkit. In: Proc. of the 3rd intl. conf. on the Internet of things (IOT 2012). IEEE; 2012. p. 159–66.

[5] Castro M, Jara AJ, Skarmeta AF. An analysis of m2m platforms: challenges and opportunities for the internet of things. In: Proc. of the 6th intl. conf. on innovative mobile and Internet services in ubiquitous computing (IMIS 2012). IEEE; 2012. p. 757–62.

[6] Chapelle O, Ji S, Liao C, Velipasaoglu E, Lai L, Wu S-L. Intent-based diversification of web search results: metrics and algorithms. Inf Retr 2011;14(6):572–92.

[7] Christophe B, Verdot V, Toubiana V. Searching the 'web of things'. In: Proceedings of the 5th IEEE international conference on semantic computing (ICSC). IEEE; September 2011. p. 308–15.

[8] Da Xu L, He W, Li S. Internet of things in industries: a survey. IEEE Trans Ind Inform 2014;10(4):2233–43.

[9] Ebrahimi M, Shafieibavani E, Wong RK, Chi C-H. A new meta-heuristic approach for efficient search in the internet of things. In: Proceedinsg of the 12th IEEE intl. conf. on services computing (SCC 2015). IEEE; 2015. p. 264–70.

[10] Geng X. Analysis and countermeasures to flight delay based on statistical data. In: 2013 5th international conference on intelligent human–machine systems and cybernetics (IHMSC), vol. 2. IEEE; 2013. p. 535–7.

[11] Haklay M, Singleton A, Parker C. Web mapping 2.0: the neogeography of the geoweb. Geography Compass 2008;2(6):2011–39.

[12] Hasemann H, Kröller A, Pagel M. Rdf provisioning for the internet of things. In: 2012 3rd international conference on the Internet of things (IOT). IEEE; 2012. p. 143–50.

[13] Horowitz D, Kamvar S. The anatomy of a large-scale social search engine. In: Proceedings of the 19th international conference on world wide web. ACM; April 2010. p. 431–40.

[14] Jansen BJ, Booth DL, Spink A. Determining the user intent of web search engine queries. In: Proceedings of the 16th international conference on world wide web. ACM; 2007. p. 1149–50.

[15] Jiang L, Da Xu L, Cai H, Jiang Z, Bu F, Xu B. An iot-oriented data storage framework in cloud computing platform. IEEE Trans Ind Inform 2014;10(2):1443–51.

[16] Kim J, Lee J, Kim J, Yun J. M2m service platforms: survey, issues, and enabling technologies. IEEE Commun Surv Tutor 2014;16(1):61–76.

[17] Kortuem G, Kawsar F, Fitton D, Sundramoorthy V. Smart objects as building blocks for the internet of things. IEEE Internet Comput 2010;14(1):44–51.

[18] Liu Y, Yang F. Initial flight delay modeling and estimating based on an improved Bayesian network structure learning algorithm. In: 2009 fifth international conference on natural computation, vol. 6. IEEE; 2009. p. 72–6.

[19] Liu Y-J, Cao W-D, Ma S. Estimation of arrival flight delay and delay propagation in a busy hub-airport. In: 2008 fourth international conference on natural computation, vol. 4. IEEE; 2008. p. 500–5.

[20] Liu Y-J, Ma S. Flight delay and delay propagation analysis based on Bayesian network. In: International symposium on knowledge acquisition and modeling, 2008, KAM'08. IEEE; 2008. p. 318–22.

[21] Ma Y, Rao J, Hu W, Meng X, Han X, Zhang Y, Chai Y, Liu C. An efficient index for massive iot data in cloud environment. In: Proc. of the 21st ACM intl. conf. on information and knowledge management (CIKM 2012). 2012. p. 2129–33.

[22] Nitti M, Atzori L, Cvijikj I. Friendship selection in the social internet of things: challenges and possible strategies. IEEE Int Things J June 2015;2(3):240–7.

[23] Ostermaier B, Römer K, Mattern F, Fahrmair M, Kellerer W. A real-time search engine for the web of things. In: Proc. of the 2nd Internet of things conf. (IOT 2010). IEEE; 2010. p. 1–8.

[24] Pang Z, Chen Q, Tian J, Zheng L, Dubrova E. Ecosystem analysis in the design of open platform-based in-home healthcare terminals towards the internet-of-things. In: Proc. of the 15th intl. conf. on advanced communication technology (ICACT 2013). 2013. p. 529–34.

[25] Perera C, Zaslavsky A, Christen P, Compton M, Georgakopoulos D. Context-aware sensor search, selection and ranking model for internet of things middleware. In: Proc. of the 14th IEEE intl. conf. on mobile data management (MDM 2013), vol. 1. IEEE; 2013. p. 314–22.

[26] Pintus A, Carboni D, Piras A. Paraimpu: a platform for a social web of things. In: Proc. of the 21st intl. companion conf. on world wide web (WWW 2012). 2012. p. 401–4.

[27] Qin QL, Yu H. A statistical analysis on the periodicity of flight delay rate of the airports in the us. Adv Transpor Stud 2014.

[28] Qin Y, Sheng QZ, Falkner NJG, Dustdar S, Wang H, Vasilakos AV. When things matter: a survey on data-centric internet of things. J Netw Comput Appl 2016;64:137–53.

[29] Qin Y, Sheng QZ, Zhang WE. SIEF: efficiently answering distance queries for failure prone graphs. In: Proc. of the 18th intl. conf. on extending database technology (EDBT). 2015. p. 145–56.

[30] Raggett D. The web of things: challenges and opportunities. Computer 2015;48(5):26–32.

[31] Rebollo JJ, Balakrishnan H. Characterization and prediction of air traffic delays. Transp Res, Part C, Emerg Technol 2014;44:231–41.

[32] Rong F, Qianya L, Bo H, Jing Z, Dongdong Y. The prediction of flight delays based the analysis of random flight points. In: 2015 34th Chinese control conference (CCC). IEEE; 2015. p. 3992–7.

[33] Shemshadi A, Yao L, Qin Y, Sheng QZ, Zhang Y. Ecs: a framework for diversified and relevant search in the internet of things. In: Proceedings of the 15th international conference on web information systems engineering (WISE). Springer; 2015. p. 448–62.

[34] Tan C, Sheng B, Wang H, Li Q. Microsearch: when search engines meet small devices. In: Indulska J, Patterson D, Rodden T, Ott M, editors. Pervasive computing. Lecture notes in computer science, vol. 5013. Berlin, Heidelberg: Springer; 2008. p. 93–110.

[35] Tang X, Liu K, Cui J, Wen F, Wang X. Intentsearch: capturing user intention for one-click internet image search. IEEE Trans Pattern Anal Mach Intell 2012;34(7):1342–53.

[36] Thoma M, Sperner K, Braun T. Service descriptions and linked data for integrating wsns into enterprise it. In: Proceedings of the third international workshop on software engineering for sensor network applications (SESENA). IEEE; 2012. p. 43–8.

[37] Tu Y, Ball MO, Jank WS. Estimating flight departure delay distributions—a statistical approach with long-term trend and short-term pattern. J Am Stat Assoc 2008;103(481):112–25.

[38] Urbanek S, Rubner Y. emdist: Earth Mover's Distance. 2012. R package version 0.3-1.

[39] Wang H, Tan C, Li Q. Snoogle: a search engine for pervasive environments. IEEE Trans Parallel Distrib Syst August 2010;21(8):1188–202.

[40] Want R, Schilit BN, Jenson S. Enabling the internet of things. Computer 2015;48(1):28–35.

[41] Welbourne E, Battle L, Cole G, Gould K, Rector K, Raymer S, Balazinska M, Borriello G. Building the internet of things using rfid: the rfid ecosystem experience. IEEE Internet Comput 2009;13(3):48–55.

[42] Whitmore A, Agarwal A, Da Xu L. The internet of things—a survey of topics and trends. Inf Syst Front 2014;17(2):261–74.

[43] Wu G, Talwar S, Johnsson K, Himayat N, Johnson KD. M2m: from mobile to embedded internet. IEEE Commun Mag 2011;49(4):36–43.

[44] Yao L, Sheng QZ. Correlation discovery in web of things. In: Proc. of the 22nd intl. comp. conf. on world wide web (WWW 2013). 2013. p. 215–6.

[45] Yao L, Sheng QZ, Ngu AH, Li X. Things of interest recommendation by leveraging heterogeneous relations in the internet of things. ACM Trans Internet Technol 2016;16(2):9.

[46] Yao L, Sheng QZ, Qin Y, Wang X, Shemshadi A, He Q. Context-aware point-of-interest recommendation using tensor factorization with social regularization. In: Proc. of the 38th intl. ACM SIGIR conf. on research and development in inf. retrieval (SIGIR). 2015. p. 1007–10.

[47] Yap K-K, Srinivasan V, Motani M. Max: human-centric search of the physical world. In: Proceedings of the 3rd international conference on embedded networked sensor systems, SenSys '05. New York, NY, USA: ACM; 2005. p. 166–79.

[48] Yoon S, Jatowt A, Tanaka K. Intent-based categorization of search results using questions from web q&a corpus. In: International conference on web information systems engineering. Springer; 2009. p. 145–58.

[49] Zhang D, Yang LT, Huang H. Searching in internet of things: vision and challenges. In: Proceedings of the 9th international symposium on parallel and distributed processing with applications (ISPA). IEEE; May 2011. p. 201–6.

MODELING RESTFUL WEB OF THINGS SERVICES

CONCEPTS AND TOOLS

3

Christian Prehofer, Ilias Gerostathopoulos

Fakultät für Informatik, Software & Systems Engineering Research Group, Technische Universität München, München, Germany

CHAPTER POINTS

- Mashup tools are widely available for creating Web of Things services in a simple and graphical way.
- Mashup tools can be compared to more expressive but also more complex model-driven approaches, as both aim for high-level modeling of services.
- Mashup tools can be extended based on model-driven approaches, while preserving the advantages of simple service creation. This is shown for generic operations on sets of things.

3.1 INTRODUCTION

The basic idea of the Internet of Things (IoT) vision is the pervasive presence of a variety of things or objects—such as Radio-Frequency Identification (RFID) tags, sensors, actuators, mobile phones, etc.—which are able to interact with each other and cooperate to reach common goals [18,1]. There is a growing interest in research on new technologies and novel applications for the IoT, as well as in related areas such as wireless sensor networks and ubiquitous and pervasive computing [46]. Web of Things (WoT) builds on this momentum and aims at an application layer for the creation of IoT services. It builds on existing Web protocols, in order to allow devices from multiple vendors to interoperate seamlessly.

In this chapter, we focus on methods and tools for the development of WoT systems. As WoT systems grow in functionality, size and management complexity, we believe that a systematic software-engineering approach towards building WoT systems becomes highly relevant. We argue that such an approach needs to combine lightweight data-flow-based IoT modeling tools, such as mashup tools, with more sophisticated model-driven engineering (MDE) methods and tools, such as UML-based design tools. Following the WoT vision, it has to be built around well-known

Managing the Web of Things. DOI: 10.1016/B978-0-12-809764-9.00004-4

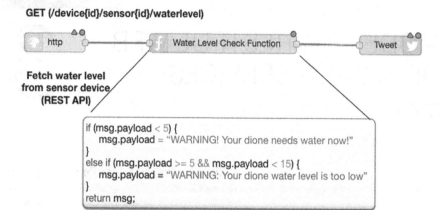

FIGURE 3.1

Model of a plant monitoring application in Node-RED

web architectural styles that allow for resource discovery and API interoperability, such as the representational state transfer (REST) style. Finally, the approach has to promote code reuse and cater for both static settings and dynamic ones, where WoT devices operate in an opportunistic fashion.

This chapter is based on earlier work towards such an integrated WoT development approach (published in [44,47,45]). We first provide an overview of *mashups*, which is a popular approach for application development in the WoT. There are several tools implementing this concept, e.g. IBM Node-RED [26], glue.things [28], WotKit [4], as well as Clickscript [20]. Such *mashup tools* allow for visual, interactive modeling of the data flow between IoT devices and Web services and are well-suited for rapid prototyping of WoT systems. As an example, Fig. 3.1 depicts the model of a simple plant monitoring application in Node-RED.

MDE methods and tools have also been proposed for the WoT/IoT, with ThingML [16] being a prominent example among other proposals [49,42,43]. Although they need more upfront effort in creating the involved models and setting up the underlying infrastructure, MDE tools allow for more expressive modeling than mashup tools, since they provide multiple views and diagrammatic notations (not just a single data flow view). Following a classical MDE approach, models created in MDE tools can be used to automatically generate code via a series of model-to-model and model-to-text transformations. These models are also typically amenable to sophisticated verification methods, both manual (e.g. model-based testing) and automatic (e.g. model checking).

MDE methods and tools can be used in the WoT in the modeling of (i) RESTful interfaces, and (ii) behavior of actuators. In case of large WoT systems with multiple sensors and actuators, the RESTful interfaces of sensors and actuators become lengthy and complex. A systematic model-driven approach to modeling and generating rich RESTful interfaces for the discovery, reading and manipulation of resources for the WoT is thus becoming important. At the same time, the behavior of actuators can be naturally modeled by state machines; this is common practice in embedded systems development.

Once WoT sensors and actuators are provided via RESTful interfaces, mashup tools can be used to model the business logic of a WoT system. In this respect, a limitation of mashup tools is that they require that all connections in the visual data flows are statically defined. At the same time, similar connections cannot be grouped together; there is no way e.g. to reuse the part of the business logic that switches on a light in one room to repeat the same action in another room. Instead, each such operation has to be modeled explicitly in a mashup tool.

To address this limitation, we propose the concept of *generic mashup operations*. In particular, we propose the extension of mashup modeling with $1 : n$ relations, which models a set of resources in a concise way. Having this in place, we can use RESTful operations to sense and actuate a whole set of resources at the same time. This provides the necessary flexibility to work with dynamic scenarios, where new resources are added to a set and are automatically considered in collective sensing and actuating. At the same time, it lifts the necessity to model identical operations explicitly, thus leads to more natural and easy-to-use programming abstractions.

The rest of the chapter is structured as follows. Section 3.2 provides the basic background and definitions of REST architectural style and WoT mashups. Section 3.3 provides an overview of mashup tools and details on three predominant tools. Section 3.4 provides a more general account on MDE methods and tools for WoT, while Section 3.5 compares them to the mashup tools. Section 3.6 explains how to model WoT applications comprised of RESTful services. Section 3.7 extends the RESTful WoT development by proposing generic mashup operations. Finally, Section 3.8 summarizes the important points of our integrated approach for WoT development.

3.2 BACKGROUND
3.2.1 RESTFUL DESIGN

The REST architectural style is aligned with the concepts used in the HTTP protocol; the work by Roy Fielding has shaped the concepts of RESTful design [15]. Following [37], the main ingredients of RESTful design are as follows:

- Identification of resources via Uniform Resource Identifiers (URI). These are hierarchically structured and each resource must have at least one URI.
- Uniform interfaces to read and manipulate the resources. These are the four basic HTTP operations GET, POST, PUT and DELETE. Other operations, e.g. HEAD and OPTIONS, deal with metadata.

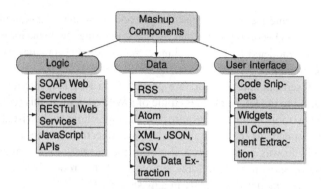

FIGURE 3.2

Classification of Mashup Components, following [12]

- Self-descriptive messages. Representation of the resources can be accessed in different formats, e.g. HTML, JSON or XML. The messages, both requests and reply, contain the complete context and are self-descriptive in this sense.
- Stateless interactions, i.e. the server does not maintain session state on the interactions with the clients. This means that all information to fulfill a request is included in the HTTP request, i.e. the resource name and message.

3.2.2 MASHUPS AND MASHUP TOOLS

A mashup is a composite application that integrates two or more existing components available on the web. These components can either be data, application logic, or user interfaces. The individual components are called "mashup component"; the gluing mechanism is called "mashup logic". The mashup logic is the internal logic which defines how a mashup operates or how the mashup components have been orchestrated [38]. It specifies which components are selected, the control flow, the data flow and data mediation as well as data transformation between different components [12].

Composition of a mashup extensively deals with the kind of components that make it up. The application stack has been broadly classified into data, logic, and presentation (user interface) layer. The mashup created accordingly is called either a data, logic, or user interface mashup.

Mashup components are the building blocks of a mashup. In practice, several technologies and standards are used in the development of mashup components. Simple Object Access Protocol (SOAP) web services [50], RESTful web services, Javascript APIs, Really Simple Syndication (RSS) [29], Comma-Separated Values (CSV) [57] etc. are some of the prominent ones. Depending on their functionality, mashup components have been broadly classified into three categories (Fig. 3.2):

1. Data components provide access to data. They can be static like RSS feeds or dynamic like web services which can be queried with inputs.

2. Logic components provide access to functionality in the form of reusable algorithms to achieve specific functions.

3. User interface components provide standard component technologies for easy reuse and integration of user interface pieces fetched from third-party Web applications within the existing user interface of the mashup application.

Mashup tools have been proposed as a simple way to develop mashups. This was supported by uniform communication protocols and APIs based on REST principles. Early mashup tools are Microsoft Popfly and Yahoo Pipes; for an overview we refer to [24]. In recent years, there has been a lot of interest in applying the same ideas to the IoT/WoT, also building on REST interfaces [5,39,19].

According to [30], mashup tools typically include data mediation. This involves converting, transforming, and combining the data elements from one or multiple services to meet the needs of the operations of another.

For connecting services, there are different concepts as discussed in [59]. The main, predominant one is modelling data flow. For others, mainly in the enterprise area, also centralized approaches with processing rules are considered. For communication, asynchronous messages are used, e.g. using REST-style communication. In general, orchestration can be described by data flow and/or workflow, or through a publish-subscribe model [59].

IoT/WoT mashup tools typically provide a graphical editor for the composition of services for one application. This models the message flow between the components. Components can be sensor nodes, processing or aggregation entities as well as external web-based services. Thus, mashup tools can also be seen as specific cases of end-user programming [58] but are however limited to the specific model of describing message flow. In addition, some mashup tools provide simulation tools and also interoperability for messaging between different platforms.

3.3 STATE OF THE ART IN MASHUP TOOLS

In this section, we detail on the most prominent mashup tools available.

3.3.1 NODE-RED

Node-RED[1] is an open-source mashup tool developed by IBM and released under Apache 2 license [26]. It is based on the server side JavaScript framework Node.js[2] (that is the "Node" in its name). It uses an event-driven, non-blocking I/O model suited to data-intensive, real-time applications that run across distributed devices.

---

[1]http://nodered.org/.
[2]https://nodejs.org/.

Node-RED provides a GUI where users drag-and-drop blocks that represent components of a larger system which can either be devices, software platforms or web services that are to be connected. These blocks are called nodes. A node is a visual representation of a block of JavaScript code designed to carry out a specific task. Additional blocks (nodes) can be placed in between these components to represent software functions that manipulate and transform the data during its passage [22]. Two nodes can be wired together by connecting the output port of a node to the input port of the other node. After connecting many such nodes, the final diagram is called a flow. An example of a flow is depicted in Fig. 3.1.

IoT solutions often need to wire different hardware devices, APIs, online web services in interesting ways. The amount of boilerplate code that the developer has to write to wire such different systems, e.g. to access the temperature data from a sensor connected to a device's serial port or to manage authentications using OAuth [11], is typically large. In contrast, to use a serial port in Node-RED, all a developer has to do is to drag on a node and specify the serial port details. Hence, with Node-RED the time and effort spent on writing boilerplate code is greatly reduced, and the developer can focus on the business logic of the application.

Node-RED flows are represented in JSON and can be serialized, e.g. in order to be imported anew to Node-RED or shared online. There is a new concept of "sub-flows" that is being introduced into the world of Node-RED. Sub-flows allow creating composite nodes encompassing complex logic represented by internal data flows.

Since in Node-RED nodes are blocks of JavaScript code, it is—technically—possible to wrap any kind of functionality and encapsulate that as a node in the platform. Indeed, new nodes for interacting with new hardware, software and web services are constantly being added, making Node-RED a very rich and easily extensible system. Lastly, the learning curve to develop a new node for the platform is low for Node.js developers since a node is simply an encapsulation of Node.js code.

To make a device or a service compatible with Node-RED, a native Node.js library capable of talking to the particular device or service is required. However, with the growing acceptance of REST style in Web and IoT systems, more and more devices and services provide RESTful APIs that can be readily used from Node-RED.

3.3.2 GLUE.THINGS

The objective of glue.things[3] is to build a hub for rapid development of IoT applications [28]. It heavily employs open source technologies for easy device integration, service composition and deployment [28]. TVs, phones, and various other home/business tools can be hooked up to this platform through a wide range of protocols like Message Queue Telemetry Transport (MQTT) [54], Constrained Application Protocol (CoAP) [54] or REST APIs over HTTP.

---

[3]http://www.gluethings.com/.

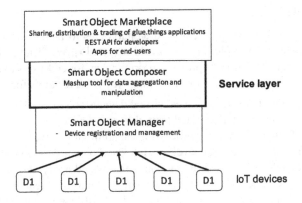

FIGURE 3.3

glue.things Architecture [28]

The development of mashup applications in glue.things goes through the following three main stages [28]:

First, the devices are connected to the platform to make them accessible using protocols like MQTT, CoAP or HTTP/TCP etc. Device registration and management is handled by the extensible "Smart Object Manager" layer in the glue.things architecture (Fig. 3.3). REST APIs provide communication capabilities and JSON data model is used for propagating device updates. These facilities are leveraged using the client libraries or, for a more intuitive experience of device addition, the web-based dashboard can be used. The dashboard also features several templates for connecting devices and simplifying the tasks for the developer.

The second stage deals with creation of mashups. The glue.things system uses a version of Node-RED that has been enhanced to support multi-users, sessions and automatic detection and listing of new registered devices. External web services like Twitter, Foursquare etc. can also be used during mashup composition. The "Smart Object Composer" layer in the glue.things architecture houses the mashup tool. This layer also has a virtualized device container for managing the registered devices.

Lastly, the created mashups are deployed as Node-RED applications including various triggers, actions and authorization settings. These deployed mashup applications are accessible via REST APIs to the developers who may want to use them in their own custom web applications. To the normal end users, they can be browsed through a collection of mashup applications which can be used after suitable alterations to the connection settings and other environment-specific values. Sharing and trading of these mashup applications is also supported by the platform. This functionality is reflected in the "Smart Object Marketplace" layer in the architecture.

3.3.3 WOTKIT

WoT aims to leverage web protocols and technologies to facilitate rapid construction of web applications exploiting real world objects [4]. WoTKit[4] is a lightweight mashup toolkit and platform that provides a simple way for end-users to find, control, visualize and share data from a variety of things [6]. WoTKit aims for:

1. Easy integration of physical devices, virtual devices and the toolkit.
2. Easy visualization of data collected from different devices.
3. Smart and efficient information processing capability for converting low level data collected from devices to high level sensible data to be used in mashups.
4. Ability to quickly combine different data streams and apply various transformations and triggers; i.e. easy service composition or mashup creation.
5. Easy sharing of created mashups and accessibility of features via APIs.

For quick visualization of data collected from different devices, WoTKit uses a JavaScript-based dashboard, which supports the creation of user-defined widgets. Every widget holds some specific set of data collected from devices and an associated visualization. The system comes with visualization plugins like Flot[5]; more visualization plugins can be hooked up into the dashboard at run-time.

WoTKit also contains an event-based data processing subsystem that processes the low-level data collected from devices and converts them into more sensible high-level data before they are fed into the system. It also features a visual programming environment (mashup tool) for mashing up different data sets. This is similar to the data flow model adopted by Yahoo Pipes. The mashup created using this environment is basically a pipe which consists of connected modules to generate new data from the input data sets. A pipe created is analogous to a flow created in Node-RED.

The toolkit supports end-user scripting to create new custom modules using Python and sharing of created pipes and devices registered in the system. It provides a RESTful API for interacting with the registered devices, thereby facilitating easy creation and integration of applications.

The high level architecture of WoTKit is depicted in Fig. 3.4. WoTKit is essentially a Java based web application developed with the Spring Framework. The "UI" part provides the dashboard to interact with the system components graphically while the "RESTful Platform API" provides access to the created mashup applications and registered devices in the system (which obtain unique APIs). The "Thing/Sensor Storage" is the repository containing all the registered devices while the data fetched from devices and pushed into the system are stored in the "Time-indexed Sensor Data Storage". The data model consists of sensors and sensor data having a unique time-stamp attached to it. The "Message Broker" is used to deliver data between different components and has been implemented with the Apache ActiveMQ message broker.[6]

---

[4]http://hub.urbanopus.net/wotkit/.

[5]**Flot:** Attractive JavaScript plotting for jQuery. http://www.flotcharts.org.

[6]http://activemq.apache.org/.

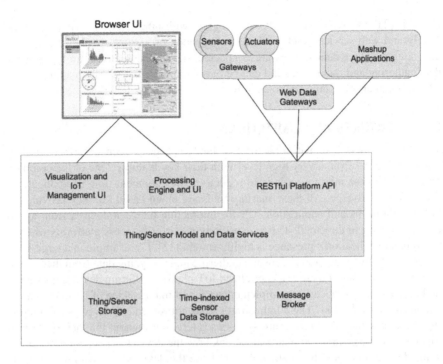

FIGURE 3.4

WoTKit architecture [6]

3.3.4 OTHER PROMINENT IOT/WOT TOOLS

Paraimpu[7] is a web-based platform which allows to add, use, share and interconnect real HTTP-enabled smart objects and "virtual" things like services on the Web and social networks [40]. User can easily create IoT applications to facilitate their devices to react to environmental changes and activities [28]. To have a unifying view on different devices, these devices are segregated based on their functionality. "Sensors" are devices/services capable of producing data in an acceptable format while "Actuators" are entities that can consume data and in the process of consumption generate some actions. Sensors and actuators communicate using the HTTP protocol and therefore it is easy to create hybrid mashups.

ThingWorx[8] platform aims to build and run applications for the IoT landscape using a so-called model-driven approach [13]. It composes services, applications and sensors as data sources and interconnects these through a virtual bus. The framework supports a wide range of connection protocols for devices like CoAP, MQTT,

---

[7]https://www.paraimpu.com/.

[8]https://www.thingworx.com/.

REST/HTTP and Web Sockets. It can integrate with other cloud providers such as Xively and web services such as Twitter, Facebook or various weather services as data sources. Once data sources are connected to dashboards, they can be used for data gathering and monitoring and can be mashed up to create mashup applications. The data can also be subjected to analytics.

3.3.5 FEATURES AND LIMITATIONS

The mashup tools and platforms for IoT landscape have been described in Sections 3.3.1–3.3.4 from a very high level with their key features. One of the common objective of these mashup tools is to reduce the development time of applications for the IoT landscape. All these mashup tools are cloud based i.e. they provide the hosting platforms and application API for interacting between devices from applications running in the cloud. This is especially good for business platforms where a centralized application's presence is highly sought [13]. For example in a large scale factory, installing temperature sensors, gathering and analyzing data from them manually is tedious. But if there is a centralized IoT platform offering device registration and management services then implementation and maintenance of an IoT scenario becomes relatively easy. The administrator need not remember the physical address of all the innumerable temperature sensors scattered throughout the factory, instead just login to the centralized platform to look how the devices are functioning, select some devices to check their data and even name the devices for easy reference and remembrance.

Although the mashup tools vary in the degree to which they strive to ease the development process, the underlying concepts they adopt is the same. Almost all tools, e.g. WoTKit or Node-RED rely on the concepts of data flow for developing an IoT application. Different data streams from different devices are connected in a logical way and data transformation is applied during the transit of the data. ThingWorx advertises to heavily rely on model-based software development approach for creating IoT applications but nevertheless we believe that the underlying concepts used and features offered by the platform largely correspondent to other existing platforms.

After careful observation of many exiting tool-kits, it is appropriate to say that they use different terminologies to denote similar concepts. Mashups are known by different names in different tool-kits but in essence they reflect the same conceptual approach. For example in Node-RED a mashup is called as a flow while in WoTKit it is called a process. The created mashups are generally deployed in a mashup run-time environment. Here the name of the run-time environment differs. For example it is called "Smart Object Marketplace" in glue.things while "RESTful Platform API module" in WoTKit. The commonality among these mashup run-time environments is that all the deployed mashup applications can be shared online and accessed by REST APIs.

Fig. 3.5 summarizes the essential features provided by these tool-kits under the banner of different terminologies. Difference arises in the features provided by these tool-kits in these three distinct layers of service. For example in "Device Manage-

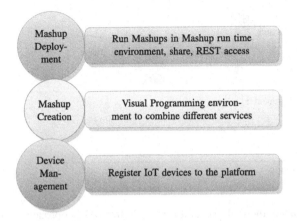

FIGURE 3.5

Conceptualization of features available in Mashup tools

ment", the protocols supported by a toolkit with which we can connect and register IoT devices vary. Almost all the tool-kits support common protocols like MQTT and CoAP. But glue.things also has support for extra protocols like PubNub (Real time publish/subscribe messaging API for web and mobile apps), Meshblu (Machine to machine instant messaging network and API), etc. Similarly, in "Mashup Creation", Node RED permits the user to embed JavaScript code while WoTKit has support for Python scripting. In "Mashup Deployment" almost all tool-kits provide the same features which include sharing of created applications and accessing them by REST APIs.

It is interesting to mention a difference between IBM Node-RED and other tools described in this Section: Node RED is just a visual programming environment and not a complete platform by itself. For instance, it does not provide a device management layer, so we cannot explicitly register IoT devices to it but it supports a wide range of connection protocols enabling it to communicate to different devices. This limitation is eliminated in glue.things which is a platform in itself. It provides support for device registration and management and uses an improved version of Node RED as its mashup tool i.e. Node RED is embedded within this tool to provide a complete IoT platform functionality.

3.4 MODEL-DRIVEN ENGINEERING FOR WOT

There is a broad range of model-driven engineering (MDE) approaches, especially including domain specific modeling languages. Here, we mainly assume general-purpose modeling languages like UML, even though many more specific approaches

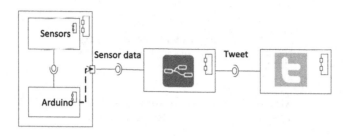

FIGURE 3.6

Component diagram

exist. For instance, there are several proposals for MDE approaches for developing IoT/WoT applications, e.g. the ThingML language [16].

The motivation for model-driven engineering is to describe a system on a higher level of abstraction. This can be done in UML and other languages by diagrams modeling specific aspects or views of a system. Typical in our setting are architecture models and state machines.

Architecture models may describe the logical role of classes by class diagrams, or the logical role of components by component diagrams. Furthermore, deployment diagrams are used to show the mapping of (software) components to physical entities (hardware).

Behavior is typically described by examples in sequence diagrams, or by state machines and activity diagrams. Activity diagrams describe the data and event flow, similar to models used in mashup tools. State diagrams are used in many embedded domains to model the behavior of specific objects. Also, state diagrams can be analyzed and verified formally (see e.g. [43]) and code can be generated automatically. In this way, it is also possible to generate code for different platforms, even though this still requires to consider the different platform APIs.

MDE development includes the following steps:

1. Model and design the application in device-independent model, here state (transition) diagrams and architecture models.
2. Code generation and compilation to device-specific, native code.

An advantage of MDE tools is that there is considerable work on semantics, which means that common understanding of diagrams is formally defined. While there are challenges in semantics for the full-featured UML [9], there exist subsets of UML which are semantically well understood [17].

On the down side, the indirection layer created by separating logical and deployment models, together with the upfront effort to set up model-to-model transformations and code generation scripts, renders MDE tools a heavyweight solution compared to mashup tools (for a detailed comparison see Section 3.5).

Consider again the Node-RED example of Fig. 3.1. In UML, we can model the logical structure of such a scenario with the component diagram of Fig. 3.6. Here,

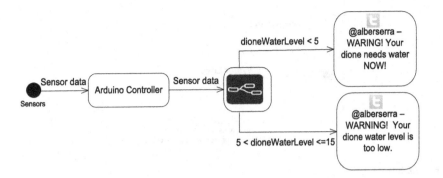

FIGURE 3.7

Activity diagram

each involved component—physical or logical—is represented by a box. Boxes are connected through channels with usual required and provided semantics. In our case, sensors and the Arduino board—gathered in the same component—produce temperature data, that are used by Node-RED for internal computation. In turn, Node-RED produces tweets, used as principal input by the Twitter component.

While the component diagram models the overall logical structure of our system, the activity diagram (Fig. 3.7) captures the data flow. In our scenario, the data coming from sensors is collected by the Arduino controller and is then sent to Node-RED. Node-RED in turn will produce a corresponding tweet published on Twitter, based on the received value.

In these diagrams, we can already note an important aspect: mashup models (e.g. the Node-RED model in Fig. 3.1) essentially correspond to activity diagrams in MDE terms, since they capture the data flow between components.

Finally, the discrete behavior of each diagram's component is usually defined in MDE through state machines. For example, the behavior of the Node-RED component (center component in Fig. 3.6) could be defined as in Fig. 3.8. In Fig. 3.8, WL(X) is an event that, when detected—i.e. we have new input data from sensors—entails the instantiation of X with the current water level and enables the two transitions—labeled with guard/action—to be, eventually, triggered.

3.5 COMPARING MASHUP AND MODEL-DRIVEN ENGINEERING APPROACHES

When comparing MDE and mashup tools for modeling WoT systems, we need to realize that MDE approaches have a much wider set of modeling techniques and a much more detailed separation of different views and concerns. Thus, we take mashup concepts as the basis and discuss how this fits in the MDE world.

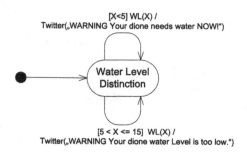

FIGURE 3.8

State machine for the Node-RED component

3.5.1 EXECUTION AND MODELING

As mentioned in Section 3.4, MDE approaches distinguish between (logical) objects and components and between the deployments of components. Components have well defined interfaces and ports, thus matching the notion of components found in mashup tools. The main motivation in MDE is to describe the system from different perspectives. For some models, in particular state machines, execution is possible. On the other hand, consistency between modeling perspectives can be an issue [53].

In contrast, mashup tools essentially define the data/message flow between components. As all data flows are described in one diagram, this also describes the system architecture by showing the connected components in the work flow. Thus, mashup tools integrate a component model with a deployment model. This is the first main difference to MDE approaches. Separating deployment from logical components in MDE creates a layer of indirection and makes prototyping less immediate, compared to mashup tools. In these, it is very easy to develop concrete systems. On the other hand, in a realistic development, applications often need to be mapped to different target deployments. For instance, in ThingML, so-called "configurations" map a logical model to a specific deployment.

Secondly, since mashup tools define a data/message flow between components, they resemble UML activity diagrams, where events are also exchanged. Activity diagrams have a semantics based on events, which drive the control flow. According to [36], there are synchronous and asynchronous semantics for control flow in activity diagrams. In almost all mashup tools, the exchanged messages are asynchronous. However, most mashup tools do not describe semantics formally.

A third difference is that components in mashup tools are either black-box entities or need to be programmed in a general-purpose programming language, e.g. Javascript, C, or Java. In contrast, modeling tools provide rich concepts to model the behavior of components. A widely used approach for developing embedded systems is to use state machines, which are also found in ThingML. From these, it is possible to generate native code for different platforms, hence avoiding execution environments for Javascript or similar languages.

3.5.2 EXPRESSIVENESS AND REFLECTING THE PROBLEM-DOMAIN

When using abstractions, as done in MDE and mashup tools, a main question is what can be expressed and whether this reflects the modeled domain in a natural way. This is essential to ensure user acceptance and long-term success of a tool.

Regarding our problem domain, mashup tools model the data flow between sensors, actuators and services. The behavior of the services however needs to be specified in some other programming language, often Javascript. In MDE approaches for IoT/WoT [16], state machines and statecharts [21] are often used for modeling the behavior of individual components as they naturally represent (logical) states of sensors and actuators. WoT modeling and development would clearly benefit by the integration of data flow modeling at the level of the system with state-based modeling at the level of individual components. This goes to the direction of *multi-paradigm modeling* [2], a concept already in use in the embedded domain in tools such as SCADE [3].

We should note that general-purpose modeling languages can be complex and, at the same time, are not ideally tailored to some specific domain. This is the reason for the considerable research on domain-specific modeling languages (DSML) [53,32], which focus on capturing the important aspects of a particular domain in the domain's idiom and abstraction level. Following this, we can see the modeling language used in a mashup tool as a DSML, since it provides the constructs needed to express the important elements of the mashups domain, i.e. the connections between device APIs and services and the data flow in the system. The syntax of such a graphical DSML provides the rules on how nodes can be connected with each other; the semantics provides the meaning of having the nodes and their connections in the data flow. For instance, in Node-RED, connecting the right side of a function node to the left side of a Twitter node is allowed and means that the output of the particular function will be tweeted. Viewed as DSMLs, mashups tools share both their benefits, i.e. expressiveness and involvement of domain experts, and limitations, mainly related to the need to learn and maintain yet another language.

Another question is the separation of platform-dependent from platform-independent code and other artifacts. MDE has taken considerable effort to separate platform specifics, e.g. deployment or low-level APIs from higher-level models. The main motivation is to produce application models that can be reused in generating code for different deployment environments (thus reducing costs by speeding up development). In some mashup tools, such separation is already in place, as there are separate mappings of logical nodes to physical ones (e.g. WoTKit [4]). On the other hand, some approaches exclusively focus on specific target platforms, e.g. Arduino. Note that this gives a very natural view on the target platform, but not as such on the problem domain and makes the code non-portable.

Another aspect is the modeling of concurrent behavior. In MDE approaches, we can model concurrent behavior in different ways, e.g. by different, parallel areas in an activity diagram or by parallel state machines. As an example, consider a controller for two lights: In this case, we can easily use two parallel state machines, one for each light. For mashup tools, concurrency is not explicitly specified; it is only assumed that asynchronous events are processed in proper order.

3.5.3 TOOL SUPPORT AND EASE OF USE

An important factor for both kinds of approaches is the tool support. While mashup approaches essentially have been tool-based from the very beginning, MDE approaches have a waste body of standards [36] and formal background and often tools implement only specific versions or subsets. Furthermore, mashup tools typically provide a rich integration with existing services (sensors, web services), as well as deployment platforms, from the very beginning.

This is a major difference to MDE approaches, which typically start from the models as such. There are many commercial tools for specific domains, especially for embedded systems. There is however considerably less tool support for the WoT/IoT domain. Regarding this, the work in [53,56] states that *"current MDE technologies are often demonstrated using well-known scenarios that consider the MDE infrastructure to be already in place. If developers need to develop their own infrastructure because existing tools are insufficient, they will encounter a number of challenges"*.

As a result, the complex MDE infrastructure that allows for model manipulation (merging, transformations), graphical editing of models and code generation is more flexible but also requires more effort to both set up and operate w.r.t. mashup tools.

3.5.4 SCALABILITY AND RUNTIME ADAPTATION

We consider scalability in terms of size of models. Generally, visual tools have issues when the views become very big. Then, abstraction or hierarchy concepts are needed. This is an issue for both approaches, as discussed in [53]. For modeling, some concepts for abstractions exist (e.g. hierarchical state machines).

Orthogonal to the scalability, adaptation should also be considered, i.e. the need for the models (e.g. data flow or behavior model) to be adapted at run-time. For instance, a new sensor or service may have to be added. Note that both kinds of tools thrive on presenting a static view of the system, i.e. a view that is invariant during execution. If systems are very dynamic, both MDE and mashup tools cannot properly represent the system anymore. In MDE, there are several approaches addressing this issue, e.g. models at run-time [33,7] as well as more generic and flexible modeling concepts [34].

3.5.5 SUMMARY

Table 3.1 summarizes this section by providing a condensed view of the similarities and differences between mashups and MDE approaches for WoT.

3.6 MODELING OF RESTFUL SERVICES

MDE methods and tools should be combined with mashup tools and concepts for an integrated development of WoT systems. In this section and in Section 3.7 we consider such a combination on the basis of RESTful design of WoT systems.

Table 3.1 Summary of Comparison Between Mashups and MDE Approaches in WoT

	Mashups	MDE approaches
Execution	Mostly asynchronous messages; no formal execution semantics	Synchronous & asynchronous messages; formal semantics
Modeling	Data/message flow diagrams	Architecture, deployment, state & activity diagrams
Expressiveness	Data/message flow; externalized specification of service behavior	Specification of both logical/physical structure and service behavior
Reflecting the Problem-Domain	Intuitive modeling of data flow between WoT sensors, actuators and services	Domain-specific modeling languages for WoT (e.g. ThingML)
Tool Support	Dedicated mashup tools for WoT (e.g. NodeRED, WoTKit)	Sophisticated tool chains with considerable configuration effort, often only subsets of standards supported in tools
Ease of Use	Low effort of setting up mashup tools, intuitive graphical editing available	High effort of setting up and working with tool chains
Scalability	Issues in representing large models	Issues in representing large models; some concepts for abstraction (e.g. hierarchical state machines)
Runtime Adaptation	No tools to capture dynamic views	Some approaches exist e.g. models at runtime

For Internet applications the paradigm of RESTful interfaces is now widely used [48], because it provides a consistent, scalable and flexible model for a large variety of interfaces. We aim to generate RESTful interfaces for WoT systems with sensors and actuators in a systematic and automatic way. This is motivated by the following two observations.

First, interfaces for larger WoT systems with multiple sensors and actuators, including discovery, reading and actuation are lengthy and complex, even using RESTful concepts (see e.g. [23]). Secondly, the WoT also includes the control of actuators. In the MDE world, it is common to model control algorithms by state machines; this is claimed to bring considerable gains in productivity [10].

For the case of complex networks of resources, modeling concepts have been proposed to describe the relations between sensors and actuators at a more high level, see e.g. [41,51]. We use common UML-based concepts to model WoT systems, and then to generate RESTful APIs from these. This way, we can describe systems at a higher level of abstraction.

While there has been some effort to use higher-level models for RESTful APIs in web applications, e.g. [60,41,51], these do not address the needs of IoT/WoT. Here, we present UML models for typical patterns of WoT systems and show how to generate REST interfaces. In particular, we use composite relations in *class diagrams* to describe physical relations of WoT devices, e.g. which sensor is in which room. This is for instance used in the recent ZigBee Smart Energy standard [23], which provides sophisticated REST interfaces for the discovery, access and recording of sensors and actuators. Secondly, we use *state machines* to model the behavior of actuators. From these models, we show how to generate rich RESTful interfaces for the discovery, reading and manipulation of resources for the WoT.

In the following subsection, we provide background on REST architectural style. Then, we introduce modeling concepts for WoT systems and show how REST interfaces can be generated from these.

3.6.1 RESTFUL DESIGN AND INTERFACES

In this section, we complement the description of the main ingredients of REST, presented in Section 3.2.1, with a high-level model of REST as in [27]. This is defined via a tuple $RS = (R, I, B, \eta, C, D)$, where R is a set of resources. I is a set of resource identifiers. $B \subseteq I$ is a finite set of root identifiers. $\eta : I \rightarrow R$ is a naming function, mapping identifiers to resources, it is a partial function which is not defined for all elements. C is a set of client identifiers and D is a set of data values, with an equivalence relation $\sim \subseteq (D \times D)$. Note that REST permits several resource identifiers to point to the same actual resource, thus we separate resources and resource identifiers.

Resources identifiers are modeled as URIs, represented as a set I, in the usual form.

```
URI = scheme ":" authority/path ["?"query]
```

Note that the authority part is optional, and also a possible fragment of the form `[ "#" fragment ]` can be added.

For the resource representation of a resource, we write (ids, d), where ids is a list of linked resources and d is a data value. For simplicity, we write just ids or d if one of these parts if empty or missing. This abstracts from typical resource representations in HTML or XML form.

We associate a partial function $deref : I \mapsto 2^I D$ with the state of the server; $deref(i)$, if defined, is the current representation of the resource $\eta(i)$ (which must be defined if $deref(i)$ is defined).

A REST communication is of the form

$$op(i, args)/rc(rvals),$$

where op is a REST operation and rc denotes the return code with return values. We use a simplified form of return codes, using OK and POSTED for successful execution, and ERROR the non successful case. A communication sequence is a sequence of communications carried out between a set of clients and the server.

We thus have the following operations as in [27]:

- $GET(i)/OK(deref(i))$: The method returns the current entity (resource representation) of the resource identified by i from the server.

- *DELETE(i)/OK*: The method dissociates the resource identifier i on the server, resulting in $deref(i)$ being undefined.
- *PUT(i, (uris, d))/OK*: The method associates a resource identified by i, if it is not already associated, and assigns a value to its corresponding entity so that $deref(i) = (uris, d)$. If this is a new association, then $S(i) = \{\}$.
- *POST(i, (uris, d))/CREATED(j)*: The method associates a fresh resource, which is identified by j, and sets $S(j) = \{\}$ and $deref(j) = (uris, d)$. The resource identified by j becomes a subordinate of the resource identified by i, and j is added to $S(i)$.
- *POST(i, d)/OK()*: This provides a data item d to a data-handling process [14]. This is the second type of POST. It does not create a new (subordinate) resource. We assume here it does not affect the linked resources. However, the state of some resources may change, as discussed later.

The last item in the above list is a very common usage of POST, originally intended for posting the content of HTML forms in HTTP requests. This is by many regarded as a different kind of usage of POST and also not included in [27]. The main author of the RESTful APIs is discussing this in a blog post, stating that a separate operation would be more suitable[9] and it is called "overloaded POST" in [48].

3.6.2 MODELING RESTFUL DESIGN AND INTERFACES

In this section, we show how to describe WoT systems with simple models and to generate REST interfaces. This will include hierarchically structured sensors and actuators, but also associated entities like sensor readings. Clearly, REST has the ambition to provide homogeneous and clean interfaces. We claim that we can give a more concise and simpler way to describe sensors and actuators, and then show how to generate RESTful interfaces from these models.

3.6.2.1 Resource Models for WoT

As a first step we discuss how to derive a resource model for WoT devices and the corresponding discovery of resources. Consider the example shown in Fig. 3.9. The description of RESTful resources by a UML model is widely used, e.g. the OData standard for RESTful Web APIs is using this [35]. Here, we focus on the IoT/WoT specifics to model the physical relations of sensors and actuators.

The diagram shows a room with several sensors and controllers, e.g. for some smart home which can be controlled based on sensor readings. The association with the room class is a composition, which expresses that the sensors and controllers are part of this room.

For the generation of a resource model, we need a root identifier, here assumed to be /. As the class *Room* is the top element of composition relation, elements of

---

[9]http://groups.yahoo.com/neo/groups/rest-discuss/conversations/topics/4732.

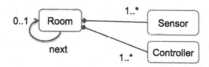

FIGURE 3.9

Class model for the WoT example

```
/
/room1
/room1/sensor1
/room1/sensor2
/room1/controller1
/room1/next
/room2
/room2/sensor1
/room2/next
```

FIGURE 3.10

Example URIs

this class will be resources under the root identifier. The other classes will then be immediate sub-resources based on the composition relation in the diagram. The other relation, *next*, between instances of the class *Room* is not a composition and is just modeled as an associated link, but not as a sub-resource. We need to assume that the composition relation in the diagram constitutes a proper tree, such that we can build a resource tree.

In a concrete example with several instances of the class diagram of Fig. 3.9, the URIs may be as depicted in Fig. 3.10.

This example assumes two rooms with associated sensors and controllers. For these URIs, we can derive the following REST operations to discover the resources in an incremental way as expected for REST. Recall that RESTful design includes the incremental, layered discovery of resources along the resource links. For instance, we have the following operations (assuming the notation [$e1, e1, \ldots$] for lists).

- *GET*(/)/*OK*([/room1/, /room2/]):
- *GET*(/room1)/*OK*([/room1/sensor1, /room1/sensor2, /room1/controller1])

Other relations between classes, here the next link, can be done by some link model in an object diagram. As an example, *GET*(/room1/next)/*OK*(/room2) returns the *next* link of *room1*, which is assumed to be *room2*.

There is already existing work on modeling resources as a UML class model, e.g. [41,51]. The main difference here is that we use the hierarchical structure inherent in

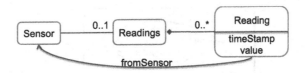

FIGURE 3.11

Class model for WoT sensor readings

our IoT/WoT application domain. Secondly, we specify not just the generic relation on the class level, but also discuss how to specify the object level relationships.

3.6.2.2 *Modeling Sensors and Sensor Readings*

Based on the resource structure of Fig. 3.9, we can now define the interfaces for sensors. Clearly, the most obvious case is reading the sensor value, which is done by a simple *GET* operation. For example, reading the room temperature from *sensor*1 may result in:

$GET(/room1/sensor1)/OK(21C)$

As discussed in Section 3.6.1, we abstract from the actual data value, which should be in a self-descriptive XML or HTML format.

The next typical step for sensors is to create new resources for specific readings, typically with a time stamp to record a specific reading and to make it available for others. This is modeled in the UML class diagram in Fig. 3.11, which shows a relation between sensors and *Reading* resources which are linked via *readings* and *fromSensor*. Note that this is not a composition, as the readings may be located in some other physical location. An example where this technique is used is the ZigBee Smart Energy standard [23].

Based on this, we get the following RESTful operations to post and to discover the readings, as well as to trace the readings back to the sensor.

- $GET(/room1/sensor1)/OK(/room1/sensor1/readings)$
- $POST(/room1/sensor1/readings, (21C, timeStamp))$
  $/CREATED(/room1/sensor1/readings/reading1)$
- $GET(/room1/sensor1/readings)$
  $/OK([/room1/sensor1/readings/reading1, /room1/sensor1/readings/reading2])$
- $GET(/room1/sensor1/readings/reading1/fromSensor)/OK(/room1/sensor1/)$
- $GET(/room1/sensor1/readings/reading1/value)/OK(21C)$

Now, the GET operation on the sensor also returns a link to the readings. Note that we have a choice here how to model the (sensor) readings resources. We model these as sub-resources of the sensors in this example.

The second example adds a new reading. This will be inserted after the most recent other reading. The third get operation yields the list of all readings. Then,

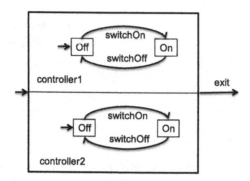

FIGURE 3.12

Actuator model for the WoT example

the get operation retrieves the associated sensor URI. Finally, the last get operation retrieves the value of the reading.

Next we can also delete readings in the expected way.

- *DELETE(/room1/sensor1/readings/reading1/)/ OK()*:
- *DELETE(/room1/sensor1/readings/)/OK()*:

Note that second delete removes all readings for this sensor. This is the usual semantics of DELETE for a composite URL.

3.6.2.3 *Modeling Actuators*

The basic case of actuators is to model an actuator by a resource [8]. In this case, we identify an actuator with a resource and use get and put to read and put values, respectively.

For more complex actuators, we show in the following how sets of actuators can be modeled by state machines. It is in fact a very common to model control algorithms by state machines in other areas like embedded systems, see e.g. [10]. While such state machines are often used for real-time control systems, we focus on control APIs which can be used locally or over a network with generic APIs.

We show a simple example of two lights in Fig. 3.12. Since the two actuators are independent, their behavior is modeled in parallel state machines. The lights themselves are modeled as sub-resources of a room.

When the state machines are translated to RESTful APIs, it is important to discuss what is modeled as resources and what operations are used for triggering state transitions. We assume here that the main objective of state machines is to abstract from the internals of a sensor and to provide an interface to trigger the transitions. These will cause internal state changes. First, it is generally accepted to use POST for triggering state transitions, see e.g. [41]. This falls into the second case of POST for invoking some processing on the server side, and does not create sub-resources on

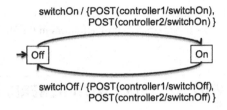

FIGURE 3.13

Example service using the actuator model

the server. Note that PUT is not suitable for implementing transitions as transitions are not idempotent.

Following this line, we choose to model transitions as subordinate resources, and state as a property to the resource. GET can be used to retrieve the possible transitions and the current state. Note that this violates the concept of hiding internals, but we have included this for completeness. It appears now that PUT can be used to write the state, yet this must be discouraged as the transitions are used to initiate actions and also may have preconditions.

The following shows a few examples, assuming the two controllers of Fig. 3.12 are in *room*1.

- $GET(/room1/)/$
  $OK([/room1/controller1, /room1/controller2])$
- $GET(/room1/controller1)/ OK([switchOff, switchOn], state = Off)$
- $POST(/room1/controller1/switchOff/)/Error()$
- $POST(/room1/controller1/switchOn/)/OK()$

3.6.2.4 *Modeling Services*

Based on the defined REST APIs, we can build services. While there is ample experience how to use RESTful services, we show here that our modeling concepts can also be used for services. As an example, consider a switch to handle all lights in one composite resource, as shown in Fig. 3.13. The state machine in this example abstracts from the state machines in Fig. 3.12 and offers simple operations to control both lights. It uses actions on the transitions which trigger transitions in the actual controller in Fig. 3.13.

The RESTful APIs enable a number of services for WoT systems, in addition to the basic functionality of reading and controlling sensors and actuators. First, we have incremental discovery of resources via GET operations to retrieve the links to (subordinate) resources. Secondly, we can search resources similar to web applications. For instance, we can limit the result of a GET request to specific kinds of sensors. Similarly, we could filter all lights which are on or off. For more details and other services like lists or transactions we refer to [48,55].

This is following the patterns of other web applications. In this way, we can achieve consistent APIs, from the sensors and actuators in the WoT to cloud services.

3.7 MODELING WOT SYSTEMS WITH GENERIC RESTFUL OPERATIONS

While the graphical presentation of the components and the message flow in a mashup tool is very attractive, it is also a limitation in itself. It essentially requires that the components and connections are statically defined. This is clearly limiting in cases where devices and services are connected dynamically. For instance, lights may be added dynamically.

A further, related problem in the WoT is that we often have multiple, almost identical devices in one scenario. Consider for instance a building with several lights and temperature sensors. With current mashup tools, all of these have to be modeled in an explicit way. As all of these operate in the same way, it is desirable to abstract from the individual device and just consider them as a set of components.

In this section, we present a novel concept for generic components which encapsulate a set of devices, for which we can define operations in a generic way. This generic behavior is specified in terms of REST interfaces, which enable one to program interactions with the components on a more abstract level. Similar to other generics concepts, we can aggregate different kinds of resources as long as they understand the same RESTful operations. Furthermore, we can also model dynamic sets of devices based on RESTful filtering on resources. For instance, we can create a new set of lights which have the property of being close to an emergency exit. Then, we can define an operation to turn on all of these lights.

There are also other approaches to lift programming of IoT devices to a more abstract level. For example, [31] proposes a reasoning-based approach where user goals are implemented based on suitable logic. Here, we focus on programming techniques, which can be combined with such reasoning engines.

3.7.1 GENERIC COMPONENTS BY 1 : n RELATIONS

In the following, we propose a simple model for generic functions using generic components. We aim to extend existing mashup concepts and employ concepts to generic or polymorphic functions as in many programming languages.

The main idea is to define a 1 : n relation for components in mashup tools, which generalizes the usual 1 : 1 relations. Based on this, the data flow can be modeled as shown in Fig. 3.14. The relation expresses that there are several light sub-resources associated with each room. Similarly, each building has 1 to n Rooms.

Operationally, the idea is to conduct REST operations over all n sub-resources in a generic way. As an example, we consider switching off all lights in a room $room1$. We can thus just write a function using the generic version of POST, denoted as

FIGURE 3.14

Generic components via $1 : n$ relations

POST*:

$$POST^*(room1/Lights/switchOFF) \qquad (3.7.1.1)$$

The implementation will then send the POST operation to all elements in *Lights*.
Similarly, we can switch off all lights in all rooms in *building*1:

$$POST^*(building1/Rooms/Lights/switchOFF) \qquad (3.7.1.2)$$

This will be translated into the following (schematic) code, ignoring error handling for now.[10]

$$for\ room\ in\ GET(/building1/Rooms): \qquad (3.7.1.3)$$
$$for\ light\ in\ GET(/building1/room/Lights):$$
$$POST(/building1/room/light/switchOFF)$$

This is similar to polymorphic or generic programming. Since, however, we deal here with distributed objects, failures cannot be easily ignored. There are different ways to handle failures. An obvious way is to handle failures locally, i.e. at each instance. Another option is to record all error messages for a generic operation in a separate aggregator object, to which a resource is added for each error that occurs, as shown in Fig. 3.15. This can be analyzed after the execution of a generic operation.

By using and extending RESTful concepts, we can integrate this approach in a more consistent and coherent way into mashup tools. First, we use the sub-resource concept to aggregate objects. Secondly, we use the concept of polymorphism via generic resources. In example (3.7.1.1), all light resources in *room*1 have to offer the operation *switchOff*. As the lights are sub-resources, we can build the URIs for the operations by appending the resource name as in example (3.7.1.3). This means to perform a generic operation over linked data structures of sub-resources.

One limitation of this approach is that each of the generic operations is executed individually. An example is to calculate the energy consumption of all devices in one room. Here, we could devise generic code like

$$SUM(GET^*(room1/Lights/currentEnergy)) \qquad (3.7.1.4)$$

---

[10]Note that we do not use multicast sending of GET messages, which is not possible for HTTP.

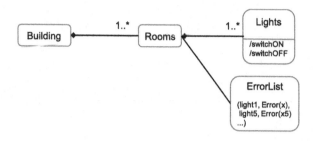

FIGURE 3.15

Generic programming and error handling

In this example, we assume GET^* returns a list, which is added up by SUM. Assuming functional languages like Haskell, one could also construct more complex operations [25]. For instance, we may want to calculate the total energy consumption and at the same time count the number of traversed resources. However, for more complex operations without such language support, we have to resort to a more explicit model, which is discussed in Section 3.7.2.

A similar concept of multicasting of REST requests is possible with CoAP multicasting [52]. However, this is designed only for requests without confirmation. As no errors or confirmations can occur, this case is easy to handle by just multicasting the request to a set of destinations. In such a case, we could of course map the construct of example (3.7.1.4) to such a CoAP multicast request.

3.7.2 GENERIC OPERATIONS VIA SUB-RESOURCES

In addition to executing functions on each device separately, there is also a need for functionality that is aware of a set of (sub-)resources. Consider, for example, rooms which have heaters and temperature sensors. In order to control the heaters, we iterate over the sensors and switch off the corresponding heater if the temperature is above 25 °C. This is shown, with simplified code, in Fig. 3.16. Note that we explicitly use the sub-resources for modeling operations on a set of sub-resources.

This could also be done by the approach described in Section 3.7.1, but would require considerable more complex programming concepts (e.g. based on function parameters).

The main advantage is that we use an explicit notation with the "$1 : n$" link to represent the link between the iterator and the set of objects. Thus, the resources relations are very explicit, and we argue that this fit better into the original concepts of mashup tools. Overall, it is more flexible and extensible compared to the multicast option. Another extension is to use a flexible generation of such components based on filtering, as shown in Section 3.7.3.

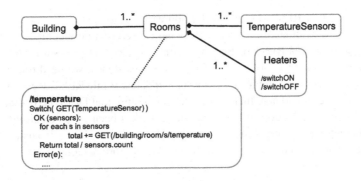

FIGURE 3.16

Generic programming with explicit sub-resources

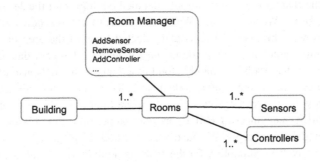

FIGURE 3.17

Managing generic components

3.7.3 MANAGING GENERIC COMPONENTS

In this section, we discuss how resources in generic components can be managed. For instance, in the building example, we may want to add or remove sensors in a room. The approach here is to have a separate *Room Manager* component which is in charge of such updates, as shown in Fig. 3.17.

In terms of a RESTful implementation, we can use sub-resources to manage a set of resources in a generic component. For instance, in the building example, we can model the sensors and controllers as a sub-resources of a room. Then, we can use POST and DELETE to manage these.

Furthermore, we can also create sets of devices based on RESTful filtering on resources, as in usual search queries. This can be implemented with the *query* option of an URL, as defined in Section 3.6.1. In the building example, we may create a set of lights with specific properties. For instance, we can create a new set of lights which have the property of being close to an emergency exit by filtering based appropriate parameters in the resources.

One issue that REST does not fully address is consistency in case of multiple simultaneous operations. For instance, a generic operation on a component may be carried out by several REST operations. Then, consider that a sensor is added while this generic operation is on the way. To ensure consistency, we need to ensure that generic operations are completed before such updates. While REST does not directly support this, we should note that REST does not require that DELETE operations are executed immediately, even if the *OK* return code has been sent. According to [14], it is sufficient that the server intends to delete the resource. Hence, in such cases, we can wait for other, complex operations to conclude before deleting.

3.8 CONCLUSIONS

The goal of the chapter was to review tools and methodologies for the development of applications for the Web of Things (WoT), as well as to propose new tool concepts. We have reviewed the main concepts and selected tools in the area of Internet of Things mashups, which focus on modeling data flow as well as easy data integration. Furthermore, mashup tools are mainly cloud based and some tools also offer device management as well as component marketplaces. Thus, these tools aim at rapid service creation with simple concepts, tailored for the Internet of Things. On the other hand, model-driven engineering (MDE) approaches permit different views and more expressive modeling concepts. We have analyzed both concepts and techniques regarding expressiveness, suitability for the problem domain as well as ease of use and scalability.

As one particular case, we show how mashup tools can be extended to more flexible, generic operations on sets of things, based on advanced modeling concepts. This includes design and code generation in the specification of the *REST APIs* of resources offered by WoT sensors and actuators, as well as the specification of *control flow* of the individual actuators.

This shows that mashup concepts can benefit from MDE approaches, but one has to carefully balance the added expressiveness with the ease of use. Thus, we believe that there is potential in improving WoT development by combining mashup tools with MDE tools and methods.

REFERENCES

[1] Atzori L, Iera A, Morabito G. The internet of things: a survey. Comput Netw: Int J Comput Telecommun Netw 2010;54(15):2787–805. http://www.sciencedirect.com/science/article/pii/S1389128610001568.

[2] Balasubramanian D, Levendovszky T, Dubey A, Karsai G. Taming multi-paradigm integration in a software architecture description language. In: Proceedings of MPM 2014, Valencia, Spain. 2014. p. 67–76.

[3] Berry G. SCADE: synchronous design and validation of embedded control software. In: Proceedings of GM R&D workshop. Springer; 2007. p. 19–33.

[4] Blackstock M, Lea R. IoT mashups with the WoTKit. In: 2012 3rd international conference on the Internet of things (IOT). 2012. p. 159–66.

[5] Blackstock M, Lea R. Iot mashups with the WoTKit. In: 2012 3rd international conference on the Internet of things (IOT). IEEE; 2012. p. 159–66.

[6] Blackstock M, Lea R. WoTKit: a lightweight toolkit for the web of things. In: Proceedings of the third international workshop on the web of things. New York, NY, USA: ACM; 2012. p. 3. http://doi.acm.org/10.1145/2379756.2379759.

[7] Blair G, Bencomo N, France R. Models@run.time. Computer 2009;42(10):22–7.

[8] Bormann C, Castellani AP, Shelby Z. CoAP: an application protocol for billions of tiny internet nodes. IEEE Internet Comput 2012;2:62–7.

[9] Broy M, Crane ML, Dingel J, Hartman A, Rumpe B, Selic B. 2nd UML 2 semantics symposium: formal semantics for UML. In: Kühne T, editor. Models in software engineering. Lecture notes in computer science, vol. 4364. Berlin, Heidelberg: Springer; 2006. p. 318–23.

[10] Broy M, Kirstan S, Krcmar H, Schätz B, Zimmermann J. What is the benefit of a model-based design of embedded software systems in the car industry? Softw Design Develop: Concepts, Methodol, Tools, Appl 2013:310.

[11] Cirani S, Picone M, Gonizzi P, Veltri L, Ferrari G. IoT-OAS: An OAuth-Based Authorization Service Architecture for Secure Services in IoT Scenarios. IEEE Sens J 2015;15(2):1224–34.

[12] Daniel F, Matera M. Mashups: Concepts, models and architectures. Berlin, Heidelberg: Springer; 2014.

[13] Derhamy H, Eliasson J, Delsing J, Priller P. A survey of commercial frameworks for the internet of things. In: 2015 IEEE 20th conference on emerging technologies factory automation (ETFA). 2015. p. 1–8.

[14] Fielding R, Gettys J, Mogul J, Frystyk H, Masinter L, Leach P, Berners-Lee T. Hypertext transfer protocol–http/1.1. Technical report, 1999.

[15] Fielding RT, Taylor RN. Principled design of the modern web architecture. ACM Trans Internet Technol 2002;2(2):115–50.

[16] Fleurey F, Morin B, Solberg A, Barais O. MDE to manage communications with and between resource-constrained systems. In: Whittle J, Clark T, Kühne T, editors. Model driven engineering languages and systems. Lecture notes in computer science, vol. 6981. Berlin, Heidelberg: Springer; 2011. p. 349–63.

[17] Foundational subset for executable UML models (FUML). http://www.omg.org/spec/FUML/Current, 2016.

[18] Giusto D, Iera A, Morabito G, Atzori L, editors. The Internet of things. New York, NY: Springer; 2010.

[19] Guinard D, Trifa V, Mattern F, Wilde E. From the internet of things to the web of things: resource-oriented architecture and best practices. In: Architecting the Internet of things. Springer; 2011. p. 97–129.

[20] Guinard D, Trifa V, Wilde E. A resource oriented architecture for the web of things. In: Internet of things (IOT), 2010. 2010. p. 1–8.

[21] Harel D. Statecharts: a visual formalism for complex systems. Sci Comput Program 1987;8(3):231–74.

[22] Health N. How IBM's node-red is hacking together the internet of things. TechRepublic.com; 2014 [Online; posted 13-March-2014].

[23] Hersent O, Boswarthick D, Elloumi O. ZigBee smart energy 2.0. In: The Internet of things: key applications and protocols. 2012. p. 209–36.

[24] Hoyer V, Fischer M. Market overview of enterprise mashup tools. In: Service-oriented computing–ICSOC 2008. Springer; 2008. p. 708–21.

[25] Hudak P, Peyton Jones S, Wadler P, Boutel B, Fairbairn J, Fasel J, Guzmán MM, Hammond K, Hughes J, Johnsson T, et al. Report on the programming language Haskell: a non-strict, purely functional language version 1.2. ACM SIGPLAN Not 1992;27(5):1–164.

[26] IBM Node-RED. A visual tool for wiring the internet of things n.d. http://nodered.org/.

[27] Klein U, Namjoshi KS. Formalization and automated verification of RESTful behavior. In: Computer aided verification. Springer; 2011. p. 541–56.

[28] Kleinfeld R, Steglich S, Radziwonowicz L, Doukas C. glue.things: a mashup platform for wiring the internet of things with the internet of services. In: Proceedings of the 5th international workshop on web of things. New York, NY, USA: ACM; 2014. p. 16–21. http://doi.acm.org/10.1145/2684432.2684436.

[29] Ma D. Offering RSS feeds: does it help to gain competitive advantage? In: 42nd Hawaii international conference on system sciences. 2009. p. 1–10.

[30] Maximilien EM, Wilkinson H, Desai N, Tai S. A domain-specific language for web apis and services mashups. Springer; 2007.

[31] Mayer S, Inhelder N, Verborgh R, Van de Walle R, Mattern F. Configuration of smart environments made simple: combining visual modeling with semantic metadata and reasoning. In: 2014 international conference on the Internet of things (IOT). 2014.

[32] Mernik M, Heering J, Sloane AM. When and how to develop domain-specific languages. ACM Comput Surv 2005;37(4):316–44. http://doi.acm.org/10.1145/1118890.1118892.

[33] Morin B, Barais O, Jezequel J-M, Fleurey F, Solberg A. Models@run.time to support dynamic adaptation. Computer 2009;42(10):44–51.

[34] Myllärniemi V, Prehofer C, Raatikainen M, Gurp Jv, Männistö T. Approach for dynamically composing decentralised service architectures with cross-cutting constraints. In: Morrison R, Balasubramaniam D, Falkner K, editors. Software architecture. Lecture notes in computer science, vol. 5292. Berlin, Heidelberg: Springer; 2008. p. 180–95.

[35] OData version 4.0. http://www.odata.org/documentation/, 2015.

[36] OMG. OMG unified modeling language TM (OMG UML version 2.5). Technical report formal/2015-03-01, http://www.omg.org/spec/UML/2.5, 2007.

[37] Pautasso C, Zimmermann O, Leymann F. Restful web services vs. big' web services: making the right architectural decision. In: Proceedings of the 17th international conference on world wide web. ACM; 2008. p. 805–14.

[38] Peltz C. Web services orchestration and choreography. Computer 2003;36(10):46–52.

[39] Pintus A, Carboni D, Piras A. Paraimpu: a platform for a social web of things. In: Proceedings of the 21st international conference companion on world wide web. ACM; 2012. p. 401–4.

[40] Pintus A, Carboni D, Piras A. Paraimpu: a platform for a social web of things. In: Proceedings of the 21st international conference on world wide web, WWW '12 companion. New York, NY, USA: ACM; 2012. p. 401–4. http://doi.acm.org/10.1145/2187980.2188059.

[41] Porres I, Rauf I. Modeling behavioral RESTful web service interfaces in UML. In: Proceedings of the 2011 ACM symposium on applied computing. ACM; 2011. p. 1598–605.

[42] Pramudianto F, Kamienski CA, Souto E, Borelli F, Gomes LL, Sadok D, Jarke M. IoT Link: an internet of things prototyping toolkit. In: 2014 IEEE 11th intl conf on ubiquitous

intelligence and computing and IEEE 11th intl conf on autonomic and trusted computing, and IEEE 14th intl conf on scalable computing and communications and its associated workshops (UTC-ATC-ScalCom). 2014. p. 1–9.

[43] Prehofer C. From the internet of things to trusted Apps for things. In: Green computing and communications (GreenCom), 2013 IEEE and Internet of things (iThings/CPSCom), IEEE international conference on IEEE cyber, physical and social computing. 2013. p. 2037–42.

[44] Prehofer C. Models at REST or modelling RESTful interfaces for the internet of things. In: 2015 IEEE 2nd world forum on Internet of things (WF-IoT). IEEE; 2015. p. 251–5.

[45] Prehofer C, Chiarabini L. From internet of things mashups to model-based development. In: 2015 IEEE 39th annual computer software and applications conference (COMPSAC). IEEE; 2015. p. 499–504.

[46] Prehofer C, Stirbu V, Satish S, Liimatainen P, Tarkoma S, Di Flora C, Van Gurp J. Practical web-based smart spaces. IEEE Pervasive Comput 2010;9(3):72–80.

[47] Prehofer C, Schinner D. Generic operations on RESTful resources in mashup tools. ACM Press; 2015. p. 1–6. http://dl.acm.org/citation.cfm?doid=2834791.2834795.

[48] Richardson L, Amundsen M, Ruby S. RESTful web APIs. O'Reilly Media, Inc.; 2013.

[49] Riedel T, Yordanov D, Fantana N, Scholz M, Decker C. A model driven internet of things. In: 2010 seventh international conference on networked sensing systems (INSS). IEEE; 2010. p. 265–8.

[50] Ryman A. Simple object access protocol (soap) and web services. In: Proceedings of the 23rd international conference on software engineering. Washington, DC, USA: IEEE Computer Society; 2001. p. 689. http://dl.acm.org/citation.cfm?id=381473. 381580.

[51] Schreier S. Modeling restful applications. In: Proceedings of the second international workshop on restful design. ACM; 2011. p. 15–21.

[52] Shelby Z, Hartke K, Bormann C. Frc 7251, the constrained application protocol (coap). https://tools.ietf.org/html/rfc7252, 2014.

[53] Straeten RVD, Mens T, Baelen SV. Challenges in model-driven software engineering. In: Chaudron MRV, editor. Models in software engineering. Lecture notes in computer science, vol. 5421. Berlin Heidelberg: Springer; 2008. p. 35–47.

[54] Thangavel D, Ma X, Valera A, Tan HX, Tan CKY. Performance evaluation of MQTT and COAP via a common middleware. In: 2014 IEEE ninth international conference on intelligent sensors, sensor networks and information processing (ISSNIP). 2014. p. 1–6.

[55] Tilkov S. Rest und http. In: Einsatz der Architektur des Web für Integrationsszenarien. Dpunkt Verlag; 2009.

[56] Wagelaa D. Challenges in bootstrapping a model-driven way of software development. In: First international workshop on challenges in model-driven software engineering (ChaMDE 2008), held in conjunction with MoDELS 2008. 2008.

[57] Wang J, Xu Z, Zhang J. Implementation strategies for CSV fragment retrieval over http. In: 2015 12th web information system and application conference (WISA). 2015. p. 223–8.

[58] Wong J, Hong JI. Making mashups with marmite: towards end-user programming for the web. In: Proceedings of the SIGCHI conference on human factors in computing systems. ACM; 2007. p. 1435–44.

[59] Yu J, Benatallah B, Casati F, Daniel F. Understanding mashup development. IEEE Internet Comput 2008;12(5):44–52.

[60] Zuzak I, Budiselic I, Delac G. Formal modeling of RESTful systems using finite-state machines. In: Web engineering. Springer; 2011. p. 346–60.

ACKNOWLEDGEMENTS

The authors are grateful to Tanmaya Mahapatra, who very actively contributed to this work. Furthermore, we would like acknowledge the input from Dominik Schinner and Luca Chiarabini to earlier publications on this topic.

A SEMANTIC-RICH APPROACH TO IOT USING THE GENERALIZED WORLD ENTITIES PARADIGM

4

Fabrizio Amarilli*, Francesco Amigoni[†], Maria Grazia Fugini[†], Gian Piero Zarri[‡]

Fondazione Politecnico di Milano, Milano, Italy*
Dipartimento di Elettronica, Informazione e Bioingegneria, Politecnico di Milano, Milano, Italy[†]
STIH Laboratory, Sorbonne University, Paris, France[‡]

4.1 INTRODUCTION

This chapter is centered around the *GWEs paradigm* [84], proposed as a conceptual framework that extends the standard IoT/WoT (Internet of Things/Web of Things) approaches [6]. Its aim is to broaden the universe of the things (more correctly, entities) that can be taken into account when automatizing a sensor-monitored environment. A definition of IoT, like the one proposed by CERP-IoT (the Cluster of European Research Projects) mentions "virtual things" as follows, "... Internet of Things ... is defined as a dynamic global network infrastructure ... where *physical and virtual things* having identities, physical attributes, virtual personalities and using intelligent interfaces are seamlessly integrated into the information network" [43]. However, the "T" of IoT/WoT is still largely assumed, in practice, to mean *physical* things. This represents a heritage of the first years of the discipline, when IoT was identified, basically, with the RFID technology [65].

Our *GWEs paradigm*, on the contrary, allows us:

- *Seamlessly modeling* in a unified way *observable, real world elementary entities*, like physical objects, humans, robots, sensors, actuators, low-level signals etc. – i.e., all the entities dealt with by the usual IoT/WoT procedures.
- Representing, moreover, structures at *higher levels of abstraction*, corresponding to general situations/actions/events/behaviors that involve lower level entities and their relationships. These high-level entities are normally left aside or dealt with in a sweeping way in an IoT/WoT context, in spite of their *pervasiveness* within any sort of real-world situations. A simple example of these high-level entities consists of the *complete, self-contained and spatio-temporally situated* description of an

event/situation where a robot or a person is trying, in real time, to reach a given object.

The unifying factor that allows us to deal with both physical and higher-level entities using a coherent set of computational tools is represented by the *unique conceptual representation of the world* used for modelling the GWEs of both types. The use of this unified approach will imply, among other things, the possibility of:

- Getting rid *in a general way* of the *interoperability problems* that notably affect the IoT domain – see in this context the so-called *silos flaw* drawback denoting the development of IoT/WoT applications under the form of *independent vertical systems*. The use of a *unique knowledge representation language, ontology-based, for IoT/WoT entities of any origin and level of conceptual complexity* guarantees then strong *semantic scalability* by allowing for smooth integration of information coming from multiple, distributed and heterogeneous sources.
- *Systematically* bridging the *semantic gap* between the values collected at the sensor level (i.e., at the *sub-symbolic level*) and their representation in conceptual, semantic format (i.e., at the *symbolic level*). Actually, the unified representation framework will be able to supply a *target symbolic representation of the original sensors' outputs independently of their level of conceptual complexity*. For example, we can move from the simple instantiation of an emergency_situation[1] concept, which follows an emergency button being pressed, to the formal modeling of a complex, structured command given to a robot moving and acting in a specific environment.
- Implementing *advanced inference techniques*, with a degree of deductive power higher than that found in usual IoT/WoT applications. This is linked with the possibility of representing in a *smoothly integrated* way – as GWEs entities making use of tools characterized by different levels of formal complexity but that are part of the same conceptual model – both the *objects* and the *contexts* (facts, events, scenarios, environments, circumstances and so on) *where these objects are immersed*. It becomes then easier, among other things, to implement those *adaptive techniques* Andersson et al. [5] particularly useful in an IoT/WoT context that concern the ability to generalize from prior knowledge/experiences, to understand the environment and to derive meaningful conclusions about actions, corrections, commands and strategies.

The chapter is organized as follows. Section 4.2 presents a comprehensive picture of the present state of the art in the so-called semantic/conceptual IoT/WoT sub-domain. Section 4.3 deepens the notions of our GWEs approach using a simple

---

[1]In this chapter, *concepts* (i.e., general notions, like emergency_situation, proper of several IoT/WoT specific applications) are represented in lower case while *individuals* (instances of concepts, like EMERGENCY_SITUATION_7) are in upper case. Moreover, the symbolic labels of concepts and individuals always include at least an underscore symbol.

example. Section 4.4 describes an architecture for GWEs-based systems. Section 4.5 introduces the operational procedures allowing for real use of the GWEs paradigm. Section 4.6 draws conclusions and outlines future developments of the approach.

4.2 STATE OF THE ART ON CONCEPTUAL/SEMANTIC IOT/WOT

Atzori and colleagues [6] identify three different visions of the IoT paradigm that, intermixed, contribute together to its definition. A first perspective is *things-oriented* referring to objects and RFID tags, with focus on the associated procedures regarding improving object visibility (e.g., the traceability of an object and its status). A second perspective consists in an *Internet-oriented* vision, promoting the Internet Protocol (IP) and its different versions, such as the network technology for connecting Smart Objects around the world. The third perspective, namely, the *semantic-oriented vision*, considers that the items involved in the Internet are many and heterogeneous. In this context, *semantic technologies* can provide solutions for modeling, describing, and interconnecting things, and for processing them in an intelligent way with limited or even no human intervention. This allows the WoT/IoT infrastructures to scale up and down as needed.

The best solution for associating semantic features to the usual IoT/WoT data and procedures has been rapidly identified, in practice, in the use of *ontologies*, as from historical papers such as [68], Toma et al. [75]. In an IoT context, ontologies are meant to represent an *abstraction technology* able to hide heterogeneity of IoT entities, acting as a *mediator* between IoT application providers and consumers, and to support their semantic matchmaking. The GWEs paradigm is no exception in this context even if, as explained in Section 4.3, the meaning we associate to the notion of ontology is neatly wider and more complete than the standard one.

4.2.1 SOME ARCHETYPAL IOT ONTOLOGIES

In this section, we briefly review the most relevant ontologies that have been employed in the literature and in real cases for scopes analogous to ours, namely attaching semantics to objects of a scenario like a smart environment. OntoSensor [63] was intended to represent a sort of general knowledge base, allowing for queries and inferences, and able to describe most of the spectrum of sensor concepts. OntoSensor can be considered as an extension of the IEEE SUMO (Suggested Upper Merged Ontology) upper-level [55] by making some OntoSensor classes extensions of classes defined in SUMO. OntoSensor includes a significant amount of sensor-related notions and is characterized by an adequate level of expressiveness. From 2008, OntoSensor is no longer under active development.

CSIRO [22] – the Australian Commonwealth Scientific and Industrial Research Organization – is an OWL ontology created for the semantic representation of sensors and for reasoning about sensors and observations. OWL/OWL 2 [14,41] is the Ontology Web Language promoted by the W3C (World Wide Web Consortium) as a standard for representing complex knowledge about things in a Semantic Web context. CSIRO, built around three sets of concepts, namely conceptual entities, domain concepts, and abstract and concrete sensor properties, gives the user the possibility to use sophisticated forms of structural and sequencing composition.

The creators of CSIRO are among the authors of [23], the official document describing the *Semantic Sensor Network* (*SSN*) ontology. SSN[2] has been developed in 2010–2011 by a specific W3C Semantic Sensor Network Incubator group (the SSN-XG) with the aim of overcoming the limits of pre-existing XML-based formats and the fragmentation of sensor ontologies into specific domains of applications. From an implementation point of view, SSN can be considered, as OntoSensor, an extension of an existing general upper level ontology, in this case DOLCE-UltraLite (DUL).[3] SSN is currently considered as a sort of standard for describing sensors and resources in sensor networks in terms of capabilities, measurement processes, observations and deployment processes. However, it does not describe domain concepts, time, locations, etc., which have to be included from other ontologies via OWL imports.

The SSN's architecture is structured according to the Stimulus-Sensor-Observation (SSO) paradigm [44], which links sensors, what they sense and the resulting observations. A stimulus is thus a sort of proxy (go-between, mediator) for an observable property or a number of observable properties. A sensor follows a method (an abstract description) describing how the sensor observes: this may be, for example, a description of the scientific method implemented by the sensor. Observations are the sticking items of the SSO patterns. They can link the act of sensing, the event that represents the stimulus, the sensor, but also a method, a result, an observed feature and a property, placing all in an interpretative context. SSN is centered on the notion of sensor and on stimulus and observations related concepts. For the concrete use of this ontology, it is then necessary to associate it with other sources of knowledge concerning, e.g., units of measurement, description of specific features and qualities and, mainly, domain ontologies (for meteorology, agriculture, commercial products, environmental data, health monitoring, safety services, military applications, emergency applications, etc.).

The IoT-Ontology[4] [46] is an extension of SSN to support the automated deployment of applications in heterogeneous IoT environments. It adds the notions of actuating, identity, and embedded devices provided by associated *software agents*. The extension is realized by adding two new ontology layers, namely the layer for representing IoT entities (IoT entities layer) and the layer for representing IoT entities alignment (IoT entities alignment layer), implemented by reusing widely accepted and agreed conceptualizations from the SSN and DUL ontologies. The decision to implement a specific layer for IoT entities alignment meets the need of assuring a true

---

[2]http://purl.oclc.org/NET/ssnx/ssn.

[3]http://ontologydesignpatterns.org/ont/dul/DUL.owl.

[4]http://purl.org/IoT/iot.

interoperability of IoT entities with minimal human involvement. The goal is then to compute and store the possible alignments *at deployment time*, in such a consistent and formal way that they could be straightforwardly utilized later on, *at runtime*, for communication among the IoT entities. [46] describes also some implementations and modalities of use of the IoT-Ontology and supply the implementation details of a specific alignment algorithm between two ontologies.

A recent work concerns the set-up of the Smart Appliances REFerence (SAREF) ontology [25]. SAREF is a shared model of consensus that facilitates the matching of existing assets (standards/protocols etc.) in the smart appliances domain. The modular architecture of this OWL-based ontology uses pre-defined building blocks that allow separation and recombination of different parts of the ontology depending on specific needs. The notion of device (saref:Device) is central in the SAREF's world. Examples of devices are a light switch, a temperature sensor, an energy meter, or a washing machine; devices are then tangible objects designed to accomplish particular tasks in households, common public buildings or offices. The modular structure of SAREF is then used to allow the definition of any device by associating, according to the function(s) that the device is designed for and the purpose for which it is used, some of the pre-defined building blocks of the ontology.

Several IoT ontologies developed after 2010 are implemented as adaptations and improvement of the SSN ontology. The OpenIoT ontology [70] describes abstraction of sensors and their integration with cloud computing concepts by integrating SSN with several existing sensor-oriented tools, such as some libraries of the Global Sensor Networks (GSN) open source project [1]. Moreover, the ontology exploits the *Linked Data* concept [67] of related sensor data sets. From the GWEs paradigm point of view, an interesting characteristic of this ontology is that sensors are assimilated to anything that can estimate/calculate a value related to a phenomenon. Thus, either a device or computational process, or a combination thereof, could play the role of a sensor. The representation of a sensor in the OpenIoT ontology links what it measures (the domain phenomena), the physical sensor (the device) and its functions and processing (the models). OpenIoT is available as a single OWL file, and provides the means for a semi-automatically generated documentation. OpenIoT is a general kind of ontology; many uses of SSN address, however, the set-up of ontologies for specific utilization domains. Compton et al. [23] mention several of these domains, e.g., the use of sensors deployed around a university campus for location-based context information, or smart consumer products that can sense, reason and communicate. A high-end automatic weather station with multiple sensing capabilities and agriculture meteorology applications are also mentioned: in the last case, microclimate sensing is used to select and breed plants for food crops.[5] Another recently implemented, interesting SSN-based work is an ontology for water quality management developed to support the classification of water quality based on different regulation authorities [4]. This paper contains noteworthy considerations about the problems

---

[5]http://www.w3.org/2005/Incubator/ssn/wiki/Agriculture_Meteorology_Sensor_Network.

triggered in a sensor context by OWL/OWL 2 (the inner support of SSN) and SWRL, the Semantic Web Rule Language [42], because of their backing of monotonic inference and open world assumption – see also, in this context, Section 4.2.3 below.

SSN is a quite complex tool to use; moreover, given its layered implementation strategy (DUL, OWL 2...), it can also be quite ineffective from a running cost point of view. We conclude, then, by mentioning the recent IoT-Lite ontology [16], a lightweight instantiation of the SSN ontology. This version allows representing and using IoT platforms without requiring excessive processing time when querying the ontology. Moreover, it represents a sort of *meta-ontology* that can be extended to represent IoT concepts in different domains. In IoT-Lite, IoT devices are classified into three main classes: sensing devices, actuating devices and tag devices. Presently, IoT-Lite focuses on sensing, although it has a high-level concept on actuation that should enable future extensions in this area.

4.2.2 PROJECTS IN THE SEMANTIC/CONCEPTUAL IOT DOMAIN

The creation of ontologies is not the only activity developed in a semantic/conceptual IoT/WoT framework. Several projects have been developed in these last years in this domain, some making use of the ontologies mentioned above (especially SSN) and others employing their own ontological/conceptual tools. Due to the weighty investments of the European Commission in the IoT domain, and in its semantic/conceptual variant in particular, Europe is playing a central and internationally recognized role in this type of developments. General information about the European activities in the IoT domain can be found on the IERC site[6]; IERC is the "European Research Cluster on the Internet of Things". The most recent view of the (European) IoT domain is collected in [78]. Some European IoT projects of interest from a semantic/conceptual point of view are now briefly surveyed in what follows.

4.2.2.1 *The Semantic Sensor Web (SSW) Applications*

One of the first (and well-known) work in a semantic/conceptual IoT/WoT context is described in [68], discussing a concrete implementation of the *Semantic Sensor Web (SSW) concept*, normally interpreted as a marriage of Sensor Web [27,36] and Semantic Web technologies. A Sensor Web consists of intra-communicating, spatially distributed sensor pods deployed to monitor and explore environments using Web services and database tools. Sensor Webs react and modify their behavior based on these data; they can also perform intelligent autonomous operations, such as responding to changing environmental conditions and carrying out automated diagnosis and recovery. The Open Geospatial Consortium (OGC) has developed a framework of (*purely syntactic*) standards (SensorML) for Sensor Web Enablement (SWE) using XML-based protocols and APIs without providing, however, neither semantic interoperability nor a basis for reasoning.

---

[6]http://www.internet-of-things-research.eu/index.html.

SSWs represent then an extension of Sensor Webs that introduces a *semantic layer* where the semantics of sensor data is specified by annotating these data with semantic meta-data according to well-defined conceptual schemas (i.e., ontologies) and formal languages. In [68], the semantic layer is implemented by annotating sensor data in the weather domain with spatial, temporal, and thematic semantic metadata. To this aim, the authors make use of one of the languages proposed in a Semantic Web context, RDFa [40], an RDF variant often used for annotation purposes. To derive additional knowledge from the semantically annotated sensor data, they utilize standard *antecedent* → *consequent* rules defined using SWRL. Follow-up of this and related work is now developed at the Kno.e.sis Center, Department of Computer Science and Engineering, Wright State University in Dayton, USA.

The European SemSorGrid4Env project[7] further develops the SSW approach by investigating and developing technological infrastructures for rapid prototyping and development of open, large-scale SSW tools for environmental management. An aspect of interest from a semantic/conceptual IoT point of view concerns the attempt of developing a semantically consistent view of several heterogeneous sensor networks as a *global data resource*. In this context, Koubarakis and Kyzirakos [47] agree with Sheth and colleagues [68] on avoiding the use of a pure RDF approach for modeling SSW metadata. They argue that RDF is only able to represent thematic metadata in a correct and exhaustive way, and that it needs then to be extended if spatial and temporal information is to be modeled. Rather than using an existing Semantic Web language like RDFa, they have chosen to develop a specific data model called stRDF and its corresponding query language stSPARQL, an extension of SPARQL [79]. The main idea underpinning stRDF's development derives from the constraint databases domain [62] and consists in representing spatial and temporal objects as quantifier-free formulas in a first-order logic of linear constraints so that spatial and temporal data can be represented in RDF using constraints. In a SemSorGrid4Env context, a stSPARQL query evaluation module, called Strabon, has been built up in order to manage thematic, spatial and temporal metadata about environmental monitoring that are stored in stRDF format in a PostGIS DBMS.[8]

Again in a SSW context, the paper by Calbimonte et al. [20] deals with the problem of coherently searching, correlating and combining sensor data while taking into account the heterogeneous characteristics of sensing environments. They propose an ontology-based querying of sensor data in a federated sensor network, making use of the SSN ontology integrated with domain-specific ontologies for effectively modeling (semantically annotating) the underlying heterogeneous sensor data sources. The query processing makes use of semantic-enriched mechanisms in the semantic expansion style. If for instance, two sensors types are named differently, temperature and thermometer for example, the query processing recognizes that they belong to the same type and include them in query results. A prototype has been built up and

---

run as the backbone of the Swiss Experiment platform,[9] a large-scale federated sensor network. This work has been developed within two European projects, PlanetData and SemSorGrid4Env and by the Spanish Ministry of Science and Innovation.

The problem of the best choice for the symbolic knowledge representation language to be used for the semantic layer in the SSW proposals is far from being definitely solved. Dietze and Domingue [29] deal with this problem in the context of an interesting study on creating a bridge, in a SSW context, between the symbolic language and the measured data collected by sensors. In particular, one needs to map a given set of arbitrary sensor data to a particular set of symbolic knowledge representations, e.g., ontology instances. The solution they propose consists in using Conceptual Spaces (CS) [35] to provide a means of representing knowledge in geometrical vector spaces in order to enable computation of similarities between knowledge entities by means of distance metrics. They propose an ontology for CS that allows refining symbolic concepts as CS and to ground instances to so-called prototypical members described by vectors. In the context of their VSAIH project, Molina and Sanchez-Soriano [53] describe a SSW application for interpreting and analyzing sensor data that summarize the behavior of hydrologic networks controlled by the SAIH system – the Spanish Automatic System Information in Hydrology. To represent sensor knowledge, they use a component-based approach formalized in many-sorted first-order logic terms [52]. The model has been implemented in Prolog. Another solution for knowledge representation has been adopted in SEMbySEM [19], an SSW European project funded by national authorities in the framework of the EUREKA-ITEA 2 programme. Because of an in-depth critical analysis about the real utility of the Semantic Web solutions for semantic-based industrial applications [86], both a specific μConcept Knowledge Representation Language and a specific μConcept Rule Language have been defined. The model defines a μconcept as a group of objects (the instances of the μconcept) that share common characteristics and are structured according to a hierarchy (an ontology). μconcept(s) are described making use of properties that are relations between a μconcept and another μconcept or a literal value. Every μconcept can define actions, which can be executed by all the instances of the μconcept. The set of properties, which can be specifically associated with actions – and that are inserted in a specific sub-branch of the Properties sub-hierarchy of the μConcept model – are Agent, Object, Source, Beneficiary, Modality, Topic and Context. Extensions are possible through more general properties (e.g., Cause, Goal, Coordination, Alternative). The μConcept Rule Language allows the SEMbySEM's users to write Business Rules in μConcept Language terms following the standard if/then production rules format. An illustrative and implemented use case of SEMbySEM concerns the management of sensors in a railway station.

---

[9]http://www.swiss-experiment.ch/.

4.2.2.2 *Virtual Entities, Integrated Abstraction, and Recent High-Level Semantic/Conceptual IoT Projects*

Semantic Sensor Web (SSW) applications have been particularly popular in the first decade of 2000. They are now more and more criticized as being either *too sensor-centric* – or, in some cases, *too knowledge-centric* – without providing any *comprehensive, integrated abstraction* for things and their high-level states. As noticed by Pfisterer and his colleagues [60], an employee looking for a free room for a meeting is mainly interested in real-world entities (meeting rooms) and their high-level states (e.g., free room) rather than in sensors (e.g., sensor 536) and their raw output (e.g., room temperature detected at time T). Moreover, this type of search refers not only to the output of sensors, but also to further machine-readable information that is available elsewhere in the Web (e.g., company maps and meeting schedules). Search engines need to integrate these different *static and dynamic data sources in a seamless way* by providing comprehensive, integrated abstractions for all sort of *concrete and virtual entities* and their high-level states, as well as the possibility of an efficient search based on such current states. *Integrated abstractions* and *virtual entities* are the new buzzwords in the semantic/conceptual IoT domain.

Let us look at the IoT-A FP7 project, defined by its proposers as the European flagship project for establishing and evolving a *federating architectural reference model* for the *Future Internet of Things*. The output of the project is a proposal called ARM (Architectural Reference Model), described in-depth in [10]. ARM consists of four (very general and abstract) parts, summarized in short below:

- The *vision*, which summarizes the rationale for an architectural reference model for the IoT.
- The *business scenarios*, defined as requirements issued by the stakeholders, who are the drivers of the architecture work.
- The *IoT Reference Model*, which provides the highest abstraction level for the definition of the IoT-A Reference Architecture. The description of this model includes, among others, an IoT Domain Model as a top-level description, an IoT Information Model explaining how IoT information is going to be modeled, and an IoT Communication Model in order to understand specifics about communication between many heterogeneous IoT devices and the Internet as a whole.
- The *IoT Reference Architecture*, which supplies views and perspectives on different architectural aspects that are of concern to stakeholders of the IoT, focusing on abstract sets of mechanisms rather than concrete application architectures.

IoT-A ARM provides then *best practices* to the organizations so that they can create compliant IoT architectures in different application domains. Those IoT architectures are seen as instances of the IoT Reference Architecture, including some specific architectural choices (*Design Choices*) like, e.g., considering strong real-time or choosing strong security features. When application domains are overlapping, the compliance to the IoT Reference Architecture ensures the interoperability of the different solutions and allows the formation of new synergies across those domains.

Within this framework, the IoT-A things dealt with in an IoT context are augmented entities formed by the association of physical entities with virtual entities (see, e.g., [11]). Physical entities correspond to sensors, actuators and any sort of possible physical devices. The introduction of virtual entities could imply an additional abstraction layer, capable of augmenting the generality level of the IoT applications. Actually, in an IoT-A context, they are simple *virtual* (in practice, computer-usable) *counterparts* of the physical ones: "Physical Entities are represented in the digital world by a Virtual Entity" [11]. More precisely, Bauer and colleagues state that virtual entities are ". . . synchronized representations of a given set of aspects (or properties) of the Physical Entity" and that ". . . each Virtual Entity must have one and only one ID that identifies it univocally". Any Virtual Entity has attributes such as a name, a type and one or more values to which meta-information, like time and location, can also be associated [11]. This vision of virtual entities as simple digital images of physical entities is largely shared in the IoT domain. See, e.g., [26], where the IoT-A physical things are called entities and the virtual things are called resources (software components) – this particular terminology derives from that introduced in the historical SENSEI project[10] – and the authors state: "a resource is the core software component that represents an entity in the digital world".

Several recent European projects are of interest from a semantic/cognitive IoT point of view; we have already mentioned, in Section 4.2.1, the OpenIoT project and its ontology, obtained by extending the SSN one.

The iCore (Internet Connected Objects for Reconfigurable Ecosystems) project uses cognitive technologies introducing *Virtual Objects* (VOs). According to their iCore definition – see also the interactions between physical and virtual entities in IoT-A – VOs are entities composed of 0 or more devices (sensors etc.) used to make observations of Real World Objects (RWOs) and phenomena and to act on them, 0 or more RWOs and phenomena observed by the previous devices and at least 1 software agent, i.e., a software responsible for the VO functionalities Sarkar and Etaläperä [66]. An abstract, general definition of a specific VO is called a VO *template*; a live replica of a VO template is called a VO *instance*. VOs give us the possibility of obtaining a semantically enriched description of the RWOs by providing a basic set of functionalities that represent the actual functions of these Real World Objects. This includes fostering the RWOs reuse and making them behaving more autonomously, e.g., by generating events, notifications and streamed sensed data that can be tailored to the needs of different applications. A characteristic of the iCore project is the implementation of concrete use cases, ranging from smart city security to smart cold chain logistic and passing through smart office and smart home applications, smart city transportation, smart human security, touristic applications, tracking of portable medical equipment in hospitals, etc.

The aim of the COMPOSE (Collaborative Open Market to Place Objects at your Service) project was the specification and implementation of a general platform for

---

[10]http://www.surrey.ac.uk/ics/research/internet-of-things/projects/completed/sensei/index.htm.

the creation of new services integrating real and virtual worlds through the convergence of the *Internet of Services* (*IoS*) with the *Internet of Things* (*IoT*). At its lower level, the platform deals with Physical External Resources – in practice, physical objects. To be managed, these physical objects should be submitted to an *abstraction process* that, in the COMPOSE case, was structured around the notions of Web Objects and Service Objects [77]. Web Objects are the key elements that provide data flows into the COMPOSE platform and communicate with the platform following a standard web-based protocol. Inside the COMPOSE platform, they assume a *virtual identity* under the form of Service Objects. These can be combined for data processing related tasks, defining then Composite Service Objects in order to be integrated in high-level applications and services: applications of the smart city and smart territory type have been implemented within the project.

The BUTLER (uBiquitous, secUre inTernet-of-things with Location and contExt-awaReness) project implements an IoT prototype of a Context-Aware information system, able to operate transparently and seamlessly across various scenarios towards a unified smart urban environment. Applications regard several use cases concerning, e.g., SmartParking and SmartTransport trials, SmartHealth, SmartShopping, etc. The interest of this project from a semantic/cognitive IoT point of view lies in the application of advanced semantic techniques in the spatio-temporal reasoning and behavior exploration domains [71]. In the first case, it enriches the usual geo-localization contextual information with semantic annotations and enables rich spatial reasoning. The semantic reasoner:

- describes the spatial characteristics of different locations in the BUTLER environment and represents sensors and their locations using the SSN ontology;
- translates location information, represented as coordinates, into semantic locations (e.g., Home_, Living_Room, etc.) and constructs semantic links between locations and activities (e.g., linking Watching_TV with Living_Room).

The semantic enrichment of geo-localization information is implemented through custom operators based on background knowledge stored in a semantic database encoding the mapping of coordinates to symbolic names (i.e., Room_); an operator in the location(x,y) style, translated into the corresponding SPARQL query, calls the semantic database to infer and retrieve the corresponding name. For semantic and spatio-temporal reasoning, the system uses a GeoSPARQL-enabled storage backend – such as Parliament, a high-performance triple store designed for the Semantic Web, or Strabon – able to supply, e.g., all possible rooms where a given user can be present. GeoSPARQL [59] is a standard used for representation and querying of geospatial linked data for the Semantic Web.

Behavioral models are semantically powerful tools that can improve the system smartness by recognizing the user contexts. To create these models, BUTLER uses algorithms that exploit the correlations between user contexts and causal information, thus enabling versatile and robust recognition of user contexts. The algorithms are based on both symbolic and probabilistic approaches; all of them should then be integrated into SAMURAI [61]. SAMURAI is a scalable and event-based stream mining architecture that integrates and exposes machine learning algorithms (learn co-occurrences of events and spatio-temporal correlations) and knowledge representation (linking positions with semantic locations and activities) as RESTful [57] services software building blocks for complex event processing (feature extraction, information fusion, notification). Each building block is integrated in a loosely coupled fashion, allowing easy deployment of multiple instances of the architecture in the cloud. A detailed description of the behavioral component of BUTLER is given in [71].

Among recent, ongoing IoT-related European projects framed in the HORIZON 2020 research framework of the European Commission, we mention here two projects of interest from a conceptual/semantic IoT perspective. The first is the BIG IoT[11] (Bridging the Interoperability Gap of the Internet of Things) project. BIG IoT aims at removing technological market entry barriers of *service* and *application* providers of the IoT by exploiting smart object platforms through *syntactic* and *semantic* interoperability. Interoperability is addressed by defining a generic, unified Web API for smart object platforms, called the BIG IoT API. The second is InterIoT[12] (Interoperability of heterogeneous IoT platform) project, designed to provide an interoperable and open IoT framework (with associated engineering tools and methodology) for seamless integration of heterogeneous IoT platforms, regardless of the application domains. Interoperability objectives are addressed at several levels (device level, networking level, middleware level...). At the data and semantics level, common interpretation of data and information is based on a *global shared ontology* integrating heterogeneous data sources.

We conclude by mentioning a recent, non-European project [28] – based on the use of *semantic annotation* procedures of sensor data making use of the Semantic Sensor Network (SSN) ontology – that is considered as an important step forward with respect to the definition of the architectures for the conceptual/semantic-oriented IoT applications. The concept of *Semantic Gateway as a Service* (SGS) is introduced as a bridge between the physical world and the high-level layers of an IoT system. According to the SGS architecture, raw sensor data are transferred from external *sink nodes* to the central *gateway node* via a multi-protocol proxy. Before being forwarded, data are *annotated* using SSN and other domain specific ontologies. Semantic annotation of sensor data provide *semantic interoperability between messages* and supply *higher-level actionable knowledge* for implementing, e.g., powerful inference procedures. The *sink nodes* (or base stations) act as low-level data collectors: all the sensor nodes send data to the different sink nodes, characterized by low computational resources, stringent energy constraints and limited communication resources. The *gateway nodes* provide connectivity among the sink nodes: they have more computing resources compared to the sink nodes and are then able to support the annotation procedures.

---

[11]http://big-iot.eu/.

[12]http://www.inter-iot-project.eu/.

4.2.2.3 *Linked Data and IoT*

Differently from the traditional Web, where documents can be crawled by following *hypertext links*, in the Linked Data (LD) Web [17,39] they are crawled by following *RDF links* to gather information stating that one piece of data has some kind of relationship to another piece of data. One popular framework is *LOD* (*Linked Open Data*) *diagram*.[13] By September 2011, this diagram had already grown to 31 billion RDF triples, interlinked by around 504 million RDF links. An updated version has been published in April 2014. According to a sensor and IoT perspective, sources of geospatial information such as GeoNames[14] and LinkedGeoData[15] are of particular importance.

From a general, architectural point of view, the LD approach has been criticized because of the necessity of associating all the exploitable data with HTTP URLs that point at RDF descriptions. Taken to its extreme consequences, this could mean that *all the real world entities should be characterized by HTTP URLs supplying RDF data when fetched*. This criticism does not nullify the practical utility of this approach in many domains, IoT included, where it is necessary to operate in a *big data* context by trying to achieve useful results through the application of *shallow surface techniques*. These are opposed to a *symbolic approach* used, e.g., in a GWEs context, and characterized by a careful exploration of the meaningful characteristics of (relatively limited) conceptual domains. Being based on RDF and making use (in general) of ontologies, the LD techniques are considered as part of the Semantic Web domain, and some information about the Linked Data IoT applications is then included in this short state of the art.

An interesting analysis of the reasons that suggest the use of LD techniques in the Sensor Web/IoT domain is given in a Patni et al. [56] paper, which supplies also the Kno.e.sis position on this matter. A number of government, corporate, and academic organizations are collecting enormous amounts of data provided by environmental sensors. However, these data are too often enfolded within these organizations and underutilized then by the greater community. A strategy to make these sensor data openly accessible consists in publishing them on the Linked Open Data (LOD) Cloud. This requires, however, the execution of a set of relatively complex operations that consist, mainly, in converting raw sensor observations to RDF and in linking the new RDF dataset with other datasets on LOD to allow querying and analysis over collected sensor descriptions and observations. The paper describes a concrete experiment including observations concerning hurricanes like Katrina, Wilma, Charley, etc. The original data, in O&M (Observation and Measurement) format,[16] have been converted to RDF using a specific API and stored on a Virtuoso RDF open source triple store.[17] Virtuoso provides then a SPARQL endpoint to query the datasets.

---

[13]http://linkeddatacatalog.dws.informatik.uni-mannheim.de/state/.

[14]http://www.geonames.org/.

[15]http://linkedgeodata.org/About.

[16]http://www.opengis.net/doc/IS/OMXML/2.0.

[17]http://virtuoso.openlinksw.com/.

In the European SPITFIRE project, illustrated in Pfisterer et al. [60], an example concerns the description of some basic possibilities of the application of LD techniques in the IoT domain. Supposing an elementary RDF graph composed of the following two RDF triples, [Sensor3 is-in ParkingSpot41] and [ParkingSpot41 is-in Berlin], and making use of standard ontological knowledge stating that is-in is a transitive property, it is possible to infer that Sensor3 is in Berlin. Assuming then that sensors are described as RDF triples, a search service based on SPARQL queries can find sensors based on meta-data such as sensor type, location, or accuracy. An application could then ask for parking spots in Berlin to calculate the city's availability of car parking places. This sort of application still refers, however, to a (limited) Semantic Sensor Web world. SPITFIRE proposes then to pass to a more complex *Semantic Web of Things*. This can be done, e.g., by integrating semantic descriptions with the LOD cloud to support semantic reasoning, by creating abstractions for things and their high-level states and assuring the integration of these abstractions with sensors, and by allowing the search for things making use of a given current state. By dynamically linking, then, arbitrary datasets on the LOD to describe complex real-world processes and to detect facts and correlations it is possible, for example, to use the parking spot sensors also to provide information about environmental pollution. Such information can be integrated with additional environmental features from http://linkedgeodata.org/ and abnormally high death rates of local population from http://www4.wiwiss.fu-berlin.de/eurostat/.

The University of Surrey (UK) hosts an important research group, the Institute for Communication Systems (ICS), heavily involved in the development of linked data applications in the IoT domain; many of their publications are popular among people working on the relationships between LD and IoT techniques. Barnaghi et al. [8] describe a linked data platform to annotate sensor data that enables users to publish their sensor description data as RDF triples, to associate any other existing RDF sensor description data, to link existing resources on publicly available linked-data repositories and make descriptions available for linked-data consumers through SPARQL endpoints. The choice of a linked data approach is justified by noticing that the usual annotation operations concern data that would be mostly processed locally according to specific domain descriptions (e.g., ontologies) and their specific properties; linking data to other resources on the Web allows us, on the contrary, to obtain more information across different domains. The platform, called Sense2Web, employs graphical user interfaces for annotation, which is performed using concepts obtained from open linked data sources (e.g., DBPedia and GeoNames) and other local domain ontologies. To demonstrate the linked-data usage and the integration of data from different sources, a mash-up application has been created by using Google Maps API.

Barnaghi et al. [9] is a general paper that provides an overview of recent developments in applying semantic technologies on various aspects of the IoT. Authors notice that the linked data principles have been applied to the IoT domain to support creation of more interoperable and machine treatable data and resource descriptions (e.g., for sensors and sensor networks). Including domain knowledge and linking IoT resources to external data (e.g., the linked open data cloud or existing knowledge bases) that describe different thematic, spatial and temporal concepts is also another key aspect in supporting effective interpretation and utilization of the IoT data. Kolozali et al. [45] describe a validation tool for the SSN ontology, i.e., a tool allowing ontologies and linked data descriptions to be validated against the concepts and properties used in the SSN model. It generates validation reports and collects statistics regarding the most commonly used terms and concepts within the ontologies. The tool can also be used to validate linked data and ontological descriptions against other reference ontologies.

4.2.3 SOME PROBLEMS LINKED WITH RECENT DEVELOPMENTS IN A SEMANTIC/CONCEPTUAL IOT DOMAIN

As illustrated so far, the semantic/conceptual IoT/WoT applications have now resolutely adopted the Semantic Web/Linked Data philosophy. This trend, thanks to the (at least relative) maturity of the Semantic Web (SW) development tools, has favored the quick development of a new breed of semantic/conceptual IoT/WoT applications, more powerful and easy to use than their XML-based ancestors. However, the SW tools are affected by theoretical and practical limitations, and we may wonder whether they can represent the ultimate support for the development of (general) IoT applications, see for the details, e.g., [85,86]. In particular:

- A first problem concerns the well-known *limited expressiveness* of the W3C languages like RDF, OWL and all their variants; an extensive literature exists about this topic. RDF(S), OWL and the similar are, in fact, *binary* languages, meaning that properties are limited to express a binary relationship linking two individuals or an individual and a value. Therefore, there is *no direct support in OWL for the (neatly more expressive) n-ary relationships*. For example, it is impossible to represent *directly* in OWL as a *single, structured and coherent conceptual unit* a *ternary* situation represented by a simple event like "John gives a book to Mary". An interesting analysis of the different (and largely unsuccessful) efforts developed in these last years to transform W3C binary tools into *n*-ary ones – RDF reification, named graphs, RDF blank nodes plus rdf:value properties, quad-tuples, *n*-ary design patterns, F-events etc. – is provided in Trame et al. [76]. OWL (and the W3C languages in general) *represents then an unsatisfactory solution for dealing with complex situations and events and for efficiently managing dynamic and real-time information.*

- A second remark relates to a *reasoning context*, which is particularly important for the IoT semantic/conceptual applications. OWL follows an open world assumption (OWA) paradigm, whilst the great majority of the practical, rule- and industry-oriented applications requires a closed world assumption (CWA). According to CWA, every fact that cannot be proven as true is implicitly assumed to be false. This happens when the existing information is believed to be complete, at least at a given moment (e.g., in the context of a running application), or when common-sense conclusions are to be drawn from existing evidence under incomplete information. Conclusions based on the absence of information can then be derived. CWA-based formalisms are typically non-monotonic. This means that updating the data/knowledge repositories may invalidate previously derived conclusions. On the contrary, OWA does not make any assumptions about the truth or falsity of a fact unless it can be proven. New information is then always additional: it can be contradictory with respect to previously asserted information, but cannot override it. Thus, if truth or falsity of some fact is unknown, nothing can be inferred about it and both scenarios must be considered, resulting in different models. This apparent flexibility is at the price of *logical inconsistencies* that are not at all admissible in an industrial/practical context. A related problem concerns the fact that OWL does not admit the *Unique Names Assumption* (UNA), which deals with two resources with different identifiers as distinct objects. This implies that, in OWL, we cannot assume the uniqueness of concept names: two different instances can refer to the same object. This is a postulate that is unacceptable in an industrial-oriented applications framework where the name of the concepts must be unique to avoid possible contradictions. The solution proposed by OWL consists in having (controversial) properties like owl:sameAs and owl:differentFrom (see, e.g., Halpin and Hayes [38]).

• More generally, standard OWL-like languages still offer limited support for building up *rules*. On the one hand, the lack of the notion of variable in OWL makes it impossible to rely on this language in its native form to build up real engines for rule processing and no support for rules and rule processing has been introduced in the original OWL specifications. On the other hand, because of their formal background, namely Description Logics (DLs) [7], all the W3C languages are based on a relatively limited reasoning paradigm, i.e., inference by inheritance. As a consequence, to give only an example, all the OWL-based so-called *reasoners* like RACER, Pellet, Fact++ or Hoolet have been created, at least originally, *to solve the most common classification (subsumption) problems rather than to execute real reasoning operations*.
Passing now from the low-level reasoners to the *rule languages* proposed in a SW context like RuleML, TRIPLE and SWRL, these last appear to be quite limited with respect to the range of their possible applications and particularly complex to be used in practice.

For example, SWRL – the Semantic Web Rule Language that, at least until recently, was considered as a sort of standard in the W3C/SW Rule domain – augments OWL by allowing a user to create if-then rules written in terms of OWL classes, properties and individuals. Because of OWA, SWRL does not support negation by failure (NAF), neither classical negation, disjunctions and non-monotonicity. SWRL is also not *decidable* (more precisely, it is semi-decidable). Therefore, SWRL rules are often written in a (more constrained) decidable subset of SWRL, DL-Safe SWRL [54]. In an industrial and practical context, efficient rule-based applications are developed then using commercial *business rules* proposals like IBM Ilog's JRules, FairIsaac's

Blaze Advisor, Oracle's Business Rule Language, RuleBurst's Rules Based Engine Solution etc., or homemade solutions implemented on top of JESS or DROOLS. Note that, being based on the use of n-ary syntactic/semantic structures more powerful and flexible than those normally used in a SW context, the adoption of the GWEs paradigm allows us to build up rules that are both more concise and expressive than the usual ones. We are no more constrained, in fact, to express the "atoms" of these rules in terms of binary clauses and these atoms can now represent directly complex and meaningful situations; a detailed paper on this topic is [85]. All the above criticisms do not mean that the GWEs paradigm rejects contribution coming from the SW world. To supply an immediate example, it is well evident that all reasonable semantic/cognitive IoT applications cannot make abstraction of the in-depth effort on the modelling of the most common IoT notions achieved in a SSN nor in a SW (and similar work) context.

4.3 DEEPENING THE GWE NOTION

GWEs are entities proper to the *digital world*, i.e., they are built up making use of one of those artificial *Knowledge Representation Languages* (KRL) created to manage some aspects of the real world *in software interpretable format*. As all the components of any possible KRL, GWEs are then supposed to represent the *digital counterpart* (the knowledge representation image) of some elements of the real world.

Fundamental constitutive elements of any KRL are *concepts* and *instances*. A concept represents a *general notion* about the real world that is *necessary to encode in digital form* to be able to create and to run computer applications in a particular domain. These notions can correspond to *very broad-spectrum concepts* (like "human being", "event", or "artefact") – proper, then, to several application domains – or to *concepts specially linked to a given application/set of applications* (like "control room operator", "level of temperature", "valve" or "heat exchanger" in some IoT applications in an industrial domain). *Instances* correspond simply to *specific, single examples* of the notions represented by the concepts.

GWEs are then *instances* of specific, single entities of any possible sort/origin that can be *recognized/described in the real world* and that can be *typified* through their association to single/multiple concepts. Considering for example a possible company called "Acme", the GWE ACME_, digital image of the real world entity "Acme", can be created as an instance of the general concept company_ thanks to the insertion of an instanceOf link associating ACME_ to this concept. GWEs are more general than *virtual entities* as they are normally conceived in an IoT context, i.e., as digital images of *chiefly physical entities* (see again Bauer et al. [12], Boussard et al. [18], Ibanez and Friess [43], etc.). GWEs represent on the contrary, in the digital world, *all the possible abstract and concrete things that can be identified (and then named) in the real world*. These correspond to physical objects, but also to humans, actions, events (e.g., "the President Obama's speech in front of the Congress"), scenarios (e.g. "going to the restaurant"), and even imaginary entities (e.g., "Gandalf" in the well-known fantasy novel The Lord of the Rings, or the "fire-breathing green-spotted dragon").

4.3.1 SAMPLE USE OF THE GWE NOTION

Let us suppose we have to encode in GWEs terms a fragment of a possible IoT scenario concerning an Ambient Assisted Living (AAL) application; in this scenario an ageing person, John, is monitored at home by a distributed control system that interacts with John via a mobile robot. This fragment reads: "On a date corresponding to April 11, 2016 at half past nine p.m., the robot reminds John, via audio warning, of the obligation to lock the front door".

In this fragment, we have several categories of entities to be mapped into GWEs of different levels of complexity:

- An animate entity, John.
- Two physical entities, the robot and the front door.
- A modality, the audio warning.
- Two elementary events, the first corresponding to the warning of the robot surface natural language verb "to remind"), the second to the information about the necessity of locking the front door (surface verb "to lock").
- The logical link between the two above events. Being able to represent this link means to be able to represent correctly the global scenario fragment in GWEs terms.

Additional information, such as the date and the obligation, must also be represented, although they do not originate specific GWEs directly, as we will see.

The entities pertaining to the first three categories do not pose any particular problem when represented in a conceptual format. They correspond, in fact, to some *stable, self-contained, a priori and basic notions* – a sort of *background terminological/definitional knowledge* – that can be considered, at least in the short term, as *a-temporal* (or *static*) and *universal*. Passing into the digital world, these entities relate then to simple concepts (human_being, audio_warning, front_door) that, along with their instances (GWEs) JOHN_, AUDIO_WARNING_1, FRONT_DOOR_1, can be denoted using a simple *binary model* like those used normally for the set-up of the existing standard ontologies. In these models, all the properties are expressed as a *binary* (i.e., accepting only two arguments) relationship linking two individuals or an individual and a value. Several ontologies expressing this sort of *background, terminological/definitional knowledge* can be freely found on the Web. For example, see, in a specific IoT context, the Semantic Sensor Network (SSN) ontology [23].

However, the situation is different when we examine the characteristics of those GWEs that represent the two *elementary events* included in the "John and the robot" fragment. In this case, the original data refer to a *particularly complex, dynamic and structured (foreground) information* denoting the *interpersonal, dynamic, unpredictable and strongly spatio-temporal characterized behaviors* proper to the ter-

minological/definitional entities (background knowledge) corresponding to "John", "robot", "audio warning" and "front door". The conceptual model to be employed to formalize this type of foreground knowledge must then necessarily utilize:

- *Conceptual predicates*, corresponding to surface verbs such as "remind" and "look". They are used to specify the *basic types* of events to be taken into account as GWEs.
- The notion of *functional role* [82], used to denote the logical and semantic function of the *background terminological/definitional entities* (representing the arguments of the conceptual predicates) involved in the different elementary events. In the situation of the robot sending a warning to John, the GWE ROBOT_1 is the SUBJ(ect) – or the AG(e)NT – of the action of sending, AUDIO_WARNING_1 the OBJ(ect) and JOHN_ the BEN(e)F(iciary) – see below for the full representation. SUBJ(ect), AG(e)NT, OBJ(ect) etc. are functional roles.
- An adequate, specific formalism to denote the *temporal and location information* and its relationships with the global representation of the elementary events.
- A way of *reifying* the global representations of the elementary events *to be able to refer to them within larger, complex scenarios/events/narratives etc.* – i.e., within GWEs of a higher level of complexity. In our example, e.g., we must specify that the GWE describing the warning corresponds to the message transmitted by the robot, where the elementary event relating the transmission of the message is represented by a different GWE.

The standard *binary* model is *quite ineffective* for taking into account the foreground, dynamic/temporally-characterized knowledge (see Section 4.2.3). An *n-ary* representation must be used then. Formal representations of this type will allow us, in fact, to assemble coherently within a *single* symbolic structure the information that is *different* even if *conceptually related*, in particular, the various *arguments of the predicate* introduced by the functional roles. Using NKRL, the *Narrative Knowledge Representation Language* [81], a KRL often employed for the conceptual representation of *high-level, structured and spatio-temporally denoted information*, the GWEs-based representation of the above fragment is given in Table 4.1. NKRL is both a KRL and a *fully operational environment*, implemented in Java and built up thanks to several European projects. It includes powerful inference engines able to carry out complex inference procedures based on analogical and causal reasoning principles. For example, an industrial, concrete application of this environment often mentioned in an applied-AI context is described in [83]. Other powerful and fully *n*-ary KRLs that could be used to implement GWEs of a high level of complexity are, e.g., Conceptual Graphs [72], Cycl, the *n*-ary representation language of the CYC project [49], Topic Maps [58], IKL, the IKRIS Knowledge Representation Language,[18] etc.

---

[18]http://www.ihmc.us/users/phayes/IKL/SPEC/SPEC.html.

Table 4.1 Examples of high-level GWEs

aal9.c11)	MOVE	SUBJ	ROBOT_1
		OBJ	#aal9.c12
		BENF	JOHN_
		MODAL	AUDIO_WARNING_1
		date-1:	11/4/2016/21:30
		date-2:	

Move:StructuredInformation (4.42)

On 11/4/2016, at 21:30, the robot reminds John through an audio message of what is described in the GWE aal9.c12.

aal9.c12)	MOVE	SUBJ	JOHN_
		OBJ	FRONT_DOOR_1: (unlocked_, locked_)
		{ oblig }	
		date-1:	11/4/2016/21:30
		date-2:	

Move:ForcedChangeOfState (4.12)

On 11/4/2016, at 21:30, John must necessarily, deontic modulator oblig*(ation), lock the front door.*

4.3.2 ADDITIONAL REMARKS ABOUT THE GWES' REPRESENTATION

According to Table 4.1, the two halves of the fragment are denoted by *two structured GWEs* expressed as *instances* of conceptual entities that, in this case, do not correspond to simple *concepts* but to *multilayered templates*. NKRL's templates correspond, in the real world, to *classes* of elementary events/states/situations like, e.g., displacement of a physical object, production of a supporting service, messages sent or received, the changed state of an entity, etc.

As it appears from the two structured GWEs of Table 4.1, templates (represented implicitly in this Table under the form of template instances) are *n-ary structures* formed of several triples of the "predicate – functional role – argument of the predicate" form. The triples are *indissolubly associated* and have the predicate in common – MOVE in Table 4.1, but also EXPERIENCE, EXIST, OWN, PRODUCE etc. [81]. Extra formal features of the *determiners/attributes* types used to supply *additional information* with respect to the (ternary) basic structure of templates and their instances. For example, the deontic modulator oblig(ation) has been employed in aal9.c12 to denote the *absolute necessity* of locking the front door. The *temporal attributes* date-1/date-2 introduce the *temporal information* proper to the original elementary events, see [81], in this context. In the template instances (structured GWEs), *semantic labels* like, e.g., aal9.c11 in Table 4.1, *reify* the global structures giving them a *name*. This sort of reification is particularly important because the semantic labels can be used to *associate together* several independent GWEs, giving then rise to the symbolic representation of *complex real world scenarios*. In Table 4.1 for example, the transmission of the message to John is represented by assuming that the symbolic label aal9.c12, denoting indirectly the content of this message, is taken as the OBJ(ect) of the transmission of information represented by the aal9.c11 GWE. This associative modality, which makes use of *Higher Order Logic (HOL) structures*, is called *completive construction* in NKRL.

Another HOL linking modality of NKRL is the *binding construction*, where several *symbolic labels* denoting elementary events are collected into a list as *arguments*

Table 4.2 A GWE denoting the robot's discovery

aal9.c13)	PRODUCE	SUBJ	ROBOT_1
		OBJ	detection_
		TOPIC	(SPECIF FRONT_DOOR_1 unlocked_)
		date-1:	11/4/2016/21:29
		date-2:	

Produce:Assessment/Trial (6.32)

On 11/4/2016, at 21:29, the robot detects that the front door is unlocked.

Table 4.3 John agrees to lock the door

aal9.c15)	BEHAVE	SUBJ	JOHN_
		MODAL	willing_
		TOPIC	aal9.c16
		{ obs }	
		date-1:	11/4/2016/21:31
		date-2:	

Behave:WillingToDo (1.321)

On 11/4/2016, at 21:31, we can see (temporal modulator obs(erve)) that John agrees about what denoted in aal9.c16.

*aal9.c16)	MOVE	SUBJ	JOHN_
		OBJ	FRONT_DOOR_1: (unlocked_, locked_)
		date-1:	
		date-2:	

Move:ForcedChangeOfState (4.12)

At some time or another, John will lock the front door.

of a particular *binding operator*. Conceptual tools of this type are, e.g., (CAUSE s_1 s_2), meaning that the event denoted by the symbolic label s_1 finds its origin in the event denoted by s_2, and (GOAL s_1 s_2), meaning that the goal of the event denoted by s_1 is the setting up of the situation denoted by s_2. For example, a new *structured GWE*, labelled as aal9.c14 and consisting in a binding construction like (CAUSE aal9.c11 aal9.c13) – where aal9.c11 still denotes the transmission of the message (see Table 4.1) and aal9.c13 is represented in Table 4.2 – could be used to indicate that the warning has been caused by the robot's discovery that the front door was unlocked. In Table 4.2, the concept detection_ is a (low level) specific term of the activity_ sub-tree of HClass (Hierarchy of Classes), the standard NKRL ontology; SPECIF(ication) is the "attributive" operator, used to introduce additional information with respect to the first argument of the operator, the FRONT-DOOR-1 (low level) GWE in our case.

We can make the encoding of the scenario even more complete by adding the aal9.c15 GWE (see Table 4.3) to denote that, immediately after the warning, John seems to be willing to execute the action detailed in the aal9.c16 structured GWE – from a formal point of view, this is another example of use of the completive construction. The two aal9.c12 and aal9.c16 GWEs are, obviously, very similar. They differ, however, with respect to the associated temporal information: aal9.c15 is marked as "uncertain" (code "*") given that no precise date is known at the time of coding for the locking operation, and its two date slots are empty.

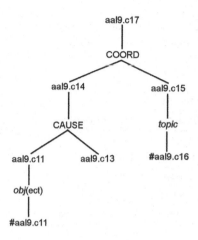

FIGURE 4.1

Graphic representation of the "John and the robot" scenario

Assembling all the formal structures introduced above we can see that the general structured GWE – let us label it as aal9.c17 – which symbolizes the "John and the robot" scenario as developed up to now can be represented under tree format, see Fig. 4.1. Its top level consists of a binding construction (COORD aal9.c14 aal9.c15): all the arguments of the binding operator COORD(ination) have equal importance from a logical/semantic point of view and must necessarily be considered together. From Fig. 4.1 it appears clearly, then, that the core of the formalized scenario is represented by two blocks of NKRL code (two structured GWEs), the first denoting the sending of the warning following the discovery of the open door, and the second denoting John's agreement to lock the door. The formalization could be made, obviously, even more complex adding, e.g., the details of the locking actions, possible new remarks of the robot, etc.

Note, to conclude, that complex situations analogous to this scenario are currently managed in an IoT context. A use case in BUTLER concerns the NFC car parking examples [15]; an analogous scenario is described in CALIPSO [51]. See also the manufacturing and traceability scenarios in EBBITS [3, 42–43], some very extended narratives that describe the IoT-A logistic and health at home scenarios [31], the weather observation experiments summarized in [68], etc. Very often, however, and opposed to what we have seen in the "John and robot case", the representations of the IoT scenarios are only partially formalized and largely expressed in natural language. This implies, among other things, reduced possibilities of adequate inference activity.

4.3.3 FINAL COMMENTS ABOUT THE GWE PARADIGM

We conclude this section by noticing that the adoption of the GWEs paradigm necessarily implies the use of a *high-level* (an *n*-ary) KRL. This rules out, e.g., the use in a GWEs context of, e.g., the so-called sensor languages [3] like the Extended Environments Markup Language, EEML, the Physical Markup Language, PML, or the Sensor Model Language, SensorML (at least without tweaks). Even if all these XML-based languages undoubtedly offer interesting solutions for IoT problems in a quite strict *physical level* context, it is difficult to see them as general solutions for representing and managing many-sided events, behaviors, intentions etc., as needed in the "John and the robot" scenario. Because of their strictly *binary-oriented representation* model and the reasons already expressed, similar considerations can be formulated about the SW tools like RDF(S), OWL, SPARQL, SWRL etc. For concise introductions to SW from an IoT point of view and indications about some actual results see, e.g., [68,2,9]. NKRL seems to represent then a reasonable solution for introducing workable semantic/conceptual features in an IoT context.

4.4 AN ARCHITECTURE FOR THE GWE PARADIGM

Several types of IoT architectures have been proposed and implemented in the past, mainly in the framework of European projects. Interactions among the different BUTLER platforms to achieve access and communication among embedded devices, servers and mobile terminals are given in [12]. The EBBITS project proposes the Service-Oriented Architecture (SOA) and its use for distributed intelligent service structures in the EBBITS platform [3]. [10] describes the architectural aspects of the IoT-A project. Several architectural solutions for IoT are illustrated in [73]. See also projects like OpenIoT, iCORE, COMPOSE, SmartSantander etc. Lempert and Pflaum [48] introduce an abstract software architecture for an integration platform for diverse smart object technologies; Barnaghi et al. [8] describe a linked-data platform to publish sensor data and link them to existing resources on the Semantic Web.

4.4.1 GENERAL CHARACTERISTICS OF THE ARCHITECTURE

As stated in the previous sections, the GWEs paradigm allows us to deal in a logically coherent *unified way* with both *physical* entities captured at the sensor level and with *higher level of abstraction* structures. From an architectural point of view, this approach must be mirrored in the design of the *middleware layer* of any IoT system implementing this paradigm. For the GWEs-based systems, the middleware has to be implemented then according to a *cognitive-oriented design largely centered on the recognition and management of Generalized World Entities* (GWEs). Fig. 4.2 illustrates, from an operational point of view, the *set of phases* (*sequence of transformations*) to be performed in the middleware layer to pass from the recognition of a change of state at the Sensors/Actuators layer (physical level) to the corresponding visualization operations at the Front End level. A general, high-level representation of the platform's architecture is represented in Fig. 4.2, where the central function of the middleware layer is emphasized. Structured according to three main layers, this architecture shows some similarities with, e.g., the cognitive OpenIoT architecture mentioned above. The three layers are:

- The *Front End* layer that is used to communicate with the users and the stakeholders to monitor and/or interact with the applications through *views* representing parts of the global system. Moreover, in the set-up phase of a specific application, the Front End addresses the users' needs by providing a set of services and features allowing, e.g., their easy recognition, the assignment of user's roles and the definition of the associated authorizations. This layer is a web-server component to which the end user connects with a XUL-compatible web-browser.[19]
- The *Core (or Middleware)* layer handles the different applications according to the GWEs paradigm. It includes the modules to be used to build and manage the GWEs, the inference engines, the ontological tools etc., and is conceived as a plug-in modular set of mechanisms allowing the inclusion/deletion of additional modules. The platform should then be *open* in order to allow, with a limited personalization effort, for an easy plug-in of: i) new general modules that could be needed to improve the functioning of the platform; ii) domain-specific GWEs applications.
- The *Sensors/Actuators* layer allows the communication between the monitoring and actuation entities (sensors, robots, services mounted on these entities) and the core layer. An external entity (a "Thing") can be accessed only through this layer. This notifies the Core about the relevant state changes concerning the input entities. Conversely, in case the final inference operations imply some modifications to the external world (close/open a door, remove an obstacle, activate an alarm...), the sensors/actuators layer receives the state changes and operations decided in the Core model and translates them into data/information/commands intelligible by the external world.

In this type of structure, for the sake of generality/flexibility and, at least as a first approximation, we have assumed that the core is executed in a single machine, while the Front End and the Sensors/Actuators layer can run on a number of remote machines. A central hypothesis is that the core ignores how many Front End and Sensors/Actuators layers are running. Conversely, the Front End and Sensors/Actuators layers only know that there is a single Core and they are aware of its location. The communication protocols between the three layers of Fig. 4.2 are the same (sets of standard messages).

4.4.2 SOME DETAILS ABOUT THE CORE LAYER MODULES

The function of (some of) the main modules of the Core are as follows:

---

[19]https://developer.mozilla.org/en-US/docs/Mozilla/Tech/XUL.

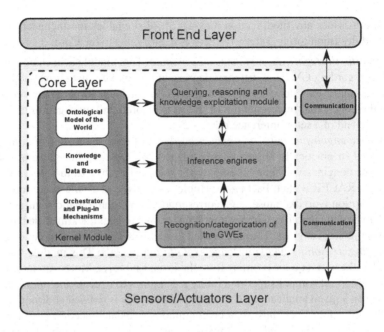

FIGURE 4.2

A schematic view of the architecture of a GWEs-based IoT platform

- *Kernel module*: it deals with the GWEs semantic/conceptual model and provides the interfaces for accessing this model. It is formed of several functional components, e.g.:

  - *Ontological Model of the World.* This component provides the tools for storing and maintaining the different GWEs' ontological structures. It assures the correct instantiation of these components to build up GWEs of different levels of complexity in accordance with the results of the *Recognition/categorization module* and by checking the logical constraints. It also updates the model according to the evolutions of the external world and the results of the inference operations.

  - *Knowledge and Data Bases.* This component manages a set of permanent data and knowledge structures storing both metadata about the maintenance of the Model of the World and knowledge about the various contexts. An important role is played by the data persistency and security/privacy functions that assure model recovery in case of failure and the description of authorizations for various roles.

  - *Orchestrator and Plug-in Mechanism.* This component is in charge of the orchestration of all the Core modules. It provides the interfaces for accessing the model of the world and deals with the notification of the changes in this model. The component must wait for the results produced by the Inference engines before it issues any modification message. It also enables the inclusion of other modules (monitoring, safety, resilience, security...) to the Core.

- *Recognition/categorization of the GWEs module*: This module is in charge of operations regarding GWEs of different degrees of complexity that correspond to new entities and events detected at the Sensor/Actuator layer level. These operations use the conceptual representation of the world stored and managed in the Kernel module and of a set of inference rules.
- *Inference engines module*: Inference procedures of diverse degrees of complexity are used in practically all the phases of the GWEs processing. Several sorts of inference engines will then be employed. These will range from tools in the SW style as RACER, Pellet, Fact++ or Hoolet to be used in all the operations of the subsumption type like those, e.g., corresponding to the automatic/semi-automatic updating of the ontology (see Section 4.5.2 below), to backtracking based, multiple reasoning-steps engines. They are needed to deal with complex examples of GWEs.
- *Querying, reasoning and knowledge exploitation module*: This module loads and handles the user's queries coming from the Front End layer. Moreover, it makes use of the different sorts of supported inference engines to execute the inference rules proper to a given application. A first set of these rules is defined at design time for each application; they must then be continuously updated according to the intermediate results. 'Knowledge exploitation' means that, starting from the conceptual representation of the world and from the results obtained using the inference engines, it is possible to improve both the *breadth* and the *depth* of the knowledge of the environment. For example, the module can get new or richer information about detected events or pro-actively move the sensors to acquire new significant information.
- *Communication module*: This enables asynchronous communications among the layers. Some internal components of the Core can however communicate directly via synchronous services or internal messaging systems.

4.4.3 FUNCTIONAL VIEW OF THE ARCHITECTURE OF A GWES-BASED SYSTEM

Fig. 4.3 supplies a functional diagram illustrating, from an operational point of view, the GWEs IoT methodology, i.e., the sequence of transformations to be performed from the recognition of a change of state at the physical level to the corresponding visualization/actuating operations at the front end level.

The conversion of the sensors' outputs into conceptual GWEs is realized by comparing their values/properties with the properties of the GWEs represented as nodes of ontological structures of different complexities. Apart from particularly simple cases, the comparison involves the use of (generalized) *if-then rules*. For example, the creation of a GWE corresponding to a movement can imply, among other things, the use of a rule intended to verify that the entity signaled in location A at time t_0 is the same identified in location B at time t_{0+x} where x depends on the context and on the type of movement. We can note that these conversion operations will prove also as

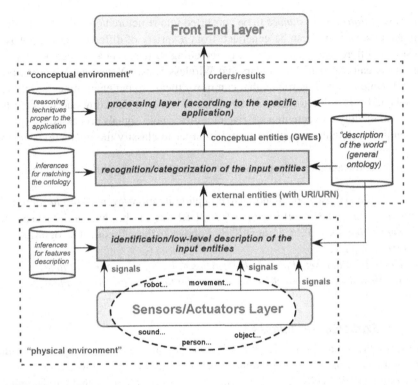

FIGURE 4.3

Functional view of the architecture of a GWE-based IoT system

particularly important when coming to bridge the *semantic gap* between the recognition of entities at the sensor/physical level and their representation/management at the conceptual level.

4.5 IMPLEMENTATION OF THE GWES PARADIGM

To provide the technological background that is needed to implement our proposed architecture, we describe in some depth the different steps of the procedure specified in Fig. 4.3; see also, e.g., [84] for more details.

4.5.1 INPUT ENTITIES

The objective concerns here the identification and the accurate characterization of all the possible *input entities* coming into a GWEs-based system from (an) external data stream(s) and to be transformed into GWEs. These entities can correspond to static objects, persons, multimedia information but also to spatio/temporally bounded *events/situations/circumstances* to be converted into structured/complex GWEs. The original data stream(s) can be generated from a variety of different hardware-based sensors of different levels of complexity, including RFIDs, contact switches and pressure mats, cameras, LIDARs, radars and Wireless Sensor Networks (WSNSs), possibly mounted on mobile robots that can move them around environments. Infrared sensors and 3-D video tracking systems can be used for detecting and tracking the presence, identity and activities of given entities; audio signals processed by speech recognition techniques can prove useful in order to classify the interactions among people, etc.

This identification/description activity means that the *original entities* must:

- *all* – including those corresponding to complex situations/events – *be characterized initially by a (provisional) identifier* (e.g., URI-like), to be changed into a specific *instance label*, like aal9.c11 or DOOR_1 above, in the subsequent recognition/categorization phase;
- *be endowed with a set of features/properties to be calculated in real time*;
- *be supplied with some interface allowing them to communicate/be integrated with other entities.*

4.5.1.1 *Extraction Techniques*

Extracting the initial *characteristic features* (identifiable attributes/properties) of the input entities by analyzing the output of several sensors – for temperature, motion, localization (RFID, GPS...), weight etc. – is a *complex activity* that can benefit of various integrated techniques. For example, with respect to the physical objects, all sorts of analytical tools like first- and second-order derivative expressions, Haar transforms, auto-regressive models and Canny–Deriche etc. filters (for edge detection), local color descriptors, global color histograms, (syntactic) pattern recognition techniques and discriminant factor analysis (for identify movements) etc. can be used. Crossed extraction – i.e., using the outputs of other sensors to reinforce the analysis proper to a given sensor – can be employed to obtain more reliable results. Use of COTS (Commercial Off-The-Shelf) tools will be envisaged whenever possible. A combination of different characteristic features extracted from the sensor data can provide accurate descriptions/characterizations for identifying the presence and properties of *entity objects* in the environment. Static and mobile objects can be detected and tracked using standard techniques (for instance, using a Viola–Jones-like approach), and by adaptively arranging the classifications.

For the detection and tracking of human beings, traditional *symbolic approaches* based on *shape analysis* techniques and grounded on parametric 3D models of humans can be utilized. These techniques use combinations of *geons* (simple 3-D geometric primitives) for the torso, the head, upper and lower arms, as well for upper and lower legs. To ensure a correct fitting, a parameterization of the geons is needed to deal with the high variability of humans due to factors like age, gender, clothing styles, etc. To improve performance, an appropriate *hierarchical approach* for classification and fitting could be used, e.g., by starting with a search for torso candidates, followed by a spatially limited search for heads in their neighborhoods, etc.

However, there have been significant, new technical progresses in recent years in the area of human tracking. Up-to-date commercial systems based on RGB-D (Red Green Blue + Depth) cameras and time-of-flight sensors and enabling advanced gesture, facial and voice recognition – such as Kinect [69], SoftKinetic, and Leap Motion – have started to appear on the market. These sensors can be used in a GWEs context. Each of these new methods, however, has limitations. For example, Kinect can track whole body motion but has low precision and cannot reliably track hands. On the other hand, Leap Motion is more precise, but it can track fingertips only. In the GWEs context, we are then going to combine the output of different sensors – supplemented by rough data about localization of a human person returned by simpler distributed sensors like infrared (IR) proximity sensors, pressure sensors, and door switches – in order to provide more complete raw data for further processing. Output of different sensors will be used as input to a *dynamic system in a state-space form*, where non-observable state variables will be estimated using Extended Kalman Filters [30].

4.5.1.2 *Uncertainty Problems*

Independently of the techniques used to identify the input entities and their type, it is evident that, for real scenarios beyond a certain level of complexity, the Sensors/Actuators layer will never be able to deliver perfect and complete information. What this layer can realistically provide is a set of low-level partial and inaccurate information (about positions, pressures, etc. and low-level events in general) with an *associated confidence* or *probability distribution*. This information can be processed with the use of statistical tools like Bayesian networks and Dempster–Shafer methods whilst delaying the selection of a final commitment to the use of high-level inference techniques.

Note, however, that Kalman filters, also called Linear Quadratic Estimation (LQE) techniques Chui and Chen [21], are today largely used for dealing with uncertainty in IoT-related applications like time series analysis in signal processing and motion planning and control and trajectory optimization in robotics [74].

A *least commitment strategy* can thus be employed in our GWEs/IoT context. Accordingly, final identification of input entities is postponed as long as possible. Different, and possibly contradictory hypotheses, will be maintained about the type of the incoming entities, their positions, their state, etc. A hypothesis is established if it has enough support from sensor data. It can be interpreted as a *voting procedure* by the sensors, which does not need the consensus of all the sensor data. Several hypotheses are then processed *in parallel*, for instance using a particle filter. For example, the expected position of an object according to its anticipated motion may differ from the position estimated by range measurements or by optical flow: all these positions are kept until later resolution of the ambiguities. Usually, there is enough time for waiting. Otherwise, if an urgent action has to be performed immediately, the action should be chosen to fit to the most probable hypotheses, and the whole algorithm can then be implemented as an anytime algorithm.

4.5.1.3 *Recognition of Entities Corresponding to Structured GWEs*

To conclude, we remark that all the above techniques can be successfully used separately to identify independent entities corresponding to *single* GWEs and their characteristic features – e.g., by reconstructing the constitutive elements, edges, corners, interest points, curvatures, etc. of a squared_object and signaling also the presence of an individual that is the subject of a MOVE action in the direction of this object. The situation is different when we must identify the characteristics of complex events, situations and circumstances and their behavioral properties that correspond to *structured GWEs* – e.g., by describing at the feature level a whole complex event that will give rise to a GWE representing an entity_ that MOVE(s) towards a squared_object. In the most complex cases, in fact, the additional execution of *inference operations* is required, implying the use of the *modelling of events and situations* components of the world model (see Section 4.5.4).

4.5.2 CONCEPTUAL REPRESENTATION OF THE WORLD

The GWEs paradigm is strongly *ontology-based*. Being able to fully recognizing/categorizing the (known or unknown) GWEs requires, in particular, the setup of a *conceptual model, namely a representation of the world in an ontological form with auto-evolving properties*.

4.5.2.1 *The two Types of Knowledge*

The design of this model must be *general enough to describe both the static/background and the dynamic/foreground characteristics/features/properties … of the GWEs*. Considering the discussion of Section 4.3, the model must take into account, at the same time:

- Those *stable, self-contained, a priori and basic notions* (terminological knowledge) that can be considered, at least initially, as *a-temporal* and *universal*. A characteristic of these notions concerns the fact that their associated definitions/descriptions in terms of properties *are not subject to change* within the framework of a given IoT application. In the following, we will refer to them as the *background knowledge*.
- The *complex and structured* (dynamic knowledge) information denoting the *multiple, interpersonal, unpredictable and strongly spatio-temporal characterized behaviors* proper to sets of logically interrelated, specific *background knowledge entities* like John, robot, message and front door in the example of Section 4.3. This dynamic knowledge is typically structured into elementary events like "The robot sends a message to John" or "John must lock the front door" (see the example). We will refer to this highly dynamic and *in fieri* knowledge as the *foreground knowledge*.

The overall model will include, classically, an *upper level* common to all the GWEs/IoT applications and (at least relatively) stable, and a *medium/lower level*, extension of the previous one and specific to the different applications – integrated, in case, with a representation of the environment (for example, based on a grid).

The modelling of the simplest, *background* GWEs like physical objects as tables, cars, bottles or vegetables – but also temperatures, light levels, pressures, etc. – can be easily obtained, as already stated, by using a standard ontology. This will use the usual conceptual relationships, namely PartOf, MemberOf and their inverses (*meronymic* relationships [80], i.e., relationships between parts and wholes) in addition to the traditional IsA (and its inverse, HasSpecialization) and InstanceOf (HasInstance) links. Important characteristics of the ontology concern:

- The possibility of supplying an *in-depth description* of the *properties* associated with its different external entities in order to *minimize the risk of false or near-matches with the characteristic features* (low-level properties) of the GWEs.
- The existence of a well-developed upper level in order to guarantee, as much as possible, that a *match will always be assured even in the absence of a precise identification* – e.g., squared_object instead of squared_table or object_grasping instead of bottle_grasping.

Ontologies of objects can be easily found on the Web. The majority of them are in RDF/OWL format or have bridges towards a SW format; in this context, the already mentioned SSN ontology can be of interest in a GWEs context. Even if a W3C/SW format is not mandatory – and its adoption could cause logical consistency problems with respect to the *n*-ary representation principles generally adopted in a GWEs context – *the adoption of an RDF(S)/OWL solution for the background knowledge could be strongly advisable*. This choice will allow us, in fact, *to profit from the several W3C/SW tools (RACER, Pellet, FaCT++ ...) existing on the market and committed to facilitating the set up and the coherence checking of standard ontologies*.

With respect now to the *modelling of the foreground knowledge (events/situations/ circumstances, etc.) where the above static entities are involved*, standard ontologies and RDF(S)/OWL solutions are not sufficient (see the discussion in Section 4.2.3). More complex and powerful conceptual structures should then be adopted to describe the *interrelationships of the elementary, basic entities involved in the events/situations/...* Examples are relations between the robot and the ageing person, or the ageing person and the door in the above example. Such conceptual structures correspond to NKRL's *templates* (see those used in the encoding of the example of Section 4.3.1 in software interpretable format). As seen, templates correspond to formal descriptions, based on the notions of *semantic predicate* (like MOVE) and *functional roles* (like SUBJ(ect), OBJ(ect)...), of *general classes of dynamic structured entities corresponding to events/situations/circumstances/behaviors*. NKRL templates are assembled into a hierarchical structure called HTemp (*hierarchy of templates*).

An advantage of this solution concerns also the fact that, in NKRL, *these structured GWEs (instances of general templates) can be associated, in turn, making use of Higher Order Logic (HOL) conceptual tools.* An example is given by the completive construction modality used in Tables 4.1 and 4.3. Another HOL linking modality of NKRL is represented by the so-called binding construction introduced in Section 4.3.2 and allowing us, e.g., to model situations in the style of "the robot is issuing a message *because* it has discovered that the front door is open" (see Table 4.2). Note that this sort of HOL mechanism is largely used in NKRL *to represent complex scenarios of the intention/willingness/behavior type.*

4.5.2.2 *Auto-Evolving Techniques*

Some simple *auto-evolving* possibilities of the ontologies – in practice, *the possibility of progressively adding new conceptual entities within these hierarchies* – must be foreseen in a GWEs context. Apart from assuring a certain degree of flexibility and generality of the ontological tools – and of providing an opportunity of *improving the model by learning from experience* – this possibility allows dealing with a very important, practical problem. This comes up when the identification of an incoming entity as a low-level, background GWE is not possible – even in an approximate way, as in the squared_object instead of squared_table example mentioned above – *because of the lack of the corresponding set of ontological entities.* In this case, because of the obvious associated *fuzziness* problems, it is appropriate to avoid the *systematic creation of the GWE to be associated with the incoming entity as an instance of the root_of the ontology* (or some other very high-level concepts).

Currently, no reliable theory/technique exists to deal with this sort of problems in a general way. A pragmatic approach to avoid the above over-generalization problem consists in:

- Keeping the provisional URI/URN associated with the incoming entity in the sensor-based description phase as the temporary *name* of the corresponding GWE. Create then a provisional father-concept for this new instance and *transfer to this last all the properties recognized for the original entity.*
- Using W3C/SW reasoners in the style of RACER, Pellet, Fact++ or Hoolet to insert in the best way, by means of a subsumption approach, the provisional concept (and its associated provisional instance/GWE) within the structures of the ontological hierarchy.
- Using (off-line, in case) free available knowledge bases like Roget's Thesaurus and WordNet, or Open-CYC, to assign the final name to new concept (and to its instance). This allows us, among other things, to import within the GWEs' ontological model all the conceptual entities that, in such large knowledge bases, are in the immediate environment of the concept corresponding to the discovered one.

Secondary problems typical of this context that concern, e.g., versioning or the recognition of deprecated concepts can be (at least provisionally) ignored, or dealt with off-line.

4.5.3 FULL RECOGNITION AND CATEGORIZATION OF THE GWES

The conceptual representation of the world mentioned above – a general ontology, including structures *for representing both static/background concepts and foreground events/situations* – will be used in association with a set of *inference rules* in order to recognize/categorize the GWEs corresponding to the input entities.

As already mentioned, in a GWEs context, recognizing/categorizing means to *establish a correspondence* (more precisely, *recognizing as instances*) between the known/unknown entities (objects, events, relationships, situations, circumstances, etc.) coming from the external world and the high level conceptual and ontological representations proper to the description of the world – incrementing these last as experiences are accumulated. Note that being able of implementing a full recognition and categorization of GWEs represents a significant improvement with respect to the state of the art. In fact, there is no guaranty in general that the information available in the external environment could be sufficient to perform the recognition task in an adequately complete way – and this independently from the level of completeness of the ontology. For instance, to return to a previous example, sensing (and inferencing) might not be capable of fully categorizing a table as such, leading then to the instance SQUARE_OBJECT_1 for an incoming GWE instead of the correct TABLE_1 or TOFFEE_BOX_1 instances. Our world model must thus be *sufficiently powerful to make up for, in case, the lack of information associated with the provisional descriptions of the GWEs with its own stored knowledge.* When stored knowledge is not sufficient for depicting a complete state of the environment, sensors can be proactively directed to get missing information – when this is possible of course, e.g., when sensors are mounted on a mobile robot.

Moreover, as stated in Section 4.5.2, the world model must be *sufficiently flexible to allow for the creation of new conceptual entities in case of impossibility of associating the description of an external incoming entity with an existing ontological entity.*

As explained in what follows, the recognition/categorization activities will be performed in two subsequent phases.

4.5.3.1 Categorization of Background Input Entities

In the first phase, the raw descriptions of the input entities pertaining to an (extended) *physical objects* category will be matched with the conceptual entities included in the *background* (standard) component of the world model introduced above. This will be done thanks, mainly, to the use of a *semantic-based reasoning system* able to unify, to the best possible extent, the low-level features (properties/attributes) attached initially to the input entities with the semantic properties of the general concepts included in this background component. This conceptual unification activity will be integrated with the usual, algorithmic machine learning techniques used to recognize an object through a comparison of the associated features with those of standard objects stored in a database. Existing methodologies are SIFT, Scale Invariant Feature Transform [50,32], SURF, Speeded-Up Robust Features [13], HOG, Histograms of Oriented Gradients [24], etc. In some tasks, like those relative to patrolling and search and rescue, this process could exploit a *representation of the environment* (see Section 4.5.2.1) to help matching the physical entities detected by sensors to the general concepts. When the match succeeds with a reasonable probability degree, the GWE is created and a new instance of the corresponding concept is added to the corresponding branch of the model.

This procedure is equivalent to *semantically annotating* input entities (input sensor data) with *concepts associated with standard ontologies*. We can note its correspondence with recent *semantic approaches* devoted to mitigate, in an IoT context, the interoperability problems originated by the use of multiple competing application level protocols. Consider, for example, to mention some open-source solutions, protocols like CoAP (Constrained Application Protocol), MQTT (Message Queue Telemetry Transport), OMA LWM2M (Lightweight M2M, a device management protocol from the Open Mobile Alliance), XMPP (Extensible Messaging and Presence Protocol). A scalable IoT architecture should, in fact, be independent of any difference among the various messaging protocol standards and should provide, on the contrary, integration and translation between them. In this context, a particularly interesting solution has been proposed in [28]. As mentioned in Section 4.2.2.2, the approach is based on the *Semantic Gateway as a Service* (SGS) as a bridge between the physical world and the high-level layers of an IoT system, and on *semantic annotation* procedures of sensor data using the *Semantic Sensor Network* (*SSN*) *ontology*. See also, in an (IoT-oriented) SW annotation context, well-known works like [68,8], etc.

4.5.3.2 *Categorization of Foreground Input Entities*

The procedures developed in a GWEs framework for recognizing the external entities represented by contexts, events, situations, circumstances – i.e., for identifying the corresponding conceptual entities described in the *dynamic/foreground* component of the world model – represent an important step towards the progressive generalization of the present IoT paradigm. They consist mainly in a *reasoning process based, in general, on the results of the previous process of recognition of the physical/static/background GWEs*. Let us suppose that a simple IoT system formed of sensors of different types – more invasive, like cameras or GPS, or less invasive, like RFID, contact switches and pressure recognition tools – could be used to hypothesize the presence of a GWE of an event of the Move:ForcedChangeOfState type. This can correspond to a situation where a human being is locking a door (see the example of Table 4.1). Before being able to add a new instance (a new GWE) of an event of this type to the dynamic component of the world model, we must:

- Identify the possible concept/instances that are candidate to fill the SUBJ(ect) and OBJ(ect) – and, in case, TOPIC, MODAL(ity), etc. – properties, i.e., the functional roles associated with the MOVE predicate that identifies the general conceptual category of this event.
- Verify that these potential fillers satisfy the constraints associated with the above roles. This means to verify that, e.g., a GWE labelled a JOHN_ in the previous,

background categorization phase, really corresponds to an instance of the human_being or robot_ concepts in the static/background component of the world model. A constraint of this type is associated, in fact, to the filler of the SUBJ(ect) role in the NKRL Move:ForcedChangeOfState template. In the same way, the filler of the OBJ(ect) role must be a GWE instance of the artefact_ concept, etc.

- Verify the *global coherence* of the new dynamic/foreground GWE with respect to the global situation we are dealing with. This means verifying that, as in the example of Table 4.1, this GWE corresponds really to the content of a message addressed to John or, in a subsequent phase, to an action carried out by John as a consequence, e.g., of the previous message.

It is also possible that a pure cognitive-driven approach *is not sufficient* to solve the correspondence problem in the most complex cases when dealing with categorization of foreground entities. Robotics-oriented solutions based, e.g., on temporal constraint propagation principle – see, e.g., those used in PEIS, Physically Embedded Intelligent Systems [64], for situation recognition – could then be associated with the cognitive ones to produce an optimized result.

4.5.4 REASONING FROM THE FULL RECOGNIZED SITUATIONS

When all the GWEs (corresponding to objects, agents, events, situations, circumstances, complex events and scenarios, behaviors, contexts, etc.) have been created, we make use of the general world description enriched with all these instances to *make decisions* (such as event processing to choose which goal to pursue, or to change the current plan). In case, *physical actions* (like opening/closing gates/doors, allowing/disallowing switches, etc.) on the external environment can also be foreseen. In a GWEs framework, these reasoning activities – represented, mainly, under the form of *inference procedures* – can be seen as *the implementation of a set of services*. These should be: i) aware of the context and of the available resources, ii) autonomously able to decide and react based on the given information, iii) and able to work together collaboratively. Moreover, they must be general enough to be used (in case, slightly adapted) in a vast range of GWEs applications: they will then be permanently stored on the platform.

4.5.4.1 *General Principles*

In an IoT context, *inferencing* is often implemented according to formalisms based on probabilistic principles as the Bayesian inference or the Dempster-Shafer theory. Techniques of this type are also used in a GWEs context to solve specific problems (see Section 4.5.1). However, in agreement with the GWEs' foundation on a high-level ontological approach, reasoning and inferencing are implemented here, mainly, according to a *symbolic approach*. GWEs' inference procedures will use a system of generalized "*if/then rules*" similar to the rule sets utilized in the commercial and open source Business Rules Engines (BREs) solutions, see also Section 4.2.3 above. An overview of the problems associated with the development of rule-based tools can be found in [37]. The common denominator for most of the BREs is the use of the Rete algorithm [33] and of its more recent versions (like Rete-2, Rete-3 and Rete-NT) to process incoming events against the stored rules.

The *rule language* to be used in a GWEs context is based on the powerful and successful NKRL inferencing system, which allows us to make use of advanced inference procedures in an "intelligent information retrieval style". For example, inference rules of the transformation type can be used to get, thanks to a sort of analogical reasoning, an *approximate answer* in case of failure of a direct query addressed to a specific knowledge base. Rules of the hypothesis type allow us to automatically find *causal connections* among structured GWEs representing situations or events, in the most general acceptation of these last terms. The antecedent and consequent components of all the above rules are represented by associations of partially-instantiated NKRL templates. Detailed descriptions of the NKRL inference techniques can be found, e.g., in [85].

4.5.4.2 *Examples of Services under the form of Inference Scenarios*

In this section, we illustrate some possible applications of the reasoning process that can be performed in our GWEs framework. These can concern, among many others:

- *Avoiding and managing critical situations*. This type of inference refers to situations like that schematically illustrated in Zarri [84], where the goal of the GWEs-based application consists in preventing a person with vision troubles (or a robot or a baby) to collide with potentially dangerous objects. This activity must be based on an in-depth knowledge of the (*a priori* unknown) GWEs in the environment to let the system decide whether a given object should be absolutely avoided (i.e., a table) or it can in principle be stepped on (a newspaper, a magazine, a puddle...). The same type of inference can be *easily generalized* in a context of homeland security, of driving control, of exploration of unknown territories by a rover, of butler robots, of crisis situations – see, e.g., in this last context [34].
- *Planning*. This set of reasoning activities could concern the optimization, e.g., of the surveillance tasks of an ageing person, or the creation of an adaptive buying path within a supermarket, or the more mundane task of preparing a cold drink. In this last case, the planning activities will consist in going to the cupboard to get a cup, going then to the fridge, opening the fridge, taking out the juice, and eventually pouring the juice into the cup. Planning includes prioritizing the goals, establishing when goals are complete, determining when the system is required to re-plan, etc. Once again, this sort of activity is proper to a very wide set of GWEs applications.
- *Monitoring*. Monitoring concerns a large class of possible applications, from that related to an elderly person in homecare after hospitalization to the prevention of terrorism activities (bomb disposal etc.), decontamination of lands and buildings, building safety, identity management, gas/oil plants inspection and supervision, etc.; see, e.g., [34]. In the elderly person case, when the system detects a fall down from stairs, it must request hospital emergency intervention and move a house care

mobile robot, embedded with a camera, to connect the (supposedly still conscious) elderly with the hospital. This is done using the camera and vital signal sensors to evaluate her/his health state while waiting for the emergency staff arrival. In all the monitoring cases, different independent GWEs of a different degree of complexity must be identified/categorized, and then aggregated/correlated to represent complex events/situations.

- *Intentions/behaviors detection.* Inferences of this type have normally (but not necessarily) GWEs of the human type as central characters. They can be associated with monitoring activities when, in the elderly monitoring situation evoked above, it is necessary to infer from her/his itinerary and actions that the old person manages to get away from the house instead of going into the kitchen/toilet, or when the unfriendly intentions of an intruder must be detected. They also concern a wide range of sociological applications such as detecting particular behaviors in young people denoting a possible pathway to social rejection, inferring attitudes towards health-related issues like the adoption of condoms, leisure, exercise or diet, carrying out perspective studies concerning the behavior of shoppers or intentions of (human/automatic) drivers, etc.

4.6 CONCLUSIONS

In spite of the notable progresses observed in recent years in the IoT/WoT domain, the semantic/cognitive capabilities of the IoT/WoT systems are still far from being fully acceptable. We can note, for example:

- The limited ability of the present IoT/WoT systems to deal with *dynamic and time varying data* (*events*).
- The limited ability to *generalize and abstract*, at the semantic/conceptual level, the observations made at the sensor physical level.
- The limited ability to infer, at the semantic/conceptual level, *hidden relationships* among entities characterized by a high degree of abstraction/complexity (e.g., human behaviors).

The *GWEs paradigm* tries to address and solve this sort of problems. It concerns an advanced interpretation of the IoT's aims where the possibilities of: i) interpreting the environmental and context information, ii) detecting information related to human intentions/behaviors, iii) enabling human-like inferences and multi-modal interactions, and eventually iv) acting on behalf of the users intentions are particularly important. The key property of GWEs concerns the fact they are not limited to *physical objects* (as it is still usual in an IoT context). Rather, this paradigm provides a *uniform formalism* (a uniform context) to represent objects, agents, events, situations, circumstances, behaviors, etc. and their evolution in time, as well as the relationships between all these entities. An architecture for GWEs-based systems has also been presented, along with a rough description of the steps needed to pass from information collected at the raw sensor level to GWEs represented at semantic/conceptual level and usable then for advanced inference procedures.

REFERENCES

[1] Aberer K, Hauswirth M, Salehi A. Infrastructure for data processing in large-scale interconnected sensor networks. In: Proceedings of the international conference on mobile data management (MDM 2007). Washington (DC): IEEE Computer Society; 2007. p. 198–205.

[2] Adorni G, Coccoli M, Torre I. Semantic web and internet of things supporting enhanced learning. JE-LKS, J E-Learn Knowl Soc 2012;8(2):23–32.

[3] Ahlsén M, Al-Akkad A, Alcaraz G, Asanin S, Checcozzo R, Franceschinis M, Hreno J, Jacobsen M, Pastrone C, Pramudianto F, Spirito M, Tomasi R, Zimmermann. Concepts and technologies in intelligent service structures 1 (EBBITS deliverable D5.1.1). Fraunhofer FIT and EBBITS consortium. Sankt Augustin; 2010.

[4] Ahmedi L, Jajaga E, Ahmedi F. An ontology framework for water quality management. In: Proceedings of the 6th international workshop on semantic sensor networks (SSN13), co-located with the 12th international semantic web conference (ISWC-2013), Aachen. CEUR workshop proceedings, vol. 1063. 2013. p. 35–50.

[5] Andersson J, de Lemos R, Malek S, Weyns D. Modeling dimensions of self-adaptive software systems. In: Self-adaptive systems. LNCS, vol. 5525. Berlin: Springer; 2009. p. 27–47.

[6] Atzori L, Iera A, Morabito G. The internet of things: a survey. Comput Netw, Int J Comput Telecommun Netw 2010;54:2787–805.

[7] Baader F, Calvanese D, McGuinness D, Nardi D, Patel-Schneider PF, editors. The description logic handbook. Cambridge: University Press; 2002.

[8] Barnaghi P, Presser M, Moessner K. Publishing linked sensor data. In: Proceedings of the 3rd international workshop on semantic sensor networks (SSN10), co-located with ISWC 2010, Aachen. CEUR workshop proceedings, vol. 468. 2010. p. 4–19.

[9] Barnaghi P, Wang W, Henson CA, Taylor K. Semantics for the internet of things: early progress and back to the future. Int J Semant Web Inf Syst 2012;8(1):1–21.

[10] Bassi A, Bauer M, Fiedler M, Kramp T, van Kranenburg R, Lange S, et al., editors. Enabling things to talk – designing IoT solutions with the IoT architectural reference model. Heidelberg: Springer; 2013.

[11] Bauer R, Köszegi ST. Measuring the degree of virtualization. Elect J Org Virtual 2003;5(2):26–46.

[12] Bauer M, Bui N, De Loof J, Magerkurth C, Nettsträter A, Stefa J, Walewski JW. IoT reference model. In: Enabling things to talk – designing IoT solutions with the IoT architectural reference model. Heidelberg: Springer; 2013. p. 113–62.

[13] Bay H, Ess A, Tuytelaars T, Van Gool L. Speeded-up robust features (SURF). Comput Vis Image Understand 2008;110:346–59.

[14] Bechhofer S, van Harmelen F, Hendler J, Horrocks I, McGuinness DL, Patel-Schneider PF, Stein LA, editors. OWL web ontology language reference, W3C recommendation 10 February 2004. 2004. http://www.w3.org/TR/owl-ref/, (accessed May 20, 2016).

[15] Benazzouz Y, Gurgen L, Hennebert C, Moreno Garcia D, Munilla C, Delsuc J, Smadja P, Atalla S, Rizzo F, Simone A, Sottile F, Nacabal F, Castanier F, Pascali S, Vilei A, Frà C, Valla M, Sancho J, Shrestha A. Smart object GW platform functional specification (BUTLER deliverable D4.3). inno TSD and BUTLER consortium. Sophia Antipolis; 2013.

[16] Bermudez-Edo M, Elsaleh T, Barnaghi P, Taylor K. IoT-lite ontology – W3C member submission 26 November 2015. https://www.w3.org/Submission/iot-lite/, 2015 (accessed May 20, 2016).

[17] Berners-Lee T. Linked data – 27 July 2006, last change 18 June 2009. http://www.w3.org/DesignIssues/LinkedData.html, 2006 (accessed May 20, 2016).

[18] Boussard M, Meissner S, Nettsträter A, Olivereau A, Salinas Segura A, Thoma M, Walewski JW. A process for generating concrete architectures. In: Enabling things to talk – designing IoT solutions with the IoT architectural reference model. Heidelberg: Springer; 2013. p. 45–112.

[19] Brunner J-S, Goudou J-F, Gatellier P, Beck J, Laporte C-E. SEMbySEM: a framework for sensors management. In: Proceedings of the 1st international workshop on the semantic sensor web (SemSensWeb 2009), co-located with ESWC (European semantic web conference) 2009, Aachen. CEUR workshop proceedings, vol. 468. 2009. p. 19–33.

[20] Calbimonte J-P, Jeung H, Corcho O, Aberer K. Semantic sensor data search in a large-scale federated sensor network. In: Proceedings of the 4th international workshop on semantic sensor networks (SSN11), co-located with the 10th international semantic web conference (ISWC-2011), Aachen. CEUR workshop proceedings, vol. 839. 2011. p. 23–38.

[21] Chui CK, Chen G. Kalman filtering with real-time applications. Berlin: Springer; 2009.

[22] Compton M, Neuhaus H, Taylor K, Khoi-Nguyen Tran K-N. Reasoning about sensors and compositions. In: Proceedings of the 2nd international workshop on semantic sensor networks (SSN09), co-located with the 8th international semantic web conference (ISWC-2009), Aachen. CEUR workshop proceedings, vol. 522. 2009. p. 33–48.

[23] Compton M, Barnaghi P, Bermudez L, García-Castro R, Corcho O, Cox S, Graybeal J, Hauswirth M, Henson C, Herzog A, Huang V, Janowicz K, Kelsey WD, Le Phuoc D, Lefort L, Leggieri M, Neuhaus H, Nikolov A, Page K, Passant A, Sheth A, Taylor K. The SSN ontology of the W3C semantic sensor network incubator group. J Web Seman: Sci, Serv Agents World Wide Web 2012;17:25–32.

[24] Dalal N, Triggs B. Histograms of oriented gradients for human detection. In: Proceedings of the 2005 IEEE computer society conference on computer vision and pattern recognition – CVPR 2005. New York: IEEEXplore; 2005. p. 886–93.

[25] Daniele L, den Hartog F, Roes J. Assets for smart appliances interoperability (D-S4: Final Report). TNO, the Hague; 2015.

[26] De S, Barnaghi P, Bauer M, Meissner S. Service modelling for the internet of things. In: Proceedings of the 2011 federated conference on computer science and information systems – 3rd workshop on software services: semantic-based software services. Los Alamitos (CA): IEEE Computer Society Press; 2011. p. 949–56.

[27] Delin KA, Jackson SP. The sensor web: a new instrument concept. Paper presented at the SPIE's Symposium on Integrated Optics (20–26 January 2001, San Jose, CA), http://www.sensorwaresystems.com/historical/resources/sensorweb-concept.pdf, January 2001 (accessed May 20, 2016).

[28] Desai P, Sheth A, Anantharam P. Semantic gateway as a service architecture for IoT interoperability. In: Proceedings of the 2015 IEEE international conference on mobile services. New York: IEEEXplore; 2015. p. 313–9.

[29] Dietze S, Domingue J. Bridging between sensor measurements and symbolic ontologies through conceptual spaces. In: Proceedings of the 1st international workshop on the semantic sensor web (SemSensWeb 2009), co-located with ESWC. CEUR workshop proceedings, vol. 468. 2009. p. 35–48.

[30] Einicke GA, White LB. Robust extended Kalman filtering. IEEE Trans Signal Process 1999;47:2596–9.

[31] Fiedler M, Meissner S. IoT in practice, examples: IoT in logistics and health. In: Enabling things to talk – designing IoT solutions with the IoT architectural reference model. Heidelberg: Springer; 2013. p. 27–36.

[32] Flitton G, Breckon TP, Megherbi N. Object recognition using 3D SIFT in complex CT volumes. In: Proceedings of the 2010 British machine vision conference. Durham: BMVA Press; 2010. p. 11.

[33] Forgy C Rete. A fast algorithm for the many pattern/many object pattern match problem. Artif Intell 1982;19:17–37.

[34] Fugini MG, Teimourikia M, Hadjichristofi G. A web-based cooperative tool for risk management with adaptive security. Future Gener Comput Syst 2016;54:409–22.

[35] Gärdenfors P. Conceptual spaces: The geometry of thought. Cambridge (MA): The MIT Press; 2000.

[36] Gibbons PB, Karp B, Ke Y, Nath S, Seshan S. IrisNet: an architecture for a world-wide sensor web. IEEE Pervasive Comput 2003;2(4):22–33.

[37] Giurca A, Gašević D, Taveter K, editors. Handbook of research on emerging rule-based languages and technologies: open solutions and approaches. Hershey (PA): Information Science Reference; 2009.

[38] Halpin H, Hayes PJ. When owl:sameAs isn't the same: an analysis of identity links on the semantic web. In: Proceedings of the linked data on the web workshop (LDOW 2010). CEUR workshop proceedings, vol. 628. 2010. http://ceur-ws.org/Vol-628/ldow2010_paper09.pdf (accessed May 20, 2016).

[39] Heath T, Bizer C. Linked data: Evolving the web into a global data space. 1st edition. San Rafael (CA): Morgan & Claypool; 2011.

[40] Herman I, Adida B, Sporny M, Birbeck M, editors. RDFa 1.1 primer. 3rd edition. 2015. Rich structured data markup for web documents, W3C working group note 17 March 2015. http://www.w3.org/TR/xhtml-rdfa-primer/, accessed May 20, 2016.

[41] Hitzler P, Krötzsch M, Parsia B, Patel-Schneider PF, Rudolph S, editors. OWL 2 web ontology language primer, W3C recommendation 27 October 2009. 2009. http://www.w3.org/TR/owl2-primer/ (accessed May 20, 2016).

[42] Horrocks I, Patel-Schneider PF, Boley H, Tabet S, Grosof B, Dean M. SWRL: a semantic web rule language combining OWL and RuleML, W3C member submission 21 May 2004. http://www.w3.org/Submission/SWRL/, 2004 (accessed May 20, 2016).

[43] Ibanez F, Friess P. Putting the internet of things forward to the next level. In: Internet of things – from research and innovation to market deployment. Aalborg: River Publishers; 2014. p. 3–6.

[44] Janowicz K, Compton M. The stimulus-sensor-observation ontology design pattern and its integration into the semantic sensor network ontology. In: Proceedings of the 3rd international workshop on semantic sensor networks, Aachen. CEUR workshop proceedings, vol. 668. 2010. p. 64–78.

[45] Kolozali S, Elsaleh T, Barnaghi P. A validation tool for the W3C SSN ontology based sensory semantic knowledge. In: Proceedings of the 2014 workshop on semantic sen-

sor networks, co-located with the international semantic web conference 2014, Aachen. CEUR workshop proceedings, vol. 1401. 2014. p. 83–8.

[46] Kotis K, Katasonov A. Semantic interoperability on the internet of things: the semantic smart gateway framework. Int J Distrib Syst Technol 2013;4(3):47–69.

[47] Koubarakis M, Kyzirakos K. Modeling and querying metadata in the semantic sensor web: the model stRDF and the query language stSPARQL. In: Proceedings of the 7th extended semantic web conference, ESWC-2010, part 1. LNCS, vol. 6088. Berlin: Springer; 2010. p. 425–39.

[48] Lempert S, Pflaum A. Towards a reference architecture for an integration platform for diverse smart object technologies. In: Proceedings of the Mobile und Ubiquitäre informationssysteme conference (MMS 2011). Bonn: Köllen Verlag; 2011. p. 53–66.

[49] Lenat DB, Guha RV, Pittman K, Pratt D, Shepherd M. CYC: toward programs with common sense. Commun ACM 1990;33(8):30–49.

[50] Lowe DG. Distinctive image features from scale-invariant keypoints. Int J Comput Vis 2004;60:91–110.

[51] Medagliani P, Leguay J, Duda A, Rousseau F, Duquennay S, Raza S, Ferrari G, Gonizzi P, Cirani S, Voltri L, Monton M, Domingo M, Dohler M, Vilajosana I, Dupont O. IP to low-power smart objects: the smart parking case in the CALIPSO project. In: Internet of things – from research and innovation to market deployment. Aalborg: River Publishers; 2014. p. 287–313.

[52] Meinke K, Tucker JV. Many-sorted logic and its applications. Chichester: John Wiley & Sons; 1993.

[53] Molina M, Sanchez-Soriano J. Modeling sensor knowledge of a national hydrologic information system. In: Proceedings of the SSW 2010 workshop, co-located with the 2nd international joint IC3K conference. Lisbon: INSTICC; 2009. p. 23–31.

[54] Motik B, Sattler U, Studer, Query R. Answering for OWL-DL with rules. J Web Semant: Sci, Serv Agents World Wide Web 2005;3:41–60.

[55] Niles I, Pease A. Towards a standard upper ontology. In: Proceedings of the 2nd international conference on formal ontology in information systems (FOIS-2001). New York: ACM; 2001. p. 2–9.

[56] Patni HK, Henson CA, Sheth AP. Linked sensor data. In: Proceedings of the 2010 international symposium on collaborative technologies and systems. New York: IEEEXplore; 2010. p. 362–70.

[57] Pautasso C, Wilde E, Alarcon R, editors. REST: advanced research topics and practical applications. New York: Springer; 2014.

[58] Pepper S. Topic maps. In: Encyclopedia of library and information sciences. 3rd edition. Abingdon: Taylor & Francis; 2010. p. 5247–60.

[59] Perry M, Herring J, editors. GeoSPARQL – a geographic query language for RDF data (version 1.0). Open geospatial consortium. 2012. http://www.opengis.net/doc/IS/geosparql/1.0 (accessed May 20, 2016).

[60] Pfisterer D, Römer K, Bimschas D, Hasemann H, Hauswirth M, Karnstedt M, Kleine O, Kröller A, Leggieri M, Mietz R, Pagel M, Passant A, Richardson R, Truong C. SPITFIRE: towards a semantic web of things. IEEE Commun Mag 2011;49(11):40–8.

[61] Preuveneers D, Berbers Y. SAMURAI: a streaming multi-tenant context-management architecture for intelligent and scalable internet of things applications. In: Proceedings of the 2014 international conference on intelligent environments. New York: IEEEXplore; 2014. p. 226–33.

[62] Revesz PZ. Introduction to constraint databases. New York: Springer; 2002.

[63] Russomanno DJ, Kothari CR, Thomas OA. Building a sensor ontology: a practical approach leveraging ISO and OGC models. In: Proceedings of the 2005 international conference on artificial intelligence (IC-AI), vol. 2. Athens (GA): CSRA Press; 2005. p. 637–43.

[64] Saffiotti A, Broxvall M, Gritti M, LeBlanc K, Lundh R, Rashid J, Seo BS, Cho YJ. The PEIS-ecology project: vision and results. In: Proceedings of the 2008 IEEE/RSJ international conference on intelligent robots and systems (IROS-08). New York: IEEEXplore; 2008. p. 2329–35.

[65] Santucci G. The Internet of things, between the revolution of the Internet and the metamorphosis of objects. Brussels: CORDIS Publications and Reports; 2010.

[66] Sarkar C, Etaläperä M, editors. Real object awareness and dissemination level – iCore Deliverable D3.2. Espoo: VTT and iCore Consortium; 2013.

[67] Shekarpour S, Lukovnikov D, Kumar AJ, Endris K, Singh K, Thakkar H, Lange C. Question answering on linked data: challenges and future directions. arXiv:1601.03541, 2016.

[68] Sheth A, Henson C, Sahoo S. Semantic sensor web. IEEE Internet Comput 2008;12(4):78–83.

[69] Shotton J, Fitzgibbon A, Cook M, Sharp T, Finocchio M, Moore R, Kipman A, Blake A. Real-time human pose recognition in parts from single depth images. In: Proceedings of the 2011 IEEE conference on computer vision and pattern recognition. New York: IEEEXplore; 2011. p. 1297–304.

[70] Soldatos J, Kefalakis N, Hauswirth M, Serrano M, Calbimonte J-P, Riahi M, Aberer K, Jayaraman PP, Zaslavsky A, Podnar Žarko I, Skorin-Kapov L, Herzog R. OpenIoT: open source internet-of-things in the cloud. In: Interoperability and open-source solutions for the Internet of things. LNCS, vol. 9001. Heidelberg: Springer; 2015. p. 13–25.

[71] Sottile F, Franceschinis M, Xiong Z, Kasinathan P, Smadja P, Enjolras P, Abreu G, Severi S, Oshiga O, Vuppala S, Poilinca S, Ramakrishnan A, Preuveneers D, Hennebert C, Tunaru I, Denis B, Suraty Filho LH, Saloranta J, Macagnano D, Destino G, Salazar M-F, Monjas M-A, Melakessou F, Andrushevich A. IoT enabling technologies and future developments – BUTLER deliverable D2.5. Torino: Istituto superiore mario boella (ISMB) and BUTLER consortium; 2014.

[72] Sowa JF. Knowledge representation: logical, philosophical, and computational foundations. Pacific Grove (CA): Brooks Cole Publishing Co; 1999.

[73] Spirito M, Pastrone C, Soldatos J, Giaffreda R, Doukas C, Stavroulaki V, Muñoz L, Gutierrez Polidura V, Gusmeroli S, Sola J, Agostinho C. Internet of things applications – from research and innovation to market deployment. In: Internet of things – from research and innovation to market deployment. Aalborg: River Publishers; 2014. p. 243–86. Chapter 7.

[74] Thrun S, Burgard W, Fox D. Probabilistic robotics. Cambridge (MA): The MIT Press; 2005.

[75] Toma I, Simperl E, Hench GA. Joint roadmap for semantic technologies and the Internet of Things. In: Proceedings of the 3rd STI Roadmapping workshop, Crete, Greece. 2009.

[76] Trame J, Kessler C, Kuhn W. Linked data and time – modeling researcher life lines by events. In: Proceedings of the 11th international conference on spatial information theory, COSIT 2013. LNCS, vol. 9001. Berlin: Springer; 2013. p. 205–23.

[77] Trifa V, Larizgoitia I, editors. Design of the object virtualization specification, COMPOSE deliverable D2.1.1. Haifa: IBM research and COMPOSE consortium; 2013.

[78] Vermesan O, Friess P, editors. Building the hyperconnected society – IoT research and innovation value chains, ecosystems and markets. Aalborg: River Publishers; 2015.

[79] The W3C SPARQL Working Group. SPARQL 1.1 overview, W3C recommendation 21 March 2013. http://www.w3.org/TR/sparql11-overview/ (accessed May 20, 2016).

[80] Winston ME, Chaffin R, Herrmann D. A taxonomy of part-whole relations. Cogn Sci 1987;11:417–44.

[81] Zarri GP. Representation and management of narrative information – theoretical principles and implementation. London: Springer; 2009.

[82] Zarri GP. Differentiating between "functional" and "semantic" roles in a high-level conceptual data modeling language. In: Proceedings of the twenty-fourth international Florida artificial intelligence research society conference, FLAIRS-24. Menlo Park (CA): AAAI Press; 2011. p. 75–80.

[83] Zarri GP. Knowledge representation and inference techniques to improve the management of gas and oil facilities. Knowledge-Based Syst (KNOSYS) 2011;24:989–1003.

[84] Zarri GP. Generalized world entities as a unifying IoT framework: a case for the GENIUS project. In: Internet of things and inter-cooperative computational technologies for collective intelligence. Heidelberg: Springer; 2013. p. 345–67.

[85] Zarri GP. Advanced computational reasoning based on the NKRL conceptual model. Exp Syst Appl (ESWA) 2013;40:2872–88.

[86] Zarri GP, Sabri L, Chibani A, Amirat Y. Semantic-based industrial engineering: problems and solutions. In: Proceedings of the 2010 international conference on complex, intelligent and software intensive systems – semantically-enabled systems engineering workshop. Los Alamitos (CA). Los Alamitos (CA): IEEE Computer Society Press; 2010. p. 1022–7.

ACKNOWLEDGEMENTS

We gratefully acknowledge the two unknown referees who reviewed a first version of this chapter for their useful suggestions that helped us to improve considerably the technical quality and the legibility of our text.

PART 2

SYSTEM BUILDING AND PRACTICES

BUILDING A WEB OF THINGS WITH AVATARS

5

A COMPREHENSIVE APPROACH FOR CONCERN MANAGEMENT IN WOT APPLICATIONS

Lionel Médini*, Michael Mrissa*, El-Mehdi Khalfi[†], Mehdi Terdjimi*, Nicolas Le Sommer[‡], Philippe Capdepuy[§], Jean-Paul Jamont[†], Michel Occello[†], Lionel Touseau[‡]

Univ Lyon, Université Claude Bernard Lyon 1, CNRS, LIRIS UMR5205, F-69622, Villeurbanne, France* Laboratoire LCIS, Université Grenoble Alpes, Valence, France[†] Laboratoire IRISA, Université de Bretagne Sud, Vannes, France[‡] Génération Robots, Bruges, France[§]

We propose the notion of avatar as a software architecture that extends a thing, in order to gain benefits from Web standards. Avatars achieve interoperability with things and expose high-level functionalities as RESTful resources, collaborate with each other and external services to form standard-compliant WoT applications.

CHAPTER POINTS

In this chapter, we highlight the following contributions:

- A generic software extension of things, called avatar. Avatars exploit things low-level capabilities, using their own protocols and encodings, to provide high-level, Web-compliant functionalities, while taking into account various concerns such as ensuring security and privacy, optimizing avatar-thing communications, locating application code or collaborating with other avatars. We present the component-based architecture of an avatar, explain its life-cycle and show how it relies on semantic Web technologies to fulfill its objectives. We also detail its components, some of them along with the architecture, the others as separate contributions.
- A RESTful disruption-tolerant support for the WoT. Resources exposed by connected things are identified by URIs and accessed through stateless services. Service requests and responses are forwarded using the store-carry-and-forward principle. We provide a complete service invocation model, allowing to perform unicast, anycast, multicast and broadcast service invocations using HTTP or CoAP.

- A multi-level, multi-dimensional context model and domain-independent adaptation process. This allows avatars to reason about contextual information and solve various adaptation requests. We show how to pre-process stable context representations, so that the adaptation process can both cope with constantly changing environments and be optimized for reducing computing load at request time.
- An approach for inter-avatar collaboration. We introduce the notion of interaction situation as the reciprocal influence that avatars have on the actions of others when they are interrelated. We also provide avatars with social and human-inspired characteristics, such as collective identity (motivations and relationships among participants) and inter-subjectivity (the avatar's ability to consider other avatars' mental states in its beliefs). We show how, using these concepts, an avatar can decide whether to participate in an avatar community.

5.1 INTRODUCTION

The Web of Things (WoT) promotes the idea of using Web technologies to support interactions with things. The benefits of this idea are twofold. First, it aims at accessing all kinds of things through standard technologies and tools, thus achieving interoperability among things and breaking silos between thing manufacturers' proprietary technologies. This will allow reusing proven platforms, technologies and user interaction techniques, ease application development and reduce time-to-market. Second, by giving things an existence as Web resources, the WoT aims at enriching the possibilities of Web applications by bridging the gap between the virtual and the physical world. Indeed, being able to control one's smart home temperature through a social network is already a reality, as well as making a flower pot tweet when its soil is getting dry. Conversely, representing a thing as a Web resource gives it an existence in the informational world. Even inanimate objects can now be added a QR-code, so that people can post comments to a bottle of wine they drank together and get back all these comments in the bottle's blog. Of course, more powerful – and useful – applications are now built to make use of things through Web technologies. But the fact is that building such applications remains a handcrafted activity.

One of the reasons is the numerous domains and technologies that a complete WoT application can require: connected things and robots are subject to specific constraints that strongly impact applications, such as physical phenomena (gravity, friction, etc.), energy management and network disconnections. As classical applications, WoT applications have functional and non-functional requirements, called concerns in the remainder of this paper, such as reliability, performance, security, privacy and usability. Moreover, "intelligent" technologies can now be added to these applications, to help objects collaborate with one another to achieve a common goal, or to learn new knowledge to be used in the application. All these interrelated concerns have to be studied, modeled and integrated in applications in order to fulfill the WoT promises. Cyber-Physical Systems (CPS) propose a global approach that aims at taking into account such various concerns. CPS applications are designed in a domain-specific, performance-driven manner; however most of them are built with a bottom-up approach and their architectures are hardly reusable. Reusable frameworks, dedicated to Machine-to-Machine (M2M) and Internet of Things (IoT) applications have been created, but they fail to meet all these challenges.

We think that WoT platforms should be able to mix these various concerns in a manner that allows all specialties to connect together and form complex and efficient, though well-architected WoT applications. To this end, we introduced in [50] the notion of avatar developed in the ASAWoO project.[1] An avatar represents the software part attached to a thing in a CPS-inspired approach. It embeds the components that implement the concerns required for the thing to participate in WoT applications through standard Web interfaces. In this chapter, we detail the notions of avatar and avatar-based WoT infrastructures that gather the common characteristics of WoT platforms able to expose things on the Web and run WoT applications using avatars. We illustrate using a realistic scenario, how avatars address concerns at different levels, such as physical constraints (network disconnections), transversal requirements (contextual adaptation) and application-level processes (inter-avatar collaboration).

CHAPTER ORGANIZATION

The chapter structure includes:

- A **motivating scenario** in the smart agriculture domain, that highlights the need for avatar-based infrastructures in the WoT
- A **description of avatar-based WoT infrastructures** that depicts the different elements of our approach: avatar architecture, common features of WoT platforms able to deploy and run avatars, and structure of interoperable WoT applications
- A **focus on contributions in three different domains**: disruption-tolerant networks, contextual adaptation and multi-agent systems; each contribution includes its own problem description, contribution and evaluation
- A **general conclusion**, including a discussion and outlook on the future of the Web of Things and avatar-based architectures

5.2 MOTIVATING SCENARIO

The WoT infrastructures presented in this chapter have applications in multiple scenarios ranging from simple home automation to more complex smart factories and service robotics settings. In this chapter, we focus on a motivating scenario in agricultural robotics that leverages the different aspects of the proposed infrastructures.

Agricultural robotics is an important trend that aims at decreasing the reliance on large machinery and human labor in favor of fleets of small autonomous robots and distributed sensors working in collaboration [58]. The objective is twofold: im-

---

[1] http://liris.cnrs.fr/asawoo/.

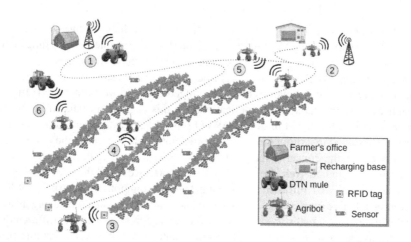

FIGURE 5.1

Illustration of the viticulture scenario

proving productivity and economic efficiency by reducing labor costs; decreasing the ecological footprint thanks to better energy efficiency and parcimonious usage of resources such as water, fertilizers and pesticides. The last aspect relies mostly on obtaining information for multiple sensors, and using smart processes for deciding how the robots should act upon these data. This is generally referred to as *precision farming* and we will refer to the involved robots as *agribots*. Such applications are already studied in the context of viticulture [54].

Fig. 5.1 depicts the application scenario that will be used for illustrating the different elements of avatar-based WoT infrastructures. This scenario takes place in a vineyard and is composed of the following elements:

1. The farmer's office from which the overall system is monitored and controlled. We assumed that it has enough available computational power for hosting a WoT infrastructure and that it provides a WiFi access point (potentially also connected to a larger network). The operator interacts with the system through a Web interface provided by the precision viticulture WoT application.
2. Recharging bases for the agribots that provide short-range radio connections.
3. Active RFID tags that mark rows and allow to know if they have been processed. These tags can be read by agribots or human workers, facilitating their interaction.
4. Low energy sensors spread all over the vineyard that monitor environmental parameters such as temperature, humidity, etc. They rely on inexpensive short-range radio communication to send their measurements.
5. Agribots of various natures that perform tasks such as weeding, irrigation, fertilization. They are equipped with sensing capabilities, computing power to autonomously achieve WoT application tasks, and network connectivity (RFID and short-range radio) to communicate with other connected things.

6. Agricultural machinery such as tractors that we herein consider as data mules. They use short-range radio to communicate with sensors and agribots and WiFi to exchange with the farmer's office.

   In the next sections, we present these infrastructures and detail how they cope with constraints such as wireless network malfunctions, adaptation to resource and environment conditions, and autonomy and coordination constraints.

5.3 AVATARS AND AVATAR-BASED WOT PLATFORMS

The WoT imposes challenges regarding the representation, interoperability and collaboration of radically different things (in our scenario: RFID tags, low energy sensors, agribots, tractors, etc.), embedding various hardware (sensors, actuators, processing and storage units, network interfaces). We herein advocate *avatars* as virtual representations of things, so that a thing and its representation form a "Web-based cyber-physical object" that proposes homogeneous and user-understandable functionalities. In this context, WoT infrastructures are platforms able to deploy and execute WoT applications by creating, using and interlinking avatars. In this section, we overview WoT challenges and show how they can be tackled with our approach.

5.3.1 REQUIREMENTS FOR WOT PLATFORMS

In the IoT field, numerous platforms have been implemented [75]. Some of them rely on existing standards (e.g. ETSI's OneM2M[2]) related to the way they connect with things. However, there is currently no standard solution to address concerns at the level of WoT software platforms. In [50], we proposed a list of design requirements for WoT software platforms to summarize the WoT main challenges. We herein complete and extend this list. A WoT platform should:

- **R1: discoverability** – allow to discover heterogeneous things [29,48], to be able to plug and unplug things to the platform
- **R2: connectivity** – take into account several communication models (request/response, message-oriented, event-based, publish-subscribe, streaming, etc.) in order to allow applications to interact with various things [40], as well as support connectivity disruptions for mobile wirelessly connected things [42]
- **R3: reactivity** – adapt its structure and behavior to its environment at runtime, such as the CityPulse[3] platform or the work in the INCOME project [4], to react to changes in the environment
- **R4: safety** – be reliable and secure so that things and applications are harmless and avoid privacy issues [29,35]

---

[2]http://www.onem2m.org/.
[3]http://www.ict-citypulse.eu/.

- **R5: interoperability** – allow WoT applications to run across heterogeneous objects [29,24], so that users can seamlessly interact with things
- **R6: delegation** – identify the most suitable location to execute each code module and deploy these modules on the thing processing unit or on a cloud infrastructure [48], instead of completely delegating computation tasks to cloud-based infrastructures (see IFTTT[4])
- **R7: scalability** – cope with high numbers of things, heavy calculation processes and/or high quantities of data [40]), as the number of things is expected to increase
- **R8: collaboration** – allow a set of things to exhibit a collective behavior [18], as seen in the SensorMeasurement[5] framework, to achieve complex functionalities
- **R9: usability** – provide high-level services, so that applications match end-users' needs [30,10]
- **R10: marketability** – design software applications and components that implement different functionalities for heterogeneous things, so that developers and industrial companies can distribute them on open online marketplaces.[6]

To the best of our knowledge, a WoT platform able to handle all these requirements for a given WoT application is missing. We think that it is possible to define such comprehensive yet realistic infrastructures for the WoT by introducing an intermediary abstraction level between the things and the platform. This way, a WoT infrastructure can delegate the management of different requirements to software artifacts at this intermediate level.

5.3.2 RELATED WORK

Since the development of Programmable Logic Controllers and robots, programming elements have been associated with things. With the advent of (wireless) networked communications, they have evolved to distributed control systems, embedded systems and more recently ambient intelligence and distributed robotics [25]. The IoT is a direct consequence of this evolution and aims at exploiting Internet's communication capabilities, nearly unlimited computing power of cloud infrastructures and modern user interfaces to provide end-users with helpful applications. The WoT builds on top of the IoT and promotes the use of Web standards.

But as soon as physical things come into play, programming such applications becomes more complex and less deterministic. Indeed, sensor data suffer from imprecisions, actuators require feedback loops, time-critical and synchronization processes need constant attention and network communications may lose data or get interrupted. CPS upholders claim that such difficulties originate from physical phenomena and must be modeled together with computer-based models and processes [44]. This

---

[4]https://ifttt.com/.

[5]http://sensormeasurement.appspot.com/.

[6]http://www.compose-project.eu/sites/default/files/publications/COMPOSE_v2_factsheet.pdf.

way, embedded system applications will allow to take into account various concerns such as reliability, safety, adaptability, scalability and usability.[7] Among the numerous CPS architectures that have been designed, many of them are component-based and include software entities that model these concerns. Some of them include semantic languages to manage their interaction workflows [3,55]. Others took advantage of the multi-agent paradigm to build more autonomous and scalable CPS [67] and mixed this paradigm with semantic technologies [45]. In these works, agents embed the algorithms that control the things and are able to communicate together to perform collaborative tasks. However, these tasks are implemented in the frameworks at design time, which makes them hardly reusable across applications.

In the WoT community, we proposed in [33] the notion of avatar to denote software artifacts attached to a thing and aggregating the necessary code to execute WoT applications. Avatars are software agents that allow collaboration between things and distribution of application code between avatars. As detailed below, avatars rely on an internal component-based architecture, so that all necessary concerns from a CPS point of view can be described. More recently, the World Wide Web Consortium (W3C) Web of Things Interest Group[8] (WoT IG) proposed the notion of "Servient" that is currently being defined to standardize software objects in WoT applications. Servients are very close to avatars: they provide access to things, can be executed on them, on gateways or on cloud infrastructures and can interact with other servients. Both also rely on semantic technologies to exchange machine-understandable data. As WoT standards must cope with a variety of use cases and platforms, servient architecture only specifies building blocks ("runtime environment", "resource model", etc.). Avatars can be seen as a specialization of servients, more focused on WoT application deployment and execution, and relying on a component-based architecture to take advantage of advances related to specific concerns and requirements in various fields.

5.3.3 **AVATARS**

Some components of the avatar architecture (Fig. 5.2) are dedicated to thing control and others implement the autonomous, self-adaptive and collaborative behavior of avatars. The physical setup is decoupled from its logical architecture: an avatar can dynamically adapt the distribution of its components to different locations (see below) to improve their efficiency. We grouped the avatar components in 8 functional modules.

The **Core Module** includes components that are used in several steps of the avatar lifecycle. The component deployment manager defines which avatar components will be instantiated wrt. the thing capabilities, and where.[9] Each avatar embeds a Rea-

---

[7]https://www.nsf.gov/funding/pgm_summ.jsp?pims_id=503286.

[8]https://www.w3.org/WoT/IG/.

[9]Avatar components can be located on the thing if it has enough computing capabilities or for time-constrained code modules, on the gateway for processes that involve inter-avatar communication, or on

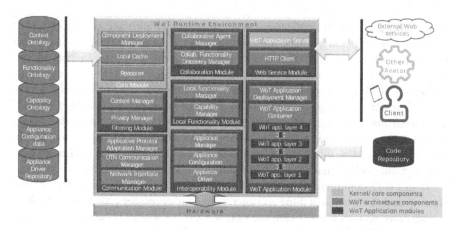

FIGURE 5.2

Architecture of the avatar software platform

soner, used by other components to process semantic information pertaining on the capabilities, functionalities and context. So is the Local Cache, that stores semantic information from diverse sources (thing, repositories, external context) and reflects the current state of the avatar. In particular, the cache loads concepts from the semantic repositories, in order to make them available to other modules through the reasoner, as shown in Section 5.5. This module is essential to address the multiple concerns targeted by the application through the avatar, while avoiding allocating unnecessary resources. As such, it participates in addressing most of the requirements, and especially (R6).

The **Interoperability module** provides the other avatar modules with a uniform interface to interact with the thing it is attached to (R1, R5). This interface consists of a set of *capabilities* that represent the thing API. It loads drivers from a platform repository and uses them to identify the communication schemes understood by the thing; eventually, it uploads onto the thing the appropriate configuration.

The **Filtering module** restricts functionality exposition and data exchanges. If, for privacy or security reason, some functionalities should not be achieved by the avatar, they will be filtered by the Privacy manager. The Context Manager has a more complex role, which is explained in Section 5.5.

The **Communication module** ensures reliable communication with the thing. It selects the appropriate network interface (Ethernet, Wi-Fi, Zigbee, etc.) and protocols (CoAP, HTTP, etc.) according to communication purposes and performance needs (throughput/energy consumption). It also supports connectivity disruptions, as explained in Section 5.4 (R4).

---

the cloud for calculation-intensive processes. This way, application components that model different CPS aspects and address different application concerns can be executed at an optimal location.

The **Web service module** allows avatars to communicate with other avatars and with the external world wrt. Web standards. By this means, avatars can: interact with the WoT platform to query repositories, respond to client requests regarding the functionalities they expose as RESTful resources, exchange data with other avatars to achieve collaborative functionalities and query external Web services to enrich their own data.

The **Local Functionality module** handles high-level *functionalities* achievable using the thing capabilities[10] (R9). It relies on semantic technologies to map the thing layer (capabilities) with the application layer (functionalities) in a declarative and loosely coupled manner, ensuring application interoperability with various things [51] (R5). When the avatar is created, the CapabilityManager queries the Interoperability module for the thing capabilities and the platform capability ontology for their semantic descriptions. It is queried by the LocalFunctionalityManager, which also loads the descriptions of functionalities and uses the reasoner to infer the avatar local functionalities.[11] For each inferred functionality, the LocalFunctionalityManager queries the Context Manager to decide if it should be exposed to clients. Exposed functionalities are bound to a registry, so that users and other avatars can find them.

The **Collaboration module** handles functionalities that require collaboration between several avatars. The CollaborativeFunctionalityDiscoveryManager queries the reasoner as described above to identify, from the local functionalities, in which higher-level ones it could participate. Then, it queries the platform functionality directory to search for the locally missing functionalities. If such functionalities are available from other avatars, it calls the Collaborative Agent Manager, which handles negotiation with these other avatars, as explained in Section 5.6 (R8). Here, (R5) and (R9) are addressed at a multi-thing level.

The **WoT Application module** provides and controls "WoT application containers" that execute code modules implementing the different aspects of a WoT application (R9). Such containers can be replicated on the thing, on the gateway and on the cloud infrastructure thanks to the deployment manager, so that modules are executed on the appropriate location (R6).

5.3.4 AVATAR-BASED INFRASTRUCTURE

As requirements R1 to R4 and R7 are also addressed by IoT platforms, existing IoT solutions can be used as a lower layer to connect things, and WoT platforms implemented as "WoT application servers" on top of these solutions. To allow deploying and running WoT applications on ubiquitous computing environnements, WoT plat-

---

[10]Functionalities provide user-understandable compositions of capabilities. For instance, a user will prefer to tell a robot to move to another part of the field, rather than to pilot each of its wheels individually.

[11]Inference processing relies on the Capability and Functionality classes, and relationships between them, expressed in our own OWL (http://www.w3.org/TR/owl2-overview/) vocabulary. Individuals expressed in other vocabularies [31] can be used and "rdf:typed" as capabilities or functionalities.

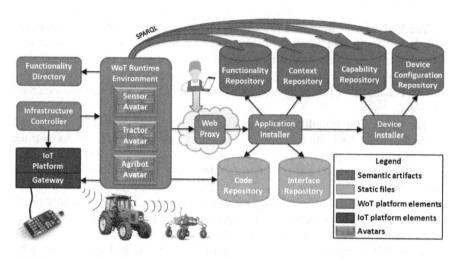

FIGURE 5.3

An Avatar-based infrastructure for the WoT

forms must provide access to information and knowledge storage facilities and to additional computing power (cloud). As we herein promote avatar-based WoT platforms, they should also support managing, executing, and (de)serializing avatars. The serialization mechanism allows scaling horizontally by replicating platforms and moving avatars between them. Vertical scaling is ensured by our multi-layer infrastructure (thing, gateway, cloud) (R7). Fig. 5.3 depicts the infrastructure of such platforms.

The main elements of this infrastructure are the *Infrastructure Controller* and *WoT Runtime Environment*. The former interacts with the IoT platform and is in charge of deciding to create,[12] update[13] or remove avatars, as things are plugged and unplugged from the IoT layer (R1, R3). The latter is the container that isolates avatars (R4) and handles their lifecycle. For performance reasons, it is also connected to the gateway, so that avatars can directly interact with things without traversing the IoT platform stack at each request (R2). Inside the container, avatars can also: access external Web resources through the *Web Proxy*, share information about the functionalities each of them exposes using the *Functionality Directory*, query the different *Semantic Repositories* to access the semantic descriptions they need to operate, and retrieve application code modules in the *Code Repository*. The *Device Installer* and *Application Installer* are in charge of populating the different repositories and are independent of the notion of avatar. Users securely interact with the platform to download thing

---

[12]Each avatar is built so that it can access the thing through the gateway. The thing capabilities are injected and the avatar components instantiated.

[13]By periodically checking the IoT platform.

drivers, install WoT applications from a marketplace (R10) or execute these applications using their Web browsers, through the proxy that blocks unidentified incoming requests (R4).

5.3.5 WOT APPLICATIONS

In order to ease WoT application design (R11) and keep it independent from the characteristics of available things (R5), a WoT application only deals with the functionality level. Hence, it mainly describes a hierarchy of functionalities, the end nodes of which graph are terminal functionalities (i.e. that have to be implemented by a thing capability[14]), and all others nodes are composed functionalities (i.e. that require sub-functionalities and query them using code modules). Some of these composed functionalities may require the capabilities of several things, and therefore, a collaboration between several avatars (R8). The top-level functionality then corresponds to the application that the end-user wishes to use (R9).

A WoT application is packaged in a compressed file, composed of: a *Manifest* file, describing its contents; the above mentioned *hierarchy of functionalities*; the *Code modules* corresponding to the algorithms that implement composed functionalities[15]; the *application context model*, containing a semantic description of the application domain and a set of adaptation rules (see Section 5.5); a set of static files that constitute the *application interface* and allow end-users to execute and control the application through their Web browser by querying avatar functionalities using Web standards (RESTful resources, WebSockets, etc.).

5.3.6 VALIDATION PROTOTYPE

The above sections show that all requirements are met by the different elements of our avatar-based WoT infrastructures. In order to validate our approach, we implemented its different components as follows. For the **IoT platform**, we chose OM2M,[16] as it relies on ETSI standards,[17] is supported by the Eclipse community and is extensible. We actually extended it by developing a module capable of introspecting things and sending semantically annotated capabilities.[18] Two versions of those **semantic annotations** have been experimented: one relying on Java annotations and one using JSON-LD files served as RESTful resources using the Hydra specification.[19] A prototype of the latter has been presented in [49], to demonstrate how avatars can

---

[14]Capabilities are semantically mapped with these terminal functionalities during avatar initialization.

[15]The R5 (interoperability) requirement imposes to these applications to be generically described, in order to be deployable and executable on diverse thing setups. Hence, we recommend describing them using declarative languages, such as state chart of finite state machines – and at installation time – pre-transpiling them into the languages of the thing, gateway and cloud platform they can be deployed on.

[16]http://www.eclipse.org/om2m/.

[17]http://www.etsi.org/technologies-clusters/technologies/m2m.

[18]http://liris.cnrs.fr/asawoo/doku.php?id=cima.

[19]http://www.hydra-cg.com/.

use semantic reasoning to dynamically compose functionalities. The **ASAWoO plat-form** has been developed in Java and runs avatars inside an OSGi (Felix[20]) container. Avatar components are implemented as OSGi services. Some of them are necessary for the avatar to function, and others depend on the concerns addressed by the application. The next sections highlight our contributions to certain concerns and detail how a given concern can be modeled and implemented in an avatar component.

5.4 DISRUPTION-TOLERANT COMMUNICATIONS

It is quite common that things involved in WoT applications cannot be connected permanently, firstly for energy saving reasons but also because of mobility. Such things – which are often equipped with short-range radio interfaces (Wi-Fi, Buetooth, Zig-Bee, etc.) – can be connected to other things or to Internet gateways while they are moving or when mobile things are passing near them. As shown in the scenario depicted in Section 5.2, communication links of such things are thus subject to frequent and unpredictable disconnections.

To cope with this issue, the communication module of avatars implements disruption-tolerant communication techniques to transport HTTP or CoAP requests and responses in partially or intermittently connected networks. These techniques do not assume that there always exists an end-to-end path between two things in the network. Mobile things can store messages, carry these messages while moving and deliver them to other things when possible.

5.4.1 RELATED WORK

The provision of REST services in partially or intermittently connected networks has been addressed in a few number of works, most of them in opportunistic networks. Opportunistic networks can be considered as a sub-category of disruption-tolerant networks, since only opportunistic contacts between mobile things are exploited to transfer data. In [20,56], the authors propose analytical models to determine the optimal number of parallel executions required to minimize the service time, without saturating the computational resources of the service providers, as well as to select the best service composition among alternative compositions based on the local knowledge of the network collected by a node through its opportunistic contacts with other nodes. The exploitation of the presence of several providers in the network and of their parallel invocation has also been investigated in [46], but with a publish/subscribe and content-based approach. The objective is to reduce the service delivery delay, and thus to provide a better response time to end-users. To reduce the response time, intermediate nodes can be used as service proxies has shown in [43]. Intermediate nodes are expected to respond on behalf of service providers, as long as that

---

[20]http://felix.apache.org/.

these intermediate nodes have in their local cache the responses for the requests they receive and the services are stateless-services. Intermediate nodes do not forward the requests towards the providers, but send back the responses to the clients directly. This solution allows to reduce drastically the network load and the response time. All these research works address the service provision in general, but do not conform to the REST architectural style, that ensures its performance, scalability and simplicity [23].

5.4.2 OVERVIEW OF THE RESTFUL DTN COMMUNICATION SUPPORT

The avatar communication module (CM) complies with the six constraints below – the sixth one is optional – defined by REST. Avatars are indeed designed as a set of distributed clients and stateless services, that interact through well-defined schemes (i.e. negotiation, functionality calls). Since the communication path between a service provider and its clients may be subject to disruptions, maintaining a session with a client can become difficult for a provider. It is consequently preferable to maintain a state on the client side. This is thus consistent with the REST approach, which is based on a loosely-coupled *client/server* (constraint 1) architecture where servers do not maintain any session state (servers must be *stateless*) (constraint 2) and are accessed through *uniform interfaces* (constraint 3).

To improve overall scalability, REST promotes a *layered system* (constraint 4) and *cacheable* responses (constraint 5). Layers consist in intermediate servers in charge of non-functional concerns such as security, load balancing or shared caches provision. By implementing the "store, carry and forward" principle, the CM stores both the service requests and service responses that have been sent in the network in the cache of clients and of intermediate nodes. Following a proxy-based approach, intermediate hosts can respond on behalf of a server if they have the response in their local cache, when this one is still valid. Such an approach allows to improve the performance and the scalability of the system, because it naturally performs load balancing and data caching on intermediate hosts, and thus fulfills the two above-mentioned requirements.

WoTApps can be partially or fully developed in Javascript, thus allowing to execute on the client side a part of the application and to reduce the computation load on the things, which complies with REST optional *code-on-demand* constraint (constraint 6).

The RESTful disruption-tolerant communication part of CM is designed to be as versatile as possible. It allows to invoke services using the HTTP and CoAP application-level protocols. It is composed of two main elements, namely an HTTP/CoAP proxy and a DTN adapter (see Fig. 5.4). Thanks to this proxy, programmers can develop HTTP and CoAP WoTApps using regular HTTP and CoAP libraries. Moreover, standard HTTP and CoAP servers do not need to be modified. This proxy can also invoke remote REST services using Internet-legacy routing protocols (i.e., TCP/IP). Application-level messages (i.e., HTTP and CoAP messages) can be encapsulated in UDP datagrams, in TCP segments or in messages of a given

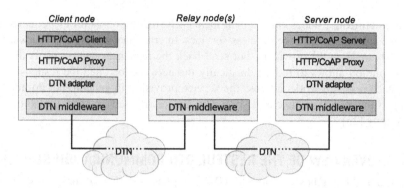

FIGURE 5.4

Overview of the architecture of the communication module

disruption-tolerant communication middleware in order to be transmitted to their destination. Different wireless technologies (e.g., Bluetooth, Wi-Fi) can be used to communicate with things.

As for the DTN adapter, it binds the proxy and the disruption–communication middleware in charge of forwarding messages in the network. Hence, the DTN adapter depends of the underlying communication system and is specifically developed for each different system. The Bundle Protocol (BP) [61], which is the standard message-based protocol over the DTN architecture [17], has been chosen as the default disruption–communication system in our current implementation. Another implementation has also been done using an opportunistic communication middleware we have developed, and which is called C3PO [42].

5.4.3 COMMUNICATION MODES

Besides providing the traditional point-to-point client/server communication model used in the Web, CM proposes alternative communication models, that are not necessarily relevant for traditional Web applications, but that are suitable for the WoT, such as anycast, multicast and broadcast transmission models. Disruption-tolerant communication systems implementing a multiple copy forwarding strategy can take advantage of these message transmission models to increase the message delivery probability and to reduce the response time. Indeed, if it exists several providers offering the same service in the environment, these providers can indifferently be invoked with the same request. If an anycast communication model is used, the communication system will only return the first received response to the client. Similarly, several sensors can simultaneously be invoked using a multicast transmission model without naming them explicitly. All responses returned by these sensors will be transmitted to the client.

In order to remain consistent with the RESTful approach, these different transmission models are specified in the scheme of the URIs used to access REST Web

Table 5.1 Examples of URIs supported by ADTRS

	URI	Method	Parameters
1	coap+dtn://agribot7/JobManager/back_to_charging_station	POST	
2	coap+dtn+acast://agribots/JobManager/weed	POST	rows=1–3
3	http+mcast://soilsensors/moisture	GET	

services. The first part of the scheme indicates the application-level protocol (i.e., HTTP, HTTPS, or CoAP) used to communicate with a remote service. +dtn must additionally be specified in the scheme if CoAP and HTTP messages must be forwarded by a disruption–tolerant communication system. By default, messages are transmitted using a unicast communication model. +acast, +mcast and +bcast specify respectively that an anycast, a multicast and a broadcast transmission model must be used in the forwarding process.

Table 5.1 gives examples of URIs that could be used in the smart vineyard scenario presented in Section 5.2. URI number 1 could be sent in unicast to order robot whose ID is agribot7 to go back to its recharging base after its current mission. Concretely, such an order is given by submitting a new job back_to_charging_station to the job manager of the avatar. This job manager is exposed as a Web service and is invoked via a POST CoAP method. Similarly, URI number 2 could be used to ask robots belonging to the agribots anycast group to weed around vine feet from rows 1 to 3 (additional parameters specified in the body of the POST request). Finally, URI number 3 allows to get the soil moisture from avatars of sensors monitoring the soil. As sensor avatars are hosted in a cloud infrastructure, they do not need to be reached in a disruption-tolerant way.

5.4.4 NON-FUNCTIONAL PARAMETERS FOR DELAY-TOLERANT COMPUTING

In delay-tolerant networks, service messages are forwarded following the "store, carry and forward" principle. The propagation delay and transmission area of messages is likely to be bounded not only to fulfill application requirements, but also to reduce the network load. Four additional parameters can be specified by service clients and service providers regarding the service delivery conditions on the one hand, and that can be exploited by disruption–tolerant communication systems in the message routing process on the other hand.

Caching parameter: Service clients can specify if their requests can be cached by intermediate nodes or not. If so, intermediate nodes will store in their cache both the request and the response associated with this request until they expire. Thus, they can reply later to a similar request sent by any node on behalf of the service provider (i.e., by returning immediately the cached response, instead of forwarding the request towards the service provider). For instance, environmental data such as air temperature at the vine feet, which is not likely to change frequently, can be cached.

Time parameters: Temporal constraints can be expressed in URIs as query strings. Two temporal constraints are considered: the message creation time, and the message expiration time, expressed relatively to the creation time.

In a service invocation request, these constraints express the fact that the client wants to get a response before the expiration time specified in the request message. The request can be forwarded in the network, and a provider of the service can answer to this request until it expires. When specifying time constraints for a response, these constraints express the lifetime of the response, and the validity duration of the data it contains. These temporal constraints are also used by the disruption–tolerant communication systems to determine how long a message can be stored in a cache or forwarded in the network.

Spatial parameters: A number of hops can additionally be specified in application-level messages to circumscribe at a coarse grain the area in which the messages can be forwarded, and to avoid that a message eternally roams in the network. Nevertheless, this limitation is not exact, and does not guarantee that a message cannot be transferred outside an expected area. As shown in [41], geographical areas can be specified in order to limit more precisely the propagation of messages in the physical environment.

Asynchronous communication: Service clients can add a callback parameter to define the URI that must be used by service providers to return the response. Clients can thus process the responses they receive asynchronously without being blocked by the reception of responses.

In our vineyard scenario, a sprinkler agribot that does not know the soil composition on the third row can ask other agribots to analyze it and send back the result. While waiting for the analysis, the agribot continues its current task (e.g., irrigating the first row). Once the soil composition analysis is received, the robot can process it and if the soil is dry, it will proceed to irrigate the row.

5.5 CONTEXT MODELING AND MANAGEMENT

An avatar must take decisions all along the lifecycle of the thing it extends, to adapt its behavior for different purposes (choose a protocol to communicate with the thing, a location to execute applicative components, etc.) and with respect to various parameters. Such parameters form the avatar context and come from various sources (thing sensors, environment, user's preferences, etc.). In this section, we build a multipurpose context adaptation framework. We discuss related work on context modeling and adaptation to show the need for such framework, and present and evaluate our context meta-model and multi-level context adaptation solutions.

5.5.1 RELATED WORK

Context is often modeled as multi-dimensional views [60,79,1] that include environmental and geospatial information, such as location, co-location (i.e. what is nearby), time, etc. [59] but also privacy [21], computing resources (availability, remaining battery power) and network information (types of connection, services in reach, distances, disconnection rates) [47,53]. Most context-aware applications give a major importance to user profiles and preferences [14,74,11] sometimes combined with network elements [73,57,76]. Context helps users with decision making [13], based on different knowledge sources [12] described in situations [19,9]. Most context information is domain-specific [52], or related to the application architecture [72,39]. Hence, existing work highlights the diversity and complexity of context that includes heterogeneous information, thus motivating our need to build a single framework that deals with any kind of context information.

Numerous self-adaptive and autonomic systems support dynamic contextual adaptation in pervasive and mobile computing environments. Most are based on a control loop, such as the autonomic computing architecture MAPE-K (Monitor, Analyze, Plan, Execute, Knowledge) [32] or the Rainbow framework [26]. Reflexive mechanisms are also used for dynamic adaptation such as in the ReMMoC [28] and CARISMA [15] middleware platforms. These centralized, problem-specific solutions are not adapted to our distributed, multi-focus setup. Different work from the IoT community perform multi-level adaptation in environments composed of cloud infrastructure and things [5,2] as well as networked cyber-physical systems [65] but does not benefit from the advantages of the Web and the collaboration between things as we provide in our avatar-based approach [33].

5.5.2 PROBLEM STATEMENT

As seen above, existing work mostly bind context models to specific scenarios and do not design them with adaptation in mind. It is currently difficult to reuse or extend these models due to their specificity, and they sometimes do not cope with WoT application requirements. Furthermore, adaptation solutions proposed in the literature do not provide abstraction for extending things and enabling collaboration between them, or do not provide multi-purpose adaptation. Some of them are also not compatible with decentralized architectures. Thus, there is a need for a solution to support flexible and interoperable context models that can be reused across applications and use-cases, as well as autonomic, decentralized and multi-purpose context adaptation. The following questions, illustrated with our agricultural scenario, must be answered to provide multi-purpose adaptation:

1. **Which protocols should be used to communicate with things?** Agribots, machineries and sensors must exchange information using adequate protocols, with respect to their heterogeneity and the network status.
2. **Where should the application code be executed?** Applicative modules can be executed either locally on agribots or remotely on the office system, which depends on their computational resources, location and availability.
3. **Which local capability should be involved in a given high-level functionality?** To move across grapefruit lines, agribots can rely on processing data from their GPS sensors or embedded cameras.

4. **Which other avatars functionalities should compose a collaborative functionality?** A sensor can select an agribot to water specific parts of the field.
5. **Which functionality should be exposed to application end-users and to other avatars?** The watering functionality would not be displayed in case of drought.

We next present our solution to instantiate reusable and flexible context models, based on both the literature and a typical WoT application architecture. We then describe how the components that compose an avatar handle, update and query an instantiated context model in order to be able to respond to the above adaptation questions.

5.5.3 CONTEXT META-MODEL

The adaptation process relies on physical, security, privacy, or other constraints, which vary according to the use-case. We have designed a context meta-model that allow avatars to instantiate domain-specific models, capable of answering different adaptation questions for a given WoT application [69]. We have organized our meta-model into levels that characterize the different parts of a WoT application.

The *Physical* level describes things, their internal states and their physical (sensed) environment. The *Application* level describes the application architecture, its state, and its configuration (*e.g.* components or services, locally stored or distributed). The *Communication* level describes network link context between application and clients, things and data sources (*e.g.* network states, bandwidth, latency, connection types). The *Social* level includes cognitive aspects related to the client's environment, which involves roles, organizations, as well as behavioral concepts and type of users (human, software).

Our meta-model is a two-dimensional matrix, that crosses pre-determined levels with a set of application-defined *Dimensions* based on the literature. Thus, it not only provides flexibility to WoT application developers by allowing the creation of any number of dimensions, but also provides reusability across WoT applications through the level/dimension view.

5.5.4 MULTI-LEVEL CONTEXT ADAPTATION

The above context meta-model allows for a single adaptation mechanism to operate across application domains. Each instantiated model supports data integration and query answering. For each dimension, data integration applies *transformation rules* to contextual data (numerical values coming from sensors or external services) in order to turn them into high-level contextual representations corresponding to the four levels of the model. Transformation rules act as filters that allow these representations to change only when the data go under significant changes. Query answering relies on SPARQL SELECT queries to get the accurate information to each adaptation question. Then, making the adaptation decisions consists in applying *adaptation rules* on the SPARQL query results. Our avatar architecture includes a context manager that populates the context model and handle the adaptation questions, as defined in [69].

5.5.5 EVALUATION

We have conducted two types of evaluations. First, we have evaluated our meta-model in [69] according to the methodology proposed in [27] and have shown its relevance and reusability across different scenarios as well as its usability in terms of performance based on the DL language it relies on. Second, we have evaluated our adaptation process in [70]. This evaluation consisted in adapting the location of application code (question #2). This code performed semantic reasoning about 2 ontologies: Fipa-Device[21] with 126 entities (schema + axioms) and IoT-O[22] with 328 entities. We have used the HyLAR [68] architecture to migrate the code between a thing (laptop mocking a drone) and a cloud (virtual machine) and to measure reasoning times. Evaluation results detailed in [70] show that our solution globally improves avatar performances for the code execution adaptation question, and that reasoning is up to 82% more effective than fixed implementations in disrupted environments for an average domain-specific ontology. This shows that our solution enables multi-purpose adaptation of avatar-based WoT applications and allows developers to declaratively define adaptation processes using high-level concepts and standardized rules.

5.6 A SOCIAL VISION OF THE WEB OF THINGS

To execute a WoT application (*i.e.* a composition of functionalities), the end-user requests its top-level functionality to an avatar that exposes it. Each avatar is responsible for the correct execution of the functionalities it exposes. To do so, it satisfies its individual *goals*. A goal can be functional or non-functional. In the first case, it corresponds to the objective of a local (resp. collaborative) functionality, handled by the *Local Functionality Module* (resp. *Collaborative Functionality Module*). In the second, it is related to other concerns, such as energy management or response time to other functionalities. The hierarchy of functionalities can be considered as a global plan to orchestrate local functionalities and produce collaborative ones. An avatar decides to provide a collaborative functionality by semantically matching the requirements of the functionality with functionalities exposed by itself and other avatars. If all sub-functionalities are available, it can start a *coalition formation* process (Fig. 5.5). A coalition is a set of self-interested avatars that agree to cooperate for executing a task [36]. The result of this process is recruiting a set of avatars in a temporary *ad-hoc* cooperation to perform a collective goal. A collective goal is the objective of a coalition of avatars (namely, the functionality that requires the collaboration). In this section, we describe how avatars can autonomously expose and fulfill collaborative functionalities and therefore, WoT applications.

---

[21]www.fipa.org/specs/fipa00091/PC00091A.html.

[22]http://www.irit.fr/recherches/MELODI/ontologies/IoT-O.owl.

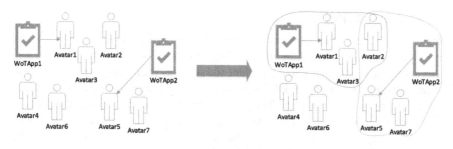

FIGURE 5.5

Coalition formation

5.6.1 TOWARDS SOCIAL CONSCIOUSNESS OF AVATARS

The smartness of a WoT system lies typically in its service composition, context-awareness, human-machine interaction, automation, semantic reasoning, data integration and analysis to name a few [8]. Still, we can more attractively exploit the potential of the Web of Things and go beyond its user-centric technical smartness. Currently, we are observing a progressive shift from things with a user-understandable smartness to things with an actual social consciousness [6]. Motivated by the same social concern, we believe that the technical smartness offered by WoT platforms and architectures is mature enough to take a further step in the evolution of everyday things into socially intelligent ones. Nonetheless, it remains difficult for a WoT system designer to manage or anticipate the heterogeneity and the complexity of interactions between things. Hence the need for a thing-centered social vision for the Web of Things. This vision cannot be easily achieved as many pieces are still missing.

While efforts to meet WoT specific challenges (listed above) are partially made, we still need an abstract high-level perspective. Recently, there has been a paradigm shift towards a social vision for the IoT/WoT. Many terms like "Social Web of Things", "Social Internet of Things", "Internet of Social Things", "Smart-its", "Everything is alive", "Cyber Physical Social Systems", "Wisdom Web of Things" have flourished attempting to make smart things as first-class citizens of the Web. However, little attention was paid to "human-inspired" social interactions between smart things. Approaching the social vision from a collective intelligence perspective [37,34,38], we consider smart things as (i) autonomous entities, i.e. operating and deciding independently according to their own agenda, (ii) exhibiting goal-directed behavior, (iii) and capable of cooperating to solve problems that go beyond the individual capabilities or knowledge of each entity.

5.6.2 COOPERATION AS AN INTENDED SOCIAL INTERACTION

Avatars can engage in many types of social interactions. The simplest form is, for example, communicative action such as sending requests or information. Cooperation is a very general form of interaction that is studied in multi-agent systems. It is established by the delegation/adoption of tasks, coordination of actions, and conflict resolution [16]. From an individual point of view, cooperation is a deliberate attitude of an avatar who decides to carry out a joint action with one or many avatars. More concretely, cooperation works through an avatar allocating a task (or sub-task) to another avatar via a specific request (offer, proposal, announcement, etc.) satisfying a commitment (help, contract, etc.) [16].

Avatars need to cooperate when they do not have the necessary skills or knowledge to accomplish their individual goals, to respond effectively to users' and other avatars' requests, but also to meet objectives of the overall system. The challenge of cooperation is the establishment and maintenance of mutually advantageous relations between avatars. This challenge is more present in the coexistence of WoT systems, unknown to each other, in the same physical environment. An avatar that belongs to one or more coalitions and that is requested by another avatar must ensure that the response to this request does not interfere in achieving its individual goals and those associated to its various coalitions.

There are several cases where "interferences" can occur:

- Incompatible goals between two avatars. An avatar A_1 delegates an action to an avatar A_2 with consequences on the environment that are not acceptable by A_2. It should be noted that this conflict has no place in a situation of competition or adversity between avatars, but occurs between avatars with collaborative attitudes.
- Cooperation with avatars having conflicting goals. When an avatar A_1 accepts requests from two avatars A_2 and A_3 in conflict, the external conflict between A_2 and A_3 will become an internal conflict to A_1. From a collective point of view, this interference transforms an external conflict between coalitions with incompatible goals into an internal conflict to the avatar agreeing to join these coalitions.
- Resource conflict between avatars. When two avatars need to use the same resource at the same time. In a cooperative setting, this interference can be considered as a scheduling constraint.

5.6.3 TOWARDS SOCIAL CONSCIOUSNESS OF AVATARS: UNDERSTANDING SOCIAL INTERACTIONS

In an open environment like the Web, systems are designed by different vendors, making it difficult for all the coexisting groups of socially conscious avatars to share the same mental attitudes (cooperative, cautious, selfish, precautious, etc.). Indeed, such coexistence can show a wide range of behaviors that may either fit the label of mutualism, cooperation, antagonism, parasitism, etc. One can also think about considering some kind of exploitive behaviour that smart things can encounter. This difference in attitudes and intentions of avatars influences the interactions between coexisting smart things. Therefore, an avatar must be able to understand the nature of its social interactions for a successful cooperation.

Identification of social interactions One of the most important prerequisites to implement a social vision of the Web of Things is to investigate the types of social

Table 5.2 Classification of Interaction Situations ([22])

Resources	Skills	Goals	Interaction Situation	
			Type	Category
Sufficient	Sufficient	Compatible	Independence	Independence
	Insufficient		Simple Collaboration	
Insufficient	Sufficient		Obstruction	Cooperation
	Insufficient		Coordinated Collaboration	
Sufficient	Sufficient	Incompatible	Pure Individual Competition	Antagonism
	Insufficient		Pure Collective Competition	
Insufficient	Sufficient		Individual Resource Conflict	
	Insufficient		Collective Resource Conflict	

interactions among things [6]. According to Ferber [22], except for independence situations where goals are compatible and the resources and skills are sufficient, the possible interaction situations are cooperation or antagonism (Table 5.2).

There have been efforts to present a taxonomy for relationships between smart things [7]: Parental object relationship, Co-location object relationship, Co-work object relationship, Ownership object relationship, Social object relationship. However, they are meant to classify agents into communities (smart things sharing the same manufacturer, environment, owner, or goal) so they can be easily navigable in social networks like the ones created by humans.

Intersubjectivity as a social process to understand social interactions Communication is the essence of multi-avatar systems. Indeed, expressing desires, setting goals and committing to joint actions require that all avatars communicate. The formation of coalitions needs, as well, some kind of communication. In this context, we point out a concept that is the basis of human communication called *intersubjectivity* [71]. Intersubjectivity – between two or more avatars in interaction – consists in considering the recognition of the intended meaning of actions and requests. From a multi-agent perspective, intersubjectivity refers to the interconnection of the self, the others and the environment. In other words, the avatar ability to take into account the mental states [62] of other avatars in its perception of the environment. Yet, we can never access the mental states of other avatars, we can only infer their existence based on what we observe, namely their performed actions, exchanged messages, requests, social links, etc. When an avatar is requested to contribute to a coalition, it is not enough to assess the cost of the provided services. The avatar should include the involvement of goals, both individual and derived from the coalitions in which the requester is involved. Additionally, in connection with its own coalitions, the avatar should construct a social representation of what we call its *Collective Identity, i.e.* any self-representational mode adopted by most of the avatars in a coalition, that they must integrate into their personal identity. Collective identity can simply be the coalition members and their common goal, or can be extended to role hierarchical structure between avatars.

5.6.4 INTENT RECOGNITION AS A MEANS FOR INTERSUBJECTIVITY

As we stated earlier, for a successful cooperation, an avatar needs to identify the type of interaction situations with its potential partners. We introduce intersubjectivity as a social process to this identification. This is where intent recognition [66] will play a very important role. There are many sub-areas that contribute to the growing field of recognizing other agents' behavior: intent recognition, goal recognition, plan recognition, activity recognition, mental state abduction, etc. But they share similar challenges and applications. This division is not meant to separate recognition into isolated research areas, they are closely related and they can transform into one another. Better than that, the resolution of one can automatically resolve others. For example, many works use goal and intention interchangeably. Likewise, intent recognition and plan recognition may have the same meaning, while some other works consider goal/intent recognition as a particular case of plan recognition.

Intent Recognition has proven useful for many research areas such as robotics, ambient intelligence, computer vision, human-machine interaction, traffic monitoring, military applications, video games and many others [66]. Several difficulties are encountered like the cost of handcrafted plan libraries [77], and partial observability of agents actions. In the absence of a plan library, agents can use action models [78] to recognize the plans that may be executed by an observed team. These techniques require a team trace, an initial state and a goal. The objective is to generate all possible plans to go from the initial state to the goal state, and keep the plans corresponding to the observed team trace. There are other techniques that do not rely on plan libraries or action models. [64] offers an approximation of a team intention considering the activities that take place between the roles of agents in a hierarchical structure (called *RoleGraph*). Agents can then match those activities between roles with rolegraphs that they already know.

5.6.5 APPLICATION TO THE VITICULTURE SCENARIO

We consider a set of agribots, RFID tags, sensors and a tractor in a vineyard. These smart things participate – through their avatars – in the satisfaction of three functionalities, grouped under a *Vineyard Management* WoT application (Fig. 5.6).

A user requests a moisture sensor avatar to achieve a *Watering* functionality, which requires several sub-functionalities, among which *water-vineyard*. To recruit an avatar that performs this functionality, the moisture sensor avatar initiates the Contract Net Protocol [63] to form a coalition. This protocol comprises four steps: (i) **Announce**: the moisture sensor avatar requests every avatar exposing a *water-vineyard* functionality, (ii) **Proposition**: the avatar of an agribot already involved in a *3D Data Analysis* functionality receives the request to provide *water-vineyard*. It knows that participating to a coalition for realizing another functionality may interfere in achieving the objective of *3D Data Analysis*. However, it can postpone the accomplishment of *3D Data Analysis* for a functionality of higher priority. For this reason, the agribot avatar requests an external service to use an intent recognition algorithm (like MARS [77] and DARE [78]) to identify the moisture sensor intention.

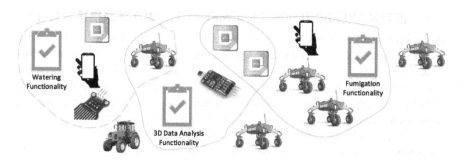

FIGURE 5.6

Coalition formation

After having determined that the moisture sensor avatar is likely seeking to realize the priority *Watering* functionality, the agribot avatar makes the decision to join the moisture sensor avatar coalition. It abandons its original plan of realizing *3D Data Analysis*, saves it for later, and responds positively to the sensor avatar proposal, (iii) **Decision**: after analysis of the positive responses, the moisture sensor avatar chooses the agribot avatar which seems to be the best candidate. (iv) **Contract**: the contract between the moisture sensor avatar and the agribot avatar that accepted to join the coalition is made. The sensor avatar can then inform the user that the collaborative functionality is being achieved.

5.7 CONCLUSION

Web of Things applications target various domains, address different concerns and will only meet global adoption by offering smart behaviors and services to their users. WoT platforms need to be sufficiently flexible to both enable interoperability between heterogeneous things and host such diverse and complex Web applications. In this chapter, we claim that such flexibility requires an abstraction layer between things and applications, and that this layer should represent things in a convenient, extensible and standard manner. To this end, we present the notion of avatar developed in the ASAWoO project and highlight several contributions.

Avatars are autonomous software artifacts that apply semantic technologies to both achieve interoperability among things and expose high-level RESTful functionalities from combinations of elementary thing capabilities. They can be connected to things using different network protocols withstanding connectivity disruptions. They can be executed and can deploy application code on the thing itself, on the gateway on which it is connected or on cloud infrastructures. They integrate a multipurpose adaptation mechanism that allows optimizing functional and non-functional processes. They can autonomously collaborate and form coalitions to provide applications composed with functionalities from avatars of multiple and heterogeneous things.

All these possibilities are provided in the avatar component-based architecture described in this chapter. We show how these contributions are put into work in the avatar architecture and more generally, how this architecture is able to efficiently handle various concerns at different levels: thing-specific constraints (*e.g.* network management), transversal requirements (*e.g.* adaptation) or application behavior (*e.g.* collaboration). This architecture has been designed to be extensible, and additional components are currently being implemented, such as a (de)serialization mechanism that will allow avatars to be saved, restored and moved between WoT platforms.

Together with the avatar architecture, we have specified an infrastructure that gathers the characteristics of avatar-based WoT platforms. Such platforms can be implemented on top of existing IoT solutions. They add support for avatar life-cycle, and act as "WoT application servers". We have also specified how to package WoT applications in a way that copes with WoT requirements and allows application designers to address domain-specific concerns while reusing existing functionalities. However, the notion of avatar does not appear in an application description; this saves developers' time and allows other WoT application specifications to be imported in our infrastructure. In any case, deploying an application in an avatar-based platform seamlessly leverages all advantages of the concerns already addressed in our avatar approach (interoperability, fine-grained deployment, network control and adaptation, collaboration). This is particularly useful when using complex things (such as robots) or heterogeneous setups. We have implemented our approach and describe the different parts of our prototype. We illustrate our contributions with a scenario inspired from agricultural robotics.

The Web of Things is currently a relatively new field. The community is large and expects promising business opportunities. Therefore, it will for sure continue to evolve and new standards will emerge. It has to deal with a multi-layered vertical stack and multiple use cases, and to combine contributions from different disciplines. This is why we have built our approach on stable and comprehensive visions from as various disciplines as cyber-physical systems, software engineering, semantic Web and artificial intelligence. In this chapter, we show first that the notion of avatar helps building multidisciplinary, efficient and user-understandable WoT applications, and second that the theoretical foundations of our approach are reusable across the languages, standards and components implemented in the avatars.

REFERENCES

[1] Abowd GD, Dey AK, Brown PJ, Davies N, Smith M, Steggles P. Towards a better understanding of context and context-awareness. In: Handheld and ubiquitous computing. Springer; 1999. p. 304–7.

[2] Alaya MB, Matoussi S, Monteil T, Drira K. Autonomic computing system for self-management of machine-to-machine networks. In: Proceedings of the 2012 international workshop on self-aware Internet of things. New York, NY, USA: ACM; 2012. p. 25–30.

[3] Arbab F. A channel-based coordination model for component composition. Rep Softw Eng 2002;3:1–35.

[4] Arcangeli J-P, Bouzeghoub A, Camps V, Canut M-F, Chabridon S, Conan D, et al. Income–multi-scale context management for the internet of things. In: Ambient intelligence. Springer; 2012. p. 338–47.

[5] Athreya A, DeBruhl B, Tague P. Designing for self-configuration and self-adaptation in the internet of things. In: First international workshop on internet of things (C-IOT), 9th international conference on collaborative computing: networking, applications and work-sharing (CollaborateCom 2013). Oct 2013. p. 585–92.

[6] Atzori L, Iera A, Morabito G. From "smart objects" to "social objects": the next evolutionary step of the internet of things. IEEE Commun Mag 2014;52(1):97–105.

[7] Atzori L, Iera A, Morabito G, Nitti M. The social internet of things (siot)–when social networks meet the internet of things: concept, architecture and network characterization. Comput Netw 2012;56(16):3594–608.

[8] Bandyopadhyay D, Sen J. Internet of things: applications and challenges in technology and standardization. Wirel Pers Commun 2011;58(1):49–69.

[9] Bazire M, Brézillon P. Understanding context before using it. Modeling and using context. 2005.

[10] Bischof S, Karapantelakis A, Nechifor C-S, Sheth A, Mileo A, Barnaghi P. Semantic modelling of smart city data. In: W3C workshop on the web of things. Jun 2014.

[11] Brézillon P. Context in artificial intelligence: II. Key elements of contexts. Comput Artif Intell 1999:1–27.

[12] Brézillon P. Representation of procedures and practices in contextual graphs. Knowl Eng Rev 2003:1–26.

[13] Brézillon P, Pomerol J. Contextual knowledge sharing and cooperation in intelligent assistant systems. Le Travail Humain 1999:1–33.

[14] Cao H, Hu DH, Shen D, Jiang D, Sun J-T, Chen E, Yang Q. Context-aware query classification. ACM Sigir 2009;106(3):3.

[15] Capra L, Blair GS, Mascolo C, Emmerich W, Grace P. Exploiting reflection in mobile computing middleware. SIGMOBILE Mobile Comput Commun Revue Oct. 2002;6(4):34–44.

[16] Castelfranchi C, Falcone R. Conflicts within and for collaboration. In: Conflicting agents. Springer; 2002. p. 33–61.

[17] Cerf VG, Burleigh SC, Durst RC, Fall K, Hooke AJ, Scott KL, et al. Delay-tolerant networking architecture. In: IETF RFC 4838. Nov. 2007.

[18] Cervantes F, Occello M, Ramos F, Jamont J. Toward self-adaptive ecosystems of services in dynamic environments. In: Proceedings of the international conference on systems science 2013, ICSS 2013. Advances in intelligent systems and computing, vol. 240. Springer; 2014. p. 671–80.

[19] Chaari T, Laforest F, Flory A, Einstein AA, Cedex V. Adaptation des applications au contexte en utilisant les services web. In: Proceedings of the 2nd French-speaking conference on mobility and uibquity computing – UbiMob '05. 2005. p. 3–6.

[20] Conti M, Marzini E, Mascitti D, Passarella A, Ricci L. Service selection and composition in opportunistic networks. In: 9th international wireless communications and mobile computing conference (IWCMC 2013). July 2013. p. 1565–72.

[21] Dey AK, Salber D, Abowd GD, Futakawa M. The conference assistant: combining context-awareness with wearable computing. In: The third international symposium on wearable computers, 1999. Digest of papers. IEEE; 1999. p. 21–8.

[22] Ferber J. Multi-agent systems: an introduction to distributed artificial intelligence, vol. 1. Reading: Addison-Wesley; 1999.

[23] Fielding RT. Architectural styles and the design of network-based software architectures. Ph.D. thesis. Irvine: University of California; 2000.

[24] Fuhrhop C, Lyle J, Faily S. The webinos project. In: Proceedings of the 21st international conference companion on world wide web. ACM; 2012. p. 259–62.

[25] Galloway B, Hancke GP. Introduction to industrial control networks. IEEE Commun Surv Tutor 2013;15(2):860–80.

[26] Garlan D, Schmerl B, Cheng S-W. Software architecture-based self-adaptation. In: Autonomic computing and networking. Springer; 2009. p. 31–55.

[27] Gómez-Pérez A. Knowledge sharing and reuse. Handbook of applied expert systems. 1998. p. 10–1.

[28] Grace P, Blair GS, Samuel S. Remmoc: a reflective middleware to support mobile client interoperability. In: On the move to meaningful Internet systems 2003: CoopIS, DOA, and ODBASE. Nov. 2003. p. 1170–87.

[29] Guinard D, Trifa V, Mattern F, Wilde E. From the internet of things to the web of things: resource-oriented architecture and best practices. In: Uckelmann D, Harrison M, Michahelles F, editors. Architecting the internet of things. New York, Dordrecht, Heidelberg, London: Springer; 2011. p. 97–129.

[30] Gyrard A. A machine-to-machine architecture to merge semantic sensor measurements. In: Proceedings of the 22nd international conference on world wide web companion. International world wide web conferences steering committee. 2013. p. 371–6.

[31] Gyrard A, Serrano M, Atemezing GA. Semantic web methodologies, best practices and ontology engineering applied to internet of things. In: 2015 IEEE 2nd world forum on Internet of things (WF-IoT). IEEE; 2015. p. 412–7.

[32] IBM. An architectural blueprint for autonomic computing. 2004.

[33] Jamont J, Médini L, Mrissa M. A web-based agent-oriented approach to address heterogeneity in cooperative embedded systems. In: Pérez JB, Rodríguez JMC, Mathieu P, Campbell A, Ortega A, Adam E, Navarro E, Ahrndt S, Moreno MN, Julián V, editors. The 12th international conference on practical applications of agents and multi-agent systems PAAMS 2014. Advances in intelligent systems and computing, vol. 293. Salamanca, Spain: Springer; Jun 2014. p. 45–52.

[34] Jamont J-P. Multi-agent approach, models and tools to collective cyber-physical system engineering. In: Habilitation thesis. Université Grenoble Alpes; 2016.

[35] Mattsson J, Göran Selander GAE. Object security in web of things. In: W3C workshop on the web of things – enablers and services for an open web of devices. June 2014.

[36] Kerr R, Cohen R. Detecting and identifying coalitions. In: International foundation for autonomous agents and multiagent systems. Proceedings of the 11th international conference on autonomous agents and multiagent systems, vol. 3. 2012. p. 1363–4.

[37] Khalfi EM, Jamont J-P, Cervantes F, Barhamgi M. Designing the web of things as a society of autonomous real/virtual hybrid entities. In: Proceedings of the 2014 international workshop on web intelligence and smart sensing. ACM; 2014. p. 1–2.

[38] Khenifar A, Jamont J-P, Occello M, Ben-Yelles C-B, Koudil M. A recursive approach to enable the collective level interaction of the web of things applications. In: Proceedings

of the 2014 international workshop on web intelligence and smart sensing. ACM; 2014. p. 1–5.

[39] Kirsch-Pinheiro M, Gensel J, Martin H. Representing context for an adaptive awareness mechanism. In: Groupware: design, implementation, and use. Springer; 2004. p. 339–48.

[40] Kovatsch M, Lanter M, Duquennoy S. Actinium: a restful runtime container for scriptable internet of things applications. In: 3rd IEEE international conference on the internet of things, IOT 2012. IEEE; 2012. p. 135–42.

[41] Le Sommer N, Ben Sassi S, Guidec F, Mahéo Y. A middleware support for location-based service discovery and invocation in disconnected MANETs. Studia Inform Universalis Sep. 2010;8(3):71–97.

[42] Le Sommer N, Launay P, Mahéo Y. A framework for opportunistic networking in spontaneous and ephemeral social networks. In: 10th workshop on challenged networks (CHANTS'2015). Paris, France: ACM; Sep. 2015.

[43] Le Sommer N, Said R, Mahéo Y. A proxy-based model for service provision in opportunistic networks. In: 6th international workshop on middleware for pervasive and ad-hoc computing (MPAC'08). Louvain, Belgium: ACM; Dec. 2008.

[44] Lee EA. Cyber physical systems: design challenges. In: 2008 11th IEEE international symposium on object oriented real-time distributed computing (ISORC). IEEE; 2008. p. 363–9.

[45] Lin J, Sedigh S, Miller A. Modeling cyber-physical systems with semantic agents. In: Computer software and applications conference workshops (COMPSACW), 2010 IEEE 34th annual. IEEE; 2010. p. 13–8.

[46] Mahéo Y, Said R. Service invocation over content-based communication in disconnected mobile ad hoc networks. In: 24th international conference on advanced information networking and applications (AINA'10). Perth, Australia: IEEE; Apr. 2010. p. 503–10.

[47] Mascolo C, Capra L, Emmerich W. Mobile computing middleware. In: Advanced lectures on networking. Springer; 2002. p. 20–58.

[48] Cuenca M, Da Cruz M, Morin R. Programming device ensembles in the web of things. In: W3C workshop on the web of things – enablers and services for an open web of devices. June 2014.

[49] Médini L, Terdjimi M. An avatar-based workflow for the semantic web of things. Communication in the WWW2016 W3C track, https://www.w3.org/2016/04/w3c-track.html, April 2016.

[50] Mrissa M, Médini L, Jamont J-P, Le Sommer N, Laplace J. An avatar architecture for the web of things. IEEE Internet Comput 2015;19(2):30–8.

[51] Mrissa M, Médini L, Jamont J-P. Semantic discovery and invocation of functionalities for the web of things. In: IEEE international conference on enabling technologies: infrastructure for collaborative enterprises. Jun. 2014.

[52] Munnelly J, Fritsch S, Clarke S. An aspect-oriented approach to the modularisation of context. In: Fifth annual IEEE international conference on pervasive computing and communications, 2007. PerCom'07. IEEE; 2007. p. 114–24.

[53] Musolesi M, Mascolo C. Car: context-aware adaptive routing for delay-tolerant mobile networks. IEEE Trans Mob Comput 2009;8(2):246–60.

[54] Neves dos Santos F, Sobreira H, Campos D, Morais R, Moreira AP, Contente O. Towards a reliable monitoring robot for mountain vineyards. In: International conference on autonomous robot systems and competitions (ICARSC 2015). Vila Real, Portugal: IEEE; Apr. 2015. p. 37–43.

[55] Papadopoulos GA, Stavrou A, Papapetrou O. An implementation framework for software architectures based on the coordination paradigm. Sci Comput Program 2006;60(1):27–67.

[56] Passarella A, Kumar M, Conti M, Borgia E. Minimum-delay service provisioning in opportunistic networks. IEEE Trans Parallel Distrib Syst 2010;22(8):1267–75.

[57] Raverdy P-G, Riva O, de La Chapelle A, Chibout R, Issarny V. Efficient context-aware service discovery in multi-protocol pervasive environments. In: 7th international conference on mobile data management, 2006. MDM 2006. IEEE; 2006. p. 3.

[58] Redhead F, Snow S, Vyas D, Bawden O, Russell R, Perez T, et al. Bringing the farmer perspective to agricultural robots. In: 33rd annual ACM conference on human factors in computing systems (CHI EA '15). Seoul, Republic of Korea: ACM; Apr. 2015. p. 1067–72.

[59] Schilit BN, Adams N, Gold R, Tso MM, Want R. The parctab mobile computing system. In: Fourth workshop on workstation operating systems, 1993. Proceedings. IEEE; 1993. p. 34–9.

[60] Schmidt A. Ubiquitous computing-computing in context. Ph.D. thesis. Lancaster University; 2003.

[61] Scott K, Burleigh S. Bundle protocol specification. In: IETF RFC 5050. Apr. 2007.

[62] Sindlar MP, Dastani MM, Dignum F, Meyer J-JC. Mental state abduction of bdi-based agents. In: Declarative agent languages and technologies VI. Springer; 2008. p. 161–78.

[63] Smith RG. The contract net protocol: high-level communication and control in a distributed problem solver. IEEE Trans Comput 1980;12:1104–13.

[64] Soon S, Pearce A, Noble M. A teamwork coordination strategy using hierarchical role relationship matching. In: Agents and computational autonomy. Springer; 2003. p. 249–60.

[65] Stehr M, Talcott CL, Rushby JM, Lincoln P, Kim M, Cheung S, Poggio A. Fractionated software for networked cyber-physical systems: research directions and long-term vision. In: Agha G, Danvy O, Meseguer J, editors. Formal modeling: actors, open systems, biological systems – essays dedicated to carolyn talcott on the occasion of her 70th birthday. Lecture notes in computer science, vol. 7000. Springer; 2011. p. 110–43.

[66] Sukthankar G, Geib C, Bui HH, Pynadath D, Goldman RP. Plan, activity, and intent recognition: theory and practice. Newnes; 2014.

[67] Sztipanovits J, Koutsoukos X, Karsai G, Kottenstette N, Antsaklis P, Gupta V, Goodwine B, Baras J, Wang S. Toward a science of cyber-physical system integration. Proc IEEE 2012;100(1):29–44.

[68] Terdjimi M, Médini L, Mrissa M. HyLAR+: improving hybrid location-agnostic reasoning with incremental rule-based update. In: WWW'16: 25th international world wide web conference companion. Apr. 2016.

[69] Terdjimi M, Médini L, Mrissa M. Towards a meta-model for context in the web of things. In: Karlsruhe service summit workshop. Feb. 2016.

[70] Terdjimi M, Médini L, Mrissa M, Le Sommer N. An avatar-based adaptation workflow for the web of things. In: WETICE 2016. Jun. 2016.

[71] Tomasello M, Kruger AC, Ratner HH. Cultural learning. Behav Brain Sci 1993;16(03):495–511.

[72] Truong H-L, Dustdar S, Baggio D, Corlosquet S, Dorn C, Giuliani G, et al. Incontext: a pervasive and collaborative working environment for emerging team forms. In: International symposium on applications and the internet, 2008. SAINT 2008. IEEE; 2008. p. 118–25.

[73] Wei Q, Farkas K, Prehofer C, Mendes P, Plattner B. Context-aware handover using active network technology. Comput Netw 2006;50(15):2855–72.

[74] Xiang B, Jiang D, Pei J, Sun X, Chen E, Li H. Context-aware ranking in web search. Sigir 2010;2010:451.

[75] Yao L, Sheng QZ, Benatallah B, Dustdar S, Shemshadi A, Wang X, Ngu AH. Up in the air: when homes meet the web of things. arXiv preprint arXiv:1512.06257, 2015.

[76] Yu Z, Zhou X, Zhang D, Chin C-Y, Wang X, et al. Supporting context-aware media recommendations for smart phones. IEEE Pervasive Comput 2006;5(3):68–75.

[77] Zhuo HH, Li L. Multi-agent plan recognition with partial team traces and plan libraries. In: IJCAI, vol. 22. 2011. p. 484.

[78] Zhuo HH, Yang Q, Kambhampati S. Action-model based multi-agent plan recognition. In: Advances in neural information processing systems. 2012. p. 368–76.

[79] Zimmermann A, Lorenz A, Oppermann R. An operational definition of context. In: Modeling and using context. Springer; 2007. p. 558–71.

ACKNOWLEDGEMENTS

This work is supported by the French ANR (Agence Nationale de la Recherche) under the grant number <ANR-13-INFR-012>.

A WOT TESTBED FOR RESEARCH AND COURSE PROJECTS

6

Mina Younan*, Sherif Khattab†, Reem Bahgat†
Computer Science Department, Minia University, Minia, Egypt* Computer Science Department, Cairo University, Cairo, Egypt†

6.1 WHAT YOU NEED TO GET STARTED

The main objective of this chapter is to gain the required practical knowledge and skills for building simple physical testbeds for the WoT, which integrates the real world into the digital world. Concrete steps for building a WoT testbed are presented in the form of four experiments and a mini-project. Testbed evaluation is out of the scope of this chapter; our work elsewhere [1] discusses evaluation of an integrated WoT testbed. This chapter focuses on the interaction between microcontrollers, sensors, actuators, and PCs using HTTP and Zigbee protocols. The required platforms and devices for running examples in this chapter are as follows:

- Platforms: C#, ASP.net, and Arduino programming language.
- Devices: Examples in this chapter are for WoT-based smart home applications and will use the components listed in Table 6.1.

6.2 INTRODUCTION

Augmenting everyday's objects (e.g., light bulbs, curtains, and appliances) with embedded computers or visual markers (e.g., LEDs and small LCD displays) allows things and information about them to be digitally accessible through the Web or mobile phones [1,2]. They become the Internet's interface to the physical world by converging the physical world into digital world [3,4]. With a partial lack of efficient and scalable communication standards, the number of devices connected to the Internet will increase rapidly as soon as IP becomes the core standard in the field of embedded devices. It is expected to reach the order of billions in 2020 [5]. The IoT

Managing the Web of Things. DOI: 10.1016/B978-0-12-809764-9.00008-1

Table 6.1 Smart Building Components

Component	Count	Description
Arduino	2	Microcontroller of type (Uno-R3 or Mega2560)
XBee Series	2	R3 Pro 3 For building a WSN using Zigbee protocol
XBee Shield	2	For installing XBee modules on Arduinos
XBee PC Shield	1	For joining PC to the network
DHT11/LM35	2	Humidity and Temperature sensors
Light Dependent Resistor (LDR)	2	LDR is sometimes called a Photoresistor or a Photocell. It is used for sensing brightness or darkness level in a certain place (e.g., room).
LEDs (2 × RGB, 2 × Blue)	4	RGB LED is a triple-light led (red, green and blue). It is used for representing power consumption levels, room state, and so on. For example, it becomes red to represent *hot* state.
Fan	2	Fan device should consume at most 5.0 voltages.
Resistors (6 × 150 Ω, 2 × 10 kΩ)	8	For adjusting voltage or current to other devices (i.e., for adjusting sensitivity of sensors (e.g., LDR)).
Bread board	2	Connection board.

Additional accessories: jumper wires for connecting components and USB programming cables for programming microcontrollers (Arduinos).

and the WoT address this challenge by using IP and IPv6 (6LoWPAN) for embedded devices [6].

From the Wireless Sensor Network (WSN) to the IoT and moving forward to the WoT, this trend has spread for the last two decades [7]. Haller [8] discusses main concepts about the IoT (e.g., SThs and EoIs). The IoT focuses on the infrastructure layer for connecting and controlling SThs through the Internet, whereas the WoT is the application layer that visualizes IoT data (sensory data) using standard web tools (e.g., HTTP) and services such as Representational State Transfer services (REST) and RESTful APIs [9]. The HTTP protocol is used in the WoT as an application protocol [10]. Some efforts have been done on HTTP libraries to be compatible with embedded devices' capabilities, so that data and services become accessible using web standards [7]. Due to web 2.0, users can get static as well as dynamic information about resources.

Using a single protocol in the WoT will not satisfy all communication needs between heterogeneous things, and HTML has to embed additional formats for representing SThs and EoIs' properties and states [11]. As a result, the WoT needs special search engines like Dyser [3] and WoTSF [12].

Muhammad et al. [13] summarize differences between the concepts of emulators, simulators, and physical testbeds. They conclude that physical testbeds provide more accurate results. Thus, building a real WoT testbed that simulates the desired set of conditions and events in certain environments produces more accurate results [2].

This chapter addresses the problem of designing and implementing testbeds for WoT research and course projects. Practical knowledge about building the WoT testbeds starts with configuring and connecting components at the IoT layer (i.e., building the WSN layer). Building the WoT follows the architecture discussed in [7]. Mini-projects in this chapter cover general services of the testbed, such as (1) getting real-time data from SThs, (2) monitoring SThs and EoIs using standard web tools and services, and getting and saving datasets. The WoT testbed can act as a simulator for the physical environment by attaching datasets to the application layer to run in offline mode like the integrated testbed environment presented in [1].

The rest of this chapter is organized as follows. The next section discusses the WoT features and challenges. Section 6.4 briefly surveys IoT and WoT testbeds. Section 6.5 discusses the hardware and software components of a WoT testbed. Section 6.6 presents concrete steps for building mini-projects and course modules, which are combined after that in Section 6.7 to build a physical testbed for the WoT. Section 6.8 summarizes the chapter.

6.3 WOT FEATURES AND CHALLENGES

Sensors can provide great benefits when their readings and states are presented in a meaningful and friendly way to users and machines. For example, users need to know the logical path representing physical location (e.g., Building X, Floor Y, Room Z) instead of sensors' longitude and latitude. The potential of the WoT lies in interconnecting and integrating services with human users in different WoT networks. Searching for SThs and EoIs is one of the most important services in the WoT, where users search in real-time in WoT datasets that are collected in different formats [3,12]. This service needs special search engines due to dynamic nature of SThs readings and EoIs states.

Due to the great interest in converting things into SThs, more challenges have been found in the WoT [14–16]. Challenges are classified in brief as follows. Firstly, some challenges are concomitant to the IoT; these are: (1) huge number and heterogeneity of connected devices; (2) no standardized naming for SThs' attributes (during registration process); (3) dynamic states (e.g., readings) and dynamic attributes (e.g., locations for movable objects on which sensors and actuators are attached); and (4) logical path not considered as a SThs's attribute. Secondly, other challenges are concomitant to the WoT; these are: (1) partially non-crawlable WoT pages; as most WoT pages host dynamic parts (e.g., coded using AJAX) for monitoring SThs and EoIs in real-time, most of search engines' spiders cannot crawl them and (2) none standardized naming for states; a single STh state is represented using different wordings that has the same semantic meaning.

Incorporating a sense of WoT challenges and features (e.g., dynamic information) in datasets generated by WoT testbeds allows for producing more accurate results. In the light of the challenges and dataset requirements (e.g., lack of information about the infrastructure layer) discussed in [2], we summarize our observations on dataset contents. If the research is only interested in SThs values or in EoIs states, the used dataset is based on the WoT level (dynamic information), whereas if the research is interested in the network infrastructure, the used dataset is based on the IoT level (static information). Because the SThs may be movable objects (i.e., their locations may be changing frequently), then the research may need an additional type of information, which is called quasi-dynamic information about SThs. In this case, such a property about SThs will be considered as a special type of their readings (dynamic information). An integrated dataset contains information about both sensor readings and network infrastructure, that is, it is based on both IoT and WoT levels.

6.4 A BRIEF SURVEY OF IOT AND WOT TESTBEDS

Several studies [13,17–19] discuss and compare between existing simulators and testbeds using general criteria, such as the number of nodes, heterogeneity of hardware, and portability, but none of them discusses WoT features, such as STh's logical path, supported formats in which EoIs' states are presented, and accuracy of the datasets generated by the testbeds.

In the following sub-sections, we briefly survey testbeds and measurement platforms that combine both IoT and WoT features.

6.4.1 IOT SIMULATION

There is no general way for simulating the IoT [13,18,19]. Moreover, there are situations in which simulators and real datasets containing raw information (e.g., sensor readings [20]) (less information about the IoT layer are present) are not enough for modeling an environment under testing. When datasets miss the sense of one or more of the WoT features or challenges (discussed above) [2], they miss main factors for accurate WoT evaluation [1]. Also, many datasets are not actually related to the problem under investigation, but were generated for testing and evaluating different algorithms or methods in other research efforts. For instance, an evaluation of WSNs' simulators according to a different set of criteria, such as the Graphical User Interface (GUI) support, the simulator platform, and the available models and protocols, concludes that there is no general way for simulating WSNs, and hence IoT and WoT [18,19]. None of these criteria addresses the previous challenges. So, it is desirable to embed the unique IoT and WoT challenges within the datasets and to make simulators address as much of these challenges as needed.

6.4.1.1 WSN Simulators

Several studies [13,18,19] summarize the differences between existing WSN simulators according to a set of criteria, such as heterogeneity, scale, user involvement, limitations, etc. The Cooja simulator gives users the ability to simulate WSNs easily using a supporting GUI [18,19] and different types of sensors (motes) for different sensor targets. For instance, sensor applications are written in the nesC [21] language then built in the TinyOS environment [22] (e.g., the RESTful client server application [23]). However, there are limitations and difficulties for testing the extensible discovery service [24] and sensor similarity search [25] in Cooja, because there is no information about the network infrastructure and entities. In particular, static information about sensors and schematics information about buildings and locations of sensors need to be presented.

6.4.1.2 *WSN Physical Testbeds*

Physical testbeds produce accurate research results [13]. Different testbeds are found in this field due to different technologies and network scales. MoteLab [26] supports two ways for accessing the WSNs, (1) by retrieving stored information from a database server (i.e., offline) and (2) by direct access to the physical nodes deployed in the environment under test (i.e., online). However, the WoT challenges mentioned previously are not fully supported in MoteLab. User access in MoteLab is similar to what is done in the WoT testbed in [2].

SmartCampus [27] tackles gaps of experimentation realism, supporting heterogeneity (of devices), and user involvement [17] in IoT testbeds. CookiLab [28] gives users (researchers) the ability to access real sensors deployed in Harvard University. However, it does not support logical paths as a property for sensor nodes and entities (WoT features).

Nam *et al.* [29] present an Arduino [30] based smart gateway architecture for building IoT testbeds, which is similar to the architecture of the testbed environment proposed in [1] and [2] (e.g., they all use periodic sensor reporting). They build an application that discovers all connected Arduinos and lists the devices connected on each Arduino. However, the framework does not cover all scenarios that WoT needs, especially for searching. For example, information of logical paths and properties of devices and entities are missing in the framework.

6.4.2 WOT SIMULATION

Using websites (e.g., [31–33]), a WoT environment can be built online by attaching SThs like Arduinos [30]. These websites monitor the states of devices and provide RESTful services (GET, PUT, UPDATE, DELETE) [9] for uploading and accessing reading feeds. Moreover, the values (sensor readings) are visualized for users. The services of the aforementioned websites are similar to services of the testbed environment in [2]. However, these websites are limited by available service usage and formats of the responses, which are hardcoded and embedded within the website code or at least not exposed to users. The testbed architecture in [1], which is built specially for testing WoT, provides more general services, such as monitoring live information fed from attached SThs, visualizing sensor readings and states of EoIs over time, controlling actuators, triggering action events, and periodic sensor reporting.

A comparison of state-of-the-art IoT and WoT Testbeds has been discussed in our previous work [1] along two main axes: (1) the infrastructure layer elements (e.g., device heterogeneity), and (2) the application-layer elements (e.g., reusability).

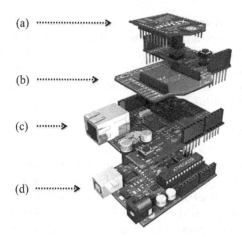

(a) ┈┈┈┈┈┈┈┈>

(b) ┈┈┈┈┈┈┈┈>

(c) ┈┈┈┈┈>

(d) ┈┈┈┈┈┈>

FIGURE 6.1

Hardware components for building IoT node: (a) XBee module of type pro S2B; (b) XBee shield; (c) Ethernet shield; and (d) Arduino board.

6.5 HARDWARE AND SOFTWARE COMPONENTS OF A WOT TESTBED

Because the WoT is foreseen as the future application of the IoT [11,23], the WoT will be built in two axes; the first axis (IoT layer) is to build the IoT layer by establishing a connection between all things (nodes) after converting them to SThs, and the second axis is to build a web application on top of the IoT layer to monitor and control SThs and EoIs that represent the set of required environmental events (WoT layer).

Building the IoT layer needs sensors, such as temperature sensor (e.g., LM35), actuators (e.g., RGB-LED), and microcontrollers, such as Arduino, Netduino, and Raspberry-Pi boards, to be connected or attached to things and objects using bread-boards. Microcontrollers act as gateways in the IoT. Building the IoT is done by implementing a certain network topology that covers the required environment. The main hardware components are Arduino, Ethernet shield and XBee module; these components are presented in the next three sub-sections followed by a brief description of Digi's configuration software (X-CTU [34,35]).

6.5.1 ARDUINO

Arduino [30], shown in Fig. 6.1(d), is the simplest type of microcontrollers, whereby its hardware and software components are open-sourced [30]. Arduino programming language is based on C++ programming language in the Arduino IDE. Arduino is considered as a tiny computer that can be programmed to perform a task, control the functionality of other components that are connected on its board (e.g., LM35 and LDR), and to process data according to program instructions. Arduino family

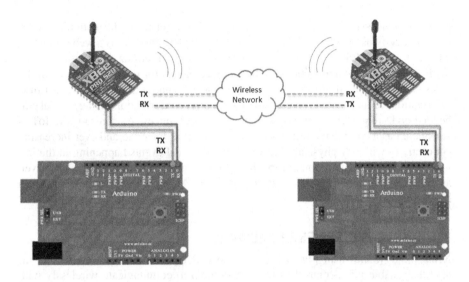

FIGURE 6.2

Two Arduinos connect wirelessly using XBee modules, which implement Zigbee protocol.

has different versions; the most famous one is of type UNO. The ATmega328 is main component of the Arduino, where it acts as a processor; it has 32KB of flash memory.

The Arduino can operate either independently (e.g., robot), connected to a computer (i.e., act as base-station), connected to other Arduinos (e.g., local area network between Arduinos, such as shown in Fig. 6.2), or connected to other controller chips. In other words, Arduino connects to the physical world through electronic sensors and actuators providing information about environmental events that sensors represent in the surrounding environment. It can use an Ethernet shield or Wi-Fi shield, so that it can act as a web server for sending and receiving data. Therefore. they can be used to represent things' states in real-time.

Arduino and Raspberry-Pi boards' families are of the most famous IoT boards for building IoT applications. Raspberry-Pi is like the Arduino, but it has more powerful features and capabilities; for example, it has bigger internal memory and can be programmed using different programming languages. But for simplicity, we will use Arduino boards (e.g., UNO and Mega2560) for building the infrastructure layer (IoT layer).

6.5.2 ETHERNET SHIELD

Monitoring components connected on Arduinos could be done in two methods. The first method is using Serial Peripheral Interface (SPI) and thread functions on base-stations (gateways), whereby sensors measure their values and Arduinos send devices' readings to base-stations, which in turn store the readings after analyzing the messages in the database. In this case, Arduino acts as a client to *push* device readings to base-stations [4]. The second method is to retrieve information from Arduinos directly using RESTful services. In this case Arduino acts as a web server [4], which provides RESTful services to control devices and *pull* device readings. Both methods require web applications (to host device pages) for monitoring states of devices connected on Arduinos and for retrieving information directly (i.e., real-time information) or indirectly from a database (i.e., stored information) using special embedded code (e.g., AJAX) in some parts of the web pages. As a result, the IoT is considered as a combination of push and pull methods for more and ever-increasing connectivity with any physical object or environmental events happening in the immediate and wider environment [36]. In order to make Arduino act as a web server, an Ethernet Shield [35] is installed on top of the Arduino board such as shown in Fig. 6.1(c).

6.5.3 XBEE PRO-SERIES2 HARDWARE

XBee [35,37], shown in Fig. 6.1(a), is a special type of small, cost-effective radios that enable microcontrollers (e.g., Arduinos) to communicate wirelessly with low power and low bandwidth. It is used with the Arduino Wireless Shield. XBee, Bluetooth, and Wi-Fi are used for allowing wireless communication between microcontrollers (gateways) in the WSN. XBee shield is a special type that is used for connecting XBee on Arduinos, as shown in Fig. 6.1(b).

As mentioned previously, the IoT is a global network of computers and sensors that communicate together through the internet using high-level (IP) or low-level (6LowPAN) protocols. So, we need to connect microcontrollers to each other forming a WSN according to a selected network topology. The XBee modules with ZigBee firmware (ZB firmware) [38] are designed to form networks with star, cluster, tree, or mesh topologies, whereby there is a hierarchy of devices and one coordinator is always necessary. For establishing wireless communication between Arduinos, radios should have the same type of firmware (e.g., ZigBee). Fig. 6.2 shows an example of communication between two Arduinos using XBee modules.

XBee uses ZigBee, 802.15.4, and DigiMesh protocols. Building a WSN using the ZigBee protocol is slower than 802.15.4 but allows for building well-structured network with nondeterministic throughput and sleeping endpoints based on a coordinator (base-station) and routers between the endpoints. The WSN that is built using ZigBee modules has three types of devices: (1) coordinator, (2) router, and (3) endpoint or end device. If the network topology is star, then the WSN contains two types only, coordinator and endpoint. The number of nodes per master node in the network may be 65,000 nodes with communication ranges from 70 meter to 300 meter (1.6 km possible).

6.5.4 X-CTU SOFTWARE (XBEE API PROTOCOL)

To configure XBee (ZigBee module) [34] as a coordinator, router, or an endpoint, we need to change the firmware files found on Digi's RF products using Digi's configuration software (X-CTU) [34,35]. X-CTU application is a Windows-based application.

It has multiple functions; each window tab in the application has a different function. For example, we can select *Range Test* tab for testing signal range between two Arduinos attached to XBee modules.

The ZigBee protocol allows setting up a radio link between the endpoints for covering a wide area by sending messages through multiple routers between endpoints. For enabling simple communication between two nodes (Arduinos with XBee modules), one of them should be configured with the coordinator firmware, and the other with router or endpoint firmware.

6.6 EXPERIMENTS FOR THE WOT

This section presents concrete steps for building a WoT testbed in the form of experiments that show how to build WoT-based smart home applications using Zigbee modules [38,39]. They are combined to eventually represent the main components of the WoT testbed. All experiments code can be downloaded [40]. The IoT layer consists of the physical network between SThs (Arduinos and sensors) and the IoT platform (also called IoT cloud) that provides services for charting sensory data in real-time using existing protocols (e.g., Xively [31] and Thingspeak [32]). The WoT enhances the IoT platform by building web applications that visualize IoT data and provide more services such as searching for SThs and EoIs [1,12]. In this section, we present experiments following the WoT architecture starting from converting things to SThs till visualizing SThs' data and EoIs' states, then these experiments are combined together forming a mini-project of a testbed for the WoT.

6.6.1 EXPERIMENT 01: CONVERTING THINGS TO STHS

Converting things to SThs is done by attaching sensors and actuators to things [7,8], so that SThs represent states of physical things online through the WoT. Integration of SThs is direct if they support IP connection and indirect if they speak other low-level protocols [41]. Converting things to SThs is the key element of the IoT [2,12, 42]. For example, converting a door to a smart door by adding a touch screen and a certain actuator allows locking and unlocking from anywhere. Representing power consumption of a building clarifies the difference between two concepts, STh and EoI. Representing power consumption could be done by converting devices to SThs through attaching special types of sensors (e.g., INA219 sensor). The building here is called an EoI, while devices attached with sensors are called SThs. The experiment for this example is simplified by using RGB-LEDs and Arduino whereby the RGB-LED becomes red when power consumption is higher than the average rate (calculated from historical data), becomes green when power consumption is in the average range, and becomes blue when power consumption is less than the average rate.

The first experiment, shown in Fig. 6.3, represents temperature state of a room using light level (brightness or diming level) of a LED located in that room. The

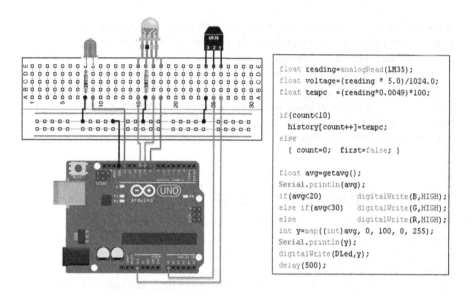

```
float reading=analogRead(LM35);
float voltage=(reading * 5.0)/1024.0;
float tempc  =(reading*0.0049)*100;

if(count<10)
  history[count++]=tempc;
else
  { count=0; first=false; }

float avg=getavg();
Serial.println(avg);
if(avg<20)        digitalWrite(B,HIGH);
else if(avg<30)   digitalWrite(G,HIGH);
else              digitalWrite(R,HIGH);
int y=map((int)avg, 0, 100, 0, 255);
Serial.println(y);
digitalWrite(DLed,y);
delay(500);
```

FIGURE 6.3

Experiment 01: Converting things and places to SThs and EoIs.

higher the dimming of the LED, the lower the room temperature, and vice versa. The RGB-LED is used as well, for representing the room state as a discrete set of states (hot, warm, and cold), where RGB-LED becomes red to represent *hot* state, green to represent *warm* state, and blue to represent *cold* state. A code segment of controlling the RGB-LED is shown in Fig. 6.3, where *getavg* is a function for calculating the average rate from sensor's historical readings, 50th percentile could be implemented by this function for getting more accurate results.

6.6.2 EXPERIMENT 02: INTEGRATING STHS AND EOIS IN THE IOT

Integrating SThs and EoIs in the IoT is done in two steps. The first step is to create profiles for newly joined SThs assigning them to EoIs. The second step is to monitor and control SThs through the Internet, forming bases of the IoT layer [4]. Creating profiles in this chapter is done manually using a configuration application (described in [1,43]), but it can be done automatically by discovering similar SThs in the IoT and selecting the most similar one, fetching its profile contents using semantics [44] and global ontologies as proposed in [45]. They propose a service-oriented middleware that abstracts things as services. Sensor similarity search could be used for this purpose [25] and the WoTSF search framework [12] enhances this process by using two-level indices; this automation is out of this chapter's scope and is planned as future work.

SThs' profiles are registered in a database, so that their static information could be retrieved. Registration is performed using a network setup application (as in [1]).

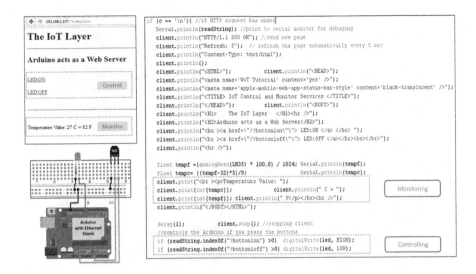

FIGURE 6.4

Experiment 02: Arduino acts as a web server supporting monitoring and controlling services for the IoT layer.

This application controls SThs and monitors EoIs locally (i.e., control is done using base-station connected to PC using SPI), and uses logical path in a smart home as an attribute for the STh [1].

The second step is monitoring SThs and EoIs in the IoT (e.g., monitoring indoor temperature) and controlling them online. This step is done (1) directly, when the Arduino gateway acts as a web server hosting its page on the attached SD-card or embedding HTML code in the response message (experiment is shown in Fig. 6.4), and (2) indirectly, by calling web services hosted on a base-station connected to the Arduino gateways, whereby the Arduinos receive commands and send raw sensory data to base-stations, which in this case are similar to the Dataset Collector application (DsC) in [1,2,46] (more details in the next sections). SThs pages are built so that they can be refreshed (i.e., reloading whole page contents) in less than a minute for monitoring SThs' states in real-time. Also, pages are coded using AJAX, so that only some parts are reloaded (partial refresh) instead of refreshing the whole page. The integrated WoT testbed in [46] codes SThs pages using AJAX.

Components in Fig. 6.3 are updated to be such as shown in Fig. 6.4, where the Ethernet shield is installed on top of the Arduino board, so that components could be monitored and controlled through the Internet, forming the IoT layer. Arduino code is also updated so that Arduino can act as a web server for monitoring room temperature using LM35 connected on pin A0, and for controlling LED connected on pin 8. GET RESTful API is implemented on the Arduino that is attached with Ethernet component and has an IP address (e.g., 192.168.1.177) by embedding HTML code in the reply message. Arduino checks if there is an available client and acts according

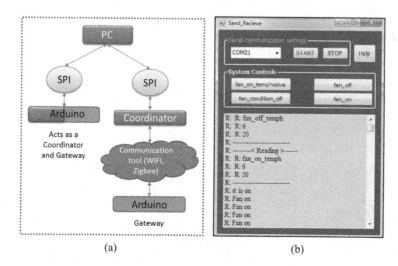

(a)   (b)

FIGURE 6.5

Experiment 03: Generating Sensory Data from the IoT. (a) Base-station architecture; (b) Dataset Collector Application (DsC) for the IoT.

to client action written in the received message, as indicated in the code segment in Fig. 6.4 for controlling the LED. Arduino's web page is refreshed or reloaded every 5 seconds.

The most appropriate method for designing a web page for visualizing STh's data despite resource constraints (allowing monitoring and controlling its state in real-time) is to implement and use APIs (RESTful services). APIs act as a middle layer between physical gateways (Arduinos) and virtual gateways (web pages). This method is preferable for building WoT applications, where it can host static and dynamic information in the same page (e.g., WoT testbed in [46]).

To sum up, the concrete steps to build a WoT are so far as follows.

1. Building the physical layer for measuring the environmental events (using sensors) and for controlling the surrounding environment (using actuators).
2. Building web pages for SThs.
3. Building APIs for sending and receiving commands between the Arduinos and their web pages. These APIs are RESTful services [15,47].

6.6.3 EXPERIMENT 03: GENERATING SENSORY DATA FROM THE IOT

The following experiment discusses how to build a base-station that contacts Arduinos in the IoT for sending commands and receiving information. The base-station runs DsC application to collect sensory data about a set of environmental events in real-time. It sends a set of configurations or commands to Arduinos in the IoT network. The base-station monitors and controls the SThs in addition to collecting the

Arduino Code	RESTful API: GET
| ```
while(Serial.available()>0)
{
   // split message into 3 parts
   (command, pin, value)
   ...
       else if(list[0]=="set_on")
       {
           state_on=true;
           cur_pin=list[1].toInt();
           cur_value=list[2].toInt();
           set_pin_state(cur_pin,
                         cur_value,
                         state_on);
       }
   ...
}
``` | ```
[WebMethod]

public string GET(string id)
{
   string url = "http://192.168.130.177/?pinG"+id;

   HttpWebRequest GETRequest =
                  (HttpWebRequest)WebRequest.Create(url);
   GETRequest.Method = "GET";

   HttpWebResponse GETResponse =
                  (HttpWebResponse)GETRequest.GetResponse();
   Stream GETResponseStream = GETResponse.GetResponseStream();
   StreamReader sr = new StreamReader(GETResponseStream);
   return sr.ReadToEnd();
{
``` |
| (a) | (b) |

FIGURE 6.6

RESTful API: (a) Arduino code for handling incoming commands; (b) RESTful API GET for getting SThs' states.

datasets. The execution of this experiment starts by establishing a connection between the base-station and gateways (Arduinos), whereby the gateways are configured to implement a certain topology (e.g., mesh or star). Base-station is implemented by attaching a microcontroller (that acts as a XBee coordinator) to a PC via SPI cable, as shown in Fig. 6.5(a). The coordinator device connects to IoT gateways using a certain connection protocol (e.g., Wi-fi or Zigbee). The DsC runs on a PC and connects to the coordinator device via serial port connection to send and receive commands and messages.

In this experiment, the collected sensory data are about the status of the fan, and there is a dependency between the fan and temperature value (Fig. 6.5(b)). The code behind the buttons of the DsC are calls for SThs' RESTful APIs. Fig. 6.6(b) shows RESTful service *GET* that monitors STh's state, where it takes STh's id as an input parameter. In this experiment, because the DsC connects directly to Arduino, it calls serial port function *writeline* to send a command message (e.g., *serialPort.Write-Line("set_on,6,20")*). On the other hand, the Arduino receives the message and executes commands, such as shown in Fig. 6.6(a). In this example, *set_on* is a command for turning on the device that is connected on *pin 6* (the fan) with degree 20 (i.e., light or speed value is 20). Maximum digital value in Arduino is 255.

Sensory data are generated in the form of dataset in order to represent device states in real-time online and offline using a web application [1]. Arduino acts as a coordinator for sending and receiving messages or commands in the network, and acts as a gateway in the same time to report states of SThs connected on it (Fig. 6.5(a)). For a larger IoT network, the coordinator contacts the main gateways, which are configured

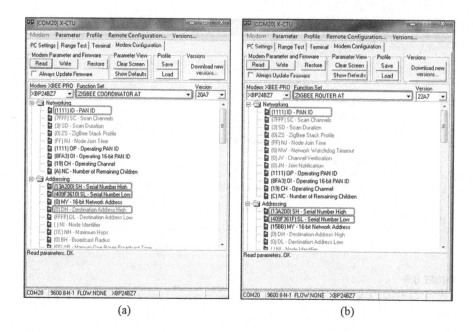

FIGURE 6.7

Experiment 04: Configuring ZigBee modules: (a) Coordinator profile and (b) Router profile.

as routers in a mesh topology, or end-devices in a star topology. Configuring the IoT network to implement a certain network topology is discussed in details in the next section.

6.6.4 EXPERIMENT 04: CONFIGURING IOT NODES USING X-CTU SOFTWARE

As mentioned previously, for building a WSN using XBee modules (i.e., using Zig-Bee firmware) [35,38], one node in the WSN should be configured as a coordinator to manage all endpoints in the WSN [39].

- **Configuring coordinator device using X-CTU.** As shown in Fig. 6.7(a), the device is configured as a coordinator by changing the function set to ZIGBEE CO-ORDINATOR AT, setting PAN ID to 1111. XBee-Shield button *XBEE/USB* should be set on *USB* selection during code burning and on *XBEE* otherwise (e.g., sending and receiving signals). Coordinator and endpoints should have the same PAN ID (default gateway in IPv4), so that all nodes send their messages directly to the coordinator or indirectly though routers (i.e., nodes that share the same PAN ID can communicate with each other [34,35]). PAN ID, high word (SH), and low word (SL) are important items in node configuration. For sending requests from the coordinator to all nodes in the network, nodes should have the same PAN ID in their configuration and Destination Address High (DH) is set to zero in the coordinator. But for building a peer-to-peer communication, DH in the coordinator is set to the value of SH in the endpoint device.

- **Configuring router device using X-CTU**. In order to enable end-point devices to send their information directly to the PC (coordinator) implementing a star topology using ZigBee modules, the XBee module attached to the PC through the USB-shield should be configured as a coordinator (Fig. 6.7(a)), and end-point devices should be configured as routers or end-point devices, as shown in Fig. 6.7(b). This figure shows configuration of Arduino-Uno, where attributes surrounded with red rectangles in this figure are kept similar in all end-point devices or router devices, while attributes surrounded with light-blue rectangles are set to different values in all end-point devices.
- **Configuring end-point device using X-CTU**. For enlarging the network (i.e., implementing a different network topology, such as mesh topology), all the remaining nodes should be configured as endpoint devices, changing the function set in Fig. 6.7(b) from ZIGBEE ROUTER AT to ZIGBEE END DEVICE AT. More details about types of configuration are in [34,35,38,48].

6.7 PROJECT: BUILDING A TESTBED FOR THE WOT

Experiments in the previous section implement main services for the WoT. These services are combined together to build a testbed for the WoT following the architecture in [1] and [2]. Main elements of this architecture are as follows.

1. IoT infrastructure, implementing appropriate network topology (e.g., star topology).
2. Network setup or configuration application: Instead of creating SThs' profiles manually, joined SThs should be discovered dynamically enabling auto generation for their profiles by searching for similar SThs [12,25]. SThs and gateways should speak the same protocol (command messages).
3. WoT web application and APIs: for representing, monitoring and controlling SThs and EoIs. Searching for SThs and EoIs in real-time (dynamic information) using simple query language is the key service in the IoT and the WoT [12].
4. Dataset collector application (DsC): for collecting sensory data in the form of datasets that could be used offline for simulating the WoT. Running the WoT testbed offline using datasets generated from physical environments enhances test results [1] as compared to simulators like Cooja [3].

6.7.1 THE IOT INFRASTRUCTURE

The project presented in this section implements a smart home application for the building architecture shown in Fig. 6.8(a). Component description of the building architecture is shown in Fig. 6.8(b). This project uses simple components indicated

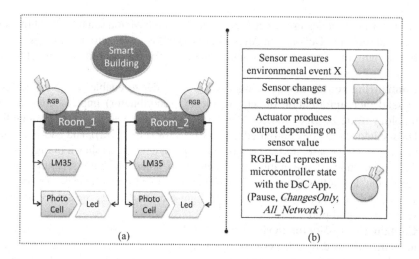

FIGURE 6.8

Smart building structure with sensors and actuators used in the project.

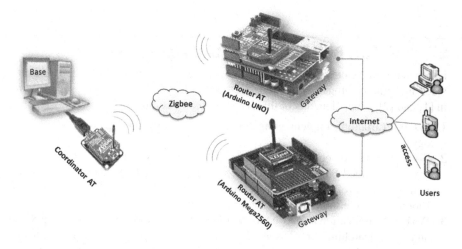

FIGURE 6.9

The IoT network of the project consists of one coordinator and two router devices (router device acts as an end-point device when the IoT implements the star topology).

in Table 6.1. For simplicity, the building has two rooms; each room has a temperature sensor, photocell and LED. Each room is represented by a physical gateway (Arduino microcontroller) and a virtual gateway (web page).

As shown in Fig. 6.9, the IoT network of the project implements a star topology to save the power consumed in message transmission (star topology configures

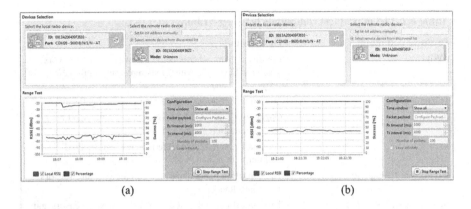

(a)   (b)

FIGURE 6.10

Measured RSSI values: (a) Arduino Mega2560 and (b) Arduino UNO.

nodes using less number of hops between coordinator and endpoint devices). In this project, the network connects two Arduinos with the coordinator wirelessly using XBee modules and Zigbee connection tools and protocols. The IoT layer consists of three nodes. The first node is of type Arduino-UNO; the second of type Arduino-Mega2560, and the third is a PC. USB-shield connects XBee module to the PC. The PC receives incoming messages wirelessly using Zigbee from Arduino-UNO and Arduino-Mega2560 then stores them in a database. As mentioned above, to implement such a WSN, Arduino-UNO and Ardunio-Mega2560 are configured as routers or end-point devices, and the PC is configured as a coordinator (base-station).

Device firmware configurations of this project are available for download [49]. Arduinos are distributed after testing Received Signal Strength Indicator (RSSI) [50, 51]. RSSI was measured in decibels using Digi's X-CTU software to determine signal noise, and its value ranges from 0 to 120; the closer it is to zero, the stronger is the signal. RSSI for Arduinos is shown in Fig. 6.10.

6.7.2 NETWORK PROTOCOLS

Internal protocols are written for managing SThs work in the IoT network (e.g., sending and receiving messages). The coordinator, routers, and end-point devices speak the same language (command messages). These commands are sent by the coordinator using DsC as in [1,2]. The list of the common messages is shown in Table 6.2.

In the project, Arduinos represent EoIs (rooms) and act as physical gateways; each Arduino is attached with two sensors (LM35 and LDR) and two actuators (LED and RGB-LED) in addition to XBee module that is connected to Arduino using XBee shield component as shown in Fig. 6.1. The Arduino circuit and a snippet of its code is shown in Fig. 6.11. This code is for the loop() function of the Arduino code. The loop() function is organized into three parts. In the first part (part 01 in Fig. 6.11), Arduino listens to all available requests (e.g., *GET*) coming from clients on the Internet

Table 6.2 List of protocol commands between Arduinos and DsC

Protocol command	Description
#Who	For discovering all connected gateways in the network, whereby they reply with a message containing their ID_Name_Type.
#Open, #Close	To turn on/off a session between DsC and gateways
#Led	Check all Connected Leds on Arduinos and send back feeds about their states
#All	Feedback about all connected devices on selected Arduinos
#Temp_on, #Temp_off	Turn on/off dependencies between temperature sensors and other devices
#LDR_on, #LDR_off	Turn on/off dependencies between Photocell sensors and other devices
#Feed_Temp_on, #Feed_Temp_off	Turn on/off feeds from temperature sensors.
#Feed_LDR_on, #Feed_LDR_off	Turn on/off light sensor (photo cell) feeds.
#Feed_Changes_Only_on	To set Arduino on change mode where it feeds information only whenever a change occurs in its objects (push method).
#Feed_Changes_Only_off	Do not feed information when a certain change occurs (poll method).
#Time = 1000	Time interval to feed their information back to DsC.
#Quick, #Normal	To initiate mode in which Arduinos send and receive signals

#Conditions_on = #Temp_on + #LDR_on (to fire all dependencies between devices).

and serves them by sending back its HTML page containing SThs readings. In the second part (part 02 in Fig. 6.11), Arduino receives and handles incoming messages (commands) from the DsC. In the third part (part 03 in Fig. 6.11), Arduino prepares all SThs readings following the configurations that are received from the DsC. In the case of the command message *All_Network*, Arduino sends all current SThs' readings, while in the case of *ChangesOnly*, Arduino sends all currently changed readings of the SThs).

6.7.3 WEB APPLICATION AND WEB SERVICES

The WoT is considered the application layer, which visualizes the IoT data using HTTP protocol and standard RESTful services. Thus, adding WoT layer to the testbed is done in two steps: (1) building the web application and (2) building SThs APIs (web services). The web application of the WoT is built using ASP.net, where each EoI (e.g., room) is represented by a web page which may contain more than one STh's link. Each STh is represented as a web page containing dynamic parts for visualizing its state in real-time (using charts). More details with code segments are in [1,2,46]. A set of web services were written in C#. The web application loads the available

```
-----------------------------<(Part-01): Handling Internet Client>
EthernetClient client = server.available();
if (client){
  while (client.connected()){
    if (client.available()) {
      //read char by char HTTP request
      //store string
      //if HTTP request has ended
      //send new page enabling monitoring & controlling services
      //stop client
      //do actions (controlling)
      ...
}}}
```

```
-------------------------<(Part-02): Handling incoming Messages>
while(Serial.available()>0)
{ reading=true; message=Serial.readStringUntil('\n');}
//Performing Incomming Message
  if(reading==true){
    //generateDataset=true
    //time:
    if((message=="#Time=0")//send SThs'changes only
    ...
    //condition
    //commands
    //Which To Feed
    ...
  }
```

```
-----------------------<(Part-03): execute rules>
if(generateDataset==true){
  if(millis()-changeTime>=Feed_Seconds){
    if(Which_To_Feed=="All") {
      if(Feed_Changes_Only) // send all changes
      else                  // send all readings
    }//end feed 'All SThs'
    ...
  }//end comparing time section
}// end dataset
```

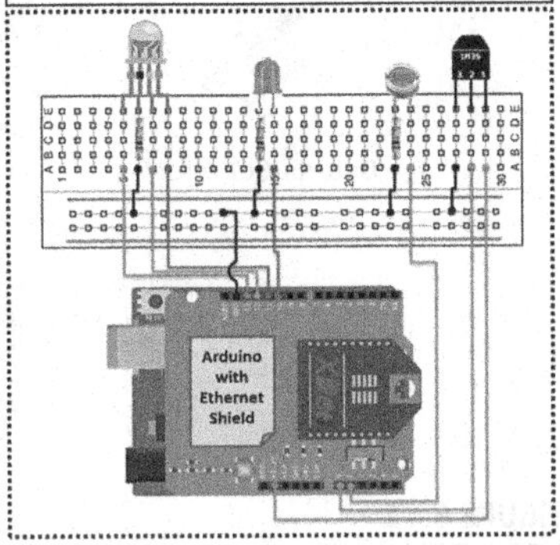

FIGURE 6.11

Arduino circuit and code snippet of its loop function: Arduino circuit represents room_1 in the building architecture.

SThs APIs dynamically. A special tag *GET#* is added as an additional service that is executed by default for the device webpage.

Because it is difficult for traditional web search engines to crawl and index pages containing dynamic information [12,16] (e.g., when pages are coded in AJAX), Google optimization rules [52] will be considered for directing spiders to index default URLs instead of parts coded in AJAX, like the WoTSF in [12]. In this project, the *GET#* service is called instead of the dynamic part. WoTSF [12] locates a server-root-file for each WoT following Google optimization rules [52] to build high-level indices, saving time in crawling and indexing dynamic pages of the WoT. Building special crawlers for WoT pages is another solution, where spiders can execute dynamic parts on the fly and index results (e.g., AJAX crawler [53]).

The main services of the web application are monitoring sensors, controlling actuators, triggering action events, and periodic sensor reporting [29]. The device page loads the RESTful services dynamically using Web Services Description Language (WSDL) [54] according to the Arduino IP and selected device ID. The web application operates in two modes: offline and online [1,2]. In offline mode, it attaches a dataset generated by the DsC (details in the next section) and simulates environmental events using historical information of real SThs, while in online mode, the web application retrieves SThs information directly from the IoT (Arduinos) in real-time.

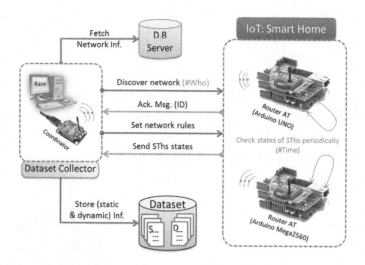

FIGURE 6.12

The architecture of the Dataset Collector Application (DsC).

6.7.4 DATASET COLLECTOR APPLICATION (DSC)

The coordinator (PC attached with XBee modules through a USB-shield) of the WoT testbed acts as a gateway by running the DsC [1,2] application for discovering and controlling SThs in the IoT. DsC generates datasets from discovered gateways by commanding the IoT using different rules, as shown in Fig. 6.12. Gateways periodically check SThs states and send back SThs information to be stored in the base-station; the period length for checking SThs states is controlled by the DsC in the beginning, whereby the DsC sends *#Time* commands to all of them (e.g., *#Time = 1000*) [46]. DsC can store SThs information written in different formats (e.g., Microformat). The main parts of the DsC are as follows.

1. Discovery part: in this part the DsC discovers all known gateways in the IoT network by sending *#Who* command (Table 6.2). It can get a list of the registered gateways from the database, where the network configuration application stores such information about the network.
2. Rule selection part: using this part, users of the WoT testbed instruct gateways about certain types of information and methods (*All_Network* or *ChangesOnly*) according to which gateways send SThs feeds. On the other hand, gateways update their settings in order to send back the required information.
3. Message analyzer part: this part handles and analyzes incoming feeds and stores information written in pre-selected format.
4. Monitoring part: it monitors the contents of the received messages, calculates the time delay of each processed message, and assesses dataset time accuracy of the generated dataset.

The DsC generates two types of information [1]: files that contain static information about building architecture and SThs profiles (i.e., static attributes of the STh) and dynamic information about SThs values and EoIs states. The network configuration application stores static information about the IoT layer (SThs profiles) in a database. DsC retrieves this type of information by implementing search queries on the database. Dynamic information is stored by IoT base-stations; this type of information is retrieved from the historical data or generated directly in real-time by requesting discovered gateways and instructing them to send their feeds following a certain dataset generation rule.

6.8 SUMMARY

In this chapter we presented the main practical knowledge and skills for building WoT applications and WoT testbeds based on a smart home application. Traditional things or daily-life objects and places are converted at first to SThs and EoIs by attaching sensors and actuators to things and attaching or locating more than one STh to represent states of the EoIs.

Building the WoT layer on top of the IoT layer needs to use current web tools and services to visualize SThs values and EoIs states. The IoT layer can have different types of nodes: coordinator, router, and end-device. Zigbee Network configuration is done using X-CTU software. For covering a wide area, building a WSN needs at least one node that acts as a coordinator and the other nodes to act as routers and end-point devices. Concrete steps for building the WoT testbed are discussed in the form of experiments and a mini-project. The experiments implement main WoT services, such as integrating SThs and visualizing their states.

The main parts of the WoT testbed project are as follows.

1. Building the IoT layer:

   - Converting things to SThs and connecting them to gateways (the IoT nodes).
   - Naming SThs: creating profiles for SThs and EoIs using network configuration application or automatically using semantic technology and SThs similarity search tools (only manual naming is presented in the chapter) [12,25].
   - Using or creating a common protocol between gateways and SThs.
   - Configuring gateways (coordinator, router, or end-device) to implement an appropriate topology (e.g., star or mesh).

2. Building the WoT application layer:

   - Building web services (connections between physical and virtual gateways).
   - Building virtual gateways (web pages) in a hierarchical structure following building or environment structure. These web pages call RESTful APIs to monitor and control SThs and EoIs.

- Discovering all available gateways, getting a list of connected devices on each gateway.
- Sending command messages (rules) to instruct the gateways to send back specific information about a specific list of devices according to a specific action or event.
- Listening to router devices following a dataset generation rule (*All_Network* or *ChangesOnly*), and analyzing incoming messages to extract SThs values.
- Storing incoming feeds (SThs states) written in the selected format (e.g., micro-format).

REFERENCES

[1] Younan M, Khattab S, Bahgat R. Evaluation of an integrated testbed environment for the web of things. Int J Adv Int Sys 2015;8(3&4):467–82.

[2] Younan M, Khattab S, Bahgat R. An integrated testbed environment for the web of things. In: ICNS 2015: the eleventh international conference on networking and services, Rome, Italy. ISBN 978-1-61208-404-6, May 2015. p. 69–78.

[3] Ostermaier B, Elahi M, Römer K, Fahrmair M, Kellerer W. A real-time search engine for the web of things. In: The 2nd IEEE international conference on the Internet of things (IoT), Tokyo, Japan. Nov. 2010. p. 1–8.

[4] Pfister C. In: Jepson B, editor. Getting started with the internet of things. 1st edn. United States of America: O'Reilly Media; 2011 [Ch. 1].

[5] Blockstrand M, Holm T, Kling L, Skog R, Wallin B. Operator opportunities in the internet of things – getting closer to the vision of more than 50 billion connected devices [Online]: http://www.ericsson.com/news/110211_edcp_244188811_c, 2011.

[6] What is DPWS and uDPWS all about [Online]: http://code.google.com/p/udpws/wiki/IntroductionGeneral, 2016.

[7] Guinard D, Trifa V. From the internet of things to web of things. In: MEAP – building the web of things. 2015. p. 1–15 [Ch. 1].

[8] Haller S. The things in the internet of things. In: Poster at the (IoT 2010), Tokyo, Japan. Nov. 2010.

[9] Elkstein M. Learn REST: a tutorial [Online]: http://rest.elkstein.org/2008/02/what-is-rest.html, 2008.

[10] Hong S. Mobile discovery in a web of things. MSc. Thesis. Swiss Federal Institution of Technology – ETH Zurich; April 22. 2010.

[11] Raggett Dave, W3C. An introduction to the web of things framework. Document [Online]: https://www.w3.org/2015/05, 2015.

[12] Younan M, Khattab S, Bahgat R. WoTSF: a framework for searching in the web of things. In: INFOS2016: the 10th international conference on informatics and systems. Egypt, Cairo: ACM; May 2016.

[13] Muhammad I, Said AM, Hasbulla H. A survey of simulators, emulators and testbeds for wireless sensor networks. In: 2010 international symposium in information technology (ITSim), vol. 2. Kuala Lumpur; June 2010. p. 897–902.

[14] Mayer S, Guinard D, Trifa V. Searching in a web-based infrastructure for smart things. In: Proceedings of the 3rd international conference on the Internet of things (IoT 2012). Wuxi, China: IEEE; October 2012. p. 119–26.

[15] Guinard D. A web of things application architecture – integrating the real-world into the web. PhD Thesis. Zürich: Computer Science, Eidgenössische Technische Hochschule ETH Zürich; 2011.

[16] Jin X, Zhang D, Zou Q, Ji G, Qian X. Where searching will go in Internet of things?. IEEE; 2011.

[17] Gluhak A, Krco S, Nati M, Pfisterer D, Mitton N, Razafindralambo T. A survey on facilities for experimental internet of things research. IEEE Commun Mag 2011;49(11):58–67. http://dx.doi.org/10.1109/MCOM.2011.6069710, inria-00630092.

[18] Miloš J, Zogović N, Dimić G. Evaluation of wireless sensor network simulators. In: The 17th telecommunications forum (TELFOR 2009), Belgrade, Serbia. 2009. p. 1303–6.

[19] Sundani H, Li H, Devabhaktuni VK, Alam M, Bhattacharya P. Wireless sensor network simulators – a survey and comparisons. Int J Comput Netw (IJCN) Feb. 2011;2(6):249–65.

[20] Bodik P, Guestrin C, Hong W, Madden S, Paskin M, Thibaux R. Intel lab data [Online]: http://www.select.cs.cmu.edu/data/labapp3/index.html, 2004.

[21] Gay D, Levis P, Culler D, Brewer E, Welsh M, von Behren R. The nesC language: a holistic approach to networked embedded systems. In: PLDI '03 proceedings of the ACM SIGPLAN 2003 conference on programming language design and implementation, New York, NY, USA. May 2003. p. 1–11.

[22] Levis P, Madden S, Polastre J, Szewczyk R, Whitehouse K, Woo A. TinyOS: an operating system for sensor networks. In: Weber W, Rabaey JM, Aarts E, editors. 1st edn. Berlin, Heidelberg: Springer; 2005. p. 115–48 [Ch. 2].

[23] Thingsquare AS IS. Contiki: the open source OS for the internet of things [Online]: http://www.contiki-os.org/, 2016.

[24] Mayer S, Guinard D. An extensible discovery service for smart things. In: Proceedings of the 2nd international workshop on the web of things (WoT 2011). San Francisco, CA, USA: ACM; June 2011. p. 7–12.

[25] Truong C, Romer K, Chen K. Sensor similarity search in the web of things. In: 2012 IEEE international symposium world of wireless, mobile and multimedia networks (WoW-MoM), San Francisco, CA. June 2012. p. 1–6.

[26] Werner-Allen G, Swieskowski P, Welsh M. MoteLab: a wireless sensor network testbed. In: Fourth international symposium on information processing in sensor networks. 2005. p. 483–8.

[27] Nati M, Gluhak A, Abangar H, Headley W. SmartCampus: a user-centric testbed for internet of things experimentation. In: 2013 16th international symposium on wireless personal multimedia communications (WPMC), Atlantic City, NJ. June 2013. p. 1–6.

[28] Mujica G, Rosello V, Portilla J, Riesgo T. Hardware-software integration platform for a WSN testbed based on cookies nodes. In: IECON 2012 – 38th annual conference on. Montreal, QC: IEEE Industrial Electronics Society; October 2012. p. 6013–8.

[29] Nam H, Janak J, Schulzrinne H. Connecting the physical world with arduino in SECE. Computer science technical reports. Columbia University, New York: Department of Computer Science; 2013. p. 6013–8. Technical reporting CUCS-013-13.

[30] Arduino. Arduino.com [Online]: http://www.arduino.cc/, 2015.

[31] LogMeIn Inc. Xively.com [Online]: http://www.Xively.com, Nov. 2014.

[32] Powered by ioBridge. ThingSpeak – the open data platform for the internet of things [Online]: http://www.thingspeak.com, 2016.

[33] XMPro. XMPro internet of things [Online]: http://xmpro.com/xmpro-iot/, 2012.

[34] Digi International Inc. Digi's xctu-software [Online]: http://www.digi.com/products/xbee-rf-solutions/xctu-software/xctu.

[35] Arduino. Arduino wireless shield with XBee series 2 radios [Online]: https://www.arduino.cc/en/Guide/ArduinoWirelessShieldS2, 2015.

[36] Kramp T, van Kranenburg R, Lange S. Enabling things to talk: designing IoT solutions with the IoT architectural reference model. Springer; 2013. p. 115–48 [Ch. 1].

[37] Faludi R. In: Jepson B, editor. Building wireless sensor networks. 1st edn. United States of America: O'Reilly Media; 2011. p. 115–48 [Ch. 1].

[38] Vedvei S. XBee wireless communication setup [Online]: https://eewiki.net/display/Wireless/XBee+Wireless+Communication+Setup, Jan. 2014.

[39] Boonsawat V, Ekchamanonta J, Bumrungkhet K, Kittipiyakul S. XBee wireless sensor networks for temperature monitoring. In: The second conference on application research and development (ECTI-CARD 2010), Chon, Buri, Thailand. May 2010. p. 221–6.

[40] Younan M. A wot testbed for research and course projects. Course project package-source codes [Online]: https://github.com/MinaYounan-CS/WoT-CourseProjects, Jan. 2016.

[41] Guinard D, Trifa V. Towards the web of things: web mashups for embedded devices. In: Workshop on mashups, enterprise mashups and lightweight composition on the web (MEM 2009), in proceedings of WWW (international world wide web conferences), Madrid, Spain. Nov. 2009. p. 1–5.

[42] McEwen A, Cassimally H. In: Hutchinson C, editor. Designing the internet of things. 1st edn. John Wiley & Sons; Nov. 2013 [Online]: https://books.google.com.eg/books?id=oflQAQAAQBAJ.

[43] Younan M. STh registration in the WoT. Code [Online]: https://github.com/MinaYounan-CS/WoT_SThRegistration, Jan. 2016.

[44] Datta SK, Da Costa RPF, Bonnet C. Resource discovery in internet of things: current trends and future standardization aspects. In: 2015 IEEE 2nd world forum on Internet of things (WF-IoT), Milan. Dec. 2015. p. 542–7.

[45] Hachem S, Teixeira T, Issarny V. Ontologies for the internet of things. In: ACM/IFIP/USENIX 12th international middleware conference, Lisbon, Portugal. Dec. 2011.

[46] Younan M. An integrated tested environment for the web of things. Source code package [Online]: https://github.com/MinaYounan-CS/WoT-Testbed-Environment, Jan. 2016.

[47] Mainetti L, Mighali V, Patrono L. A software architecture enabling the web of things. IEEE Int Things J Dec. 2015;2(6):445–54. http://dx.doi.org/10.1109/JIOT.2015.2477467.

[48] Digi International Inc. Official XBee website-connect devices to the cloud [Online]: http://www.digi.com/xbee, Jan. 2015.

[49] Younan M. IoT XBee pofiles [Online]: https://github.com/MinaYounan-CS/IoTXBeeProfiles, Jan. 2016.

[50] Wikipedia. Packet transfer delay [Online]: https://en.wikipedia.org/wiki/Packet_transfer_delay, Apr. 2011.

[51] Randolph G, Hirsch N. PIC32MX: XBee wireless round-trip latency [Online]: http://hades.mech.northwestern.edu/index.php/PIC32MX:_XBee_Wireless_Round-trip_Latency, Mar. 2010.

[52] Google. Search engine optimization (SEO) – starter guide. Jan. 2010.

[53] Suganthan PGC. AJAX crawler. In: 2012 international conference on data science & engineering (ICDSE). Cochin, Kerala: IEEE; 2012. p. 27–30.

[54] Wikipedia. Web services description language [Online]: http://en.wikipedia.org/wiki/Web_Services_Description_Language, Nov. 2014.

USING REFERENCE ARCHITECTURES FOR DESIGN AND EVALUATION OF WEB OF THINGS SYSTEMS*

7

A CASE OF SMART HOMES DOMAIN

Muhammad Aufeef Chauhan[*,†,#], **Muhammad Ali Babar**[*,‡]

Software and Systems Section, IT University of Copenhagen, Copenhagen, Denmark[*] Department of Applied Mathematics and Computer Science, Technical University of Denmark, Lyngby, Denmark[†] Centre for Research in Engineering Software Technologies, School of Computer Science, The University of Adelaide, Adelaide, SA, Australia[‡]

CHAPTER POINTS

This chapter presents following key contributions:

- A methodology for analysis, design, evaluation and evolution of Internet of Things (IoT) subsystems and Web of Things (WoT) system using a selected IoT Reference Architecture (RA).
- An approach for analysis and evaluation of the key business requirements and quality constraints of the IoT subsystems.
- Guidelines on using architectures of the concrete IoT subsystems as a source for evolution of an IoT RA.
- A comprehensive case study on application of the presented approach for smart homes domain.

---

[*]This chapter describes a method for software architecture design, analysis, evaluation and evolution of individual Internet of Things (IoT) subsystems and how individual IoT subsystems can be used for design of Web of Things (WoT) systems.

[#]Muhammad Aufeef Chauhan is a Postdoctoral researcher at IT University of Copenhagen and Technical University of Denmark. His research interests include software architecture for distributed and cloud-based systems, security of the cloud-based system, global software development and software evolution. He can be contacted at muac@itu.dk.

Managing the Web of Things. DOI: 10.1016/B978-0-12-809764-9.00009-3

7.1 INTRODUCTION

Web of Things (WoT) aims to provide a platform for smart and connected things also referred as Internet of Things (IoT) including sensors and actuator networks, embedded devices, digitally enhanced objects and decision support systems [1]. Whilst the IoT research primarily focuses on providing connectivity in a variety of networked environments, WoT focuses on the application layer [1]. Although IoT subsystems constituting a WoT system for managing multiple IoT devices and device management systems are designed and developed by numerous independent organizations, the IoT subsystems need to operate as part of a specific WoT ecosystem (domain). Designing the IoT subsystems to manage the sensors and the devices in a manner that the IoT subsystems can comply with essential business requirements and quality constraints is not trivial. The requirements can be related to general quality of the software systems such as security of data [2] and services [3], as well as infrastructure (on which the data and services are hosted) specific quality requirements such as availability, scalability, Service Level Agreement (SLA) compliance and interoperability [4]. As different IoT subsystems constituting a WoT ecosystem can be designed and developed independently, there is a need to have a standardization mechanism that can facilitate the analysis, design, evaluation and evolution of IoT subsystems' architecture.

A Reference Architecture (RA) is used to provide either a standardisation of the concrete architectures or to propose a preliminary architecture that can be used for designing the concrete architectures [5]. A RA consist of not only different elements of the architecture in terms of architecturally significant requirements, architecture components and architecture views [6] but also consists of the process for designing, evaluating and instantiating a RA into concrete architectures [5]. As a RA encompasses a complete life cycle of instantiation of a specific type of RA into multiple concrete architectures, choosing a RA-centric approach for architectural standardisation of the IoT subsystems' architecture in a WoT system can facilitate achieving architectural quality standardisation.

In this chapter, we present a RA-centric process-based approach for analysis, design and evaluation of the multiple concrete IoT subsystems' architectures driven by a single RA. We also provide insight on how the detailed design and instantiation of the concrete IoT architectures can lead to the evolution of the RA. We have considered smart home IoT subsystems as a specific case of WoT systems for the application of the proposed approach. In particular, we have addressed the following research objectives:

- We have presented a RA-centric process-based approach that focuses on using a single RA for design of the concrete architectures of all the encompassing IoT subsystems for a given WoT system domain. The presented approach also focuses on identifying variability and evolvability points in the RA that can change and evolve with the evolution of the concrete IoT systems' architecture.

- We have analysed the benefits of participation of architects involved in concrete architecture design of IoT subsystems to streamline core business and quality requirements of the domain and corresponding architecture design tactics adopted to satisfy the requirements.
- We have demonstrated application of the proposed approach for security and devices' management (energy management) in the smart-home IoT subsystems as well as the corresponding WoT system.

The chapter is organized as follows. Section 7.2 provides details on the proposed RA-centred architecture analysis, design, evaluation and evolution approach. Section 7.3 provides details on the case study of application of the approach for designing ten IoT subsystems, which lead to design of a WoT system for smart-homes. Section 7.4 describes the related work. Section 7.5 concludes the chapter and provides insight to the experiences and lessons learned.

7.2 ARCHITECTURE DESIGN CONSIDERATIONS FOR WEB OF THINGS SYSTEMS

In the Web of Things (WoT) concepts, smart things and their associated services are fully integrated by leveraging technologies and patterns that are used to develop traditional web-based systems [1]. As a result the things and services constituting WoT has to be compliant with a core set of quality requirements. A compromise in the core quality requirements by any one of the IoT subsystems constituting a WoT system, can result in compromise on the quality of whole WoT system. Hence, it is important to consider quality in the architecture design of each of the subsystems. In this section, we first describe the key architecture quality concerns for WoT with reference to IoT. We then describe design guidelines for architecting the individual IoT subsystems using the RA and using the IoT subsystems for architecting a WoT system, strategies for evaluation of the architectures and how concrete architecture design can be used for the evolution of the RA. Fig. 7.1 shows the pictorial representation of the analysis, design, evaluation and evolution process.

7.2.1 KEY ARCHITECTURE QUALITY CONSIDERATIONS

As things and services constituting a WoT concept operate in a composite manner, to achieve the quality in the WoT concept, all the things and services need to adhere to a core set of quality requirements. Absence of quality in software of any of the participating IoT subsystems (things or service) can negatively impact the quality of the whole WoT system. Hence it is important to select a minimum set of quality attributes that can be eligible for consideration while designing the WoT concepts. The quality attributes can be related to design-time and run-time quality of the things and services, quality of deployment infrastructure and quality of communication infrastructure. In this section, we provide an overview of the key quality attributes to be

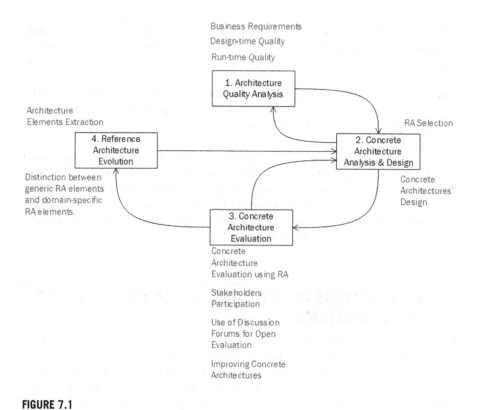

Business Requirements
Design-time Quality
Run-time Quality

Architecture
Elements Extraction

RA Selection

Distinction between
generic RA elements
and domain-specific
RA elements.

Concrete
Architectures'
Design

Concrete
Architecture
Evaluation using RA

Stakeholders
Participation

Use of Discussion
Forums for Open
Evaluation

Improving Concrete
Architectures

FIGURE 7.1

Architecture analysis, design, evaluation and evolution process

considered while designing IoT and WoT systems. The presented quality attributes can be related to each other. For example, different dimensions of security and scalability can be leveraged to achieve multi-tenancy in a WoT system.

7.2.1.1 *Security*

Security is a key quality attribute of every distributed system [4] and guarantees that the things and services are secured from un-authorised access, and data and messages are secured from being corrupted while transmission and are persisted according to required security parameters of a specific system. The security quality attribute for an IoT subsystem and a WoT system can be broken down into three main sub-attributes: (i) *Access Control*, (ii) *Communication Security* and (iii) *Persistence Security*. *Access Control* guarantees that things and services are accessible only by authenticated client services to protect these from unauthorised access and only the allowed level of information is revealed to the clients based upon their access level in the authorization hierarchy. *Communication Security* guarantees that the data and messages are encrypted while transmission so that these are protected from stealing. *Persistence*

Security guarantees that the data is stored in an encrypted manner both by the things and by the services, and encryption keys are securely handled so that even if some of the things or services are confiscated, the data is protected from malicious use.

7.2.1.2 *Availability*

The WoT concepts primarily focus on the application layer [1] and require to guarantee the availability of all the composite things and services. Hence, an IoT or a WoT architecture has to ensure smooth operation of the services even if some of (i) the things and services are out of operation, (ii) the communication channels are broken or (iii) the things, services and communication channels are attacked by an insider (e.g., by any of the thing or service) or by an outside (e.g., a hacking attack or a denial of service attack [7]). Availability is also important from deployment perspective. If the things and services in IoT cannot perform the desired operation, then new things are to be activated and new service instances are to be deployed and instantiated on hosting infrastructure.

7.2.1.3 *Scalability and Elasticity*

Scalability and elasticity of an IoT or a WoT system is required to complement the availability. The number of active devices in an IoT system can vary and the data that is generated by the devices can increase or decrease. As a result, the corresponding server side services need to be scaled up or down. There can be a large number of things and services in a WoT system as well as the users that interact with the things and services. A highly scalable and elastic infrastructure such as Infrastructure as a Service (IaaS) cloud can be viable option to achieve scalability and elasticity [4] in the WoT systems.

7.2.1.4 *Reliability*

Guaranteeing reliability of the things and services in an IoT or a WoT system can play a vital role in adoption of the system. Reliability requires that a specific configuration of the things and services in a WoT system can be able to complete the desired operations and the produced results are correct. Therefore, an IoT or a WoT system should allocate services to the things in an IoT mesh according to the requirements of the operations and should have redundancy mechanisms in place to guarantee variability of the produced results. Fault tolerance approaches such as Byzantine Fault Tolerance model can be used for reliability verification [8].

7.2.1.5 *Multi-tenancy*

Multi-tenancy is an important characteristic of the system and requires providing isolation among the data and services belonging to different tenants (user groups). Multi-tenancy is handled in different manners including: (i) Access control based on the tenants' roles that they can perform in a system and the type of data they can access [9,3]. (ii) Sharing services among the tenants having similar quality constraints [10]. (iii) Scheduling tasks on the resources that can achieve the desired quality [11]. (iv) Periodic monitoring of the services for their suitability to the tenants' requirements [12]. An IoT or a WoT system has to comply with the multi-tenancy requirements.

7.2.1.6 *Interoperability*

Interoperability quality enables a software system to work with other software systems [13]. Interoperability of things and services in a WoT system is important to facilitate their composition and provisioning. Interoperability is also critical from infrastructure perspective that is used to host the services in a WoT system. For example, if heterogeneous IaaS cloud infrastructures are used to host the services, their capability to host the IoT subsystems constituting a WoT system is important so that an appropriate IaaS cloud, which matches the security and reliability constraints can be chosen. A number of architecture tactics can be adopted in the IoT subsystems architectures and the corresponding WoT system architecture to support interoperability. For example, proxies and services' facades can hide the internal details of how the subsystems are deployed and migrated among IaaS clouds during their lifecycle [14]. Autonomous conversion of information associated with an IoT service semantics into service syntax can facilitate services' interoperability [15]. Adopting a layered architecture approach can be useful to compartmentalise the IoT subsystems' services and to provide interoperability among the services belonging to similar layers of the federated clouds [16]. A strategy to delegate tasks to the optimal services configuration and dynamically allocating hosting IaaS cloud resources can facilitate the process of achieving interoperability [17].

7.2.2 CONCRETE ARCHITECTURE DESIGN

An architecture design process guides the analysis and design of a software architecture [18]. The architecture analysis and design process for WoT systems needs to consider all possible things and services for a specific domain for which a particular WoT system is envisioned. As a WoT system aims to provide re-usability and adaptability of the IoT subsystems (things and services), the design process needs to focus on providing a standardization. A starting point to have a standardised system design is to analyse design of the IoT subsystems by using a common reusable architecture template, which is known as a Reference Architecture (RA) [5]. There are two main stages for WoT architecture design: (i) selecting an appropriate RA that is compliant with desired quality requirements and (ii) using the selected RA for analysis and design of the concrete IoT subsystems' architectures.

7.2.2.1 *Selecting an Appropriate Reference Architecture*

While selecting the RA as a tool kit for standardization that is to be used as a baseline for analysis and design of the concrete IoT subsystem architectures, the first step is to analyse the essential quality requirements of the domain. Once the essential quality requirements are determined, all of the candidate RAs should be analysed for (i) whether a RA under consideration support the essential quality requirements or (ii) whether the RA supports addition of new components or modification of existing components corresponding to a specific quality attribute without impacting the overall quality of the architecture (for scenarios) when there is no direct support for a specific quality attribute in the RA. A RA providing a closest match with respect to the above mentioned conditions can be selected for the analysis and design of the IoT subsystems' architectures.

7.2.2.2 *Using the Selected RA for Analysis and Design of Concrete IoT Subsystems and WoT System*

Once a RA is selected, it can guide the analysis and design of the concrete architectures of the IoT subsystems, which then can lead to the concrete architecture of a WoT system. First step after selecting a RA is to analyse it for its adoption for the given IoT domain with respect to the core business and quality requirements. The analysis includes identification of the RA's subsystems and components that can be incorporated in the concrete architecture. There can be three cases for the analysis: (i) Identification of the RA elements (subsystems and components) that can be incorporated in the concrete architecture without tailoring and modification. (ii) Identification of the RA components that can be incorporated in the concrete architectures but require tailoring. (iii) Identification of the elements that are not presented in the RA but are needed because of the IoT domain and critical quality requirements.

Based upon the analysis, individual IoT subsystems can be designed using the IoT RA. Then the IoT RA along with the additional elements that are incorporated in each of the IoT subsystems, are used for the design of the concrete WoT system's architecture, which can facilitate interaction of things and services across multiple IoT subsystems. While designing additional elements (which are not presented in the RA) for the concrete architectures, existing design patterns [19] and architecture styles as well as architecture patterns can be used [20].

7.2.3 CONCRETE ARCHITECTURE EVALUATIONS

Once the IoT subsystems' architectures are designed, the next step is to evaluate the architecture for business, functional and quality requirements of the selected IoT domain. Software architecture evaluation guarantees that the system design is compliant to the desired quality. A number of software architecture evaluation methods are proposed including Architecture Trade-off Analysis Method (ATAM) [21], Software Architecture Analysis Method (SAAM) [22] and Quality-driven Architecture Design and Analysis Method (QADA) [23]. ATAM, SAAM and QADA can be used to perform specific architecture evaluation activity e.g., identifying risks and non-risks of architecture design decisions, identifying sensitivity and trade-off points, performing trade-off analysis for conflicting design decisions and quality driven analysis of the architecture for its quality completeness [21–23]. However, for architecture evaluation of the IoT subsystems, a specialized meta architecture evaluation strategy is required.

We propose the use of the RA as a baseline for evaluation and involving stakeholders (architects who are involved in the design of the related IoT subsystems) in the architecture evaluation process. The architecture evaluation sessions need to be organized in such a manner that architecture is evaluated by not only the stakeholders of an IoT subsystem that is being evaluated but also by the stakeholders of other IoT subsystems. Consequently, the architecture of the WoT system should be enhanced based on the evaluation results of the IoT subsystems. Tailored ATAM, SAAM and QADA methods can be used to perform specific evaluation activities. The IoT subsystems' architectures should be distributed among the participants of the sessions well in advance. The feedback from the evaluation sessions is needed to be analysed in a joint evaluation debriefing session to make sure that the design decisions made during multiple architecture evaluation sessions are harmonious. We also propose the use of discussion forums to share design decisions across evaluation teams to mitigate the risk of conflicting evaluation decisions.

7.2.4 REFERENCE ARCHITECTURE EVOLUTION

The RA used as a baseline for the concrete architecture design needs to be evolved to cater the emerging requirements of a specific IoT domain. Albeit a clear distinction should be made between generic RA elements and domain specific RA elements. The additional elements (as described in Section 7.2.2.2) from the concrete WoT architecture and each of the concrete IoT architectures should be extracted and added into the RA. The RA evolution facilitates the design of new concrete IoT subsystems constituting a WoT system and facilitates their evaluation as the RA already includes findings from the evaluations of the previous IoT subsystems (design and evaluation activities of the RA's concrete instances). However, only the elements associated with the domain's business or quality requirements should be included in the RA. Elements related to functional requirements should not be included in the RA unless these are related to core domain functionality.

7.3 A CASE STUDY ON APPLICATION OF THE APPROACH IN SMART HOMES DOMAIN

We have used the architecture design considerations presented in Section 7.2 for design of a concrete WoT system's and multiple IoT subsystems' architectures for smart homes domain. A case study was conducted with participation of thirty five master level course students and 3 course instructors. The students were divided into group of at least three participants each and were given a task to design a concrete IoT subsystem's architecture for a particular dimension of smart home domain (e.g., smart home's security or safety) using a given IoT reference architecture. The students were given a brief description of the smart homes domain and were asked to choose a specific subsystem as per their preference and knowledge of the domain. Whereas, the instructors participated in design of WoT architecture that can facilitate interaction of multiple smart home subsystems via web-based protocols. All the participating students had a bachelor degree in information technology related discipline and had

Table 7.1 IoT Subsystems and Quality Attributes

IoT Subsystems	Groups IDs	Quality Attributes
Devices and Appliances Management	Group 1, Group 4, Group 5, Group 6, Group 7, Group 8, Group 9, Group 10	Performance, Usability, Reliability, Security, Modifiability, Interoperability, Multi-tenancy, Availability, Scalability, Elasticity
Fire and Safety Management	Group 2, Group 3, Group 5	Availability, Reliability, Scalability, Performance, Failure Recovery, Interoperability, Modifiability, Security
Home Access and Security	Group 3, Group 6, Group 7, Group 8, Group 9	Interoperability, Availability, Modifiability, Performance, Security, Reliability, Usability
Monitoring and Surveillance	Group 7, Group 10	Security, Reliability, Performance, Usability, Elasticity, Interoperability, Multi-tenancy

an industrial experience with design and development of web-based systems. Two of the course instructors had PhD in software engineering and one course instructor had a master degree in software engineering. The course instructors had extensive experience with architecture design and development of distributed and web-based software systems.

7.3.1 STREAMLINING BUSINESS AND QUALITY REQUIREMENTS

First step of the concrete IoT subsystems' architectures design is to streamline core business and quality requirements of a specific IoT subsystem. As the students group were given a choice to select an IoT subsystem domain (e.g., smart home's security or safety) for the concrete design of the architecture, they chose different aspect of a smart home. Each group had been assigned a number from 1 to 10 (e.g., Group 1). Table 7.1 shows the different IoT subsystems core functionality chosen by each group. The subsystems can correspond to core business requirements of the smart home IoT. As some groups selected more than one aspects of smart home domain (e.g., Group 5 chose management of different appliances in smart homes and safety management in case of an incident of fire), such groups are shown corresponding to multiple subsystems in Table 7.1.

Streamlining quality requirements in individual IoT subsystems is important so that a collective set of quality requirements for a WoT system (to facilitate an individual IoT subsystem's management) can be determined. A two faceted approach was adopted to determine a set essential quality requirements. At first stage, the individual groups identified the quality requirements specific to the IoT subsystem they selected for the architecture design. At second stage, a public discussion forum was used to discuss the quality requirements of the IoT subsystems that two and more of the groups considered for the design. Table 7.1 shows the finally agreed quality requirements for different IoT subsystems. It is clear from Table 7.1 that core quality requirements (Security, availability, scalability/elasticity, Reliability, Multi-tenancy and Interoperability) presented in Section 7.2.1 were considered for all the IoT subsystems.

7.3.2 SELECTING AND USING AN IOT REFERENCE ARCHITECTURE FOR PRELIMINARY ARCHITECTURE DESIGN

The next step is to select an IoT Reference Architecture (RA) that provides support and flexibility to design concrete IoT architectures by incorporating desired quality attributes (characteristics) in the RA and by tailoring the RA in terms of adding additional components and excluding undesired components from a concrete IoT architecture. Our analysis of the RAs for IoT revealed that Bauer et al. [24] have presented a comprehensive RA for IoT domain. We selected their RA and enhanced it based on our domain knowledge and analysis of the related IoT concrete architectures. We used the enhanced architecture as a baseline for design and analysis of the concrete architectures for IoT subsystems and subsequently for WoT architecture design, which can manage individual IoT subsystems. Fig. 7.2 shows the enhanced IoT RA based upon the one presented in [24]. The project groups used the enhanced RA as a baseline to design their concrete IoT subsystems' architectures.

The RA shown in Fig. 7.2 presents a layered view of the subsystems and components of the IoT RA. The *Devices Layer* represents IoT devices that are a part of an IoT system. The *Network Layer* represents communication protocols and components that support integration among the devices as well as integration between the devices and *IoT Middleware*. The *IoT Middleware* represents components and subsystems used for managing IoT processes, security handling and deployment of the resources on underlying *Hardware Infrastructure Layer*. The *Service Layer* represents back-end IoT services as well as management services. The *Interface Layer* provides interfaces to the IoT services and management services. The *Application Layer and Administrative Graphical User Interfaces Layer* include management applications and front-end interfaces.

7.3.2.1 *Using IoT RA Architecture for Design of Concrete IoT Subsystems for Smart Homes*

After selecting the IoT RA, the students groups were asked to use the RA as a baseline for the design of the concrete IoT architectures for the specific business and quality requirements (as elaborated in Section 7.3.1). Following design strategies were adopted for designing the concrete architectures.

- IoT RA layers were analysed to identify main layers of the IoT subsystems' architectures.
- The components of the IoT RA that could be directly adopted in the concrete IoT architectures were analysed and adopted. For example, *Authentication* and *Authorisation* components from the *Security* layer were adopted directly into the concrete architectures.

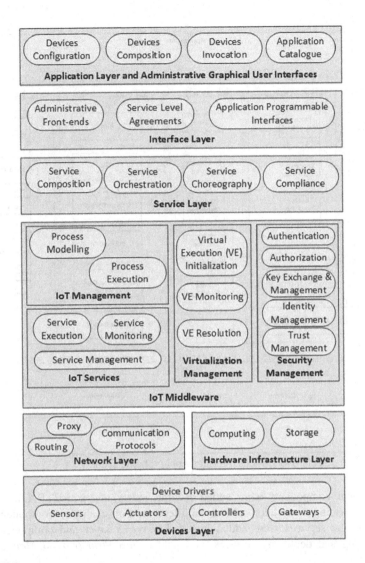

FIGURE 7.2

Internet of Things (IoT) reference architecture – an enhanced version of [24]

- The components that required tailoring or specialisation were modified according to the requirements of the target concrete architectures. For example, *Communication* layer of the IoT RA is used to identify the components for end-to-end communication, network communication and hop-to-hop communication. These components were needed to have specializations for the specific types of communication protocols that were to be used by the concrete IoT architectures.

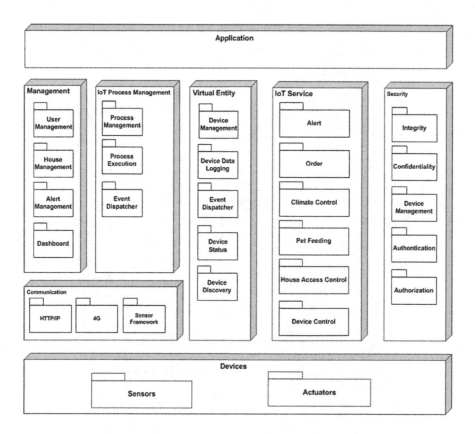

FIGURE 7.3

IoT system architecture for devices management and home security

- Additional components were added for the layers of the IoT RA that were only providing a skeleton of the architecture. For example, components for the specific services were added into *IoT Services* layer and components for managing and deploying services were added into *Virtualization Management* layer.
- To incorporate the desired quality attributes in the concrete IoT architectures, multiple architectures styles and patterns [20] as well as design patterns [19] were used.

Fig. 7.3 shows a representative concrete IoT system architecture for management of the devices in the smart homes designed to achieve business and quality requirements related to devices management in the smart homes. As shown in the figure, the layers and components from the IoT RA have been tailored and modified. *Devices* layer provides interfaces to connect to and receive information from different types of the sensors. This layer also provides interfaces through which devices and actuators in smart homes can be controlled. *Communication* layer includes components

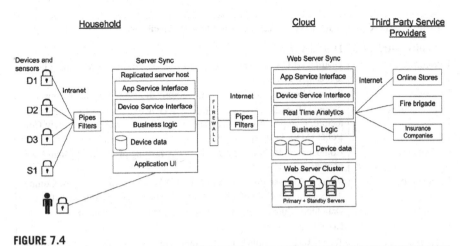

FIGURE 7.4

IoT system distribution and interaction

for *Http and TCP/IP, Mobile communication* (such as 4G) and *Sensor Framework* (to accommodate device specific communication protocols). Other layers of the architecture interacts with the devices via *Communication* layer.

Security layer includes components for *Authentication, Authorization, Integrity* verification, *Confidentiality* handling of the data and secured collection of data from the devices (via *Device Management* component). *IoT Service* layer includes components corresponding to specific devices in the smart homes. For example, *House Access Control* component manages access to the home by the householders, *Climate Control* components control indoor temperature and *Pet Feeding* components put food and water into pet food utensils. *Virtual Entity* layer manages devices (turning the devices on and off), data and event logging, and recovery of system configuration if some of the devices malfunction. *IoT Process Management* layer handles definition and execution of the rules and processes for management of the smart homes. *Management* layer provides Graphical User Interfaces (GUIs) and tools, which users can use to manage and control the devices.

Fig. 7.4 shows deployment configuration of the IoT subsystem in a distributed arrangement, in which the components are hosted on in-house infrastructure as well as on external hosting platforms to adequately handle system failure scenarios. The devices and sensors can be connected to only in-house components. The communication between internally hosted and externally hosted components is filtered through a firewall to protect the locally hosted subsystem from undesired access. Connection to the external systems (e.g., online stores for ordering of the items) is managed by externally deployed components to minimize internal system exposure to the external world.

A number of architecture and design patterns were used to achieve quality attributes. Table 7.2 lists commonly used architecture and design patterns in different IoT subsystems.

Table 7.2 Design Tactics Used to Achieve the Quality Attributes

Quality Attributes	Design Tactics
Performance	Distributed Components, Pipes and Filters, Prioritized Message Queues and Data Indexes
Security	Secured Proxies, Authentication, Authorization, and Session Tokens
Modifiability	Adapter, Facade, Loosely-coupled Layers/Components, Layered Architecture, Components/Services-based Architecture and Model View Controller (MVC) Pattern
Availability	Components' Redundancy and In-house hosting of Critical System Components
Reliability	Monitor Analyse Plan Execute (MAPE) Pattern, Redundancy of Components and Data, and Hybrid Cloud Infrastructure for hosting Systems
Scalability	Data Input Queues, Hybrid Deployments and Load Balancing
Auditing	Event Logs
Multi-tenancy	Tenant-specific Publisher/Subscriber Architecture, and Tenant Profiling and Management
Interoperability	Components' Facade and Broker Pattern

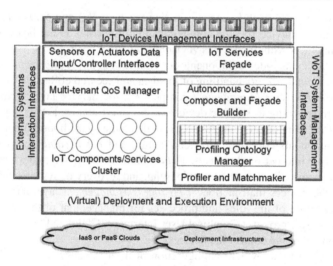

FIGURE 7.5

Web of things system architecture

7.3.2.2 *Web of Things Architecture to Manage Constituting IoT Subsystems*

Contrary to concrete IoT smart home architectures, which focus on providing different types of smart home services, connectivity with the respective devices and sensors; Web of Things (WoT) architecture focuses on the application layer [1]. Fig. 7.5 shows a high level view of the WoT system architecture designed to support smart home IoT subsystems. The WoT system architecture was designed using concrete IoT subsystem architectures and abstracting the application layer. The WoT system architecture focuses on provisioning of the IoT subsystems' components and services on the suitable hosting infrastructure, provide interfaces for interaction of the subsystems with external systems, managing Quality of Service (QoS) [4] parameters that are used for provisioning and composing IoT subsystems to provision a system configuration that can satisfy desired business, functional and quality requirements. The concrete IoT subsystems can either be hosted using a WoT system or can be managed using a WoT system.

The WoT architecture presented in Fig. 7.5 was designed following separation of concerns and layered architecture approaches [20]. The architecture has three interface layers named as *IoT Devices Management Interfaces*, *External System Interaction Interfaces* and *WoT System Management Interfaces*. *IoT Devices Management Interfaces* are used to receive input from the sensors of an IoT system and controlling devices and actuators. For example, in an IoT subsystem used for temperature control in a smart home, the hosted components and services can receive temperature readings from temperature sensors and can turn on heating or cooling system accordingly. *External System Interaction Interfaces* are used to connect hosted IoT subsystem services with external systems. For example, in an IoT smart home subsystem for security management, the subsystem interacts with emergency police services and notify home owners in case of a break-in or burglary. *WoT System Management Interfaces* are used to define tenants, their desired QoS parameters and specify Service Level Agreements (SLAs) [4] of the IoT subsystem.

The core WoT system components are classified into two categories: (i) the components that are responsible for IoT subsystems selection and their composition for desired QoS parameters and (ii) the components that are responsible for the provisioning of the subsystems' components/services on dedicated or virtualized infrastructure. *Profiler and Matchmaker* component maintains profiles of all the components/services of the hosted IoT subsystems using *Profiling Ontology Manager*, autonomously compose components/services and build on-the-fly interfaces using *Autonomous Service Composer and Facade Builder*. Ontology meta-models and service selection ontologies [25] can be used for profiling of the components/services. The interfaces are exposed via *IoT Services Facade* and *Sensors or Actuators Data Input/Controller Interfaces* intermediate layers. *Multi-tenant QoS Manager* is used to maintain desired QoS parameter for each specific tenant so that the services can be composed and provisioned accordingly. *Deployment and Execution Manager* is used to deploy the IoT subsystem components on either dedicated or virtualized infrastructure (e.g., IaaS or PaaS clouds [4]). *Deployment and Execution Manager* can be tailored using the RA for services selection and deployment on the cloud [25]. For cases in which some components/services of an IoT system are partially deployed on in-premise infrastructure and partially on off-premise infrastructure, the locally hosted and remotely hosted components can interact via *IoT Services Facade*.

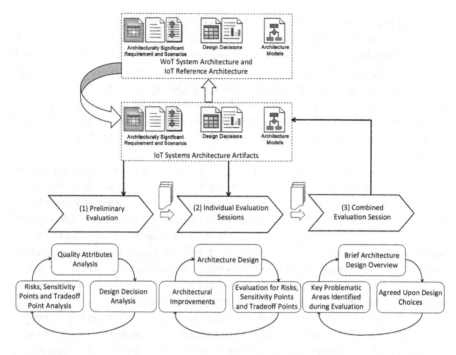

FIGURE 7.6

Evaluation process overview

7.3.3 EVALUATION OF IOT SUBSYSTEMS ARCHITECTURES

Evaluation of the software architectures plays a critical role to verify quality of a software system. A number of approaches have been proposed to carry out specific software architecture evaluation activities including but not limited to ATAM [21], SAAM [22] and QADA [23] as discussed in Section 7.2.3. As the aim of the IoT subsystem architecture design activity was to carry out design of the IoT subsystems corresponding to different high-level business requirements and quality requirements, the architecture evaluation activities had to verify compliance of the IoT subsystems to agreed upon standardized quality requirements (as discussed in Section 7.3.1) and design choices (as discussed in Section 7.3.2.1) that are not contradictory to each other. Hence, the evaluation activities are to be carried out in a way that the stakeholders involved in the design of an IoT subsystem can have maximum insight into the design of the other IoT subsystems. The following subsections describe the details on the evaluation activities and how the IoT subsystems evaluation can lead to the evaluation of WoT system architecture as well as evolution of the IoT RA. An overview of the evaluation process is presented in Fig. 7.6.

7.3.3.1 *Organization of the Evaluation Sessions*

Evaluation sessions for the evaluation of the IoT subsystems' architectures were organized in a way that stakeholders involved in the design of an IoT architecture covering one part of the domain (business requirements), evaluate IoT architecture designed to satisfy another part of domain (business requirements). For example, as presented in Table 7.1, Group 1 focused on IoT subsystem for management of devices and appliances in smart homes to have efficient utilization of electricity and water, Group 2 focused on IoT subsystem for safety management and fire extinguishing process in case of a fire incident, and Group 3 focused on IoT subsystem for access control and security of the smart homes. Group 1's architecture was evaluated by Group 2, and Group 2's architecture was evaluated by Group 3 so that Group 2 can have insight to both of the device management and security subsystems. The architecture design documents were shared with the group who was to evaluate the architecture before the evaluation session. For example, Group 1's architecture documentation was shared with Group 2 and Group 2's architecture documentation was shared with Group 3.

7.3.3.2 *Architecture Evaluation Activities*

Architecture evaluation activities consisted of three stages. (i) Before the evaluation session, the groups prepared a short architecture evaluation questionnaire on quality attributes considered in the architecture design, key architecture design decisions, strengths and weaknesses of the design decisions, sensitivity and trade-off points, and risks and non-risks in the architecture [26]. (ii) During the evaluation sessions, the group whose architecture was evaluated presented the architecture while the group who was evaluating the architecture asked questions based upon their initial preparation as well as from integration perspective of their own architecture. During the architecture presentation, design artefacts were analysed for evaluation of the IoT subsystem architectures as well some new artefacts specific to architecture evaluation such as architecture utility trees [21] were generated to present architecture design decision corresponding to quality attributes. During the architecture evaluation sessions, sensitivity points, trade off points, architecture risks and architecture non risks were discussed. (iii) After the individual architecture evaluation sessions, a joint session was conducted in which each group briefly presented their IoT subsystem architecture, quality attributed those were considered in the architecture and feedback it received during the individual architecture evaluation session. Each group member also prepared a written report on the evaluation of the architecture that the group member had evaluated in the architecture evaluation session. The report was shared with teaching staff, who was responsible for design and analysis of the WoT architecture. Table 7.3 shows commonly reported missing quality requirements, risky design decisions, sensitivity and trade-off points, and common improvements suggested in the IoT subsystem architectures during the evaluation sessions.

Table 7.3 Summary of the Points Discussed in the Evaluation Sessions

Dimension	Details
Risks	Using same communication protocol for inter-system and intra-system communication can make failure safety procedures difficult. Using broker pattern can result in selection of services not fully compliant with QoS constraints. Data storage on centralised persistence units is a risk for availability. Communication overhead of using Publisher/Subscriber pattern.
Sensitivity and Trade-off Points	Maintaining Facade for continuously evolving services. Using Singleton pattern instead of Message broker pattern for multi-tenant session management. Negative impact of layered pattern on performance. Trade-off between performance and modifiability by using either publisher scriber or layered pattern. Misuse of Pipes and Filter pattern where Broker pattern can be used. Trade-off is needed for Security versus Performance.
Commonly Missing Quality Attributes	Safety on Failure. System availability when Internet connection is not available.
IoT RA Shortcomings	Architecture and design patterns for implementing different elements of the IoT RA are not specified in the IoT RA.

7.3.3.3 *Improvements in IoT Subsystems Architectures*

All the groups improved IoT subsystems architectures of their respective subsystems based upon the changes suggested during architecture evaluation sessions. While improving the architectures, the findings from the individual evaluation sessions as well as joint follow up evaluation session were considered (as described in Section 7.3.3.2). A change log was maintained by each group to track (i) what changes had been made in the architecture, (ii) what was the source that triggered the change (i.e., feedback from individual evaluation session or finding from joint session) and (iii) traces to the relevant place of the architecture documentation where changes had been made.

7.3.4 EVOLUTION OF WEB OF THINGS SYSTEM AND INTERNET OF THINGS REFERENCE ARCHITECTURE

The improved architecture artefacts generated as a result of architecture evaluation of IoT subsystems were used for improvements in the WoT system architecture and evolution of the IoT RA. Because architecture of WoT system was designed based on the IoT subsystems (as described in Section 7.2.2.2), the newly added components were included in the WoT system and modified components were changed. The concrete IoT subsystem architectures can also lead to the evolution of the selected IoT RA for a specific type of domain. A large-scale empirical study on challenges with designing and using RAs have revealed that unavailability of the details on design decisions and how to materialize the decisions using architecture styles and patterns can lead to problems while using the RA for concrete architecture design [27]. Same challenge was also reported by the teams who were designing IoT subsystems architectures using the IoT RA (as discussed in Section 7.3.3.2). Hence, including architecture design decisions rationale and corresponding architecture and design patterns in the IoT RA can facilitate its adoption. For example, including architecture and design patterns (presented in Table 7.2) in the IoT RA (presented in Fig. 7.2) can facilitate its adoption for smart homes domain. However, variability points in the RA architecture should be considered while doing so to keep generic elements of the RA and domain specific elements of the RA distinguishable.

7.4 **RELATED WORK**

Since the inception of the software architecture [26], a number of methods have been proposed for architecture design. Most prominent of these methods are Attribute Driven Design method [28], Siemens Four Views method, Rational Unified Process [6], Business Architecture Process and Organization and Architectural Separation of Concerns method [18]. All these methods have three common activities: architecture analysis, architecture synthesis and architecture evaluation [18]. Architecture analysis and synthesis activities include identifying architecturally significant requirements, developing architecture scenarios, designing architecture elements using architecture patterns and representing architecture using multiple views [6]. Generic architecture evaluation methods include Architecture Trade-off Analysis Method (ATAM) [21], Software Architecture Analysis Method (SAAM) [22] and Quality-driven Architecture Design and Analysis (QADA) method [23]. These methods focus on evaluating software architectures with respect to specific quality attributes by evaluating architecture strengths and weaknesses, sensitivity and tradeoff points, and completeness of a given architecture.

Other than generic architecture design methods, the methods for designing and evaluating specific technology paradigms have also been proposed. The methods for Service Oriented Architectures (SOA) focus on transforming system elements in to software services, communication among the services, and exception handling and fault recovery strategies [29–31]. The methods for cloud-based systems focus on satisfying Quality of Service (QoS) requirements (e.g., availability, security and safety), incorporating cloud specific quality requirements (e.g., multi-tenancy and cloud-interoperability) and selecting appropriate cloud resources or cloud-hosted services that satisfy Service Level Agreements (SLAs) [4,32].

The increase in the complexity of the software systems has raised the need to have methods for reusable architecture solutions. Hence, the RAs design and analysis methods are devised [5]. A RA focuses on capturing generic business and architecture requirements and corresponding architectural representations. For example, a RA for cloud-based tools focuses on tools selection, tools provisioning, providing semantic integration among the tools and raising awareness of the operations that are performed using the integrated suite of tools [25]. However, using a RAs to design concrete architectures and evolving the RAs as the domain for which the RA is designed evolves, is a challenging undertaking [27]. The research presented in this chapter has attempted to bridge this gap by proposing an analysis and design approach on top of the existing approached.

The related work on architectures for WoT focus on discovery, selection, provisioning, integration, interoperability and management of the things and services in a WoT system. Guinard et al. [33] have proposed a Service Oriented Architecture (SOA) to support integration of services in an Internet of Things (IoT) system. The proposed architecture consists of two tiers: one tier can be deployed on the local premise and other tier can be deployed on a cloud-based infrastructure. The local tier facilitates integration with the devices with help of the local proxies. The data received from the devices is sent to the cloud-based infrastructure. The cloud infrastructure monitors all the incoming requests and delegates the requests to the services assigned to handle the requests after analysis of the nature and type of the requests. Akribopoulos et al. [34] have proposed an architecture to support integration of things in a WoT System with the help of small programmable objects. The data from the IoT devices is delegated to the programmable objects using a centralized controller. The controller provides proxies for integration with the client devices and authenticate all the incoming requests. The controller also uses web services to expose the interfaces for accessing the devices and the programmable objects. Mrissa et al. [35] have proposed an avatar-based infrastructure for the WoT. The infrastructure maintains package repositories for end user applications, functionality services and appliance drivers, and facilitate a WoT system's composition for varying user requirements.

Some of the related work focus on providing solutions for addressing the challenges specific to IoT architectures. Guinard et al. [36] have proposed a resource oriented architecture to support integration among the devices using smart gateways and RESTful interfaces. The proposed architecture facilitates direct interaction among the web clients and the IoT devices by abstracting the communication protocols of the IoT devices. Gronli et al. [37] have proposed a layered architecture for managing the things in a WoT system. The architecture is consisted of interface, management, service and application layers. Mainetti et al. [38] have proposed an architecture for visual composition of the services in a WoT system. The proposed architecture abstracts the wireless sensor network using a proxy server (web socket) and provides interfaces for the visual designer. Xu et al. [39] have presented a SOA for IoT based upon the industries best practices. The SOA for IoT is consisted of sensing, network, service and interface layers. These layers correspond to different elements of a WoT system. Yashiro et al. [40] have presented an IoT architecture for embedded appliances. The architecture puts a Constrained Application Protocol (CoAP) in the middle of end user applications and IoT censor hardware. The CoAP provides concrete communication mechanisms for the constrained networks. Zhou et al. [41] have proposed a cloud-based IoT architecture for dynamic service composition. The architecture is consisted of hardware, infrastructure, platform, service composition middleware and application layers.

Whilst the related work on WoT architecture focus on describing detailed architectures to manage different aspect of a WoT system, the research presented in this chapter is focused on how elements from standardized reference architectures (which are designed using a number of concrete IoT or WoT architectures) can be used for designing a specific type of a WoT system.

7.5 CONCLUSIONS AND LESSONS LEARNED

In this chapter, we suggested using a Reference Architecture (RA) centred approach for the detailed analysis, design, evaluation and evolution of the Internet of Things (IoT) and Web of Things (WoT) systems. After discussing the key architecture quality attributes for designing IoT and WoT systems (i.e., security, availability, scalability, reliability, multi-tenancy and interoperability), we argued that selection of the RA for concrete IoT system design should be based upon the RA's support for the desired quality attributed or its ability to support addition of architectural elements that can support the desired quality attributes. We have proposed to directly use the selected RA for design of the concrete IoT systems (i.e., using RA as a baseline for designing IoT systems) and indirectly use the RA for design of concrete WoT system (i.e., using IoT systems as a baseline for designing WoT systems). Concrete IoT architectures can be evaluated using existing software architecture evaluation methods and the common components from the concrete architectures can be included into the RA to have a domain-specific representation of the RA (e.g., for smart home domain). We have also shown applicability of the proposed approach for design and evaluation of ten smart home IoT subsystems architectures and a corresponding WoT system architecture. In this chapter, we have presented application of the proposed approach for IoT and WoT systems domain, however the approach is generic and can be applied on other domains.

We have made a number of observations while applying the approach for smart homes domain as follows. If different subsystems of an IoT system are being designed by independent teams, it is important to *streamline core quality requirements for all the IoT subsystems* so that conflicting and contradictory architectural design decisions can be avoided. Using a core set of quality requirements in the subsystems and using discussion forums that are accessible to all teams can be a good practice in this regard. Considering the generic nature of the RAs, the RAs always need to be tailored for adoption in a specific domain. Hence, *the selected RA should be flexible to accommodate components specific to functional requirements as well as additional quality requirements*. Contrary to using a RA directly for analysis and design of WoT system for IoT subsystems, *using concrete IoT architectures as a baseline for WoT architecture can provide a better opportunity for analysis* of the common application components and their inclusion in the WoT system. *Maintaining a log of all the design decisions, and architecture patterns and design patterns* used in the concrete IoT subsystems' design can facilitate not only design of the IoT subsystem but also evolution of the RA for future use in similar systems. Organization of the individual evaluation sessions for different IoT subsystem in a way that ensures *maximum participation of the teams* involved in designing other subsystems can lead to common understanding of the domain. *Maintaining variability points in a RA* when it is evolved by incorporating domain specific elements from the concrete IoT subsystems can guarantee separation of the generic RA elements and domain specific RA elements.

We foresee that the presented approach can be used for design and evaluation of the complex WoT systems, and can be beneficial for researchers and practitioners. In the future we plan to conduct more case studies on usage of the reference architectures for other IoT and WoT domains to analyse effectiveness of the proposed approach.

REFERENCES

[1] Guinard D, Trifa V, Mattern F, Wilde E. From the internet of things to the web of things: resource-oriented architecture and best practices. In: Architecting the internet of things. Springer; 2011. p. 97–129.

[2] Yahya F, Chang V, Walters RJ, Wills GB. Security challenges in cloud storages. In: 2014 IEEE 6th international conference on cloud computing technology and science (Cloud-Com). IEEE; 2014. p. 1051–6.

[3] Almorsy M, Grundy J, Ibrahim AS. Tossma: a tenant-oriented saas security management architecture. In: 2012 IEEE 5th international conference on cloud computing (cloud). IEEE; 2012. p. 981–8.

[4] Chauhan MA, Babar MA, Benatallah B. Architecting cloud-enabled systems: a systematic survey of challenges and solutions. Software: practice and experience.

[5] Angelov S, Grefen P, Greefhorst D. A framework for analysis and design of software reference architectures. Inf Softw Technol 2012;54(4):417–31.

[6] Kruchten PB. The 4 + 1 view model of architecture. IEEE Softw 1995;12(6):42–50.

[7] Huang W, Ganjali A, Kim BH, Oh S, Lie D. The state of public infrastructure-as-a-service cloud security. ACM Comput Surv (CSUR) 2015;47(4):68.

[8] AlZain MA, Soh B, Pardede E. A byzantine fault tolerance model for a multi-cloud computing. In: 2013 IEEE 16th international conference on computational science and engineering (CSE). IEEE; 2013. p. 130–7.

[9] Bernabe JB, Perez JMM, Calero JMA, Clemente FJG, Perez GM, Skarmeta AFG. Semantic-aware multi-tenancy authorization system for cloud architectures. Future Gener Comput Syst 2014;32:154–67.

[10] Moens H, Truyen E, Walraven S, Joosen W, Dhoedt B, De Turck F. Cost-effective feature placement of customizable multi-tenant applications in the cloud. J Netw Syst Manag 2014;22(4):517–58.

[11] Fehling C, Leymann F, Mietzner R. A framework for optimized distribution of tenants in cloud applications. In: 2010 IEEE 3rd international conference on cloud computing (CLOUD). IEEE; 2010. p. 252–9.

[12] Sousa FR, Machado JC. Towards elastic multi-tenant database replication with quality of service. In: Proceedings of the 2012 IEEE/ACM fifth international conference on utility and cloud computing. IEEE Computer Society; 2012. p. 168–75.

[13] Maximilien EM, Ranabahu A, Engehausen R, Anderson L. IBM altocumulus: a cross-cloud middleware and platform. In: Proceedings of the 24th ACM SIGPLAN conference companion on object oriented programming systems languages and applications. ACM; 2009. p. 805–6.

[14] Ribeiro LS, Viana-Ferreira C, Oliveira JL, Costa C. Xds-i outsourcing proxy: ensuring confidentiality while preserving interoperability. IEEE J Biomed Health Inform 2014;18(4):1404–12.

[15] Rezaei R, Chiew TK, Lee SP, Aliee ZS. A semantic interoperability framework for software as a service systems in cloud computing environments. Expert Syst Appl 2014;41(13):5751–70.

[16] Charalabidis Y, Koussouris S, Ramfos A. A cloud infrastructure for collaborative digital public services. In: 2011 IEEE third international conference on cloud computing technology and science (CloudCom). IEEE; 2011. p. 340–7.

[17] Flores H, Srirama SN. Mobile cloud middleware. J Syst Softw 2014;92:82–94.

[18] Hofmeister C, Kruchten P, Nord RL, Obbink H, Ran A, America P. A general model of software architecture design derived from five industrial approaches. J Syst Softw 2007;80(1):106–26.

[19] Shalloway A, Trott JR. Design patterns explained: a new perspective on object-oriented design. Pearson Education; 2004.

[20] Buschmann F, Henney K, Schmidt DC. Pattern-oriented software architecture, on patterns and pattern languages, vol. 5. John Wiley & Sons; 2007.

[21] Kazman R, Klein M, Barbacci M, Longstaff T, Lipson H, Carriere J. The architecture tradeoff analysis method. In: Fourth IEEE international conference on engineering of complex computer systems, proceedings. 1998. IEEE; 1998. p. 68–78.

[22] Kazman R, Bass L, Webb M, Abowd G. Saam: a method for analyzing the properties of software architectures. In: Proceedings of the 16th international conference on software engineering. IEEE Computer Society Press; 1994. p. 81–90.

[23] Matinlassi M, Niemelä E, Dobrica L. Quality-driven architecture design and quality analysis method, a revolutionary initiation approach to a product line architecture, VTT Technical Research Centre of Finland, Espoo.

[24] Bauer M, Boussard M, Bui N, De Loof J, Magerkurth C, Meissner S, Nettsträter A, Stefa J, Thoma M, Walewski JW. Iot reference architecture. In: Enabling things to talk. Springer; 2013. p. 163–211.

[25] Chauhan MA, Babar MA, Sheng QZ. A reference architecture for a cloud-based tools as a service workspace. In: 2015 IEEE international conference on services computing (SCC). IEEE; 2015. p. 475–82.

[26] Gorton I. Essential software architecture. Springer Science & Business Media; 2006.

[27] Angelov S, Trienekens J, Kusters R. Software reference architectures-exploring their usage and design in practice. In: European conference on software architecture. Springer; 2013. p. 17–24.

[28] Bass L, Klein M, Bachmann F. Quality attribute design primitives and the attribute driven design method. In: International workshop on software product-family engineering. Springer; 2001. p. 169–86.

[29] Razavian M, Lago P. A frame of reference for soa migration. In: European conference on a service-based internet. Springer; 2010. p. 150–62.

[30] Razavian M, Lago P. Towards a conceptual framework for legacy to soa migration. In: Service-oriented computing. ICSOC/ServiceWave 2009 workshops. Springer; 2010. p. 445–55.

[31] Lewis G, Morris E, O'Brien L, Smith D, Wrage L. Smart: the service-oriented migration and reuse technique (no. cmu/sei-2005-tn-029), Pittsburgh: Software Engineering Institute.

[32] Chauhan MA, Babar MA. Towards process support for migrating applications to cloud computing. In: 2012 international conference on cloud and service computing (CSC). IEEE; 2012. p. 80–7.

[33] Guinard D, Trifa V, Karnouskos S, Spiess P, Savio D. Interacting with the soa-based internet of things: discovery, query, selection, and on-demand provisioning of web services. IEEE Trans Serv Comput 2010;3(3):223–35.

[34] Akribopoulos O, Chatzigiannakis I, Koninis C, Theodoridis E. A web services-oriented architecture for integrating small programmable objects in the web of things. In: Developments in E-systems engineering (DESE), 2010. IEEE; 2010. p. 70–5.

[35] Mrissa M, Médini L, Jamont J-P, Le Sommer N, Laplace J. An avatar architecture for the web of things. IEEE Internet Comput 2015;19(2):30–8.

[36] Guinard D, Trifa V, Wilde E. A resource oriented architecture for the web of things. In: Internet of things (IOT), 2010. IEEE; 2010. p. 1–8.

[37] Grønli T-M, Ghinea G, Younas M. A lightweight architecture for the web-of-things. In: International conference on mobile web and information systems. Springer; 2013. p. 248–59.

[38] Mainetti L, Mighali V, Patrono L, Rametta P, Oliva SL. A novel architecture enabling the visual implementation of web of things applications. In: 2013 21st international conference on software, telecommunications and computer networks (SoftCOM). IEEE; 2013. p. 1–7.

[39] Da Xu L, He W, Li S. Internet of things in industries: a survey. IEEE Trans Ind Inform 2014;10(4):2233–43.

[40] Yashiro T, Kobayashi S, Koshizuka N, Sakamura K. An internet of things (iot) architecture for embedded appliances. In: Humanitarian technology conference (R10-HTC), 2013 IEEE region 10. IEEE; 2013. p. 314–9.

[41] Zhou J, Leppänen T, Harjula E, Ylianttila M, Ojala T, Yu C, Jin H. Cloudthings: a common architecture for integrating the internet of things with cloud computing. In: 2013 IEEE 17th international conference on computer supported cooperative work in design (CSCWD). IEEE; 2013. p. 651–7.

ACKNOWLEDGEMENTS

We acknowledge contribution of Software Architecture 2015 course students at IT University of Copenhagen for their participation in design and evaluation of IoT subsystems architectures for smart homes. In particular we acknowledge Henrik Buch-Larsen, Michael Poulin Mortensen and Rasmus Løbner Christensen for their contribution to Fig. 7.3; and Abdulrashid Mas'ab Mohammed, Diana Elena Giosanu, Gediminas Kucas and Vitor Dominguez Pintos for their contribution to Fig. 7.4. We also acknowledge Tan Phong Phan, a teaching staff member for the course, for his participation in evaluations of the IoT subsystems architectures and design of the WoT system architecture.

EFFICIENT AND SECURE PULL REQUESTS FOR EMERGENCY CASES USING A MOBILE ACCESS FRAMEWORK

8

Corinna Schmitt, Claudio Anliker, Burkhard Stiller

Communication Systems Group, Department of Informatics, University of Zurich, Zurich, Switzerland

CHAPTER POINTS

- To secure collected data and the privacy request of data owners, a fine-grained privilege management solution was developed to restrict pull requests to authorized persons or organizations only.
- Secure Pull Requests (SPR) are send toward the respective WSN-based constrained device using the TinyIPFIX data format, which is also used to answer the request by sending a full data set back to the framework.
- Assuming the requester is only allowed to see parts of the data, a filtering process, shifted to the server side of the framework, selects relevant data and saves the limited resources of WSN devices to ensure a longer lifetime of the network deployed.

8.1 INTRODUCTION

Today more and more devices and systems are connected building the Internet-of-Things (IoT). The range of devices is as manifold as application areas and includes constrained devices, especially sensor nodes forming Wireless Sensor Networks (WSN) [23,2]. Those devices are constrained in memory, computational capacity and power, making it typically difficult to implement all desired functionality (*e.g.*, periodical push-based data collection and transmission, security operations, and aggregation) at the same time. Thus, any solutions, supporting aforementioned functionalities, need a lightweight design to ensure a long system lifetime and less manual input. In addition, users desire (1) user-friendly interfaces, (2) flexible and intuitive

Managing the Web of Things. DOI: 10.1016/B978-0-12-809764-9.00010-X solutions, (3) security support concerning access and data storage, and (4) mobility support. Especially, the last two requirements become essential upon the inspection of data collected within WSNs. This data can include sensitive information (*e.g.*, GPS, medical information, address, or identifiers) allowing profiling of the data source, which is stands in contrast to user's privacy request and, thus, needs to be protected and their access to be controlled.

The developed Secure Pull Requests (SPR) solution in this chapter was motivated by an Ambient Assisted Living (AAL) scenario: A house is equipped with intelligent carpets including pressure sensors, which are connected to an emergency response system and which perform periodical measurements in predefined reporting intervals (*e.g.*, 5 minutes). This setting allows for a behavior monitoring of inhabitants and sending out emergency calls, if required, especially in case a person falls and does not get up again within that predefined measurement interval. This monitoring ensures a secure feeling for inhabitants and especially allows elderly people to stay at home without having to live in a retirement home. The key drawback of this setting in current implementations is that unnecessary emergency calls can be generated: Assuming an external person (*e.g.*, a family member or technician) visits the inhabitant, the system recognizes this due to periodical measurements showing unexpected changes of carpet pressure values, which do not match the inhabitant's estimated values for weight or movement patterns. Obviously, in this case an emergency call is not required. In order to avoid exactly such calls to happen, the pull functionality in the system provides an observer (*e.g.*, doctor, fire department, police, or health care center) the chance to request measurements explicitly and independently of any predefined intervals in order to apply a short human-centric analysis of the data. Thus, it can be decided, if an ambulance has to called directly (no visitor in place) or if the inhabitant needs to be called back only to check his status. Thus, SPR was applied to a mobile access framework for evaluation purposes.

The pull functionality allows the user to request immediate and selected sensor data (*e.g.*, "pressure of node 2") independent of any predefined reporting intervals of a push-based solution. This solution is designed in a general manner (specification of destination node and specific sensor value) in order to make it applicable to different applications and uses a set of existing SecureWSN [36] framework components where to integrate pull support: The data format TinyIPFIX [35], the CoMaDa (Configuration, Management, and Data handling) framework [34], and the Web-MaDa (Web-based Mobile access and Data handling) framework [24]. Within the frameworks of CoMaDa and WebMaDa authentication and fine-grained privilege management solutions are integrated.

The remainder of this chapter – based on [6] – is structured as followed: Section 8.2 presents selected work for AAL monitoring solutions, a solution to query sensor networks, and introduces reference frameworks and the SecureWSN framework, where the proposed SPR solution is integrated. The SPR implementation is presented in Section 8.3 including an updated architecture of SecureWSN. Finally, the SPR solution is analyzed in Section 8.4 with the focus on a functional proof and performance values in terms of latencies induced by SPRs. Section 8.5 summarizes and concludes the work.

8.2 RELATED WORK

This section contains three parts: First, monitoring solutions are described in the area of AAL that inspired the extension of the existing framework SecureWSN [36] with pull functionality. Therefore, an efficient solution for handling queries in general is required. Second, two frameworks – Sentilo and FIWARE – are introduced. They have been chosen as reference projects. Finally, all relevant components of the existing SecureWSN infrastructure are introduced leading to the discussion of key requirements for the pull support.

8.2.1 MONITORING SOLUTIONS

The field of WSNs has a wide range. Most deployed networks have in common that sensor devices measure environmental data in predefined intervals and directly send them out to the final destination (usually the sink) [23,2]. The data is then analyzed corresponding to the research questions, stored, and visualized. To the best of the authors' knowledge, no solution exists that allows selective pull requests independent from predefined intervals and without interval updates in the installed code on the devices. This section focuses on related work that inspired our scenario selection and our solution design.

When looking into the area of AAL, all applications and solutions have common goals: (1) Allowing elderly people to stay at home as long as possible, (2) to make them feel save in their surroundings, and (3) to inform departments or people in emergency cases [7]. To achieve those goals, WSNs are a good solution, because they monitor the environment or personal medical data with less impact on the person. Several other solutions for environmental monitoring in houses work with noise sensors and video cameras [22]. A quite new approach is the intelligent carpet system [22,5,14,32,21], which is a textile-based sensor system. The carpet is equipped with piezoelectric and weight sensors, which are connected to a central station for analysis purposes. Based on the collected data and the known weight of the inhabitants, the movement of the inhabitants as well as their position in the room can be predicted. Monitoring data is usually done by Wireless Body Area Networks (WBAN) [28,4, 31,38], which measure values like heartbeat, blood pressure, and temperature periodically and transmit them to a gateway forwarding the data to a doctoral office or health care center. Based on the analysis' result an emergency call can be placed.

Based on the provided brief description of the above solutions, it can be recognized that all those solutions work on a push basis, meaning the measurements are performed in predefined intervals and, therefore, in an automatic manner. The arising question is if the measurements are trustworthy at any time. Do we really need to call an ambulance, if the blood pressure rises for some minutes or if the heart rate sinks, because a person is sleeping? In order to answer this question interval-independent measurements are required.

8.2.2 REFERENCE PROJECTS

The two selected reference projects Sentilo [8] and FIWARE [19] have an academic nature and do not focus on concrete application scenarios. Instead, they are extensible multi-purpose frameworks to build smart applications of various kinds. This is important for the smart city context (including the assumed emergency cases in this chapter), which is defined by manifold interactions between arbitrary smart applications and sensor networks of all kinds, no matter if they are wired or wireless. Smart city is a buzzword and its definition depends on the context of usage as pointed out by Albino et al. [3]. All of these definitions can be interpreted to include WSN technology as well. Openness and interoperability are important to deploy WSNs in the smart city context.

Similar to [3] the developers of the framework Sentilo realized the importance of openness as well and promote Sentilo as "an open source sensor and actuator platform designed to fit in the Smart City architecture of any city who looks for openness and easy interoperability" [8]. It is a generic framework to integrate the management of applications based on WSNs into smart cities. Sentilo is actively used in Barcelona [10]. The company Effilogics uses Sentilo in an energy management system, a so-called *smarty energy solution* to measure and analyze data, *e.g.*, temperature values, and to regulate remote devices [11]. Sentilo provides features, amongst others, a front-end for message processing, an administration console, a high performance memory database, and a non-SQL database to achieve higher flexibility and scalability [9].

Sentilo's architecture is extensible, such that core code does not need to be modified to support new, customized applications. In the context of Sentilo, smart city applications consist of three layers or tiers. The top tier is the application itself, utilizing sensor data it receives from Sentilo, which is the middle tier. The bottom tier contains applications that encapsulate sensor networks. These applications must implement Sentilo's interface to provide sensor measurements and WSN metadata to Sentilo. Its position already indicates that Sentilo is not a concrete application, but can be considered as a broker, connecting sensor networks with smart applications. The interfaces between the tiers use Representational State Transfer (REST) [12] over the Hyper Text Transfer Protocol (HTTP) [13].

FIWARE is "an open initiative aiming to create a sustainable ecosystem to grasp the opportunities that will emerge with the new wave of digitalization caused by the integration of recent Internet technologies" [19]. The FIWARE platform provides a set of public and royalty-free APIs to simplify smart application development. The FIWARE Lab provides a sandbox environment to test applications using data published by organizations and cities. FIWARE is getting increasingly important in the smart city context [17] and announced a connector for the SIGFOX IoT network [18].

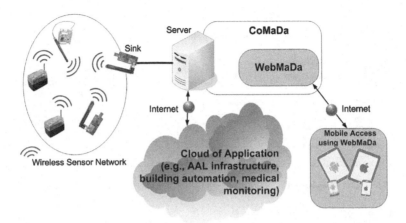

FIGURE 8.1

SecureWSN architecture

FIWARE's architecture is too complex to be discussed in detail here. The most interesting part for this work is the IoT architecture, i.e., how FIWARE integrates smart applications with sensor networks, and WSNs in particular. FIWARE's IoT architecture provides two kinds of interfaces [20]. The northbound interface defines communication between a smart application of choice and the Context Broker. The Context Broker is the main-front end for developers and provides the IoT data as attributes of entities, which represent IoT devices. The IoT Agent Manager allows connecting and monitoring a set of IoT Agents. The deployed IoT Agents define the protocols (*e.g.*, CoAP [37] and MQTT [30]) used on the southbound interface to connect to sensor networks. The mentioned protocols are dedicated to define communication with low-resource sensor networks. This makes it possible to connect WSNs directly to FIWARE, without the need for any intermediary applications.

8.2.3 COMPONENTS OF SECUREWSN

SecureWSN is a two-parted framework existing of a WSN part and a server part as illustrated in Fig. 8.1. In the following paragraphs the TinyIPFIX for data transmission within the WSN and the GUIs CoMaDa and WebMaDa are briefly described. It is assumed that the communication within the WSN and towards the sink is done in a secure way using standard approaches of public key infrastructure (PKI) or special developed algorithms in order to achieve a two-way authentication of the communication partners by performing handshakes (*e.g.*, TinyDTLS [25] or TinyTO [29]) resulting in new keying material and secured communication channels. This chapter will not address this security issue in detail here.

Within the WSN (shown in the left part) constrained devices are deployed with a maximum memory capacity of 48 kByte RAM [1] performing data collection in a

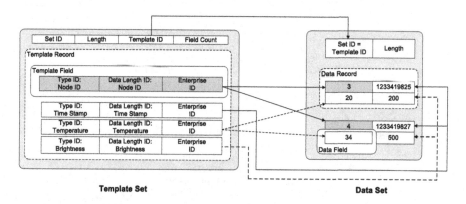

FIGURE 8.2

TinyIPFIX template and data record relationship

push manner using TinyIPFIX. **TinyIPFIX** [35] was inspired by the Internet Proto-col Flow Information Export (IPFIX) solution standardized under RFC 7011 [16]. In WSNs it is common that each message includes meta information of the sensor (*e.g.*, temperature or brightness) and the measured value (*e.g.*, an integer or floating point number). Due to the fact that the meta information of a sensor never changes, it pro-duces redundancy. In additional, the maximum transmission unit (MTU) over IEEE 802.15.4 is very limited (*e.g.*, 127 Byte for RF transceiver CC2420 [15]) [27,26], and, therefore, space for relevant data should be saved. Thus, the meta information should be deleted to save space in the message and, therefore, it makes sense to split the traditional sensor messages into two parts, which brought IPFIX to our mind.

IPFIX works with a template-based design in a push manner. A message is split into its components – meta information and measured value – resulting in a template and data record. When a device boots up, it first announces its template record to the network including a reference number (Template ID) and different template fields. The latter includes all required information (Type ID, Data Length ID, and Enterprise ID) building the meta information for each sensor in a unique manner. This template record is stored by all relevant intermediate nodes, which need to touch the data in any way, like an aggregator, and by the server. Next, the device is able to collect the sensor data and create the data record referring to the corresponding Template ID and send it out automatically according to the push characteristic of IPFIX. The second step can now be repeated periodically, which results in small messages without redundant information. All intermediate nodes and the server are able to translate the received data record when the template record is known. Fig. 8.2 illustrates the relationship between template and data record realized in TinyIPFIX [35]. The template record is re-sent periodically in order to insure this translation process, because routes might change or an unreliable transmission protocol (like UDP) is used [35,33].

In order to apply IPFIX to WSNs, TinyIPFIX was developed [35]. Therefore, templates and Enterprise IDs were specified matching sensor requirements. One

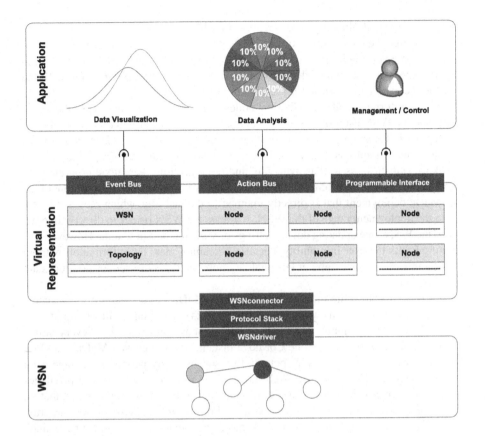

FIGURE 8.3

Architecture of CoMaDa

drawback of IPFIX is the additional overhead of 20 Byte caused by the headers of IPFIX messages, which is overcome by replacing those headers with a new header of 3 Byte length, leaving enough space for essential data in the message. Details about the message structure can be found in [33]. In order to optimize the usage of the MTU, TinyIPFIX also supports aggregation [35]. Summarizing, TinyIPFIX is an efficient and flexible protocol as proven by [33,35] and shows a push characteristic, which is the classic manner for WSNs with periodic measurements in predefined intervals. However, TinyIPFIX does not support pull functionality yet, which becomes interesting when requesting data immediately.

The GUIs CoMaDa and WebMaDa build the server part of SecureWSN. **CoMaDa** [34] was developed in order to answer the users' desire to have a user-friendly and highly flexible GUI for WSNs, independent from a device's vendor and data types. This GUI should allow configuration, management, and data handling (*e.g.*, storage and visualization) for any kind of WSN data. Thus, a unified framework was implemented allowing further extensions like WebMaDa (cf. Section 8.3.2). Fig. 8.3 illustrates the architecture of CoMaDa. The deployed WSN is located on the bottom layer. Via three components (WSN driver, Protocol Stack, and WSN connector) the received data of the WSN enters the gateway running CoMaDa. Based on the received data, a virtual representation of the data is established in real-time, including information about individual nodes (*e.g.*, ID, sensor equipment), the topology, and the WSN itself (*e.g.*, size or events). Linked to this virtual representation are different busses and interfaces supporting applications, like data visualization (*e.g.*, measurement graphs and network topology), and data analysis (*e.g.*, routing and package statistics), as well as managing and/or controlling (*e.g.*, node programming and tunnel setup) [34]. CoMaDa requires that the WSN owner has to sit in front of the CoMaDa deployment that is directly mapped to the gateway, which means the user is in the deployment range of the WSN. It allows the WSN owner to directly interact with the WSN, like updating device settings or viewing measured data. However, this setting limits the user in mobility, because he cannot view the information without sitting in front of the computer terminal anymore. Notions of users or privileges are not defined.

In order to close the mobility gap, the **WebMaDa** (Web-based Mobile Access and Data Handling) framework was developed [24]. WebMaDa allows monitoring many WSNs using mobile devices (*e.g.*, smartphones, tablets) where every single WSN is managed by exactly one CoMaDa instance. However, WebMaDa is a globally accessible web application, potentially used by many people to manage a lot of registered WSNs. Therefore, WebMaDa needs to introduce users and privileges to control which WSNs and measurements are accessible to whom. For that matter, WebMaDa provides a basic privilege system. For example, a WSN owner can grant access to all his WSNs to another person, but he cannot assign more fine-grained privileges to restrict access to a subset of the measurements (*e.g.*, only temperature values).

8.2.4 REQUIREMENTS FOR SPR SUPPORT

In view of the related work, Sentilo and FIWARE are both frameworks offering a middleware solution that handles incoming requests both from users and networks. This functionality is already offered by the CoMaDa component of SecureWSN. Sentilo uses HTTP for data transfer between interfaces. SecureWSN uses WebMaDa to transfer data across the Internet. In order to perform a secure data transmission between user, WebMaDa, and CoMaDa HTTPS is used instead of HTTP as done by Sentilo. To host data, a database solution is required as done by Sentilo and FIWARE. This storage issue is already addressed by CoMaDa storing data on the local CoMaDa instance. FIWARE includes an IoT Agent Manager offering the functions of connecting and monitoring of IoT devices. In SecureWSN the connecting part is relayed with CoMaDa and the monitoring is supported by CoMaDa and WebMaDa to ensure monitoring support during absence to the monitoring area when traveling. As of today, Sentilo, FIWARE, and SecureWSN do not support pull functionality. Thus, amongst others, to reduce false alarms in emergency cases as outlined above the Se-cureWSN special enhancements are fulfilled by extending the existing components of CoMaDa, WebMaDa, and TinyIPFIX.

Since the current setup of the SecureWSN framework does not allow measurements beyond predefined reporting intervals, immediate measurements in a pull manner require the extension of existing components with the following functionality:

1. Integration of a fine-grained privilege management
2. Extension of the Template Record of TinyIPFIX with a type field
3. Verification of pull requestor credentials and rights
4. Visualization of pull data in a user-friendly manner in CoMaDa and WebMaDa
5. Translation of pull requests into the TinyIPFIX format for processing in the WSN
6. Filtering of received answers in CoMaDa before publishing data in WebMaDa

Functionality 1 results from the general request of data owners to obtain control over data collected. Especially, the determination of who is allowed to see what information is essential, *e.g.*, a family member can access data every time, in comparison to a doctor or an ambulance, which only can do so in emergency cases. Functionality 2 is needed to distinguish between predefined interval records (push packet) and pull answers to coordinate the packet handling in CoMaDa. Functionality 3 ensures that external persons must prove their given credentials and rights to access data at all times. This becomes essential in cases when a data owner revokes access rights, excludes persons, or updates their rights (*e.g.*, only see pressure values, no pull right anymore). It is relevant for the existing components CoMaDa and WebMaDa to provide for a user-friendly visualization of data (functionality 4). Similarly, functionalities 5 and 6 are justified, since the reuse of existing components and software avoids the integration of resource-hungry algorithms that consume even more resources of constrained devices and, thus, reduce the lifetime of the WSN.

8.3 DESIGN OF THE SPR SOLUTION

Two major features in the course of this work have extended CoMaDa and WebMaDa: The pull mechanism was developed and integrated. Second, WebMaDa was extended by the privilege management system to provide WSN owners with a tool to control access to their WSNs and collected data.

8.3.1 PRIVILEGE MANAGEMENT

The **fine-grained privilege management solution** (privilege management in short) is a component integrated in the WebMaDa web application. It enables WSN owners to share access to their WSNs with other users. An owner can give family members the right to view all data, but can restrict the access for doctors or ambulance to relevant data in emergency cases only. This includes access to previous measurements and to the pull mechanism. To achieve that, an owner can assign two kinds of privileges:

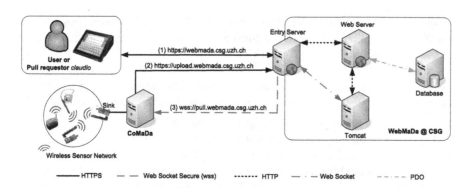

FIGURE 8.4

Communication interfaces for pull support of WebMaDa

- **Push privileges** allow users to see data, which has been pushed by the WSNs push mechanism in predefined intervals.
- **Pull privileges** enable users to pull data by themselves. This means, they can query the WSN to get up-to-date measurements independently of the nodes' configurations. Besides pulling data, pull privileges also give a user view rights on the data he is allowed to pull.

The privileges are stored in the WebMaDa database and checked at two occasions. First, whenever the WebMaDa user interface shows measurements to the user, filtering based on the user's privileges is applied to prevent unauthorized data disclosure. Second, the pull query is compared with the corresponding user's privileges to prevent unauthorized pull attempts whenever the pull mechanism is used. This is important, since pull queries are constructed on the client side and, thus, might be manipulated. The implementation of the privilege management is intuitive to use. First, the user interface allows selecting one of the owner's WSNs. In a next step, a username must be chosen in a drop down menu. Push and pull privileges can then be granted using checkboxes for the chosen user in the selected WSN.

8.3.2 SPR TRIGGERED BY WEBMADA

WebMaDa provides the pull mechanism to users over the Web. While the privilege management is part of WebMaDa, it enables owners to assign privileges and, thus, to share access to their WSNs with others. The WebMaDa database schema was improved to maintain WebMaDa user accounts, their privileges, as well as the data and metadata of registered WSNs. WebMaDa provides the following three communication interfaces as shown in Fig. 8.4.

The **user interface** (cf. Fig. 8.4 (1) https://webmada.csg.uzh.ch)) is used to maintain and access WSNs after successful authentication. Maintaining WSNs includes registration, reset, and deletion of WSNs. WSN registration means to create a representation of the corresponding WSN in the database schema of the WebMaDa web application. Successful WSN registration produces credentials bound to this WSN and is the prerequisite for communication between CoMaDa and WebMaDa, since the credentials must be used to authenticate at the pull and upload interfaces. A WSN reset deletes data and metadata of a WSN. However, it does neither invalidate the credentials bound to this WSN nor does it revoke any privileges assigned to other users. Thus, the WSN can be reused. In contrast, deleting a WSN leads to a complete and irreversible cleanup. This means, the credentials are invalidated, and cannot be used by CoMaDa anymore. Accessing WSNs embraces pulling data from this WSN and to view previously uploaded data. This access is regulated by the privilege management introduced in Section 8.3.1.

The **upload interface** (cf. Fig. 8.4 (2) https://upload.webmada.csg.uzh.ch) can be accessed using HTTP POST and uses a set of well-defined JSON messages. After a successful authentication, the communication is as follows: CoMaDa provides data and requests an upload. WebMaDa checks the requestor's authentication status (i.e., if an authenticated session has been established). If this is the case, it executes the upload procedure immediately. Finally, it confirms the operation or sends an error code. Different message types can be used to upload different types of data and meta data.

The **SPR interface** (cf. Fig. 8.4 (3) wss://pull.webmada.csg.uzh.ch) is used by WebMaDa to send pull queries to CoMaDa. Therefore, the server initiates communication to the client. The WebSocket protocol is suitable for this task and used to implement the SPR interface. After successful authentication, the communication on the SPR interface is completely one-directional: CoMaDa listens for pull queries transmitted by WebMaDa. On a pull query reception, CoMaDa forwards requests to WSN nodes. The above-mentioned upload interface is used to upload resulting measurements. The SPR interface was implemented as a Java servlet on Apache Tomcat. To submit pull queries, WebMaDa communicates with the servlet internally over HTTP POST. The Web server is configured to block HTTP POST access to the servlet over the Internet to prevent pull query submissions over HTTP POST from the outside, which prevents circumvention of WebMaDa's the privilege management.

8.3.3 SPR AND ANSWER TRANSLATED BY COMADA

Using CoMaDa alone restricts the mobility of the user, since it does neither allow mobile access nor secure sharing of WSN access at all. For this matter, CoMaDa can be used in conjunction with WebMaDa. To achieve that, the CoMaDa user must have a WebMaDa user account and register a WSN in WebMaDa as explained in Section 8.3.2. WebMaDa provides credentials to use the pull and upload interface in return. CoMaDa can be configured with these credentials and communicate with WebMaDa over the mentioned interfaces. Meta data and data of the WSN can be uploaded and pull queries can be received. One must state at this point, that CoMaDa blindly trusts WebMaDa, since the interfaces, and in particular WebMaDa's identity, are cryptographically protected by TLS (HTTPS and WSS).

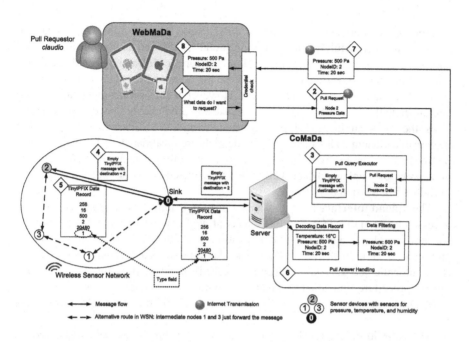

FIGURE 8.5

Handling of SPRs

CoMaDa contains a **Pull Query Executor** that transforms received pull query strings into requests for the respective nodes. Pull queries are stored in a queue and handled one-by-one by a worker thread. This restricts the pull traffic in the WSN and prevents the need for increased coordination in case of almost concurrent pull queries. This is beneficial, because TinyIPFIX uses UDP and does not handle message collisions at all.

8.3.4 SPR HANDLING USING TINYIPFIX

In order to establish an efficient solution for the SPR handling the TinyIPFIX message format (cf. Section 8.2.3) is re-used. Thus, no additional resources, especially memory, are required from constrained nodes and no computational overhead occurs, because all nodes can answer the SPR in the traditional manner as needed for a predefined interval reporting. The respective message flow is illustrated in Fig. 8.5 and consists of the following steps under the assumption that node 2 is the destination node:

1. The pull requestor defines which information of a special node he wants to pull via WebMaDa (*e.g.*, pressure from node 2).
2. Assuming that the pull requestor, a family member or a doctor, owns the correct credential, checked within WebMaDa, the request is forwarded to CoMaDa.

3. Within CoMaDa the information is translated into a TinyIPFIX message consisting of an empty payload addressed to the destination node.
4. Via the WSN's sink the TinyIPFIX message is routed through the WSN to the destination node.
5. The destination node immediately requests measurements of all available sensors and constructs a common TinyIPFIX message including all information as in the case of a predefined interval report, being send back to the sink.
6. CoMaDa now decodes the data record with the help of the referred to template record [35] and filters all values received based on the concrete SPR.
7. The filtered information is forwarded to WebMaDa and,
8. After a credential check, the result is displayed to the pull requestor.

Usually, within Step 5 the data answering the SPR is expected to be smaller than the usual report size of a predefined interval report. Thus, the node would need to create new templates with updated information each time a request is done. This computational overhead due to constructing the template, announcing it to the network, and to create the corresponding data record can be saved. Additionally, further memory required due to the saving of the new template record meanwhile can be saved, too, including the savings of energy to perform these aforementioned steps. To be as efficient as possible constrained nodes are relieved from the additional burden of operations and resource consumptions of the filtering process, which is shifted in full to CoMaDa. This leads to a very straightforward design that the requested node answers with its common TinyIPFIX message including all possible data. Consequently, in Step 6 CoMaDa decodes the data record with the help of the referred to template record [35] and filters values received based on the concrete SPR. Finally, Step 7 forwards the filtered information to WebMaDa and after a credential check the result is displayed to the pull requestor. This credential check is required, since rights granted may have been updated or revoked in the meantime.

As a consequence of this data handling process, the existing TinyIPFIX message style can be re-used by introducing one new pull message format (empty payload). Thus, no further modification on the node is required and limited memory resources can be saved. The use of TinyIPFIX allows even for future extensions, in particular, it allows the sink to separately send metadata and data by itself, providing a possibility to define new pull message formats on-the-fly.

8.4 EVALUATION

The SRP solution was implemented as a prototype deployed in a home scenario, where WSN owners granted (a) full access to family members including pull rights and (b) restricted access to doctors or ambulances.

The changes to the software running TinyIPFIX on the deployed sensor nodes have been reduced to an absolute minimum, due to the memory being constrained. Nodes only listen for pull requests, indicated by an empty payload in the TinyIPFIX

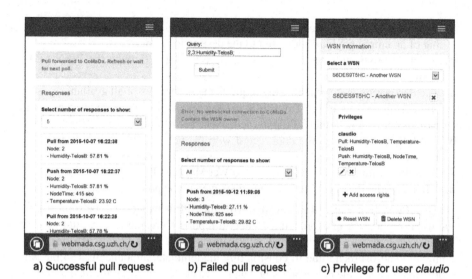

a) Successful pull request   b) Failed pull request   c) Privilege for user *claudio*

FIGURE 8.6

WebMaDa usage via Smartphone

message, to perform the same algorithm for sensor measurement request used by the push mechanism in TinyIPFIX to measure and transmit data periodically. All other extensions to process data or to manage privileges relate to CoMaDa and WebMaDa. Since these two components do not run on restricted devices, but on a laptop and a Web server, investigating power consumption and memory management is not of that high relevance in this environment. However, latency is different, since it is affected by the restricted nodes as well.

CoMaDa allows users to setup and manage a physical WSN and to collect its data. The corresponding WSN can be registered in WebMaDa for a location-independent access over the Web. WebMaDa creates credentials as part of this registration procedure. These credentials can be used to configure CoMaDa accordingly, such that CoMaDa can authenticate itself to WebMaDa. In turn, CoMaDa is able to upload measurements and metadata over the upload interface and to receive pull queries from WebMaDa over the SPR interface. WebMaDa's privilege management gives full access control over uploaded data to the WSN owner. This improves privacy compared to the previous WebMaDa solution, in which the administrator of the system was able to assign arbitrary privileges, which provided him with access to all data. The access to the pull mechanism is also controlled by WebMaDa's privilege management.

Pulling was tested in a network consisting of 20 TelosB nodes. Fig. 8.6 shows three example screenshots of the WebMaDa user interface on a Nokia Lumia 925 running Windows Phone 8. Message panels are used to provide the user with success and error messages, as illustrated in Fig. 8.6a and Fig. 8.6b respectively. A successful pull is shown in Fig. 8.6a. The pulled values are visible in the top-most data entry.

WebMaDa can only pull data from a running CoMaDa instance. If CoMaDa is terminated, the corresponding WebSocket connection with WebMaDa terminates as well. In this case, the user is informed over the user interface as shown in Fig. 8.6b, where the error message suggests contacting the WSN owner. Fig. 8.6c shows the privilege management used by the WSN owner. It lists different pull and push privileges assigned to users, like *claudio* in this case. Buttons can be used to add, modify, and delete user privileges.

In the current setup, latency is defined by the 3 seconds update interval of the WebMaDa user interface. In case the user interface (UI) update is timed unluckily, i.e., immediately after a pull query submission, new results might not be available yet. This increases the latency to more than 3 seconds. But the consumers of this data are humans only, this latency is acceptable. If latency is considered to be more critical in the future, the solution can be improved such that the database triggers the update of the WebMaDa user interface whenever new measurements are available. This reduces latency significantly. The implemented solution does not assume encryption inside the WSN. However, tests have been made with TinyTO [29] to encrypt the communication from the nodes to the sink. It has been shown in [29] that TinyTO needs 9.28 ± 0.18 seconds to sign a message, i.e., to cryptographically ensure its integrity, and 9.41 ± 0.18 seconds to encrypt it, i.e., to ensure confidentiality. This increases the latency on the path from the node to the sink to almost 20 seconds on average. This implies a tradeoff between latency and WSN-internal security, as the feeling of a real-time pull mechanism suffers substantially with a delay of 20 seconds. Due to the hardware constraints of the TelosB node, memory is too scarce to deploy secure channels bi-directionally using current TinyTO implementation. Thus, SPRs are still sent in clear text from the sink to collector nodes. Hypothetical encryption and authentication on this path would increase the latency, since signature verification alone takes 18.41 seconds in average using TinyTO on TelosB [29], whereas decryption has never been tested due to those mentioned resource constraints.

The developed SPR solution reached two main efficiency goals: (1) No further overhead for constrained devices is introduced and (2) a reduction of false alarms in emergency cases was reached. The overhead minimization with respect to resource consumption was reached by reusing the existing message structure within the WSN. Thus, the TinyIPFIX message structure was re-used without modifications to answer SPRs. The destination node (cf. node 2 in Fig. 8.5) is triggered by the TinyIPFIX message with an empty payload received. In this case the node performs a general sensor request, it creates TinyIPFIX messages as done for predefined interval reports, and sends the data out to the sink and CoMaDa, respectively. The only difference within this TinyIPFIX message send back to the sink is that the "type field" is set to 1, indicating the SPR?s answer. Thus, this workflow does not require any further computational overhead or resource consumption, making it fully comparable to the creation of a predefined interval report.

The reduction of false alarms was reached, since a human interaction (e.g., service assistant like police, doctor, or nurse) is required before reacting on an emergency call (*e.g.*, sending out police or ambulance). Before sending data to the observer, for each measurement acceptable value ranges (intervals) were specified by the sensor owner, and reported to the observer (*e.g.*, doctor, fire department, police, or health care center) for comparison purpose of upcoming measurements. Examples for those acceptable intervals are 50–100 heartbeats per minute or a room temperature above 40 centigrade. When a WSN is deployed, measurements are send to the observer in predefined intervals (*e.g.*, 5 minutes or 1 hour), stored in a database, and compared to the given value range. If a deviation occurs, an alarm is send automatically to authorized observers instead of sending directly an emergency call out. The authorized observers can now request an immediate measurement by applying SPR. This can be repeated, if needed, several times to obtain more measurements allowing for a correct analysis of the situation, (a) resulting in an emergency call or (b) ignoring the current deviation, because values are back in acceptable interval.

8.5 SUMMARY AND CONCLUSION

This chapter introduced a SPR solution in an efficient manner for applications in WSNs, especially for emergency cases in AAL scenarios. The pull support is an extension of a deployed, flexible, and operational SecureWSN approach. The SPR extension required modifications to existing components of TinyIPFIX, CoMaDa, and WebMaDa to ensure efficiency and secure access. While the structure of SPR follows the existing TinyIPFIX message structure and, at the same time, allows a requestor to ask several nodes synchronously for individual sensor readings, CoMaDa handles these requests, directs them to individual nodes, and filters the answer received to provide selected information to the original requestor. WebMaDa supports by now a fine-grained privilege management in control of the WSN generation and publication mechanism as well as individual rights of end users. Privilege changes (*e.g.*, pull and viewing rights) are processed immediately, especially important if an access is updated or even denied. Finally, based on the prototypical implementation of SPRs, the encryption in the WSN has been tested with TinyTO, showing that securing communication channels between nodes and the sink is possible in theory, but substantially increases the latency in practice.

Concluding, the designed and prototyped SPR solution is efficient, because (1) it does not introduce any overhead to the code running on constrained devices answering SPRs and (2) reduces false emergency alarms due to human interaction requested before an emergency call is really performed. The SPR solution is sensor device-independent, due to the flexible structure of TinyIPFIX data formats. Thus, SPR can be applied to very different IoT applications and sensor settings, besides the Ambient Assisted Living scenario. The fine-grained privilege management and its handling of different roles can be adapted to other application requirements than in the AAL case, giving the data owner full and detailed control of his sensor data. This enables a wide range of access solutions with a high flexibility offering data owners a trustworthy environment. Thus, the dedicated AAL scenario sees key advantages in practical operations with this new WebMaDa's feature of efficient SPRs.

REFERENCES

[1] Advantic Sistemas y Servicios S.L.: TelosB CM5000-SMA datasheet. Barcelona, Spain, 2015, http://tinyurl.com/cm5000sma. Online accessed: 24.8.2016.

[2] Akyildiz IF, Su W, Sankarasubramaniam Y, Cayirci E. A survey on sensor networks. IEEE Commun Mag August 2002;40(8):102–14. http://dx.doi.org/10.1109/MCOM.2002. 1024422. New York, NY, USA.

[3] Albino V, Berardi U, Dangelico R. Smart cities: definitions, dimensions, performance, and initiatives. J Urban Technol 2015;22(1):3–21.

[4] Alemdar H, Ersoy C. Wireless sensor networks for healthcare: a survey. Elsevier J Comput Netw 2010;54(15):2688–710. http://dx.doi.org/10.1016/j.comnet.2010.05.003.

[5] Ando B, Baglio S, La Malfa S, Pistorio A, Trigona C. A smart wireless sensor network for AAL. In: IEEE international workshop on measurements and networking. October 2011. p. 122–5.

[6] Anliker C. Secure pull request development for TinyIPFIX in wireless sensor networks. Master thesis. Zurich, Switzerland: University of Zurich, Communication Systems Group, Department of Informatics; November 2015.

[7] Augusto CA, Huch M, Kameas A, Maitland J, McCullagh P, editors. Handbook of ambient assisted living, technology for healthcare. Rehabilitation and well-being. Amsterdam, Netherlands: IOS Press; January 2012.

[8] Barcelona City Council: Sentilo. http://www.sentilo.io. Online accessed: 24.8.2016.

[9] Barcelona City Council: Sentilo Website: API documentation. Sentilo Website. http://www.sentilo.io/xwiki/bin/view/APIDocs/WebHome. Online accessed: 24.8.2016.

[10] Barcelona City Council: Sentilo website: Barcelona sentilo deployment reaches the 300 million transactions milestone. Sentilo website, May 2015. http://www.sentilo.io/wordpress/?p=1215. Online accessed: 24.8.2016.

[11] Barcelona city council: effilogics' energy management systems now compliant with sentilo. Sentilo website. June 2015. http://www.sentilo.io/wordpress/?p=1258. Online accessed: 24.8.2016.

[12] Bayer T. REST web services. Orientation in objects GmbH, 2002. http://www.oio.de/public/xml/rest-webservices.htm. Online accessed: 24.8.2016.

[13] Berners-Lee T, Fielding R, Frystyk H. Hypertext transfer protocol – HTTP/1.0. IETF, Fermont, CA, USA, RFC 1945, May 1996. https://tools.ietf.org/html/rfc1945. Online accessed: 24.8.2016.

[14] Cantoral-Ceballos JA, Nurgiyatna N, Wright P, Vaughan J, Brown-Wilson C, Scully PJ, et al. Intelligent carpet system, based on photonic guided-path tomography, for gait and balance monitoring in home environments. IEEE Sens J January 2015;15(1):279–89. http://dx.doi.org/10.1109/JSEN.2014.2341455.

[15] Chipcon AS SmartRF: CC2420 preliminary datasheet (rev 1.2). December 2015. http://inst.eecs.berkeley.edu/~cs150/Documents/CC2420.pdf. Online accessed: 24.8.2016.

[16] Claise B, Trammell BH, Aitken P. Specification of the IP flow information export (IPFIX) protocol for the exchange of IP traffic flow information. IETF, RFC 7011, Fermont, CA, USA, September 2013. https://tools.ietf.org/html/rfc7011. Online accessed: 24.8.2016.

[17] FIWARE Consortium: FIWARE at the smart city 360 summit – 14, 15 October in Toronto (Canada). The FIWARE website, 2015, https://www.fiware.org/news/fiware-at-the-smart-city-360-summit-1415-october-in-toronto-canada/. Online accessed: 24.8.2016.

[18] FIWARE and SIGFOX. SIGFOX and FIWARE announce open-source connector for SIGFOX internet of things network. The FIWARE website. 2015, http://tinyurl.com/open-source-connector. Online accessed: 24.8.2016.

[19] FIWARE consortium: The FIREWARE homepage, https://www.fiware.org. Online accessed: 24.8.2016.

[20] FIWARE consortium: FIWARE website: connection to the Internet of things. https://www.fiware.org/devguides/connection-to-the-internet-of-things/. Online accessed: 24.8.2016.

[21] Glaser R, Lauterbach C, Savio D, Schnell M, Karadal S, Weber W, et al. Smart carpet: a textile-based large-area sensor network. In: 21st international conference on advanced information networking and applications. New York, NY, USA: IEEE; May 2007.

[22] HAW Hamburg – Department Informatik: Smart Home – Living Place Hamburg. June 2015. http://tinyurl.com/HAWsmartliving. Online accessed: 24.8.2016.

[23] Karl H, Willig A, editors. Protocols and architectures for wireless sensor networks. Hoboken, NJ, USA: John Wiley and Sons Inc.; 2007.

[24] Keller M. Design and implementation of a mobile app to access and manage wireless sensor networks. Master thesis. Zurich, Switzerland: University of Zurich, Department of Informatics, Communication Systems Group; November 2014.

[25] Kothmayr T, Schmitt C, Hu W, Brünig M, Carle G. DTLS based security and two-way authentication for the Internet of things. J Ad Hoc Netw 2013;11(8):2710–23. http://dx.doi.org/10.1016/j.adhoc.2013.05.003.

[26] Kushalnagar N, Montenegro G, Schumacher C. IPv6 over low-power wireless personal area networks (6LoWPANs): overview, assumptions, problem statement, and goals. IETF, Fermont, CA, USA, RFC 4919, August 2007. http://tools.ietf.org/html/rfc4919. Online accessed: 24.8.2016.

[27] Montenegro G, Kushalnagar N, Hui J, Culler D. IPv6 over low power wireless personal area networks (6LowPAN). IETF. Fermont, CA, USA, RFC 4944, September 2007. http://www.ietf.org/rfc/rfc4944.txt. Online accessed: 24.8.2016.

[28] Movassaghi S, Abolhasan M, Lipman J, Smith D, Jamalipour A. Wireless body area networks: a survey. IEEE Commun Surv Tutorials March 2014;16(3):1658–86. http://dx.doi.org/10.1109/SURV.2013.121313.00064. New York, NY, USA.

[29] Noack M. Optimization of two-way authentication protocol in internet of things. Master thesis. Zurich, Switzerland: University of Zurich, Department of Informatics, Communication Systems Group; August 2014.

[30] OASIS website: MQTT 3.1.1 becomes an OASIS standard. OASIS. https://www.oasis-open.org/news/announcements/mqtt-version-3-1-1-becomes-an-oasis-standard. Online accessed: 24.8.2016.

[31] Ragesh GK, Baskaran K. A survey on futuristic health care system: WBANs. Proc Eng 2012;30:889–96. http://dx.doi.org/10.1016/j.proeng.2012.01.942.

[32] Rodríguez RV, Lewis RP, Mason JSD, Evans NWD. Footstep recognition for a smart home environment. Int J Smart Home, Sci Eng Res Supp Soc April 2008;2(2):95–110.

[33] Schmitt C. Secure data transmission in wireless sensor networks. Ph.D. Thesis. Munich, Germany: Network Architectures and Services (NET), Technische Universität München, Fakultät für Informatik, Network Architectures and Services; ISBN 3-937201-36-X, July 2013.

[34] Schmitt C, Freitag A, Carle G. CoMaDa: an adaptive framework with graphical support for configuration, management, and data handling tasks for wireless sensor networks. In: 9th international conference on network and service management. Zurich, Switzerland: CNSM; October 2013. p. 211–8.

[35] Schmitt C, Kothmayr T, Ertl B, Hu W, Braun L, Carle G, et al. TinyIPFIX: an efficient application protocol for data exchange in cyber physical systems. J Comput Commun January 2016;74:1503–11. http://dx.doi.org/10.1016/j.comcom.2014.05.012. Elsevier.

[36] Schmitt C, Stiller B. Secure and efficient wireless sensor network (SecureWSN). University of Zurich, Department of Informatics, Communication Systems Group, Zurich, Switzerland; http://www.csg.uzh.ch/research/SecureWSN.html. Online accessed: 24.8.2016.

[37] Shelby Z, Hartke K, Bormann C, editors. The constrained application protocol (CoAP). Fermont, CA, USA: IETF; June 2014. RFC 7252, https://tools.ietf.org/html/rfc7252. Online accessed: 24.8.2016.

[38] Yuce MR. Implementation of wireless body area networks for healthcare systems. Sens Actuators A, Phys 2010;162(1):116–29. http://dx.doi.org/10.1016/j.sna.2010.06.004.

GLOSSARY

CoMaDa is a Configuration, Management, and Data handling framework. It allows the data owner to configure the sensor devices in his WSN, to manage the deployed network, and to handle the collected data (*e.g.*, storing, preprocessing, publishing).

Constrained device is a device with limited resources for memory, power, and computational capacity. It collects data with its sensors like temperature, pressure, humidity, or brightness.

Data owner is the person who owns a WSN a wants to control the data access to the collected data.

Internet-of-Things (IoT) is a network where any kind of devices independent of their resources are connected with each other using wired and wireless communication.

TinyIPFIX is a data format to transport collected data in an efficient manner using a template-based design.

WebMaDa is a Web-based Mobile access and Data handling framework.

Wireless Sensor Network (WSN) is a network built of constrained devices with different resources and sensors.

ACKNOWLEDGEMENTS

The presented efficient and secure pull request solution in this chapter was supported partially by FLAMINGO and SmartenIT, funded by the EU FP7 Program under Contract No. FP7-2012-ICT-318488 and No. FP7-2012-ICT317846, respectively.

DATA INTEGRATION AND ANALYTICS

AUTOMATIC INTEGRATION AND QUERYING OF SEMANTIC RICH HETEROGENEOUS DATA

9

LAYING THE FOUNDATIONS FOR SEMANTIC WEB OF THINGS

Muhammad Rizwan Saeed, Charalampos Chelmis, Viktor K. Prasanna

Ming Hsieh Department of Electrical Engineering, University of Southern California, Los Angeles, CA, United States

> *The suite of technologies developed in the Semantic Web, such as Ontologies, Semantic Annotation, Linked Data and Semantic Web Services, can be used as principal solutions for the purpose of realizing the IoT.*
>
> **–Barnaghi et al. [1]**

CHAPTER POINTS

- Introducing key concepts of Semantic Web.
- Applying the principles of Semantic Web to Internet of Things (IoT) and Web of Things (WoT) to build Semantic Web of Things (SWoT).
- Using SWoT to achieve the vision of Smart Oilfields and Smart Cities.

9.1 INTRODUCTION

Recent developments in embedded devices and sensors have led to smart devices increasingly becoming a part of daily activities. These smart devices include sensors, mobile devices, vehicles, appliances and other devices which are uniquely addressable and possess the capability of collecting and exchanging data. A network of such devices is conceptualized as Internet of Things (IoT) [2]. The research in this area mainly focuses on exploring efficient ways to connect such smart devices for creating data networks in a variety of challenging and constrained networking environments [3]. Due to various vendors involved in manufacturing smart devices and multiple hardware and software architectures, developing multi-platform applications on top of this network is a challenging task as it requires expertise across vendors and systems. A promising next step is to build the Web of Things (WoT) on top of the basic network of devices [4].

To understand this, consider the example of Internet which is a scalable network of networks that successfully connects heterogeneous devices. On top of the Internet, at the application layer, the Web provides an information exchange (using open protocols e.g. HTTP) where uniquely identifiable documents and web resources can be accessed by users worldwide using URLs, irrespective of the underlying networking infrastructure. Similarly, the Web of Things (WoT) aims to integrate real-world smart devices into the realm of Web so that the devices, their services and data become searchable [4,5]. Multiple web-oriented service standards have been proposed to integrate physical devices and their services into information systems, allowing access through APIs, resulting in a web of heterogeneous data generating sources [6–8]. However, there is an inherent drawback of the Web itself. Currently, the Web can more appropriately be called the web of documents [9]. Like real files, users skim through web documents to extract relevant information which is cumbersome to do manually, given the huge number of documents on the Web. Without giving a meaningful structure to web documents (or resources), it is difficult for the machines to understand their contents automatically. Similarly in WoT, the Web APIs can be used to acquire data which often is presented as documents (JSON, XML). The selection of relevant APIs and identifying required data to poll can be difficult and time-consuming, if done manually. There is a need for a way to model the information produced or consumed, so that it can be automatically gathered, integrated and shared [10].

An improvement for the Web has been proposed as Semantic Web [11] which aims to build a web of data on top of the existing web of documents. The objective is to give meaning to data and provide the flexibility of linking multiple data sources together. This enables machines to comprehend information and rapidly integrate multiple data sources. Based on the principles of Semantic Web, Semantic Web of Things (SWoT) has been proposed for Web of Things (WoT) [1]. The goal of SWoT is to associate semantically rich and easily accessible information to real-world objects, locations and events by modeling and integrating the data acquired from underlying sensor networks.

The purpose of this chapter is to introduce Semantic Web technologies as an enabler of Semantic Web of Things and discuss how different techniques developed as part of Semantic Web suite can address challenges related to discovering, modeling, integrating and accessing data from networks of devices. In Section 9.2, we present a brief introduction of Semantic Web and its key concepts and briefly discuss the challenges faced in realizing SWoT. In that context, in Section 9.3, we discuss various Semantic Web based techniques that can address those challenges. Finally, in Section 9.4, we discuss how Semantic Web technologies through SWoT can pave way for smart applications such as Smart Oilfields and Smart Cities.

9.2 BUILDING THE SEMANTIC WEB OF THINGS (SWOT)

According to an estimate,[1] there will be 21 billion IoT devices by 2020. The goal then becomes to provide capability of interlinking massive streams of data and services provided by such devices and to make them discoverable and queryable by users (machines and humans). The term "Semantic Web of Things" (henceforth referenced by its abbreviation SWoT) has been recently coined to formally lay the groundwork for applying Semantic Web technologies to the domain of IoT (and WoT) [12]. Before we discuss the challenges in realizing SWoT, we present a brief introduction of Semantic Web along with some of its key concepts.

9.2.1 WHAT IS SEMANTIC WEB?

As discussed in Section 9.1, the Web can be categorized as a web of documents and hence is geared more towards direct human consumption. However, the next version of Web, labeled "Semantic Web" [11], aims at creating a web of data that is understandable by machines. The main idea behind Semantic Web is to augment HTML with more suitable language such that some structure (context) can be added to the content of a web document. This way, in addition to carrying content and formatting information, the web documents are able to carry information about their content. Such representation is easier to process for machines. The information about content is referred to as metadata – data about data. This is where the term semantic comes from in Semantic Web i.e., capturing meaning of data [13].

As an example, consider the sentence "Barrack Obama was born in Hawaii" appearing in a web document. Although this sentence is readily understandable by human readers but holds no specialized meaning for a computer. If we add metadata identifying different entities within this sentence, we can add context to it for a machine. We define Barrack Obama as an instance of class Person, Hawaii as an instance of class State and link the two instances using a property, say, born-in. This makes it easier for a machine to understand the context of the information in the web document and be able to answer more complex queries. For example, by annotating multiple similar sentences (or web documents), a machine can answer query asking for list of all people born in Hawaii (i.e., all instances of class Person that are linked through the property born-in with the entity Hawaii). To achieve this way of representing information we require (i) identification and modeling of concepts (Person, City, State, Movie, Actor, Vehicle etc.) and properties (acted, directed, born-in, lives-

---

[1]http://www.technocracy.news/index.php/2016/02/02/internet-of-things-devices-to-expand-to-21-billion-by-2020/.

in, works-at, founded etc.) in the document and (ii) a set of formal languages to do so. This understanding of the domain is captured through the use of ontologies.

9.2.1.1 *Conceptualizing Domains through Ontologies*

In the domain of Semantic Web, ontologies (or vocabularies) define the concepts and relationships used to describe and represent an area of concern. The role of ontologies in Semantic Web is to facilitate data organization and integration [14]. This integrated data (known as Linked Data) which can be used for reasoning or simply querying is the main strength of the Semantic Web. Most of the applications employing Semantic Web technologies are essentially based on the accessibility and integration of Linked Data at various levels of complexities. Ontologies can play a crucial role in enabling automatic knowledge processing, sharing, and reuse among applications. An ontology typically contains a hierarchy of concepts (or classes) along with their attributes (or properties) related to an area of interest. From our example regarding birthplace of Barrack Obama, we need to create (or reuse) an ontology that models such biographical content using classes such as Person, City, State and Country (to name a few) along with relationships among them. Moreover, literals such as age, salary etc. can also be modeled through ontological constructs called data (or datatype) properties and linked to respective classes.

9.2.1.2 *Resource Description Framework (RDF)*

An ontology is a formal conceptualization of a particular domain and is described using RDF[2] syntax. The Resource Description Framework (RDF) is used for expressing information about resources, their attributes and relationships with other resources. A resource can be anything, including a document, person, object or an abstract concept. RDF allows us to make statements about these resources. These statements always follow a simple structure:

```
<subject> <predicate> <object>
```

For example: A statement that shows the entities "Barrack Obama" and "Hawaii" linked through the property "birthPlace" is formally represented in RDF as:

```
<http://example.org/BarrackObama>
<http://schema.org/birthPlace>
<http://example.org/Hawaii>.
```

Moreover, we can add more context about the entities "Barrack Obama" and "Hawaii" such as:

```
PREFIX rdf:
<http://www.w3.org/1999/02/22-rdf-syntax-ns#>
```

---

[2]http://www.w3.org/RDF/.

```
<http://example.org/BarrackObama> rdf:type
<http://schema.org/Person>.

<http://example.org/Hawaii> rdf:type
<http://schema.org/State>.

<http://example.org/BarrackObama>
<http://schema.org/name>
"Barrack Obama".

<http://example.org/Hawaii> <http://schema.org/name>
"Hawaii".
```

In RDF subjects, predicates and objects are represented using URIs (Uniform Resource Identifiers). URIs are used to identify resources irrespective of their location on the web. Readers interested in understanding more about Semantic Web and its constituent concepts should consult some of the introductory material such as [13] and [15].

9.2.2 CHALLENGES IN REALIZATION OF SWOT

Barnaghi et al. [1] present the challenges in fully realizing the semantic-oriented vision towards IoT. We present some of those challenges here. Later, in Section 9.3, we see how they can be addressed through Semantic Web technologies.

9.2.2.1 *IoT Data Modeling and Integration*

One of the key visions of Semantic Web is to model information on the Web so that it can be automatically understood, organized and retrieved by machines. The IoT devices exchange data with each other and with users on the Web. In order to facilitate automated interactions among devices and users, some context is needed to be built around data. In the domain of Semantic Web, context is provided through use of ontologies. Ontologies encode domain knowledge in terms of concepts (or classes), attributes (or properties) and rules to model a given domain. Using ontologies, we can model how data is being generated, how it interacts with other sources and how metadata and other attributes are managed. Ontologies can facilitate identification of different types of data streams. In essence, ontologies are reference maps that are used to model similar entities across domains, promoting standardization. Moreover, heterogeneous data from multiple sources can be integrated together to create complete view of an environment or an entity (e.g. energy consumption, temperature and occupancy data can be used to characterize a building). In an effort to standardize publishing of ontologies and data, W3C (World Wide Web Consortium) has provided some guidelines [16] which are summarized here:

- Publish the domain knowledge (ontology, dataset and rules) online.
- Write labels or comments at least in English.

- Dereferencing URIs: If a URI does not point to a document, then it should point to an ontology (not to 404 error page).
- Use semantic validation tools to fix errors in the ontology.

In order to promote standardization, there needs to be an agreement among the different stakeholders over ontological definitions which, in real world, is seldom the case due to the decentralized design of the Web. For example, museums around the world have built databases about the artworks they host using different schemas without consideration for interoperability with other museums [17]. If, for instance, each of these museums model similar entities such as a Painting or an Artist using classes from independently developed ontologies, it will be difficult to query paintings by the same artist across museums without first performing the process of ontology alignment [18] and record linkage [19]. In Section 9.3.1, we discuss more about how ontologies can be used to model and integrate heterogeneous data.

9.2.2.2 *IoT Resources Search and Discovery*

As more and more IoT data become available through web-oriented services, it becomes difficult to manually keep track of and locate relevant services. Semantic annotation of IoT resources and services are key to supporting the search and discovery of such resources. In Section 9.3.2, we discuss different approaches of semantic modeling of web services and linking to LOD (Linked Open Data).

9.2.2.3 *IoT Data Querying*

Once the data has been modeled through ontologies, the users require knowledge of Semantic Web and query languages to access it. In the literature, several approaches have been proposed that allow non-expert users to access information without having the pre-requisite knowledge of Semantic Web principles. In Section 9.3.3, we present multiple techniques to facilitate querying over semantic repository.

9.3 SEMANTIC WEB AS ENABLER OF SWOT

The realization of SWoT essentially relies on multiple concepts related to Semantic Web. In this section, we discuss different techniques built as part of the Semantic Web suite and how they can be applied to sensors and data (and IoT in general) to address the challenges presented in Section 9.2.2.

9.3.1 ONTOLOGY-BASED DATA MODELING AND INTEGRATION

The purpose of creating the ontologies and integrating data is to organize heterogeneous data sources for simplifying on-demand information access and enable complex analytics to be performed on the integrated knowledge bases. In the domain of IoT, data from various devices along with metadata can be integrated using the principles of Semantic Web. In the particular example of sensor networks, Semantic Web technologies have been applied to model oceanographic measurements [20], ecological surveys [21], external corrosion detection [22] and smart grids [23]. For example, in [23] authors propose an extensible model that caters to the information diversity in Smart Grids with provision to integrate new information sources and concepts. It is shown that such a model can facilitate dynamic Demand Response (DR) planning for the utilities as it is capable of presenting and integrating electric consumption data, weather data, building occupancy data etc., to create a unified view of the environment needed for decision making. Such studies show the benefits of the approach in terms of integration and contextualization of data. These representations can not only explicitly reveal relationships between facts but also be used to drive methods to infer hidden or implicit relationships between entities. For instance, it is shown by authors in [24] that reasoning capabilities over semantic data allows certain queries to be issued that cannot be composed using SQL.

In the domain of Semantic Web everything is uniquely identifiable through URIs and hence can be made accessible via HTTP protocol. Using RDF statements, these URIs can be linked to other URIs using different properties. This linking can provide intra-domain as well as inter-domain integration. However, in reality, researchers modeling data in their areas of interest seldom follow standardized vocabularies and create their own custom ontologies. To solve this issue, ontology mapping/matching techniques have been proposed in literature. Such techniques link together same concepts modeled differently in two ontologies on the basis of (i) names of the concepts and attributes and (ii) comparison of the instances of the concepts under review [25–27]. For the sake of discussion in this chapter we limit ourselves to standardized ontologies only, used in the domain of sensors. One commonly used such ontology is Semantic Sensor Network (SSN) ontology which is presented in next section.

9.3.1.1 *Semantic Sensor Network (SSN) Ontology and Sensor Cloud Ontology (SCO)*

Semantic Sensor Network (SSN) ontology [28], shown in Fig. 9.1, focuses on domain independent sensing applications by integrating sensor data (measurements) and sensor specific data (sensing principles, quality etc.). The ontology provides a number of concepts and attributes to model sensors and sensor observations and measurements. The ontology can describe sensors, accuracy, ranges, frequency, units and hierarchies of sensors etc. Users can derive their own custom domain ontologies by creating subclasses of classes described by SSN ontology. Another related ontology is the Sensor Cloud Ontology (SCO) [21] which extends SSN ontology by adding provisions for the parameters being sensed as separate entities instead of just metadata and explicitly introduces the concept of time series. The ontology provides a unified view of data collected from multiple sensor networks and organizes sensors hierarchically i.e., *Network → Platform → Sensor → Phenomenon → Observation*. This means that a network can have multiple platforms. Each platform has multiple sensors attached to it and each sensor measures a particular phenomenon and the measured results are stored as observations.

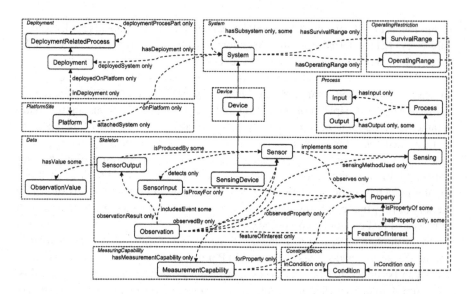

FIGURE 9.1

Overview of the Semantic Sensor Network (SSN) Ontology [28]. Some of the key concepts of SSN ontology are shown, which are split into conceptual modules. These concepts model sensors, measurements, features being measured etc. The concepts not depicted here are related to metadata about devices and observations such as operating ranges, accuracy, precision, resolution etc.

Müller et al. [21] have used SCO ontology for (offline[3]) modeling and integration of sensor data acquired through REST API. The Commonwealth Scientific and Industrial Research Organization (CSIRO[4]) provides access to data of a large number of terrestrial and marine sensors through a Web API implemented using RESTful principles. These sensors measure parameters such as temperature, salinity and rainfall. The data is available as JSON documents. The URL of each document depicts the hierarchical organization (network, platform names etc. e.g. network1/platform1/sensor1/data.json etc.) for a given sensor. By creating instances of classes such as Network, Platform and Sensor from the SCO ontology, the hierarchical information can be mapped to corresponding concepts in RDF format. The data itself as well as the measured phenomenon (rainfall, in this case) can be modeled using `ObservedPhenomenon`, `ObservationResult` and `TimeSeriesObservedValue`. This allows to create a single linked RDF graph from a set of JSON documents acquired through REST API. Once the data

---

[3]Offline techniques usually constitute extraction of entire data from a source, bulk conversion to RDF and then use this converted data for querying. Alternatively, online approaches deal with modeling services and can perform data modeling on the fly, discussed in Section 9.3.2.
[4]http://www.csiro.au.

is linked, users can extract relevant data by issuing SPARQL queries like the one, shown in Box 9.1, that retrieves a list of sensors and their observations along with observation quality information.

Box 9.1: SPARQL Query Example

```
SELECT DISTINCT ?sensingDevice ?observation ?obsMetadata
?qualityInfo ?methodType WHERE
{
    ?sensingDevice a ssn:Sensor.
    ?sensingDevice sco:hasObservedPhenomenon ?observation.
    ?observation sco:hasMetadata ?obsMetadata.
    ?obsMetadata md:dataQualityInfo ?qualityInfo.
    ?qualityInfo dq:report ?report.
    ?report dq:evaluationMethodType ?methodType.
}
```

–From RESTful to SPARQL: A Case Study on Generating Semantic Sensor Data [21]

9.3.1.2 *Modeling of Time Series Data*

A time series is a temporally ordered sequence of observations. Usually, the observations in the sequence have the same feature of interest and observed property. For example, time-stamped sequence of kWh values obtained from an electricity meter (sensor) forms a time series representing energy consumption (observed property) for a particular house (feature of interest for the sensor). In order to ensure that the observations that constitute a time series are populated correctly in an RDF graph, usage of OWL (Web Ontology Language) based rules have been proposed [29]. Such rules ensure that all the observations in a single time series have the restriction of having same feature of interest and the same observed property. One such example is shown here:

Box 9.2: Using OWL Property Restrictions

Assuming an ontology that models kWh consumption data for residential buildings, the OWL syntax fragment below represents that House2717KWhObservation is subclass of Observation with a restriction that all instances of the former will have energyConsumption as value of the property observedProperty and House2717 as value of the property featureOfInterest. This is to ensure that when the RDF graph is created from raw data, only those observations that meet these two criteria become instances of the class House2717KWhObservation.

```
<owl:Class rdf:about=
    "http://www.energydata.org#House2717KWhObservation">
    <rdfs:subClassOf rdf:resource="#Observation"/>
    <rdfs:subClassOf>
        <owl:Restriction>
            <owl:onProperty rdf:resource="#observedProperty"/>
            <owl:hasValue rdf:resource=
            "http://www.energydata.org#energyConsumption"/>
```

```
        </owl:Restriction>
    </rdfs:subClassOf>
    <rdfs:subClassOf>
        <owl:Restriction>
            <owl:onProperty rdf:resource="#featureOfInterest"/>
            <owl:hasValue rdf:resource=
                "http://www.energydata.org#House2717"/>
        </owl:Restriction>
    </rdfs:subClassOf>
</owl:Class>
```

9.3.1.3 *Dealing with Heterogeneous Data*

Nowadays, data is not only being generated by sensor networks, but also a large amount of it is coming from human and machine users. A sensor observation has so far been modeled keeping in mind its numeric nature. However, due to new forms of data generating entities, data may comprise of images, videos, text (structured and unstructured), drawings etc. In such scenarios it is useful to abstract the data generating entities and focus on the data itself. Due to recent focus on data sciences, complex analytical models are commonly being applied to observed data to detect patterns, learn hidden correlations and find new facts. This derived data needs to be integrated with the raw data for querying and future analysis. SOFOS (Smart Oil Field Ontology) [22] is designed for data and event-centric modeling. Entities are viewed as data sources (including both raw data and metadata). Like SSN and SCO, discussed earlier, there is a Measurement class, but the nature of measurement is not limited to numeric data. It includes anything from an image to a descriptive observation (e.g. comments). The observed data is linked to analyzed data through inter-class relationships. Based on critical thresholds, events (e.g. low/high alarms, warning/critical alarms etc.) can be generated based on observed and derived data. The events are modeled using classes derived from PoEM (Process-oriented Event Model) [30] for event modeling. Bridging the two ontological models together results in linking of data streams, event detection and event-based goal planning, promoting the re-usability aspect of Semantic Web.

9.3.2 DISCOVERING AND MODELING WEB SERVICES

So far we have discussed how different techniques have been applied to model raw data and devices to build semantic data. Other than raw data, IoT data is also available through WoT approach, which builds a layer of web services on top of the IoT devices so that the devices, their services and data become browsable. There are examples, in the literature, of modeling data acquired from web services [20,31,32]. However, creating a solution or scheme that models only a particular web service is inefficient. Also some of the approaches extract all available data from such services and convert them into RDF (offline approaches such as [21], discussed in Section 9.3.1.1). There

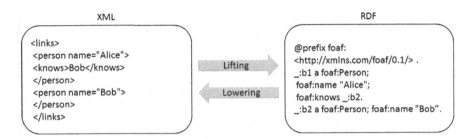

FIGURE 9.2

Lifting and Lowering. Conversion of information related to the relationship between two entities Alice and Bob from XML to RDF (Lifting) and back (Lowering)

were more than *"9000 Web APIs that were available in 2013, up from 105 in 2005"*.[5] Offline processing is not a viable solution for such a large number of web services and also can lead to data freshness issues, as the process of data extraction and modeling may need to be repeated to keep the data up-to-date. This necessitates having mechanisms for automatic and generalized way of discovering and modeling services and making them available for querying. Before we discuss some of the proposed approaches, it will be worthwhile to understand the concept of *Lifting* and *Lowering*. It is possible that a user application that issues SPARQL queries (that match RDF graph patterns) may have to access web service that provides data as XML or JSON. As shown in Fig. 9.2, the process of *Lowering* converts the user provided RDF graph pattern into the input needed by the web service. The process of *Lifting* converts the XML/JSON result into RDF format [33]. This should happen seamlessly so that from the user's perspective he only deals with RDF data.

Several approaches have been developed to integrate Web APIs with the Linked Data cloud. One approach is to semantically annotate attributes provided by the web services using known ontologies and make them available as Linked Data (on a Semantic Service registry). Users can query the registry using SPARQL queries to find out relevant web services that provide the data they need [34–36]. An example of a SPARQL query for service discovery is:

Box 9.3: Service Discovery SPARQL Query Example

This example is for services which have been annotated using SAWSDL[a] and MSM (Minimal Service Model) [35] ontologies. The query finds services that take dbpedia:City as input and return dbpedia:State as output.

```
SELECT ?url WHERE
{
    ?s rdf:type msm:Service; msm:hasOperation ?o.
```

---

[5]http://en.wikipedia.org/wiki/Web_API.

```
    ?o rdf:type msm:Operation;  rest:hasAddress ?url;
    msm:hasInput ?in;  msm:hasOutput ?out.
    ?in rdf:type msm:MessageContent; msm:hasPart ?par.
    ?par rdf:type msm:MessagePart; sawsdl:modelRefrence ?m.
    ?m rdf:type dbpedia:City.
    ?out rdf:type msm:MessageContent; msm:hasPart ?par2.
    ?par2 rdf:type msm:MessagePart; sawsdl:modelRefrence ?m2.
    ?m2 rdf:type dbpedia:State.
}
```
---
[a]http://www.w3.org/TR/sawsdl-guide/.

Another approach [37] proposes to build an RDF template (using known ontologies) on the server side that links together different attributes provided by the service. This is essentially a wrapper built on the server side. In this way, there will be no lowering and lifting, since the HTTP requests will be accepting and replying in RDF patterns. For existing services, automatic modeling and conversion of XML/JSON data into RDF format has been proposed. For instance, in [38] authors present an approach that first invokes a Web API several times to get a list of attributes along with examples of different invocations of the service. Using ontology matching, it matches the names of the fields in the data recieved to concepts and attributes in well-known or user-specified ontologies. Once the model is finalized, the software acts as an intermediary between the client and the server and performs automatic lowering and lifting for subsequent queries.

9.3.3 QUERYING SEMANTIC-RICH HETEROGENEOUS DATA

The Resource Description Framework (RDF) and the SPARQL query language have been recognized as two of the key technologies of the Semantic Web. An RDF repository is a collection of triples, denoted as <subject, predicate, object>, and can be represented as a graph. The vertices of this graph denote subjects and objects, and edges denote predicates. SPARQL allows users to write queries against data repositories that follow the RDF specification of the World Wide Web Consortium (W3C) by creating queries that consist of triples, conjunctions, disjunctions, and optional patterns. Although SPARQL is a standard way to access RDF data, it remains tedious and difficult for non-expert users because of the complexity of the SPARQL syntax and the RDF schema [39]. To automatically generate SPARQL query, a system would have to (i) separate the user input into syntactic markers and tokens, (ii) map tokens to concepts in the ontology, (iii) link identified concepts based on relationships in the ontology, and (iv) issue the query to collect the results.

In this section, we present a discussion on some of the systems that aim to convert user query intention into formal query syntax through different approaches.

9.3.4 STATE OF THE ART

Part of the Semantic Web vision is to provide Web-scale access to semantically annotated content [11,40]. This implies understanding users' information needs accurately enough to allow for retrieving a precise answer using semantic technologies. An ideal system would allow end-users to benefit from the expressive power of Semantic Web standards while at the same time hiding their complexity behind an intuitive and easy-to-use interface [41,42]. For this reason, NLP and ontology-based approaches for translation of end-user queries into formal queries have been significantly explored [39,43–46]. Systems based on natural language can imply semantic relationships between keywords using a whole sentence [47]. Additionally, some existing natural language based approaches limit input to a subset of natural language rules by introducing a pre-specified vocabulary, grammar or sentence structure that must be followed while constructing a query [48].

Approaches that avoid the challenges of natural language processing rely on controlled environments by guiding the user step by step with suggestions of terms that are connected in the ontology [49,50], formulating queries interactively. Querix [50] translates natural language queries into SPARQL. In case if the NL query translates into multiple semantic queries, Querix relies on clarification from the users via dialog boxes. Ginseng (Guided Input Natural language Search Engine) [49] allows users to query RDF knowledge bases using a controlled input language. The system provides suggestions through pop-up lists for each word in the user entry. These pop-up menus offer suggestions on how to complete the current user-entered word or present the options for the next word. The possible choices get reduced as the user continues to type. Entries that are not part of these suggested lists are not accepted by the system. Ginseng translates the entry to SPARQL query, executes it against the ontology model using Jena[6] and displays the SPARQL query and answer to the user.

Another approach [39] requires predefined SPIN (SPARQL Inferencing Notation) rules to be stored in the semantic repository. SPIN rules are essentially SPARQL statements stored as part of the RDF graph. Approaches that rely on predefined rules limit the ability of users to formulate new queries on demand and rely on involvement of IT experts or database admins to add new queries to the library [51]. In [52] authors perform offline processing to map natural language phrases to top-k possible predicates in an RDF dataset in order to form a paraphrase dictionary which is later used in the online phase of semantic query formulation. This approach of maintaining pre-processed mappings (called templates) of NL phrases to RDF predicates and later using them for the basis of RDF Q/A systems is also called template-based approach [53,54].

Since a user query does not need to be syntactically correct but must contain a minimum set of "relevant" concepts, a keyword-based interface eliminates the need of pre-processing natural language phrases into discernible tokens before matching such keywords to concepts and attributes in the ontology. The keyword-based approach is the basis for Automatic SPARQL Query Formulation (ASQFor) technique [55] which takes the <key, value> pairs approach to solve the problem of querying a semantic data repository. This is similar to the way arguments are passed to

---

[6]https://jena.apache.org/.

functions in high level programming languages such as Java. ASQFor framework is a reusable and extendable domain independent approach that requires virtually no end-user training to facilitate semantic querying over a knowledge base represented in RDF. ASQFor's simple and intuitive tuple-based interface accepts <key, value> inputs and translates them into a formal language query (currently SPARQL). Generated queries are then executed against the semantic repository and the results are returned to the user. The main objective of this approach is to develop a domain independent framework that provides a simple but powerful way of specifying complex queries and automatically translates them into formal queries on the fly (i.e., does not rely on predefined rules and can instantaneously adapt to changes in the ontology).

9.3.4.1 *ASQFor: Automatic SPARQL Query Formulation*

The main goal of ASQFor is to enable end-users to formulate queries over semantic data in terms of classes and properties while being oblivious to the actual structure of the data. To achieve that, ASQFor generates SPARQL queries in three steps. First, the user provided keywords are mapped to concepts and attributes in the ontology O. Each key in the user provided input maps to a node u in O. Second, the algorithm determines the minimum number of nodes and edges from O needed to connect all the nodes u to form the query subgraph Q. A semantic relationship between two nodes (or keys from the input) can be simple (i.e., a single triple) or complex (i.e., represented by a path). To construct the semantic query graph Q, the lowest common ancestor r of all the mapped nodes u is computed. This step is necessary to establish the smallest set of relationships between concepts and attributes in the query that lie on different branches of O. Then the paths that connect all nodes u to r are traced (r is the root of the query subgraph Q). The SPARQL statements are generated while traversing these paths to r by populating statements that correspond to semantic relations and intermediate nodes at each step. Finally, the SPARQL query is executed on the semantic repository and results are returned to the user.

9.3.4.2 *Semantic Search of 1990 US Census Data*

To show how ASQFor can be incorporated into a semantic search system, we developed a simple user interface (Fig. 9.3) that supports a combination of semantic search and exploration queries. From the user's perspective, he only needs to know what kind of information is available in the database irrespective of how it is organized. This has led to our minimalist design which allows users to pick and choose the concepts that are relevant for the query, specify filtering values and get the desired results. After selecting the required attributes, the user can optionally specify filtering values. The filtering values can be entered concatenated with comparison operators e.g. < 500. The results of the query are returned in CSV format. The selection and filtering values in Fig. 9.3 correspond to a query asking for *people with more than 16 years of education who are employed and making more than $100,000/yr.* Unlike other visual query interfaces, our primary focus is to abstract the details of SPARQL and schema ontologies from the end users, providing them only the data attributes to choose from. Furthermore, this interface can be dynamically generated

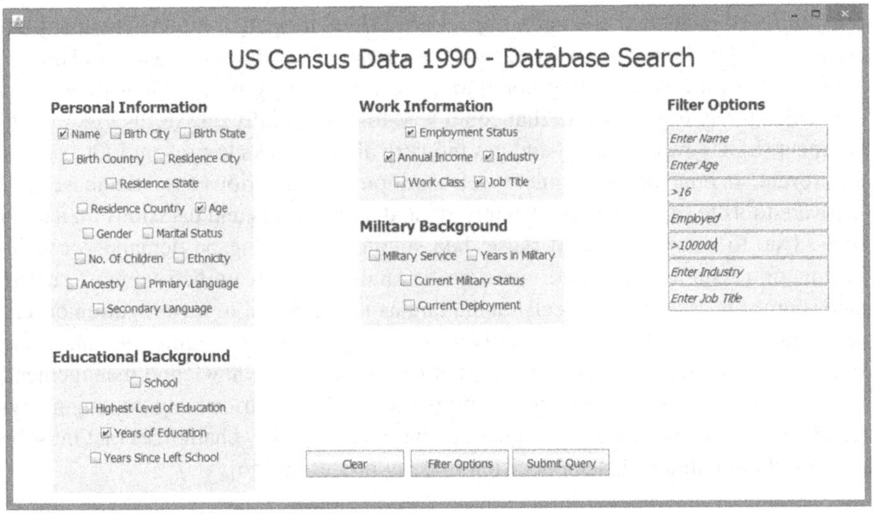

FIGURE 9.3

ASQFor based Application. US Census 1990 – Database Search: The users simply selects from the attributes that are available in the database. The formal query is generated by the system on the fly, executed and the results are returned to the user

from a schema ontology, resulting in a portable application that only requires access to the semantic repository (which must contain schema ontology along with data) to build a functional-to-SPARQL query translator and a GUI on the fly.

9.4 CASE STUDIES: SMART APPLICATIONS

9.4.1 SMART OILFIELDS

One environment characterized by data heterogeneity, where Semantic Web technologies are being used for discovering, modeling, integrating and sharing knowledge is the Smart (or Digital) Oilfield. Multiple processes on oil and gas facilities generate vast volumes of data. The data can be generated by variety of sensors and process controllers or manually gathered through inspections. This gathered data is often located in multiple independent repositories and undergoes further processing by different users by performing analytics and other domain-specific activities that result in generation of derived data. For example, engineers working in the oilfields often create or re-use different simulation models [56] such as geographic models, reservoir simulation models, network models, integrated (coupled) simulation models etc., all of which produce and consume vast amounts of data. Another area where effective decision making is critical is Asset Integrity Management, where assets are continuously monitored to ensure that they perform their required functions effectively while operating within defined safe operating ranges. Asset integrity is affected by many parameters [22] including normal wear and tear, weather, production, repair, and human factors etc. In a rare operating condition, these seemingly independent parameters may collectively trigger a fault that could lead to a potentially disastrous loss of containment (LOC) event. The oil and gas industry always seeks to prevent LOC events. To prevent such incidents, engineers rely on inputs from various asset databases and software tools to make important safety-related assessments and decisions on a daily basis. Due to heterogeneity of these data sources, providing on-demand access to information with an integrated view can be challenging. A unified view of current data sources is desirable for decision making as it could lead to identification of telltale signatures of LOC events. However, manually cross-referencing and analyzing such data sources is labor intensive. Another challenge is knowledge management, which refers to a systematic way to capture the results of various engineering analyses and prediction models. To summarize, there are three key challenges that must be addressed to facilitate all such decision making processes [56]:

- **Integrated view of the information:** For effective decision making, there needs to be a system that presents a comprehensive and continuous view of the assets and processes. Useful information may reside in multiple databases or files. Having scattered information makes it difficult to connect the dots and come up with actionable information. Hence, integration of multiple data sources is a crucial step.
- **Knowledge management:** As the models (e.g. for modeling production or external corrosion) are constantly being used and improved with passage of time (due to availability of more data), the rationale behind the changes and decisions are generally lost. Such knowledge could be extremely useful for auditing and training purposes.
- **Efficient access to information:** It is critical for the decision maker (production engineer, asset integrity manager etc.) to have access to relevant pieces of information required to make an informed decision. For example, an asset integrity manager who is looking for solution to a problem can benefit from a database of surveys conducted on other facilities to look for similar problems and associated recommendations or solutions.

9.4.1.1 *Semantic Model of Asset Integrity Data*

Semantic Web technologies can be used for an expressive representation of various heterogeneous data sources to deal with aforementioned challenges. First of all, the data streams need to be modeled using appropriate ontological models that capture the relevant domain knowledge, as is done through SOFOS (Smart Oilfield Ontology) and ECD (External Corrosion Detection) ontologies in [22]. The ontologies capture physical entities and their inter-relationships as well as the associated observed data, metadata and derived data. Once all the entities in the data streams have been identified, the next step is to perform record linkage across data streams. Different types of data may be recorded for same assets in different databases. The key idea is to integrate and present a unified view of the environment. Fig. 9.4 shows data orga-

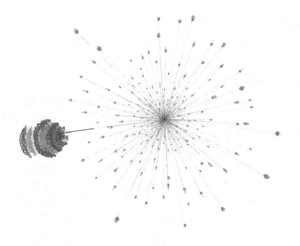

FIGURE 9.4

Integrated asset integrity data. Data from one oil and gas facility is organized as a graph where the center node represents the facility. Each group of nodes represents all information related to a single equipment organized in a hierarchical way. A hierarchy of data for a single equipment is shown in the expanded view

nized as an integrated RDF graph where raw data was originally stored as multiple CSV files, databases, images and text files. Data from multiple sources is integrated into a central repository serving as a single endpoint for maintaining and retrieving knowledge. Asset integrity managers can query previously separate databases to issue meaningful queries e.g. *all work orders for assets that have been labeled severely corroded in the most recent survey.* This query requires data from work orders database and inspection database, which have now been linked together after the integration process. This way data from disjoint repositories can be combined to provide actionable information. This is, essentially, an end goal for any enterprise to not just store and manage vast amounts of data, but also get actionable insights faster for robust decision making process. Other automatic and semi-automatic approaches of using ontologies for organizing data and metadata into semantic repositories are discussed in [56] and [57].

9.4.1.2 *Accessing Integrated Information*

Once we have the integrated repository, the data become available for querying. However, non-expert users require IT experts to build applications or create queries to be used. Our definition of a non-expert user is someone who is not familiar with the concepts of databases, querying, Semantic Web and ontologies but is an expert in his area of specialization e.g. an asset integrity manager or a production engineer. To do his job that person only requires access to data irrespective of underlying techniques of data organization and retrieval. For such users, ASQFor algorithm (discussed in Section 9.3.4.1) aims to abstract Semantic Web concepts (such as ontologies, RDF,

SPARQL) and allows them to formulate queries at a higher level which the system then translates into formal SPARQL queries automatically.

9.4.2 SMART CITIES

Currently, a wide variety of devices such as computers, mobile devices, surveillance equipment, sensors, actuators, displays, vehicles, home appliances and so on, have the capability of generating and exchanging data. The IoT framework (along with its application layers: WoT and SWoT) enables the development of applications that harness that information to provide new services to individuals and organizations (both public and private) [58]. In this context, the beneficial role of Semantic Web technologies becomes even clearer in linking together variety of data. For example, Intelligent Transport Systems can automatically create alerts to be sent out or displayed along the highways in case of flood, fog or snow forecast. Based on traffic data, such systems can, in real-time, update the arrival times of buses and taxis. Smart Buildings can adjust their air-conditioning systems based on the ambient conditions. Smart Neighborhoods or a group of Smart Buildings can optimize their energy consumption based on occupancy, weather and short and long-term consumption patterns. Healthcare Systems can issue alerts (flu season etc.) based on impending weather conditions. Health Monitoring Systems through remote-sensing equipment at ports of entry or popular areas can be used as predictor of epidemics [59]. The realization of such applications is only possible if IoT data can be harnessed effectively in order to enable intelligent systems (that constitute a Smart City) to make such data-driven decisions.

9.4.2.1 *Challenges*

IoT devices, which form the basis of a Smart City, offer heterogeneous data. For instance, in an IoT network, the devices can be measuring speed, light, temperature, sound etc. and usually have varying degrees of sampling frequencies. Different sensors provide different forms of data at varying rates and even with varying levels of quality and availability. The applications need to be built in a way that they interact with devices that are trustworthy and discard the noisy data. In these types of large-scale highly dynamic environments, the process of discovering, modeling, integrating and efficiently querying data are complex tasks [60]. Various aspects of Semantic Web technologies (discussed in Section 9.3) can help to some extent, enabling valuable services towards the goal of achieving Smart Cities. One such approach is described next.

9.4.2.2 *Automated Complex Event Implementation System (ACEIS)*

ACEIS [61] acts as a middleware between IoT data and Smart City applications and performs real time discovery and integration of data streams automatically. The data streams are modeled using SSN ontology (discussed in Section 9.3.1.1). User queries are translated into "semantically annotated complex event service requests". These event requests are modeled using Complex Event Service (CES) ontology, which is an extension of OWL-S.[7] The event requests are processed by ACEIS core to determine the data streams that are to be discovered and integrated. It uses an algorithm [62] to create composition plans to detect the complex events specified in event requests. Candidate sensors are determined by querying semantically annotated sensors capabilities (modeled using `ObservedProperty` and `FeatureOfInterest` from SSN ontology). The query transformer then transforms the composition plans into set of streaming queries to be executed on a streaming query engine. This mechanism can work with actual sensors as well as virtual sensors (social media streams) to detect complex events for users.

9.5 CONCLUSION

We have discussed some aspects of Semantic Web and its applications to data discovery, modeling, integration and querying. These principles have been applied to the IoT (and WoT) paradigm to pave path for Semantic Web of Things (SWoT). The purpose is to bring data from "Things" to the realm of the Web in fully integrated and discoverable fashion for consumption by humans and machines and build cross-domain applications. In this context, ontologies are needed to model the instances of "Thing", its data, metadata, services and all other relevant information. The reasoning capabilities of the description languages along with other data analytics techniques can be used to infer implicit relationships and to fill the gaps in data. The role of standardized ontologies such as SSN is to facilitate semantic interoperability among various domains and data sources. Due to the scale of data being generated by IoT devices and the dynamic nature of IoT devices, we believe that Semantic Web technologies will play a key role in addressing the challenges faced in realization of smart environments such as Smart Oilfields and Smart Cities due to their ability of giving meaning to data for machine-readability, describing data using ontologies, re-using and sharing of domain knowledge and inferencing. However, as noted in [1], most of the Semantic Web technologies have been developed with Web in mind and, hence, do not adequately address the dynamic, resource-constrained and distributed environment of physical devices. To address that, the future research work should focus on the dynamicity and scalability issues when adapting the principles of Semantic Web technology for the domain of IoT.

REFERENCES

[1] Barnaghi Payam M, Wang Wei, Henson Cory A, Taylor Kerry. Semantics for the internet of things: early progress and back to the future. Int J Semantic Web Inf Syst 2012;8(1):1–21.

---

[7]https://www.w3.org/Submission/OWL-S/.

[2] Atzori Luigi, Iera Antonio, Morabito Giacomo. The internet of things: a survey. Comput Netw 2010;54(15):2787–805.

[3] Gubbi Jayavardhana, Buyya Rajkumar, Marusic Slaven, Palaniswami Marimuthu. Internet of things (iot): a vision, architectural elements, and future directions. Future Gener Comput Syst 2013;29(7):1645–60.

[4] Guinard Dominique, Trifa Vlad. Towards the web of things: web mashups for embedded devices. In: Workshop on mashups, enterprise mashups and lightweight composition on the web. Proceedings of WWW (international world wide web conferences). 2009. p. 15.

[5] Mattern Friedemann, Floerkemeier Christian. From the internet of computers to the internet of things. In: From active data management to event-based systems and more – papers in honor of Alejandro Buchmann on the occasion of his 60th birthday. 2010. p. 242–59.

[6] Guinard Dominique, Trifa Vlad, Wilde Erik. A resource oriented architecture for the web of things. In: Proceedings of the 2010 Internet of things (IOT). 2010.

[7] Stirbu Vlad. Towards a restful plug and play experience in the web of things. In: Proceedings of the 2th IEEE international conference on semantic computing. 2008. p. 512–7.

[8] Mathew Sujith Samuel, Atif Yacine, Sheng Quan Z, Maamar Zakaria. Web of things: description, discovery and integration. In: 2011 IEEE international conference on Internet of things (iThings) & 4th IEEE international conference on cyber, physical and social computing. 2011. p. 9–15.

[9] Berners-Lee Tim. The web of things. Special theme on the future web. Ercim news – the European research consortium for informatics and mathematics. http://ercim-news.ercim.eu/en72/keynote/the-web-of-things, 2008. Accessed: 2016-05-15.

[10] Guinard Dominique, Trifa Vlad, Karnouskos Stamatis, Spiess Patrik, Savio Domnic. Interacting with the soa-based internet of things: discovery, query, selection, and on-demand provisioning of web services. IEEE Trans Serv Comput 2010;3(3):223–35.

[11] Berners-Lee Tim, Hendler James, Lassila Ora. The semantic web. Sci Am May 2001;284(5):34–43.

[12] Scioscia F, Ruta M. Building a semantic web of things: issues and perspectives in information compression. In: IEEE international conference on semantic computing, 2009. Sept 2009. p. 589–94.

[13] Wooldridge Michael. An introduction to multiagent systems. John Wiley & Sons; 2009.

[14] Decker Stefan, Melnik Sergey, van Harmelen Frank, Fensel Dieter, Klein Michel CA, Broekstra Jeen, Erdmann Michael, Horrocks Ian. The semantic web: the roles of XML and RDF. IEEE Internet Comput 2000;4(5):63–74.

[15] Manola Frank, Miller Eric, McBride Brian, et al. RDF Primer. W3C Recommend 2004;10(1–107):6.

[16] Gyrard Amelie, Bonnet Christian, Boudaoud Karima. Domain knowledge interoperability to build the semantic web of things. 2014.

[17] Szekely Pedro A, Knoblock Craig A, Yang Fengyu, Zhu Xuming, Fink Eleanor E, Allen Rachel, Goodlander Georgina. Connecting the Smithsonian American art museum to the linked data cloud. In: The semantic web: semantics and big data. Proceedings of the 10th international conference. 2013. p. 593–607.

[18] Shvaiko Pavel, Euzenat Jérôme. Ontology matching: state of the art and future challenges. IEEE Trans Knowl Data Eng 2013;25(1):158–76.

[19] Winkler William E. The state of record linkage and current research problems. In: Statistical research division. US Census Bureau. Citeseer; 1999.

[20] Cameron Mark A, Wu Jemma, Taylor Kerry, Ratcliffe David, Squire Geoffrey, Colton John. Semantic solutions for integration of federated ocean observations. In: Pro-

ceedings of the 2nd international workshop on semantic sensor networks (SSN09). 2009. p. 64–79.

[21] Müller Heiko, Cabral Liliana, Morshed Ahsan, Shu Yanfeng. From RESTful to SPARQL: a case study on generating semantic sensor data. In: Proceedings of the 6th international workshop on semantic sensor networks co-located with the 12th international semantic web conference. 2013. p. 51–66.

[22] Saeed Muhammad, Chelmis Charalampos, Prasanna Viktor K, House Robert, Blouin Jacques, Thigpen Brian. Semantic web technologies for external corrosion detection in smart oil fields. In: SPE western regional meeting. 2015.

[23] Zhou Qunzhi, Natarajan Sreedhar, Simmhan Yogesh, Prasanna Viktor K. Semantic information modeling for emerging applications in smart grid. In: Ninth international conference on information technology: new generations. 2012. p. 775–82.

[24] Skjæveland Martin G, Lian Espen H, Horrocks Ian. Publishing the Norwegian petroleum directorate's factpages as semantic web data. In: The semantic web, ISWC 2013. Proceedings of the 12th international semantic web conference, Part II. 2013. p. 162–77.

[25] Zhang Yinuo, Panangadan Anand V, Prasanna Viktor K. UFOM: unified fuzzy ontology matching. In: Proceedings of the 15th IEEE international conference on information reuse and integration. 2014. p. 787–94.

[26] Shvaiko Pavel, Euzenat Jérôme. Ontology matching: state of the art and future challenges. IEEE Trans Knowl Data Eng 2013;25(1):158–76.

[27] Choi Namyoun, Song Il-Yeol, Han Hyoil. A survey on ontology mapping. SIGMOD Rec 2006;35(3):34–41.

[28] Compton Michael, Barnaghi Payam, Bermudez Luis, García-Castro Raúl, Corcho Oscar, Cox Simon, Graybeal John, Hauswirth Manfred, Henson Cory, Herzog Arthur, Huang Vincent, Janowicz Krzysztof, David Kelsey W, Le Phuoc Danh, Lefort Laurent, Leggieri Myriam, Neuhaus Holger, Nikolov Andriy, Page Kevin, Passant Alexandre, Sheth Amit, Taylor Kerry. The {SSN} ontology of the {W3C} semantic sensor network incubator group. J Web Semant: Sci, Serv Agents World Wide Web 2012;17:25–32.

[29] Henson CA, Neuhaus Holger. An ontological representation of time series observations on the semantic sensor web. In: 1st international workshop on the semantic sensor web, Greece. 2009. p. 79–94.

[30] Om Prasad Patri, Sorathia Vikrambhai S, Panangadan Anand V, Prasanna Viktor K. The process-oriented event model (poem): a conceptual model for industrial events. In: The 8th ACM international conference on distributed event-based systems. 2014. p. 154–65.

[31] Page Kevin R, De Roure David, Martinez Kirk, Sadler Jason, Oles Kit. Linked sensor data: restfully serving RDF and GML. In: Proceedings of the 2nd international workshop on semantic sensor networks. 2009. p. 49–63.

[32] Janowicz Krzysztof, Bröring Arne, Stasch Christoph, Schade Sven, Everding Thomas, Llaves Alejandro. A restful proxy and data model for linked sensor data. Int J Digital Earth 2013;6(3):233–54.

[33] Lopes Nuno, Polleres Axel, Passant Alexandre, Decker Stefan, Bischof Stefan, Berrueta Diego, Campos Antonio. Rdf and xml: towards a unified query layer. In: Proc. W3C workshop on RDF next steps. 2010.

[34] Pedrinaci Carlos, Domingue John. Toward the next wave of services: linked services for the web of data. J UCS 2010;16(13):1694–719.

[35] Pedrinaci Carlos, Liu Dong, Maleshkova Maria, Lambert David, Kopecky Jacek, Domingue John. iserve: a linked services publishing platform. In: CEUR workshop proceedings, vol. 596. 2010.

[36] Villalba Álvaro, Luis Pérez Juan, Carrera David, Pedrinaci Carlos, Panziera Luca. Servioticy and iserve: a scalable platform for mining the iot. Proc Comput Sci 2015;52:1022–7. The 6th international conference on ambient systems, networks and technologies (ANT-2015), the 5th international conference on sustainable energy information technology (SEIT-2015).

[37] Norton Barry, Krummenacher Reto. Consuming dynamic linked data. In: Proceedings of the first international workshop on consuming linked data. 2010.

[38] Taheriyan Mohsen, Knoblock Craig A, Szekely Pedro A, Ambite José Luis. Rapidly integrating services into the linked data cloud. In: The semantic web. Proceedings of the 11th International Semantic Web Conference, Part I. 2012. p. 559–74.

[39] Sander Malte, Waltinger Ulli, Roshchin Mikhail, Runkler Thomas. Ontology-based translation of natural language queries to sparql. In: AAAI fall symposium series 2014. 2014.

[40] Cardoso Jorge. The semantic web vision: where are we? IEEE Intell Syst September/October 2007;22(5):84–8.

[41] Kaufmann Esther, Bernstein Abraham. Evaluating the usability of natural language query languages and interfaces to semantic web knowledge bases. J Web Semant: Sci, Serv Agents World Wide Web 2010;8(4):377–93.

[42] Lopez Vanessa, Unger Christina, Cimiano Philipp, Motta Enrico. Evaluating question answering over linked data. J Web Semant 2013;21:3–13.

[43] Wang Chong, Xiong Miao, Zhou Qi, Panto Yong Yu. A portable natural language interface to ontologies. In: The semantic web: research and applications. Springer; 2007. p. 473–87.

[44] Damljanovic Danica, Agatonovic Milan, Cunningham Hamish. Freya: an interactive way of querying linked data using natural language. In: The semantic web: ESWC 2011 workshops. Springer; 2012. p. 125–38.

[45] Ulli Waltinger, Tecuci Dan, Olteanu Mihaela, Mocanu Vlad, Sullivan Sean. USI answers: natural language question answering over (semi-)structured industry data. In: Proceedings of the twenty-fifth innovative applications of artificial intelligence conference. 2013.

[46] Lehmann Jens, Bühmann Lorenz. Autosparql: let users query your knowledge base. In: The semantic web: research and applications. Springer; 2011. p. 63–79.

[47] Freitas André, Curry Edward, Oliveira João Gabriel, Seán O'Riain. Querying heterogeneous datasets on the linked data web: challenges, approaches, and trends. IEEE Internet Comput 2012;16(1):24–33.

[48] Ferré Sébastien. Expressive and scalable query-based faceted search over SPARQL endpoints. In: The semantic web. Proceedings of the 13th International Semantic Web Conference, Part II. 2014. p. 438–53.

[49] Bernstein Abraham, Kaufmann Esther, Kaiser Christian. Querying the semantic web with ginseng: a guided input natural language search engine. In: 15th workshop on information technologies and systems. 2005. p. 112–26.

[50] Kaufmann Esther, Bernstein Abraham, Zumstein Renato. Querix: a natural language interface to query ontologies based on clarification dialogs. In: The semantic web. 5th international semantic web conference. Springer; 2006. p. 980–1.

[51] Kharlamov Evgeny, Solomakhina Nina, Lütfü Özçep Özgür, Zheleznyakov Dmitriy, Hubauer Thomas, Lamparter Steffen, Roshchin Mikhail, Soylu Ahmet, Watson Stuart. How semantic technologies can enhance data access at siemens energy. In: The semantic web. Proceedings of the 13th International Semantic Web Conference, Part I. 2014. p. 601–19.

[52] Lei Zou, Huang Ruizhe, Wang Haixun, Xu Yu Jeffrey, He Wenqiang, Zhao Dongyan. Natural language question answering over RDF: a graph data driven approach. In: International conference on management of data. 2014. p. 313–24.

[53] Höffner Konrad, Unger Christina, Bühmann Lorenz, Lehmann Jens, Ngonga Ngomo Axel-Cyrille, Gerber Daniel, Cimiano Philipp. User interface for a template based question answering system. In: Knowledge engineering and the semantic web. Proceedings of the 4th international conference. 2013. p. 258–64.

[54] Zheng Weiguo, Zou Lei, Lian Xiang, Xu Yu Jeffrey, Song Shaoxu, Zhao Dongyan. How to build templates for RDF question/answering: an uncertain graph similarity join approach. In: Proceedings of the 2015 ACM SIGMOD international conference on management of data. 2015. p. 1809–24.

[55] Saeed Muhammad. Charalampos Chelmis, and Viktor Prasanna. Asqfor: automatic sparql query formulation for the non-expert. CS Department technical report 16-967. University of Southern California; 2016. Accessed: 2016-09-06.

[56] Soma Ramakrishna, Bakshi Amol, Prasanna Viktor, DaSie William J, Colbert Bourgeois Birlie, et al. Semantic web technologies for smart oil field applications. In: Intelligent energy conference and exhibition. Society of Petroleum Engineers; 2008.

[57] Chelmis Charalampos, Zhao Jing, Sorathia Vikrambhai S, Agarwal Suchindra, Prasanna Viktor, et al. Semiautomatic, semantic assistance to manual curation of data in smart oil fields. In: SPE western regional meeting. Society of Petroleum Engineers; 2012.

[58] Zanella A, Bui N, Castellani A, Vangelista L, Zorzi M. Internet of things for smart cities. IEEE Int Things J Feb 2014;1(1):22–32.

[59] Bagavathiappan S, Saravanan T, Philip J, Jayakumar T, Raj B, Karunanithi R, Panicker TM, Korath MP, Jagadeesan K. Infrared thermal imaging for detection of peripheral vascular disorders. J Med Phys Jan 2009;34(1):43–7.

[60] Bischof Stefan, Karapantelakis Athanasios, Nechifor Cosmin-Septimiu, Sheth Amit P, Mileo Alessandra, Barnaghi Payam. Semantic modelling of smart city data. https://www.w3.org/2014/02/wot/papers/karapantelakis.pdf, 2014. Accessed: 2016-05-15.

[61] Gao Feng, Intizar Ali Muhammad, Mileo Alessandra. Semantic discovery and integration of urban data streams. In: Proceedings of the fifth workshop on semantics for smarter cities a workshop at the 13th international semantic web conference. 2014. p. 15–30.

[62] Gao Feng, Curry Edward, Bhiri Sami. Complex event service provision and composition based on event pattern matchmaking. In: The 8th ACM international conference on distributed event-based systems. 2014. p. 71–82.

BUILDING ENTITY GRAPHS FOR THE WEB OF THINGS MANAGEMENT

10

**Lina Yao*, Quan Z. Sheng[†], Anne H.H. Ngu[‡], Xue Li[§], Boualem Benatallah*,
Xianzhi Wang***

*School of Computer Science and Engineering, University of New South Wales, Sydney, NSW,
Australia* Department of Computing, Macquarie University, Sydney, NSW, Australia[†]
Department of Computer Science, Texas State University, San Marcos, TX, United States[‡] School
of Information Technology and Electrical Engineering, University of Queensland, Brisbane,
QLD, Australia[§]*

10.1 INTRODUCTION

Since its birth in the early 1990s, the World Wide Web has been the heart of the research, development, and innovation in the world. Indeed, it has changed our world and society so quickly and profoundly over the last two decades by sharing knowledge and connecting people. Very recently, the World Wide Web is beginning to connect ordinary things in the physical world, also called the "Web of Things" (WoT) [5, 9,17,3,36]. As indicated by the inventor of the World Wide Web, Tim Berners-Lee, "*it isn't the documents which are actually interesting; it is the things they are about!*".[1] WoT aims to connect everyday objects, such as coats, shoes, watches, ovens, washing machines, bikes, cars, and even humans, plants, animals, and changing environments, to the Internet to enable communication/interactions between these objects. Being widely regarded as one of the most important technologies that are going to change our world in the coming decade, the ultimate goal of WoT is to enable computers to see, hear, and sense the real world.

While such a ubiquitous WoT environment offers the capability of integrating information from both the physical and virtual worlds, which leads to tremendous business and social opportunities (e.g., efficient supply chains, independent living of elderly persons, and improved environmental monitoring), it also presents significant challenges [8,2,30,26,22]. With many things connected and interact over the Web,

---

[1] http://ercim-news.ercim.eu/en72/keynote/the-web-of-things.

Managing the Web of Things. DOI: 10.1016/B978-0-12-809764-9.00013-5

there is an urgent need to efficiently index, organize, and manage these things for object search, recommendation, mash-up, and effectively revealing interesting patterns from things.

Before effectively and efficiently classifying, managing, and recommending ubiquitous things, a fundamental task is to discover relations among things. Indeed, finding implicit correlations among things is a much more challenging task than finding relations for documents, web pages, and people, due to the following unique characteristics of things on the Web.

- **Lack of uniform features**. Things are diverse and heterogeneous in terms of functionality, access methods, or descriptions. Some things have meaningful descriptions while many others do not [6,40]. As a result, it is quite challenging to discover the implicit correlations among heterogeneous things. Things cannot be easily represented in a meaningful feature space. They usually only have very short textual descriptions and lack a uniform way of describing the properties and the services they offer [11].
- **Lack of structural interconnections**. Correlations among things are not obvious and are difficult to discover. Unlike social networks of people, where users have observable links and connections, things often exist in isolated settings and the explicit interconnections between them are typically limited. Such high-level structural interconnection information (e.g., a water tap and a cutting board are likely to be used together when cooking) are implicit in general [38].
- **Contextual uncertainty**. Things are tightly bound to contextual information (e.g., location, time, status), as well as user behaviors (e.g., activities involving things), as things usually provide functionality-oriented services (e.g., washing vegetables for a water tap). Unfortunately, contextual information associated with things is highly dynamic (e.g., the location of a moving person changes all the time) and has no obvious, easily indexable properties, which is unlike those static, human-readable texts in the case of documents [9,39]. Capturing discriminative contextual information carried by things, therefore, is of paramount importance in effective things management.

To illustrate the conception of Internet of Things and implication of multiple relationships, we firstly take the *Tony's One Day* as an illustrative story to demonstrate the typical heterogeneous interactions in Internet of Things (see Fig. 10.1).

Tony's home is a typical smart home (① in Fig. 10.1), where all the home appliances are already connected and enabled to the Internet and can be acknowledged and controlled by the Web interface. Tony goes to work around 7:00 am before he leaves for work, he usually sets the rules for the air conditioner, *when the temperature reaches to* 30 °C, air conditioner in the house will be automatically turned on to cool down his house. He also sets the cleaner and washing machine to begin to work around 10:00 am.

When he arrives near to his workplace, he needs to check the parking availability through his mobile phone. It is hard to find an available one efficiently, usually people

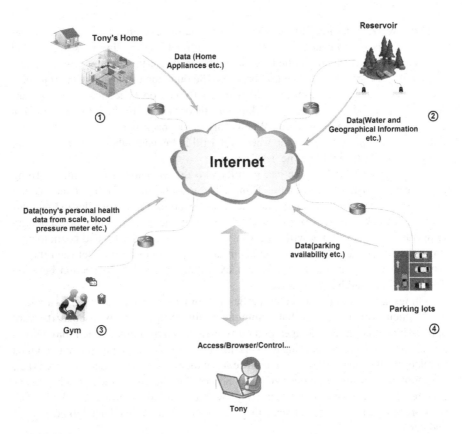

FIGURE 10.1

An illustrative scenario of Internet of Things: Tony's one day

have to drive around to find it. Thanks to the Smart Parking system (② in Fig. 10.1), Tony only needs to subscribe this smart parking system, he can retrieve the latest status of parking lots in real-time, in the meanwhile, Tony's location can also be collected by the parking system through his GPS. The parking planner can guide and recommend him to the most appropriate parking space.

After settling down in his office, Tony is a hydraulician and needs to monitor and track the information every day from the reservoir about the water and other related information. Thanks to Internet of Things, even though the reservoir is in a remote suburb, Tony can easily obtain desirable information, which is harvested by the sensors installed around the reservoir and in the water, and the sensor values are transmitted to Tony's office. Then tony can use these data for analyzing and modeling about the research (④ in Fig. 10.1). Around 11:00 am, Tony received a Tweet notifying from his washing machine and vacuum that cleaning and washing are already finished.

After work, Tony goes to the Gym for his routine exercise, he wears the monitoring devices which generate his personal health data during the working out, and the data can be sent to an online medical analyzer in real-time so that his coach can adjust Tony's exercise plan instantly based on the outcome of the analyzer. Tony also likes to share his working-out record with his friends on Facebook, where he authorizes his friends to access his working out records so as to share the information amongst friends (③ in Fig. 10.1). When Tony drives back home, he turns the automatic warming program to let the warm water fill in his bath tub, so that he can have a comfortable bath right after he gets home.

From *Tony's One Day*, we can identify two different levels of Thing-to-Thing relationships existing in Internet of Things. The most basic one is direct and explicit connections between things. For example, Tony specifies a series of rules in his smart home. Taking the simplest example, when the thermometer detects the corresponding temperature (i.e., 30 °C), it will trigger air conditioner to power on and begin to cool down the house. Another one is the latent and implicit connection between things, which can not be observed directly. For example, what is the connection between Tony's vacuum and his microwave?

Things may exhibit similar properties to humans when interacting in a social environment. Smart objects that communicate in co-operation with context-aware applications, may affect changes in their real-world environment which may have a significant impact on underlying networking structures. We argue there are two kinds of relationships: one is the explicit connection which can be direct and observed (i.e., thermometer and air conditioner in Tony's home). Another one is the implicit connection, recall the relationship between Tony's vacuum and his microwave. This kind of relationship is our main target since they can not be observed and need to be learned and derived.

The regularities of users' interactions can be recorded as things usage events in our work. Things usage events are growing data repository: every time people has interaction with an object, it will generate an event item. With the development of ubiquitous computing techniques, including wireless sensor network, RFID, and Web Services etc., monitoring and tracking the objects usage events are becoming handier. The things usage events logs have been becoming popular and significant like the click-through data in web mining or check-in records in location-based research. The ever growing objects use events can contribute to many research areas including mining the relationships of objects and human behavior analysis by mining the people's objects use records. In this chapter, we will use the things usage events as the only source to exploit the implicit relationships among ubiquitous things.

Therefore, the problem targeted in this chapter can be formulated as discovering the latent correlations among things by exploiting observable things usage events with the goal of automatically distinguishing strong correlations of things from the weak ones. A thing usage event happens when a person interacts with a particular thing (see solid lines in Fig. 10.1). View from thing in the usage events, it carries three-dimensional information: location, time, and user. These usage events can be captured explicitly (Section V-B), e.g., via RFID and sensor readings), and provide

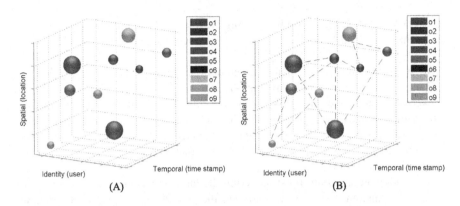

FIGURE 10.2

(A) Things usage and contextual attributes (B) Correlation discovery. Different colors of balls denote different things/objects, and the size represents the usage frequency. (For interpretation of the references to colour in this figure legend, the reader is referred to the web version of this chapter.)

rich information to discover implicit connections (i.e., correlations) among things (dotted lines in Fig. 10.2(B)).

Some research efforts have proposed to explore things similarity and relations from semantic Web perspective [18,5]. In such cases, explicit relations of things can be characterized by using keyword-based, textual-level calculations. However, physical things also hold *implicit* relations due to their more distinctive structures and connections in terms of functionalities (i.e., usefulness), as well as non-functional attributes (i.e., availability). Different things provide different functionalities (e.g., microwave and printer), and might be of interest to different groups of people. With the recent development of technologies such as radio frequency identification (RFID), wireless sensors, and Web services, human-thing interactions can be easily recorded and obtained (e.g., RFID readings). These interactions are not completely random. They carry rich information that can be harnessed and utilized to uncover the implicit relations. Although correlations between things are implicit, we argue that they can be captured by exploring regularities of user interactions with similar things.

This work targets mining useful information for unveiling implicit correlations of things from the contextual information of human-thing interactions. Our proposed method, *DisCor-T* (**dis**covering **cor**relations of **t**hings), should be *effective* in capturing and reflecting the hidden structure of things from things usage events in the modeling stage and *efficient* in inferring the related things in the inferring stage. Specifically, we present a novel approach that converts the things usage events into a *relational graph of things* (RGT) by extracting three-dimensional contextual information contained in event history. The RGT graph underpins many important applications. We particularly present an application scenario to show its benefits in serving things clustering and annotation. To the best of our knowledge, no previous work has systematically studied mining the relationships of ubiquitous objects in WoT. The main contributions of our work can be summarized as follows:

- We study the problem of managing ubiquitous things in the emerging Web of Things environment, which have unique characteristics (e.g., short descriptions, diverse, dynamic and noisy). We propose to investigate human-thing interactions from three contextual aspects: user, temporal, and spatial. Accordingly, we develop two graph presentations that approximate corresponding relationships from user-thing interactions. These graphs lay the foundation for uncovering latent correlations among things.
- We develop an algorithm for discovering the latent correlations among things by applying Random Walk with Restart over the two contextual graphs. The learned correlations are used to construct the relational graph of things (RGT), which can help in a number of important applications on things management. In particular, we focus on two fundamental use cases of entity graph on *things annotation* and *recommendation* to showcase the effectiveness of our approach.
- We establish a testbed environment where things are tagged by RFID and sensors and things usage events are collected in real-time. Using this real-world data with ~20,000 records collected from the testing environment over a period of four months, we conduct extensive experimental studies to demonstrate the feasibility of our proposed approach.

10.2 BACKGROUND

In this section, we first describe several application scenarios underpinned by the techniques discussed. We then formally formulate the research problems target by our work.

10.2.1 MOTIVATING APPLICATIONS

Discovering underlying similarities except keyword-based similarity allows for more meaningful and accurate things recommendation, classification and even context-aware activity recognition. We briefly discuss some of the areas where things contextual similarity can be applicable.

- **Recommendation.** Things recommendation is a crucial step for promoting and taking full advantage of the Web of Things (WoT), where it benefits the individuals, businesses, and society on a daily basis in terms of two main aspects. On the one hand, it can deliver relevant things to users based on users' preferences and interests. On the other hand, it serves to optimize the time and cost of using WoT in a particular situation [39]. The underlying correlations of things can enhance the performance of the generalized recommendation systems in the Web of Things in terms of two main points. Firstly, due to the sparsity of thing-user interactions, widely used collaborative filtering recommendation systems fail to find similar users or things, since these methods assume that two users have invoked at least some things in common. Moreover, users who have never used any things can not be fed good results in the first place (i.e., the cold start problem). Secondly, physical things have more distinctive structures and connections in terms of functionalities in real life (i.e., usefulness), as well as non-functionalities (i.e., availability), which are saliently highlighted in the contextual information of human-thing interactions.

- **Searching.** Developing efficient searching approaches is a crucial challenge with the rapid increase of a vast amount of things connected to the Web. Our approach adds one additional dimension to assist and reinforce current search techniques. For instance, existing semantic-based solutions do not make full use of the rich information contained in users' historical interactions with things (e.g., implicit relations of different things). Our approach can effectively capture such information, which can be integrated into existing search solutions, whereas the strength of latent connections between things/objects can be leveraged to predict which things will possibly co-occur. In this way, it would be complimentary to many semantic-based solutions for better performance, which usually require preparation of prior knowledge such as defining the descriptions of things and their corresponding characteristics and concepts. Our primary work on searching with entity graph for the Web of Things can be found at [38].

- **Context-aware Activity Recognition.** Recognizing human activities from sensor readings has recently attracted much research interest in pervasive computing due to its potential in many applications, such as assisted living of older people and healthcare. This task is particularly challenging because human activities are often performed in a not only simple (i.e., sequential) but also complex (i.e., interleaved or concurrent) manner in real life [34]. Our proposed approach provides a new useful means to infer human activities by taking advantages of reasoning relationships of globally unique object instances. For example, dense sensing-based activity monitoring learns human activities by detecting and analyzing human-object interactions. By discovering correlations of objects, we can cluster and organize things into differently structured groups based on their underlying relationships. In many cases, an activity could involve multiple relevant things including not only the things with similar functionalities but also things with complementary functionalities, which can be effectively uncovered by our proposed approach. Pairwise things with strong correlations indicate either they have similar functionalities (i.e., microwave and toaster) or them have a higher likelihood to be used together. For instance, a water tap and a chopping board are both in use when we prepare meals since most of the time we need to wash cooking ingredients (e.g., vegetables) before cutting them.

10.2.2 PROBLEM STATEMENT AND DEFINITIONS

The only data source used in our work is human-thing interactions, namely *things usage events*. Each event happens when a person interacts with a particular thing, which carries three kinds of information: location, timestamp, and user. Each usage event record can be defined as a quadruplet *ThingID, UserID, Timestamp, Location* described as follows.

Definition (Things Use Log). Each thing use log happens when a person interacts with a particular thing. Let $\mathbf{O} = \{o_1, ..., o_n\}$, $\mathbf{U} = \{u_1, ..., u_m\}$, $\mathbf{Ts} = \{ts_1, ..., ts_p\}$ and $\mathbf{Loc} = \{loc_1, ..., loc_q\}$ represent the set of things, users, timestamps and locations, respectively. A usage event of a thing o_i, denoted by $h \in \mathbf{H} = \{h_1, ..., h_i\} = \{< o, u, ts, loc > | o \in \mathbf{O} \wedge u \in \mathbf{U} \wedge ts \in \mathbf{Ts} \wedge loc \in \mathbf{Loc}\}$, indicates that user u has used a particular thing o located in a specific location loc.

The problem targeted in this article can be therefore formulated as discovering the *latent correlations* among things by exploiting observable *human-thing interactions* with the goal of automatically distinguishing strong correlations of things from the weak ones. As illustrated in Fig. 10.2, each node denotes a thing (represented as a ball) in a three-dimensional space of identity, spatiality, and temporality. Things are discrete without distinctive and explicit correlations (Fig. 10.2(A)). However, our proposed approach can derive latent connections among these things and form a relational graph of things, where their implicit relatedness can be revealed (Fig. 10.2(B)). Therefore, our goal can be formulated as follows in Problem 10.1. The derived latent relations are a set of real-valued numbers between 0 and 1 in this work.

Problem 10.1 (Things Implicit Correlation Discovery). Given a set of human-thing interactions of quadruplets (thing, user, timestamp and location), discovering the latent relations between things.

To complete this goal, there are two sequential subproblems we need to solve, which are defined as Subproblem 10.1.1 and Subproblem 10.1.2, respectively.

Subproblem 10.1.1 (Modeling). Given a collection of things usage events $\mathbf{H}$, construct two graphical models $\mathbf{G}_m$ capturing relations between things and their spatial-temporal information, and $\mathbf{G}_u$ capturing relations between things and users.

Subproblem 10.1.2 (Inferring). Given the constructed graphs induced from things usage events collection $\mathbf{H}$, infer the similarities among things.

10.3 PROPOSED METHODOLOGY

Our approach for correlation discovery of things involves two main stages corresponding to two subproblems defined in Section 10.2.2. First, we extract two types of graphs, namely the *location-time-thing* graph (Fig. 10.3(A)) and the *user-thing* graph (Fig. 10.3(B)). The graphs are deduced from thing usage events, which reflect object and its three related information in terms of spatiotemporal and social aspects. Then we perform a random walk on these two graphs respectively to inference relationships of pairwise things and sum them up as the overall pairwise correlations of things.

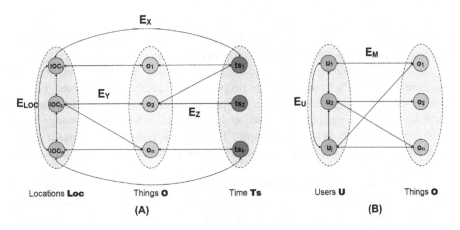

Locations **Loc**   Things **O**   Time **Ts**   Users **U**   Things **O**

(A)   (B)

FIGURE 10.3

Two graphs induced from things usage events: (A) spatio-temporal graph $\mathbf{G}_m$ (B) social graph $\mathbf{G}_u$

The first stage centers around building two graphs from things usage events. As illustrated in Fig. 10.3, the *spatio-temporal* graph in Fig. 10.3(A) captures the relations between things and their temporal and geographical influence, while the *social* graph in Fig. 10.3(B) captures the social influence among users on interacting things. The technical details on how to construct these graphs will be described in Section 10.3.1 and Section 10.3.2 respectively. In the second stage, our goal is to derive the pairwise relevance scores for things. To achieve this, a random walk with restart (RWR) [33] is performed on the two constructed graphs. A relevance score is produced for any given node to any other node in the graph, presented as a converged probability. The value of the relevance score reflects the correlation strength between a pair of things. Based on the relevance scores, a top-*k correlation graph of things* can be constructed, upon which many advanced things management problems such as annotation and clustering can be solved by tapping the wealth of literature in graph algorithms. The technical details on this part can be found in Section 10.3.3.

10.3.1 SPATIO-TEMPORAL GRAPH CONSTRUCTION

A spatiotemporal graph such as the one shown in Fig. 10.3(A) reflects the temporal pattern and spatial information hidden in the things usage events. In our approach, the spatial and temporal information of things usage events is treated as inseparable since they are mutually influential on detecting the correlations among things. Unlike virtual resources such as web pages, music or images, physical things such as restaurants and cookware usually provide more distinguished functionalists, and are more connected with people's daily lives. Some such distinctive features of physical things are their physical locations and functioning times. For example, kitchenware is more frequently used during dining times and they have higher likelihood to stay in a kitchen or similar locations (e.g., a dining room). We specifically explore the integrity of spatial and temporal information in the ubiquitous things environment via finding the periodical pattern between time and locations.

Generally, the timing of access to similar things may be similar. For example, restaurants are likely to be visited by people during lunch or dinner times. For the spatial information, we also argue in this paper that *geographical influence* to user activities cannot be ignored, i.e., a user tends to interact with the nearby things rather than the distant ones [41]. For example, if a user is at her office, she has a higher probability of using office facilities such as telephone, desktop computer, printer, and seminar rooms.

A spatiotemporal graph has three sets of nodes, namely locations, things, and timestamps. It contains one type of intra-relation (i.e., representing similarities between locations) and three types of inter-relations between locations, things, and timestamps. Edges between times and things can be obtained from usage events, say, the weight of edge $<loc, o> \in \mathbf{E_Y}$ and $<ts, o> \in \mathbf{E_Z}$ is proportional to the number of times objects o is used in a location loc and at timestamp ts. The inter-relation between location and time $<loc, ts> \in \mathbf{E_X}$, indicates the periodical patterns. Formally, we define the spatio-temporal graph $\mathbf{G}_m$ as the following:

Definition (Spatio-Temporal Graph). A spatio-temporal graph is denoted by $\mathbf{G}_m = <\mathbf{V}_m, \mathbf{E}_m>$. Here $\mathbf{V}_m = \mathbf{Loc} \cup \mathbf{Ts} \cup \mathbf{O}$ where $\mathbf{Loc}$, $\mathbf{Ts}$ and $\mathbf{O}$ are the sets of locations, timestamps and things respectively. Edges $\mathbf{E}_m = \mathbf{E_{Loc}} \cup \mathbf{E_X} \cup \mathbf{E_Y} \cup \mathbf{E_Z}$, where $\mathbf{E_{Loc}} = \{(loc, loc') : (loc, loc') \in \mathbf{Loc} \times \mathbf{Loc}\}$ and the weight of each edge $E_{loc}(i, i') \in \mathbf{E_{Loc}}$ is associated with the similarity between location i and i'. $\mathbf{E_X} = \{(loc, ts) : (loc, ts) \in \mathbf{Loc} \times \mathbf{Ts}\}$ and the weight of each edge $E_X(i, j) \in \mathbf{E_X}$ is associated with a binary value, referring to whether location loc_i has periodic relationship with time interval ts_j. $\mathbf{E_Y} = \{(loc, o) : (loc, o) \in \mathbf{Loc} \times \mathbf{O}\}$ and the weight of each edge $E_Y(i, j) \in \mathbf{E_Y}$ is associated with the frequency that thing o_j in location loc_i is accessed. $\mathbf{E_Z} = \{(ts, o) : (ts, o) \in \mathbf{Ts} \times \mathbf{O}\}$ and the weight of each edge $E_Z(i, j) \in \mathbf{E_Z}$ is associated with the frequency that thing o_j is accessed in time interval ts_i.

The corresponding weight matrix $\mathbf{W}_m$ of graph $\mathbf{G}_m$ can be formulated as:

$$\mathbf{W}_m = \begin{bmatrix} \mathbf{W_{Loc}} & \mathbf{W_X} & \mathbf{W_Y} \\ \mathbf{W_X^T} & \mathbf{W_{Ts}} & \mathbf{W_Z} \\ \mathbf{W_Y^T} & \mathbf{W_Z^T} & \mathbf{W_O} \end{bmatrix} \tag{10.1}$$

where each of the entries in Eq. (10.1) can be obtained as the following. $\mathbf{W_{Loc}}$ indicates the similarity of each pair of locations. Given two locations, we measure their similarity using the Jaccard coefficient between the sets of things used at each location:

$$\mathbf{W_{Loc}}(i, j) = \frac{|\Gamma_i^o \cap \Gamma_j^o|}{|\Gamma_i^o \cup \Gamma_j^o|} \tag{10.2}$$

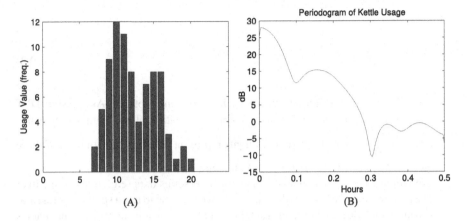

FIGURE 10.4

(A) Usage history of a kettle in the kitchen area over 24 hours within one week (e.g., the kettle was used 12 times at 10am); (B) Periodogram of the kettle usage

where Γ_i^o and Γ_j^o denote the set of used things at location i and location j respectively. $\mathbf{W_{Ts}}$ and $\mathbf{W_O}$ should be 0 since we do not consider the relationships between timestamps and the ones between things. $\mathbf{W_Y}$ and its transpose $\mathbf{W_Y^T}$ are integers, indicating how often a thing is accessed at a location. Similarly, $\mathbf{W_Z}$ and its transpose $\mathbf{W_Z^T}$ are integers, which indicate how often a thing is accessed at a particular time.

For defining relationship between time stamps and locations and their corresponding weight $\mathbf{W_X}$ of graph $\mathbf{G}_m$, we propose *periodic patterns* between locations and timestamps. Given a sequence of locations $Loc = \{loc_1, ..., loc_n\}$, our aim is to find their corresponding time period. To obtain relationship between time and location, we analyze the potential periods for each location and find the periodical pattern between locations and timestamps. A periodic pattern represents the repeat of certain usage event at a specific location with the certain time interval(s).

Periodic patterns can be extracted by analyzing things usage events. In particular, we build a time series dataset for each location where the elements of the time series data are the number of time slots (e.g., 0 for the period of 0:00–1:00; 1 for 1:00–2:00 and so on) that a thing at a location is invoked. We can clearly observe such periodic pattern from the example relating to a kettle in the kitchen from Fig. 10.4(A) and its periodogram in Fig. 10.4(B).

Given a sequence of locations, we adopt the Discrete Fourier Transform (DFT) method to detect the time periods in this discrete time-series sequence [31]. For each location, we define an integer sequence $A = \{a_1 a_2 ... a_n\}$, where $a_i = 1$ if the thing is used at this location at time i, and 0 otherwise. Essentially, this sequence can be transformed into a sequence of n complex numbers $X(f)$ from the time domain to the frequency domain:

$$X(f_{k/N}) = \frac{1}{\sqrt{N}} \sum_{n=0}^{N-1} a_n e^{-\frac{j2\pi kn}{N}}, k = 0, ..., N-1 \tag{10.3}$$

where k/N denotes the frequency that each coefficient captures. As a result, DFT transforms the original sequences as a linear combination of the complex sinusoids $s_f(n) = \frac{e^{j2\pi fn/N}}{\sqrt{N}}$. The Fourier coefficients represent the amplitude of each of these sinusoids after sequences S is projected on them.

We aim at capturing the general shape of time-series data (e.g., thing usage over time) as "economically" as possible. To do so, we propose to use a spartan representation[2] from which one could reconstruct the signal using just its dominant frequencies (i.e., the ones that carry most of the signal energy). A popular way to identify the power content of each frequency is by calculating the *power spectral density* (PSD) of the sequence which indicates the signal power at each frequency in the spectrum. A well-known estimator of the PSD is the *periodogram*. The periodogram P is a vector comprised of the squared magnitude of the Fourier coefficients $X(f_{k/N})$:

$$P(f_{k/N}) = \|\dot{X}(f_{k/N})\|^2, k = 0, 1, ..., \left\lceil \frac{N-1}{2} \right\rceil \tag{10.4}$$

The k dominant frequencies appear as peaks in the periodogram (and correspond to the coefficients with the highest magnitude). In order to specify which frequencies are important, we need to set a threshold and identify those frequencies higher than this threshold. Each element of the periodogram provides the power at frequency k/N or, equivalently, at period N/k. That is, coefficient $X(f_{k/N})$ corresponds to periods $[\frac{N}{k}, ..., \frac{N}{k-1})$. Interested readers are referred to [31].

When obtaining the periodogram of each location, we can decide their corresponding peak points based on preset threshold. From the periodogram, we can find the location and its corresponding time range. One benefit of using the periodogram is that we can visually identify the peaks as the k most dominant periods (period = 1/frequency). For automatically returning the important periods for a set of location sequences, we can simply set a threshold in the power spectrum to distinguish the dominant periods.

10.3.2 SOCIAL GRAPH CONSTRUCTION

Users' relations (e.g., friendships) can have a significant impact on things usage patterns. Personal tastes are correlated. Research in [10] shows that friendships and

---

[2]Inspired by the frugal lifestyle of the ancient Spartans, a spartan representation means an economic way of representing a dataset in a smaller size [35].

relations between users play a substantial role in human decision making in social networks. For instance, people usually turn to a friend's advice about a commodity (e.g., hair straighter) or a restaurant before they go for them. For exploring the impact social links between users on things' correlation discovery, we also construct a social graph, which is an augmented bipartite graph representing user interactions with things based on things usage events. As shown in Fig. 10.3(B), such a graph contains two sets of entities, users **U** and things **O**. There is one type of intra-relation between users (also called social connections) and one type of inter-relations: edges between users and things that can be obtained from usage events. Formally, the social graph is defined as the following:

Definition (Social Graph). A social graph, denoted by $\mathbf{G}_u = <\mathbf{V}_u, \mathbf{E}_u>$, is an augmented undirected bipartite graph. Here $\mathbf{V}_u = \mathbf{U} \cup \mathbf{O}$ where $\mathbf{U}, \mathbf{O}$ are the sets of users and things respectively. Edges $\mathbf{E}_u = \mathbf{E}_U \cup \mathbf{E_M}$, where $\mathbf{E}_U = \{(u, u') : (u, u') \in \mathbf{U} \times \mathbf{U}\}$ denotes the user social links (friendship) and each edge $E_U(i, i') \in \mathbf{E_M}$ is associated with the similarity between user u_i and user u'_i. $\mathbf{E_M} = \{(u, o) : (u, o) \in \mathbf{U} \times \mathbf{O}\}$. In this graph, each edge between users and things $E_M(i, j) \in \mathbf{E_M}$ is associated with the frequency that thing o_j is accessed by user u_i.

The corresponding weight matrix $\mathbf{W}_u$ of graph $\mathbf{G}_u$ can be formulated as:

$$\mathbf{W}_u = \begin{bmatrix} \mathbf{W}_U & \mathbf{W}_M \\ \mathbf{W}_M^T & \mathbf{W}_O \end{bmatrix} \tag{10.5}$$

The entries in Eq. (10.5) can be obtained as follows: $\mathbf{W}_M$ and its transpose $\mathbf{W}_M^T$ should be proportional to the number of times of a thing being used by the users. $\mathbf{W}_O$ should be zero since we do not consider relationships between things. The weight $\mathbf{W}_U$ of edges $\mathbf{E}_M$ indicates the user similarity influenced by the social links between users, reflecting the homophily meaning that similar users may have similar interests. We use the cosine similarity to calculate $\mathbf{W}_U$ as follows:

$$\mathbf{W}_U(i, j) = \frac{e^{\alpha cos(b(i), b(j))}}{\sum_{k \in \Omega(i)} e^{\alpha cos(b(i), (b(k))}} \tag{10.6}$$

where $cos(b(i), b(j)) = \dfrac{b(i) \cdot b(j)}{\|b(i)\| \|b(j)\|}$, $\Omega(i)$ is the set of the user i's friends (i.e., $j \in \Omega(i)$), $b(i)$ is the binary vector of things used by user i, $\| \cdot \|$ is the L-2 norm of vector $b(\cdot)$, and α is a parameter that reflects the preference for transitioning to a user who interacted with the same things.

10.3.3 CORRELATION INFERENCE

After the two graphs $\mathbf{G}_m$ and $\mathbf{G}_u$ are constructed, we can perform the random walk with restart (RWR) [33] to derive the correlation between each pair of things. RWR provides a good relevance score between two nodes in a graph and has been successfully used in many applications such as automatic image captioning, recommendation systems, and link prediction. The goal of using RWR in our work is to find other things that have top-k highest relevance scores for a given thing. The values of the relevance scores imply the strength of the correlations among things. In the following, we focus on using RWR on the spatiotemporal graph $\mathbf{G}_m$ for discovering correlations between things.

We assume the random walker starts from a thing node o_i on $\mathbf{G}_m$. The random walker iteratively transits to other nodes which have edges with o_i, with the probability proportional to the edge weight between them. At each step, o_i also has a restart probability c to return to itself. We can obtain the steady-state probability of o_i visiting another vertex π_i when the RWR process is converged. The RWR process can be formulated as

$$\pi_i = (1 - c)\mathbf{P}\pi_i + c\mathbf{e}_i \tag{10.7}$$

where $\pi_i \in \mathbb{R}^{N \times 1}$, and weight matrix from graph $\mathbf{G}_m$ is $\mathbf{W}_m \in \mathbb{R}^{N \times N}$ (Section 10.3.1), $\mathbf{e}_i \in \mathbb{R}^{N \times 1}$ with i-th entry is 1, all other entries are 0. Eq. (10.7) can be further formulated as:

$$\pi_i = c(\mathbf{I} - (1 - c)\mathbf{P}_m)^{-1}\mathbf{e}_i = \mathbf{Q}\mathbf{e}_i \tag{10.8}$$

where $\mathbf{I}$ is an identity matrix and $\mathbf{P}_m \in \mathbb{R}^{N \times N}$ is the transition matrix, which can be obtained based on weight matrix $\mathbf{W}_m$ of $\mathbf{G}_m$ by row normalization:

$$\mathbf{P}_m = \mathbf{W}_m \mathbf{D}_m^{-1} \tag{10.9}$$

where $\mathbf{D}_m$ is a diagonal matrix with $\mathbf{D}_m(i, i) = \sum_j \mathbf{W}_m(i, j)$. The random walker on thing o_i traverses randomly along its edges to the neighboring nodes based on the transition probability $\mathbf{P}_m(i, j), \forall j \in N(i)$, and the probability of taking a particular edge $< o_i, o_j >$ is proportional to the edge weight over all the outgoing edges from o_i based on Eq. (10.9).

In Eq. (10.8), $\mathbf{Q} = c(\mathbf{I} - (1 - c)\mathbf{P}_m)^{-1} = c \sum_{t=0}^{\infty} (1 - c)^t \mathbf{P}^t$ defines all the steady-state probabilities of random walk with restart. $\mathbf{P}^t$ is the t-th order transition matrix, whose elements p_{ij}^t can be interpreted as the total probability for a random walker that begins at node i and ends at node j after t iterations, considering all possible paths between i and j. Since in our case we only consider relevance score between two things, if we vary the value of t, we can explicitly explore the relationship between two things at different scales. The steady-state probabilities for each pair of nodes can be obtained by recursively processing Random Walk and Restart until convergence. The converged probabilities give us the long-term visiting rates from any given node to any other node. This way, we can obtain the relevance scores of all pairs of thing nodes, denoted by $R_m(o_i, o_j) \in \mathbf{R}_m, \forall o_i, o_j \in \mathbf{O}$. It should be noted that the results can be calculated more efficiently by using the Fast Random Walk with Restart implementation [29] via low-rank approximation and graph partition.

Similarly, the transition probability matrix $\mathbf{P}_u$ for the social graph $\mathbf{G}_u$ can be obtained using:

$$\mathbf{P}_u = \mathbf{W}_u \mathbf{D}_u^{-1} \qquad (10.10)$$

where $\mathbf{D}_u$ is a diagonal matrix with $D_u(i, i) = \sum_j \mathbf{W}_u(i, j)$. Accordingly, we can obtain the relevance scores of things on this graph $R_u(o_i, o_j) \in \mathbf{R}_u, \forall o_i, o_j \in \mathbf{O}$.

The overall relevance score (i.e., the correlation value) of any pair of things can be calculated using

$$R(o_i, o_j) = \alpha R_m(o_i, o_j) + \beta R_u(o_i, o_j) \qquad (10.11)$$

where $\alpha \in [0, 1]$ and $\beta \in [0, 1]$, which are regulatory factors affecting the weight on the social influence and the spatio-temporal influence.

With obtained correlation values, we could construct a top-k *correlation graph of things* by connecting each thing with the things that have top-k overall correlation values $R(o_i, o_j)$. Formally, the graph is defined as the following:

Definition (Relational Graph of Things (RGT)). RGT is denoted by $\mathbf{G} = (\mathbf{O}, \mathbf{E})$. For each thing $o_i \in \mathbf{O}$, let $\mathbf{O}_i^k$ denote the top-k set of correlative things to o_i. $\mathbf{E} = \{e(x, i) | \forall o_i \in \mathbf{T}, o_x \in \mathbf{O}_i^k\}$, where $e(x, i)$ is an edge from o_x to o_i. Each edge is associated with a weight w_{o_x, o_i} with the correlation value R_{o_x, o_i}.

10.4 APPLICABILITY OF DISCOR-T: THINGS CLASSIFICATION

The top-k correlation graph $\mathbf{G}$ is essentially a *graph* representing the relationships among things. For instance, from our experiment, we found that the top four things most close to a three-seated sofa are a modular sofa, leather chair, high chair, and wooden chair. Using the constructed $\mathbf{G}$, many problems centered around things management (e.g., things discovery, search, and recommendation) can be solved and explored further by exploiting existing graph algorithms. In this section, we will showcase the feasibility and effectiveness of our proposed DisCor-T by detailing one important research problem, *automatic things annotation*, which will be used later to evaluate the performance of our proposed approach to correlation discovery.

Automatically predicting appropriate tags (i.e., category labels) for unlabeled things can save manual labeling workload and has important research significance. Although some things have been labeled with useful tags (e.g., cooking, office), which are crucial for assisting users in searching and exploring new things, as well as recommending them, some other things may not have any meaningful labels at all. Furthermore, a thing might be associated with multiple categories. For instance, a microwave oven can be categorized in Cooking and also Home Appliance.

The aim of things annotation is that when given a new thing, the classifier automatically decides whether this thing belongs to the category of the corresponding labels. The algorithm can be divided into two stages: i) extracting features from the top-k correlation graph $\mathbf{G}$ and things, and ii) performing multi-label classification of things. We extract three kinds of features $\mathbf{F_L}$, $\mathbf{F_S}$ and $\mathbf{F_C}$ from RGT in terms of label property, link structures and node attributes respectively.

EXTRACTING FEATURE $\mathbf{F_L}$

This feature represents the label probabilities for unknown things, which can be computed using generative Bayesian rules from $\mathbf{G}$, where each unknown thing o^* is to be assigned one or multiple labels $l_k \in \mathbf{L} = \{l_1, ..., l_k\}$. We propose to formulate our solution as posterior probability $Pr(l_k|o^*)$. Once we know these probabilities, it is straightforward to assign o_i the label having the top-K largest probabilities,

$$Pr(l_k|o^*) = \frac{Pr(o^*|l_k)Pr(l_k)}{\sum_{j=1}^{K} Pr(x|l_j)Pr(l_j)} \propto Pr(o^*|l_k)p(l_k) \qquad (10.12)$$

where the prior distribution probability $Pr(l_k)$ can be easily calculated from the training dataset. Let $\mathbf{o}^{l_k} = o_1^{l_k}, ..., o_{M_k}^{l_k}$ be the training dataset, having M_k things with label k. Then $Pr(o^*|l_k)$ can be calculated using:

$$Pr(o^*|l_k) = \frac{1}{Z} \sum_{m=1}^{M_k} Pr(o^*|o_m^{l_k}, l_k)Pr(o_m^{l_k}|l_k)$$

$$= \frac{1}{Z \times M_k} \sum_{m=1}^{M_k} Pr(o^*|o_m^{l_k}, l_k) \qquad (10.13)$$

where Z is a normalizing constant and the conditional probability $Pr(o^*|o_m^{l_k}, l_k)$ indicates the relevance score between testing thing o^* and things in the training dataset $o_m^{l_k}$. $Pr(o^*|o_m^{l_k}, l_k) \approx \pi_{o^*}$ denotes the steady state probability between o^* and $\mathbf{o}^{l_k} = o_1^{l_k}, ..., o_{M_k}^{l_k}$, which can be obtained from Eq. (10.8) in our RWR process. The distribution $p(o_m^{l_k}|l_k)$ is set as a uniform distribution $1/M_k$. The probability $p(o^*|l_k)$ can be predicted in Eq. (10.13), and the labels with different posterior probabilities can be assigned to the testing thing. As a result, we can get the label probabilities for each testing object.

EXTRACTING LATENT FEATURE $\mathbf{F_S}$

With RGT, we can easily extract features of things that indicate the things relationship with different communities on $\mathbf{G}$. In reality, things usually hold multiple relations. For instance, a thing might be shared among its owner, owner's friends, co-workers, or family members. It might also be connected to other things based on functionality or non-functionality attributes. Detecting such relations from RGT, which can be used as a structural feature for things annotation, is naturally related to the task of *modularity-based community detection* [15]. Modularity is to evaluate the goodness of a partition of undirected graphs. The reason that we choose this method is that modularity has been shown to be an effective quantity to measure community structure in many complex networks [28].

Modularity Q is like a statistical test that the null model is a uniform random graph model, where one vertex connects to others with uniform probability. It is a measure of how far the interaction deviates from a uniform random graph with the same degree distribution. Modularity is defined as:

$$Q = \frac{1}{2m} \sum_{ij} \left[\mathcal{A}_{ij} - \frac{d_i d_j}{2m} \right] \delta(s_i, s_j) \tag{10.14}$$

where $\mathcal{A}_{ij}$ is the adjacent matrix on the graph RGT, m is the number of edges of the matrix, d_i and d_j denote the in-degree of vertex i and out-degree of vertex j, and $\delta(s_{t_i}, s_{t_j})$ are the Kronecker delta function that takes the value 1 if node t_i and t_j belong to the same community, 0 otherwise. A larger modularity Q indicates denser within-group interaction. So that, the modularity-based algorithm aims to find a community structure such that Q is maximized. In [20], Newman proposes an efficient solution by reformulating Q as:

$$Q = \frac{1}{2m} \mathcal{S}^T \mathbf{B} \mathcal{S} \tag{10.15}$$

where $\mathcal{S}$ is the binary matrix indicating which community each node belongs to. $\mathbf{B}$ is the modularity function, is defined as the following:

$$\mathcal{B}_{ij} = \mathcal{A}_{ij} - \frac{d_i d_j}{2m} \tag{10.16}$$

Since our relational graph of things (RGT) is a weighted and directed graph, we need to make some modifications on Q to solve the equation. This involves two steps.

In the first step, we extend $\mathcal{B}$ to directed graphs. Based on [15], we rewrite the modularity matrix $\mathcal{B}$ as the following:

$$\mathcal{B}'_{ij} = \mathcal{A}_{ij} - \frac{d_i^{in} d_j^{out}}{2m} \tag{10.17}$$

where $d_i^{in} d_j^{out}$ are the in-degrees and out-degrees of all the nodes on the RGT graph. In the second step, we extend $\mathcal{B}'$ to weighted graphs. To do so, we conduct further modification based on Eq. (10.17). It can be rewritten further as below:

$$\mathcal{B}''_{ij} = \mathcal{W}_{ij} - \frac{w_i^{in} w_j^{out}}{2m} \tag{10.18}$$

where $\mathcal{W}_{ij}$ is the sum of weights of all edges in the RGT graph replacing the adjacency matrix $\mathcal{A}$, w_i^{in} and w_j^{out} are the sum of the weights of incoming edges adjacent to vertex t_i and the outgoing edges adjacent to vertex t_j on the RGT graph respectively. After these two steps, it should be noted that different from undirected situation, $\mathcal{B}''$ is not symmetric. To use the spectral optimization method proposed by Newman in [20], we restore symmetry by adding $\mathcal{B}''$ to its own transpose [15], thereby the new $\mathcal{Q}_{new}$ is:

$$\mathcal{Q}_{new} = \frac{1}{4m} \mathcal{S}^T (\mathcal{B}'' + \mathcal{B}''^T) \mathcal{S} \qquad (10.19)$$

We are then able to calculate all the eigenvectors corresponding to the top-k positive eigenvalue of $\mathcal{B}'' + \mathcal{B}''^T$ and assign communities based on the elements of the eigenvector [21]. We take the obtained modularity vectors as the latent features, which indicate things relationships to communities (i.e., a larger value means a closer relationship with a community).

EXTRACTING FEATURE $\mathbf{F}_C$

It is the set of content-based features extracted from thing descriptions. We convert the keywords vectors into tf-idf format, which assigns each term x a weight in a thing's description d. $tf - idf(x, d) = tf(x, d) \times idf(x)$, where $tf(x, d)$, the number of times word x occurs in the corresponding thing's description d, and idf is the inverse text frequency which is defined as : $idf(x) = \log \frac{|N|}{df(x)}$, where $|N|$ is the number of texts in our dataset, and $df(x)$ is the number of texts where the word x occurs at least once.

Based on our experience in ontology bootstrapping for Web services [25], we exploit Term Frequency/Inverse Document Frequency (TF/IDF)—a common method in IR for generating a robust set of representative keywords from a corpus of documents—to analyze things' descriptions. It should be noted that the common implementation of TF/IDF gives equal weights to the term frequency and inverse document frequency (i.e., $w = tf \times idf$). We choose to give higher weight to the idf value (i.e., $w = tf \times idf^2$). The reason behind this modification is to normalize the inherent bias of the tf measure in short documents.

Finally, the set of feature vectors for the N things in the dataset $\tilde{\mathbf{v}} = [\vec{v}_1, ..., \vec{v}_N]$ where $\vec{v}_i \in \mathbb{R}^m$ is the feature vector for each thing, m is the size of vocabulary we produced. For better performance, we perform a cosine normalization for tf-idf vectors: $\hat{\mathbf{v}} = \frac{\vec{v}}{\|\vec{v}\|_2}$ [24].

BUILDING A DISCRIMINATIVE CLASSIFIER

After obtaining the features based on attributes of **G** and things, we combine the features ($\mathbf{F}_L + \mathbf{F}_S + \mathbf{F}_C$) together and feed them into a discriminative classifier.

Our method is a very flexible feature-based method, where the structural features can be put into any discriminative classifier for classification. In this paper, we evaluate our method based on SVM and Logistic regression. Specifically, we adopt LibSVM [4] for one-vs-rest classification.

DISCUSSION

The high and real-time streams of interactions between human and ubiquitous things call for online processing techniques that are suitable to large-scale datasets and can be rapidly updated, adapted to reflect the constantly evolving the contextual similarities due to changing contextual information of things (e.g., social networks, status, locations etc). Our proposed model can be easily extended to deal with large-scale IoT data streams with online processing and incremental techniques due to the following characteristics of the model:

- We characterize each thing as a discriminative feature descriptor including static features (e.g., content-based features) and easily integrated dynamic features (e.g., locations, and instantaneous status of things). The feature vectors can be continuously updated with users' interactions with things in a real-time manner. It is noted that we only focus on training an offline model with the mixture of static and dynamic features, which provides the possibility of online learning, such as partaking in an incremental activity learning a framework that is able to continuously update and learn newly seen data.
- Our proposed model does not require any explicit input from users. All the contextual information is automatically obtained from users' social networks, localization techniques and sensor technologies in a non-obtrusive way.
- The process of contextual similarity calculation works based on the random walk techniques, which has been successfully used in large-scale online search engines. This type of techniques can be easily parallelized (e.g., using Hadoop framework for improving performance) and processed in real time.

10.5 APPLICABILITY OF DISCOR-T: THINGS RECOMMENDATION

Things recommendation is a crucial step for promoting and taking full advantage of Internet of Things (IoT), where it benefits the individuals, businesses, and society on a daily basis in terms of two main aspects. On the one hand, it can deliver relevant things to users based on users' preferences and interests. On the other hand, it can also serve to optimize the time and cost of using IoT in a particular situation. Physical things, in reality, have multiple unique attributes. For example, they have stated (e.g., in use or not in use; expired or not expired). When a certain thing is in use, it can not be used simultaneously by another user. Under this circumstance, a recommender system can refer the user to a list of things which have same or similar functionalities. For example, if microwave 1 is in use, microwave 2 will be recommended to a user who would like to warm her food.

In this section, we briefly introduce a probabilistic model for effective Thing-of-Interest recommendation over the entity graph, RGT. More details can refer to [39]. Fig. 10.5 shows our model that fuses social network, things correlations and user-

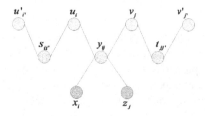

FIGURE 10.5

Our model: x_i and z_j are the explicit features (e.g., textual descriptions) of users and things respectively; $s_{ii'}$ and $t_{jj'}$ denote users friendship and things correlations, while y_{ij} denote interactions between users and things; u_i, $u'_{i'}$, v_j, $v'_{j'}$ are the latent factors induced from the three relationships

thing interactions, and incorporates three relationships: user-user connections $s_{ii'}$, thing-thing correlations $t_{jj'}$ (obtained from RGT) and user-thing interactions (thing usage) y_{ij} with shared factors u_i and v_j. We describe how to encode these two relationship matrices.

ENCODING USER FRIENDSHIPS

User affinity can directly adopt the method in Section 10.3.2. We construct a directed weighted graph $\mathbf{G}_u = (V_u, E_v)$, whose vertex set V_u corresponds to users set $\{u_1, ..., u_m\}$, edges set E_v represents the friendships between users and the range of their associated weight are in $[0, 1]$. Bigger weights represent stronger ties between users. W_u indicates the user similarity influenced by the social links between users, reflecting the *homophily* (i.e., similar users may have similar interests). We use the cosine similarity to calculated $s_{ii'}$ as follows:

$$s_{ii'} = \frac{e^{\alpha \cos(b(i), b(i'))}}{\sum_{k \in \Omega(i)} e^{\alpha \cos(b(i), (b(k)))}} \qquad (10.20)$$

where $\cos(b(i), b(i')) = \dfrac{b(i) \cdot b(i')}{\|b(i)\| \|b(i')\|}$, $\Omega(i)$ is the set of the user i's friends (i.e., $j \in \Omega(i)$), $b(i)$ is the binary vector of things used by user i, $\| \cdot \|$ is the L-2 norm of vector $b(\cdot)$, and α is a parameter that reflects the preference for transitioning to a user who interacts with the same things.

After we obtain the users friendship matrix from $\mathbf{G}_u$, we factorize users' friendship matrix to derive a high-quality, low dimensional feature representation to user-based latent features vectors $u_i \in \mathbb{R}^{1 \times m}$ and factor-based latent feature vectors $u'_{i'} \in \mathbb{R}^{1 \times m}$ on analyzing the social network graph $\mathbf{G}_u$. The conditional probability of $s_{ii'}$ over the observed social network is determined by:

$$s_{ii'} \sim Pr(s_{ii'}|u_i^T u'_{i'}; \sigma_s)$$
$$\text{where} \quad u_i \sim \mathcal{N}(0, \sigma_u^2), u'_{i'} \sim \mathcal{N}(0, \sigma_{u'}^2) \qquad (10.21)$$

Similar to the Web link adjacency [43], if a user i has lots of links to other users, the trust value of $s_{ii'}$ should be decreased. Whereas if a user i is trusted by many other users, the trust value of $s_{ii'}$ should be increased, since the user can be considered as local authority. $s_{ii'}$ should be adjusted as:

$$s_{ii'}^* = \sqrt{\frac{d^{in}(i')}{d^{out}(i) + d^{in}(i')}} \times S_{ii'} \qquad (10.22)$$

where $d^{out}(i)$ represents the outdegree of node i, while $d^{in}(i')$ indicates the indegree of i'. Eq. (10.21) can be reformulated as:

$$s_{ii'}^* \sim Pr(s_{ii'}^* | u^T u'; \sigma_s) \qquad (10.23)$$

ENCODING USER-THING INTERACTIONS

User-thing interactions y_{ij} are embodied by the usage frequency of thing i by user j in a certain time frame. We can map the usage frequency to interval [0, 1] by using function $f(x) = (x - y_{min})/(y_{max} - y_{min})$ without loss of generality, where y_{max} and y_{min} are the maximum and minimum usage values respectively. The dyadic relationship between a user and a thing does not only depend on their latent factor $U^T V$, whose vulnerability is that it makes use of past interactions and can not handle brand new things well, i.e., cold start problem. To tackle this issue, we use the explicit features directly by profiling users observable features $x_i \in \mathbb{R}^c$ (i.e., age, gender, location etc.) and things observable features $z_j \in \mathbb{R}^d$ (i.e., textual description of things functionalities). Here, c and d are the dimensionalities of users observable features and things observable features respectively. The dyadic relationship (thing usage value) depends on not only the inner product of latent factors of users and things, but also their observable features. Things usage value y_{ij} can be defined as the following conditional probability:

$$y_{ij} \sim Pr(y_{ij} | u_i, v_j, x_i, z_j, \sigma_y^2) \qquad (10.24)$$

We adopt the bilinear product to specify the similarity between user observable features and thing observable features [7]. The pairwise similarity between x_i and z_j can be denoted as:

$$r_{ij} = \mathbf{w}^T (x_i \otimes z_j) \qquad (10.25)$$

where $\mathbf{w}$ is a column vector of entries $\{w_{mn}\}$, $x_i \otimes z_j$ denotes the Kronecker product of x_i and z_j. Eq. (10.25) can be rewritten as:

$$r_{ij} = x_i^T W z_j \qquad (10.26)$$

where matrix $W \in \mathbb{R}^{m \times n}$ is a weight coefficients capturing pairwise associations between user i's explicit feature vector and thing j's explicit feature vector. The thing usage value depends on both the inner product of user and thing latent factors and the bilinear product of user observable features and thing observable features. Eq. (10.24) can be reformulated as:

$$y_{ij} \sim Pr(y_{ij}|u_i^T v_j + r_{ij}, \sigma_y^2) \tag{10.27}$$

MODEL LEARNING

Given a training dataset for $\mathbb{O} = \{\mathbb{O}_y, \mathbb{O}_s, \mathbb{O}_t\}$, the joint posterior probability of model parameters Σ can be obtained through Bayes' theorem:

$$Pr(\Sigma|\mathbb{O}) \propto Pr(\mathbb{O}|\Sigma)Pr(\Sigma) \tag{10.28}$$

Maximizing Eq. (10.28) can be converted to minimizing the negative logarithm of $Pr(\mathbb{O}|\Sigma)Pr(\Sigma)$ via:

$$\min_{\Sigma} L(\Sigma) = \min \lambda_y \sum_{ij \in \mathbb{O}_y} \ell(y_{ij}, u_i^T v_j + r_{ij})$$
$$+ \lambda_s \sum_{ii' \in \mathbb{O}_s} \ell(s_{ii'}^*, u_i^T u_{i'}') + \lambda_t \sum_{jj' \in \mathbb{O}_t} \ell(t_{jj'}, v_j^T v_{j'}')$$
$$+ \lambda_{\mathbf{w}} \|\mathbf{w}\|^2 + \lambda_u \|u\|^2 + \lambda_{u'} \|u'\|^2 + \lambda_v \|v\|^2 + \lambda_{v'} \|v'\|^2 \tag{10.29}$$

where $\ell \cdot$ is a loss function (we adopt the most widely used ℓ_2 loss), and $\lambda = \{\lambda_y, \lambda_s, \lambda_t, \lambda_{\mathbf{w}}, \lambda_u, \lambda_{u'}, \lambda_v, \lambda_{v'}\}$ are trade-off parameters. A gradient descent process can be implemented to solve the parameters. Given a training dataset $\{y_{ij}\}$, the objective function in Eq. (10.29) can be found by performing gradient descent in u_i, v_j and w_{mn}.

$$u_i \rightarrow u_i - \delta \times (\frac{\partial \ell}{\partial u_i}(y_{ij}, u^T v + r_{ij})v_j + u_i^T u_i)$$

$$v_j \rightarrow v_j - \delta \times (\frac{\partial \ell}{\partial v_j}(y_{ij}, u^T v + r_{ij})u_i + v_j^T v_j)$$

$$w \rightarrow w - \delta \times (\frac{\partial \ell}{\partial w}(y_{ij}, u^T v + r_{ij})u_i v_j^T + w^T w)$$

$$u'_{i'} \rightarrow u'_{i'} - \delta \times (\frac{\partial \ell}{\partial u'_{i'}}(s_{ii'}^*, u_i^T u'_{i'})u_i + u'^T_{i'} u'_{i'})$$

$$v'_{j'} \rightarrow v'_{j'} - \delta \times (\frac{\partial \ell}{\partial v'_{j'}}(t_{jj'}, v_j^T v'_{j'})v_j + v'^T_{j'} v'_{j'}) \tag{10.30}$$

where δ is the learning rate. After we obtain the optimal parameters Σ^*, we can use them to predict the given testing data $\{\tilde{i}, \tilde{j}, y_{\tilde{i}, \tilde{j}}\}$

$$y_{\tilde{i}\tilde{j}} = u_{\tilde{i}}^T v_{\tilde{j}} + \sum_{mn}^{cd} x_{\tilde{i}n} z_{\tilde{j}m} w_{mn}^* \tag{10.31}$$

Table 10.1 Dataset			
No.	**Category**	**# Things**	**# Labels**
1	Entertainment	28	118
2	Office	20	51
3	Cooking	25	103
4	Transportation	11	24
5	Medicine/Medical	10	18
6	Home Appliances	33	83

10.6 EXPERIMENTS

10.6.1 EXPERIMENT SETUP

Due to the lack of experimental public data sets, we set up a testbed that consists of several different places in the first author's home (e.g., bedroom, bathroom, garage, kitchen etc), where approximate 127 physical things (e.g., couch, laptop, microwave, fridge etc.) are monitored by attaching RFID and sensors. Table 10.1 presents the statistics of things used in this paper. The details in regards to this testbed can refer to [37]. To collect the records of things usage events, we need to figure out i) how to detect a usage event when it is happening; and ii) how to retrieve this thing's corresponding three contextual information. There are two ways to detect usage events of things with two identification technologies used, namely *senor-based state changes* and *RFID-based mobility detection.*

To conduct experimental studies, we manually labeled 127 things with 397 different labels. It should be noted that some things belong to multiple categories, therefore having multiple labels. For example, a *Wii* device belongs to category label *Entertainment* as well as *Home Appliance*. This dataset serves as the ground-truth dataset in our experiments for performance evaluation. Ten volunteers participated in the data collection phase by interacting with RFID tagged things for a period of four months, generating 20,179 records on the interactions of the things tagged in the experiments.

10.6.2 EVALUATION ON THING ANNOTATION

We randomly removed the category tags of a certain percentage, ranging from 10% to 50%, of things from each category of the ground-truth dataset. These things were used to test our approach while the rest were used as the training set. We iterated five times for each training percentage and took the averaged value as the final result. Our algorithm produces a vector of probabilities, representing the assignment probabilities of all labels for an unknown object. In our experiments, we ranked these probabilities and chose the top k labels to compare with the ground truth labels. The k value was set to the number of ground truth labels for each unknown object and it varies from object to object. The parameters α and β were set as 0.5 each.

We particularly compared the annotation performance by using i) the features obtained from **G**, ii) the features obtained from thing descriptions (i.e., content features

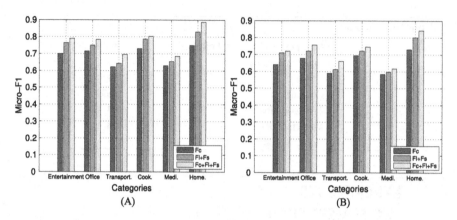

FIGURE 10.6

Overall performance comparison: (A) Micro-F1, (B) Macro-F1

$\mathbf{F_C}$), and iii) the combination of the both. Each process was repeated 10 times and the average results were recorded. Similar observations were obtained for different testing percentages. Fig. 10.6 shows the result when we removed 30% of things from each category of the ground-truth dataset. Descriptions of things are normally short and noisy, it is therefore not surprising that the performance based on content features only is worse than the one based on implicit structural features (i.e., $\mathbf{F_L} + \mathbf{F_S}$) in most categories. The consistent good performance from the latent features also indicates that our top-k correlation graphs $\mathbf{G}$ is able to capture the correlations among things well. From the figure, we can see that by combining the two together, the performance of all six categories is increased and is the best consistently among the three.

10.6.3 EVALUATION ON RECOMMENDATION

We compare the prediction accuracy of our approach based on fusing social networks and things correlations (FST) with some state-of-the-art approaches based on probabilistic factor analysis: Probabilistic Matrix Factorization (PMF) [23], SoRec [16] and SVD++ [12]. This experiment evaluated our approach, in particular, its capability in handling the cold start problem, which refers to providing accurate prediction when some users only use few things or even have no usage historical records at all. In order to verify the capability of our approach to predicting the usage value of things that have not been used, we randomly selected and marked off $p\%$ of data ($p = 10$, 20 and 50) from our dataset as training data and different number of latent factors (5 and 10) to test all the methods. The experimental results are shown in Table 10.2.

From the table, it is clear that our approach outperforms other methods on different training ratios and different number of factors, especially when the training data is small. PMF is a pure probabilistic factor model. Relying heavily on user-thing usage matrix, it can not deal with the circumstance where little interactions

Table 10.2 MAE Comparison with Other Approaches						
Training Data	10%		20%		50%	
# of Factors	5	10	5	10	5	10
PMF	0.8635	0.8544	0.8245	0.8153	0.7662	0.7495
SVD++	0.8425	0.8311	0.8004	0.7982	0.7410	0.7273
SoRec	0.8103	0.7978	0.7872	0.7723	0.7317	0.7168
FST	**0.7303**	**0.7246**	**0.7112**	**0.6948**	**0.6631**	**0.6406**

information is available. SoRec works better than PMF and SVD++ because of its aggregation of user-user internal information (social links). Our approach not only incorporates users and things internal information, but also defines the explicit features (i.e., content) for users (e.g., users profile) and things (e.g., description of things functionalities), which makes our approach performing better when there is a cold start problem. The experimental result further demonstrates the effectiveness on improving the recommendation accuracy by incorporating things correlations.

10.7 RELATED WORK

Finding related and similar things is a key service and the most straightforward method of finding related things is the traditional keyword-based search, where user querying keyword is matched with the extracted description of things including textual descriptions on thing's functionalities and non-functional properties. For example, in Microsearch [27] and Snoogle [32], each sensor is attached to a connected object, which carries a keyword-based description of each object. Following an ad hoc query consisting of a list of keywords, the system returns a ranked list of the top k entities matching this query. As we pointed out, this method can not work well for ubiquitous things due to unique characteristics, e.g., insufficient description of things, the inconsistency of the meaning of the textual information, more importantly, this solution does not make use of implicit inter-correlations between things and their rich contextual information.

Another mainstream solution is via semantic Web-related techniques. Such solutions typically use the metadata annotation (e.g., details related to a sensor such as sensor type, manufacturer, capability and contextual information), then use a query language to search related available things [18,5]. Online sensors such as Pachube,[3] GSN [1], Microsoft SensorMap [19] and linked sensor middleware [13] support search for sensors based on textual metadata that describes the sensors (e.g., type and location of a sensor, functional and non-functional attributes, object to which the sensor is attached), which is manually entered by the person who deploys the sensor. Other users can then search for sensors with certain metadata by entering appropriate

---

[3] https://pachube.com/.

keywords. Unfortunately, these ontology and their use are rather complex and it is uncertain whether end users can provide correct descriptions of sensors and their deployment context without the help from experts. In other words, such methods require extensive prior knowledge. There are efforts to provide a standardized vocabulary to describe sensors and their properties such as SensorML[4] and the Semantic Sensor Network Ontology (SSN),[5] but not widely adopted.

The above solutions are time-consuming and require expert knowledge. For example, the descriptions of things and their corresponding characteristics and ontology need to be predefined under a uniform format such as Resource Description Framework (RDF) or Schema.org.[6] In addition, the methods do not make full use of the rich information on users' historical interactions with things, which may imply containing implicit relations of different entities. For example, if some users have the similar usage pattern on certain things, it may indicate some close connections among these things. Existing solutions can not capture such information well. We propose to extract the underlying connections between things by exploiting the human-thing interactions in the ubiquitous environment. Our method not only takes rich contextual information of human-thing interactions into account but also utilizes the historical pattern by analyzing the past human-thing interactions.

10.8 CONCLUSION

Recent advances in radio-frequency identification (RFID), wireless sensor networks and Web services have made it possible to bridge the physical and digital worlds together, where ubiquitous things are becoming an integral part of our daily lives. Despite the exciting potential of this prosperous era, there are many challenges that persist. In this paper, we propose a novel model that derives latent correlations among things by exploiting user, temporal, and spatial information captured from things usage events. This correlation analysis can help solve many challenging issues in managing things such as things search, recommendation, annotation, classification, and clustering. The experimental results demonstrate the utility of our approach.

We view the work presented in this paper as a first step towards effective management of things in the emerging Web of Things (WoT) era.

There are a few interesting directions that we plan to work in the future:

- *Real-time things status update.* In the real situation, physical things are more dynamic compared to traditional Web resources. Examples of such dynamic features include availability, and changing attributes (e.g., geographical information, status). We plan to improve our model so that it can adaptively propagate up-to-date

---

[4]http://www.opengeospatial.org/standards/sensorml.
[5]http://www.w3.org/2005/Incubator/ssn/ssnx/ssn.
[6]http://schema.org/.

information from things correlations network and make more accurate recommendations.

- *Scalability.* We plan to improve the scalability of our approach by adopting constraints in searching a local area. This can be realized by applying generalized clustering algorithms on hypergraphs. The search space can be significantly pruned in this way. We also plan to evaluate the improved approach using real-world large-scale WoT datasets. We notice that some parameters (e.g., α and β) in our approach need to be tuned in a category specific way. This might be a burden to apply the algorithm to other WoT datasets. We will investigate ways to reduce the workload of parameter tuning e.g., by some meta-feature based methods or multi-task learning [14,42].
- *Thing-to-Thing communications.* Our current model works based on human-thing interactions to extract the latent connections between things. The communications between things are getting more prevalent with the development of communication technologies, which represent a rich source to exploit for making our current model more robust. Extending our model by analyzing and exploring the thing-to-thing communications is another future work.

REFERENCES

[1] Aberer K, Hauswirth M, Salehi A. A middleware for fast and flexible sensor network deployment. In: Proc of the 32nd intl conference on very large data bases. 2006. p. 1199–202.

[2] Baresi L, Mottola L, Dustdar S. Building software for the internet of things. IEEE Internet Comput 2015;19(2):6–8.

[3] Barnaghi P, Sheth A, Henson C. From data to actionable knowledge: big data challenges in the web of things. IEEE Intell Syst Nov 2013;28(6):6–11.

[4] Chang C, Lin C. Libsvm: a library for support vector machines. ACM Trans Intel Syst Technol (TIST) 2011;2(3):27.

[5] Christophe B, Verdot V, Toubiana V. Searching the web of things. In: Proceedings of the 5th international conference on semantic computing (ICSC). IEEE; 2011. p. 308–15.

[6] Christophe B, Verdot V, Toubiana V. Searching the web of things. In: Proc of the 5th IEEE intl conf on semantic computing. 2011. p. 308–15.

[7] Chu W, Park S-T. Personalized recommendation on dynamic content using predictive bilinear models. In: Proc of the 18th intl world wide web conf (WWW). 2009.

[8] Ferscha A. 20 years past Weiser: what's next? IEEE Pervasive Comput 2012;11(1):52–60.

[9] Guinard D, Trifa V, Mattern F, Wilde E. From the internet of things to the web of things: resource-oriented architecture and best practices. In: Architecting the Internet of things. Springer; 2011. p. 97–129.

[10] Kameda T, Ohtsubo Y, Takezawa M. Centrality in sociocognitive networks and social influence: an illustration in a group decision-making context. J Pers Soc Psychol 1997;73(2):296.

[11] Kindberg T, et al. People, places, things: web presence for the real world. Mob Netw Appl 2002;7(5):365–76.

[12] Koren Y. Factorization meets the neighborhood: a multifaceted collaborative filtering model. In: Proc of the 14th ACM SIGKDD intl conf on knowledge discovery and data mining. 2008.

[13] Le-Phuoc D, Quoc HNM, Parreira JX, Hauswirth M. The linked sensor middleware–connecting the real world and the semantic web. In: Proceedings of the semantic web challenge. 2011.

[14] Lee S-I, Chatalbashev V, Vickrey D, Koller D. Learning a meta-level prior for feature relevance from multiple related tasks. In: Proceedings of the 24th international conference on machine learning. ACM; 2007. p. 489–96.

[15] Leicht E, Newman M. Community structure in directed networks. Phys Rev Lett 2008;100(11).

[16] Ma H, Yang H, Lyu M, King I. Sorec: social recommendation using probabilistic matrix factorization. In: Proceedings of the 17th ACM conference on information and knowledge management. 2008. p. 931–40.

[17] Mathew SS, Atif Y, Sheng QZ, Maamar Z. The web of things: challenges and enabling technologies. In: Bessis N, Xhafa F, Varvarigou D, Hill R, Maozhen L, editors. Internet of things and inter-cooperative computational technologies for collective intelligence. Springer; 2013. p. 1–23.

[18] Mietz R, Groppe S, Römer K, Pfisterer D. Semantic models for scalable search in the internet of things. J Sensor Actuator Netw 2013;2(2):172–95.

[19] Nath S, Liu J, Zhao F. Sensormap for wide-area sensor webs. IEEE Comput 2007;40(7):90–3.

[20] Newman M. Finding community structure in networks using the eigenvectors of matrices. Phys Rev E 2006;74(3).

[21] Newman M, Girvan M. Finding and evaluating community structure in networks. Phys Rev E 2004;69(2).

[22] Qin Y, Sheng QZ, Falkner NJ, Dustdar S, Wang H, Vasilakos AV. When things matter: a survey on data-centric internet of things. J Netw Comput Appl 2016;64:137–53.

[23] Salakhutdinov R, Mnih A. Probabilistic matrix factorization. In: Proc of the 21st intl conf on neural information processing systems (NIPS). 2007.

[24] Salton G, Buckley C. Term-weighting approaches in automatic text retrieval. Inf Process Manag 1988;24(5):513–23.

[25] Segev A, Sheng QZ. Bootstrapping ontologies for web services. IEEE Trans Serv Comput 2012;5(1):33–44.

[26] Sheng QZ, Li X, Zeadally S. Enabling next-generation RFID applications: solutions and challenges. IEEE Comput 2008;41(9):21–8.

[27] Tan CC, Sheng B, Wang H, Li Q. Microsearch: a search engine for embedded devices used in pervasive computing. ACM Trans Embed Comput Syst 2010;9(4):43.

[28] Tang L, Liu H. Relational learning via latent social dimensions. In: Proceedings of the 15th ACM SIGKDD international conference on knowledge discovery and data mining. ACM; 2009. p. 817–26.

[29] Tong H, Faloutsos C, Pan J. Fast walk with restart and its applications. In: Proceedings of the 6th international conference on data mining (ICDM'06), Hong Kong, China. December 2006.

[30] Vitali M, Pernici B. A survey on energy efficiency in information systems. Int J Coop Inf Syst 2014;23(3).

[31] Vlachos M, Meek C, Vagena Z, Gunopulos D. Identifying similarities, periodicities and bursts for online search queries. In: Proceedings of the 2004 ACM SIGMOD international conference on management of data. ACM; 2004. p. 131–42.

[32] Wang H, Tan CC, Li Q. Snoogle: a search engine for the physical world. In: Proceedings of the 27th conference on computer communications (INFOCOM 2008). IEEE; 2008.

[33] Xia J, Caragea D, Hsu W. Bi-relational network analysis using a fast random walk with restart. In: 2009 ninth IEEE international conference on data mining (ICDM'09). Miami, USA: IEEE; 2009. p. 1052–7.

[34] Yao L, Benatallah B, Wang X, Tran NK, Lu Q. Context as a service: realizing internet of things-aware processes for the independent living of the elderly. In: International conference on service-oriented computing. Springer; 2016. p. 763–79.

[35] Hristopulos DT. Spartan Gibbs random field models for geostatistical applications. SIAM J Sci Comput 2003;24(6):2125–62.

[36] Yao L, Sheng QZ, Dustdar S. Web-based management of the internet of things. IEEE Internet Comput July/August 2015;19(4):60–7.

[37] Yao L, Sheng QZ, Dustdar S. Web-based management of the internet of things. IEEE Internet Comput 2015;19(4):60–7.

[38] Yao L, Sheng QZ, Falkner NJ, Ngu AH. Thingsnavi: finding most-related things via multi-dimensional modeling of human-thing interactions. In: Proceedings of the 11th international conference on mobile and ubiquitous systems: computing, networking and services. ICST (Institute for Computer Sciences, Social-Informatics and Telecommunications Engineering); 2014. p. 20–9.

[39] Yao L, Sheng QZ, Ngu AH, Li X. Things of interest recommendation by leveraging heterogeneous relations in the internet of things. ACM Trans Internet Technol 2016;16(2):9.

[40] Yao L, et al. A model for discovering correlations of ubiquitous things. In: Proc of the 13th IEEE intl conf on data mining (ICDM). 2013.

[41] Ye M, Shou D, Lee W, Yin P, Janowicz K. On the semantic annotation of places in location-based social networks. In: Proceeding of the 17th ACM SIGKDD international conference on knowledge discovery and data mining, San Diego, CA, USA. August 2011.

[42] Zhang Y, Yeung DY. Multi-task learning in heterogeneous feature spaces. In: 25th AAAI conference on artificial intelligence and the 23rd innovative applications of artificial intelligence conference. Proceedings of the national conference on artificial intelligence. 2011.

[43] Zhou D, Schölkopf B, Hofmann T. Semi-supervised learning on directed graphs. In: Proc of the 18th conf on neural information processing systems (NIPS). 2004.

BUILDING INTEROPERABLE AND CROSS-DOMAIN SEMANTIC WEB OF THINGS APPLICATIONS

11

Amelie Gyrard*, **Martin Serrano***, **Pankesh Patel**[†]

*Insight Centre for Data Analytics, IoT Unit, National University of Ireland, Galway, Ireland**

ABB Corporate Research, Bangalore, KN, India[†]

CHAPTER POINTS

- The evolution from IoT and Web of Things to Semantic Web of Things is explained.
- Semantic web technologies applied to the Internet of Things domain are presented.
- This chapter mainly focuses on extending the semantic part for the Web of Things.
- We explain the proposed M3 framework and how to assist developers and system integrators in easily integrating semantic web technologies.
- We focus on semantically annotating data, inferring meaningful information from WoT data and reusing knowledge expertise to build smarter WoT applications.

11.1 INTRODUCTION: UNDERSTANDING TRENDS AND THE EVOLUTION

The **Internet of Things (IoT)** vision is to connect sensors embedded into devices with the Internet and exploiting their services and functional capabilities [1,3]. The multiple number of IoT applications are likely to revolutionize every aspects of our lives. For instance, Oral-B[1] connected to the toothbrush controls dental hygiene. The Apple HealthKit[2] tracks fitness, nutrition and sleep. However, the existing IoT applications largely focus on building dedicated scenarios and this limit the evolution

---

[1]http://connectedtoothbrush.com/, Last visited: September 2016.
[2]http://goo.gl/n2V42g, Last visited: September 2016.

Managing the Web of Things. DOI: 10.1016/B978-0-12-809764-9.00014-7

of the IoT because each time new resources/devices are added, technical skills and ad-hoc adaptations are required using their own protocols and their proprietary data formats. Since such applications are already deployed and operating for a particular purpose, the main challenge is working on data interoperability in order to make the applications interoperable with each other. The main benefits are the possibility to compose simple applications to build more complex ones, but also to combine heterogeneous applicative domains to build innovative applications that co-exist with the already deployed ones.

On the other hand, in the last two decades the Web technologies have become very popular. In many areas, web solutions are the only option to make business, mainly because its potential capacity for ecosystem expansion of the number of users and because it is relatively simple to use, reliable and portable to multiple technology platforms (i.e. smart phones, smart TVs, tablets, laptops, computers, etc.). The most important aspect of the Web is the loose coupling between applications and computing servers. An example is HTTP that decouples a server and an application that accesses the server, the developer can change the functionality of the server without breaking the system. The **Web of Things (WoT)** [2,18] has been already considered a part of the core activities in the Internet of Things – *leveraging what made the Web so successful and applying their principles to the physical devices* [4]. The Web of Things is what makes possible that Internet of Things (IoT) developments and data can be accessible to a large number of Web developers and business designers and thus re-using the already available knowledge on the web to enhance IoT applications. System integrators and solution providers benefit from this accessibility and enable new and innovative cross-domain IoT applications.

Recently, the combination of features and functional characteristics around the Internet of Things and the current demands in computing and processing capacity relay in the use of the cloud as the medium to solve interoperability issues, erroneously the cloud has been claimed as an interoperability facilitator, together with the Web technologies and the existing interoperability data services the cloud is making the IoT data manageable at the edge and particularly when IoT interoperability is required at the device level. This is called Fog of The Internet of Things or simply **Fog of Things** [34]. Fog of things aims for providing value to the data before making it available to the web facilitating the interoperability of the devices at the edge and preparing the managed data for further applications to be interoperable. This approach has demonstrated that the decoupling between physical devices and the web and bringing the computing capacity of the cloud down to the device is possible, explaining in details the Fog of Things is out of the scope in this chapter but it is mention here as a matter of comprehensive summary and consideration in the IoT evolution.

Following the evolution, and the main objective of this chapter to identify methodologies for building cross-domain interoperability, not less important is the new trend following the integration of semantic web technologies to enhance the data and promote its use in multiple and diverse applications, also called **Semantic Web of Things (SWoT)** [13,14]. SWoT is independent of any domain, data can be generated by one domain and used in complementary domains. The best example here is an open data portal, where the data is offered to any developers to make use of it. The data format is specified and mostly generic, thus multiple use applications can be developed. For example, a data set containing information about the number of available spaces in a car park, can be used in different applications: for offering available spaces, but also for pre-booking or simply for estimating the occupancy of the place, etc. Semantic web technologies bring several benefits: 1) Semantically annotating sensor datasets to unify heterogeneous data and explicitly describe metadata, 2) enriching semantic sensor datasets with external knowledge graphs available on the Web to add value to them and most important operate them in a more knowledge-based manner, and 3) performing analytics on data by means of applied logic and reasoning mechanisms to deduce meaningful additional information from data.

In this chapter, we will focus on this last trend, assuming that Internet of Things and Web of Things have resolved the challenging aspects of transparently sharing information with a defined format amongst devices. In the next section, we describe a simple SWoT application, more complex ones could have been included but the main intention is to simplify the understanding process and highlight advantages when using semantic web technologies. The scenario is relevant when we observe the added capabilities for cross-domain usage and interoperablity of the information. It is also the main objective to use this simple approach to illustrate characteristics and motivation for building interoperable and cross-domain SWoT applications based on those identified characteristics. Annotated and metadata aggregations are considered here as part of the methodologies to enable interoperability.

A thermometer could be plugged into the Web to retrieve data and an application on the Web will show statistical and analytical information to make the user of the thermometer aware of the conditions. Most of the existing Internet of Things applications would just enable the visualization of the data produced by the thermometer in the form of a "dashboard" including location on where and when data was collected, trends and perhaps some forecasting on what could happen based on historical and other external sensor data information (i.e. humidity, pressure, etc.). Beyond that non-special solution, the example in this case is the need for building an application that assists the humans to automatically interpret the visualized data and combines analytical and statistical data while reusing knowledge databases designed by specialist experts. This mean the usage of healthcare databases to define if the temperature reported by the thermometer located in a room is affecting the body temperature of the people. For instance, people having asthma will be more prone to have problems if the temperature is not controlled adequately. The Web of Things will work to have all the thermometers "talking" with each other and via web applications. It will also simplify the decision making of the building manager by taking the most optimal average temperature according to pre-defined conditions such as period of the year (e.g., summer, winter, spring) or the time of the day (e.g., morning, evening, etc.). The Semantic Web of Things application would additionally help to identify the patterns that has been reported historically as problematics and based on specific periods and use of the data to correlate with current knowledge databases that report similar symptoms. The developers using SWoT approach can design such applications to combine the data produced by the body thermometer with the healthcare knowledge databases. More services can be offered for example when there is detected an increase in the normal body temperature. Not only healthcare knowledge databases can be used but also additional ones to suggest causes and home remedies. This example shows the necessity of making not only two different domains interoperable: Healthcare and Food but it also highlights the need for reusing domain-knowledge expertise (e.g., models to structure data and reasoning mechanisms to add value to data) available on the Web. This example emphasizes on integrating a reasoning mechanism specific to cross-domain knowledge databases but also the need to add value to data which is the main objective of using SWoT.

At this point, we have described the evolution and the main differences in the Internet of Things mayor trends, i.e. Internet of Things, Web of Things, Fog of Things and Semantic Web of Things. In the next section, we focus on describing application development requirements to build cross-domain Semantic Web of Things applications.

The remainder of this chapter is organized as follows: Section 11.2 reviews the related work that applies Semantic Web to IoT and work towards identifying the most common challenges for enabling cross-domain interoperability. Moreover, a study about the limitations of the existing work and the justification about the need of a comprehensive framework for SWoT is explained. Section 11.3 presents our contributions and the M3 framework that focuses on the semantic part of the WoT and which primary objective is for assisting developers in designing SWoT applications. Section 11.4 summarizes this chapter and describes briefly some future directions for the SWoT area and the refinement of the M3 framework.

11.2 RELATED WORK AND CHALLENGES IDENTIFICATION

This section introduces the most relevant work that could be applied to WoT regarding data interoperability, its modeling and reasoning mechanisms integrating semantic web technologies and addressing the research challenges towards enabling SWoT interoperability.

11.2.1 TECHNICAL REQUIREMENTS

In this section, we review application development requirements as learned from the analysis of application examples, research studies and based on practical implementation of Internet of Things solutions and Web of Things modeling in the context of OpenIoT framework[3] and VITAL platform[4] and FIESTA-IoT portal.[5] The

---

[3] http://www.openiot.eu/, Open Source Middleware for the Internet of Things.
[4] http://vital-iot.eu/, The future of connecting IoT smart city systems.
[5] http://fiesta-iot.eu/, Federated Semantic interoperability for Internet of Things systems.

projects have been coordinated and the implementations and developments lead by consortium technical team. We focus in providing a selection of challenges based on identified solutions on how to build cross-domain interoperability.

Ensuring interoperability among heterogeneous data. Devices are not interoperable with each other since data is exchanged following non standardized protocols using proprietary data formats and they do not use common taxonomies or vocabularies. Usually, IoT devices provide unformatted data names as "raw" sensor data. This "raw" sensor data does not contain any additional description or metadata and requires specialized knowledge and manual effort in order to build cross-domain applications.

Deducing meaningful information from raw data. Users are primarily interested in real-world entities (such as people, places and things) and their high-level knowledge (e.g., deriving snowfall from temperature and precipitation measurements, a body temperature is abnormal or not) rather than raw output data produced by sensors attached with these entities.

Reusing and integrating the domain knowledge already available on the Web to enable WoT data. Knowledge already available in the web can be used to simplify complex knowledge operations, for instance, knowledge bases already designed for smart homes could be reused to describe a smart home which comprises thermometers, smoke detectors, humidity sensors and their related actions to take. This reusability is crucial in the Web of Things in order to enable data interoperability.

Ensuring interoperability among WoT projects. Taking inspiration from "*sharing and reuse*" approaches, an effort should be done to reuse data, vocabularies, designs, and softwares already done in the past to encourage reusability but also to build composite and interoperable applications that uses annotated data for enabling the creation of more WoT services. There is a need to study the existing projects and find a common pattern of the components constantly redesigned (e.g., the model to structure data or the reasoning mechanisms).

Combining different application domains. Combining different domains could enable smarter applications. It requires an interoperable domain knowledge to easily navigate from one domain-specific knowledge graph to another. This approach takes inspiration from the Semantic Web community designing Ontology Design Patterns (ODPs) [5] and Ontology Networks [9].

In addition to the listed requirements, achieving such challenges would help to enable a more directional approach towards building interoperable solutions, best SWoT practices are founded to encourage replicability. The most important is to work on:

- *Reducing the time spent for developing WoT applications.* In order to create interoperable and cross-domain SWoT applications, developers have to perform various tasks such as designing an application, semantically annotating data and interpreting data. To perform these tasks, developers have to learn semantic web technologies and tools, a time consuming process, which can take several months. Reducing this gap as much as possible can be done by empowering a framework that assist developers in designing interoperable applications without learning semantic web technologies.

• *Reducing the learning curve required by WoT developers to integrate semantic web technologies.* Fast prototyping of semantic-based WoT applications by hiding the use of semantic web technologies as much as possible is required to avoid the developers burden on designing ontologies, semantic annotators and reasoning mechanisms to enrich their data. An extensive work with Web frameworks (e.g., Drupal, Wordpress) has been done to design pre-defined templates to automatically generate web sites to avoid users dealing with Web technologies. Based on this idea, pre-defined templates to design SWoT applications can be created.

11.2.2 SEMANTICALLY ANNOTATING DATA

This section presents approaches that leverage the semantic web technologies for annotating data and achieve data interoperability.

Semantic Sensor Web is designed to semantically annotate sensor data with Semantic Web languages such as Resource Description Framework in Attributes (RDFa) [22]. Semantic Sensor Web uses and defines ontologies to support interoperability over heterogeneous environments and to describe concepts and units related to applicative domain. It also introduced the idea to reason over semantic sensor data to infer new knowledge in two domain-specific scenarios: weather and healthcare. For instance, in the weather domain "Potentially Icy", "Low Visibility" and "High Winds" can be deduced. Semantic Sensor Web leads to a set of tools such as SemSOS [23] and IntelligO [12]. SemSOS has been designed for accessing and querying sensor data on the web. SemSOS uses the 52° North's SOS[6] implementation and enriches the SOS service with semantic annotations. Both tools uses semantic web technologies to manage sensors measurements.

Linked Sensor Data is an approach to semantically annotate the MesoWest weather dataset to publish a unified dataset on the web available as Linked Data [24]. Linked Open Data (LOD) is an open-based sharing and reusing approach for publishing, sharing, reusing and combining data on the Web [25]. It is based on Sensor Web Enablement (SWE) [16] standards to retrieve sensor measurements, convert data encoded with O&M[7] into RDF,[8] and then publish semantic sensor datasets on the Web. The datasets comprise 20,000 sensors, 160 million sensor observations and 1.7 billion RDF statements. Datasets have been enriched with contextual information using the GeoNames dataset to deduce regions, etc. Real sensor datasets have been semantically annotated to design specific applications without having in mind application interoperability.

---

[6]http://52north.org/communities/sensorweb/sos/.

[7]O&M stands for Observations and Measurements, http://www.opengeospatial.org/standards/om.

[8]RDF stands for Resource Description Framework, http://www.w3.org/TR/REC-rdf-syntax/.

Linked Sensor Middleware is an open source middleware where more than 110,000 sensors from open data endpoints are included. LSM follows the W3C[9] SSN extended Group recommendations. The SSN ontology, [15] is one of the main outcome of the extended group and was originally designed for agriculture, ocean observations, smart vineyard and smart farm scenarios which have been extensively used in IoT domains.

LD4Sensors is an approach to semantically annotate sensor data coming from different platforms (e.g., from different weather stations) and link data together [6]. This mechanism is called "Linked Data for Sensors" and enables aggregating same kind of data generated by heterogeneous devices using heterogeneous terms. The LD4Sensors approach also attaches explicit metadata to raw data by using semantic web technologies and enables publishing "linking sensor data" on the web, so other users can reuse it to build innovative applications.

11.2.3 KNOWLEDGE DISCOVERY: REUSING DOMAIN KNOWLEDGE

To ease interoperability among WoT applications and services, reusing existing ontologies is highly encouraged. In this section, semantic search engines and ontology & dataset repositories for reusing the background knowledge available on the Web are briefly studied and presented.

11.2.3.1 Semantic Search Engines

The **Neon** project provides ontology methodologies, and suggests semantic web search engines to find and reuse domain ontologies [9]. Since the integration of semantic web technologies within IoT is emerging, frequently, a new ontology is redesigned instead of reusing the existing ones as preconized by Noy et al.: "an ontology is designed to be shared and reused" [10]. Semantic search engines such as **Sindice** [35], **Watson** and **Swoogle** [38] cannot reference relevant domain ontologies for WoT since they are not published online most of the time. There is a real need to spread semantic web best practices within the IoT community. A comprehensive survey of the best practices for publishing, sharing and reusing IoT ontologies is summarized [7]. For instance, tools to automatically document ontologies are referenced, and recommendations for adding ontology metadata and publishing the ontology online with a good namespace are given.

11.2.3.2 Ontology and Dataset Repositories

Datalift [8] is a project assisting people in semantically annotating and linking data, but not in IoT area and it does not provide any vocabularies relevant for IoT. Datalift provides the **Linked Open Vocabularies (LOV)** [17], an ontology catalogue, mainly known by semantic web experts. LOV lacks of ontologies relevant for IoT, and does not accept new ontologies if they do not follow semantic web best practices.

---

[9]W3C stands for World Wide Web Consortium.

DataHub is a dataset catalogue and does not provide quality checking when submitting a new dataset which leads to interoperability issues when consumers want to reuse and combine datasets.

11.2.4 DEDUCING MEANINGFUL INFORMATION FROM DATA

To interpret IoT data, the existing approaches explained in this section are mainly based on machine learning based approaches such as clustering to extract useful information from data. However, as previously mentioned in Section 11.2.2, some projects used semantic web technologies to annotate data. From a more practical point of view, it would be easier to use Semantic Web Rule Language (SWRL)[10] and reasoning/inference engines to reason on data.

IntellegO is a semantic perception approach to interpret and reason on sensor data [12]. IntellegO uses an abductive logic framework and Parsimonious Covering Theory (PCT) to interpret data based on an "ontology of perception". The development and reuse of the background knowledge (i.e., domain knowledge designed by domain experts for instance in healthcare) required for interpreting data is a difficult task and is not considered in this work.

Knowledge Acquisition Toolkit (KAT) enables pre-processing and cleansing of data to reduce the traffic in network communications [33]. KAT is composed of three components: 1) An extension of Symbolic Aggregate Approximation (SAX) algorithm, called SensorSAX, 2) abductive reasoning based on the Parsimonious Covering Theory (PCT), and 3) temporal and spatial reasoning. KAT is based on machine learning techniques (k-means clustering and Markov model methods). However, KAT neither deduces meaningful information from sensor data nor exploits domain-specific background knowledge relevant for IoT, which is already available on the web.

11.2.5 RELEVANT SEMANTIC-BASED WOT PROJECTS

In this section existing approaches and projects working on interoperability by integrating semantic web technologies to WoT platforms are described: Spitfire, Open-IoT, CityPulse, VITAL, and FIESTA-IoT.

SPITFIRE introduced the Semantic Web of Things concept to integrate semantic web technologies to the Web of Things [26]. SPITFIRE connected the real world of things and the Web by proposing concepts, methods and software infrastructure. Spitfire provided tools such as smart-service-proxy, LD4Sensors for linking sensor data presented above, Web-based Task Assignment and execution (WebTAsX), visualizer server and gateway connection mapper.

OpenIoT[11] is an open-source IoT platform enabling the semantic interoperability of IoT services in the cloud [27]. OpenIoT introduced the *"Sensing-as-a-Service"*

---

[10]https://www.w3.org/Submission/SWRL/.
[11]http://www.openiot.eu/, Last visited: September 2016.

principle by converging cloud infrastructures with IoT applications facilitating IoT service creation and deployment. OpenIoT has been successfully demonstrated and implemented by means of using semantic web design and this is a major advancement over the IoT/cloud infrastructure state-of-the-art. Previously, the state-of-the-art was characterized by an essential lack of semantic interoperability and integration across the diverse IoT applications and sensor data streams. OpenIoT brings IoT applications, Semantic Web design and Cloud infrastructure technologies all together. The OpenIoT platform is a joint effort of awarded open source contributions associated with popular RFID and Wireless Sensor Networks (WSN) such as the Global Sensor Networks (GSN) [36], and the Linked Sensor Middleware (LSM) [37] to connect heterogeneous sensors for real-time processing. OpenIoT has been applied, but not limited, to four scenarios: smart cities by enabling crowd sensing for air quality analysis, smart agriculture for monitoring large-scale deployments, intelligent manufacturing for optimizing logistic processes and traceability of material, and the smart building in a university campus for indoor sensing and booking resources for specific activities associated with students study rooms.

CityPulse[12] is mainly focused on large-scale analysis and real-time intelligence to extract meaningful knowledge and perceptions from heterogeneous data streams [28]. CityPulse works on designing and developing a framework, which supports the development of 101 applications for smart cities (e.g., public parking space availability prediction). CityPulse contains tools which can be used for discovering, processing and interpreting the data sources (e.g. weather data, traffic data, etc.) and social data streams (e.g. Facebook, Twitter, Google) by using Complex Event Processing (CEP) techniques. CityPulse works on bridging the gap between the application technologies on the WoT and the real world data streams.

VITAL[13] is a platform that focuses on reducing the development and deployment costs of smart city applications [21,29] by exploiting the functionality for interconnect legacy data with IoT sensor collected data by using semantics. VITAL has deployed demonstrators in two cities: Istanbul and London. VITAL platform reuses the work achieved in OpenIoT and the W3C SSN-XG in terms of ontologies. VITAL follows a specific model enabling for the first-time an operating system that works across the cities and provides software tools based on semantic annotation and complex event processing to integrate heterogeneous IoT systems (legacy) and ensures data integration, and interoperable IoT services.

FIESTA-IoT,[14] stands for Federated Interoperable Semantic IoT/cloud Testbeds and Applications, is a project, that reuses the previous work done in European project such as OpenIoT, CityPulse, VITAL, and SmartSantander. The FIESTA-IoT project works on integrating IoT platforms, testbeds, data, and associated silo applications. FIESTA-IoT aims for opening up new opportunities in the development and deployment of experiments that exploit data and capabilities from multiple

---

[12]http://www.ict-citypulse.eu/page/, Last visited: September 2016.

[13]http://vital-iot.eu/, Last visited: September 2016.

[14]http://fiesta-iot.eu/, Last visited: September 2016.

testbeds. The FIESTA-IoT infrastructure looks at enabling experimenters to use a single Experiment-as-a-Service (EaaS) API for executing experiments such as reasoning on sensor data or sensor data discovery. Such experiments are conducted over multiple IoT federated testbeds in a testbed agnostic way i.e. like accessing a single large scale virtualized testbed. The main goal of the FIESTA-IoT project is to open new horizons in the development and deployment of IoT applications and experiments at a global scale, based on the interconnection and interoperability of diverse IoT platforms and testbeds. FIESTA-IoT project's experimental infrastructure is targeting to be the entry point for European experimenters in the IoT domain with the unique capability for accessing to and sharing IoT datasets in a testbed-agnostic way. It enables the execution of experiments across multiple IoT testbeds, based on a single API for submitting the experiments.

11.2.6 LIMITATIONS OF EXISTING APPROACHES

Most of the existing WoT projects and tools described above are using Semantic Web principles and available technologies for integrating semantic-enabled WoT services. The state-of-the-art analysis reveals that interoperability issues remain open since existing projects constantly redesign their own models to structure data, semantic annotators, semantic based IoT data analytics mechanisms, and domain-specific IoT applications. Based on this study, important notes can be addressed such as follows. There are new methods inspired from the Linked Open Data (LOD) approach to reuse existing efforts in order to help WoT developers to interpret IoT data and ease interoperability among applications. To ensure interoperability, the reuse of efforts and background knowledge already designed is highly encouraged. The following research directions regarding reusing background knowledge are highlighted: 1) Extracting domain knowledge (ontologies, datasets and rules), 2) combining domain knowledge, 3) new ontology mapping, alignment and merging tools adapted to IoT ontologies, 4) make the domain knowledge interoperable by using semantic web methodologies and best practices, 5) integrate a semantic reasoning engine and reuse "IF THEN ELSE" rules already designed, and 6) an assistance for IoT application development using semantic web technologies. Overcoming such challenges will enable providing interoperability among semantic-based WoT applications and providing a uniform guideline to the application developers.

11.3 CONTRIBUTIONS AND M3 FRAMEWORK

We propose a comprehensive Machine-to-Machine Measurement (M3) framework that provides the entire data workflow generated by devices to build SWoT applications. This framework creates meta data models and semantically annotates sensor data, deduces meaningful information out of data, reuses the domain knowledge available on the Web. More specifically, the M3 addresses the semantic-related requirements, discussed in Section 11.2.1, as follows:

- "Ensuring interoperability among heterogeneous data" is addressed by using a taxonomy to unify terms and deal with issues such as synonyms and abbreviations, thus semantic web technologies for *unifying* data are used.
- "Deducing meaningful information from raw data" is addressed by using reasoning mechanisms such as logic-based inference engine (e.g., if temperature is 38 °C then hot).
- "Reusing and integrating the domain knowledge already available on the Web to enrich WoT data" is addressed by classifying domain knowledge as a new dataset.
- "Ensuring interoperability among WoT projects" is addressed by ensuring interoperability among data, models to structure data and reasoning mechanisms.
- "Combining different application domains" is addressed by generating rules and use them for domain knowledge control.

To overcome the limitations of the WoT enabling semantic interoperability, the Machine-to-Machine Measurement (M3) framework has been designed to assist developers in designing semantic WoT applications. "Measurement" explains that M3 is mainly focused on data interoperability. M3 is a framework, a semantic engine and a methodology to define an entire workflow exploiting data produced by devices to: 1) Semantically annotate data, 2) reason over data to infer new knowledge, and 3) provide Semantic Web of Things (SWoT) templates to ease the task of WoT developers who are not familiar with semantic web technologies to easily develop semantic-based applications. The M3 framework and its four sub-components explained thereafter addresses the following challenges (introduced in Section 11.2.1), as depicted in Fig. 11.2.

11.3.1 A SEMANTIC ENGINE FOR WOT

The Fig. 11.1 summarizes the M3 semantic engine workflow [20], and at the same time it maps the use case described in the introduction of this chapter showing same data (e.g., temperature 38.7 °C) produced by a thermometer from two different applicative domains: Path A (upper side in the figure) for healthcare and path B (lower side) for weather forecasting. This example highlights the necessity to 1) Explicitly add description to sensor measurements, 2) interpret data, and 3) combine domains to design cross-domain applications. The first box, called "WoT data" returns sensor descriptions such as temperature 38.7 °C. In the second box, called "Semantic data", previous data is semantically annotated according to the M3 language, implemented as an ontology, which is required for the future steps.

In the box called "Semantic Rule, new domain concept", the S-LOR approach is exploited, and a set of interoperable rules compliant with the M3 language to infer new knowledge used. In path A, S-LOR deduces the concept "fever", whereas in path B, S-LOR deduces the concept "hot". In the boxes called "Domain ontologies" and "Domain datasets" the results of the reasoning provided by S-LOR are linked to the M3 interoperable domain ontologies and datasets used in the SWoT templates. Such interoperable domain knowledge has been extracted from the LOV4IoT dataset.

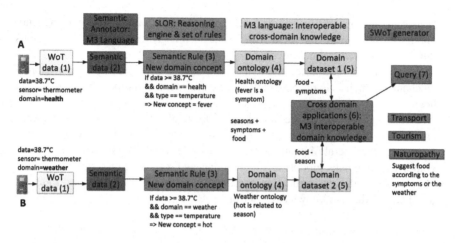

FIGURE 11.1

The M3 semantic engine workflow

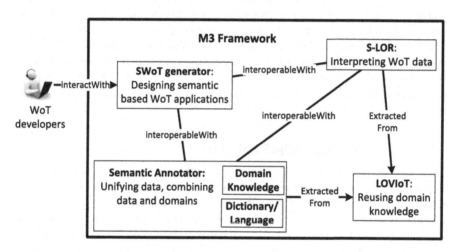

FIGURE 11.2

The M3 Framework and functional relations

In step 6), "Cross domain applications", the M3 interoperable domain knowledge is used to combine domains and provide suggestions. For instance, food related to the fever symptom in path A, and food related to season in path B. Since food referred to the same namespace in both domain knowledge, it is easy to combine domains. Finally, in step 7), a request queries the M3 interoperable cross-domain knowledge to get smarter data and suggestions as result of a SPARQL query for example. All of these steps can be done by loading the SWoT template provided by the SWoT generator and a Java skeleton that we provide[15] to easily build semantic-based IoT applications and enrich IoT data. The provided results will be later parsed and exploited in the final application such as the naturopathy application which suggests home remedies when a high temperature (which could be a potential fever) is detected. The final application could be a user-friendly interface or could even send notifications, alerts or could send order to actuators.

11.3.2 MAIN FUNCTIONALITY AND SEMANTIC VALUE

In the following section, we describe essential functionalities for enabling data interoperability in the context of using the M3 framework [30] and its semantic orientation towards data interoperability. The cross domain nature comes across as result of following the requirements described in previously introduced in Section 11.2.1.

- **SWoT generator**, produces templates to the developers to ease their task in development. The template contains the files required to execute the semantic functionality and passes this to the semantic annotator and SLOR. SWoT is explained in detail in Section 11.3.3,
- **Semantic Annotator**, explained in Section 11.3.4, comprises a dictionary/language to semantically annotate data in a unified way compliant with the M3 framework, a cornerstone component for the well execution of the S-LOR reasoning engine.
- **Sensor-based Linked Open Rules (S-LOR)**, explained in Section 11.3.5, is the inference engine executing the dataset of interoperable rules to deduce meaningful information from semantic data.
- **Linked Open Vocabularies for Internet of Things (LOV4IoT)**, explained in Section 11.3.6, is a dataset and a set of APIs to retrieve domain knowledge required. This domain knowledge has been manually redesigned to be interoperable and used by the M3 language, SLOR and SWoT generator.

In this section, we present the M3 framework, and explained its functional relations.

11.3.3 SWOT GENERATION

The SWoT generation or SWoT Generator is a necessary process in any SWoT Application with the objective to ease the task of WoT developers in designing semantic-based WoT applications [31]. The SWoT generation provides the domain knowledge required to build semantic-based WoT applications by reducing development costs. Developers can interact with SWoT generator though Application Programming Interface (API) or Graphical User Interface (GUI).

---

[15]http://sensormeasurement.appspot.com/?p=end_to_end_scenario.

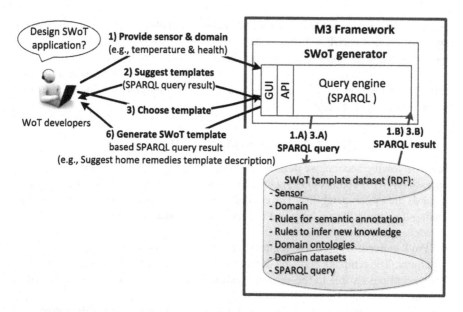

FIGURE 11.3

The SWoT generator and its semantic-based IoT templates generation cycle

Fig. 11.3 shows that developers interact with the SWoT generator by providing sensors used within the IoT application that they want to develop and in which domain the sensors are deployed (e.g., thermometer in healthcare). The SWoT generator interacts with a RDF template dataset through SPARQL queries and returns several SWoT templates matching the requirements. The template dataset has been manually designed and implemented with RDF. The current dataset contains 33 templates to design semantic-based applications. The developers choose one template (e.g., suggest home remedies template to interpret body temperature), a new SPARQL query is done to return the description of one specific template. Each template enables building semantic-based WoT applications and indicates: 1) The sensors employed in the application, 2) the applicative domains, 3) the rules to semantically annotate data, 4) the rules to deduce new knowledge from data, 5) the domain knowledge comprised of ontologies and datasets to build domain-specific or cross-domain applications, and 6) the SPARQL query to request smarter data enriched with semantic web technologies and inferred data produced once the reasoning engine is executed.

Once the description of the template is returned by the SPARQL query engine, SWoT generator produces a template with interoperable ontologies, rules and datasets to: 1) Semantically annotate data, 2) run a reasoning mechanism over data, and 3) combine applicative domains by linking data. The main novelty of this research approach and tool is that developers do not need to be familiar with semantic web technologies. Moreover, another important aspect is that the SWoT generator will provide interoperability among semantic-based WoT applications.

11.3.4 MACHINE-TO-MACHINE MEASUREMENT LANGUAGE

M3 language is used by the Semantic Annotator for unifying WoT data coming from heterogeneous projects, platforms and testbeds. The M3 language can be seen as a dictionary to describe and unify: 1) Sensor type, 2) unit, 3) sensor measurement type, and 4) applicative WoT domain [41]. The M3 language enables dealing with heterogeneous terms used in different projects such as synonyms. This language has been designed by extracting popular terms from LOV4IoT explained in Section 11.3.6. For instance, the M3 language deals with interoperability of terms when describing sensors: Precipitation sensor or rainfall sensor or delete ambiguities by explicitly adding the meaning of the data (e.g., body temperature differs from a room temperature). This is also an essential step to later easily interpret data and infer new information. Using the M3 compliant 'Semantic Annotator', data become compatible with the M3 language, an essential step for an easy interpretation of data. The M3 language has been implemented through the M3 ontology[16] (V1) or the M3-lite taxonomy (V2),[17] more precisely they are extensions of the popular W3C Semantic Sensor Networks (SSN) ontology. The M3 ontology is mainly focused on the interoperability of data, by extending the `ssn:ObservationValue` concept and by providing subclasses of `ssn:Sensor` and `ssn:FeatureOfInterest`. M3 language is a cornerstone to enable interlinking cross-domain knowledge, a set of interoperable ontologies, datasets and rules reused by the SWoT generator to design cross-domain applications (e.g., smart home and weather forecasting).

11.3.5 SENSOR-BASED LINKED OPEN RULES

Sensor Based Linked Open Rules (S-LOR) is a sharing and reusing based approach, inspired from the Linked Open Data approach, to share the knowledge on the Web. S-LOR provides a dataset of interoperable rules used to infer new knowledge from WoT data (e.g., fever deduced from a body temperature) [32]. The rules have been written manually but extracted from the LOV4IoT dataset explained in Section 11.3.6. The rules are compliant with the M3 ontology mentioned previously and the Jena framework,[18] more precisely the Jena inference engine.[19] Previously, the developer uses the M3 language to semantically annotate IoT data to produce M3-compliant data. Then, the data is enriched with new information thanks to the logic based reasoning engine S-LOR and the rules loaded that have been provided by the SWoT template as depicted in Fig. 11.4. Enriched M3 data is queried through a

---

[16]http://sensormeasurement.appspot.com/m3#, Last visited: September 2016.

[17]http://ontology.fiesta-iot.eu/ontologyDocs/fiesta-iot/doc, Last visited: September 2016.

[18]https://jena.apache.org/.

[19]https://jena.apache.org/documentation/inference/.

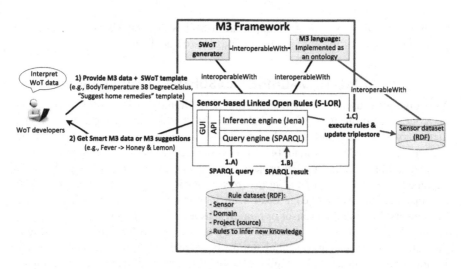

FIGURE 11.4

The S-LOR cycle for IoT data Interpretation

SPARQL query also provided by the SWoT template to provide domain-specific or cross-domains suggestions to the developer. For instance, S-LOR will deduce new information "fever" from the measurement body temperature 38 °C and will combine it to healthcare and naturopathy ontologies and datasets provided by the template. Finally, the developer will display results in a user-friendly interface, send alerts or even order actuators (e.g., open or close a door).

S-LOR has some limitations, it only deals with simple devices such as thermometer and not complicated sensors such as accelerometer or electrocardiograms (ECG).

11.3.6 LINKED OPEN VOCABULARIES FOR INTERNET OF THINGS

To facilitate application development and its interoperability, the **Linked Open Vocabularies for Internet of Things (LOV4IoT)** dataset[20] has been designed [39,40]. The main purpose of this dataset is to reuse the domain knowledge expertise already designed and available on the Web. LOV4IoT references 300 ontology-based projects exploiting sensors in various domains such as healthcare, building automation, food, agriculture, tourism, security, transportation, and smart city. Projects have been identified, studied and referenced since: 1) Devices are being used, 2) domain knowledge can be re-used in another context to design cross-domain use cases (e.g., the naturopathy application combines health, weather and smart kitchen domains), 3) ontologies and their evaluations have been designed, 4) ontologies or datasets can be re-used to ease interoperability and reduce development costs, 5) rule-based systems have been

---

[20]http://sensormeasurement.appspot.com/?p=ontologies, Last visited: September 2016.

designed, 6) papers have been published in conferences or journals, and 7) the explanations of why semantic web technologies are integrated are provided. However, the LOV4IoT dataset has some limitations since a lot of ontologies referenced lack of interoperability and best practices which hinder automation tasks. The LOV4IoT dataset has been mainly exploited to build the M3 language, SLOR interoperable rule dataset and the interoperable domain knowledge mainly exploited by the templates generated by the SWoT generator. A major challenge would be to automatically extract the domain knowledge from LOV4IoT and automatically re-design it to make it interoperable and enrich the SWoT generator with additional templates.

11.3.7 VALIDATION WITHIN FIESTA-IOT

In the context of the FIESTA-IoT project (Federated Interoperable Semantic IoT/ cloud Testbeds and Applications – introduced in Section 11.2.5) it is required to go beyond WoT. FIESTA-IoT focuses on interoperability of data, but also on the integration of testbeds (e.g., smart cities producing data) and experiments (e.g., WoT applications). The data workflow that has been presented in Section 11.3.1, is being applied within FIESTA-IoT to address data interoperability issues. It is currently extended to design a generic approach, called SEG 3.0 methodology, to ensure data interoperability from data to end-user applications that could be applied on other domains than WoT [19]. The SWoT generation is used to design and implement the concept "Experiment-as-a Service" (EaaS), mainly addressing interoperability of applications and services within IoT. LOVIoT has been used to easily find and reuse existing IoT ontologies to build the FIESTA-IoT ontology, which reuses, extends and aligns W3C SSN, IoT-Lite, and M3-lite ontologies. S-LOR is used to deduce meaningful information from data provided by testbeds (e.g., smart cities) registered within FIESTA-IoT.

11.4 SUMMARY AND FUTURE WORK

Summary. In this chapter, we presented a comprehensive study about the main WoT challenges, highlighting those that rely on combining heterogeneous IoT data for the design of smarter services and applications and that benefit from data interoperability. We discussed about the limitation of the existing work in the Web of Things and the justification about the need for a comprehensive framework. We presented the most relevant projects and tools working on semantic interoperability for annotating, linking and reasoning over Web of Things (WoT) data. To overcome some of the actual limitations of the existing WoT projects, the M3 framework has been designed and explained in detail. This chapter is mainly focused on assisting WoT developers in understanding the integration of semantic web technologies in order to deduce meaningful information from WoT data to build smarter WoT applications.

Future work. Future activities focus on the refinement of the M3 framework and automatize as much as possible each component. For instance, LOV4IoT could be automatized to reuse, combine and extract the domain knowledge to easily deduce meaningful information from data. This knowledge is mainly reused to build interoperable semantic-based WoT applications and services provided by the SWoT generator. SWoT generator could be extended by investigating *Semantic Web Services* and *Linked Open Services* to enable the composition of simple services to provide more sophisticated WoT applications.

REFERENCES

[1] Aggarwal C, Ashish N, Sheth A. The internet of things: a survey from the data-centric perspective. In: Managing and mining sensor data. Springer; 2013. p. 383–428.

[2] Guinard D, Trifa V, Wilde E. A resource oriented architecture for the web of things. In: Internet of things (IoT). IEEE; 2010. p. 1–8.

[3] Vasseur J-P, Dunkels A. Interconnecting smart objects with ip: the next internet. Morgan Kaufmann; 2010.

[4] Guinard D, Trifa V, Mattern F, Wilde E. From the internet of things to the web of things: resource-oriented architecture and best practices. Springer; 2011.

[5] Gangemi A, Presutti V. Ontology design patterns. In: Handbook on ontologies. Springer; 2009.

[6] Leggieri M, Passant A, Hauswirth M. inContext-Sensing: LOD augmented sensor data? In: Proceedings of the 10th international semantic web conference (ISWC 2011). Springer; 2011.

[7] Gyrard A, Serrano M, Atemezing G. Semantic web methodologies, best practices and ontology engineering applied to internet of things. In: WF-IOT 2015, world forum on internet of things. Springer; 2015.

[8] Scharffe F, Atemezing G, Troncy R, Gandon F, Villata S, et al. Enabling linkeddata publication with the datalift platform. In: Proc. AAAI workshop on semantic cities. 2012.

[9] Suarez-Figueroa M-C. NeOn methodology for building ontology networks: specification, scheduling and reuse. 2010.

[10] Noy N, McGuinness D. Ontology development 101: a guide to creating your first ontology. Stanford knowledge systems laboratory technical report KSL-01-05 and Stanford medical informatics technical report SMI-2001-0880, 2001.

[11] Gyrard A. Designing cross-domain semantic web of things applications. Eurecom; 2015.

[12] Henson C. A semantics-based approach to machine perception. Wright State University; 2013.

[13] Barnaghi P, Wang W, Henson C, Taylor K. Semantics for the internet of things: early progress and back to the future. Int J Semantic Web Inf Syst 2012;8(1):1–21. IGI Global.

[14] Jara A, Olivieri A, Bocchi Y, Jung M, Kastner W, Skarmeta A. Semantic web of things: an analysis of the application semantics for the IoT moving towards the IoT convergence. Int J Web Grid Serv 2014;10(2):244–72. Interscience.

[15] Compton M, Barnaghi P, Bermudez L, Garcia-Castro R, Henson C, Herzog A, et al. The ssn ontology of the w3c semantic sensor network incubator group. J Web Semant: Sci, Serv Agents World Wide Web 2012. Elsevier.

[16] Botts M, Percivall G, Reed C, Davidson J. OGC sensor web enablement: overview and high level architecture. GeoSensor networks. Springer; 2008. p. 175–90.

[17] Vandenbussche P-Y, Atemezing G, Poveda-Villalon M, Vatant B. LOV: a gateway to reusable semantic vocabularies on the web. Semant Web J 2015.

[18] Zeng D, Guo S, Cheng Z. The web of things: a survey. J Commun 2011;6(6):424–38.

[19] Gyrard A, Serrano M. Connected smart cities: interoperability with SEG 3.0 for the Internet of things. In: 30th IEEE international conference on advanced information networking and applications workshops, 2016. 2016.

[20] Gyrard A, Bonnet C, Boudaoud K. Enrich machine-to-machine data with semantic web technologies for cross-domain applications. In: WF-IOT 2014, world forum on internet of things. 2014.

[21] Petrolo R, Loscri V, Mitton N. Towards a smart city based on cloud of things, a survey on the smart city vision and paradigms. Transactions on emerging telecommunications technologies. Wiley Online Library; 2015.

[22] Sheth A, Henson C, Sahoo SS. Semantic sensor web. IEEE Internet Comput 2008;12(4):78–83.

[23] Henson C, Pschorr J, Sheth A, Thirunarayan K. henson2009semsos. In: International symposium on collaborative technologies and systems, 2009. CTS'09. IEEE; 2009. p. 44–53.

[24] Patni H, Henson C, Sheth A. Linked sensor data. In: 2010 international symposium on collaborative technologies and systems (CTS). IEEE; 2010. p. 362–70.

[25] Bizer C, Heath T, Berners-Lee T. Linked data-the story so far. Int J Semantic Web Inf Syst 2009;5(3):1–22. IGI Global.

[26] Pfisterer D, Romer K, Bimschas D, Kleine O, Mietz R, Truong C, Hasemann H, Kroller A, Pagel M, Hauswirth M. SPITFIRE: toward a semantic web of things. IEEE Commun Mag 2011;49(11):40–8.

[27] Soldatos J, Kefalakis N, Hauswirth M, Serrano M, Calbimonte J-P, Riahi M, Aberer K, Jayaraman P, Zaslavsky A, Zarko I. OpenIoT: open source internet-of-things in the cloud. In: Interoperability and open-source solutions for the internet of things. Springer; 2015. p. 13–25.

[28] Barnaghi P, Tonjes R, Holler J, Hauswirth M, Sheth A, Anantharam P. CityPulse: real-time IoT stream processing and large-scale data analytics for smart city applications. In: European semantic web conference (ESWC) 2014. Springer; 2014.

[29] Petrolo R, Mitton N, Soldatos J, Hauswirth M, Schiele G. Integrating wireless sensor networks within a city cloud. In: 2014 eleventh annual IEEE international conference on Sensing, communication, and networking workshops (SECON workshops). IEEE; 2014. p. 24–7.

[30] Gyrard A, Datta S, Bonnet C, Boudaoud K. Cross-domain internet of things application development: M3 framework and evaluation. In: FICLOUD 2015, 3rd international conference on future internet of things and cloud. IEEE; 2015.

[31] Gyrard A, Bonnet C, Boudaoud K, Serrano M. Assisting IoT projects and developers in designing interoperable semantic web of things applications. In: IEEE international conference on internet of things 2015 (iThings). IEEE; 2015.

[32] Gyrard A, Bonnet C, Boudaoud K. Helping IoT application developers with sensor-based linked open rules. In: SSN 2014, 7th international workshop on semantic sensor networks in conjunction with the 13th international semantic web conference (ISWC 2014). Springer; 2014.

[33] Ganz F, Barnaghi P, Carrez F. Automated semantic knowledge acquisition from sensor data. IEEE systems. IEEE; 2016.

[34] Prazeres C, Serrano M. SOFT-IoT:Self-OrganizingFOGofThings. In: 30th IEEE international conference on advanced information networking and applications (IEEE AINA-2016) workshop on pervasive internet of things and smart cities (PITSaC). ACM; 2016.

[35] Tummarello G, Delbru R, Oren E. Sindice.com: weaving the open linked data. Springer; 2007.

[36] Calbimonte J-P, Sarni S, Eberle J, Aberer K. XGSN: an open-source semantic sensing middleware for the web of things. In: 7th international workshop on semantic sensor network. Springer; 2014.

[37] Le-Phuoc D, Quoc H, Ngo Q, Nhat T, Hauswirth M. Enabling live exploration on the graph of things? In: International semantic web conference – proceedings of the semantic web challenge. Springer; 2014.

[38] Ding L, Finin T, Joshi A, Pan R, Cost R, Peng Y, Reddivari P, Doshi V, Sachs J. Swoogle: a search and metadata engine for the semantic web. In: Proceedings of the thirteenth ACM international conference on information and knowledge management. ACM; 2004. p. 652–9.

[39] Gyrard A, Bonnet C, Boudaoud K, Serrano M. LOV4IoT: a second life for ontology-based domain knowledge to build semantic web of things applications. In: 4rd international conference on future internet of things and cloud (FiCloud 2016). IEEE; 2016.

[40] Gyrard A, Atemezing G, Bonnet C, Boudaoud K, Serrano M. Reusing and unifying background knowledge for internet of things with LOV4IoT. In: 4rd international conference on future internet of things and cloud (FiCloud 2016). IEEE; 2016.

[41] Gyrard A, Datta SK, Bonnet C, Boudaoud K. Standardizing generic cross-domain applications in internet of things. In: Third workshop on telecommunications standards, part of IEEE globecom 2014. IEEE; 2014.

ACKNOWLEDGEMENTS

The activity presented in this chapter is partially funded by the European project "Federated Interoperable Semantic IoT/cloud Testbeds and Applications" (FIESTA-IoT) from the European Union's Horizon 2020 Programme with the Grant Agreement No. CNECT-ICT-643943. This chapter is extended from the authors' past work particularly from the PhD thesis [11] under the supervision of Prof. Christian Bonnet and Dr. Karima Boudaoud. We specially thank Prof. Amit Sheth for providing feedback and valuable comments regarding this work.

WEB OF THINGS DATA STORAGE

12

Hongming Cai*, Athanasios V. Vasilakos[†]

School of Software, Shanghai Jiao Tong University, Shanghai, China* Department of Computer Science, Electrical and Space Engineering, Luleå University of Technology, Luleå, Sweden[†]

CHAPTER POINTS

- On the purpose of building a clear insight for different WoT applications and techniques, a WoT data storage framework with multi-layer structure is given which describes related techniques from the view of data disposing process.
- Data isolation and multi-tenant data storage are discussed to provide a critical and accurate view of current WoT data management in cloud platform.
- Some open issues are given from the considerations of complex data model, semantic data management and real-time data disposing in order to provide a future tendency for WoT data storage techniques.

12.1 INTRODUCTION

With the wide spread of Web of Things (WoT) technology, massive data have been generated by huge amounts of distributed sensors and different applications. WoT applications have emerged as an important area for both engineers and researchers. As a consequence, how to acquire, integrate, store, dispose and use these data has become an urgent and important problem for enterprises to implement their business applications such as intelligent transportation, smart home, intelligent manufacturing and wisdom medical system.

The features of WoT data can be summarized as follows:

- Highly heterogeneous data: WoT data are acquired from different sorts of distributed sensors and applications. The data types vary from structured data such as table data, semi-structured like eXtensible Markup Language(XML) or Resource Description Framework(RDF), and unstructured data like images and videos.
- Massive dynamic data: WoT applications are always connected to a huge quantity of sensors or devices. Communications between different objects always generate a large volume of real-time, high-speed, uninterrupted data streams, which change rapidly.

Managing the Web of Things. DOI: 10.1016/B978-0-12-809764-9.00015-9

- Weakly semantic data: WoT data are event-driven low-level data with little semantic meaning. We could find little business value unless these raw data are integrated and processed.

For the reason that WoT data are always distributed, unstructured, event-based and time-related, interoperability between massive data generated by heterogeneous WoT objects brings new challenges, especially in cloud environment. Different requirements are given for these massive data processing covering different levels of data representation, data storage, data analysis and data utility. Traditional data storage focuses on resource measurement, management and provision in web-based environment. Therefore, Service Level Agreement (SLA) factors such as performance, scalability, availability, management and price are mainly concerned by owners of information infrastructure. Aiming to trace the latest progress in WoT-based data storage systems, a comprehensive process of WoT data applications and various relevant topics are discussed thoroughly.

First, based on data processing functional analysis, a framework is provided to identify the representation, storage, management, and processing areas of WoT data. Several associated functional modules are defined and described in terms of their key characteristics and capabilities.

Then, current researches in WoT data storage are classified and compared. This paper proposes a timely research of the current WoT data storage methods especially in cloud platform, and gives a timely survey which describe the state-of-the-art techniques from the view of data disposing process.

Next, some WoT data storage techniques are given to enable WoT applications to move into cloud platforms. Some key techniques related to WoT data storage, for the purpose of archiving higher availability and flexible resource provision, are discussed to provide an overview and essential information for current Cloud-based WoT applications.

As WoT technologies are evolving, a substantial amount of related applications have been founded in many industries. Based on research analysis, some future technical tendencies are also described and discussed.

12.2 THE FRAMEWORK OF WOT DATA STORAGE

A common WoT framework consists of perception layer, network layer and application layer. Based on the process of WoT data disposing, a framework of cloud-based data storage system for WoT application is given. The framework consists of several modules covering data storage, data representation, data management, inner or external data processing, and also a optimization module based on cloud platform, as Fig. 12.1 shows.

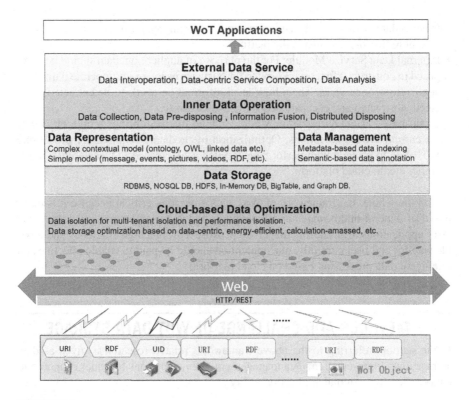

FIGURE 12.1

A framework of WoT-based storage systems in Cloud Computing

Descriptions of modules are given as follows:

- Data Storage Module: Considering WoT data can be structured, semi-structured, and unstructured format, effective data storage should combine different kinds of data storage type into one body so as to build intelligent complex WoT applications.
- Data Representation Module: How to define and describe heterogeneous data from distributed and mobile devices is a fundamental problem for the data disposing process. Therefore, simple models such as event, message, rdf and other data format, and complex models such as contextual information and semantic relations are both required to represent WoT data.
- Data Management Module: For the reason that data from sensors are always raw or low-level data, different data management approaches are implemented based on data index, metadata, semantic relations and linked data, so as to retrieve and access data from distributed data sources with high efficiency.
- Inner Data Operation Module: For the purpose of disposing data in the distributed platform, massive data processing mechanisms are constructed for parallel and dis-

tributed data processing. And querying and reasoning operations can be carried out in a more flexible way inside the platforms.
- External Data Service Module: For the purpose of application, data should be composed to construct a functional service for business users, or interoperate with other applications or services. Then, high-level information needs to be extracted, classified, abstracted and encapsulated for end-user utility.
- Cloud-based Data Optimization Module: Cloud platform brings a high efficiency for current WoT applications. Optimization methods are required for processing WoT data to provide high performances, such as decreased I/O, scalability, availability etc. in cloud platform.

On the whole, the framework of WoT data storage is critical because it is composed of general middlewares and functional models to implement real large-scale WoT applications. Considering that cloud platforms bring a high efficiency and flexible way for end-user currently, much attention should be paid to enable effective and intelligent data processing based on cloud platform.

12.3 METHODS AND CHALLENGE OF WOT DATA STORAGE

In the section, referring to the above framework, related research is given as data storage, data representation, data management, data operations for inner support and data services for external application utility.

12.3.1 DATA STORAGE TYPE

After being attained from different data sources, WoT data can be persisted for further disposing. There are several data storage types. Relational database management system (RDBMS) is the basic and traditional storage type, which use Structured Query Language (SQL) as its basic query language. Based on RDBMS, lots of storage type arc extended or developed, such as Not only SQL (NoSQL) database, database based on Hadoop Distributed File System (HDFS), In-Memory database, Bigtable database, and Graph database. Based on these different data type, the features are given and discussed as follows.

12.3.1.1 Relational Database Management System

Relational database management system has been a popular data storage type for a long time, which was proposed in 1970 in [1]. This model protects users from the details about data organization in machines, and only provides a high level accessing-query language to operate data. However, as the development of Web 2.0 and cloud computing, RDBMS has its shortage. With static schema [2], no linear query execution time and unstable query plan, RDBMS is poor in scalability. For faster and more efficient operations for big data, the authors of [3] provided Cache Augmented Database Management System (CADBMS), improving speed of queries that read and write a certain part of data by caching. CADBMS is very useful for social network applications and others systems with high read-write ratio.

Traditional database queries follow a simple policy that defined constraints must satisfied by each tuple in the query result. This policy is computationally efficient, as the database system can evaluate the query conditions on each tuple individually. However, many practical real-world problems require a collection of result tuples to satisfy constraints collectively, rather than individually. In [4], a new query model named package queries is presented to extend traditional database queries to handle complex constraints. They design PaQL, a SQL-based query language that supports the declarative specification of package queries.

12.3.1.2 *NoSQL Database*

NoSQL database is also called non-relational database. Data in NoSQL database has no explicit types or patterns, they are in different buckets and related data are linked to each other. In fact, NoSQL database is a general designation, people usually divide them into three main categories: key-value stores, document-based and column-oriented. Data are stored as key-value pairs in key-value database like Amazon's SimpleDB, which supports both structured and unstructured data storage. Document-based databases such as MongoDB and Apache CouchDB store data as a collection of documents, usually JSON-based. Any fields of any length can be added, any type of data can be easily stored. As for column-oriented databases, fairly related data would be linked as an extensible column, which is different to the strictly structured table in RDBMS.

In [5], the authors said that NoSQL database systems nowadays need to make trade-off among consistency, availability and partition tolerance to optimize for their applications. While a hybrid database system can use various kinds of database softwares and take advantage of their features for individual applications and workloads, how to make the database software work together to achieve the highest performance is still a challenging problem. They also provide an extensible database interface for integrating NoSQL databases and adding database operations.

NoSQL databases are mostly non-relational, distributed, open-source and horizontally scalable. The main characteristics of these databases are schema-free, no join, non-relational, easy replication support, simple API and eventually consistent.

12.3.1.3 *HDFS-Based Database*

Hadoop is now one of the most popular MapReduce data storage solution. However, the programming model of Hadoop is very low level, which makes developers unable to reuse and hard to maintain these programs. Then HDFS [6] comes up. This distributed file system can run on daily-used devices with low cost and high tolerant. The high throughput makes applications with big data set more available and efficient.

Hive [7] is another open-source big data storage solution on the basis of Hadoop. What makes Hive different is that it provides HiveQL, a SQL-like declarative language. Hive compiles HiveSQL into MapReduce jobs executed using Hadoop. The language includes type system and allows user-defined script and custom type. Hive also provides schemas and statistics functions, which make it more useful in query optimization, query compilation and data exploration.

Still, the result of [8] experiments in throughput over the numbers of files, and shows that Hadoop performs poorer when the number grows larger. The bottlenecks are the size of files used, the number of data nodes available and the number of reducers used.

12.3.1.4 *In-Memory Database*

In-memory database management systems (IMDBMS) are designed for analysis usage like On-Line Transaction Processing (OLTP) and On-Line Analysis Processing (OLAP). MonetDB and Vectorwise are traditional OLAP engines. Nowadays more modern engines occur, including Microsoft Hekaton, HStore/VoltDB, Shore-MT etc. Recently, following the trend of executing OLTP and OLAP within same system on same database state, SAP's Hana and HyPer are developed [9].

In-memory database offers great performance for data with high update rates, thus it can be used in many daily services. One usage scenario of IMDBMS is Location-Based Service (LBS) which plays an important role in different area of WoT applications. In [10], the authors combined a series of techniques to implement in-memory storage for LBS with high inserting efficiency.

Another scenario is managing vector spatial data, which is similar to the former one. The authors of [11] concentrated on reducing the cost of I/O and improving algorithm efficiency by designing and realizing a spatial data access system on the basis of in-memory database.

In-memory database can process large in-memory datasets entirely due to the growth of main memory space currently. However, the speed of main memory operations can not be as fast as CPU's for now. Therefore, the bottleneck of main-memory techniques lies in the process of moving data from memory to CPU caches. The main-stream research aspect turns to near memory computation capabilities by making good use of hardware advantages. A near data processing accelerator named JAFAR [12], is presented for pushing "select" queries down to memory instead of pulling data into caches. By this mean, select operations in column-based data system can enjoy an improvement up to nine times as before.

12.3.1.5 *BigTable*

BigTable is a distributed storage system which is designed by Google, just as its name, it is proposed to deal with data in large scale. Different from another popular system HDFS, BigTable only supports structured data. Thanks to the distributed features of BigTable, developers and researchers can easily get a cloud storage solution for large-scale data task with no need to build clusters by themselves. However, the public cloud service also becomes a concern for users. How to ensure the integrity of data in cloud becomes a big issue in BigTable.

BigTable serves quantities of projects at Google [13]. Data sizes of these projects can be several petabytes in different data centre and different server. BigTable has been always satisfying the demands on large data scale and low latency.

Aiming to enhance BigTable by providing an integrity solution, the authors of [14] present iBigTable. iBigtable consists of a series of security protocols based on designed data structure and BigTable. These protocols efficiently assure that the data returned by BigTable are integral. Moreover, iBigtable inherits great features of BigTable and has a great compatibility, which allows existing BigTable applications transferring to iBigTable with little change of code.

BigTable provides a flexible, high-performance solution for various products. It is implemented by three significant components: many tablet servers, a master server and a client-based library. Tablet servers manage a set of tablet, including dealing with reading and writing operations on loaded tablets and splitting super large tablets into small ones. These servers are added or removed dynamically from a cluster to accommodate changes in workloads. The master server assigns each tablet to a tablet server in cluster, detects the change in tablet servers, balances load of tablet-servers, collects garbage of files in Google file system and handles schema changes such as creating a table or a column family.

12.3.1.6 *Graph Database*

Graph database utilizes features of graph to provide a scalable data storage. The queries are based on nodes, properties and edges that represent or store data. Recently, more focus is put in graph for the usability in complicated structure modelling.

In [15], some experiments on graph database Neo4j and relational database MySQL are carried out. The result shows that graph database have great advantage over relational database on structured type queries and full-text searches.

Graph databases have no schema, which is very suitable for XML document storage and biological or chemical data storage. Compare to storage in graph, retrieving data efficiently from large graph database via indices is more difficult and desirable.

Aiming to realize graph mining, a novel solution of indexing graph called gIndex [16] is proposed. Distinguished from existing methods based on path, gIndex utilizes frequent substructure as the basic indices. Frequent substructures have high stability during updates and show the intrinsic features of data, which make it ideal for graph indices. However, the size of indices will grow large in a large data warehouse, so two techniques are proposed to reduce the size, size-increasing support constraint and discriminative fragments. Besides the elegant solving in graph indexing, gIndex also illustrates that data mining can do great help to indexing and query processing, especially frequent pattern mining.

To query graph database is a big issue. Query navigation is the most important part and is heavily used in graph databases. For now, using reachability patterns with regular constraints is widely adopted for query. XPath-like languages is an example [17]. XPath is widely used in XML navigation for its ability to express queries of interest, easy query evaluation for fragments and close connection to yardstick database query languages.

Inspired to use graph to represent genome data, the authors of [18] carry out an investigation in graph-based database and are inspired to use graph to represent genome data. Researchers may build a database based on the adapted graph model storing genome data, which makes genome data storage and retrieval efficient and stable.

12.3.1.7 *Comparison Between Different Data Storage Types*

Based on the above references analysis, a comparison is given as Table 12.1.

From the table, we could find that WoT data storage is similar to other application data. As a traditional data storage type, RDBMS have many complex restrictions which ensure the reliability and consistency, but also make it lack scalability. However, SQL query language still makes great effect in both SQL and NoSQL database. NoSQL database has no tabular relations like traditional RDBMS does, but it owns a unique mechanism for data storage and retrieval. For the NoSQL database, HDFS-based database and BigTable perform great in distributed storage system. In big data era, they will be significant components. In-memory DB improves the performance on frequently updated data, and will show its power in geographical information systems or location-based applications. Graph database is useful for graph storage and retrieval, which makes a significant effort to social networking and semantic web applications [19].

In general, aiming to adapt to the high heterogeneity of WoT data from distributed data sources, it is a popular way to combine different data types such as RDBMS integrated with HDFS, so as to construct a scalable data storage for WoT applications.

12.3.2 DATA REPRESENTATION

Data Representation models are always fundamental for WoT applications. Based on the data disposing level, we divided these data model into three types: simple data model, integrated data model and semantic data model. Simple models are connected with sensor devices, such as messages, events, pictures, videos, and other data. Integrated model is composed of several simple models to construct an integrated view. Semantic model is a combination of simple models, model relationships with related contextual data.

12.3.2.1 *Simple Data Model*

The authors of [20] demonstrated the most significant factors in WoT: physical entity, resource and service, which can be concluded as physical entities and relationships between them. To describe these key concepts more accurately, the authors built an interlinked metadata model using micro-format such as RDF and micro-data to break the limitation of HTML format and enhance the surface representation metadata.

The authors of [21] explored a well-defined model with good extensibility for WoT information representation and organization. Based on the proposed three mainstream data type as object-cored organizing data, event-based explaining data and knowledge-based using data, the authors presented a model framework. It using two data types as different layers: the object layer and the event layer, to make an improvement over using single type only. The object layer using object-based organizing data represents all objects and relations between them. The event layer contains event-

Table 12.1 Comparison Between Data Storage Types

Product	RDBMS	NoSQL database			HDFS-based database	In-memory database	BigTable	Graph database
	MySQL	MangoDB	FB Cassandra	HBase	Amazon SimpleDB	SAP's Hana	Google BigTable	Neo4j
Data Model	Relational database	Document Oriented	Column database	Column database	Document Oriented	Multi-column database	Column database	Graph database
Interface	TCP/IP	TCP/IP	TCP/IP	HTTP/REST	TCP/IP	TCP/IP	TCP/IP	HTTP/REST
Data Storage	Disk	Disk	Disk	HDFS	S3 (Simple Storage Solution)	Memory and disk	GFS	Disk
Query Method	SQL	Map/Reduce	Map/Reduce	Map/Reduce	String-based query language	SQL and MDX	Map/Reduce	Cyphe query language
Replication	Asynchronous	Asynchronous	Asynchronous	Asynchronous	Asynchronous	Synchronous	Asynchronous/ Synchronous	Asynchronous
Concurrency Control	Locks	Locks	Multi Version Concurrency Control	Locks	None	–	Locks	Locks
Transactions	Local	No	Local	Local	No	No	Local	Local
Written In	C, C++	C++	Java	Java	Erlang	–	C, C++	Java
Characteristics	Static Schema Consistency High Availability Partition Tolerance Persistence	Consistency Partition Tolerance Persistence	High Availability Partition Tolerance Persistence	Consistency Partition Tolerance Persistence	High Availability Scalability	High Availability	Consistency High Availability Partition Tolerance Persistence	High Availability Scalability

based explaining data which is extracted from raw detailed data processed by the object layer. The event layer regulates events and relations between them based on event semantic link network model with a given reasoning rule set.

The authors of [22] focused on the extraction of event information from heterogeneous and massive raw data. They proposed an approach that can effectively extract events and internal links between them from large dataset based on existing event types in a particular domain. The conceptions of event, event type, link type, and event schema are introduced and a three-layered model which consists of the data-collecting-layer, the event-extracting-layer and the presenting-layer is raised to compress the redundant data.

Aiming to describe dynamic entities in WoT applications, the authors of [23] proposed a specification model to specify the entity services. The model extends OWL-S with service status ontology to illustrate information involved in the services. The extension issues entity status in real-time and releases the information as dynamic services to requesters. With this method, the model constructs and executes transactions intelligently.

12.3.2.2 *Integrated Data Model*

The authors of [24] proposed an approach of creating ontological models to describe connected objects to implement support of WoT and finally to achieve unified communication between objects. Moreover, a framework is presented to allow seamless integration of semantic models and objects of web applications.

Thing Broker [25] integrates WoT objects with different characteristics, based on different protocols, providing different interfaces and constraints, meanwhile kept simple and flexible to meet the requirement from different applications. Thing Broker provides a uniform Twitter-like RESTful interface to different WoT objects. By giving one abstraction containing configurable attributes to represent each WoT object, Thing Broker manages to involve all kinds of objects in WoT, from physical entities to high-level services.

The authors of [26] delivered a formal model that provides a formal ontology representation of relations between geographic events and observations. The model exploits SEGO, a mechanism based on rules, to reason information about events via in-situ observations, and it illustrates the scenario that ontological vocabularies can be well utilized by a reasoning and querying approach to retrieve events data and sensing information.

12.3.2.3 *Semantic Data Model*

The authors of [27] proposed an ontology-based WoT data model called the continuum model to reflect entities evolving as space and time change. This model is important in studying the history and predicting future trends and it can track spatial entities evolving through the time and space, which play an important role in capturing semantics of modelled phenomena. This model well combines the spatial functions and temporal capabilities.

The authors of [28] proposed a general methodology that develops consumable semantic data models for smart cities. It transfers large city data of different sources into a uniformed and integrated semantic data model (RDF/OWL) by using different engineering approaches, and it enables semantic interoperability at the concept level and support application developers to design advanced city services and applications.

12.3.2.4 *Comparison Between Different Representative Data Models*

Based on the above references from the complex level, a comparison is given as Table 12.2.

In short, data representation is used for further WoT data disposing. Simple models such as event, RDF combined with REST API provide a common format for WoT applications. Aiming to support intelligent interaction for WoT in a contextual level, the data representation should focus on integrated model by the integration of multiple simple model such as sensors, event, RDF and other format. Considering not only the data content, but also data relationships, the semantic model based on ontology and linked open data is a promising new model for web-based applications especially with social network.

12.3.3 DATA MANAGEMENT

WoT enables billions of smart things to be accessible based on the RESTful architecture and protocols like HTTP and Constrained Application Protocol (CoAP). Meanwhile, seamless integration and wide scale interoperability are the critical challenges of data management of WoT. The WoT data management can be divided into two kinds: Metadata-based data index methods and semantic-based model annotation methods.

12.3.3.1 *Metadata-Based Data Indexing*

Metadata is a kind of special data defined for data management. It can make data easily organized and understood by users without being involved with everything concerning the accessing solution.

In [29], an efficient distributed metadata management scheme was proposed for data management in cloud platform. It uses the technique of metadata distribution based on parent directory path, hierarchical directory structure, cooperative double layer cache mechanism to access the distributed data with reduced latency.

Mobile Metadata [30] were proposed to build a mobile code agent supporting image retrieval based on client in web-based computing environments. Both the data model and mapping functions as a mashup and moves them to the client side. The model provides clear object model and view construction based on client, quick query response time and better exploit of network resources, and it is flexible in expansion.

By means of embedding metadata to represent smart things, a system was developed to control and monitor the state of WoT application environment [31]. The system produces a machine-readable state description of application environment. A Web request will be generated when a smart device reach this state, then an appli-

Table 12.2 Comparison Between Representative Data Models

	Article	Aim	Basic Data Structure	Main Methods	Representation Type
[21]	An extensible and active semantic model of information organizing for the Internet of Things	intelligent reasoning	Object and event	Object-cored organizing data, event-based explaining data, and knowledge-based using data	Simple data model
[22]	Constructing the web of events from raw data in the web of things	to integrate heterogeneous and massive raw data	event	extracting events and their internal links from large scale data	Simple data model
[23]	An OWL-S based specification model of dynamic entity services for Internet of Things	to construct and execute the transactions intelligently	OWL	extending OWL-S with Service Status ontology to describe information involved in the services	Simple data model
[24]	Semantic surface representation of physical entity in the WEB of things	to enhance the metadata elements of surface representations	RDF	describing physical entities, resources and services by means of an interlinked metadata model	integrated data model
[25]	Thing Broker: A Twitter for Things	to integrate WoT objects with different characteristics for further disposing	protocols, interfaces	providing a uniform Twitter-like RESTful interface to different IoT objects	integrated data model
[26]	A formal model to infer geographic events from sensor observations	to infer information about geographic events from these observations	Ontology-based	exploiting a rule-based mechanism called SEGO to infer information about events	integrated data model
[27]	Continuum: A spatio temporal data model to represent and qualify filiation relationships	entities evolving in space and time	ontology-based spatiotemporal data model	tracking the evolution of spatial entities or objects through the time, and combining the spatial functions provided by GeoSPARQL	Semantic data model
[28]	A Smart City Data Model based on Semantics Best Practice and Principles	to enable semantic interoperability at the concept level	RDF, OWL	transferring large city data sources of different nature into RDF/OWL	Semantic data model

cation will implement related operations to reconfigure the user's smart environment automatically. Therefore, intelligent application is implemented by means of meta-data even huge quantity requests are involved.

12.3.3.2 *Semantic-Based Model Annotation*

The authors of [32] presented a framework for semantic and location-based services exploiting enriched maps. In particular, the framework contains mainly an approach for semantically annotating crowd-sourced cartographic data, and an innovative ontology-based function for semantic-based searching and disposing capabilities in current navigation systems.

To extract and link related concepts from raw sensor data and represent them as a topical ontology, a clustering approach extended k-means was used on the basis of rules extracted from external sources. The authors of [33] introduced a knowledge acquisition technique for real-world data processing aiming at topical ontologies creation and evolution. Then, these concepts are marked to make them understandable for user for the purpose of data analysis and data reasoning, and a related system is proposed for software support.

On handing unstructured models, the authors of [34] provided a semi-automatic semantic annotation in visualization scene based on three-layer ontology. The three-layer ontology including general ontology, domain ontology and scene ontology is constructed to form a comprehensive knowledge representation for semantic annotation. It is effective for large scale model management.

In short, metadata and simple index are good for structured data management. However, since WoT data are always unstructured or semi-structured in a dynamic and contextual environment, semantic-based techniques are widely studied, designed and applied to overcome these challenges in the past few years. With the rapid increase in the amount of data and their correlation, automatic metadata generation, ontology generation and evolution, and efficient, low cost and dynamic-updating semantic notation for WoT data indexing and model annotation have attracted great attention.

12.3.4 DATA OPERATIONS FOR INNER PLATFORM SUPPORT

In the WoT applications, data produced and consumed are mostly composed of the sensory data and generated data in stream. Based on data disposing process, related researches can be divided into data collection, data pre-disposing, information fusion and distributed data disposing.

12.3.4.1 *Data Collection*

A data collection protocol named EDAL [35] is modelled similarly to the open vehicle routing problem which is proved to be NP-hard. The EDAL is efficient in energy using, aware of delay and balancing in lifetime and used to collect data in wireless sensor network (WSN) domain.

The authors of [36] constructed a universal mobile data collection framework for WoT services. They addressed four basic requirements that are task specification, task managing, status sensing and data managing. Architecture for a general-purpose mobile data collection is also proposed which separates the whole system into two parts: one is the back-end operating on server sides and the other is font-end on mobile devices.

Aiming to carry out data stream analytic, OpenWoT approach [37] was proposed. It designs an event and clustering analytic server to collect sensor data from mobile devices and serves as an interface for data stream analysis. In detail, it uses intelligent servers and edge servers for real-time data collection, annotation and processing and adds some extensions for WoT data streams.

A sensor data stream delivery system was proposed with different delivery cycles for WoT environments [38]. When connected to servers and delivering sensor data stream, the system could provide a dynamic computational and communication performance according to the different requirement of clients.

The authors of [39] presented a hybrid system based on RFID and WSN called HRW, which integrates the traditional RFID systems and WSN systems for efficient data collection. HRW has a set of smart nodes which have both RFID and WSN functions and take place of RFID readers to gather data. Moreover, an enhanced data transmission algorithm which avoids the data redundancy and unnecessary overhead in transmission and security mechanisms which avoid data manipulation and data selective forwarding are proposed.

12.3.4.2 *Data pre-Disposing*

Considering that redundant information will be generated among nodes close to each other, a spatial correlation model [40] was proposed to minimize total consumption in process of data preservation. The problem of data preservation with data correlation can be transformed to the minimum cost flow problem, thus a more efficient and optimal solution than the greedy algorithm is proposed.

To solve the low efficiency and data redundancy of communications in integration, a data-cleaning algorithm called cross-redundant algorithm was proposed to archive higher performance. The authors of [41] proposed a five-layer system architecture for the integration of WSN and RFID, and chose Bluetooth and ZigBee as the communication protocols.

The authors of [42] proposed a classification method for the data streams based on some supervised classification techniques like SVM (Support Vector Machine) and reduces the volume of data by simple aggregation and approximation density. The former classification and labelling steps are the fundamentals of knowledge discovery in data stream.

A framework processing raw RFID data was proposed to reduce the uncertainty of data [43]. This framework is composed of two parts: a model tracking global objects and a model cleaning local RFID data. The former one is implemented with a Markov-based model and the latter one is implemented with a particle filter based approach.

For the purpose of communication and data collection among devices in heterogeneous network interfaces, a middleware that consists of a Multiple Protocol Transport Network (MPTN) gateway and a coordinated model was proposed [44]. Messaging and data alignment among multiple networks are implemented for concurrent data stream collections.

The authors of [45] proposed a technique preserving privacy while collecting data that can be used in healthcare applications with sensor and RFID. It assures secrecy of data via a data privacy protection mechanism and has been tested to pass various attacks. Moreover, it can be adapted for different scales of network.

12.3.4.3 *Information Fusion*

In [46], the authors applied OLAP techniques on sensor data to integrate data from different sources and to gather the correlative information for analysis and decision-making. An on-the-fly generating solution is proposed with metadata using the W3C semantic sensor network ontology and W3C RDF data cube vocabulary for generating multidimensional data cubes.

An automatic segmentation methodology [47] was proposed for real-time high-level activity prediction. The end of the predicated activity can be automatically marked and the training dataset can be divided into segments according the previous tagging.

In [48], the authors presented an online sensor data segmentation methodology for real-time activity recognition. A two-layer strategy composed of sensor correlation and time correlation manipulation is introduced to facilitate dynamic segmentation.

A data stream clustering algorithm [49] was proposed, which makes use of sliding window and micro-clusters merging in order to batch the similar quality farm products in the agricultural WoT platform.

The authors of [50] proposed an approach to implement some operations such as inquiries for heterogeneous sensor data that is in the format of RDF. The approach can process multiple data resources at the same time on the basis of ontology and can also integrate heterogeneous sensor data. It can construct SPARQL query statements automatically and query sensor data semantically according to the requirements of users.

12.3.4.4 *Distributed Data Processing*

In WoT data environment, data are changing on types, states and analysis purposes. Other than centralized master-server implementations, a parallel and particle data processing framework is need to enable the execution of MapReduce pattern in dynamic information infrastructures.

MapReduce is not perfect for every large-scale analytical task, and the cost of high communication and redundant processing makes a big challenge on WoT application. An approach which uses the MapReduce framework for large-scale graph data processing was given in [51]. The approach relies on a density-based partitioning to build balanced partitions of a graph database over a set of machines. The experiments show that the performance and scalability are satisfying for large scale data processing. However, in [52], a technical framework for improving MapReduce was given.

In [53], a parallel distributed processing system was proposed for data analysis. The system manages dependent relations between data and data, as well as data and analytic programs. The system aims to illustrate dependency and uses Hadoop Streaming for distributed parallel processing requirement. There are certain repeated executions in a program and may be executed with distinguished data each time. The specification filters these executions and check dependencies separately at each execution.

In [54], a storage system with high security and scalability on the basis of revised secret sharing scheme was proposed. The system is composed of two scalable, flexible and reliable layer: data layer and system layer. Using secret sharing scheme can avoid the complicated key management when using traditional cryptographic algorithms. Moreover, multiple storage servers for WoT data work together to achieve large storage capacity. However individual servers can still join or leave flexibly at system layer.

In [55], the authors proposed vRead, a programmable framework connecting HDFS I/O flows to the application data directly. vRead supports VMs to 'read' data node in disk images, which improves I/O flow without the overhead of virtualization.

12.3.4.5 *Comparison Between Data Operations Inside the Platform*

Data operations plat a fundamental role for inner platform support. Based on disposing steps, a comparison is given as Table 12.3.

(1) Data collection is always the first step in WoT applications. Considering WoT Data is often large-scale, dynamic, and at high sampling rates, some researches focus on how to organize the data collection tasks. And also a big part of researches focus on data transmission [35,38,49]. The authors of [36] built a general mobile data collection framework and talked about four basic requirements and some open issues in current mobile data collection framework. The authors of [37] made use of the OpenWoT middleware and designed an intelligent server for real time acquisition. Moreover, some researches paid attention to some open issues in data collection, such as privacy [45].

(2) Data pre-disposing is carried out for further data operation. With different disposing purposes, data pre-disposing methods can be divided into data preservation [40], data cleaning [41,43], data alignment [44] and so on. The authors of [42] proposed a classification method for the data streams based on some supervised classification approaches like Support Vector Machine (SVM) and reduced the volume of data.

(3) After collecting data from sensors, how to dispose the semi-structured, streaming data to extract information is another problem. The authors of [22] proposed an approach to extract event information from heterogeneous and massive raw data. The authors of [47,48] proposed some methods of data segmentation in order to recognize and predict human activities. And the authors of [49] designed a new data stream

Table 12.3 Comparison Between Data Disposing Methods

Researches	Data Resources	Semi-Structured Data	Data Stream	Generic	Main Methods	Topics
EDAL [35]	Data in WSN (Wireless Sensor Network) Domain	✓		✓	1. Modelled like OVR problems. 2. A centralized meta-heuristic. 3. A distributed heuristic.	Data Collection
Mobile Data Collection Framework [36]	Mobile Sensor Data	✓		✓	#4 Basic Rqrmnts + Additional Issues	Data Collection
A Sensor Data Stream Delivery System [38]	Sensory Data Stream	✓	✓		A sensor delivery system for flexible delivery cycles for different clients.	Data Collection (Data Stream Delivery)
Data Collection for Large-Scale Mobile Monitoring Applications [39]	Sensory Data with tag	✓			Methods to improve data transmission efficiency and to protect data privacy and avoid malicious data selective forwarding in data transmission.	Data Collection
Data Alignment for Multiple Temporal Data Streams [44]	Data Stream in Heterogeneous Network	✓	✓		1. A MPTN gateway for messaging and data alignment among multiple networks. 2. A coordinated model to collect concurrent data streams and convert time.	Data Collection (Data Alignment)
Constructing the web of events from raw data in the web of things [22]	Heterogeneous and Massive Raw Data	✓		✓	1. Conceptions (Event, Event Type, Link Type). 2. A Three-layered Model.	Data Pre-disposing (Information Extraction)
Data Preservation in Data-Intensive Sensor Networks with Spatial Correlation [40]	Sensory Data	✓		✓	Considering spatial correlation to reduce the redundant information.	Data Pre-disposing

(continued on next page)

Table 12.3 (continued)

Researches	Data Resources	Semi-Structured Data	Data Stream	Generic	Main Methods	Topics
Data Cleaning for RFID and WSN Integration [41]	RFID Data	✓		✓	1. A five-layer system architecture developed to integrate WSNs and RFID 2. Bluetooth and ZigBee are selected as communication protocols. 3. ICRDC is used for redundant data elimination.	Data Pre-disposing (Data Cleaning)
A Novel Learning Method to Classify Data Streams in the Internet of Things [42]	High Volume of Multi-dimensional Unlabeled Data Stream	✓	✓		1. Data Stream Classification methods based on SVM. 2. Dimension Reduction methods based on SAX Density.	Information fusion (Data Classification and Labelling)
Automatic Sensor Data Stream Segmentation for Real-time Activity Prediction in Smart Spaces [47]	Sensor Data Stream and Time Window	✓	✓		Automatic segmentation methods based on the peak value of JWD.	Information fusion (Activity Prediction)
A new Clustering Algorithm for sensor Data Streams in an Agricultural IoT [49]	Various Types of Sensor Data Stream in Agricultural IoT	✓	✓		A new data stream clustering algorithm based on sliding window and micro-clusters merging.	Information fusion (Data Stream Clustering)
Dynamic sensor event segmentation for real-time activity recognition in a smart home context [48]	Sensory Data	✓	✓		An online sensor data segmentation with two-layer strategy: sensor correlation and time correlation.	Information fusion (Data Segmentation)
Parallel, distributed, and differential processing system [53]	Sensory Data	✓		✓	managing dependent relations between data and data, data and analytic programs	Distributed data disposing

clustering algorithm in the agricultural WoT platform. Some of these researches take use of sliding windows to implement real-time processing.

(4) Despite its evident merits such as scalability, fault-tolerance, and flexibility, MapReduce [51] has limitation in interactive or real-time processing on handling distributed WoT data disposing. It is not perfect for every large-scale analytical task [54], and the high communication cost and redundant processing make a big challenge for IoT application. Therefore, some optimization work on WoT data are still needed for a large-scale processing purpose.

To sum up, the researches for WoT data operation are mainly concentrated on the following respects.

Firstly, researchers will pay more attention to disposing of different characteristics of WoT data, such as the elimination of redundant data, the alignment and merging of heterogeneous data, and online analysis for dynamic data. Secondly, researchers will take the integrations with existing technologies into consideration. On grounds that data in WoT applications are always at large-scale and with high sampling rate, the data disposing in WoT will be combined with the technologies of distributed computing, and streaming computing, such as Hadoop and Storm [56]. Thirdly, researchers will focus on more usage scenarios, such as activity recognition, complex cooperation, etc.

12.3.5 DATA SERVICE FOR EXTERNAL APPLICATION INTEROPERATION

Data service are used to provide functional support for WoT applications. The purposes of data service construction can be divided into three functional aspects as data interoperability, data-centric service composition and data analysis.

12.3.5.1 *Data Interoperability*

Although data interoperability development keeps innovative, some challenges exist. The researchers proposed a hub-centric framework [57] on interoperability and validated this framework in a large-scale WoT environment.

A novel Semantic WoT framework was proposed based on the Constrained Application Protocol (CoAP) [58]. The framework supports annotated resources retrieval and logical ranking on the basis of semantic matchmaking services with non-standard interface. To detect high-level events and specify them using machine-readable metadata, the framework also includes some approaches on data mining to deal with raw data gathered.

The authors of [59] proposed SAMPLES to classify network traffic generated by mobile applications. SAMPLES is composed of an offline part and an online part. The offline part is a training system in charge of rule generation and the online part is an engine for application identification and traffic classification. For each input flow, a subset of conjunctive rules is applied to the flow on the basis of pre-filtering conditions. Conjunctive rules are decided by context of lexica and a unique identifier of application in HTTP header.

12.3.5.2 *Data-Centric Service Composition*

Mashup tools [60] are used for the development of WoT applications, which can connect the dataflow between applications and devices in a graphical way. RESTful interfaces are generated from the WoT data models, which represent a set of sensors and actuators. Generic components extend existing mashup concepts and employ concepts to polymorphic functions as in many programming languages.

By means of the composition of web services with data streams from WoT devices [61], WoT devices are connected with web service in an efficient and extensible way. Thus real-time communication, device integration and data stream mashups are elaborated.

DiscoWoT [62] provided a semantic discovery service that supports semantic discovery of the functionality of smart things by human and machines. On the basis of multiple discovery strategies, the service provided by DiscoWoT supports all strategies using RESTful interface created or updated by users at runtime.

12.3.5.3 *Data Analysis*

To make WoT smarter [63], data mining was introduced into applications. A system architecture for WoT and big data mining system was proposed, in which lots of WoT devices are integrated into this system to perceive the world and generate data continuously. The system focuses on the integration with devices and data mining technologies, where data mining functions will be provided as service.

Condor [64] was proposed to handle data-parallel style execution of analysis algorithms in WoT system. The analytic processes are naturally data-parallel but the executions are not. Therefore, how to execute these processes in fixed time simultaneously becomes an important challenge. The architecture of the framework allows to synchronously execute any algorithms considering them as black boxes.

In [65], an overview of related issues and challenges in aspect of big data provenance research was presented, like Accessing Big Data, Minimum Computational Overhead Requirement and so on.

To sum up, RESTful service is the main form for external applications support. Application integration across heterogeneous and distributed environments is implemented by means of RESTful service. Thus, a flexible application construction and execution environment is provided for application interaction. However, how to combine REST APIs with inner distributed disposing environment for massive data analysis is not an easy task.

12.4 WOT DATA STORAGE IN CLOUD PLATFORM

In WoT applications, massive data from sensors consume large storage space. Meanwhile, since different roles and tenants require different service and security levels, data should be isolated for various requirements of performance and safety. How to share and isolate these data in cloud platform are the main challenges in WoT data storage.

12.4.1 THE INTEGRATION OF WEB OF THINGS WITH CLOUD COMPUTING

The development in cloud computing and WoT provides a hopeful way for the increasing WoT applications. CloudWoT [66] was proposed to integrates Cloud computing and WoT to bridge the gap between Cloud and WoT, which brings new opportunities in both technology and business areas.

The conception of Database-as-a-Service (DBaaS) [67] was constructed to move operational burden from database users to service operators, which means how to configure, adjust performance, backup and so on are not responsible for database users but the service users. Early DBaaS such as Microsoft SQL Azure and Amazon RDS always try to provide such services but do not pay much attention to multi-tenancy, flexible scalability challenge and database privacy.

A new vehicular data cloud with multiple layers [68] was presented under the support of cloud computing and WoT techniques. Two fresh and original cloud services: smart parking service and vehicular data mining service, were also presented to analyze vehicle warranty in the WoT environment. Two models integrating all available sensors or devices in vehicles and road based on Naïve Bayes and logistic regression models were proposed.

Links as a Service (LaaS) [69] was proposed to act as an innovative abstraction in cloud aspect. It provides isolation of network links to decrease interference in the cloud network. A unique link set is assigned to tenants and a virtual fat-tree is formed by these links. With these links, tenants feel just like it is the only one application in the shared cloud by getting the same bandwidth and delay. Finally, the forwarding mechanism will perfectly fit each tenant.

A transactional DBaaS named Relational Cloud [70] was introduced to solve the challenge of DBaaS. Relational Cloud has three significant technical characteristic: workload awareness, graph-based data partition and adjustable security. Firstly, the Cloud has multiple tenant and the system implements an approach identifying co-located workloads on server to gain good performance and high consolidation. Secondly, by exploiting a data partitioning algorithm based on graph, the system achieves near-linear flexible scale-out no matter the transactions are simple or complicated. Thirdly, the system provides an adaptable security scheme that allows certain queries to access encrypted data under secure situations. The concept of workload awareness is an underlying key of the system design. By supervising data accesses and query patterns, the system gathers useful information for sorts of optimization and security functions, which eliminates the effort of configuration for users and operators.

As adoption of cloud-based WoT is hindered by severe privacy concerns, to make users widely apply it in different areas, the authors of [71] presented a comprehensive privacy solution. In this approach, the potentially sensitive data are protected before uploaded to the cloud, the privacy functionality are packed as a service, whether the information is private is decided by users instead of developers, and users can configure privacy easily with transparent interfaces.

12.4.2 PERFORMANCE ISOLATION FOR MULTI-TENANT DATA STORAGE IN CLOUD PLATFORM

Aiming to assure the isolation within tenants, the authors proposed an approach based on a fitness function [72] and made some optimization to gain accurate weights to reflect different requirements.

An abstraction data model for performance isolation named SQLVM [73], was presented by the researchers at Microsoft. It is implemented in the condition of reserving key resources for tenants on database server, including CPU, I/O and memory. The main issue is that in a relational database system resource allocation is static, but the abstraction needs to allocate resources dynamically to tenants. Meanwhile, the overheads need to be low and the scale may grow very large. So the overhead and scalability are also great challenge. SQLVM can effectively isolate the performance of a tenant from the others while these tenants are co-located in same database server. And multiple scripted scenarios and a framework of data collection and visualization are applied to demonstrate the abstraction of SQLVM on performance isolation.

The authors of [74] focused on performance isolation when executing multi-tenant SaaS applications. They proposed a middleware architecture that uses a scheduler and a profiler known by tenant on the basis of tenant-specific SLAs to enhance performance isolation. The prototype they implemented reveals satisfying primary results.

In [75], the authors presented a resource allocation method in multi-tenant cloud environments by understanding the subtle interference between network, compute, and storage resources. The experiments provide insight that help cloud administrators know how to best distribute virtual cores to physical cores considering the effect of advanced virtual network technologies on remote block I/O performance.

To compare different performance isolation strategies, a standard metric is needed to quantitatively measure the capability of performance isolation in cloud. The metric should treat the cloud environment as a black box by running external benchmarks. In [76], the authors proposed three different metrics and applied them to a stimulant case mocking various tenants sharing one SaaS application instance.

The authors of [77] presented a tenant-isolated and fair system where every tenant in a data centre is isolated and shares key-value storage averagely. The previous resource allocation strategies rely on per-VM allocations and fix rate limits to make whole workloads achieve a high level. Pisces proposed by the authors corresponds to the weight of each tenant to assign the shared resources and services. The approach also works on the co-located situation and works when the request for many partitions is skewed time-varying or bottlenecked by different server resources.

In [78], the authors implemented an adaptive middleware that enables SaaS providers to efficiently enforce different and competing performance constraints in multi-tenant Software-as-a-Service(SaaS) applications. It can manage a combination of performance constraints in terms of latency, throughput and deadlines at a fine-grained level, and enables rapid response on changing circumstances, while preserving the resource usage efficiency of application-level multi-tenancy.

In short, the problem of sharing and isolating these data in cloud platform is still a main challenge in WoT data storage considering characteristics of different applications. There is still great contradiction between user authority and performance flexibility. Performance isolation has to be implemented in different levels with a consideration of different data types. Therefore, how to implement a data management model that solves the contradiction between secured sharing and performance isolation is the difficulty in current study of data management in cloud computing.

12.5 **TENDENCY FOR WOT DATA STORAGE TECHNOLOGY**

Currently, we are stepping into a new stage of Web3.0, which attracts more widely cooperation and crowd-sourcing both in information creation and information consumption. Therefore, data storage techniques for WoT applications have also move forwards to a new stage. Future technical tendency and some open issues are given from aspects of complex data representation, data storage and management, and real-time disposing mechanism, such as smart contextual models for data representation, big linked data for semantic data storage and management, and data stream mining for real-time data analysis and application.

12.5.1 **SMART CONTEXTUAL MODELS FOR COMPLEX DATA REPRESENTATION**

WoT data as a service faces the issues of interoperability and re-usability for massive heterogeneous sensor data and data services. Therefore, how to develop a smart device as an intelligent and self-organizational contextual model in the cloud platform is an important open issue.

The authors of [79] designed a developed platform named Semantic Web of Things (SWoT). The platform can provide semantic-based WoT application templates for developers so as to construct interoperable SWoT applications. And high-level abstractions are carried out to add sensor measurements into templates which help to reuse background or domain knowledge. Therefore, a unified platform for the implementation of interoperable semantic-based WoT applications is provided easily.

Considering complex data associations are generated from different sources or complex data structure, extracting relevant information in multilingual context from massive amounts of unstructured, structured and semi-structured data is a challenging task. Various theories have been developed and applied to ease the access to multicultural and multilingual resources. With the development of intelligent WoT applications, enhanced intelligence and contextualization models will enrich WoT with more expressive semantic association and support social interaction reasoning between smart things. It will facilitate smart things to construct a convenient and powerful devices or environment for intelligent WoT applications.

12.5.2 BIG LINKED DATA FOR SEMANTIC DATA STORAGE AND MANAGEMENT

Linked Data is defined as relationships or connections between data from different data sources such as databases and the Web. For the purpose of effective data management, semantic annotation based on linked data provides a new issue in a massive, complex associated and contextual application scene. These associated and contextual data play a critical role for intelligent application.

The authors of [80] described and annotated WoT data stream by means of linked-data. A novel semantic model containing the observation and measurement data is built to create expressive descriptions of sensor streams. And the semantic model is proved to be efficient, which can reduce the size of the representations of the stream data.

In short, driven-by semantic technology such as linked data and ontology, we could predict that semantic data processing approaches will get a great improvement in the near future. And a more natural and meaningful way with high-level information will be common in different WoT areas. Combined with Natural Language Processing, the semantic technology will be used to create more intelligent applications.

12.5.3 DATA STREAM DISPOSING FOR REAL-TIME DATA OPERATION

Unstructured data such as video data can not be stored into a structured database system for analysis purpose. And data mining on data stream form different data sources with non-persisted association is a new but important issue. There are several different directions to process data stream with some dynamic methods, for example, to retrieve features from continuous data stream so as to build data association, or to process the whole body of a fragment of data stream by function transformation.

In [81], WoT infrastructure should focus on real-time interaction in the future research. Therefore, a WoT micro-benchmark is designed to combine cloud computing, service decomposition and multi-threading programming. And the benchmark is evaluated over a real WoT system.

The Streaming Linked Data (SLD) framework [82] provides a pluggable system for analysis of RDF streams. By means of a set of visualization widgets, data streams could be collected and analysed based on semantic techniques. And the Streaming Linked Data Format can be used in distributed environments with flexibility.

Data Stream mining involves uncertain reasoning based on partition data and utilizes intermediate result for high efficiency. When unstructured and semi-structured data are also involved in the processing process, there are lots of researches and technical problems left to do.

12.6 CONCLUSION

As WoT technologies are evolving and acting an important role in many applications, the article surveys the timely literatures to give an overview of WoT data storage researches.

For the purpose of providing a clear insight for different WoT systems and techniques, a WoT data storage framework with multi-layer structure is given firstly. Then related techniques are described and discussed from the view of data disposing process such as data representation, storage, management, inner data operations and external data services and so on.

Cloud platform is a popular information infrastructure for current WoT applications. Data isolation and multi-tenant data storage are discussed to provide a critical and accurate knowledge of the current WoT data management in cloud platform. It is significant for current WoT applications to achieve higher availability and flexible resource provision in cloud platform.

Aiming to provide a future tendency for WoT data storage techniques, some open issues are given from the considerations of complex data model, semantic data management and real-time data disposing.

In short, data storage techniques can be utilized to offer competitive advantage to the intelligent WoT applications. However, lots of efforts still need to be made to respond to the high heterogeneous, massive dynamic, weak semantic features of WoT data.

REFERENCES

[1] Codd Edgar F. A relational model of data for large shared data banks. Commun ACM 1970;13(6):377–87.

[2] Padhy Rabi Prasad, Patra Manas Ranjan, Satapathy Suresh Chandra. Rdbms to nosql: reviewing some next-generation non-relational databases. Int J Adv Eng Sci Technol 2011;11(1):15–30.

[3] Ghandeharizadeh Shahram, Yap Jason. Cache augmented database management systems. In: Proceedings of the ACM SIGMOD workshop on databases and social networks. ACM; 2013. p. 31–6.

[4] Brucato Matteo, Beltran Juan Felipe, Abouzied Azza, Meliou Alexandra. Scalable package queries in relational database systems. Proc VLDB Endow 2016;9(7):576–87.

[5] Huang Han-Sheng, Hung Shih-Hao, Yeh Chih-Wei. Load balancing for hybrid nosql database management systems. In: Proceedings of the 2015 conference on research in adaptive and convergent systems. ACM; 2015. p. 80–5.

[6] Bui Dinh-Mao, Hussain Shujaat, Huh Eui-Nam, Lee Sungyoung. Adaptive replication management in hdfs based on supervised learning. IEEE Trans Knowl Data Eng 2016;28(6):1369–82.

[7] Thusoo Ashish, Sarma Joydeep Sen, Jain Namit, Shao Zheng, Chakka Prasad, Zhang Ning, Antony Suresh, Liu Hao, Murthy Raghotham. Hive-a petabyte scale data warehouse using hadoop. In: 2010 IEEE 26th international conference on data engineering (ICDE). IEEE; 2010. p. 996–1005.

[8] Dipayan Dipayan, Patgiri Ripon. Performance evaluation of hdfs in big data management. In: 2014 international conference on high performance computing and applications (ICHPCA). IEEE; 2014. p. 1–7.

[9] Leis Viktor, Kemper Alfons, Neumann Thomas. Exploiting hardware transactional memory in main-memory databases. In: 2014 IEEE 30th international conference on data engineering (ICDE). IEEE; 2014. p. 580–91.

[10] Ray Suprio, Blanco Rolando, Goel Anil K. Supporting location-based services in a main-memory database. In: 2014 IEEE 15th international conference on mobile data management (MDM), vol. 1. IEEE; 2014. p. 3–12.

[11] Yao Xiao, Qiu Qiang, Zhang Mengfei, Chen Cuiting, Fang Jinyun. Research on vector spatial data access based on main memory database. In: 2015 IEEE international geoscience and remote sensing symposium (IGARSS). IEEE; 2015. p. 4704–7.

[12] Babarinsa Oreoluwatomiwa O, Idreos Stratos. Jafar: near-data processing for databases. In: Proceedings of the 2015 ACM SIGMOD international conference on management of data. ACM; 2015. p. 2069–70.

[13] Chang Fay, Dean Jeffrey, Ghemawat Sanjay, Hsieh Wilson C, Wallach Deborah A, Burrows Mike, Chandra Tushar, Fikes Andrew, Gruber Robert E. Bigtable: a distributed storage system for structured data. ACM Trans Comput Syst (TOCS) 2008;26(2):4.

[14] Wei Wei, Yu Ting, Xue Rui. ibigtable: practical data integrity for bigtable in public cloud. In: Proceedings of the third ACM conference on data and application security and privacy. ACM; 2013. p. 341–52.

[15] Vicknair Chad, Macias Michael, Zhao Zhendong, Nan Xiaofei, Chen Yixin, Wilkins Dawn. A comparison of a graph database and a relational database: a data provenance perspective. In: Proceedings of the 48th annual southeast regional conference. ACM; 2010. p. 42.

[16] Yan Xifeng, Yu Philip S, Han Jiawei. Graph indexing: a frequent structure-based approach. In: Proceedings of the 2004 ACM SIGMOD international conference on management of data. ACM; 2004. p. 335–46.

[17] Libkin Leonid, Martens Wim, Vrgoč Domagoj. Querying graph databases with xpath. In: Proceedings of the 16th international conference on database theory. ACM; 2013. p. 129–40.

[18] Graves Mark, Bergeman Ellen R, Lawrence Charles B. Graph database systems. IEEE Eng Med Biol Mag 1995;14(6):737–45.

[19] Barceló Baeza Pablo. Querying graph databases. In: Proceedings of the 32nd symposium on principles of database systems. ACM; 2013. p. 175–88.

[20] Yu Haining, Fang Binxing, Yu Xiangzhan, Chen Juan. Semantic surface representation of physical entity in the web of things. In: 2012 IEEE 2nd international conference on cloud computing and intelligent systems (CCIS), vol. 3. IEEE; 2012. p. 1032–6.

[21] Sun Yunchuan, Jara Antonio J. An extensible and active semantic model of information organizing for the internet of things. Pers Ubiquitous Comput 2014;18(8):1821–33.

[22] Sun Yunchuan, Yan Hongli, Lu Cheng, Bie Rongfang, Zhou Zhangbing. Constructing the web of events from raw data in the web of things. Mob Inf Syst 2014;10(1):105–25.

[23] Qu Chao, Liu Fagui, Tao Ming, Deng Dacheng. An owl-s based specification model of dynamic entity services for internet of things. J Ambient Intell Humaniz Comput 2016;7(1):73–82.

[24] Christophe Benoit. Semantic profiles to model the "web of things". In: 2011 seventh international conference on semantics knowledge and grid (SKG). IEEE; 2011. p. 51–8.

[25] Perez de Almeida Ricardo Aparecido, Blackstock Michael, Lea Rodger, Calderon Roberto, do Prado Antonio Francisco, Guardia Helio Crestana. Thing broker: a twitter for things. In: Proceedings of the 2013 ACM conference on pervasive and ubiquitous computing adjunct publication. ACM; 2013. p. 1545–54.

[26] Devaraju Anusuriya, Kuhn Werner, Renschler Chris S. A formal model to infer geographic events from sensor observations. Int J Geogr Inf Sci 2015;29(1):1–27.

[27] Harbelot Benjamin, Arenas Helbert, Cruz Christophe. Continuum: a spatiotemporal data model to represent and qualify filiation relationships. In: Proceedings of the 4th ACM SIGSPATIAL international workshop on GeoStreaming. ACM; 2013. p. 76–85.

[28] Consoli Sergio, Mongiovic Misael, Nuzzolese Andrea G, Peroni Silvio, Presutti Valentina, Reforgiato Recupero Diego, Spampinato Daria. A smart city data model based on semantics best practice and principles. In: Proceedings of the 24th international conference on world wide web companion. 2015. p. 1395–400. International World Wide Web Conferences Steering Committee.

[29] Wang Yixue, Lv HaiTao. Efficient metadata management in cloud computing. In: 2011 IEEE 3rd international conference on communication software and networks (ICCSN). 2011. p. 514–9.

[30] Beatty Daniel, Lopez-Benitez Noé. Mobile metadata for web-based image query services. In: 2010 eleventh international conference on mobile data management (MDM). IEEE; 2010. p. 53–8.

[31] Mayer Simon, Basler Gianin. Semantic metadata to support device interaction in smart environments. In: Proceedings of the 2013 ACM conference on pervasive and ubiquitous computing adjunct publication. ACM; 2013. p. 1505–14.

[32] Scioscia Floriano, Binetti Mario, Ruta Michele, Ieva Saverio, Di Sciascio Eugenio. A framework and a tool for semantic annotation of pois in openstreetmap. Proc, Soc Behav Sci 2014;111:1092–101.

[33] Ganz Frieder, Barnaghi Payam, Carrez Francois. Automated semantic knowledge acquisition from sensor data. IEEE Syst J 2016;10(3):1214–25.

[34] Cai Hongming, Shi Mengwei, Xu Boyi, Yu Mingjiu. Semantic annotation for web3d scene based on three-layer ontology. Integr Comput-Aided Eng 2015;22(1):87–101.

[35] Yao Yanjun, Cao Qing, Vasilakos Athanasios V. Edal: an energy-efficient, delay-aware, and lifetime-balancing data collection protocol for heterogeneous wireless sensor networks. IEEE/ACM Trans Netw 2015;23(3):810–23.

[36] Cao Paul Y, Li Gang, Chen Guoxing, Chen Biao. Mobile data collection frameworks: a survey. In: Proceedings of the 2015 workshop on mobile big data. ACM; 2015. p. 25–30.

[37] Hromic Hugo, Le Phuoc Danh, Serrano Martin, Antonic Aleksandar, Zarko Ivana P, Hayes Conor, Decker Stefan. Real time analysis of sensor data for the internet of things by means of clustering and event processing. In: 2015 IEEE international conference on communications (ICC). IEEE; 2015. p. 685–91.

[38] Yoshihisa Tomoki, Ishi Yoshimasa, Mako Kodai, Kawakami Tomoya, Teranishi Yuuichi. A sensor data stream delivery system with different delivery cycles for iot environments. In: 2015 10th international conference on P2P, parallel, grid, cloud and internet computing (3PGCIC). IEEE; 2015. p. 748–53.

[39] Shen Haiying, Li Ze, Yu Lei, Qiu Chenxi. Efficient data collection for large-scale mobile monitoring applications. IEEE Trans Parallel Distrib Syst 2014;25(6):1424–36.

[40] Crary Nathaniel, Tang Bin, Taase Setu. Data preservation in data-intensive sensor networks with spatial correlation. In: Proceedings of the 2015 workshop on mobile big data. ACM; 2015. p. 7–12.

[41] Wang Li, Xu Li Da, Bi Zhuming, Xu Yingcheng. Data cleaning for rfid and wsn integration. IEEE Trans Ind Inform 2014;10(1):408–18.

[42] Khan Muhammad Asad, Khan Ajmal, Khan Muhammad Nasir, Anwar Sohel. A novel learning method to classify data streams in the internet of things. In: 2014 national software engineering conference (NSEC). IEEE; 2014. p. 61–6.

[43] Ma Jiangang, Sheng Quan Z, Xie Dong, Chuah Jen Min, Qin Yongrui. Efficiently managing uncertain data in rfid sensor networks. World Wide Web 2015;18(4):819–44.

[44] Shih Chi-Sheng, Yang Chan-Ming, Cheng Yen-Chien. Data alignment for multiple temporal data streams without synchronized clocks on iot fusion gateway. In: 2015 IEEE international conference on data science and data intensive systems. IEEE; 2015. p. 667–74.

[45] Rahman Farin, Williams Doug, Ahamed Sheikh Iqbal, Yang Ji-Jiang, Wang Qing. Pridac: privacy preserving data collection in sensor enabled rfid based healthcare services. In: 2014 IEEE 15th international symposium on high-assurance systems engineering (HASE). IEEE; 2014. p. 236–42.

[46] Mehdi Muntazir, Sahay Ratnesh, Derguech Wassim, Curry Edward. On-the-fly generation of multidimensional data cubes for web of things. In: Proceedings of the 17th international database engineering & applications symposium. ACM; 2013. p. 28–37.

[47] Cho Hyunjeong, An Jihoon, Hong Intaek, Lee Younghee. Automatic sensor data stream segmentation for real-time activity prediction in smart spaces. In: Proceedings of the 2015 workshop on IoT challenges in mobile and industrial systems. ACM; 2015. p. 13–8.

[48] Wan Jie, O'Grady Michael J, O'Hare Gregory MP. Dynamic sensor event segmentation for real-time activity recognition in a smart home context. Pers Ubiquitous Comput 2015;19(2):287–301.

[49] Wu Mingze, Wang Yitong, Liao Zhicheng. A new clustering algorithm for sensor data streams in an agricultural iot. In: 2013 IEEE 10th international conference on high performance computing and communications & 2013 IEEE international conference on embedded and ubiquitous computing. IEEE; 2013. p. 2373–8.

[50] Zhang Xiaoming, Zhao Yunping, Wang Xiang, Pan Dongyu. An approach to provide visual data service for heterogeneous sensor data based on ssn ontology. In: 2015 international conference on identification, information, and knowledge in the internet of things (IIKI). IEEE; 2015. p. 254–7.

[51] Aridhi Sabeur, d'Orazio Laurent, Maddouri Mondher, Nguifo Engelbert Mephu. Density-based data partitioning strategy to approximate large-scale subgraph mining. Inf Sci 2015;48:213–23.

[52] Doulkeridis Christos, Nørvåg Kjetil. A survey of large-scale analytical query processing in mapreduce. VLDB J 2014;23(3):355–80.

[53] Toda Takamichi, Inoue Sozo, Li Lin. Parallel, distributed, and differential processing system for human activity sensing flows. In: Proceedings of the 2013 ACM conference on pervasive and ubiquitous computing adjunct publication. ACM; 2013. p. 689–700.

[54] Jiang Hai, Shen Feng, Chen Su, Li Kuan-Ching, Jeong Young-Sik. A secure and scalable storage system for aggregate data in iot. Future Gener Comput Syst 2015;49:133–41.

[55] Xu Cong, Saltaformaggio Brendan, Gamage Sahan, Kompella Ramana Rao, Xu Dongyan. vread: efficient data access for hadoop in virtualized clouds. In: Proceedings of the 16th annual middleware conference. ACM; 2015. p. 125–36.

[56] Toshniwal Ankit, Taneja Siddarth, Shukla Amit, Ramasamy Karthik, Patel Jignesh M, Kulkarni Sanjeev, Jackson Jason, Gade Krishna, Fu Maosong, Donham Jake, Bhagat Nikunj, Mittal Sailesh, Ryaboy Dmitriy. Storm@twitter. In: Proceedings of the 2014

ACM SIGMOD international conference on management of data, SIGMOD '14. ACM; 2014. p. 147–56.

[57] Blackstock Michael, Lea Rodger. Toward interoperability in a web of things. In: Proceedings of the 2013 ACM conference on pervasive and ubiquitous computing adjunct publication. ACM; 2013. p. 1565–74.

[58] Ruta Michele, Scioscia Floriano, Pinto Allan, Di Sciascio Eugenio, Gramegna Fabiana, Ieva Saverio, Loseto Giuseppe. Resource annotation, dissemination and discovery in the semantic web of things: a coap-based framework. In: Green computing and communications (GreenCom), 2013 IEEE and internet of things (iThings/CPSCom), IEEE international conference on and IEEE cyber, physical and social computing. IEEE; 2013. p. 527–34.

[59] Yao Hongyi, Ranjan Gyan, Tongaonkar Alok, Liao Yong, Mao Zhuoqing Morley. Samples: self adaptive mining of persistent lexical snippets for classifying mobile application traffic. In: Proceedings of the 21st annual international conference on mobile computing and networking. ACM; 2015. p. 439–51.

[60] Prehofer Christian, Schinner Dominik. Generic operations on restful resources in mashup tools. In: Proceedings of the 6th international workshop on the web of things. ACM; 2015. p. 3.

[61] Kleinfeld Robert, Steglich Stephan, Radziwonowicz Lukasz, Doukas Charalampos. glue.things: a mashup platform for wiring the internet of things with the internet of services. In: Proceedings of the 5th international workshop on web of things. ACM; 2014. p. 16–21.

[62] Mayer Simon, Guinard Dominique. An extensible discovery service for smart things. In: Proceedings of the second international workshop on web of things. ACM; 2011. p. 7.

[63] Chen Feng, Deng Pan, Wan Jiafu, Zhang Daqiang, Vasilakos Athanasios V, Rong Xiaohui. Data mining for the internet of things: literature review and challenges. Int J Distrib Sens Netw 2015;2015(12).

[64] Mukherjee Arijit, Dey Swarnava, Paul Himadri Sekhar, Das Batsayan. Utilising condor for data parallel analytics in an iot context—an experience report. In: 2013 IEEE 9th international conference on wireless and mobile computing, networking and communications (WiMob). IEEE; 2013. p. 325–31.

[65] Cuzzocrea Alfredo. Provenance research issues and challenges in the big data era. In: 2015 IEEE 39th annual computer software and applications conference (COMPSAC), vol. 3. IEEE; 2015. p. 684–6.

[66] Botta Alessio, de Donato Walter, Persico Valerio, Pescapé Antonio. Integration of cloud computing and internet of things: a survey. Future Gener Comput Syst 2016;56:684–700.

[67] Lehner Wolfgang, Sattler Kai-Uwe. Database as a service (dbaas). In: 2010 IEEE 26th international conference on data engineering (ICDE 2010). IEEE; 2010. p. 1216–7.

[68] He Wu, Yan Gongjun, Xu Li Da. Developing vehicular data cloud services in the iot environment. IEEE Trans Ind Inform 2014;10(2):1587–95.

[69] Zahavi Eitan, Shpiner Alexander, Rottenstreich Ori, Kolodny Avinoam, Keslassy Isaac. Links as a service (laas): guaranteed tenant isolation in the shared cloud. In: Proceedings of the 2016 symposium on architectures for networking and communications systems. ACM; 2016. p. 87–98.

[70] Curino Carlo, Jones Evan PC, Popa Raluca Ada, Malviya Nirmesh, Wu Eugene, Madden Sam, Balakrishnan Hari, Zeldovich Nickolai. Relational cloud: a database-as-a-service for the cloud. In: 5th biennial conference on innovative data systems research, CIDR 2011. 2011. p. 235–40.

[71] Henze Martin, Hermerschmidt Lars, Kerpen Daniel, Häußling Roger, Rumpe Bernhard, Wehrle Klaus. A comprehensive approach to privacy in the cloud-based internet of things. Future Gener Comput Syst 2016;56:701–18.

[72] Krebs Rouven, Schneider Philipp, Herbst Nikolas. Optimization method for request admission control to guarantee performance isolation. In: Proceedings of the 2nd international workshop on hot topics in cloud service scalability. ACM; 2014. p. 4.

[73] Narasayya Vivek, Das Sudipto, Syamala Manoj, Chaudhuri Surajit, Li Feng, Park Hyunjung. A demonstration of sqlvm: performance isolation in multi-tenant relational database-as-a-service. In: Proceedings of the 2013 ACM SIGMOD international conference on management of data. ACM; 2013. p. 1077–80.

[74] Walraven Stefan, Monheim Tanguy, Truyen Eddy, Joosen Wouter. Towards performance isolation in multi-tenant saas applications. In: Proceedings of the 7th workshop on middleware for next generation internet computing. ACM; 2012. p. 6.

[75] Ruth Paul, Mandal Anirban, Castillo Claris, Fowler Robert, Tilson Jeff, Baldin Ilya, Xin Yufeng. Achieving performance isolation on multi-tenant networked clouds using advanced block storage mechanisms. In: Proceedings of the 6th workshop on scientific cloud computing. ACM; 2015. p. 29–32.

[76] Krebs Rouven, Momm Christof, Kounev Samuel. Metrics and techniques for quantifying performance isolation in cloud environments. Sci Comput Program 2014;90:116–34.

[77] Shue David, Freedman Michael J, Shaikh Anees. Performance isolation and fairness for multi-tenant cloud storage. In: Presented as part of the 10th USENIX symposium on operating systems design and implementation (OSDI 12). USENIX; 2012. p. 349–62.

[78] Walraven Stefan, De Borger Wouter, Vanbrabant Bart, Lagaisse Bert, Van Landuyt Dimitri, Joosen Wouter. Adaptive performance isolation middleware for multi-tenant saas. In: 2015 IEEE/ACM 8th international conference on utility and cloud computing (UCC). IEEE; 2015. p. 112–21.

[79] Bizer Christian. The emerging web of linked data. IEEE Intell Syst 2009;24(5):87–92.

[80] Barnaghi Payam, Wang Wei, Dong Lijun, Wang Chonggang. A linked-data model for semantic sensor streams. In: Green computing and communications (GreenCom), 2013 IEEE and internet of things (iThings/CPSCom), IEEE international conference on and IEEE cyber, physical and social computing. IEEE; 2013. p. 468–75.

[81] Gomes Márcio Miguel, da Rosa Righi Rodrigo, da Costa Cristiano André. Future directions for providing better iot infrastructure. In: Proceedings of the 2014 ACM international joint conference on pervasive and ubiquitous computing: adjunct publication. ACM; 2014. p. 51–4.

[82] Balduini Marco, Della Valle Emanuele, Dell'Aglio Daniele, Tsytsarau Mikalai, Palpanas Themis, Confalonieri Cristian. Social listening of city scale events using the streaming linked data framework. In: The semantic web–ISWC 2013. Springer; 2013. p. 1–16.

APPLICATIONS, SECURITY AND SOCIAL IMPACT

WOX: MODEL-DRIVEN DEVELOPMENT OF WEB OF THINGS APPLICATIONS

13

Adriana Caione*,†, **Alessandro Fiore***,†, **Luca Mainetti***,†, **Luigi Manco***,†, **Roberto Vergallo***,†

Department of Innovation Engineering, University of Salento, Lecce, Italy* *VidyaSoft s.r.l., Spin-off company of Salento University, Lecce, Italy*†

CHAPTER POINTS

- Web of Topics (WoX) is a Cloud platform for the Internet of (every) Thing.
- WoX APIs allows companies and organisations to realise robust and high-maintainable IoT-based services, while minimising deployment costs and the time-to-market.
- Its model-driven approach guarantees a great end-user experience and a seamless integration among the heterogeneous IoT entities.

13.1 INTRODUCTION

During the last few years we have witnessed the Internet of Things reaching the market level, so that it is definitely entering our homes, cars, offices, and cities. Gartner, Inc. forecasts that 6.4 billion connected things will be in use worldwide in 2016, up 30 percent from 2015, and will reach 20.8 billion by 2020. In 2016, 5.5 million new things will get connected every day [1]. Unfortunately, most IoT vendors attempt to lock the users onto their platforms, keeping their solutions siloed and not interoperable. This approach clashes with the smart city evolution fundament: for a connected community to succeed there needs to be a mix of large corporations, startups, community groups and government agencies working together. The smart citizen is becoming aware of the siloed IoT, especially when comparing the IoT experience with the Web experience. Free Web-based services like "If This Then That" (IFTTT) allows users to create chains of simple conditional statements involving heterogeneous Web services such as Gmail, Facebook, Instagram, Pinterest, and Dropbox. In the IoT instead, when crossing the borders of silos, users must open a

Managing the Web of Things. DOI: 10.1016/B978-0-12-809764-9.00017-2

new app, talk a new language, pay with a new wallet. IFTTT is a benchmark for the future IoT. The IoT looking at IFTTT is called Internet of Everything (IoE) and will be supported by XaaS (anything/everything as a Service) infrastructures. In the IoE, not only physical devices but also "virtual" data streams are available. The Web of Things (WoT) paradigm plays a key role in the IoE: everything is a Web resource. But it is not enough. Sharing a common application layer protocol on top of the physical "things" does not guarantee interoperability. Defining REST APIs for the IoT objects remains in charge of the system integrator, whose aim is to develop the best fitting APIs for the specific use case. Other related issues are: technological needs may vary as long as new sensing technologies gain popularity; IoT applications should be fast-developed, robust and easily evolvable; stakeholders are often interested in aggregated environment features, rather than the specific networked or virtual thing. To overcome these open issues, we think that it is needed an additional abstraction level between the WoT and the application layer. This should be model-driven – in order this to be adequately agreed by all the IoT stakeholders – and topic-based – because of the event-driven nature of the IoT. In this work we propose Web of Topics (WoX), a Cloud platform for the IoE. WoX APIs allows companies and organisations to develop robust and high-maintainable IoT-based services, while minimising deployment costs and the time-to-market. The WoX model-driven approach guarantees a great end-user experience and a seamless integration among the heterogeneous IoT entities. In WoX, the key entity between who needs and who offers IoT capabilities is the WoX Topic, which wraps the value of a Feature of interest (taken from a discrete taxonomy, e.g. presence, temperature, or even higher concepts such as crowd or power saving), in a URI-identified Location. A WoX entity declares its Role within a Topic by specifying its technological (source/executor/function) and collaborative (capability/need) dimensions. We built the WoX architecture on top of an EPCglobal implementation. We published the WoX APIs on the WSO2 Enterprise Service Bus (ESB) in order to exploit the key benefits of an enterprise architecture: security, scalability, interoperability, etc. WoX brings two main advantages:

- WoX defines a standard, effective and efficient way of connecting the real world to the applications: not only concrete things but also 'virtual' things can be easily wired to develop innovative scenarios. WoX concepts are close to the people: anyone can design and deploy custom scenarios;
- WoX accelerates the development of the applications, by taking care of the communication with the heterogeneous WoT things. It hides the protocol details, while letting designers/developers concentrate on their business.

This chapter is organized as follows. Section 13.2 reports on the existing standards, guidelines and initiatives currently esteemed in the IoT, as well as a scientific literature in the matter of IoE. Section 13.3 outlines the open issues and challenges. Section 13.4 describes the WoX model. Section 13.5 describes the design and implementation of the Cloud architecture supporting the WoX model. As a proof of concept, Section 13.6 shows how we implemented an original IoT scenario using the

WoX concepts, APIs and architecture. Section 13.7 sketches the conclusions as well as the future work.

13.2 STATE OF THE ART
13.2.1 IOT AND WOT STANDARDS

In the IoT domain, anyone can propose an own architecture and an own communication protocol, due to a wide variety of requirements to which each architecture should be compliant. Then, each solution could propose a reference model and encourage clients to use it. Some consortium of universities and companies working in IoT have proposed the birth of few common reference models. A common reference model for the IoT domain and the identification of reference architectures can help to a faster, more focused development and an exponential increase of IoT-related solutions. WoX architectural model is developed looking at two IoT standards IoT-A and ITU-T, which we present in the next sections. Moreover we will also analyze two data representation formats: SensorML and Observation&Measurement.

The IoT-A Reference Model

The European Lighthouse Integrated Project has addressed for three years the Internet-of-Things Architecture (IoT-A) [2] and created an architectural reference model together with the definition of an initial set of key building blocks. It wants to promote a common ground between architectures so that they can interoperate even a more levels. IoT-A has achieved that thanks to two steps:

- Establishing a Reference Model;
- Providing a Reference Architecture.

The IoT-A ARM (Architecture Reference Model) (Fig. 13.1) consists of four parts:

- Vision: summarizes the rationale for providing an architectural reference model for the IoT;
- Business scenarios: define requirements provided by stakeholders that are the drivers of the architecture. They allow the architecture to be validated;
- The IoT Reference Model, which provides the highest abstraction level for the definition of the IoT-A Architectural Reference Model. It promotes a common understanding of the IoT domain. It includes the description of domain, communication and information model;
- The IoT Reference Architecture, which is the reference for building compliant IoT architectures. It provides views and perspectives on different architectural aspects that are of concern to stakeholders of the IoT.

An important aspect is the compliance of their technologies with standards and best practices, so that interoperability across organizations is ensured. If such compli-

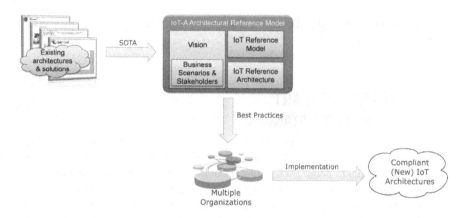

FIGURE 13.1

IoT-A ARM. *Source:* IoT-A project

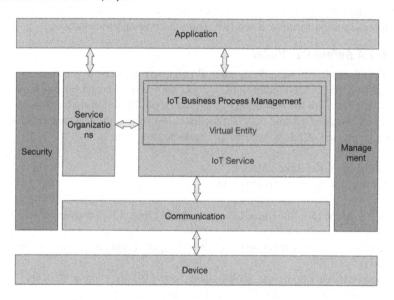

FIGURE 13.2

IOT-A Information Model. *Source:* IOT-A project

ance is given, the ecosystem allow every stakeholder to create new businesses entities that "interoperate" with already existing entities. Fig. 13.2 shows a high level information model derived by the IoT-A architecture. This model is so abstract that can represent any generic IoT solution. In particular, the device layer represents each device that interacts with the architecture and the communication layer represents mechanism to do it.

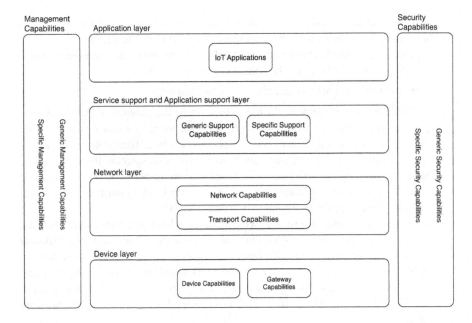

FIGURE 13.3

ITU-T Reference Model. *Source:* ITU-T project

ITU-T

The ITU Telecommunication Standardization Sector (ITU-T) [3] is one of the three sectors of the International Telecommunication Union (ITU). It coordinates standards for telecommunications. The main products of ITU-T are Recommendations (ITU-T Recs) standards defining how telecommunication networks operate and interwork. ITU-T Recs have non-mandatory status until they are adopted in national laws. ITU-T recommendations are guidelines to develop IoT application. They have a deeply impact both for implementation phase and for validation stage in IoT software architectures. Fig. 13.3 shows the IoT reference model. It is composed of four layers as well as management capabilities and security capabilities which are associated with the four layers: the application layer, the service support and application support layer, the network layer, and device layer.

In particular, the device layer capabilities can be logically categorized into two kinds of capabilities:

- Device capabilities, which include but are not limited to:
  - Direct interaction with the communication network: Devices are able to gather and upload information directly (i.e., without using gateway capabilities) to the communication network and can directly receive information (e.g., commands) from the communication network.

- Indirect interaction with the communication network: Devices are able to gather and upload information to the communication network indirectly, i.e., through gateway capabilities. On the other side, devices can indirectly receive information (e.g., commands) from the communication network.

• Gateway capabilities, which include but are not limited to:

- Multiple interfaces support: At the device layer, the gateway capabilities support devices connected through different kinds of wired or wireless technologies, such as a controller area network (CAN) bus, ZigBee, Bluetooth or Wi-Fi. At the network layer, the gateway capabilities may communicate through various technologies, such as the public switched telephone network (PSTN), second generation or third generation (2G or 3G) networks, long-term evolution networks (LTE), Ethernet or digital subscriber lines (DSL).

- Protocol conversion: There are two situations where gateway capabilities are needed. One situation is when communications at the device layer use different device layer protocols, e.g., ZigBee technology protocols and Bluetooth technology protocols, the other one is when communications involving both the device layer and network layer use different protocols e.g., a ZigBee technology protocol at the device layer and a 3G technology protocol at the network layer.

SensorML

The SensorML standard is originated from the work of Sensor Web Enablement (SWE) activity. Its primary focus is to provide a framework for defining processes and components associated with the measurement processes for sensors. The standard specifies models and an XML implementation, and provides a common framework for describing any process. Processes are entities that take one or more inputs and through the application of well defined methods and configurable parameters, they produce one or more outputs. SensorML can be used to describe a wide variety of processes, not only sensors, but also actuators and generic data transformation processes. SensorML also supports explicit linking between processes and thus supports the concept of process chains, networks, or workflows, which are themselves defined as processes using a composite pattern. Interoperability within and between various sensor communities is greatly improved through the definition of shared community-specific semantics (within online dictionaries or ontologies) that can be utilized within the framework.

Observation & Measurement

O&M (OGC Observation and Measurement) is a standard model of SWE for encoding observations and measurements from sensors. This model provides guidelines for accessing and exchanging observations without the need of supporting specific data formats. O&M propose also an implementation of the aforementioned standard. It was firstly proposed the use of an XML encoding, but a JSON encoding has been recently adopted. It guarantees a lightweight format to exchange data with web services and optimized memory resource thanks to the compact encoding. The OGC defines an Observation as the act of observe a property of a feature at a certain instant of time. The output of this action is a result that reports a value describing some phenomenon. Therefore, the observation is modeled as an object with a set of properties:

- Feature of interest: the property to classify;
- Observed property: a description of the observed property;
- Result: a value (numerical or not) that describes the result of the observation;
- Procedure: the process that make possible to do the observation;
- Phenomenon time: the timestamp associated to the observation;
- Result time: the timestamp associated to the instant the phenomenon happened;
- Validity time: the timestamp during which the result is valid.

13.2.2 IOT AND WOT RESEARCH WORKS

In the literature, the interest in design and development of WoT software architectures, using different approaches, is very deep. Several Web platforms are emerging with the aim to abstract the heterogeneity of the physical embedded devices in order to facilitate their integration and interoperability. Most of the existing architectures belong to two main categories:

- Architectures based on international standards. They enjoy several benefits arising from compliance with international standards, but they are very close to the physical layer. Therefore, using these architectures requires expert knowledge of physical technologies and significant familiarity with programming languages. Furthermore, they are generally focused on a specific use cases and are not horizontal enough to support the integration of heterogeneous technologies.
- Horizontal architectures, which are explicitly designed to integrate heterogeneous protocols and standards. Semantic architectures, for example, belong to this category. Generally, these architectures are not compliant with international standards, but have the considerable advantage of being closer to the developer's mental model, who is not required to know about the involved physical technologies nor specific programming languages.

Regarding the first category, in [8] authors propose an IoT framework, based on the EPCglobal [4] architecture, which is able to integrate the transducer capability of IEEE 1451 standards [9]. As the original EPCglobal definition only supports C-1 Gen-2 RFID tag identification, authors propose to extend the framework to support more readers, tags, and transducers in versatile IoT applications. EPCglobal Application Level Events (ALE) middleware is provided with transducer capability of IEEE 1451. Regarding the second category, the Semantic Web of Things (SWoT) is an emerging activity in Information and Communication Technology (ICT), joining together the Semantic Web and the Internet of Things. Its goal is to associate semantically rich and easily accessible information to real-world objects, locations and events, by means of a service infrastructure that makes easy the deployment and use of semantic applications involving Internet of Things devices, as described in [10].

A widely used tool for the development of semantic architectures is Smart-M3 [11]. It is a content-based, semantic subscribe-notify, and open-source middleware able to provide a Semantic Web information-sharing infrastructure among software entities and devices. The main goals of Smart-M3 is the sharing interoperable information in smart environment applications and making information in the physical world available for smart services. Authors in [12] describe their own vision a middleware for the Internet of Things, with the aims of creating a new generation middleware platform which will enable self-managed complex systems, in particular industrial ones, consisting of distributed, heterogeneous, shared and reusable components of different nature. Grounding on semantic and Multi-Agent System technologies and methodologies, they analyze and design such middleware and demonstrate how it is possible to enable various components to automatically discover each other and to configure a system with complex functionalities based on the atomic functions of the components. Another interesting horizontal approach is presented in [13], where authors propose a software architecture to easily mash-up CoAP resources. The architecture is able to discover the available devices and to virtualize them outside the physical network. These virtualizations are then exposed to the upper layers by a RESTful interface, so that the physical devices interact only with their own virtualization. The architecture is designed to establish a bidirectional communication channel, allowing not only to monitor but also to control the devices. The achieved platform, also, provides simplified tools allowing the development of mash-up applications to different-skilled users. Relating to Enterprise Service Bus for IoT, the study in [14] proposes an architecture for an effective integration of the Internet of Things in enterprise services: the architecture exposes real-world devices with embedded software to standard IT systems by making them accessible in a service-oriented way. The author in [15] shows a new IoT sensing service system based on ED-SOA (Event Driven SOA) architecture to support real-time, event-driven, and active service execution. The study also provides a new IoT browser that uses augmented reality technology to display IoT resource, obtaining the superposition presentation of the physical world and abstract information. Despite these interesting approaches, in literature there is a lack of integrated platforms that can provide a cloud access to IoT resources along with a semantic management of them. There is the need of IoT architecture that can manage smart devices with the support of knowledge processing tools and, at the same time, that allow end-users to interact with them as Web resources, adopting a model-driven approach typical of the Web engineering sector. Moreover, WoX approach differs from existing solutions thanks to its independence from specific hardware constraints, since it grounds on a software architecture enabling the inter-connection of any kind of IoT real and virtual devices, as described later in the chapter. The WoX architecture tries to satisfy both the requirements.

13.3 **OPEN ISSUES AND CHALLENGES**

As we observed in the state of the art section, several service platforms propose standardized and integrated architectures for IoT, but their complexity and, above all, the lack of well-known tools makes them usable only by a small group of expert developers and, hence, their usage in applications is rather limited. Current IoT implementations, when standard-based, are well-performing and scalable, but lack in configuration simplicity. On the other hand, semantic-based implementations are highly flexible and close to human language, but the compatibility with the IoT technologies is poor and must be implemented on a per-use basis. Existing solutions are too strictly focused on specific concepts such as "sensors" and "actuators", so requiring developers to bridge several technological gaps. The WoT model has shortened the distance between the IoT and humans (both developers and users) and it has ensured the compatibility with the existing IoT technologies through the design and implementation of specific adaptors. Even using RESTful architectures, the informative unit is often the IoT device, not the topic (i.e. information item) of interest. It is reasonable instead that talking the human language is the key for the IoT to get closer to the stakeholders, hence satisfying diverse users needs by the means of the same tools. The need for a novel IoT model, compatible with the existing one, also comes out when analyzing the possibility for an IoT node not only to provide data but also to request data to other peers, including peers of heterogeneous technologies. In fact, it is plausible to think at the IoT devices of the future not as super-equipped nodes with extreme processing capabilities, but as entities with different and shareable functionalities, that can autonomously cooperate and self-organize to accomplish both pre-determined and completely new tasks. The extreme heterogeneity of such nodes requires a powerful and flexible model to wrap their blended nature. As an immediate consequence of such perspective, every thing can be considered a sensor: a crawler in a Web site or even an "onclick" trigger in an HTML page. An IoT application can be seen as an IoT entity with no environmental capabilities but with computation capabilities, e.g. the possibility to perform an energy-consuming algorithm on behalf of passive IoT nodes. On the basis of these considerations, a new IoT model is needed to bridge the gap between the design domain and the solution domain: customers talk in terms of features; engineers talk in terms of sensors and actuators. Developing IoT scenarios should be as fast as drawing its sketches instead. Research challenges can be summarized as follows:

- To provide an IoT modeling technique that can abstract all the complexity and the diversity of the IoT data and service provider;
- Such modeling technique should be adapt to express not only the human–machine interaction, but also the machine–machine interaction;
- The IoT modeling technique should let IoT stakeholders concentrate on the innovative experience to be delivered, not on the physical details;
- Heterogeneous smart environments should be compliant with the novel IoT model: smart cities, smart education, smart grid, smart building, smart metering, etc.;

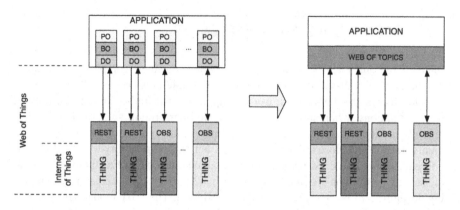

FIGURE 13.4

WoX reference model. WoX simplifies the application layer: the specific Presentation Objects (PO), Business Objects (BO) and Data Objects (DO) for each (OBServable) resource are wrapped in WoX, hence significantly reducing the application volume

- Diverse kinds of stakeholders should take advantage of the novel IoT model: experience designer, developers, end users, policy makers.

13.4 THE WEB OF TOPICS (WOX) MODEL

Web of Topics (WoX) is the model-driven approach for the IoE we propose. In WoX, the key entity between who needs and who offers IoT capabilities is the Topic, wrapping the value of a Feature of interest (e.g. presence, temperature, light, or even higher concepts such as crowd or coffee-making), in a URI-identified Location. IoT entities declare their Roles for Topics of interest by specifying their technological (source/executor/function) and collaborative (capability/need) dimensions. WoX brings two main advantages:

- Not only concrete things but also virtual things can be easily wired up to develop innovative scenarios. WoX concepts are close to the people: anyone can design and deploy custom IoE scenarios.
- WoX accelerates the development of applications, by taking care of the communication toward the heterogeneous IoT things. It hides the communication protocol details, letting designers/developers concentrate on their business.

WoX can be seen as an abstraction layer put between the WoT and the user applications (Fig. 13.4). WoX provides ready-to-use IoE Business Objects (BO) and Data Objects (DO), while leaving to the developer the only duty to display or handle the upcoming data. In the next section we describe the WoX analytical model. The reader could deepen the WoX concepts in [16].

13.4.1 ANALYTICAL FORMULATION

WoX refers to both IoT hardware nodes and IoT applications generically as IoT entities. In WoX, the "sensor" and "actuator" concepts are hidden. The main concept is the Topic. A WoX Topic is about an information of interest – called feature – in a certain location. More rigorously, a feature is any characteristic or entity of the environment that can be perceivable, definable, measurable and/or controllable. Some bare examples of feature are: temperature, humidity, presence. A crowd of people can be a feature too, as well as an alarm. Also a mathematical function – e.g. sum, min, max – can be a feature. The set of WoX features is the following:

$$F = \{f_i\} \tag{13.1}$$

The location is expressed hierarchically following the URN (Uniform Resource Name) scheme, e.g. "urn:italy:salento:highschool:firstfloor:phylab:desk1" or "urn:usa:california:la:westwood:overlandavenue:2801". The set of WoX locations is the following:

$$L = \{l_i\} U LOC_A NY, LOC_S ELF \tag{13.2}$$

where L also includes two special locations:

1. LOC_ANY, i.e. a wildcard for any location;
2. LOC_SELF, i.e. a reference to the current location.

Hence WoX define T as the set of couples feature-in-location:

$$T = \{t_{i,j} = (f_i, l_j) \in F \times L\} \tag{13.3}$$

As we said, in WoX the topic is the key between who asks for services and who provides services. Separating the twos, WoX reaches the maximum abstraction possible. In fact, IoT designers can focus on concepts (features) rather than on hardware. An IoT entity will link itself to a topic in different ways, depending on its nature. In WoX, such nature is captured in two dimensions:

1. Collaborative dimension. It includes two aspects: (i) the capability to perform a service within the topic, and (ii) the need for other entities who can perform a service.
2. Technological dimension. It includes the legacy (i) sensor and (ii) actuator distinction, as well as a generic (iii) function service.

Hence WoX defines the following two dimensions sets:

$$D_C = \{Capability, Need\} \tag{13.4}$$

$$D_{TECH} = \{Source, Executor, Function\} \tag{13.5}$$

Then, WoX defines the set of WoX roles R included in the following Cartesian product:

$$R = D_C \times D_{TECH} = \{SN, EN, FN, SC, EC, FC\} \tag{13.6}$$

The items in the curly brackets respectively state for: sensor capability, actuator capability, function capability, sensor need, actuator need, function need. The generic IoT entity z can be modeled as a set of couples role-topic belonging to the following Cartesian product:

$$E_z = \{(r_k, t_{i,j}) \in R \times T\} \tag{13.7}$$

By this way, WoX is able to model any device or app in the IoE, even the most complex or abstract. An example of IoE node implementing the WoX model is a personal enhanced RFID tag which need to know the temperature in the current room, is capable to perform a comparison between float numbers and can activate a LED alarm.

13.4.2 THE INFORMATION ARCHITECTURE

End-users applications as well as core architectural components (e.g. data analysis) need to aggregate information that will not be directly available from the IoT physical layer. This is because the physical layer generates raw sensor data that need to be compared, intersected, cross checked, reasoned before being available for the upper layers. Particularly, we can distinguish the following information types, as depicted in Fig. 13.5:

- Raw data coming from the specific IoT technology (sensor). This is wrapped in the specific technology protocol message, and may vary in format (int, float, Boolean, binary, string), semantics and timing of availability/update;
- Event, described by a unified information schema that encapsulates the raw data and specifies meta-data such as: time, location, (technological) source. Event messages mask the inherent technology complexity. Such events are typically fired by middleware. Despite the uniformity of the event definition among different IoT technologies, events still wrap technology-specific information. Moreover, different events could describe the same situation (e.g. more events incoming from different IoT technologies could say that someone is entering a place);
- Topics, updated by events. A topic wraps a value and it is identified by providing its Feature and Location. We can distinguish in:
  - Low level topics, for example, an application may be interested in someone entering a place, no matter which technology originates this event;
  - High level topics, which retain the information inferred by interpreting the relations among more topics and data sources. Such relations can be statically foreseen;
- Facts and Patterns. The topic is a synchronous entity (its value continuously changes at every event incoming from the lower layers or from low level topics). A Fact is the snapshot of a topic at a certain time. Facts for one or more topics can be stored for future analysis. Such analysis can use heuristics in order to find recurring Patterns. That is, we can find "a-posteriori" topic relations. Domain experts

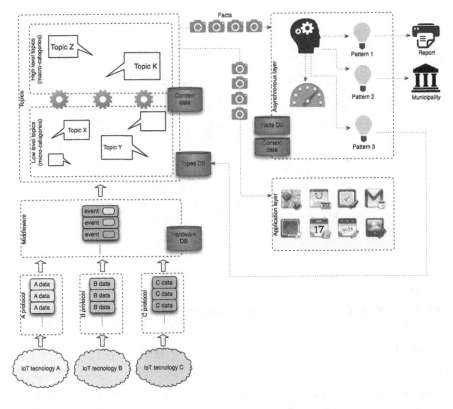

FIGURE 13.5

WoX information architecture

can decide what to do with the elicited patterns: print reports, define new high level topics, send alerts, etc.

13.4.3 EXPECTED BENEFITS

A number of stakeholders will benefit from the WoX model's abstraction power:

• The end-user does not want to waste money in buying non-interoperable hardware that delivers few pre-defined scenarios. For instance, the end-user expects that when s/he is going back home, the air conditioner will automatically turn on, no matter how the user location is picked, no matter what the air conditioner manufacturer is.

• IoT inventors (e.g. developers and makers) want to shorten the distance between the idea and the solution. Unfortunately, currently they spend most of their time

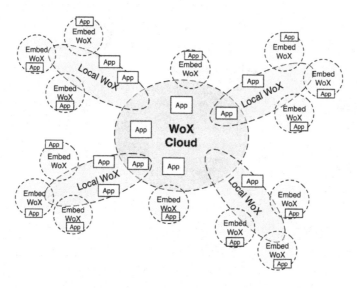

FIGURE 13.6

WoX is supported by a fractal architecture spearing the WoX Topics Domain. We detected three kind of topics domain: Ccloud, Llocal (e.g. topic living in the smartphone), and eMmbedded (topics living in embedded systems). Each can choose whether to forward topic information the upper hierarchical level, or retaining it for itself

in focusing on the implementation details (often reinventing the wheel) rather than the core concepts of their ideas.

- Business organizations want to minimize the cost of their solutions as well as the time-to-market. They want to concentrate on the business models and on the business logic rather than burning their efforts on study different protocols and deal with implementation details.

13.5 DESIGN AND IMPLEMENTATION

WoX adopts a fractal architecture, that is every WoX entity is a broker for other WoX entities (Fig. 13.6). We group WoX topics in three domains: the WoX Cloud, the Local WoX (L-WoX, e.g. mobile devices), and eMbedded WoX (M-WoX, e.g. embedded devices). Every entity talk about WoX topics. Being a topic a feature of the environment in a specific location holding the current value of information anyone having data about a topic will perform the update hence sharing its knowledge. According to the deployed scenarios, every entity decides if forwarding topic updates to the parent entities or not. As a consequence, WoX entities at the edge of the architecture talk about few very specific topics, while entities near the core retain the master knowledge. Entity types include: apps, devices (sensors/actuators), knowledge processors (KP), business processes (BP), any piece of software in general. WoX delegates to the entities the responsibility of interacting with the topics, whether they have "capabilities" toward the specific topic (i.e. providing services) or "needs" (i.e. requesting services). Such interaction is performed using APIs. Different APIs exist for different entity types. Apps use iOS/Android APIs. IoT devices use C/C++ APIs. Software in general uses Java/Python/.NET APIs. Entities of any kind always talk about the same concepts: capabilities or needs towards one or more topics. Such model-driven approach brings two main advantages: (i) minimizes the language distance between people and technology, and (ii) abstracts the many-to-many complexity in a hierarchical publish-subscribe architecture. As a side benefit, different topics can be combined together, or with external data sources, in order to provide new knowledge, that is new "high-level" topics. KPs accomplish this task. When end-users create a new scenario, they choose the topics they are interested in, connect them and publish the scenario in the cloud. Behind the scene, the WoX app and the WoX core will work in symbiosis for running the scenario. In the next sections we show how we practically implemented the WoX information model on top on an EPCglobal instance and over the WSO2 Enterprise Service Bus.

13.5.1 REFERENCE ARCHITECTURE

The WoX model requires a robust ICT architecture capable of facing the extremely high number of IoT entities and Topics, the intense exchange of messages, and the heterogeneity of the IoT technologies. WoX architecture is built as instance of the publish-subscribe (pub/sub) software design pattern. Pub/sub is an enterprise integration pattern where senders of messages, called publishers, do not know a priori what are the specific receivers of messages, called subscribers. Instead, published messages are characterized into classes, without knowledge of subscribers identity. Similarly, subscribers express interest in one or more classes, and only receive messages that are in their scope, without knowledge of publishers' identity. The modelling of the pub/sub architecture starts from the Topic class. In Fig. 13.7 the UML dependence diagram is shown. The Observer software design pattern implements the main WoX idea. The Topic class has the Feature and Location member variables, as well as two other member variables, to hold respectively the topic's actual value and preferred value: the actual value contains the most recent value for the feature in the location; the preferred value is used to send and receive requests about the desired topic value (e.g. the desired temperature in a room).

Every time an IoT node shows up, it handshakes with the WoX architecture, i.e. it declares its roles according to the formula (13.7). The corresponding subscriber classes are instanced and get attached to the Topic instance. When the Topic's actual value gets updated, SN subscribers (i.e. information consumers) get notified. Vice versa, when the Topic preferred value is modified, AC subscribers are notified so they can absolve their tasks. If the Topic's feature is a function, the topic's preferred value is ignored and the actual value is used both to pass function parameters as

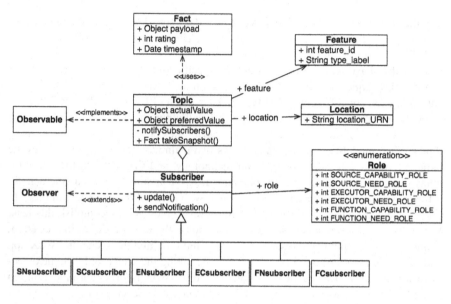

FIGURE 13.7

WoX UML dependency diagram

well as to obtain the function result. In the first case, FC subscribers get notified; in the second case, FN subscribers get notified. The pub/sub architectural pattern centralizes the core information separating who provides data from who consumes it. IoT-based apps perform a one-time subscription to the topic(s) of interests, without perceiving the hardware layer. Subscribing to topics is easy also for "stupid" IoT nodes (e.g. RFID tags). Moreover, the total number of exchanged messages is drastically reduced because of dropping all the point-to-point connections between IoT entities. The whole enterprise architecture depends on the WoX model, as presented in the previous section. The platform receives the raw data from sensors and it elaborates them in order to extract complex information. The workflow of data within the application is basically depicted in Fig. 13.8. The WoX logical architecture introduces two kinds of topics, both compliant with the definition of Topic, but referring to different levels of abstraction:

1. Low-Level Topic: it is related to data belonging to observable/controllable IoT entities without any semantic connotation;
2. High-Level Topic: it represents a refined information semantically characterized and interpreted.

The other components in the logical architecture are:

1. Enterprise Service Bus (ESB): it is the solution adopted to connect the various component of the application. It is compliant to Service-Oriented Applications

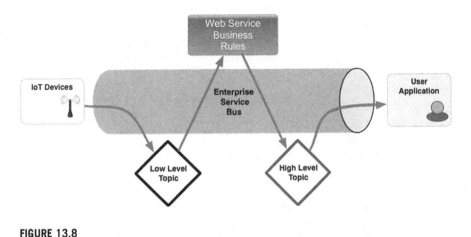

FIGURE 13.8

Enterprise System Logic Workflow

(SOA) architectural pattern and it guarantees the interoperability among hetero-geneous technologies.

2. Business Rules Web Service: it is a middleware component with the specific func-tion of Knowledge Processor (KP). The module subscribes to the Low-Level Topic and applies the business rules on row data deriving information from it, in order to draw events of interest and to update the corresponding High-Level Topic;

3. User Application: high abstraction level module. Its role is to subscribe the High-Level Topic and to notify the user when an event of interest occurs.

The Low Level Topic is used to catch data provided by sensors, to control actua-tors and, generally, to process row data in an IoT network. The High Level Topic is used to treat elaborate information mined from raw data according to the logic rules imposed by the KP. Once a High-Level Topic changes its own internal state, that is some event of interest has occurred, it notifies the User Application component as any other topic too.

13.5.2 PHYSICAL ARCHITECTURE

WoX uses an EPCglobal middleware (ETH Zurich's Fosstrak [5] implementation) and WSO2 ESB [6]. Fig. 13.9 shows the WoX technical architecture. A pub/sub architecture alone cannot satisfy the requirements of hardware abstraction, event fil-tering, and standard-compliant persistence of an IoT middleware. To this aim, the pub/sub architecture is put on the top of an EPCglobal middleware. Such design choice guarantees quality and performance to the whole architecture. As aforemen-tioned, the WoX architecture grounds on the Fosstrak. It is made up of four main layers:

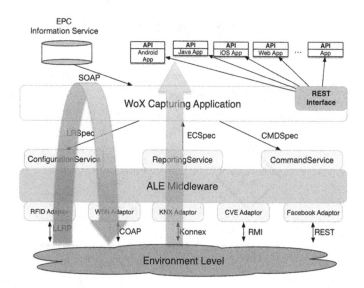

FIGURE 13.9

The WoX technical architecture, based on the EPCglobal standard and its open source implementation (Fosstrak). The arrows indicate the possible flows of information in WoX: node-to-node and node-to-app

1. **Environment Level:** it comprises the physical layer as well as any virtual environment that can generate events. Social networks chats or other virtual data generators can be source of events too.

2. **ALE middleware:** it is responsible of querying/piloting the Environment Level and packing event reports for the upper layers. It also normalizes the events and filters duplicated data. On the bottom side, a series of adaptor is present for each IoT technology, both physical (e.g. RFID, WSN, KNX, etc.) and virtual (social networks, virtual environments, etc.). On the top level, three SOAP (Simple Object Access Protocol) Web services are needed to send hardware configuration (when needed), receive event reports formatted with the ECSpec (Event Cycle Specification) schema, and to send data to the technologies using the respective technology formats.

3. **WoX Capturing Application:** it is the architectural level implementing the WoX model. It instances the topics, updates them, updates the topic map, and makes such data available to the end-user apps by a set of REST interfaces.

4. **End users applications** use the WoX APIs to subscribe topics; they can run on any kind of device. For testing purposes, in the current work, Java and Android APIs have been used, but APIs in other programming language will be developed in the next steps. An additional element, the EPCIS (EPC Information System), persists IoT events for asynchronous usage.

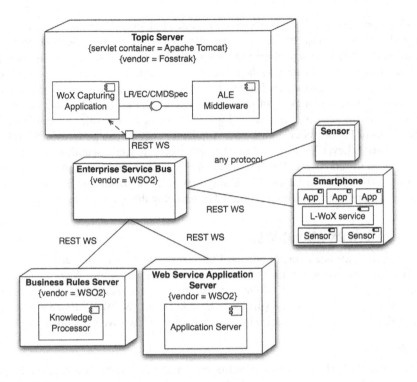

FIGURE 13.10

The WoX physical architecture

Fig. 13.9 evidences the two possible flows of information: (i) node-to-node, the curved arrow, i.e. any IoT node can request services to other nodes (even of different technology), and (ii) node-to-app, the straight arrow, i.e. any app can receive data from any node, and vice-versa. The cornerstone of each information exchange is the WoX Capturing application, where the WoX model is implemented and the topics are instanced.

Referring to Fig. 13.10, most part of the architecture is implemented using WSO2 technologies. Particularly, WSO2 implements the following components: Enterprise Service Bus, Business Rules Server and Web Service Application Server. The module for managing topics is implemented on the top of Fosstrak EPCGlobal implementation and is deployed on a dedicated server. The different modules in the architecture communicate by way of RESTful interfaces, in accordance with WSO2 guidelines. The sensor component sends the data describing the state of the environment to the Enterprise Service Bus. The ESB sends the data from sensors to the Fosstrak Capturing Application component, where a specific instance of Low-Level Topic encapsulates the data from the sensor. The Application Server implemented on the WSO2 Web Service Application Server subscribes all the topic instances in the Capturing Application, firing different actions depending on the type of topic. In case of Low-Level Topic subscription, the Application Server receives notifications from it in conjunction with sensor updates and it forwards the information included in the topic to the Business Rule Server. In the latter component there is a Web service equipped with a Knowledge Processing Engine. It acts as Knowledge Processor and computes the received data. f an event of interest has occurred, the Business Rule Server updates the corresponding High-Level Topic. The business logic rules are implemented by means of Drools tool [7]. Since the Application Server can perform subscriptions also to High-Level Topic, an event of interest occurrence is seamless notified to it and, so, to the end users. The Business Rules Server exposes the logic rules as Web services. Therefore, it is possible adding new rules or modifying existing ones by means of http requests, without the need of redeploy the application.

13.5.3 L-WOX AND M-WOX

As we said at the beginning of Section 13.5.1, three WoX topics domains exist: (i) the Cloud domain, more general and horizontal with respect to the WoX applications, (ii) the Local WoX (L-WoX) domain, which lives in intelligent user devices such as smartphones and tablets, and (iii) the Embedded WoX (M-WoX) domain, related to embedded devices. In this section we describe the last two WoX declinations.

L-WoX

The Local WoX (L-WoX) is a subset of the whole architecture running on the personal user device (smartphones and tablets). In L-WoX, the personal device works as an aggregator towards local WoT entities. Allowing to retain and manage some topics locally on the device is more efficient in some circumstances. For example, multiple mobile apps on the same device may be interested to the same topic, and its value is updated by an onboard sensor (e.g. the accelerometer). Another example consists in two mobile apps interested in two different topics, updated using the same onboard sensor. As an example, the accelerometer can feed both the "ATHLET_TRAINING" topic and "ELDERLY_PERSON_FALL" topic. In L-WoX we have the following components:

1. The L-WoX service, instanced as a singleton in the mobile operating system, retaining the topic instances;
2. The mobile apps, subscribing to the local topics after binding to the L-WoX service;
3. The native sensors APIs, offered by the mobile operating system to access the available sensors;
4. A set of WoX adaptors, which use the values incoming from the sensors to update specific topics.

Notice that the Location values for the local topics is often LOCATION_SELF. As for the Cloud case, the mobile app developer decides what to do with each local topic value. In addition, s/he decides if updating a Cloud topic (hence acting as a capability entity) or not.

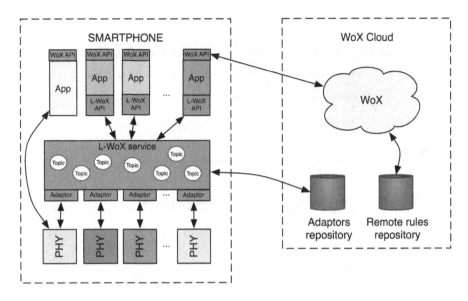

FIGURE 13.11

Local WoX integration with WoX apps

Fig. 13.11 reports the L-WoX architecture. It is evidenced how to connect both existing and new App to the WoX Cloud.

The legacy app talks directly to the physical layer, using its own application layer protocol. In order for the legacy app to share its existing services, it should use the WoX APIs in order to translate the proprietary event to the common WoX topic. If necessary, the app forwards the new topic information to the global WoX architecture, else the information will remain in the specific app context. New IoT apps (not legacy) can directly uses all the L-WoX advantages.

M-WoX

No matter which IoT technique/technology – even passive – is considered, the specific IoT entity should be able to tell peers, gateways and apps its WoX profile, according to formula (13.7). The WoX profile exchange message format is called M-WoX. When possible, implementing the M-WoX data format protocol allows a seamless dialogue between different kind of devices, in a P2P fashion. The M-WoX application protocol is independent from the specific IoT device nature/brand, because its purpose to format the message payload rather than defining how the devices are networked. It can be used to format the payloads of BLE beacons/connections, QR codes, NFC tags, and so on. Given the constrained – even self-powered – of IoT nodes, it is obvious that such message should be composed bit by bit. M-WoX is based on and expands the user memory mapping proposal presented in the BRIDGE

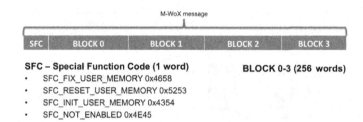

FIGURE 13.12

The M-WoX message format

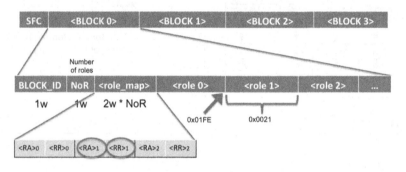

FIGURE 13.13

The M-WoX single block

Project[1] Actually, if we consider the passive RFID as the most constrained IoT technology, we can use the WORD variable as the atomic piece of information. A WORD is composed of 4 HEX digits, i.e. 16 bit (e.g. AAAA, 0123, BCFF). In Fig. 13.12 the high level WoX message format is depicted.

The message starts with a Special Function Code (SFC) (1 WORD), by which the entity memory can be fixed, reset or initialized. The entity itself can also tell that it is not available in a certain moment. After the SFC, there is a succession of 236 WORDs blocks. The blocks division is foreseen in order to face the constraints of some IoT technologies, which does not allow to read all the retained information at once. Every block is self-consistent (i.e., it is not mandatory to read all the blocks in order to understand the single block content). In Fig. 13.13 the single block details is depicted.

Each block contains the serialized version of the WoX entity profile, as defined in formula (13.7). Here we describe the block format in detail. The first field is the NoR (Number of Roles).

---

[1] BRIDGE Project, http://bridge-project.eu/.

Table 13.1 The Number of Roles (NoR) Field	
FIELD	LENGTH
NoR[a]	1 word

[a] *NoR: Number of Roles, i.e. the number of roles wrapped in the block.*

Table 13.2 The roleAddress and roleRange Fields Details	
FIELD	LENGTH
roleAddress[a]	1 word
roleRange[b]	2 word

[a] *roleAddress: hex address (in WORDs) of the role inside the whole message.*
[b] *roleRange: length of the role, in number of WORDs.*

Table 13.3 The Capability Case Fields	
FIELD	LENGTH
DATA	1 word
NUM_INTERVAL	1 word
LIMIT_HI	1 word
LIMIT_LO	1 word
NEGATIVE_OFFSET	1 word
INTERVAL	1 word
COUNT	1 word
TIMESTAMP	2 words
STARTTIME	2 words
LOGCTRL	1 word
LOGSTAT	1 word
ROLE_TYPE	1 word
FEATURE_ID	1 word
TOTAL	15 words

The NoR (Number of Roles) is the number of roles wrapped in the block. A role can be: (i) source capability; (ii) source need; (iii) executor capability; (iv) executor need, (v) function capability, (vi) function need. Then, the block contains the role map, which is a field having NoR couples roleAddress-roleRange, i.e. the memory address (expressed in WORDs) and the role size for each role.

The roleAddress is the hex address (in WORDs) of the role inside the whole message. The roleRange is length of the role, in number of WORDs. Then, each role must be described (serialized). Such serialization varies if it is a capability or a need.

In Table 13.3 there are shown the capability case fields. The fields meanings:

- FEATURE_ID: it is the unique identification number of the WoX feature (temperature, light, fall, ...)
- ROLE_TYPE: defines the role type. The value is one of the following:

Table 13.4 The LOGSTAT Register Details

LOGSTAT						
Type	RFU	RFU	LHV	LLV	RFU	F

Table 13.5 The LOGCTRL Register Detail

LOGCTRL							
RFU	RST	L	D	TL	LHM	LLM	RFU

```
SOURCE_CAPABILITY_ROLE = 0;
SOURCE_NEED_ROLE = 1;
EXECUTOR_CAPABILITY_ROLE = 2;
EXECUTOR_NEED_ROLE = 3;
FUNCTION_CAPABILITY_ROLE = 4;
FUNCTION_NEED_ROLE = 5;
```

- LOGSTAT: a register containing the status flags (memory_full, upper_limit_violation, lower_limit_violation) as well as information about the feature data type. The Type field contains the data type, which could be one of the following:

  - 0000 = signed 16-bit integer
  - 0001 = unsigned 16-bit integer
  - 0010 = signed 32-bit integer
  - 0011 = unsigned 32-bit integer
  - 0100 = float, IEEE 754 Single-precision (32 bit)
  - 0101 = fixed point Q10.6
  - 1111 = Bitwise presentation (manufacturer specific)

The other LOGSTAT fields are:

  - F = Memory Full flag
  - LLV = Limit Low Violation flag
  - LHV = Limit High Violation flag

- LOGCTRL: a configuration register defining the behavior of the specific feature. In Table 13.5 there are shown the LOGCTRL fields details.

  - RST = Reset
  - L = Sensor monitoring activated
  - D = Data logging activated
  - TL = Timestamp activated
  - M = Mode

    - 0 = Continuous logging
    - 1 = Event logging

Table 13.6 The Need Case Fields

FIELD	LENGTH
DATA	1 word
locationMD5	1 or 8 words
NUM_INTERVAL	1 word
LIMIT_HI	1 word
LIMIT_LO	1 word
NEGATIVE_OFFSET	1 word
LOGCTRL	1 word
LOGSTAT	1 word
ROLE_TYPE	1 word
FEATURE_ID	1 word
TOTAL	10 or 17 words

- LHM = Limit High Monitoring (on/off)
- LLM = Limit Low Monitoring (on/off)

- STARTTIME: UNIX timestamp holding the beginning of logging (if the technology supports logging)
- TIMESTAMP: timestamp (UNIX time).
- COUNT: quantity of data record in memory. If data logging is not active, the value of COUNT is 1.
- INTERVAL: interval of sampling, in seconds (not needed if logging)
- NEGATIVE_OFFSET: the negative offset to be added to LIMIT_LO or LIMIT_HI to obtain the real limits (avoiding to face negative values).
  Example. If: NEGATIVE_OFFSET = 20, LIMIT_LO = 0, LIMIT_HI = 30, then the real limits are:
  (real) LIMIT_LO = −20 (i.e. LIMIT_LO + (−NEGATIVE_OFFSET))
  (real) LIMIT_HI = 10 (i.e. LIMIT_HI + (−NEGATIVE_OFFSET))
- LIMIT_LO: the lower measure limit range
- LIMIT_HI: the upper measure limit range
- NUM_INTERVAL: defines the number of steps in which the interval (LIMIT_HI – LIMIT_LO) is sampled.
- DATA: data generated by the source (sensor) or to be forwarded to the executor (actuator)

The "need" case is reported in Table 13.6.

The common fields have the same meaning as for the capability case. A specific comment is needed for the following field:

- locationMD5: The location URN in which the entity wants its need to be satisfied. When the URN is the same location where the entity resides (LOC_SELF), or any location (LOC_ANY), then the location URN field is 1 WORD long. Else, 8 WORDS.

13.6 PROOF OF CONCEPTS

In this section, we describe how the WoX model-driven approach and implementation helped us developing the airport's Kiss&Fly parking service.

13.6.1 THE KISS&FLY SCENARIO

The Kiss&Fly zone is a short-stay parking area located near the airports' terminals. Tipically, the total time of free pass and/or stay in this area is 10 minutes. For a stay of over 10 minutes users are charged for some price. The innovative scenario we want to develop includes the use of a smartphone to detect the entrance/exit of the user in the parking lot. Considered sensing technologies are:

- NFC. The user will tap its device to the entrance and exit gates;
- A mobile app. The user will tap manually the "I'm entering" and "I'm exiting" buttons.

The use of two different sensing technologies (very different from each other, the first one is physical, the second one is virtual) demonstrates the independence of the scenario from the specific hardware involved. We developed a unique physical gate for both entering and exiting the parking lot. We implemented it using an Arduino Mega 5360, expanded with a Seed Studio NFC Shield. The Arduino also has a relay which is needed to lift up and bring down the park barrier. Besides the mobile device and the Arduino, another IoT entity is needed: the billing system. It listens for users entering and exiting the parking lot, takes the event times, decides whether to charge or not the user, and settle the transaction if needed. In order to simulate the user status (inside or outside the parking lot), we use a light bulb connected to the Arduino relays instead if a real barrier. For this scenario we used the following topic: feature BARRIER, location: "it:apulia:brindisi:casale:parking:kissFly". The value of the topic is formatted with a JSON String like this: {"user" : "user_id", "lifted" : true}. Then, for each IoT entity (node or app) involved, we defined its role(s):

- The mobile app has an executor need role, because of both the "I'm entering" and "I'm exiting" buttons and the NFC tap possibility;
- The billing system has a source need role, because it want to know about the status of the barrier topic;
- The Arduino has both an executor capability (because it can lift up the barrier) and a source capability (because it can say that the barrier is lifted up or not after the execution).

```
10  public class MainActivity extends Activity {
11
12      public static Boolean preferredBarrierStatus = false;
13      private static Topic t;
14      private static Button b;
15
16⊖    @Override
17      protected void onCreate(Bundle savedInstanceState) {
18          super.onCreate(savedInstanceState);
19          setContentView(R.layout.activity_main);
20          b = (Button) findViewById(R.id.button1);
21
22          //initialize WoX
23          WoXmanager.getInstance().setAppId("kissFlyBDS");
24          //topic instance
25          t = new Topic(Topic.FEATURE_BARRIER, "it:brindisi:airport:parking:kissFly01");
26      }
27
28⊖    public static void toggleKissFly(View v) {
29          preferredBarrierStatus = !preferredBarrierStatus;
30          b.setText(preferredBarrierStatus? R.string.btn_exit : R.string.btn_enter);
31          //change topic preferred value
32          t.setPreferredValue(preferredBarrierStatus);
33      }
```

FIGURE 13.14

The Android mobile app code. WoX needs only 3 lines of code

In Fig. 13.14 it is shown the mobile app code we wrote for the Android platform. As readers can see, most code is about UI and variables updates. WoX needs only three instructions. L-WoX takes care of the NFC interaction.

Fig. 13.15 shows the Arduino firmware code. We used the M-WoX.h library we developed for embedded systems. Even here it is noticeable how short is the development effort. The smartphone's L-WoX instance and the Arduino's M-WoX instance silently uses the M-WoX application protocol to exchange data over the NFC link. The developer's only duty is to specify the callback function for each WoX role.

Generally, a billing system is already present at the business location. In this case, system integrators can use WoX APIs to add IoT functions to the system. For the considered scenario, we developed a sample billing system as a Java stand-alone application. In Fig. 13.16 we show a couple of code snippets of the billing system.

In Fig. 13.17 we show the prototyped barrier, whose status is simulated by a light bulb turning on and off. The reader can see the presence of the NFC shield and antenna, mounted on top of the Arduino, as well as the relays.

The light turns on/off in two cases: the user taps the button in the mobile app (hence the WoX Cloud is dragged in), or the user moves close the smartphone to the NFC antenna (direct M-WoX interaction, then the Arduino updates the WoX Cloud).

13.7 CONCLUSIONS AND FUTURE WORK

In this section we sketch our conclusions as well as future research directions.

```
void setup() {
  ports_init();
  pinMode(13, OUTPUT);

  //init WoX
  wox_init(2, roles);

  //first WoX role: BARRIER EXECUTOR CAPABILITY
  wox_EC_default(0);
  roles[0].feature_id = FEATURE_ID_BARRIER;
  roles[0].location_MD5 = wox_location("it:brindisi:airport:parking:kissFly01");
  roles[0].callback=&manage_barrier;

  //second WoX role: BARRIER SENSOR CAPABILITY
  wox_SC_default(1);
  roles[1].feature_id = FEATURE_ID_BARRIER;
  roles[1].location_MD5 = wox_location("it:brindisi:airport:parking:kissFly01");
  roles[1].callback=&sense_barrier;

  wox_write_roles();
}

void loop() {
  wox_work();
  delay(1000);
}
```

FIGURE 13.15

The Arduino firmware code snippet

```
45      WoXmanager.getInstance().setAppId("kissFlyBDS");
46      t = new Topic(Feature.BARRIER, "it:brindisi:airport:parking:kissFly01");
47      t.subscribe(new BarrierObserver());

93⊖    public class BarrierObserver implements Observer {
94
95         Date d1, d2;
96         Timer timer;
97
98⊖        @Override
99         public void update(Observable arg0, Object arg1) {
100
101            Topic t = (Topic) arg0;
102            Boolean barrierStatus=Boolean.valueOf(arg1.toString());
103
104            if(barrierStatus) {
105                //...
```

FIGURE 13.16

A snippet of the WoX code we written for the billing system

13.7.1 CONCLUSIONS

In this work we have presented the Web of Topics (WoX) approach, a novel design model that facilitates the design and development of innovative IoT scenarios. De-

 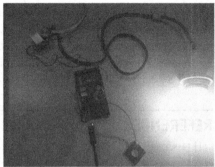

FIGURE 13.17

The entrance/exit gate for the Kiss&Fly scenario. The user status (inside or outside the parking lot) is simulated by a light bulb

spite the great spread of IoT devices in different context, nowadays IoT stakeholders face considerable difficulties in designing IoT applications without running into significant gaps with the solution domains. Moreover, there is a need to ease the access to the IoT nodes services also among physical nodes, particularly when they are technologically heterogeneous. The proposed model is based on the concept of Topic. Just like humans, IoT nodes and applications can talk and exchange information about a certain topic of interest. This kind of abstraction level ensures a lightweight configuration for physical nodes, and an intuitive metaphor for the IoT stakeholders, including the developers. The WoX model has been implemented on top of the EPCglobal architecture, which gives scalability, efficiency and robustness. The WoX reference model fills the gap between the Web of Things paradigm and the IoT apps. WoX aggregates data and events incoming from the WoT, providing ready-to-use information and concepts. This simplifies the mechanics behind the upper application levels as well as all the levels of knowledge base, ontology and knowledge discovery enriching the IoT and making it valuable for the people. WoX puts the basis for the definition of an interactive dialogue model between people and smart environments.

13.7.2 OPEN ISSUES AND FUTURE CHALLENGES

WoX is inspired by the standard architectures proposed in the state of the art section, but it is not fully compliant yet. The main future work in this direction is the adoption of the O&M standard to describe the topics payload. Indeed, current topic payloads are primitive values (integer, float, string, boolean, etc.). Currently we are working on the development of the L-WoX app and process for the Android and iOS platforms. We are using the reflective architecture paradigm to let services dynamically downloading and installing adaptors from the repository. From the non-technical stakeholders' side, it is needed a WoX dialogue model intuitive notation allowing anyone to design their own IoT-based experience by the means of a simple authoring tool. we will build the WoX Author Web interface to let the users draw their scenarios and deploying them onto the Cloud. Another research direction will be the release of more programming languages WoX interfaces with an enhanced set of exposed APIs, as demanded by the developers involved in the experimentation.

REFERENCES

[1] Osservatori.net – digital innovation. http://www.osservatori.net. Accessed: 2016-09-01.

[2] Internet of things architecture. http://www.iot-a.eu/. Accessed: 2016-09-01.

[3] Internet of things global standards initiative. http://www.itu.int/en/ITU-T/gsi/iot/Pages/default.aspx. Accessed: 2016-09-01.

[4] EPCGlobal. http://www.gs1.org/epcglobal. Accessed: 2016-09-01.

[5] Fosstrak. Open source RFID platform. https://code.google.com/p/fosstrak/. Accessed: 2016-09-01.

[6] WSO2. Open source, SOA, web services, cloud computing, Java PaaS, middleware projects for developers/architects. http://www.wso2.com. Accessed: 2016-09-01.

[7] Drools – business rules management system (JavaTM, open source). http://www.drools.org/. Accessed: 2016-09-01.

[8] Tseng CW, Lin YS, Lu WH, Huang CH. Extending EPCglobal ALE middleware to integrate transducer capability of IEEE 1451 standards. In: Proceedings of the 6th international conference on ubiquitous and future networks (ICUFN 2014). 2014. p. 289–94.

[9] Song EY, Lee K. Understanding IEEE 1451-networked smart transducer interface standard – what is a smart transducer? IEEE Instrum Meas Mag 2008;11(2):11–7.

[10] Pfisterer D, Romer K, Bimschas D, Kleine O, Mietz R, Truong C, Hasemann H, Kröller A, Pagel M, Hauswirth M, et al. SPITFIRE: toward a semantic web of things. IEEE Commun Mag 2011;49(11):40–8.

[11] Honkola J, Laine H, Brown R, Tyrkko O. Smart-M3 information sharing platform. In: Proceedings on the IEEE symposium on computers and communications (ISCC). 2010. p. 1041–6.

[12] Katasonov A, Kaykova O, Khriyenko O, Nikitin S, Terziyan VY. Smart semantic middleware for the internet of things. In: Proceedings of the fifth international conference on informatics in control, automation and robotics, intelligent control systems and optimization (ICINCO). 2008. p. 169–78.

[13] Mainetti L, Mighali V, Patrono L. A software architecture enabling the web of things. IEEE Int Things J 2014;2(6):445–54.

[14] Spiess P, Karnouskos S, Guinard D, Savio D, Baecker O, de Souza LMS, Trifa V. SOA-based integration of the internet of things in enterprise services. In: Proceedings of the IEEE international conference on web services. 2009. p. 968–75.

[15] Lan L, Li F, Wang B, Zhang L, Shi R. An event-driven service-oriented architecture for the internet of things. In: IEEE Asia-Pacific services computing conference. 2014. p. 68–73.

[16] Mainetti L, Manco L, Patrono L, Sergi I, Vergallo R. Web of topics: an IoT-aware model-driven designing approach. In: 2015 IEEE 2nd world forum on Internet of things (WF-IoT). 2015. p. 46–51.

ACKNOWLEDGEMENTS

The work was partially supported by Vidyasoft S.r.l. Spin-off company of University of Salento.

SECURITY ISSUES OF THE WEB OF THINGS

14

Saad El Jaouhari, Ahmed Bouabdallah, Jean-Marie Bonnin

Institute Mines-Telecom/TELECOM Bretagne, Network, Multimedia and Security Department,
Cesson Sévigné, France

14.1 INTRODUCTION: FROM IOT TO WOT

The progress in the embedded devices, introduced the concept of smart object, with interesting communication capacities and autonomy in one hand and low power and computation capabilities in the other hand. Wireless sensors and actuators are able to interact with humans and other smart objects through low-power network protocols such as Bluetooth, ZigBee, Z-Wave, and so on. By definition the *smart Things* (or *smart objects*) are physical objects, enhanced with micro-controller, sensor and/or actuator, communication capability, and low energy consumption. Examples of smart objects are illustrated by smartphones, smart TVs, temperature/light/presence sensors, and so on and so forth. Hence, the Internet of Things (IoT) is defined as a network of smart objects, where each smart object is uniquely identified in the infrastructure. The idea of the IoT is to connect a myriad of embedded devices worldwide through the Internet. According to IP for Smart Objects (IPSO), more and more objects will be able to support the IP protocol, i.e., support direct connectivity to the Internet. Those smart objects can be discovered, monitored, controlled and able to interact with other humans and eventually other objects over the Internet.

Those smart objects, usually called "*Things*", extend the world we live in today by enabling a whole new range of applications. Moreover, they are now publicly available and very cheap, which explains the exponential growth of their number. The range of the Things can vary from a very simple tagged product (NFC, RFID, QR codes or bar codes), to more powerful, complex and elaborated objects such as smart cars and smart cities. However, building a global ecosystem gathering the different IoT platforms, where Things can communicate seamlessly is a difficult task. Since each IoT platform uses its own stack of communication protocols, they usually are not able to work across the many available networking interfaces, which creates silos of users and Things. Complexity and the proprietary tools may also become a hindrance toward the creation of a global and interoperable environment. In order to concrete such vision, a single universal application layer protocol enabling the various Things to communicate with each other in seamless way is needed. Hence the idea of using the standards and the APIs of the web as a universal platform, on

Managing the Web of Things. DOI: 10.1016/B978-0-12-809764-9.00018-4

389

top of the Internet and for all the smart objects [1]. And this is what *Web of Things* (WoT) is all about, applying the existing and emerging tools and techniques used on the Web to the development of different innovative IoT scenarios. The advantage of using such approach is that we can reuse the available and widely popular Web protocols without the need of reinventing another complex protocol, which by the way may not bring the full interoperability for the IoT.

In the WoT, connecting the Things becomes simpler. Adapting the web technologies provides an abstraction of the complexity of the low-level protocols. For instance, HTTP and WebSocket can be reused by the smart objects. Moreover, developers can write applications that can interact with the smart objects in the same way as with any other Web service, in particular using the RESTful architectures. Concretely, Things can have a public URL accessible through the Web. However, this approach requires an embedded web server running inside the constrained environment of the smart object [2,3]. Arduino Uno[1] and Raspberry Pi[2] are examples of devices that can be equipped with web servers.

However, the WoT inherits not only the specific properties of the IoT, but also many security and privacy issues. Those problems are mainly related to the heterogeneous and the constrained nature of the Things, the identity management (identification and authentication), the privacy, the physical and the digital access to the device and the trust. Indeed, the vision of a pervasive communication, anytime and anywhere, needs to deal with those problems. Yet unfortunately, security and privacy studies on the WoT are few and still to mature.

In this chapter we will give a survey of the current advancements in this field. The chapter is structured as follows. Section 14.1 introduces the main building blocks involved in the security of the Internet, provides a list of the main security properties, investigates the security of the smart objects during their life cycle and finally exposes the threats and the security requirements in the current IoT architecture. Section 14.3 begins with an introduction about the security of the WoT, and lists the currently proposed security architectures in the WoT mainly the identity management, data confidentiality and integrity, the authorization and the access control.

14.2 THE EXISTING SECURITY MODELS

The IoT is seen as the next "industrial revolution" by many experts, where billions of connected devices are able to exchange information between them and with other computing devices. Thence, these devices will constantly generate a huge amount of data, that will be exchanged via Internet. For this reason, we have first to go through some general security properties and threats to which systems are exposed when they are connected to the Internet. Naturally, since more and more data are exchanged

---

[1]https://www.arduino.cc/en/Main/ArduinoBoardUno.
[2]https://www.raspberrypi.org/.

over the Internet, they are susceptible to undergo different kinds of attacks including hijacking, eavesdropping, tampering, etc., where the attacker doesn't have to be physically present to take control over the device, a simple corrupted package can do the work. Indeed an eventual attacker can be present in any host connected to the Internet (including the device itself), and it becomes more challenging to prevent them [4].

In this section, we will first introduce the main security properties related to the Internet. The main interest of this subsection, is (1) to give a formal definition to some keywords that will be used all over this chapter; and (2) to have a brief idea of the main security properties required in the Internet in general, and in the IoT and the WoT in particular. Next we will take an interest in the SO itself. We will analyze the different security and privacy mechanisms deployed by the SO to be able to securely communicate with the outside world. And finally we will provide a general security analysis in IoT, including the different threats and vulnerabilities that IoT is exposed to and some security requirement that should be considered while building an IoT application.

14.2.1 SECURITY PROPERTIES

- Confidentiality: guarantees that the information exchanged by the users, will not be revealed to a third unauthorized party. A restricted access to the information must be applied and allows only the authorized ones to consult them.
- Integrity: guarantees that the information exchanged between two parties will not be altered or modified by unauthorized third party. It also involves maintaining the consistency, accuracy, and trustworthiness of data over its entire life cycle. It requires direct authorization by the owner of the data, and cryptographic mechanisms to check the integrity such as a hash function (e.g., SHA and MD5), checksums, etc.
- Availability: ensures that the data are always accessible by a legitimate user. Together with the confidentiality and the integrity they form the so called CIA triad, and they are the most crucial components of security.
- Authentication: is a way of identifying users, traditionally by requiring the user to provide valid credentials (e.g., username, password, etc.). The credentials provided are then compared to those already stored in the authentication server database. The credentials are proper to each user and must not be revealed to others. More elaborated authentication processes are required especially for critical systems, for instance using biometric authentication (e.g., fingerprint, eye, etc.), or requiring strong authentication (i.e., authentication with more than one identity factor).
- Authorization: usually following a successful authentication process, users are granted authorization to execute certain task or getting certain information depending on the defined policies. Mainly, who can access the resource? what resource? what action can be performed and for how much time?
- Accounting/Auditing: Accounting consists in the measures of the quantity of resources consumed by a given user during his access, including the amount of system time and the amount of data exchanged. It merely concerns system man-

agement. It serves for collecting information in order to do statistics on resource utilization, authorization control and for economical purpose such as trend analysis and billing.

Together with the authentication and the authorization they form the **AAA** [5], which essentially define a framework for coordinating these individual disciplines across multiple networks, technologies and platforms. Hence, allowing an intelligent and efficient access control to computer resources, enforcing policies, auditing usage and providing the information necessary for services requiring billing. These combined processes are required for any effective security and network management.

- Non-repudiation: guarantees that the author of an information cannot deny its ownership. For example, a user who signed a document with his/her private key cannot deny his/her signature.

Before going deeper into the security mechanisms defined in IoT and WoT, we need to investigate first the critical aspects related to the security of the smart objects. The next section is dedicated to the different security and privacy properties that need to be preserved during the life-cycle of a smart object.

14.2.2 SECURITY OF SMART OBJECTS

An attacker who has physical access to the smart object (SO) is able to gather lots of private information. Moreover, if the attacker succeeds to recover the private keys, he/she can decrypt all the traffic flowing from and into this SO, or he/she can inject some malicious codes to other endpoints. Hence, this is a very serious problem and also a critical point in the architecture of WoT and IoT.

In this subsection we will go through the different security and privacy properties that has to be preserved in order to secure the SO, by exploring an architecture proposed in [6].

First we will expose some of the important concepts that will be used in the architecture, some are related to the security and other are for discovery. We will begin with the notion of identity in IoT, since a lot of definitions can be found in the literature, mainly about the identity and the partial identity of objects. In the IoT, SOs are considered as independent entities, with communication and computation capabilities, and with the ability to act on behalf of the user. Traditional identity management becomes obsolete and needs to be extended in order to deal with those changes. Identity will allow in one hand to distinguish the different objects inside the network, and in the other hand to verify their origins. Same as any identity management architecture, in order to create a trust environment, those identifiers must be unique.

Another kind of identity called partial identity can be also used to authenticate objects. Partial identity is mainly used for anonymity purpose. They contain a subset of attributes of a global identity, those attributes can either be chosen by the user or by the identity provider. Pseudonym is an example of partial identity. Those partial identities can be attributed to the users and eventually the objects depending on the situation and the context. Thus we can use either global identity (or identity in general) or partial identity to identify each of the objects according to the context and the environment.

Objects discovery is also one of the concerns in the current architectural research. Objects have to be addressable, named and also discovered. This is a very complex problem especially for the mobility, the availability and the constrained nature of the objects. Many proposals have been introduced in order to address such problems, in particular: IoT Addressing, IoT Naming and IoT Discovery [7,8]. Those problems need a suitable infrastructure such as X.509 [9] or Lightweight Directory Access Protocol (LDAP) [10]. In the solution described bellow they prefer to use the Handle system (HS) [11], because of its advantages such as, simplicity, search capability, interoperability with the others systems, security features and the distributed administration and service model. Handle system is a distributed information system for secure global name service on the network. HS supports secure handled resolution, enabling storing names in a distributed manner, and guarantees access control, data confidentiality, integrity and non-repudiation [11].

Now we will go through the proposed security architecture. This document adds in fact a security layer to an European project called IoT-A focusing on the design of an Architectural Reference Model (ARM) [12], aiming at bringing interoperability between the different IoT domains. This proposal intends to extend the security functions in ARM, particularly the security and privacy in the different stages of the smart object life cycle.

In this architecture, the life cycle of a smart object is divided into three phases: the first one is the *Bootstrapping and Registration* phase where the smart object is installed, commissioned and connected to the network. The second phase is the *Discovery and Provisioning* process, where a smart object tries to access the resources of another one. And finally the *Operation* phase, where the smart object is able to communicate with the destination in a secure manner.

Every step in the previous life cycle needs to provide security and privacy of the users. The information and resources of the smart object must also be protected. Before going deeper into the security aspects of the different phases, a security hypothesis was assumed. Every smart object needs to be statically configured with a cryptographic material such as a X.509 certificate or equivalent, called *root identity*, in order to execute some security computation later in the different phases. Those materials could be provided either by the manufacturer or by its owner. Next we will inspect the security and privacy analysis of the different phases and also the proposed mechanisms.

The first step in the life cycle of a smart object is the *Bootstrapping*, where the smart object is installed and needs to be connected to the network. First the smart object needs to be authenticated and authorized before deployed. Naturally not every smart object is allowed to act in the network, otherwise malicious frameworks starting to deploy infected objects in the network may be problematic. This authentication and authorization can be performed using a lightweight protocol respecting the constraints related to the computation capabilities and energy consumption of the

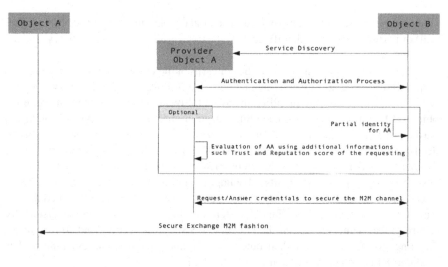

FIGURE 14.1

Discovery and operation phases

objects. Different protocols were mentioned such as Host Identity Protocol Diet EX-change (HIP-DEX) [13], Protocol for carrying Authentication for Network Access (PANA) [14], and 802.1X an IEEE standard for port-based network access control [15]. The proposed solution in [6] can use either PANA or EAP methods [16]. Once this operation done, the smart object can be registered and ready to be discovered, this is done using the resolution infrastructure Handle system discussed before. Additional privacy aspects can be done at this level, in case of successful authentication and authorization. For example, the smart object can compute other cryptographic materials, for anonymity purpose for instance by computing a partial identity. One more thing before going into the next step, is that the credentials are mainly exchanged using a Key Encapsulation Mechanism (usually a public key algorithm), in order to provide a symmetric key material, that will be used later to encrypt the future messages exchanges.

The second step is *Discovery and Provisioning* where the requester object wants to get resources from an other Object. Hence service discovery should check the authentication and the authorization of the requester object. And the final step is the *Operation*, where an Object A tries to communicate with an Object B. Fig. 14.1 shows the messages exchanged between the different objects to create a secure communication channel. It regroups the two previous steps.

As shown, first B has to discover if the provider has such kind of service. If it is the case, B will have to authenticate itself, either by providing its full identity, or using a partial identity for privacy-preserving purposes or anonymity. The selection of the identity is done according to the Object B policies and also to the contextual data. Once the authorization and the authentication are successfully done, B requests credentials from the provider to create a secure communication with A. The credentials are formated as a DCapBAC token [17]. The authentication, the authorization, and token exchanges parts can be done using PANA, and the exchanges between the object B and the provider can be secured using HTTPS or CoAP/DTLS [18]. As for the access control, it can be done via XACML technology [19]. Finally, with this DCapBAC token, a secure CoAP-DTLS [20,21] channel can be created between the Object A and the Object B, hence providing a secure M2M communication.

Now that we analyzed the security of the smart object, in what follows we will analyze briefly some of security and privacy properties in the IoT. First we will go through the different threats and vulnerabilities that the IoT is exposed to, then the main security requirements for an IoT system, and finally we will present an example of an authorization framework.

14.2.3 THE SECURITY IN THE INTERNET OF THINGS

The huge number of smart objects that can be integrated into the Internet thanks to the IoT, and the number of users becoming more reliant on these interconnected devices, raises several security and privacy issues. In order to fully understand those issues, we structured this subsection as follows: (1) We will go through the main threats and vulnerabilities encountered in the IoT. To do so, we firstly present a risk analysis and the origins of those risks. And then, we present the most important attacks surface area, and the top ten IoT's vulnerabilities according to OWASP.[3] (2) We will present the main security requirements that should be fulfilled by an IoT application. (3) And we will conclude with an example of security model dedicated to the IoT.

14.2.3.1 *Threats and Vulnerabilities*

In order to secure an IoT application, several points need to be considered:

- Firstly, with the device itself, since those devices apply relatively weak security mechanisms due to their constrained nature, and also they can be either physically accessible or they can simply be malicious. Hence all these possibilities need to be treated, as explained in 14.2.2.
- Then, the different communication protocols used to communicate with the smart devices. Several vulnerabilities appear (such as Ghost attack in ZigBee [22], usurpation, Sybil attack and Sinkhole attack in 6LoWPAN [23], etc.), which can compromise the devices and the infrastructure.
- Next, the threats coming from the external entities. Attacks such eavesdropping, tampering, DoS attacks, phishing attacks or code injection attacks can occur.
- And finally, problems related to the privacy and trust from the device owner perspectives. Naturally private information needs to be confidential, protected and also guaranteed to be destined only to the legitimate person or device. Hence security and privacy requirements need to be set and applied to protect IoT.

---

[3]https://www.owasp.org/index.php/OWASP_Internet_of_Things_Project.

Related works in this field considered the analysis of IoT's specific properties, to be able to analyze the security and privacy challenges, and this is the objective of this section.

A research study in HP [24] conducted on the security risks on the IoT devices, by viewing 10 of the most popular devices in some of the most common IoT architectures, shows that:

- 90% of devices collected at least one piece of personal information via the device, the cloud, or its mobile application such as name, address, data of birth, health information, and even credit card numbers.
- Six out of 10 devices that provide user interfaces raised security concerns and were vulnerable to a range of issues such as persistent XSS and weak credentials.
- 70% of devices do not encrypt communications to the Internet and local networks.
- 70% of devices along with their cloud and mobile application enable an attacker to identify valid user accounts through account enumeration.
- 80% of devices along with their cloud and mobile application components failed to require passwords of a sufficient complexity and length, hence weak passwords.

According to HP and OWASP those problems are mainly due to insufficient authentication and authorization, lack of transport encryption, insecure web interface and insecure software and firmware. Deeper analysis of those problems will be threatened in what follow. OWASP Internet of Things (IoT) Project,[3] an Open Web Application Security Project explores and exposes the security risks associated with the IoT in order to help developers, manufacturers or any entity of interest to understand and make better decision when dealing with IoT technologies. This project is structured into sub-projects mainly the IoT attack surface area and the top IoT vulnerabilities.

The IoT attack surface[4]:

The IoT attack surface is pretty wide and exposes an exhaustive list of attacks surfaces and their correspondent vulnerabilities. In this section, we will go through the most important ones which will give us the essential background to continue the exploration of the advancements in the field of IoT security researches:

- Ecosystem Access Control: This area focuses on the problems related to control the access to the device, mainly the problems related to the implicit trust between the components, the enrollment security and the lost access procedures.
- Device Web Interface: it covers all the web attacks that the device's web interface may be exposed to such as SQL injection attacks, Cross-site scripting, username enumeration and weak passwords etc.

---

[4]https://www.owasp.org/index.php/OWASP_Internet_of_Things_Project#tab=IoT_Attack_Surface_Areas.

- Device Network Services: covering the network attacks that may threat the device, such as Denial of Service, poorly implemented encryption, unencrypted services, buffer overflow, relay attacks, etc.
- Local Data Storage: since the resources in the device need to be protected, several vulnerabilities may occur mainly in case of unencrypted data or data encrypted with discovered keys, lack of data integrity checks or the use of same static encryption/decryption keys.
- Mobile Application: vulnerabilities such as lack of transport encryption, lack of two-factors authentication, weak passwords, etc.
- Network Traffic: covers all the problems related to the communication protocols specially the wireless ones (WiFi, Zigbee, Bluetooth) and the application of fuzzing protocols to test the IoT applications.
- Authentication/Authorization: one of the most important problems, not only in the IoT but also in the WoT. The vulnerabilities are mainly related to the authentication/authorization related values (credentials, session keys, tokens, etc.), device to device authentication, device to mobile application authentication and the lack of dynamic authentication.
- Privacy: user data disclosure, user/device disclosure and differential privacy are the main vulnerabilities that an IoT user may be exposed to.
- Hardware (Sensors): and last but not least all the problems related to the electronic devices itself such as sensing environment manipulation, tampering and damaging the device physically.

Covering all the vulnerabilities provided by OWASP needs a lot of times. In the discussion that follows we will focus on the top ten vulnerabilities provided by OWASP. They are present in many attacks surface areas, and they form also the basis of the previous statistics made by HP.

IoT's top ten vulnerabilities[5]:

1. Insecure Web Interface: it's a threat that can be initiated either by an internal or an external attacker, exploiting the problems related to weak credentials or by the enumeration of users accounts. In term of exploitability and detectability, it is rated as EASY, which means that attacks of this type can be discovered just by manually examining the interface or by using automated testing tools. Also other issues can be identified using those tools such as cross-site scripting. The impact of an unsecured web interface may lead to data loss or corruption, denial of access and even complete device takeover. This is why it is rated as SEVERE regarding the impact.

2. Insufficient Authentication/Authorization: since access to the device's resource must be prohibited for unauthenticated or unauthorized entities, insufficient authentication or authorization mechanism is rated as SEVERE concerning the impact on the data and the device itself (data loss and corruption and even complete compromise of

---

[5]https://www.owasp.org/index.php/Top_IoT_Vulnerabilities.

the device and/or the user accounts). The attacker can take advantage of the lack of granular access control and weak credentials, since authenticating entities with weak credentials may not be sufficient. In term of exploitability it is rated as AVERAGE and EASY in term of detectability.

3. Insecure Network Services: checking vulnerabilities related to open ports such as DoS, buffer overflow, and fuzzing attacks are very commune, since anyone who has access to the device via a network connection may attack the device, thus only the necessary ports need to be exposed and protected. Also, abnormal request traffic need to be blocked. Several DoS attacks have been proven to be efficient on the IoT devices [25,26] specially when unsecured network services are available, rendering the device unavailable or inaccessible to the user. In term of exploitability and detectability it is rated as AVERAGE. However, the impact is rated as MODERATE.

4. Lack of Transport Encryption: eavesdropping and tampering can be easily set by an attacker in case of unencrypted data sent over the network, since it is prevalent that the traffic in the local networks is assumed to be not widely visible hence the lack of transport encryption. However, traffic can be visible in case of a mis-configured local wireless network which may result in data leak or loss. Many propositions for end-to-end encryption using DTLS or a lightweight cryptography have seen the light [27]. In term of exploitability it is rated as AVERAGE and EASY in term of detectability. The impact is rated as SEVERE.

5. Privacy Concerns: protecting the user's private information is an important requirement in any system. In IoT case, the attacker can take advantage of a weak authentication, lack of transport encryption or unsecured network to gather personal non-protected information. This scenario can be crucial in case of confidential and sensitive information such as credit cards information or health information. Thus data anonymization, authorization and encryption need to be guaranteed in such environments. In term of exploitability it is rated as AVERAGE and EASY in term of detectability. As for the impact, it is rated as SEVERE.

6. Insecure Cloud Interface.

7. Insecure Mobile Interface.

8. Insufficient Security Configurability are also critical aspects that must be taken into account while dealing with such environment.[4]

9. Insecure Software/Firmware: even if the exploitability of this kind of vulnerabilities is DIFFICULT, its impact is considered as SEVERE, since it can lead to compromission of user's data and even to take control over the device. The device needs to be able to perform updates regularly, specially when vulnerabilities are discovered. The updates need also to be protected, since software/firmware updates files delivered on insecure network connection are susceptible to altering attacks. Consequently, encryption and integrity checks need to be performed. This vulnerability can be EASILY detected by inspecting the network traffic during the update and check the encryption.

10. Poor Physical Security: finally, physical attacks are widely used to access the operating system and the sensitive data stored in the device such as the encryption keys and the credentials, by disassembling it and accessing the storage medium. Precautions can be made by encrypting the stored data and ensuring that the USB ports can not be used maliciously. In term of exploitability and detectability it is rated as AVERAGE.

14.2.3.2 *Security Requirements for the IoT*

The exponential growth of the number of deployed devices and the size of data that will be exchanged on the network raised several challenges in order to achieve a global architecture. Those challenges concern not only the operational part, but also, and most importantly, the security and the privacy in such environment [28]. What makes the uniqueness of the IoT are the properties that need to be treated in order to define the security and the privacy challenges. Such properties, as explained in [29], are the result of the analysis of many related researches in the IoT field, they are mainly four properties: 1) *Uncontrolled environment* which is natural for an environment such as the Web especially when dealing with mobile Things (from one domain to another), physically accessible and requiring the establishment of trust relationships in order to exchange sensible information. 2) *Heterogeneity* since the IoT environment may integrate various types of entities coming from different origins. 3) *Scalability* related to the plethora of Things that need to be interconnected, hence a highly scalable protocols need to be applied and 4) *Constrained resources* in term of energy, computation capabilities and storage space. The same analysis shows that the security requirements can be grouped into five main sections: Network Security, Identity Management, Privacy, Trust, and Resilience.

Network Security:

Preventing eavesdropping, tampering, spoofing, denial of service, and so on, of sensitive information when they are sent via the Internet, either from a Thing to another or from a Thing to human, is an important requirement for network security. *Confidentiality* requires the establishment of a secure communication for the IoT's smart objects, specially when they communicate through the Internet. Traditionally, several technologies such as IPSec and TLS have been proven to fulfill the requirement, however they require significant cryptographic computations that exceed the capacities of the current IoT devices. Thus, dedicated secure network stack for the IoT needs to provide strong and lightweight encryption, so that the constrained devices can benefit from the same security functionalities that are typical of unconstrained domains. Most of the solutions trend to use a trusted unconstrained node to offload the computationally intensive tasks such as the calculation of the master session key. Another property guaranteed by the encryption is the *Integrity* of the data to ensure they are not altered during their way to the destination. While *Authenticity* provides proof that a connection is established with an authenticated entity, it can also include the integrity. And finally, the Things need always to be available meaning that the connectivity of a Thing should persist even under link failure, referring to the *Availability* property. *Secure routing* is also one of the issues that can occur in the network, and it can be instantiated through the implementation of secure routing with a strong protocol such as RPL [30].

Identity Management:

First of all, each object needs to be aware of its own resources such as identity, constraints, security requirement, etc. Due to the enormous number of devices deployed in the Internet, and the complex relationships that they can have with each other, appropriate identity management mechanisms need to be present. Still identity management alone is not sufficient showing the importance of authentication, authorization, accountability and revocation mechanisms. *Authentication* is very important to IoT and is likely to be the first operation carried out by a node when it joins a new network, which appears in first deployment or mobility cases as examples. Usually authentication is performed using an authentication server with a network access protocol such as PANA or Extensible Authentication Protocol (EAP) [16]. As for the management of the access *authorization* and the ownership of resources, federated authorization such as Kerberos and OAuth have the possibility to provide delegation of access across domains and provide quick revocation. A presentation of an authorization framework is presented in 14.2.3.3. As for the *Accountability*, it needs to deal with the massive amount of data that will be exchanged. Also mechanisms to manage the identity of the nodes and a key management with protocols such Authenticated Key Exchange (AKE) can be compatible with IoT [16].

Privacy:

Objects dealing directly with the private information of individuals and organizations raise a challenging privacy issue in IoT. The environment needs to provide data privacy for the data transmitted in the Internet, in the sense that traffic sniffed containing those data will not reveal/expose its content. For this reason mechanisms for data anonymity, pseudonimity and unlinkability need to be used to guarantee the privacy of the data in on hand and the entity itself (human or device) in the other hand.

Trust:

Giving a proper definition of the Trust specially in a distributed architecture such IoT is still a challenge, since any trusted entity can become malicious either intentionally or after being compromised. However, the Trust in this case can be separated into three parts. The first part is the *Device Trust*, since a prior trust cannot always be established due to the mobility and the distributions properties of IoT. However, approaches such as trusted computing [31] and computational trust [32] can solve the problem. The second part is the *Entity Trust* referring to the expected behavior of the different entities. This part presents more challenges. Solutions based on the behavior analysis and the application of proper policies need to be investigated. The last part is the *Data Trust*, which can use the previous established trust relationships to judge the trustworthiness of the data e.g., data originating from a trusted entity might be also trusted.

Resilience:

And finally the Resilience requirement, where the IoT applications need to ensure the availability of the resources in case of system failure, and also to have robustness against the different attacks.

14.2.3.3 *Example of Security Model in IoT: OAuth-Based Authorization Service*

Authorization as we defined it previously, is a critical aspect in accessing the objects in a secure way, and preventing unauthorized users form extracting information, in particular the private ones. Many innovative architectures have been proposed in the last years. One of the main problems related to the authorization process (for example with OAuth) is the limited computational power and the communication constraints of the smart objects, since some cryptographic primitives such as computing checksums or digital signatures require both processing power and energy consumption. Moreover, if the access policies for the services provided by the Smart Object reside on the Smart Object itself, it could be extremely hard to dynamically update them once they have been deployed. The proposed architecture, described below, solves this issue by deploying an external authorization service based on OAuth.

OAuth-Based Authorization Service for IoT (IoT-OAS), is a framework based on HTTP/CoAP services to provide an authorization framework, in order to protect the privacy of the personal information. This authorization is based on the protocol OAuth allowing a secure authorization form third-party applications, and benefiting from the advantages of using such delegated authorization protocol such as lower processing load, fine-grained customization of access policies and scalability. The proposed framework uses the access token in order to access the IoT application resources, and also a delegation approach [33].

Now that we have a global overview of the threats and the security requirements in the IoT, we will introduce the security of the WoT by listing the currently proposed models, mainly the identity management, data confidentiality and integrity, the authorization and the access control.

14.3 SECURITY IN THE WEB OF THINGS

Privacy, security, and trust issues in WoT require special attention and further investigations and ameliorations. To briefly clarify these issues, lets consider the example of an object accessible over the web. The privacy involves handling issues raising from sharing this object with others on the web, allowed only to the authorized ones, the concealment of personal information as well as the ability to control what happens with this information. The security deals with issues related to who will have access to the object and what he/she can do while he/she has the access. And trust concerns the issues related to the interactions between the different WoT entities in the Web. The use of REST-based API in WoT makes it possible to layer the entire interactions using HTTPS protocol. Since Things on the Web will be accessible and shared among many users, researches in this area are essential for a successful and widespread use of the WoT. Until recently, researches dealt only with IoT issues [34,35], thus WoT security is yet to be explored [36].

In this section we will first go through the problematics related to the identity management, we then focus on data confidentiality and integrity, and finally we explore the authorization and the access control models.

Generally, openness and sharing in any ecosystem come always with security and privacy issues, same applies to the WoT. Things' shared resources and data need to be protected against vulnerabilities raised from malicious intervention and inadvertent errors. In the last few decades, several Web services based solutions have been proposed to address those privacy and security issues. However, those solutions in most of the time are not compatible with the constrained environment such as the WoT. Moreover, it does introduce new dimensions of risk due to its heterogeneous nature. Some of the main threats related to WoT can be summarized in the following list:

- **Impersonating a Server or a Thing**: the server acts as a proxy to deliver requests to the right destination, Things discovery or other purposes. An attacker can take control of the server and present itself as a valid server. Hence, all the traffic going through it will be compromised by the attacker including credentials and users/objects identities. Furthermore, an impersonated Thing can reveal personal information, or send malicious code that can be injected in the requester side.
- **Tampering attacks** against Things' resources.
- **Unauthorized access** to the Things' resources.
- **Eavesdropping** of the traffic flowing between the different entities in the WoT environment, hence compromising the privacy property.
- **Denial of Services attacks**, which aim the unavailability of the Objects in the Web, by submerging it with excessive amount of network traffic.

To face such threats, WoT needs to provide some security and privacy guarantees while taking into account the mobility and the size of the Network. It is necessary to protect the Things private resources and critical information from being accessed, modified or inserted by unauthorized entity. Thus, Authentication, Authorization and Access control are indispensable requirements for the WoT, combined with efficient Identity management and policies can provide a strong security and privacy architecture. Other security properties need to be also taken into account such data integrity and confidentiality which can be provided through secure communication through encrypted channels inside the WoT ecosystem. The rest of the section provides an overview of the different security mechanisms that are actually proposed or that are under development.

We will start with how the identity is managed in the WoT architectures, the different identity management models and we will conclude with an example in Section 14.3.1. Then in Section 14.3.2, a study on providing confidentiality and integrity of data through securing the channels between the communicating devices. Then in Section 14.3.3, we introduce the authorization approach that can be applied to a WoT architecture. We conclude in Section 14.3.4 with the analysis of the access control mechanisms that can be deployed in a WoT environment.

14.3.1 **IDENTITY MANAGEMENT IN WOT**

Controlling users identity is an important process in any application and system. Such control includes authenticating users and verifying their access permissions to the desired information. This process is also applied on the user's data inside an ecosystem, since personal information such as identity, credentials, social security, etc., must be protected against unauthorized access. Consequently, several mechanisms have been exposed in the literature allowing such control such as the Identity Management mechanisms [37]. Kim Cameron in [38] refers to the set of guidelines related to the digital identity systems, including the design principles and rules to achieve security and dependability properties.

The Identity management defines the rules to identify individuals in a given system, through their identities and depending on the circumstances. The system controls user's access to its resources by attributing respective rights and restrictions. Defining the appropriate policy is also important in the identity management by defining if the entity (devices or user) is authorized on the network or not, what it can accomplish, in what circumstances, if it have the privileges and probably other factors.

However in our case the encountered problem is identifying the smart objects in the WoT. Undoubtedly in WoT, we will have interactions of the form object-to-object where an object A will send information to object B without human intervention, and object-to-human, where sensors will send their results to the human. So obviously for security reasons, identity control in these use cases is crucial, since we exchange and entrust more and more personal information to the smart objects, that are directly exposed to Internet.

In fact several questions raise such as: How to uniquely identify objects in WoT? And how to provide these identities in the object-to-object use case, and the object-to-human use case? Finally, how safe the identity of the users and objects in the WoT ecosystem is? We will answer these questions in the next sections of this chapter by exploring some researches in this domain and through some real-life use cases deploying such techniques.

14.3.1.1 *Identity Management Models*

The general architecture of the identity management models in the WoT ecosystem is composed of an Identity Provider (IdP), a Service Provider (SP) and the user/object. In this section we will provide a brief sketch of the existing identity management models [39].

- **Centralized federation model**: where there is a unique trusted IdP responsible for collecting and provisioning users with identity information. Usually located in a secure domain, this model enables Single Sign On (SSO), and sharing the users identity information with different SP. However, the IdP suffers from the problem of single point of failure, if this part fails the entire identity management system will fail.
- **Decentralized federation model**: the IdP's functions are distributed among several IdPs, and in different secure domains. This model needs to establish a trust

relationships between the SPs and the IdPs, in order to provide SSO to users affiliated to different IdPs and SPs. However in this model, the user does not have the full control of his identity information, since they are stored in the IdP, and they can be disclosed to a third party without his permission.

- **User-centric model**: this model solves the problem of controlling the user's identity, by providing the user with full control of all the transactions involving his identity. Concretely, the user needs to explicitly approve the use of his identity. The user/object can have one or more identities issued by one or more Identity Provider. Such system needs to guarantee several properties, some of the basic ones are the confidentiality, the integrity and the unlinkability. The complete taxonomy of properties related to the user control is illustrated in [39]. An example of user centric IdM is illustrated in [40].

14.3.1.2 *Real-Life Identity Management Case Study: E-Health*

A new E-Health approach combining remote medical assistance, with the use of smart objects in order to continually monitor patients suffering from chronicle illnesses or age-related diseases, can be brought by the WoT concepts. This kind of remote medical assistance is called *Ambient Assisted Living* (AAL). Some examples of smarts objects used in the health domain are peacemakers, remote vital signs and motor activity monitoring with wearable smart objects, and so on. They have direct and real-time access to the medical data of the patient. Communicating with those objects can be performed using two methods: directly, which needs powerful devices embedded with web servers or indirectly using a Smart Gateway that allows web interaction with different kinds of smart objects usually using different communication technologies [36]. The indirect method is the one used in this case study [41].

However, accessing private medical information by the objects raises serious security and privacy related problems. Generally in order to access health information by authorized people (relatives, professionals involved in the treatment), the patient's consent must be provided. Due to the high sensitivity of the information, these embedded devices needs to ensure privacy and security requirement, specially when they are directly exposed on the web. Thus authentication and access controls mechanisms needs to be deployed for this purpose. The use of an Authentication and Authorization Infrastructure (AAI) [42], can perfectly satisfy these requirements by providing the Identity Management to the platform together with guaranteeing the identification of the user/object and the quality of the identity information.

As we discussed above, several types of identity management can be deployed depending on the circumstances. In this case where the patient private information needs to be controlled by himself, the user-centric model is the most suitable choice, for authenticating users and devices and also for establishing a trust relationship between the different actors of the system, by adopting the OpenID Connect framework. It is a simple identity layer on top of OAuth2.0, providing identity verification of variant types of users, smart objects, applications, mobiles, etc., based on the authentication performed by the authorization server, or what we usually call IdP. It allows also to obtain a basic identity information about the requester in an interoperable and REST-like manner [43]. Furthermore some security requirements need to be provided by the WoT in addition to the identity management, such as secure exchanges between the entities, data confidentiality and integrity, secure network access just by the authorized objects and the protection of the objects against tampering and physical attacks.

The identity management in this case study helps to control the access to the medical information of the patient, in one hand by identifying the authorized users/devices, and in the other hand by countering the unauthorized people/devices through the use of OpenID Connect combined with policies based on the user-attribute located in the Smart Gateway [41].

14.3.2 DATA CONFIDENTIALITY AND INTEGRITY

Securing the communication between the different components of the Web of Thing environment is mandatory, in order to preserve data confidentiality and integrity and to prevent a third party from eavesdropping and intercepting information exchanged between the different entities of the system. However, encryption in a constrained environment such as WoT can be problematic since cryptographic computation usually requires memory and energy which are not always available in the smart devices. In what follows we will go through two examples of end-to-end encryption, the first one is based on securing the communication at the transport-layer, and the second one for securing the communication at the application layer.

14.3.2.1 *End-to-End Security in CoAP's Transport-Layer*

Several security-related issues are raised in [44], on how to allow secure communications on the WoT, either for Thing-to-Thing communication or for Human-to-Thing, since most of the applications currently envisioned for the WoT require strong security assurances while taking into consideration the constrained environment of the smart objects. Those issues need to be handled before it can realistically be considered ready for deployment.

For this objective, an experimental evaluation of the different mechanisms proposed to secure end-to-end web communications with IPv6-capable sensing applications and devices have been realized in [44]. Those experiments are based on the analysis of Constrained Application Protocol (CoAP) protocol [18] maintained by CoRE (Constrained RESTful Environments), by using the Representational State Transfer (RESTful) web services with IPv6-enabled sensing devices. In CoAP the security is not integrated at the application-layer protocol itself, but rather directly applied to all CoAP messages at the transport layer of the protocol. Thus deploying DTLS in protecting communications at the transport layer appears as a logical choice, since currently 6LoWPAN environments employ UDP, at least from the standardization's standpoint. CoAP proposes three security modes based on the usage of DTLS to secure web communications with smart objects: 1) RawPublicKey, 2) Pre-SharedKey, and 3) Certificates all employing the CoAPs scheme when contacting a DTLS-enabled CoAP server [18]. The RawPublicKey and Certificates modes employ Elliptic Curve Cryptography (ECC) by using the Elliptic Curve Digital Signature Algorithm (ECDSA) for devices and messages authentication, and the Elliptic Curve Diffie–Hellman (ECDH) for the key agreement. The PreSharedKey mode used in the case where the smart devices already store some predefined keys either provided by the manufacture or the developer or simply by the user. Those keys will be used to secure the communications with other devices.

The experiments done in [44] analyze the impact the different CoAP's security modes on the network-layer payload space, the memory footprint and the computation and the energy overhead of the smart devices deploying theses security modes.

From the first analysis on the overhead on network-layer payload space, they concluded that even if the impact of CoAP security on the payload space available to applications is visible (up to 33% of the payload), it may be considered viable for applications that are thrifty with respect to payload space requirements. However, fragmentation is unavoidable in case where the applications requires a larger payload.

From the second analysis on the memory footprint of CoAP security, they concluded also that hardware-level encryption does not come without a non-negligible overhead on memory, especially the ROM memory (in the best case 78.9% will be needed in the Certificate mode). They also identified a major limitation that there is not enough ROM memory available to support the RawPublicKey mode. RAM is potentially a problem in this case, since 88.6% of memory usage in case of RawPublicKey mode may compromise the usage of other required applications in the device. Elaborated sensing devices with more memory will be required in the future to appropriately support ECC-based security modes. The remaining CoAP security modes appear to be valid in this case.

The last analysis concerns the computational and energy overhead of CoAP security, the outcome is that a significant impact of ECC on the performance and energy of current sensing platforms, inevitably influences the lifetime of sensing applications and its maximum achievable transmission rate. The advantage of hardware-based cryptography is again expressed by the values obtained from the PreSharedKey mode, therefore a good choice when pre-deployment and configuration of security-related parameters on sensing devices is desired. For scenarios where public-key cryptography is required, the Certificate mode appears again the best alternative to ECC.

The analysis concluded that the modes deploying the Elliptic Curve Cryptography consume more memory and energy, and cannot be used for high transmission rate. However in the future the ECC approach can become very promising with the evolution of the capacities of the smart devices due to the strong cryptographic properties proposed.

14.3.2.2 End-to-End Security in CoAP Application-Layer

Indeed, application-based security have been proved to have the capability of interpreting and interacting directly with the information contained in the payload portion of a datagram such as the application proxies used in most firewalls for FTP transfers. These proxies have the ability to control and restrict the use of certain commands even if they are contained within the payload part of the package. Moreover, lower-layer security protocols like DTLS do not have this capability. They can encrypt the commands for confidentiality and authentication, but they cannot apply restriction and policies for their use.

Hence, deploying such security in the transport layer in CoAP misses all the advantages available in the usage of security at the application layer. Another analysis, done in [45], focusing this time on the security of the end-to-end communications between devices at the application-layer rather than the transport layer of the protocol. Respecting the limitation brought by the WoT applications, this mechanism is employable in the context of a general security architecture supporting web-enabled sensors (Things).

Historically, several approaches were proposed to address in particular the end-to-end communications security between 6LoWPAN wireless sensing devices and Internet hosts. However, most of them are not compatible with the current vision of WoT using CoAP and 6LoWPAN as standards. We mention Sizzle [46] which is one of the smallest web server providing HTTP accesses secured using SSL's 160-bit ECC keys, for key negotiation and authentication, but requiring a reliable transport-layer protocol and therefore was incompatible with CoAP and 6LoWPAN at that time. However since then researches have evolved enough so that CoAP can now provide reliable transmission of messages according to the RFC7252 (Section 4.2 in [18]), by adding the *Confirmable* option to the CoAP's header. This would be a possibility to a future analysis of using Sizzle with the current CoAP. However, another issue with Sizzle is that it does not support two-way authentication which is required by many Machine-to-Machine (M2M) applications on the WoT environment. As an alternative, Sensor Networks for All-IP world (SNAIL) [47] secured using a lightweight SSL (SSNAIL) is another solution proposed to solve the two-way authentication using an ECC-enabled handshake instead of RSA [48], also requiring a reliable transport-layer protocol that was not available at that moment. This reliability can also be brought by CoAP, thus extra analysis can be done to check the compatibility of SNAIL in the WoT environment. More in line with the security in the application layer, a proposed solution for the integration of security with CoAP using options for the activation/deactivation of security contexts and for the protection of CoAP messages have been proposed and abandoned in an IETF draft [49].

The proposed mechanisms integrate and evaluate the security at the application-layer with the CoAP, by adding new security options to CoAP. The first option is *SecurityOn* which precises if the received CoAP message is protected with an application-layer security or not. This option states which security is applied (encrypted, signed or both) in the SecurityApplied field; the Destination Entity identifies the actor CoAP URI that the destination must handle, this option can be employed several times in the same CoAP messages to enable the traversal of different trust domains and possibly using different encryption keys; the timestamp to verify the legitimacy of the message; and finally the Context identifier enabling the receiver to contextualize the message in term of security, in particular deciding the appropriate ciphers and keys.

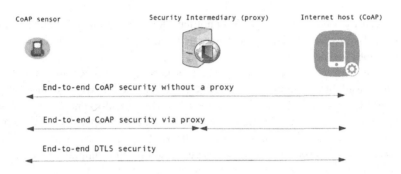

FIGURE 14.2

CoAP and DTLS security end-to-end usage scenarios [45]

The second option is the *SecurityToken* enabling the use of authorization and identity mechanisms. With this option, the requester may identify itself to obtain the access to a given CoAP resource. This option enables also request authorization based on a per message basis. Using the "TokenType" field, the requester can precise the authentication mechanism, that can be either a simple authentication process using its Username and Password or with a more sophisticated authentication process using its public-key, its X.509 certificate referred by a URI, or a kerberos ticket obtained from a domain server.

The last one is the *SecurityEncap* option. It transports the security related information required for the processing of the CoAP message, which depends on the content of the SecurityOn option. If only an encryption is required in the SecurityOn message (SecurityApplied set to 0), this message may transport a nonce plus the number of options followed by the encrypted data. If the SecurityOn requires a signature (SecurityApplied set to 1) this message may be used to transport an encrypted MAC plus a nonce value for freshness purpose. If the SecurityOn message requires both encryption and signature (SecurityApplied set to 2) a nonce, a MAC, a number of options and encrypted data may be transported with this option. More details on these new CoAP's security options can be found in [45].

An evaluation of the deployment of these options have been achieved to evaluate the impact the end-to-end security on the CoAP payload, the lifetime and the communication rate of the sensing application. The test platform is composed of a CoAP sensor (TelosB), an Internet host using CoAP and a CoAP intermediary (a forward proxy) that will be used for security processing. Via the SecurityToken option, the intermediary will provide authorization of CoAP clients and access control to the resource. As explained in Fig. 14.2.

The first evaluation is the impact of end-to-end security on the payload space of a CoAP packet, it computes the space needed to add security in the application layer. The analysis shows that the usage of the CoAP security intermediary in the encryption and the signature performs even better than using only CoAP with DTLS in the transport-layer. Thus the usage of the intermediary allows offloading the security computation, and guaranteeing a very small impact on CoAP's payload space. The analysis also shows that in the worst case when using encryption, signature and authentication, 65% of the original 6LoWPAN payload is still available. Hence, this approach is viable from the payload space point of view.

The second evaluation is on the lifetime of sensing application, by computing the energy consumption of the device when using such security options. It shows that the usage of the CoAP security intermediary in the encryption and the signature perform even better than using only CoAP with DTLS in the transport-layer. However, end-to-end CoAP security without an intermediary has bigger impact on the expected lifetime, specially for lower communication rates where the cumulative impact of AES/CCM encryption in the default CoAP security context is lower compared to the impact of the energy required to process and transmit CoAP security options. Consequently the obtained results show that CoAP security provides acceptable lifetime values in all usage scenarios, particularly considering the WoT applications natively designed to require low or moderate wireless communications rates.

Finally concerning the impact of end-to-end encryption on the communication rate of sensing applications, the study shows that using CoAP signing and encryption of all messages (as using DTLS) provides inferior performance. However, the results are still clearly above the requirements for the number of CoAP protected messages per second of most CoAP wireless sensing applications envisioned for the WoT, even in the worst case.

The overall evaluation of the proposed mechanism shows that CoAP application-layer security may perform similarly or better than transport-layer security. This approach brings new security to CoAP messages that are not possible in the transport layer to allow secure end-to-end communication for WoT wireless sensing applications, but still needs further investigation specially in term of key management and synchronization mechanisms [45].

14.3.3 AUTHORIZATION IN WOT

Allowing fine-grained and flexible access control to only authorized parties is crucial to an open ecosystem such as WoT, where objects are part of the World Wide Web and easily discovered. Traditional cryptographic algorithms and protocols might not be feasible due to the constrained nature of smart objects. Most of the actual solutions aim at setting a distributed authorization architecture, where a back-end server deals with the complicated tasks, which needs processing resources while letting the constrained devices handle the minimum of messages. The server is usually located between the smart device and the requesters. However, the device also needs to be able to distinguish the different requests coming from different entities and to apply the right authorization decision.

At the same time, several lightweight cryptographic algorithms such as (SEA, PRESENT, OAuth [50]) appeared specially to satisfy this purpose. Another solution is Delegated CoAP Authentication and Authorization Framework (DCAF) [51], allowing the delegation of the complex cryptographic computation to external entities, and establishing a secure DTLS channel between resource-constrained nodes. This protocol can be used to delegate authentication of communicating peers and authorization management to a trusted third party with more computation power, memory and energy [52].

As discussed in the previous sections, constrained environment needs to be treated differently than the normal environment. Moreover, those constrained nodes are expected to be present in various aspects of everyday life, hence they will be entrusted with large amount of personal data very likely susceptible to various attacks. For this reason, authentication and authorization are required for a secure WoT.

In some cases, static configuration of the authentication and the authorization process can be efficient, just as the case of prefixed silos of users or purposes, by statistically defining the access lists and the trusted entities when first deployed or by the manufacturer. However in case of flexible access to already deployed Things available to various number of users through the Web, this options seems to be obsolete and inefficient. In addition, authorization and privileges may change depending on the circumstances and the policies of the environment such as modifying the privileges of a black listed malicious entity.

For this end, an authorization and authentication architecture is proposed in [53] exclusively for constrained environments, where complicated security tasks will be assigned to another trusted entity, or by getting help from less constrained actors in the system. In this architecture, each entity will be assigned a constrained level ("constrained level", "less-constrained level", etc.). The less constrained nodes, also called Authorization managers, will perform the complex security tasks on behalf of their respective managed nodes, such as managing keys, enforcing authorization policies, etc. Fig. 14.3 shows the overall authorization architecture:

The components deployed in this architecture with their roles are such as follow:

- The *Resource Server (RS)* is hosting and representing a resource. It can be a SO or a traditional server (less constrained device).
- The *Client (C)* is an endpoint requesting a resource on the resource server (RS). The endpoints may or may not have a trust relationships, it can also be a constrained device (Thing) or not.
- The *Authorization Server (AS)* is in charge of creating and approving the authorization and the authentication data for the RS. It's a less constrained level of the architecture (in term of memory, energy and processing). Plays the role of backup for the RO and acts on behalf of it to handle the access requests to the RS. Authorization and authentication mechanisms can be deployed also between AS and CAS in order to further relieve the constrained level.
- And finally the *Client Authorization Server (CAS)* in charge of creating and approving the authorization and the authentication data for the Client. It is also a less constrained level of the architecture and play the role of backup for the RqP and act on behalf of it to handle the access requests to the Client.
- The *Resource Owner (RO)* is the entity (principle) that owns and controls the resource and also grants permissions using mechanisms such as OAuth [50] and

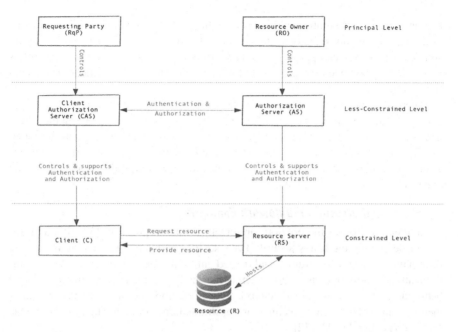

FIGURE 14.3

Overall authorization architecture [53]

User-Managed Access (UMA) [54]. The RO controls and makes authorization decision for the RS. Basically if an entity is not authorized by the RO it cannot access the resource R, hence performing authorization in the RS side.

- The *Requesting Party (RqP)* is the principal in charge of the Client, it controls requests that the client makes and the acceptance of the received responses. Precisely, it controls the interactions that the Client may operate with other endpoints and makes authorization decisions on behalf of the Client. Basically the client cannot exchange information (requests/responses) with a resource without the authorization of RqP, hence performing authorization in the requester side. Furthermore RqP may provide enough information to CAS to autonomously negotiates the access to RS with AS on behalf of the requesting Client.
- The *Principal* it can be either an RqP or a RO.

To summarize the aim of the overall architecture, the interactions between the constrained nodes must be controlled via the less-constrained level entities (AS and CAS) that act on behalf of the respective principals of the endpoints (RqP ans RO). Securing this interaction together with the control messages, by the bias of cryptographic keys, is also a requirement. The connection between the constrained nodes and the less-constrained nodes should be protected using a symmetric pre-shared keys and credentials. Also, protecting the connection between constrained nodes needs to be considered. This solution addresses also the confidentiality, the integrity and the availability problems since only the authorized entity has the right to access the resources, hence less charge on the system. Moreover, adding authentication to this architecture guarantees the accountability property and the authentication/verification of third parties.

There are other variants for this architecture depending on the scenario, for example some components can be merged in a single entity, such as combining the Client and the CAS if the Client has enough capabilities. A deeper analysis can be found in [53]. In what follows, we will present two authorization frameworks, the first one is a concrete implementation of the overall architecture presented above, and the second one is a token based mechanism.

14.3.3.1 *Authorization Framework Example 1*

An implementation of the previous architecture was proposed in [52]. It's a protocol for delegating the heavy security tasks such as authentication and authorization information to a less constrained and trusted entity. It relies on the DTLS to send authorization information and shared secrets (basically symmetric cryptographic keys) between nodes in a constrained network. It uses the notion of access token to implement the authorization architecture for constrained environment such as WoT. This protocol is called DCAF [52].

The goal of DCAF is mainly to setup a secure DTLS channel between two constrained nodes using the symmetric pre-shared key (PSK) cryptography, where the most sophisticated tasks are handled by the less constrained nodes. Moreover, DCAF ensures secure transmission of authorization tickets and enforces the authorization policies defined by the respective principal of the constrained node. Another advantage of the protocol is the support of implicit authorization where no authorization information are exchanged, hence a simplified authorization mechanism.

The actors of this implementation remain the same, with a difference in the terminology:

- Server (S) referring to the "Resource Server (RS)".
- Client (C) remains the same.
- Server Authorization Manager (SAM) referring to the "Authorization Server (AS)".
- Client Authorization Manager (CAM) referring to the "Client Authorization Server (CAS)".
- Authorization Manager (AM) which can be either a SAM or a CAM.
- Client Overseeing Principal (COP) referring to the "Requesting Party (RqP)".
- Resource Overseeing Principal (ROP) referring to the "Resource Owner (RO)".

Fig. 14.4 is a global overview of the proposed architecture, it summarizes the main interactions.

As explained before in the authorization architecture, each server (S) (which is a constrained environment that hosts a resource and it can be a Thing) is controlled by a Server Authorization Manager (SAM) that will perform the authorization and

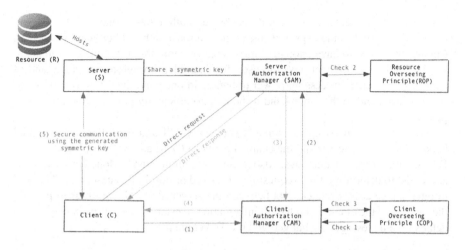

FIGURE 14.4

DCAF's overall authorization architecture

authentication process on its behalf. They both have already a pre-shared symmetric key that was exchanged initially using a key exchange mechanism.

When a client requests an access to the server's resources, he/she has first to ask the SAM for an "Access Ticket". The client can be either a constrained device (a Thing) or a less constrained device. In the case of a less constrained client, he/she can directly request the access ticket from the SAM, that will perform the "Check 2" to verify if the client is authorized to access the server's resource, by consulting the Resource Overseeing Principle (ROP) policies. Once the check is done correctly, the client will get an access ticket that contains a PSK, and also some details for the access permission in case of explicit authorization. Using this PSK, the client can directly and securely communicate with the server.

In the second case where the client is a constrained device, in order to get the access ticket he/she needs to go through a CAM that will act on his behalf, represented as step 1. The CAM will perform "Check 1" to verify if the server is an authorized source for the wanted resource, by consulting the policies defined by the COP, and then will forward the request to SAM (the step 2). Similarly, SAM will perform the "Check 2" to verify if the client is authorized to access the server's resource, by consulting ROP's policies. Once the check is done correctly, it will return an access ticket that contains a PSK and also some details for the access permission in case of explicit authorization which is represented by the step 3. Another check is done by CAM to verify if the permission in the access ticket complies with COP's authorization policies for the client ("Check 3"), then sends the ticket to the client which is shown in step 4. Finally, the client can use the PSK to directly and securely communicate with the server in step 5.

Some requirement has to be fulfilled by the authorization manager (SAM and CAM) in order to be able to provide the authorization and the authentication services. Mainly, they need to have enough storage space to store the different credentials, to be able to directly interact with the user, for example, through an interface, and of course have enough processing power to handle in one hand the different authorization requests, and in the other hand to be able to efficiently generate the PSK for a given client.

For security purposes, the channels between CAM and the Client, the channel between SAM and Server and the channel between CAM and SAM are encrypted by DTLS using the pre-shared keys. Also an authentication must be done between SAM and CAM to determine if the request is authorized or not. In this case, CoAP is used to interchange access-related data between the server and SAM in order to provide the server and the client with enough information to establish a secure channel. More details on the messages exchanged and the Ticket are presented in [52].

14.3.3.2 *Authorization Framework Example 2*

The second authorization framework complements IoT-OAS, an authorization service architecture based on OAuth for secure services in IoT scenarios [33] as we explained in 14.2.3.3, by introducing access token mechanism to access the IoT resources. The analysis is also based on the delegation approach to authorization introduced by IoT-OAS, which can also manage fine-grained access to web resources in the WoT.

The proposed system is composed of four parts: the smart objects, the owner, the external user who wants to access the object and the delegation authorization service IoT-OAS. A preliminary process is the authentication of users into IoT-OAS using one of the known authentication mechanisms (Google login, Tweeter login, Facebook login, etc.), once logged the user will be granted an access token to authorize him to interact with IoT-OAS.

The permission hence will be expressed by the tuple $< res, act, exp >$ where res is the URI of the object, act is the REST method that will be sent to the object and exp is the expiration time. The full method and messages are expressed in [55].

In fact owners prefer not only to restrict access to their object's resources, but also want to be able to grant access to authorized parties. In this case we distinguish two possible access policies:

1. Owner-to-Owner authorization: where the owner explicitly gives permission to himself to access or control an object. This type of authorization can be addressed using the OAuth 2.0 protocol [50]. The owner reads the UUID of the object, and sends a register request to IoT-OAS, which verifies if the object belongs to someone else, if not, will bind the object to the owner and grant him an all-access token allowing him to execute any operation on the object. The full message flow is explained in Fig. 3.a of [55].
2. Owner-to-Any authorization: where the owner can grant authorization to access one of his/her objects to other parties. This type of authorization in the web can also be addressed by the OAuth 2.0 protocol using the User-Managed Access

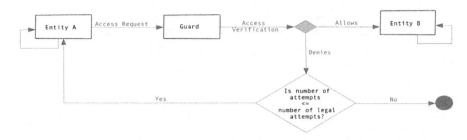

FIGURE 14.5

Basic access control

(UMA) profile. This type of authorization can be either *Reactive*, where the external user asks the owner for permission, as explained in Fig. 3.b of [55], or *Proactive* where the owner gives directly the authorization to the external user, as explained in Fig. 3.c of [55].

14.3.4 ACCESS CONTROL IN THE WOT

Traditional access control focuses on the protection of data based on the identity and attributes of the users. And generally the access control is used to protect front-end and back-end data and system resources by adding restrictions on who can access the data, what users can do, which resource they have access to and what operations are allowed to be performed on the data. Ideally, access control prevents unauthorized users from viewing, modifying or copying the data. The basic model of access control can be summarized in Fig. 14.5, where mainly an entity A wants to access entity's B resources, this request must go through a guard that will either allow or deny the access. The deny use case has also two branches, if the number of attempts of the same user reaches the legal one, the system will automatically drop his request and can also be black listed, else the user can resend an access request.

The WoT context enables the smart objects to publish and exchange their information over the Web. However, some security preventions needs to be taken into account, in order to deal with threats regarding the information exchanged over the Web. In particular regarding the access permission for the Things information and resources, such threats can be malicious clients, unwanted data sharing, divers attacks, etc. Hence the question of how to allow Things to grant clients secure access to their resources in such environment?

For computer network systems and in order to facilitate the access control, standard authorization models, such as Access Control List (ACL), Subject/object access control matrix [56], Multilevel security using information flow [57], Role-base access control (RBAC) [58] and Attribute-based access control (ABAC) [59], dynamic authorization model have been suggested [60] and capability-based systems must be deeply analyzed before applying them in the WoT. The selected mechanism needs to respect the constrained nature of the WoT, the autonomy (since the objects in-

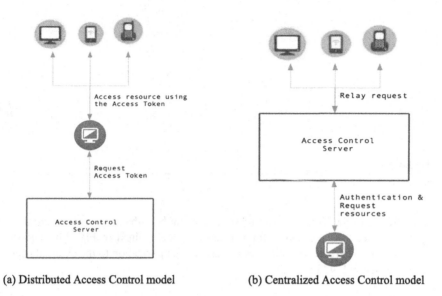

(a) Distributed Access Control model   (b) Centralized Access Control model

FIGURE 14.6

Access Control models

side needs to be able to communicate with each others over the web without humans intervention) and the security requirement.

In the literature, there are two ways to implement the access control for WoT: (1) A distributed fashion, where an access control server authenticates the user and grants him the appropriate access token, allowing him to access the Thing's resources for a certain period of time or permanently depending on the deployed policy, such as shown in Fig. 14.6.a. And (2) a centralized architecture where all the user's requests go through an access control server that authorizes and relays them to the right destination. In this case, there is no direct interaction between the communicating parties, such as shown in Fig. 14.6.b. Most of the access control models can be implemented in both fashions. The centralized model is interesting in the WoT since all the complexity can be carried out by the server. However, this will create the single point of failure, impersonation and privacy problems since all the requests and eventually responses are monitored by the server. The distributed architecture provides better scalability and privacy in the system, however it can be complicated to implement models such as RBAC and ABAC in WoT constrained environment since the Things themselves needs to check the received access token.

As stated in [61], the access control for WoT should have the following requirements: each object may publish its information as one or more web resource(s) over the web, those resources can be accessed via a basic HTTP/REST request. Finally permissions assignment can have a web resource representation, according to it, a permission grant decision can be made. In what follows we will provide two access control architectures, the first one is resource-oriented architecture, and the second one is a role-based access control architecture.

14.3.4.1 *Example 1: Access Control Through Resource-Oriented Architecture of the WoT*

A decentralized access permission control using resource-oriented architecture for the WoT has been proposed in [62]. It adopt the REST-style to allow Things and users to manage access privileges to their own web resources, which are accessible through a unique URI. They propose 5 steps to control and assure any resource access request coming from an external user. Those requests must be transported via a secure channel. As it is explained is the same paper, the first step to control the access to the resource is by filtering TCP/IP packets, especially filtering out the unallowable domain access. The second step is to parse the HTTP/REST request by filtering out the invalid requests and the abnormal parameters. The third step is to checks the HTTP header for basic authentication purpose so that the unverified users will be blocked. The fourth step is to check whether the requested resource exists or not, since requests for expired or irrelevant resource must be automatically dropped. And finally, the system needs to check the assigned access permission for the request operation. Unassigned access permission for a requested operation must be filtered.

The study focuses on the CRUD operations that can be applied on the object's resources, where a specific permission policy can be applied to each REST request. This permission policy, expressed using XML, can contain the requester information such as IP address, domain, host name, etc, and also some contextual information about the object itself, such as the time duration, localization, hardware state, capabilities, etc. An example of access rights for each CRUD operation to an object is shown in (14.1):

$$Permission\_Flag\_C[/R/U/D] = \{X\} \cap \{Y\} \quad [62] \qquad (14.1)$$
$$X = Condition\_about\_subjects$$
$$Y = Condition\_about\_the\_requested\_object$$

Handling the rules that have more than one condition has to be settled by the implementation. Assuming that all the conditions have the same priority to grant permission. There are two cases, either all the conditions need to be met or at least one of them. A more precise representation can be applied by dividing the condition part into two categories: inclusive and exclusive. In this paper the chosen rule was: "Permission is granted if any of inclusive conditions meets when any of exclusive condition does not meet" [62]. Then, the expression can be represented as shown in (14.2):

$$Permission\_Flag\_C[/R/U/D] = \{X\} - \{Y\} \quad [62] \qquad (14.2)$$
$$X = Union\_of\_inclusive\_conditions$$
$$Y = Union\_of\_exclusive\_conditions$$

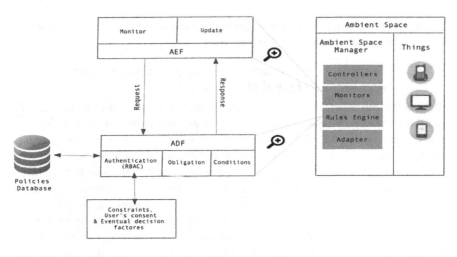

FIGURE 14.7

RBAC/WoT architecture

14.3.4.2 *Example 2: Role-Based Access Control*

Another example of access control is presented in [63], introducing the use of the RBAC [58]. It specifies the access policies for the plethora of data published by Things in the Web, and also how to access them and how the access can continue or should terminate. Cryptographic keys are also deployed to enforce those policies. The benefits from using RBAC reside in supporting a set of important security properties such as data abstraction, least privilege and the simplicity of adding access rights to users as long as the existing roles are used.

Generally each *User* is assigned a *Role* and each role is assigned to a *Permission*, hence users acquire permission to access a particular data depending on theirs roles. The user can have many roles and a role can be assigned to many users, same for the role which can have many permission, a permission can be assigned to different roles. And finally, each assignation needs to take into account the different constraints, for example to enforce conflict of interest policies that Thing's owner may employ to limit the number of users able to access Thing's resources. A more elaborated analysis can be found in [64].

However, RBAC suffers from the *role proliferation* problem related to the issues of dealing with a large amount of data, for instance granting permission to a big number of users to access a Thing's dataset, where each permission depends on the user's affiliation to the system. More precisely, the problem lies in handling the task of assigning a single role to each user which can be complicated in this case. *Role parameterization* have been proved to be an efficient solution in these types of scenarios [65]. The global proposed RBAC/WoT architecture, as explained in the paper, can be summarized in Fig. 14.7.

The proposed security architecture in Fig. 14.7 aims at integrating RBAC model into a WoT-based environment by mapping the RBAC entities with the WoT entities. Where the Things in WoT are represented as users in the RBAC model, with a set of permission that will grant privileges to the users and eventually the Objects. Also a set of RBAC authorization rules needs to be respected in order to access any WoT entity (user/object). The access control of the object's resources is done centrally. To enforce the specified access policies in WoT, RBAC needs to use the concept of *reference monitor* (RM), a process continuously running inside a trusted computer base, referring to the core control mechanism for the access and the usage of digital information. The reference monitor, located in the ambient space manager, is composed of two main components 1) the Access Control Enforcement Facility (AEF), located in the Monitors section and the 2) Access Decision Facility (ADF), located in the Rules Engine section. The two components interact with each other in order to approve or block an access request. Mainly, the AEF intercepts the different requests, and asks the ADF for a decision. The decision is then enforced in the AEF. More details can be found in the RM standard and [63].

14.3.5 SUMMARY

In this section we went through the currently proposed architectures for securing the WoT in the literature. We started with, how the identity is managed in the WoT, by listing the different identity management models currently proposed. Then, how the data is secured during the communication between the different components of the WoT system, in order to guarantee the integrity and the confidentiality of the data. The majority of the proposals are related to the security of CoAP, which is considered as the ideal communication protocol for the constrained devices. Next, we presented the authorization frameworks that allow a fine-grained and flexible access control to the SO's resources. And we concluded by presenting two models of implementing an access control mechanism in a WoT ecosystem. The first one is a centralized model, where all the access requests go through a server that decides either to authorize or to block the access. And the second one is a decentralized model where the device itself decides either to authorize or to block the access. With this summary, we concluded our overview of the security aspects in the WoT. We believe that the security and privacy in the WoT in particular, and the IoT in general, are a critical aspects that needs to be considered when developing new architectures. We noticed more and more interest by the working groups and the researchers. We hope that the future proposed solutions will be mature enough to cover most of the security and privacy properties, so that we can fully unlock the potential of the IoT/WoT.

14.4 CONCLUSION

Almost all the technologies are now available to implement a strong WoT and IoT infrastructure, starting from the first deployment of the Things until the step where each

Thing is able to interact autonomously with other entities (either humans or objects). Indeed the revolution of the WoT will not stop here. Periodically, innovative ideas of smart objects appear, aiming at covering all the aspects of our daily life. However, the main reason why it has not been widely implemented is the lack of sufficient security and privacy protections. Users are worried about their personal data that they will share with the smart objects and more importantly who can access them. They prefer to have full control of their personal information and to have enough security mechanisms to protect their data inside and outside the infrastructure. In this chapter, we covered the advancement in the WoT security and the privacy mechanisms that are currently proposed by the researchers. We mentioned four main aspects.

The first one is about the *Identity management* that includes also the authentication of the users. As a remainder each WoT entity needs to be identifiable inside the ecosystem. Within this identity the requester can authenticate itself and ask for permissions to access resources. There is still a lot of work to do in this part, especially since the few current proposed models do not at least fulfill some privacy requirements such as the anonymity and the unlinkability. The second aspect covers the *End to end encryption* in order to guarantee the confidentiality and the integrity of the communication between the entities. Currently, the IETF working group are on the different security mechanisms related to CoAP. The third aspect is about the current *authorization* models. They are based on the use of a third entity to execute the excessive tasks in term of memory, energy and computation capabilities. This can be seen as one possible solution to the authorization. However, this solution introduces it's own security concerns such as the MITM attacks. Maybe in the future, objects will have enough capacities to perform this task autonomously without the intervention of a third party, or that new mechanisms will be proposed. Finally the existing *Access control* solutions suffer from the same restrictions as the authorization ones. The only proposed architectures are based on a third party. Moreover well defined policies needs to take place in order to enforce this mechanism.

In our point of view, security and privacy models still needs to mature, and other aspects needs to be taken into account. Mainly the problems related to the trust relationship between the different entities of the environment. And finally, since undoubtedly vulnerabilities will appear, those systems need to be resilient, in order to prevent any threat and dysfunctionality in the future.

REFERENCES

[1] Guinard BD. A web of things application architecture-integrating the real-world into the web. PhD th. Zurich: ETH; 2011. p. 220. [Online]. Available: http://webofthings.org/dom/thesis.pdf.
[2] Guinard D, Trifa V, Wilde E. A resource oriented architecture for the web of things. In: Internet of things (IOT), Tokyo, Japan. Nov 2010. p. 1–8.
[3] Guinard D, Trifa V. Towards the web of things: web mashups for embedded devices. In: Workshop on mashups, enterprise mashups and lightweight composition on the web. Proceedings of WWW (international world wide web conferences). 2009. p. 15.

[4] Kruegel C. Internet security. In: The industrial communication technology handbook. 2005.

[5] Metz C. Aaa protocols: authentication, authorization, and accounting for the internet. IEEE Internet Comput Nov 1999;3(6):75–9.

[6] Skarmeta A, Hernández-Ramos JL, Bernabe JB. A required security and privacy framework for smart objects. In: ITU kaleidoscope: trust in the information society. Dec 2015. p. 1–7.

[7] Lee S, Jeong JP, Park JS. Dnsna: Dns name autoconfiguration for internet of things devices. In: 18th international conference on advanced communication technology (ICACT). Jan 2016. p. 410–6.

[8] Yan Z, Kong N, Tian Y, Park YJ. A universal object name resolution scheme for iot. In: IEEE international conference on green computing and communications and IEEE internet of things and IEEE cyber, physical and social computing. Aug 2013. p. 1120–4.

[9] Cooper D, Santesson S, Farrell S, Boeyen S, Housley R, Polk W. Internet X.509 public key infrastructure certificate and certificate revocation list (CRL) profile. RFC 5280 (proposed standard), internet engineering task force, updated by RFC 6818 [Online]. Available: http://www.ietf.org/rfc/rfc5280.txt, May 2008.

[10] Yeong BW, Howes T, Kille S. Lightweight directory access protocol. RFC 1777 (historic), internet engineering task force, obsoleted by RFC 3494. [Online]. Available: http://www.ietf.org/rfc/rfc1777.txt, Mar 1995.

[11] Sun S, Reilly S, Lannom L, Petrone J. Handle system protocol (ver 2.1) specification. RFC 3652 (informational), internet engineering task force [Online]. Available: http://www.ietf.org/rfc/rfc3652.txt, Nov 2003.

[12] Bassi A, et al. Enabling things to talk. In: Designing IoT solutions with the IoT architectural reference model. 2013. p. 163–211.

[13] Hummen R, Moskowitz R. Hip diet exchange (dex). IETF, Internet-Draft; 2015 (Expires: September 22, 2016).

[14] Forsberg BD, Ohba Y, Patil B, Tschofenig H, Yegin A. Protocol for carrying authentication for network access (PANA). RFC 5191 (proposed standard), internet engineering task force, updated by RFC 5872 [Online]. Available: http://www.ietf.org/rfc/rfc5191.txt, May 2008.

[15] Pack S, Choi Y. Pre-authenticated fast handoff in a public wireless lan based on IEEE 802.1 x model. In: Mobile and wireless communications. Springer; 2003. p. 175–82.

[16] Aboba BB, Blunk L, Vollbrecht J, Carlson J, Levkowetz H. Extensible authentication protocol (EAP). RFC 3748 (proposed standard), internet engineering task force, updated by RFCs 5247, 7057 [Online]. Available: http://www.ietf.org/rfc/rfc3748.txt, Jun 2004.

[17] Ramos JLH, Jara AJ, Marin L, Skarmeta-Gómez AF. Dcapbac: embedding authorization logic into smart things through ECC optimizations. Int J Comput Math 2016:345–66.

[18] Shelby BZ, Hartke K, Bormann C. The constrained application protocol (CoAP). RFC 7252 (proposed standard), internet engineering task force [Online]. Available: http://www.ietf.org/rfc/rfc7252.txt, Jun 2014.

[19] Sinnema BR, Wilde E. eXtensible access control markup language (XACML) XML media type. RFC 7061 (informational), internet engineering task force [Online]. Available: http://www.ietf.org/rfc/rfc7061.txt, Nov 2013.

[20] Raza S, et al. Lithe: lightweight secure coap for the internet of things. IEEE Sens J 2013;13.

[21] Chavan AA, Nighot MK. Securing coap using enhanced dtls for the internet of things. Int J Innovat Res Comput Commun Eng December 2014;2(12).

[22] Cao X, Shila D, Cheng Y, Yang Z, Zhou Y, Chen J. Ghost-in-zigbee: energy depletion attack on zigbee based wireless networks. IEEE Int Things J 2016.

[23] Pongle P, Chavan G. A survey: attacks on rpl and 6lowpan in iot. In: International conference on pervasive computing (ICPC). Jan 2015. p. 1–6.

[24] Internet of things research study 2015 report. Hewlett Packard; Nov 2015. [Online]. Available: http://www8.hp.com/h20195/V2/GetPDF.aspx/4AA5-4759ENW.pdf.

[25] Kasinathan P, Pastrone C, Spirito MA, Vinkovits M. Denial-of-service detection in 6lowpan based internet of things. In: IEEE 9th international conference on wireless and mobile computing, networking and communications (WiMob). 2013. p. 600–7.

[26] Sonar K, Upadhyay H. A survey: Ddos attack on internet of things. Int J Eng Res Develop 2014.

[27] Shemaili MB, Yeun CY, Mubarak K, Zemerly MJ. A new lightweight hybrid cryptographic algorithm for the internet of things. In: International conference for internet technology and secured transactions. Dec 2012. p. 87–92.

[28] Company WR, Security in the internet of things lessons from the past for the connected future, White paper, 2015.

[29] Vasilomanolakis E, Daubert J, Luthra M, Gazis V, Wiesmaier A, Kikiras P. On the security and privacy of internet of things architectures and systems. In: International workshop on secure internet of things. 2015. p. 49–57.

[30] Tsao BT, Alexander R, Dohler M, Daza V, Lozano A, Richardson M. A security threat analysis for the routing protocol for low-power and lossy networks (RPLs). RFC 7416 (informational), internet engineering task force. [Online]. Available: http://www.ietf.org/rfc/rfc7416.txt, Jan 2015.

[31] Iliev A, Smith SW. Protecting client privacy with trusted computing at the server. IEEE Secur Priv 2005;3(2):20–8.

[32] Audun J, Roslan I, Colin B. A survey of trust and reputation systems for online service provision. Decis Support Syst 2007;43(2):618–44.

[33] Cirani S, et al. Iot-oas: an oauth-based authorization service architecture for secure services in iot scenarios. IEEE Sens J Feb 2015;15(2):1224–34.

[34] Weber RH. Internet of things – new security and privacy challenges. Comput Law Secur Rev 2010:23–30.

[35] Medaglia CM, Serbanati A. An overview of privacy and security issues in the internet of things. In: The internet of things: 20th Tyrrhenian workshop on digital communications. New York, NY: Springer; 2010. p. 389–95.

[36] Mathew SS, Atif Y, Sheng QZ, Maamar Z. The web of things – challenges and enabling technologies. In: Internet of things and inter-cooperative computational technologies for collective intelligence. Stud comput intell, vol. 460. Springer; 2013. p. 1–23.

[37] Ferdous MS, Poet R. A comparative analysis of identity management systems. In: 2012 international conference on high performance computing and simulation (HPCS). 2012. p. 454–61.

[38] Cameron K. The laws of identity. Microsoft Corp 2005.

[39] Bhargav-Spantzel A, Camenisch J, Gross T, Sommer D. User centricity: a taxonomy and open issues. J Comput Secur 2007;15(5):493–527.

[40] van Thuan D, Butkus P, van Thanh D. A user centric identity management for internet of things. In: International conference on IT convergence and security (ICITCS). IEEE; Oct 2014.

[41] Domenech MC, Comunello E, Wangham MS. Identity management in e-health: a case study of web of things application using openid connect. In: IEEE 16th international

conference on e-health networking, applications and services (healthcom). Oct 2014. p. 219–24.

[42] Lopez J, Oppliger R, Pernul G. Authentication and authorization infrastructures (aais): a comparative survey. Comput Secur 2004:578–90.

[43] Sakimura N, Bradley J, Jones M, de Medeiros B, Mortimore C. Openid connect core 1.0 incorporating errata set 1. 2014.

[44] Granjal J, Monteiro E, Silva JS. On the feasibility of secure application-layer communications on the web of things. In: 2012 IEEE 37th conference on local computer networks (LCN). Oct 2012. p. 228–31.

[45] Granjal J, Monteiro E, Silva JS. Application-layer security for the wot: extending coap to support end-to-end message security for internet-integrated sensing applications. In: Wired/wireless internet communication. Proceedings of 11th international conference. 2013. p. 140–53.

[46] Gupta V, Wurm M, Zhu Y, Millard M, Fung S, Gura N, Eberle H, Shantz SC. Sizzle: a standards-based end-to-end security architecture for the embedded internet. Pervasive Mob Comput March 2005;1(4):425–45.

[47] Jung W, et al. Ssl-based lightweight security of ip-based wireless sensor networks. In: 23rd international conference on advanced information networking and applications, AINA, workshops proceedings. 2009. p. 1112–7.

[48] Jonsson BJ, Kaliski B. Public-key cryptography standards (PKCS) #1: RSA cryptography specifications version 2.1. RFC 3447 (informational), internet engineering task force [Online]. Available: http://www.ietf.org/rfc/rfc3447.txt, Feb 2003.

[49] Yegin A, Shelby Z. Coap security options. expired IETF internet-draft 2014.

[50] Hardt BD. The OAuth 2.0 authorization framework. RFC 6749 (proposed standard), internet engineering task force [Online]. Available: http://www.ietf.org/rfc/rfc6749.txt, Oct. 2012.

[51] Gerdes S, Bergmann O, Bormann C. Delegated authenticated authorization for constrained environments. In: IEEE 22nd international conference on network protocols. Oct 2014.

[52] Gerdes S, et al. Delegated coap authentication and authorization framework (dcaf). In: IETF, Internet-draft. 2014 (Expires: April 21, 2016).

[53] Gerdes S, Seitz L, Selander G, Bormann C, et al. An architecture for authorization in constrained environments. In: IETF, Internet-draft. 2015 (Expires: September 2, 2016).

[54] Maler E, Catalano D, Machulak M, Hardjono T. User-managed access (uma) profile of oauth 2.0. In: IETF, Internet-draft. 2015 (Expires: July 29, 2016).

[55] Cirani S, Picone M. Effective authorization for the web of things. In: IEEE 2nd world forum on internet of things (WF-IoT). Dec 2015. p. 316–20.

[56] Lampson BW. Protection. SIGOPS Oper Syst Rev 1974:18–24.

[57] Myers AC, Liskov B. A decentralized model for information flow control. In: ACM symp oper syst principles (SOSP). Oct 1997. p. 129–42.

[58] Sandhu RS, Coyne EJ, Feinstein HL, Youman CE. Role-based access control models. Computer Feb 1996;29(2):38–47.

[59] Al-Kahtani MA, Sandhu R. A model for attribute-based user-role assignment. In: Proceedings of the 18th annual computer security applications conference. IEEE; 2002. p. 353–62.

[60] Liu J, Liu C, Jiao D, Chen J. The research of a multi-factor dynamic authorization model. In: IEEE ninth international conference on e-business engineering, Hangzhou, China. 2012. p. 201–5.

[61] Oh SW, Kim HS. Study on access permission control for the web of things. In: 17th international conference on advanced communication technology. 2015. p. 574–80.

[62] Oh SW, Kim HS. Decentralized access permission control using resource-oriented architecture for the web of things. In: 16th international conference on advanced communication technology (ICACT), Pyeongchang, South Korea. 2014. p. 749–53.

[63] Barka E, Mathew SS, Atif Y. Securing the web of things with role-based access control. In: Codes, cryptology, and information security – first international conference. Proceedings – in honor of thierry Berger. 2015. p. 14–26.

[64] Ferraiolo DF, Sandhu R, Gavrila S, Kuhn DR, Chandramouli R. Proposed nist standard for role-based access control. ACM Trans Inf Syst Secur Aug 2001;4(3):224–74.

[65] Müldner T, Leighton G, Miziołek JK. Parameterized role-based access control policies for xml documents. Inf Security J: A Global Perspec 2009;18(6):282–96.

ACKNOWLEDGEMENT

This work has received funding from the European Union's Horizon 2020 research and innovation program under grant agreement No 645342, project reTHINK.

A WEB OF FITNESS "THINGS": AN EXPLORATION OF SOCIAL IMPACTS & VULNERABLE POPULATIONS

15

Kayla M. Booth, Elizabeth V. Eikey, Eileen M. Trauth

The College of Information Sciences and Technology, The Pennsylvania State University, University Park, PA, United States

CHAPTER POINTS

- In what ways can the WoT make individuals and societies healthier?
- What are some potential challenges or unintended consequences in terms of public health, particularly when considering vulnerable populations?
- How can we empower users and advocate for designers to consider vulnerable groups?
- Health and technology is often painted as a "double-edged sword." How can WoT alleviate potential challenges and unintended consequences while capitalizing on potential benefits?

15.1 WEB OF THINGS AND HEALTH: AN INTRODUCTION

The Web of Things (WoT) phenomenon has been looked at in several domains, including "smart homes and cities", health, automobiles, transportation, environmental and energy initiatives. While each of these domains is important, this chapter is interested in the WoT and health. In particular, this chapter explores the *social implications* of the WoT's application in a health context. Broadly speaking, many stakeholders in healthcare stand to benefit from the capabilities and opportunities of the WoT. While these possible benefits are important to discuss, so too are the potential unintended consequences of the WoT. While there are obviously technical challenges to having devices connect and communicate with one another, our focus is on the social issues around WoT. This chapter explores the WoT and the potential

Managing the Web of Things. DOI: 10.1016/B978-0-12-809764-9.00019-6

425

benefits and challenges in relation to health, particularly when it comes to vulnerable populations.

The conversation surrounding connected "things" and health initially began with the Internet of Things (IoT), or the notion of separate devices connected to one another. Technology media company Tech Target recently pointed out that "patients and providers both stand to benefit from [the Internet of Things] carving out a bigger presence in healthcare. Some uses of healthcare IoT are mobile medical applications or wearable devices that allow patients to capture their health data. Hospitals use IoT to keep tabs on the location of medical devices, personnel and patients" (Tech Target). As we transition in our discourse from the Internet of Things (IoT) to the WoT, we must examine the potential social impacts of this additional application layer. The connections of heterogeneous "things" and the movement (WoT) to have these "things" integrate and interact have implications across domains and users, especially when it comes to health. The WoT is significantly engaged in this domain – for good and (potentially) bad.

Even "health" is an enormous domain in which there are a myriad of stakeholders and perspectives. While this chapter talks about health at a high level, its detailed level of analysis is particularly interested in fitness. For the purpose of this chapter "fitness" encompasses physical exercise and nutrition. Fitness (and associated topics such as weight loss, body image, eating disorders, etc.) is a particularly interesting subtopic of health when it comes to technology. The ways in which fitness is depicted and discussed varies globally; this particular discussion and analysis focuses on a United States context.

Within the United States, there is a general awareness about paying attention to health, especially when it comes to diet and exercise. Poor nutrition and lack of physical activity are often linked to chronic and sometimes deadly diseases and conditions. Multiple stakeholders are addressing these concerns. For example, government agencies release guidelines as to how many servings of fruit, vegetables, grains, and proteins are optimal. Healthcare professionals often encourage patients to exercise daily. Amid these messages, technology is playing a significant role in these interventions. For example, some organizations, employers require employees to wear fitness trackers and subsequently base their health insurance benefits on each person's "healthy" recorded behaviors.

While there are a plethora of government, healthcare, and organizational initiatives geared towards improving health, there are also significant efforts employed by individual users. Many users are utilizing their smartphones and other devices to monitor their health. Sixty-four percent of United States adults have a smartphone, which is an increase of almost 100% from 2011 [1]. With the increasing prevalence of smartphones and tablets, mobile health applications or "apps" are becoming increasingly popular [1,2]. In terms of health apps, weight loss, diet, and physical activity tracking apps are the most popular [2]. Younger people are more likely to own a smartphone and download a health app than older adults [2]. In fact, 85% of young adults ages 18–29 are smartphone owners, and about 75% of them have used their smartphone to find health information [1]. Twenty-one percent of teens ages 13–18 have used mobile health apps [3]. Of those teens, 7% of them say they have changed their behavior as a result of using the app [3].

There is a rapidly expanding number of fitness "things" available and employed by the myriad of stakeholders invested in public health. From individuals to government agencies to employers and insurance companies, these devices and applications are increasingly embedded in United States citizens' everyday lives. This chapter explores how the WoT in a fitness context may impact vulnerable users, both positively and negatively. This narrative begins by considering the history of the relationship between the web and fitness. This starting point serves to explore the rich context in which WoT is entering.

The second point of discussion is exploring the ways in which users are made vulnerable within these contexts, setting the stage for the bulk of the chapter, which explores the potential positive and negative implications of the WoT within a fitness context. These sections consider how the application of and connection between "things" may help and/or harm: 1) users with less access to health resources and 2) users who may suffer from health conditions surrounding food or exercise, such as eating disorders. This exploration of social implications serves to help 1) consider users who are often overlooked during design and integration and 2) maximize possible benefits while minimizing potential harm by empowering vulnerable users.

15.1.1 A HISTORY OF THE WEB & FITNESS: UNDERSTANDING CONTEXT

While wearable trackers and apps are somewhat new phenomena, there is a long history studying the relationships between food, exercise, and technology, even if "fitness" is a newer term. The extant research paints a landscape in which there are benefits as well as unintended negative consequences of the ways in which users utilize technology in accordance with their exercise and dietary needs. For example, studies have found that online health-related communities can be beneficial for users trying to lose weight and maintain weight loss [4]. Virtual forums can provide spaces in which users motivate one another and exchange information and experiences [5]. These interactive spaces allow users to find support in their journeys, share and receive information, while often having the option of anonymity. While these forums and communities may be beneficial to many users, there are also communities in which disordered behavior is promoted in the same ways as healthy behaviors. For example, there are numerous online communities devoted to eating disorders. While some users come to these spaces to aid in their recovery, some use them to perpetuate and exacerbate their conditions. There have been numerous studies exploring "pro-ana" (pro-anorexia) and "pro-mia" (pro-bulimia) communities that promote eating disorders as a lifestyle choice that values thinness, rather than a medical condition [6]. Within these spaces, users often provide one another with encouragement to lose or maintain a low weight and continue with their symptoms, which can range from and include self-starvation, severe calorie restriction, cycles of bingeing and purging, and extreme exercise. Out of these communities grew the term "thinspiration" (sometimes abbreviated as "thinspo"), which refers to content that inspires viewers to be thin and can take the form of text, photos, videos etc. One "thinspiration" slogan most commonly associated with the "pro-ana" movement is the phrase "nothing tastes as good as skinny feels." Studies across decades depict a landscape in which users interact with one another via technology to encourage, motivate, and exchange information surrounding their nutrition and exercise habits and goals, which can range from healthy to disordered.

While there is this long history of users utilizing technology to discuss and monitor their nutrition and exercise, "fitness" is currently becoming an increasingly popular topic online, particularly on social media platforms such as Facebook, Instagram, YouTube, and Pinterest. A 2015 national study at Northwestern University in the Unites States found that teenagers look up fitness and nutrition information more than any other type of health information [3]. There is a current and evolving research stream explores the types of messages and content on the web (particularly social media and mobile apps) surrounding fitness [7–9] as well as how different groups are interacting with this content [10–12]. While this information is accessible to many and may help users live a healthier lifestyle, there are potentially negative and harmful messages often embedded within this content.

Within current social media research that focuses on fitness content, scholars discuss the similarities and differences between "pro-ana", "pro-mia", and thinspiration messages and new online movements. For example, when a user searches "thinspiration" on Pinterest, a link to the national eating disorder association's web page is made available. The term is not allowed as a hashtag on Instagram. Currently, however, there is a new movement labeled "fitspiration," which is meant to inspire viewers to be "fit" rather than skinny by eating nutrient dense food and exercising regularly [9]. This search term does not come with a warning and is not banned on Instagram, yet scholars have found that content with this label is likely to contain messages that promote weight-related guilt, encourages food restriction [13] negatively affect body image [9], decrease mood and self-esteem [8]. These scholars point out that there are numerous similarities between thinspiration and fitspiration, yet the latter is portrayed as healthy, seemingly focusing on fitness rather than thinness. While the former is often associated with the slogan "nothing tastes as good as skinny feels," the latter is often associated with "strong is the new skinny." While the words and messages are different, both movements often include photographs of women with idealized, often unattainable body types. This growing research landscape presents a continued depiction from earlier research: a double-edged sword in which users are able to access fitness-related information via social media platforms and monitor their progress via mobile apps, but are also interacting with disordered content. The current state is complex and nuanced in that disordered content is not always clearly labeled, is often embedded with healthy information (making it difficult to discern between healthy and disordered), and is often masked as "healthy."

This history of the ways in which users have interacted with technology to discuss and monitor their nutrition and exercise, in ways both healthy and disordered, is important to examine because it helps us understand context. While this long history exists, there are currently emerging topics across disciplines, such as "fitspiration" and other online movements that span across online communities, apps, and social media. This combination of rich history and emerging issues at the intersection of technology and fitness creates a larger narrative in which the WoT plays a pivotal role. If the WoT is to use the web and connect "things" in ways that are meaningful in a health and fitness domain, then it will do so within an already-existing context. Understanding this context is crucial if we are to consider the social implications of this new layer of application.

15.1.2 FRAMING THIS CHAPTER: WHY VULNERABILITY MATTERS

This particular chapter is interested in the *social impacts* of WoT and fitness. This chapter explores both the potential positive implications, as well as potential challenges, when it comes to the WoT and public health within a particular emphasis on vulnerable populations. Vulnerability is essential to examine in this chapter for two reasons: 1) When considering unintended consequences of technology, it is imperative to consider those who are often overlooked during design and integration processes. Those who are not considered "typical" or "target users" are historically most often those who are disenfranchised or negatively impacted by technological advancement, 2) "Health," and fitness in particular, as a context is fraught with inequality, especially for the "have-nots" of societies [14]. While this is often the case globally, this particular chapter will focus on the context of the United States. Within the United States, vulnerabilities exist in numerous ways across geographic and social dimensions.

This chapter explores both *societal* vulnerabilities as well as *contextual* vulnerabilities related to fitness (e.g. body image, disordered behavior, and eating disorders). Societal vulnerabilities refer to ways in which users are made vulnerable by larger systems in society (e.g. educational institutions, local economies, etc.). Contextual vulnerabilities refer to ways in which users are vulnerable based on the specific context of health and fitness. In other words, this perspective considers how users' negative relationships with food and exercise may affect their relationship to fitness information. The web is a space that researchers consistently paint as a double-edged sword when it comes to health and fitness, especially for vulnerable populations. How can WoT alleviate this tension and accentuate possible benefits while mitigating potential unintended consequences? This chapter explores how the WoT impacts these vulnerable populations as shown in Fig. 15.1.

15.2 POTENTIAL POSITIVE IMPLICATIONS FOR HEALTH

The relationship between public health and technology is a topic healthcare professionals and academic researchers have been deeply invested in for decades [15]. This raises the question: How can technology help make individuals and societies healthier?

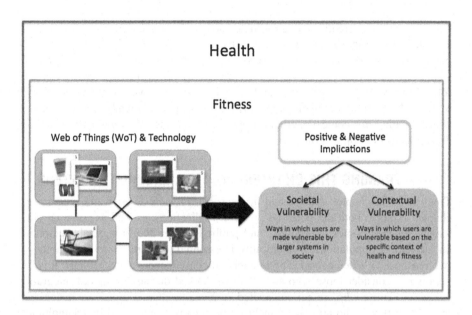

FIGURE 15.1

The relationship between WoT and societal and contextual vulnerability within the fitness context. All images used under Creative Commons License 2.0 (https://creativecommons.org/licenses/by/2.0/); Modifications: border added and cropped; https://www.flickr.com/photos/healthgauge/9504072114/in/photolist-bmEm6E-jEYN7t-jK2Ly9-hrWijP-iZUNXZ-hUCVZe-iq6t9n-jmusUB-iQ4dVo-jNVqyM-juBUYj-i7yZMx-jyK8ja-jBMzmG-k3X2w8-ftQRwj-jFHC61-iU13BP-j5Hdey-iRSUkW-hVMAz9-i3qi6T-jpCXba-jLvrwv-ic3CNh-j6Um6r-jsq5Vg-jr39nr-hvgyrM-jeCh42-ijc4KW-k67beB-ifaMrC-htN8pn-hD1r15-ihWEkw-jRHRrD-hmyDkL-hB9zyz-i1RmHT-incrAt-igKTHx-iKyrLp-i8P5Tk-jweSL3-jAhWzC-hZ3MQC-iGKGP8-hzHxB3-i4Wj6d/; Health Gauge (www.healthgauge.com/portfolio-tag/apps/); https://www.flickr.com/photos/alejandropinto/10671377545/; Alejandro Escamilla; https://www.flickr.com/photos/121483302@N02/15489204048/; Global Panorama; Image Courtesy: US CPSC (www.flickr.com/photos/uscpsc/13104103473); https://www.flickr.com/photos/kaeru/15608476720/; Kars Alfrink; https://www.flickr.com/photos/shardayyy/5920707858/; Shardayyy; https://www.flickr.com/photos/29638108@N06/5618665304/; Jennifer C.; https://www.flickr.com/photos/kendrickmeekdotcom/4950927627/; Kendrick Meek; https://www.flickr.com/photos/67272961@N03/6123892769/; jfcherry

In the United States, there are a myriad of diseases and conditions that are linked to poor diet and lack of exercise. United States First Lady Michelle Obama herself has launched a massive campaign, "Let's Move," to encourage children to eat healthier and exercise. This operation aims to combat childhood obesity and its relationship to serious health conditions such as heart disease, asthma, diabetes, high blood pressure, and cancer. Technology is taking a prominent role in helping people address the risk factors associated with these severe health issues. Mobile apps are available to map caloric intake and calories burned during exercise. Primary care physicians can set

Table 15.1 The Relationship Between WoT and Implications in Terms of Vulnerability in the Context of Fitness

	Societal Vulnerability	Contextual Vulnerability
Potential Positive Implications	Ease time, travel, and financial burdens that act as barriers to healthcare	Provide users access to healthcare resources and peer support
	Connect users with healthcare professionals or experts otherwise unavailable to them	Connect healthcare professionals with users and even other healthcare professionals
	Provide an opportunity for users to monitor their health and share their behaviors with providers who can identify indicators of health	Help reduce the stigma associated with eating disorders
	Empower users to learn skills and access resources	Connect different types of data to create a more holistic view of health

up appointments via online systems and communicate with their patients via Skype or Facetime. Over time there has been an increase in users' connections to "things" that will help measure and monitor their health. Removable heart rate monitors are strapped around an athlete's chest, connected to a watch, connected to a treadmill, and their activities are reviewable on their internet profiles. Mobile apps are designed to gage running and walking distance, speed, and can be linked to microchips in running shoes. Athletes and everyday individuals are using Fitbits, Apple Watches, and other devices or "things" and the connections between them to reach their health and fitness goals. These "things" can be particularly helpful by showing users where they can improve, keeping track of their progress, monitoring their behavior, and encouraging consistency [16]. Table 15.1 shows the potential positive implications of WoT.

15.2.1 SOCIETAL VULNERABILITY

When exploring the social implications of technology, whether it be a singular device, algorithm, or a technological movement, it is important to examine how these relate to, impact, and affect not just the dominant populations but minority and vulnerable populations and users as well. While there are a myriad of dimensions in which populations are made vulnerable, there is a significant number of studies that explore the relationships between socioeconomic status (SES) and health. Researchers often refer to this relationship between SES and health as "the gradient." This term describes the well-documented phenomenon in which the more privileged or "better off" a person is, the better their health [14,17]. In their 2012 review of the extant literature exploring the gradient, Evans et al. explain that this phenomenon exists across all countries and nearly all ages, yet the cause of disparities in health are not clear. Cutler et al. [14] explore this lack of clarity, arguing that SES consists of several dimensions that all have relationships with health, including "income, education, occupation, race, and ethnicity," (pg. 2).

The WoT has the potential to ease this gradient. Evans et al. [17] discuss income as one of the dimensions of SES, indicating that this can affect the quality of medical care and food, along with types of housing, toys, childcare, and neighborhoods (pg. 23). In terms of costs, the WoT may be able to alleviate some of the costs often associated with healthcare by connecting them to 1) professionals with lower costs, 2) digestible information. Visiting a healthcare professional requires both time and money in numerous ways. Doctors' offices are often open during working hours, which means that to keep an appointment requires adults or parents to take off work (which can be financially devastating). Visiting a doctor or specialist can also require travel, which demands time and money for transportation (gas, car payments, public transportation); for those who do not live close to a professional in general or one covered by their insurance, this may be a several day affair. Similar to time commitments, many jobs do not offer health insurance or pay enough to supply individuals and/or families with insurance. Even those who do have insurance often have to pay pricey co-pays and deductibles. In addition, many healthcare plans do not cover preventative, nutrition-based, or exercise-based healthcare. While poor diet and lack of exercise are linked to numerous diseases and conditions, gym memberships, nutritionists, personal trainers, and access to other types of dietary or fitness expertise are all often considered luxuries. Those between jobs or unable to find employment also experience tremendous hardship with these issues. The WoT may be able to ease the financial burdens of healthcare if they can connect with professionals digitally, either synchronously or asynchronously. By connecting asynchronously, this could ease the financial burden of time and travel. For those who offer synchronous, digital connection this could afford families to establish a relationship with a healthcare professional without the same monetary costs. Similarly, if a patient with a serious condition was able to monitor and log their relevant information (e.g. heart rate, blood sugar levels, emotional health, etc.), then having this information connected to their primary physician or caretaker may be able to alert them if something is wrong. This may decrease the need for expensive checkups, but increase quality of care. WoT stands to increase the connection to healthcare providers in affordable ways that give users the tools to learn and apply healthy strategies.

Another dimension of SES outlined in the literature is education. While education is an expansive topic, some scholars suggest that there may be a relationship between SES and the ways in which users evaluate the health information they interact with online. For example, in their review of extant literature surrounding youth and Information Quality, Gasser et al. [18] suggest that there may be a relationship in young users' "evaluative ability" and SES, particularly when it comes to education. While young people of lower SES are less likely to use the internet for information [18–20], they are more likely to use social networking sites than their higher-income peers.

While there is a cost barrier to accessing nutritionists, gym memberships, and personal trainers, users are turning to and utilizing technology to search for, interact around, and monitor their diet and exercise. As discussed in the introduction section, there is an increasing amount of fitness-related content on social networking sites (SNS). While this information is easily accessible for those who have the access and skills to navigate such sites, these spaces are not monitored by experts or healthcare professionals. These spaces have several benefits to users (lack of medical jargon may be perceived as more approachable, photographs and blogs may be more entertaining, perceived freedom of expression, lack of judgment, etc.). While there are significant benefits, the absence of a "traditional gatekeeper" on these sites means that disordered content is readily available, and sometimes it is difficult for users to discern between healthy and disordered messages [21]. If these SNS and devices through which users are interacting with this information were also connected to healthcare professionals, users could ask experts or share with their providers the spaces they most often search for and interact with health-related information. For instance, a person with diabetes could share where they most often find recipes with a nutritionist, who would be able to screen ingredient lists and teach their client how to do the same. A person recovering from an injury may be able to share a workout plan with a physical therapist, who can discuss or share a checklist as a means of evaluating a plan for re-integrating exercise. Users can learn through these connections and become empowered in ways that they define and can control. While income and education are only two of several dimensions of SES, examining them in relation to the WoT helps illustrate how this notion of connection and application may help ease the SES health gradient (see Table 15.1). The WoT has the potential to ease barriers that perpetuate the SES health gradient, as well as empower users to manage and make decisions about their health.

15.2.2 CONTEXTUAL VULNERABILITY

While the WoT may be beneficial to those who are made vulnerable by the SES health gradient, it may also be beneficial for those who are contextually vulnerable (see Table 15.1). That is, those who suffer from disorders or conditions directly related to our context of fitness.

The *Diagnostic and Statistical Manual of Mental Disorders (DSM)*, which is the standard classification of mental disorders used by mental health professionals in the United States, provides standard criteria for the classification of mental disorders, including eating disorders [22]. According to the *DSM-V*:

"Eating and feeding disorders are characterized by a persistent disturbance of eating or eating-related behavior that results in the altered consumption or absorption of food and that significantly impairs physical health or psychosocial functioning" (p. 329) [22].

Eating disorders provide an interesting health example because they encompass not only aspects of mental health, but also nutrition and fitness. Not only do eating disorders deal with behaviors associated with food, but they also are related to behaviors associated with exercise. For instance, with restricting type of anorexia nervosa, individuals lose weight through dieting, fasting, and/or excessive exercise [22]. Exercise may also be used as a compensatory behavior to avoid weight gain, such as in the case of bulimia nervosa [22]. Users with eating disorders are particularly important to study given that these conditions affect roughly 30 million people. Twenty million females and 10 million males in the United States have an eating disorder, and many more have unhealthy eating behaviors [23,24]. These numbers are concerning and the prevalence of these eating disorders has been continuously increasing [23]. Approximately 1 in 200 females will develop anorexia nervosa, and 1–3 in 100 will develop bulimia nervosa [25]. Since 1930, the rate of anorexia nervosa has increased each decade for 15–19 year olds, and between 1988 and 1993, the rate of bulimia nervosa has tripled for 10–39 year olds [26]. Anorexia nervosa can lead to serious medical conditions, such as heart failure, loss of bone density, malnutrition, and depression [22]. Similarly, bulimia nervosa can lead to heart problems, other psychological disorders, and suicide [22]. There is increased risk of mortality with anorexia and bulimia nervosa either from medical complications or suicide [22].

These statistics demonstrate the importance of considering users with eating disorders as we move forward in the ways we connect health and technology. The WoT can be especially helpful to users with eating disorders. Having connected devices can improve access to healthcare resources and support for eating disorder recovery from not only other users, but also healthcare professionals. Technologies that can be used for eating disorder recovery and support include internet-based recovery programs and telemedicine, online communities, forums and blogs dedicated to recovery, social media platforms, and health apps for eating disorder recovery. These can allow easy and often cheap (or free) access to help and support [27]. Additionally, these devices can also allow different types of healthcare professionals (such as nutritionists, therapists, and primary care physicians), fitness instructors, and parents/significant others/other family members/friends to communicate with one another and the user in order to provide the best course of treatment. The internet has given us the ability to access novel treatment programs. Internet-based interventions, including both synchronous and asynchronous communication tools, have been shown to have positive effects on a number of mental health outcomes [28] and may have advantages over face-to-face therapy [29].

Internet-connected technologies that allow users to interact with one other can provide social support to their users and offer users a space to express their thoughts about eating disorders, diet, and fitness. Some studies have considered the use of mobile technology for treatment [30–35]; however, there have been mixed findings on the development and effectiveness of such technology. A quick search on the Google Play or iTunes reveals a number of eating disorder recovery apps. However, many of these apps do not take advantage of smartphone capabilities and do not adhere to evidence-based principles [30].

One exception is Recovery Record (see [36]), which is one app available on the App Store and Google Play. Developed by a team of psychologists, engineers and entrepreneurs, Recovery Record builds on cognitive behavioral therapy and self-monitoring techniques and also compliant with The Health Insurance Portability and Accountability Act of 1996 (HIPAA) [37]. In the United States, HIPAA defines privacy rules that protect the confidentiality, integrity, and security of protected health information and includes penalties for violations of the rules [37]. Recovery Record begins to take advantage of the WoT because unlike many apps, it connects to healthcare professionals, such as psychologists, medical doctors, nutritionists, licensed clinical social workers, dietitians, counselors, psychiatrists, and nurse practitioners, so that users can get access to needed healthcare and tailor their treatment plan to their specific needs. Healthcare professionals have access to a different interface than users but can deliver care directly through the app.

Some researchers have focused on online communities for eating disorder recovery and support [38–50]. Online communities have the potential to be therapeutic for those with eating disorders [41]. The main function of these communities is often to communicate encouragement, promote self-esteem, and provide information and support related to diagnosis, treatment, and interaction with healthcare professionals and other users [44]. Research has shown that online communities can provide new information about health conditions, concerns, and treatments and give users the ability to help others with the same condition or issue [51]. Online spaces can be safe spaces for discussing or finding information about stigmatized conditions, such as eating disorders [51–55]. With more connected devices, the opportunity to receive and give support grows.

While some of these online communities have expert moderators and healthcare professionals who may specialize in eating disorder recovery and support, one concern is that these professionals do not always play an active role in the forums [42]. WoT can potentially help address this concern by providing healthcare professionals technology that easily connects to and communicates with the technology users are already using. This would also help make the technologies more personal and relevant to each user's unique needs.

Much of the research on eating disorder recovery technologies has focused on technologies intended specifically to help users with eating disorders. However, users may be using technology not specific to eating disorders to aid in their recovery. That is, some users are employing technologies to help them recover that were not designed for that purpose. To date, little academic research has examined how users trying to recover from eating disorders are using these types of technology. There is a recent initiative to address this gap, exploring how women with eating disorders are utilizing non-eating disorder-specific technology, such as mobile weight loss and fitness apps, to aid in their recovery [56]. While this topic is newly emerging in an academic space, several popular media sources have discussed how some users are using social media to recover from eating disorders [57,58]. Some teens and young women have turned to Instagram in search of a support and recovery community. For example, an article on BuzzFeed.com explained how a 16-year-old with anorexia nervosa uses Instagram to document her recovery [57]. She largely posts images of food she consumes to promote others to eat a balanced diet instead of heavily restricting both amount and types of foods. Currently, she has over 1,000 followers. These types of communities can offer support to users with eating disorders while still offering a degree of anonymity. With the increasing prevalence of smartphones and mobile devices, accessing these communities is becoming easier and easier.

WoT can not only provide more access to eating disorder care, but it can also help reduce the stigma around eating disorders. Having these various devices connected to one other can help shed light on how many people are struggling with disordered eating behaviors. While it is estimated that 20 million females in the United States have an eating disorder, this number is far larger considering many more have unhealthy eating behaviors [23,24]. These technologies can allow users to connect with one other, as well as healthcare professionals without ever leaving their home. This ability to increase access to needed healthcare resources and support has the potential to reduce stigma by making these issues less "taboo" to discuss. Through technology, we can encourage more people to talk about eating disorders and thus perhaps reduce the feelings of isolation often associated with eating disorders.

Another advantage of connecting different technologies (i.e., health apps, activity and heart rate trackers, connected medications, connected food and weight scales, internet refrigerators, online forums, social media accounts) is the potential for users and healthcare professionals to get a more holistic understanding of the user's health. Each of these connected devices in the WoT provides different types of information and data about a user and her experiences.

Imagine a young woman may use a variety of technologies, each of which shows something different about her life. On her health app, she may record her calorie intake and her exercise, but because she feels guilty when she overeats, she does not always record her binge episodes or her weight. With a connected refrigerator, however, there is data on the foods she has consumed. Her medicine cabinet and medications are also connected, so there is data showing she has been using laxatives frequently, especially after she has not recorded any foods in her health app. Her wearable activity tracker and heart monitor shows that her heart rate has been lower than normal. Her connected scale tells us she has weighed herself a lot lately and has lost weight. It also has data on her bone density and muscle mass, which has been decreasing over the last year. She also uses an app to track her moods as well as Instagram to search for fitness information. When all of this data comes together, we can see a larger picture of her behaviors and her health. While some of these devices' data alone may hint at a health problem, in isolation, the data does not show a full picture of her health. For instance, you look at her Instagram account; it is full of fitness information and inspiration. It looks like she is trying to be healthy. But you look at her activity and heart rate monitor. Does she have a heart problem? Her medicine cabinet and medications indicate she may have a digestive issue. Together, though, the data tells a different story and may indicate that she is suffering from an eating disorder.

15.3 POTENTIAL CHALLENGES AND UNINTENDED CONSEQUENCES FOR SOCIAL HEALTH

While there are a myriad of possible benefits the WoT provides to socially and contextually vulnerable users, there are also significant challenges or potential "unintended

Table 15.2 Negative Implications of WoT in Terms of Societal and Contextual Vulnerability

	Societal Vulnerability	Contextual Vulnerability
Potential Negative Implications	Exacerbate existing digital and healthcare divides	Exacerbate disordered behavior and/or unintentionally negatively affect users
	Worsen healthcare outcomes if they are dependent on connectivity	Compromise user privacy and anonymity
	Discourage users with limited connectivity	Allow for intentional misuse of the technology
	Widen the education gap in technology skill and use	Provide too much data

consequences" to consider moving forward. The term "unintended consequences" refers to unforeseen or unpredicted results to a specific action [59]. This is common in discussing technological impact, especially related to health information technology. These consequences can be positive, negative, or neutral.

At a high level, scholars have discussed several challenges from multiple perspectives. For example, in their discussion of the Internet of Things and healthcare, Tech Target points out the potential for overload from multiple perspectives and stakeholders, stating "there's the danger of overloading physicians with too much data and distracting them from their mission of treating patients," [60]. They also point out that "Some hospitals are still tweaking their security policies to keep up with the technological advancements of the BYOD and mHealth era. Stories in this guide explore how much securing healthcare IoT operations will add to an IT department's workload," [60]. While this relates to the IoT, the same concerns remain as this application layer is applied to the WoT. While the goal of this chapter is to articulate the ways in which WoT may empower users, it is important to note that these issues surrounding cognitive overload and security may unintentionally negatively affect patients, healthcare professionals, and other stakeholders (caretakers, loved-ones, etc.).

In terms of our context, these "fitness things" and the connections among them enable individuals to take charge of and manage their health in ways previously unattainable. However, as with all areas of technological progress, there are some potentially dangerous implications for certain populations and individuals, which are summarized in Table 15.2. What happens when access to these devices or the connections they offer is no longer a possibility? What if it is only a possibility some of the time?

15.3.1 SOCIETAL VULNERABILITY

As scholars consider this application layer, it is also important to discuss how to avoid exacerbating existing divides. As previously discussed, there is a divide in access to and quality of healthcare based on socioeconomic status. The WoT may lessen the disparity between the "haves" and "have nots" in terms of health, but we must consider another type of disparity: connection. While the WoT may aid in easing health disparities, these same groups are also often under connected which may block access to these connected "things" in the first place.

For decades, technologically-centered research has explored differences between populations and subpopulations with and without access to technology, the internet in particular. Often referred to as the "digital divide," this research has evolved from exploring those with and without access to now exploring differences in use, skills, and connectivity [61,62]. In many developed nations, the divide surrounding internet access is diminishing, while the gaps in knowledge, types and use, and continuous connectivity persist and become more pronounced [61].

In their nationally representative survey of 1,191 US low-income parents with children ages 6–13, Rideout & Katz [62] found that the question of a "divide" extends beyond internet access and instead falls on a spectrum of connectivity. While 94% of the families had some kind of internet access, many of them were "underconnected." This spectrum of connection depends on several factors, including: sole internet access via a mobile device, interrupted service, sharing devices with others and thus having limited time with connection, slow internet access, service cut off as a result of non-payment, and reaching their data limits.

If all applications and stakeholders are connected via the web and that becomes the standard for health-related interaction, what happens to users when their connections are interrupted, unreliable, or erratic? How is their care, which may be reliant on access and connection, affected? What happens if they are on a dietary or nutrition plan that requires access to record, monitor, or complete? What happens if they are monitoring or tracking a condition? Will irregular connection prevent some users from knowing about and/or pursuing these options in the first place?

In order to empower users who are made vulnerable by the SES health gradient, as well as avoid exacerbating existing divides, we must consider how to manage connectivity issues. While in an ideal world this connectivity spectrum would be dismantled, it is crucial to consider how intermittent or unreliable connectivity could negatively impact access to or quality of care users who are already disadvantaged by the SES health gradient experience. Similarly, while individuals and families may have smartphones or computers with internet connection, they may not have other expensive health-related devices (fitness trackers, heart-rate monitors, etc.). An expectation that all users can record this type of data may negatively impact those who cannot do so and ultimately discourage them from monitoring their health. Similarly, education needs to be considered. While these connections may empower users to seek resources, where are they learning to do that? Are these devices and connections available and taught in school? Do they have practice using it? Or do only the wealthiest users learn how to operate and maximize the potential of the WoT?

15.3.2 CONTEXTUAL VULNERABILITY

In the same way there are potential unintended consequences for those who fall on the lower end of the socioeconomic spectrum, WoT poses potential challenges for users with eating disorders. While the WoT may amplify the benefits of monitoring weight, food consumption, and exercise, with these affordances also comes a potential to also exacerbate obsessive and disordered behaviors. Obsessive and compulsive behaviors are central components of eating disorders, both traditional and emerging. For example, one eating disorder currently receiving a lot of attention is "orthorexia," which health professionals define as an obsession with eating foods a person considers "healthy." While considering which foods are the most nutritious is often encouraged by experts, these considerations can become disordered when they monopolize a person's thoughts and actions. Similarly, there is an emerging focus on excessive exercise and the extreme bodily harm it may cause.

Debates about the line between healthy fitness behaviors and obsession (as well as the role technology plays in disambiguating the two) are emerging across disciplines, particularly when it comes to social media. Over a decade ago, scholars discussed the ramifications of online communities that are devoted to encouraging anorexia ("pro-ana") and bulimia ("pro-mia") as a lifestyle choice, rather than eating disorders [6]. In the last two years, this conversation and research space has expanded to explore how harmful messages promoting obsessive, disordered behavior are subtler. Messages once clearly labeled "pro-ana" (pro-anorexia) or "pro-mia" (pro-bulimia) are now mixed amongst general content and labeled "healthy" on popular social media sites [8,63]. Often called "fitspiration" (inspiration to be "fit"), users without professional training are posting nutrition and exercise tips that range from "healthy" to dangerous.

Information Communication Technology (ICT) users, especially youth, carry around mobile phones and interact with these messages all day long, regardless of physical setting. Conversely, a recent Buzzfeed article featured interviews with young women across the world who are using these same platforms to overcome and recover from their eating disorders [57]. Research and popular culture show us how these spaces can be used to exacerbate disordered behavior, but also to aid in recovery and improved health. Exploring these trends across social media helps us understand how these dichotomies emerge. While social media is the connection of people, the connection of things (i.e., web of things) may (or may not, with interventions) reproduce the same patterns.

Unfortunately, with great potential comes a number of challenges. Although WoT can help provide a more holistic view of a user's health, there are many privacy and ethical concerns around having that much information about users. Do users want all of their data linked? How much do users want to reveal about themselves? Who gets to view and use this data? How is this data going to be used? What happens if their data is leaked? These are important questions we need to address as the WoT becomes more prevalent.

Returning to the aforementioned hypothetical user, assume a holistic view of her data across devices suggests she may have an eating disorder. Now imagine her data is reported directly to her physician. Her physician recognizes that her behaviors may be indicative of anorexia nervosa, but the user does not want treatment. What obligations does the physician have? Would the physician be required to send her information and data to a specialist? Would she be forced into treatment? Would this information have to be relayed to her insurance provider? How would that impact her life? The lives of her loved ones, especially if some of them are dependent upon her (ex: children, elderly parents, etc.)?

There are numerous dangers in having all of this information and these systems connected for users with eating disorders. As more technologies are connected, more data is available on users, reducing their anonymity. If this information is revealed, then it is more easily tied to an individual and may have real consequences (such as impacting their mental health, job, personal relationships, etc.) As mentioned before, there is stigma associated with eating disorders and other mental health conditions, and many people suffering from eating disorders experience other mental health conditions, such as depression [22]. Users may worry that others will perceive them differently based on their eating disorder, which could result in feelings of deeper isolation and separation as well as anxiety about others knowing about private aspects of their lives. There are also often real consequences to revealing this type of information about themselves. For instance, what if employers get access to this information? An article published in the Daily Mail in 2015 highlighted some of the potential negative consequences of employers having access to this information. The article details the story of one woman who said she was fired from her teaching job after staff realized she had anorexia nervosa [64]. These reports are not uncommon, in which people with eating disorders have said they have been bullied, passed up for promotions, and fired from their jobs once their conditions became common knowledge in the workplace.

One way to address these concerns is to provide users with the option to record and link this data and the ability to decide who accesses it. Imposing data sharing may be problematic, especially in areas of stigmatization. Whether or not it is positive or negative, the user should have the power to decide. Otherwise, we risk users not trusting and ultimately not using these technologies, which may be providing them some form of help and support for their eating disorders and other conditions. By not giving users agency to make their own decisions about their data, we may actually negatively affect these users.

As WoT becomes increasingly popular, the opportunity for unintended uses and unintended negative consequences increases. When considering how technology may be used in unintended ways or result in unintended consequences, scholars are encouraged to consider what is already known about these types of technologies individually.

There has been a great deal of research on how users have created blogs, websites, and online communities to enable, promote, and maintain eating disorders. Traditionally, much of this research has focused on pro-eating disorder sites and communities, such as "pro-ana" and "pro-mia". On pro-eating disorder sites and forums, users share information on how to lose weight and essentially maintain the symptomatology of eating disorders [6]. While pro-eating disorder communities can offer emotional support and a sense of community, the messages and content focus on sustaining disordered eating not recovery [6,65]. Many researchers have found that pro-eating disorder communities have negative effects on their users. Some researchers believe that these sites are a façade of "support" but actually are anti-help-seeking and anti-recovery [66]. These communities actually exacerbate their symptoms [65,66] and perpetuate unhealthy habits, such as extreme food restriction and purging [67].

While these spaces were once the primary spheres promoting disordered behaviors and content, extant literature suggests that the line between "healthy" eating and exercise content and disordered content is continuously becoming less distinct [8,63]. This means that "health" technologies (i.e., health apps and diet and activity trackers) and even technology not specific to health and fitness (i.e., Instagram, Facebook, Twitter) may negatively impact users.

Although there is limited research on the use and misuse of health apps in relation to eating disorders, some popular media articles report that health apps and diet and activity trackers can be dangerous [68–71]. Currently, some academic research aims to examine how using mobile health apps impact women with eating disorders [56,72]. As part of this work, healthcare professionals are explaining how health apps can trigger and feed into eating disorders by focusing too much on the numbers and data around calories and weight [72]. Users may be intentionally using these types of technologies to enable their eating disorders. However, even when users have intentions of utilizing health apps in a healthy way, they may go too far and develop disordered eating behaviors [72].

Other types of technology, such as social media, may unintentionally negatively impact users' body image and disordered eating behaviors [73–77]. For example, Kim and Chock [78] conducted an online survey to examine Facebook's impact on drive for thinness. They found engaging in social behaviors such as checking friends' profiles, leaving messages, and commenting on profiles is correlated with drive for thinness in both females and males [78]. Fardouly et al. [74] studied the effects of Facebook on female university students' body image and found frequency of Facebook use was related to body image concerns. Other researchers have studied hashtags and photos on sites such as Instagram and Twitter. For instance, Tiggeman and Zaccardo [8] discuss how "fitspiration" can have unintended negative effects on college-aged girls. In her analysis of fitness blogs and media culture, Stover [63] argues that "fitspiration" is dangerous in that the images and text are more "culturally acceptable" than those that showcase emaciated subjects.

In addition to concerns about the effects of connected systems, WoT increases the amount of data available, and in the context of health, this may be problematic. From health apps and activity trackers to self-diagnosing online, users play a bigger role in their health than ever before. With more and more connected "things" in the WoT, an abundance of user data is created. While all of this data may reveal important health information, healthcare professionals' time is already limited. More physicians are explaining how WoT is impacting their work and their interactions with their patients. In many cases, physicians may only have 15 minutes with their patients, and the amount of data patients want to go over is just too much. So how can we possibly interpret all of this data? Although automation and machine learning methods may reduce the burden, we still face a huge challenge in being able to use all of this data in a meaningful way. Yet with all of this data, the context may still get lost, resulting in misunderstandings about what the data actually means.

Although WoT can provide a number of benefits to users, caution should be taken, especially when thinking about vulnerable populations, such as people with eating disorders. In addition to examining the privacy issues surrounding WoT, researchers need to continue to study unintended uses, unintended users, and unintended consequences (both positive and negative) of different types of technology in order to understand how they will impact users. Before connecting devices and integrating different forms of data, it is important to know not only potential effects on users but also how to use the data in a meaningful and ethical way. Ideally, WoT can help users, and we can empower users by giving them the choice to record, connect, and use data pertaining to their health.

15.4 IMPLICATIONS

The WoT has the potential to benefit all different types of users when it comes to health. Perhaps most notably, it has the potential to benefit those who are often most vulnerable in a health context in the United States. Those who are considered of lower socioeconomic status typically suffer from poorer health, yet the WoT may alleviate hardships and eliminate barriers that prevent individuals and families from accessing quality medical care and resources. Similarly, the WoT and its layer of application being connected could potentially give agency to users in ways that did not previously exist for people without access to medical care; the WoT can empower and enable them to learn strategies for monitoring their own care. While these potential benefits are exciting, there are also unintended consequences to consider that may negatively impact vulnerable users. For those for whom connectivity is not always guaranteed, but instead is erratic or unpredictable, how do we ensure their care is not compromised? Similarly, how do we ensure users have the skills to maximize the potential of WoT? How do we avoid exacerbating the gap between the haves and have nots in terms of technology education, skills, and use?

For persons struggling with eating disorders, which are seminal to this context given their relationship to food and exercise, the WoT may provide several benefits. By having access to multiple types of healthcare providers and the ability to monitor their behavior, users may be able to use technology to facilitate their recovery. The WoT enables users to engage with a myriad of perspectives, while healthcare providers are able to access a holistic view of their patient's health. Conversely, however, there are significant privacy concerns surrounding health and technology. This is particularly true of heavily stigmatized conditions, such as eating disorders and other conditions that fall under the category of "mental health." While the ability for users to be empowered and in control of their health while having access to the resources they find valuable is a benefit of WoT, the potential for a loss of control over personal data and sensitive information is of serious concern. Similarly, many of the behaviors that benefit people without eating disorders (counting calories, tracking food, monitoring exercise, etc.) may exacerbate the conditions of users who do suffer from these disorders. As we move forward, how can we take into account the needs of these users?

This chapter does not claim to answer all of these questions. Rather, it serves as a launch pad by discussing the potential benefits and unintended consequences of the WoT, specifically in regard to vulnerable populations and health. We hope to facilitate a discussion that emphasizes the importance of considering these elements as we move forward to a more connected world.

REFERENCES

[1] Smith Aaron. U.S. smartphone use in 2015. 2015.
[2] Fox Susannah, Duggan Maeve. Mobile health 2012. Pew internet & American life project. 2012.
[3] Wartella E, Ridout V, Zupancic H, Beaudoin-Ryan L, Lauricella A. Teens, health, and technology: a national survey. In: Center on media and human development. School of Communication Northwestern University; 2015. p. 1–56.
[4] Harvey-Berino Jean, Pintauro Stephen, Buzzell Paul, Gold Elizabeth Casey. Effect of internet support on the long-term maintenance of weight loss. Obesity Res 2004;12(2):320–9.
[5] Hwang KO, Ottenbacher AJ, Green AP, Cannon-Diehl MR, Richardson O, Bernstam EV, Thomas EJ. Social support in an internet weight loss community. Int J Med Inform 2011;79(1):5–13.
[6] Sharpe Helen, Musiat Peter, Knapton Olivia, Schmidt Ulrike. Review pro-eating disorder websites: facts, fictions and fixes. Health (San Francisco) 2011;10(1):34–44.
[7] Boepple Leah, Thompson J Kevin. A content analytic comparison of fitspiration and thinspiration websites. Int J Eating Disord 2016;49(1):98–101.
[8] Tiggemann Marika, Zaccardo Mia. Exercise to be fit, not skinny: the effect of fitspiration imagery on women's body image. Body Image 2015;15:61–7.
[9] Tiggemann Marika, Zaccardo Mia. 'Strong is the new skinny': a content analysis of # fitspiration images on instagram. J Health Psychol 2016.
[10] Booth Kayla M, Trauth E. Do this, not that: how teens make decisions about contradictory health information on social media. In: America's conference on information systems, San Diego, CA. 2016.
[11] Booth Kayla M. Teens and information quality: an intersectionality-based dissertation in progress exploring fitness information and social media. In: 2016 ACM SIGMIS conference on computers and people research (doctoral consortium). Washington, D.C.: ACM; 2016. p. 5–6.
[12] Booth Kayla M. From "weight loss tips" to "fastest exercise to get abs:" how teens search for fitness information across social media platforms. In: 2016 ACM SIGMIS conference on computers and people research pages (poster session). Washington, D.C.: ACM; 2016. p. 23–4.
[13] Boepple Leah, Thompson Joel Kevin. A content analysis of healthy living blogs: evidence of content thematically consistent with dysfunctional eating attitudes and behaviors. Int J Eating Disord 2014;47(4):362–7.

[14] Cutler David M, Lleras-Muney Adriana, Vogl Tom. Socioeconomic status and health: dimensions and mechanisms. 2008.

[15] Magnuson JA. Introduction to public health informatics. 2014.

[16] Benefits of fitness trackers. 2013.

[17] Evans William, Wolfe Barbara, Adler Nancy. The SES and health gradient: a brief review of the literature. In: Biological consequences of socioeconomic inequalities. 2012. p. 1–37.

[18] Gasser U, Cortesi S, Malik M, Lee A. Youth and digital media: from credibility to information quality. In: The Berkman center for internet & society research publication series. 2012. p. 1–150.

[19] Peter Jochen, Valkenburg Patti M. Adolescents' internet use: testing the "disappearing digital divide" versus the "emerging digital differentiation" approach. Poetics 2006;34:293–305.

[20] Wartella E, Rideout V, Zupanic H, Beaudoin-Ryan L, Lauricella A. Teens, health, and technology: a national survey. Media Commun 2016;4(3):13–23.

[21] Syed-Abdul Shabbir, Fernandez-Luque Luis, Shan Jian Wen, Li Chuan Yu, Crain Steven, Huei Hsu Min, Chin Wang Yao, Khandregzen Dorjsuren, Chuluunbaatar Enkhzaya, Nguyen Phung Anh, Ming Liou Der. Misleading health-related information promoted through video-based social media: anorexia on youtube. J Med Internet Res 2013;15(2).

[22] American Psychiatric Association, editor. Diagnostic and statistical manual of mental disorders (DSM-5). 5th edition. Washington, D.C. and London, England: American Psychiatric Publishing; 2013.

[23] Wade TD, Keski-Rahkonen A, Hudson J. Epidemiology of eating disorders. In: Textbook in psychiatric epidemiology. 3rd ed., M Tsuang edition. New York: Wiley; 2011. p. 343–60.

[24] Reba-Harrelson L, Von Holle A, Hamer RM, Swann R, Reyes ML, Bulik CM. Patterns and prevalence of disordered eating and weight control behaviors in women ages 25–45. Eating Weight Disord 2009;14(4).

[25] Neumark-Sztainer Dianne. "I'm like, SO fat!": helping your teen make healthy choices about eating and exercise in a weight-obsessed world. Number 1–338. New York, NY: The Guilford Press; 2005.

[26] Engel Bridget, Staats Reiss Natalie, Dombeck Mark. Prevalence, onset and course of eating disorders. 2007.

[27] Olsen Elin, Kraft Pål. ePsychology: a pilot study on how to enhance social support and adherence in digital interventions by characteristics from social networking sites. In: Persuasive '09. Claremont, CA: ACM; 2009. p. 1–6.

[28] Mohr David C, Burns Michelle Nicole, Schueller Stephen M, Clarke Gregory, Klinkman Michael. Behavioral intervention technologies: evidence review and recommendations for future research in mental health. Gen Hosp Psych 2013;35:332–8.

[29] Taylor C Barr, Luce Kristine H, Taylor C Barr, Luce Kristine H. Computer- and internet-based psychotherapy intervention. Curr Dir Psychol Sci 2003;12(1):18–22.

[30] Juarascio Adrienne S, Manasse Stephanie M, Goldstein Stephanie P, Forman Evan M, Butryn Meghan L. Review of smartphone applications for the treatment of eating disorders. Eur Eating Disord Rev 2015;23:1–11.

[31] Norton Margo, Wonderlich Stephen A, Myers Tricia, Mitchell James E, Crosby Ross D. The use of palmtop computers in the treatment of bulimia nervosa. Eur Eating Disord Rev 2003;11:231–42.

[32] Bauer Stephanie, Percevic R, Okon E, Meermann R, Kordy H. Use of text messaging in the aftercare of patients with bulimia nervosa. Eur Eating Disord Rev 2003;11:279–90.

[33] Shapiro Jennifer R, Bauer Stephanie, Andrews Ellen, Pisetsky Emily, Bulik-Sullivan Brendan, Hamer Robert M, Bulik. Cynthia M. Mobile therapy: use of text-messaging in the treatment of bulimia nervosa. Int J Eating Disord 2010;43:513–9.

[34] Heron Kristin E, Smyth Joshua M. Ecological momentary interventions: incorporating mobile technology into psychosocial and health behaviour treatments. Br J Health Psychol 2010;15:1–39.

[35] Robinson S, Perkins S, Bauer S, Hammond N, Treasure J, Schmidt U. Aftercare intervention through text messaging in the treatment of bulimia nervosa: feasibility plot. Int J Eating Disord 2006;39:633–8.

[36] RecoveryRecord.

[37] Health Information Policy.

[38] Flynn Mark A, Stana Alexandru. Social support in a men's online eating disorder forum. Int J Men's Health 2012;11(2):150–69.

[39] Gulec Hayriye, Moessner Markus, Mezei Agnes, Kohls Elisabeth, Túry Ferenc, Bauer Stephanie. Internet-based maintenance treatment for patients with eating disorders. Prof Psychol: Res Pract 2011;42(6):479–86.

[40] Johnsen Jan-Are K, Rosenvinge Jan H, Gammon Deede. Online group interaction and mental health: an analysis of three online discussion forums. Scand J Psychol 2002;43:445–9.

[41] Keski-Rahkonen Anna, Tozzi Federica. The process of recovery in eating disorder sufferers' own words: an internet-based study. Int J Eating Disord 2005;37:580–6.

[42] Kummervold Per E, Gammon Deede, Bergvik Svein, Johnsen an-Are K, Hasvold Toralf, Rosenvinge Jan H. Social support in a wired world: use of online mental health forums in Norway. Nordic J Psychiat 2002;56(1):59–65.

[43] Ljotsson B, Lundin C, Mitsell K, Carlbring P, Ramklint M, Ghaderi A. Remote treatment of bulimia nervosa and binge eating disorder: a randomized trial of Internet-assisted cognitive behavioural therapy. Behav Res Ther 2007;45:649–61.

[44] McCormack Abby. Individuals with eating disorders and the use of online support groups as a form of social support. CIN: Comput, Inform, Nursing 2010;28(1):12–9.

[45] Stommel W, Koole T. The online support group as a community: a micro-analysis of the interaction with a new member. Discourse Stud 2010;12(3):357–78.

[46] Stommel Wyke, Meijman Frans J. The use of conversation analysis to study social accessibility of an online support group on eating disorders. Global Health Promot 2011;18(2):18–26.

[47] Stommel Wyke. Mein Nick bin ich! Nicknames in a German Forum on eating disorders. J Comput-Mediat Commun 2008;13:141–62.

[48] Walstrom Mary K. "You know, who's the thinnest?": combating surveillance and creating safety in copy with eating disorders online. CyberPsychol Behav 2000;3(5):761–83.

[49] White Marsha, Dorman Steve M. Receiving social support online: implications for health education. Health Edu Res 2001;16(6):693–707.

[50] Whitlock Janis L, Powers Jane L, Eckenrode John. The virtual cutting edge: the internet and adolescent self-injury. Dev Psychol 2006;42(3):407–17.

[51] Mo Phoenix KH, Coulson Neil S. Empowering processes in online support groups among people living with HIV/AIDS: a comparative analysis of 'lurkers' and 'posters'. Comput Hum Behav Sep 2010;26:183–1193.

[52] Buchanan Heather, Coulson Neil S. Accessing dental anxiety online support groups: an exploratory qualitative study of motives and experiences. Patient Edu Counsel 2007;66(3):263–9.

[53] Coulson Neil S, Knibb Rebecca C. Coping with food allergy: exploring the role of the online support group. CyberPsychol Behav Feb 2007;10(1):145–8.

[54] Davison KP, Pennebaker JW, Dickerson SS. Who talks? The social psychology of illness support groups. Am Psychol Feb 2000;55(2):205–17.

[55] Pereira J, Bruera E, Macmillan K, Kavanagh S. Palliative cancer patients and their families on the Internet: motivation and impact. J Pal Care Jan 2000;16(4):13–9.

[56] Eikey Elizabeth V. The use of weight loss apps by women with eating disorders (doctoral consortium). In: SIGMIS. Alexandria, VA: SIGMIS; 2016. p. 1–2.

[57] Krishna Rachael. Meet the teen girls using instagram to recover from anorexia. 2015.

[58] Mirhashem M. Overcoming an eating disorder with instagram. 2015.

[59] Campbell RH, Sittig EM, Ash DF, Guappone JS, Dykstra KP. Types of unintended consequences related to computerized provider order entry. J Am Med Inform Assoc 2006;13(5):547–56.

[60] TechTarget. A guide to healthcare iot possibilities and obstacles. 2013.

[61] van Dijk J. Digital divide research, achievements and shortcomings. Poetics 2006;34(4–5):221–35.

[62] Rideout VJ, Katz VS. Opportunity for all? Technology and learning in lower-income families. In: A report of the families and media project. New York: the Joan Ganz Cooney center at sesame workshop. 2016. p. 2016.

[63] Stover Cassandra Marie. Elements of a sensibility: fitness blogs and postfeminist media culture. Master of arts. The University of Texas at Austin; 2014.

[64] Siebert V. Teacher claims she was fired from her Catholic school after seeking treatment for anorexia by 'villainous' headmistress who 'humiliated' her about her condition. 2015.

[65] Csipke E, Horne O. Pro-eating disorder websites: users' opinions. Eur Eating Disord Rev 2007;15:196–206.

[66] Rouleau Codie R, Von Ranson Kristin M. Potential risks of pro-eating disorder websites. Clin Psychol Rev 2011;31(4):525–31.

[67] Ransom Danielle C, La Guardia Jennifer G, Woody Erik Z, Boyd Jennifer L. Interpersonal interactions on online forums addressing eating concerns. Int J Eating Disord 2010;43(2):161–70.

[68] Miller Anna Medaris. The dark side of activity trackers. 2015.

[69] Mahdawi A. The unhealthy side of wearable fitness devices. Jan 2014.

[70] Thorpe JR. 4 problems with activity trackers that can trigger eating disorders – and how to fix them. 2015.

[71] Larson S. Are fitness trackers dangerous for people with eating disorders? 2015.

[72] Eikey Elizabeth V. Providers' perceptions of the impact of weight loss apps on users with eating disorders (poster). In: SIGMIS. Alexandria, VA: ACM; 2016. p. 1–2.

[73] Andsager Julie L. Research directions in social media and body image. Sex Roles 2014;71:407–13.

[74] Fardouly Jasmine, Diedrichs Phillippa C, Vartanian Lenny R, Halliwell Emma. Social comparisons on social media: the impact of Facebook on young women's body image concerns and mood. Body Image 2015;13:38–45.

[75] Mabe Annalise G, Forney K Jean, Keel Pamela K. Do you "like" my photo? Facebook use maintains eating disorder risk. Int J Eating Disord 2014;47:516–23.

[76] Meier Evelyn P, Gray James. Facebook photo activity associated with body image disturbance in adolescent girls. CyberPsychol Behav Soc Netw 2014;17(4):199–206.

[77] Stronge Samantha, Greaves Lara M, Milojev Petar, West-Newman Tim, Barlow Fiona Kate, Sibley Chris G. Facebook is linked to body dissatisfaction: comparing users and non-users. Sex Roles 2015;73:200–13.

[78] Kim Ji Won, Chock T Makana. Body image 2.0: associations between social grooming on Facebook and body image concerns. Comput Hum Behav 2015;48:331–9.

INDEX

Symbols

μConcept rule language, 112

A

Abstraction, 23, 29, 31, 88, 105, 109, 118, 121, 167, 334, 346, 390
  level of, 5, 84, 89, 105, 127, 372
Access control, 208, 221, 390, 395, 401, 402, 408, 415
Access permission, 403, 413
Access policies, 401, 418, 419
Access token, 401, 412, 414, 416
Activity diagrams, 84
Actuators, 4, 8, 19, 20, 29, 63, 73–75, 81, 87, 89–91, 94–96, 100, 105, 114, 155, 156, 181, 183, 186, 187, 189, 197, 219, 268, 317, 344, 362, 365, 368, 389
Adaptation, 88, 109, 155, 166, 167, 175
Adaptation process, 152, 168
Agents, 112, 139, 157, 172, 173
Agribots, 154, 155, 165–168, 173
Airports, 50
Ambient assisted living (AAL), 6, 28, 122, 230, 404
Analysis, flight delay, 39, 49, 68
Application development, 74, 100, 268, 320, 366
Application domains, 4, 7, 8, 108, 113, 116, 121, 161, 168, 309, 315
Application layer, 73, 159, 182, 198, 206, 209, 218, 219, 224, 252, 326, 358, 361, 405, 407, 437
Application programming interfaces (APIs), 3, 44, 77, 110, 117, 158, 192, 252, 314, 317, 359, 371, 374, 389
Applications
  context-aware, 278
  cross-domain, 309, 318
  design software, 156
  intelligent, 337, 348
  mash-up, 118, 364

  military, 108, 173
  naturopathy, 317, 320
  novel, 49, 73
  semantic-based, 315
  sensor, 184
  sensor network, 23
  smart, 232, 233, 253, 265
  social network, 329
Apps, 368, 371, 375, 377, 382, 426, 427, 429, 434–436
Architectural reference model (ARM), 113, 359, 393
Architecture
  physical, 373
  pub/sub, 371
  semantic, 363
  WoX technical, 373
Architecture analysis, 210, 223
Architecture design, 207, 221
Architecture trade-off analysis method (ATAM), 211, 223
Arduino boards, 85, 182, 187, 191, 382
Artificial intelligence, 175
Attacker, 391, 392, 396, 398, 402
Attacks, 391, 395, 397, 402
Authentication, 64, 78, 217, 238, 239, 243, 390–395, 400, 402, 404, 407, 409, 410, 412, 414, 420
  two-way, 233, 407
Authorization, 129, 217, 390–396, 398, 400–402, 408–412, 414, 415, 420
  architecture, 410, 412
  explicit, 413
  framework, 395, 400, 401, 412, 419
  information, 412
  OAuth, 400, 401, 404, 409, 410, 414
  PRESENT, 409
  SEA, 409
Authorization managers, 410, 412, 414
Automatic SPARQL query formulation (ASQFor), 263

449

Printed in the United States
By Bookmasters